Readings in
Animal Behavior

Readings in Animal Behavior

SECOND EDITION

Edited by

Thomas E. McGill

Williams College
Williamstown, Massachusetts

HOLT, RINEHART AND WINSTON, INC.

New York   Chicago   San Francisco   Atlanta
Dallas   Montreal   Toronto   London   Sydney

ACKNOWLEDGMENTS

The articles making up this collection are reprinted with the kind permission of the authors and the following publishers and copyright holders:

AMERICAN ASSOCIATION FOR THE ADVANCEMENT OF SCIENCE: Terman, M., & Terman, J. S., Circadian rhythm of brain self-stimulation behavior, *Science,* 1970, *168,* 1242–1244. Rosenblatt, J. S., Nonhormonal basis of maternal behavior in the rat, *Science,* 1967, *156,* 1512–1514. Levine, S., & Mullins, R. F., Jr., Hormonal influences on brain organization in infant rats, *Science,* 1966, *152,* 1585–1592. Bronson, F. H., & Desjardins, C., Aggression in adult mice: Modification by neonatal injections of gonadal hormones, *Science,* 1968, *161,* 705–706. Fuller, J. L., Experiential deprivation and later behavior, *Science,* 1967, *158,* 1645–1652. Marler, P., and Tamura, M., Culturally transmitted patterns of vocal behavior in sparrows, *Science,* 1964, *164,* 1483–1486. Pratt, C. L., and Sackett, G. P., Selection of social partners as a function of peer contact during rearing, *Science,* 1967, *155,* 1133–1135. Sackett, G. P., Monkeys reared in isolation with pictures as visual input: Evidence for an innate releasing mechanism, *Science,* 1966, *154,* 1468–1473. Burghardt, G. M., Chemical-cue preferences of inexperienced snakes: Comparative aspects,

Science, 1967, *157,* 718–721. Smith, W. J., Messages of vertebrate communication, *Science,* 1969, *165,* 145–150. Kellogg, W. N., Communication and language in the home-raised chimpanzee, *Science,* 1968, *162,* 423–427. Frisch, K. von, Honeybees: Do they use direction and distance information provided by their dancers? *Science,* 1967, *158,* 1072–1076. Wenner, A. M., & Johnson, D. L., Reply to von Frisch, *Science,* 1967, *158,* 1076–1077. Wenner, A. M., Wells, P. H., & Johnson, D. L., Honey bee recruitment to food sources: Olfaction or language? *Science,* 1969, *164,* 84–86. Dawkins, R., Bees are easily distracted, *Science,* 1969, *165,* 751. Landreth, H. F., & Ferguson, D. E., Newts: Sun-compass orientation, *Science,* 1967, *158,* 1459–1461. Grant, D., Anderson, O., & Twitty, V., Homing orientation by olfaction in newts (*Taricha rivularis*), *Science,* 1968, *160,* 1354–1356. Bresler, D. E., & Bitterman, M. E., Learning in fish with transplanted brain tissue, *Science,* 1969, *163,* 590–592. Chesler, P., Maternal influence in learning by observation in kittens, *Science,* 1969, *166,* 901–903. Wilcoxon, H. C., Dragoin, W. B., & Kral, P. A., Illness-induced aversions in rat and quail: Relative salience of visual and gustatory cues, *Science,* 1971, *171,* 826–828. LeBoeuf, B. J., & Peterson, R. S., Social status and mating activity in elephant seals, *Science,* 1969, *163,* 91–93. Washburn, S. L., Jay, P. C., & Lancaster, J. B., Field studies of Old World monkeys and apes, *Science,* 1965, *150,* 1541–1547. Tinbergen, N., On war and peace in animals and man, *Science,* 1968, *160,* 1411–1418. Copyright 1964, 1965, 1966, 1967, 1968, 1969, 1970, 1971 by the American Association for the Advancement of Science.

AMERICAN GENETIC ASSOCIATION: Collins, R. L., On the inheritance of handedness: I. Laterality in inbred mice, *Journal of Heredity,* 1968, *59,* 9–12.

AMERICAN PHILOSOPHICAL SOCIETY: Miller, N. E., Laws of learning relevant to its biological basis, *Proceedings of the American Philosophical Society,* 1967, *111,* 315–325.

AMERICAN PSYCHOLOGICAL ASSOCIATION: Hodos, W., & Campbell, C. B. G., *Scala naturae:* Why there is no theory in comparative psychology, *Psychological Review,* 1969, *76,* 337–350. Lockard, R. B., Reflections on the fall of comparative psychology: Is there a message for us all? *American Psychologist,* 1971, *26,* 168–179. Moltz, H., Contemporary instinct theory and the fixed action pattern, *Psychological Review,* 1965, *72,* 27–47. Hirsch, J., Behavior-genetic, or "experimental" analysis: The challenge of science versus the lure of technology, *American Psychologist,* 1967, *22,* 118–130. Wimer, R. E., Symington, L., Farmer, H., & Schwartzkroin, P., Differences in memory processes between inbred mouse strains C57BL/6J and DBA/2J, *Journal of Comparative and Physiological Psychology,* 1968, *65,* 126–131. Hutchinson, R. R., & Renfrew, J. W., Stalking attack and eating behaviors elicited from the same sites in the hypothalamus, *Journal of Comparative and Physiological Psychology,* 1966, *61,* 360–367. Essman, W. B., Differences in locomotor activity and brain-serotonin metabolism in differentially housed mice, *Journal of Comparative and Physiological Psychology,* 1968, *66,* 244–246. DeFries, J. C., Weir, M. W., & Hegmann, J. P., Differential effects of prenatal maternal stress on offspring behavior in mice as a function of genotype and stress, *Journal of Comparative and Physiological Psychology,* 1967, *63,* 332–334. Arling, G. L., & Harlow, H. F., Effects of Social deprivation on maternal behavior of rhesus monkeys, *Journal of Comparative and Physiological Psychology,* 1967, *64,* 371–377. Meyer, M. E., Stimulus control for bird orientation, *Psychological Bulletin,* 1964, *62,* 165–179. Bitterman, M. E., Phyletic differences in learning, *American Psychologist,* 1965, *20,* 396–410. Boice, R., Avoidance learning in active and passive frogs and toads, *Journal of Comparative and Physiological Psychology,* 1970, *70,* 154–156. Campbell, B. A., & Jaynes, J., Reinstatement, *Psychological Review,* 1966, *73,* 478–480. Reprinted by permission of the American Psychological Association.

AMERICAN SOCIETY OF ICHTHYOLOGISTS AND HERPETOLOGISTS: Emlen, S. T., Territoriality in the bullfrog, *Rana catesbeiana, Copeia,* 1968, *2,* 240–243.

AMERICAN SOCIETY OF ZOOLOGISTS: Ehrman, L., Courtship and mating behavior as a reproductive isolating mechanism in *Drosophila, American Zoologist,* 1964, *4,* 147–153. Rothenbuhler, W. C., Behavior genetics of nest cleaning in honey bees. IV. Responses of F_1 and backcross generations to disease-killed brood, *American Zoologist,* 1964, *4,* 111–123, Rabb, G. B., Woolpy, J. H., & Ginsburg, B. E., Social relationships in a group of captive wolves, *American Zoologist,* 1967, *7,* 305–311.

BAILLIÈRE, TINDALL & CASSELL LIMITED: Jaynes, J., The historical origins of "ethology" and "comparative psychology," *Animal Behaviour,* 1969, *17,* 601–606. Lott, D., Scholz, S. D., & Lehrman, D. S., Exteroceptive stimulation of the reproductive system of the female ring dove (*Streptopelia risoria*) by the mate and by the colony milieu, *Animal Behaviour,* 1967, *15,* 433–437. Scudder, C. L., Karczmar, A. G., & Lockett, L., Behavioural developmental studies on four genera and several strains of mice, *Animal Behaviour,* 1967, *15,* 353–363. Bateson, P. P. G., & Reese, E. P., The reinforcing properties of conspicuous stimuli in the imprinting situation, *Animal Behaviour,* 1969, *17,* 692–699. Wilz, K. J., Causal and functional analysis of dorsal pricking and nest activity in the courtship of the three-spined stickleback *Gasterosteus aculeatus, Animal Behaviour,* 1970, *18,* 115–124.

JOHN WILEY & SONS, INC.: Lindzey, G., Thiessen, D. D., & Tucker, A., Development and hormonal control of territorial marking in the male Mongolian gerbil, *Developmental Psychobiology,* 1968, *1,* 97–99.

J. B. LIPPINCOTT COMPANY: Davidson, J. M., Activation of the male rat's sexual behavior by intracerebral implantation of androgen, *Endocrinology,* 1966, *79,* 783–794.

MACMILLAN (JOURNALS) LIMITED: Denenberg, V. H., & Rosenberg, K. M., Nongenetic transmission of information, *Nature,* 1967, *216,* 549–550. Salzen, E. A., & Meyer, C. C., Imprinting: Reversal of a preference established during the critical period, *Nature,* 1967, *215,* 785–786. Michael, R. P., & Keverne, E. B., Pheromones in the communication of sexual status in primates, *Nature,* 1968, *218,* 746–749.

NATURAL HISTORY: Geist, V., A consequence of togetherness, 1967, *76,* 24–30. © *Natural History,* 1967.

PAUL PAREY: Dawkins, R., The ontogeny of a pecking preference in domestic chicks, *Zeitschrift für Tierpsychologie,* 1968, *25,* 170–186. Fabricius, E., Crucial periods in the development of the following response in young nidifugous birds, *Zeitschrift für Tierpsychologie,* 1964, *21,* 326–337. Klopfer, P. H., & Klopfer, M. S., Maternal "imprinting" in goats: Fostering of alien young, *Zeitschrift für Tierpsychologie,* 1968, *25,* 862–866. Grant, E. C., Mackintosh, J. H., & Lerwill, C. J., The effect of a visual stimulus on the agonistic behaviour of the golden hamster, *Zeitschrift für Tierpsychologie,* 1970, *27,* 73–77.

PERGAMON PRESS LIMITED: Manning, A., Evolutionary changes and behaviour genetics, *Genetics Today,* 1964, Proceedings XI International Congress of Genetics, 807–813. McClearn, G. E., Genotype and mouse behaviour, *Genetics Today,* 1964, Proceedings XI International Congress of Genetics, 795–805. Ursin, H., Sundberg, H., & Menaker, S., Habituation of the orienting response elicited by stimulation of the caudate nucleus in the cat, *Neuropsychologia,* 1969, *7,* 313–318.

THE PSYCHOLOGICAL RECORD: Gulick, W. L., & Zwick, H., Auditory sensitivity of the turtle, 1966, *16,* 47–53. Reprinted from *The Psychological Record.*

PSYCHONOMIC JOURNALS, INC.: Denenberg, V. H., Paschke, R. E., & Zarrow, M. X., Killing of mice by rats prevented by early interaction between the two species, *Psychonomic Science,* 1968, *11,* 39.

SOCIETY FOR THE EXPERIMENTAL ANALYSIS OF BEHAVIOR, INC.: Catania, A. C., On the visual acuity of the pigeon, *Journal of the Experimental Analysis of Behavior,* 1964, *7,* 361–366. Copyright 1964 by the Society for the Experimental Analysis of Behavior, Inc.

Preface to the First Edition

The science of animal behavior is rapidly becoming a distinct academic discipline. This is evidenced by the following: the growing number of colleges and universities that offer undergraduate courses in animal behavior; the formation of several graduate departments of animal behavior; the existence of research laboratories and institutes devoted exclusively to the study of the behavior of animals; recent "summer institutes" designed to train college teachers in the subject; and several scientific journals and "associations" that specialize in animal behavior.

Historically, new sciences developed by disengagement from larger disciplines. The science of animal behavior, however, is being formed in a slightly different way: by the recombination of parts of several sciences into one discipline.

The rather eclectic nature of the new science creates special problems for those engaged in teaching the subject. It is axiomatic that advanced undergraduates and graduate students should have experience in reading journal articles and other primary sources. However, it is very difficult to arrange for the availability of such source material in an area where major contributions have come from a great diversity of academic specialties. Endocrinologists, ethologists, geneticists, physiologists, psychologists, zoologists, among others, have contributed to the field. Consequently, the reports have appeared in a bewildering variety of journals and books, and the instructor finds it difficult to arrange an adequate and representative "reserve shelf." *Readings in Animal Behavior* was designed to meet this need—to serve as an aid, either as core text or as collateral reading, in the teaching of advanced-undergraduate and graduate courses in animal behavior. It is hoped that the book may in this way contribute to the development of the science.

Four criteria were used in selecting the readings that are included in this volume. First, an effort was made both to secure a representation from a wide variety of disciplines and to obtain a broad sample of animal subjects. Second, whenever possible, contributions were selected that illustrate a *program* of research—the long-range work of one scientist or one laboratory. A third criterion was recency of publication; only three of the articles appeared before 1956, and the median publication date is 1961. Finally, an attempt was made to include representative samples of both theoretical reviews and reports of specific experiments.

The stylistic idiosyncrasies of the various sources have been maintained in the reproductions that make up this volume. For example, if the summary or abstract preceded the article proper in the original journal, it does so in the reprinted version; if titles were omitted in the original reference list, they are omitted in the reproduction. This procedure should serve to familiarize the student with a variety of journal styles.

A difficult problem encountered in the preparation of a book of readings is organization, determining the categories for major sections and the ordering of studies within each section. It is obvious that many papers could logically be placed in any of several sections. Thus any particular arrangement must be arbitrary. Further, although a given arrangement may suit one instructor, others may find the sequence completely unworkable. For this reason, a simple alphabetical or chronological order was considered. But because this seemed a bit faint-hearted, if not downright cowardly, the decision was made to provide a scheme of classification for the material. It is the editor's sincere hope that at least some of his colleagues in the teaching of animal behavior will find the present organization useful.

Each major section and individual reading is preceded by an editor's introduction. The introductions to sections contain outlines of major problems in the areas covered, general introductions to the studies included, and suggestions for further reading. The introductions to the the individual papers contain, in various combinations, necessary information on the background of the problem or author, cross-references to related studies in the book, definitions of abbreviations or terms used in the paper, aspects of the paper the student should note particularly or questions he should keep in mind as he reads the article, and suggestions for further reading.

In preparing this book the editor has repeatedly imposed on many of his busy colleagues with requests for suggestions, reprints, permissions, photographs, and moral support. To these most gracious and patient gentlemen, most of whose names appear in the Table of Contents—thank you. The editor is also grateful to his Williams colleagues, Professors William C. Grant, Jr. and Richard O. Rouse, Jr., for careful criticism of the introductions.

T. E. McG.

Williamstown, Mass.
July 1965

Preface to the Second Edition

This book is not so much a "second edition" as it is "Volume II," since none of the readings in the current edition appeared in the previous one. There were two reasons for electing to publish a completely new collection. First, the existence of the first edition makes the articles included in it that much more readily available to students. Second, in a rapidly developing discipline the goal of presenting the current state of the science is best met by including the more recent publications. Thus, none of the articles in the present collection were originally published prior to 1964 and the median publication date is 1967. Obviously, it is not my intention to imply that anything published prior to 1964 is unworthy of inclusion. Rather, I wish to show the student that he can read effectively in the modern literature and to stimulate discussions oriented around such topics as "What questions are still unanswered?" and "What is the next logical experiment to perform?" This procedure encourages in the student the notion that he too might make a contribution to the discipline and, ideally, leads him to try out his ideas in experiments of his own.

This second edition has been published in paperback and produced by a process whereby the original articles are photographed. Both of these changes were made in an effort to keep the cost of the book within reasonable limit. The photographic process has the additional benefit of introducing to the student the stylistic ideosyncrasies of the various journals; a goal that was partially met in the first edition.

The change in the manner of producing the book necessitated certain other modifications in this edition. The first is that the brief introductions to the individual readings are included with the general introduction to each major section. The second is that all acknowledgments to publishers and copyright holders have been gathered into a single section.

The organization of the book, its goals, and my hopes for its usefulness remain as expressed in the preface of the first edition.

In the preparation of this book I have been impressed once more by the kindness, generosity, and willingness to help that characterize the scientists who wrote the original articles. I am very grateful to them.

T. E. McG.

Williamstown, Mass.
July 1972

Contents

VII. Social Behavior   405

Readings in Animal Behavior

PART 1 Introductory Readings

Why does an organism behave as it does? What determines its behavior? How can we account for the fact that within particular species certain behavior patterns appear identical from individual to individual, whereas others show large individual differences? The question of behavioral determination, or causality, is one of the most basic and recurrent problems in animal behavior. Historically, the answers to questions concerning the causes of behavior have taken two main forms. On the one hand were the hereditarians, who claimed that behavior is largely the result of genotype: "Like begets like." "He's a chip off the old block." On the other hand were the environmentalists, who maintained that most behavior is the product of experience: ". . . as the twig is bent, so is the tree inclined."

Scientific and philosophical opinion as to which of these two schools of thought is "correct" has varied greatly over the years.

Fortunately, with the passage of time, experimentation tended to replace mere speculation, and most (but not all) scientists came to the realization that this "nature–nurture controversy," as it came to be called, was largely a pseudoproblem. The wrong questions had been asked. To ask whether a given bit of behavior is learned or innate is both misleading and restrictive. It states an either / or dichotomy that does not allow for *interaction* between the variables or for the operation of variables that could be described as *neither* innate nor learned.

Two major branches of the science of animal behavior, which for the most part developed independently of one another, can trace their origins to different theoretical positions on the nature–nurture dichotomy. First, consider behavioral research in the United States during the last forty years. Under the combined influences of Watsonian behaviorism and the common interpretation of Freud's theory of personality, this research has been largely "environmental" in its approach. Most studies have been concerned with conditioning and learning (emphasized by the behaviorists) or with the effects of early experience on later behavior (emphasized by the Freudians).

In Europe, on the other hand, under the influence of Darwinism, a school of animal behavior known as "Ethology" has developed. The primary emphasis of the ethologists has been on "innate" patterns of behavior, their function and their evolution. The following table compares, in a rather crude and general fashion, these two major branches of the science of animal behavior.

	Comparative Psychologist	Ethologist
Geographical location	North America	Europe
Training	Psychology	Zoology
Typical subjects	Mammals, especially the laboratory rat	Birds, fish, insects
Emphasis	"Learning," the development of theories of behavior	"Instinct," the study of the evolution of behavior
Method	Laboratory work, control of variables, statistical analysis	Careful observation, field experimentation

It is obvious that the two approaches are complementary and that both are necessary (but probably not sufficient) for a complete understanding of behavior. After a period of sometimes vitriolic disagreement, these two "schools" have largely merged into one. But, as will be apparent from some of the readings included in the present volume, the merger is not yet completed.

The first reading in Part 1 presents a history of ethology and comparative psychology. The origins of the two disciplines are traced to an early nineteenth-century controversy in French science. Julian Jaynes, the author of this paper, was one of the first psychologists to conduct laboratory investigations of modern ethological concepts. Several different examples of such laboratory studies are included in Part 4.

Readings 2 and 3 are critical articles directed at the conceptual basis of Comparative Psychology. First, Hodos and Campbell consider the concept of a continuous "phylogenetic scale" within the animal kingdom. This scale, originally proposed by Aristotle, conceives of an orderly evolutionary progression through the animal phyla. Thus man becomes the most "highly evolved" of all the animals. The authors attack this notion and make specific suggestions for the selection of animal subjects in comparative research.

In the next reading, Robert Lockard continues the critique of comparative psychology by citing ten premises that "would have been widely accepted [by comparative psychologists] in the 1950s." After reviewing the history of behavioral biology, he provides an interesting discussion of these premises and the results of their uncritical acceptance in several different areas of psychological research.

After finishing Readings 2 and 3, the reader may feel that psychologists should retire from the animal behavior business and leave the field to those better capable of handling it, ethologists for example. Reading 4 is included at this point to dispel, at least partially, any such notion. In this paper, Howard Moltz considers one of the basic concepts of ethological theory, the "fixed action pattern." He critically discusses the significance of the empirical and theoretical properties of the fixed action pattern and proposes an alternative, "epigenetic" approach to the concept.

REPRINT No. 149 from *Animal Behaviour*, **17**, 4, November, 1969

Anim. Behav., 1969, **17**, 601–606

THE HISTORICAL ORIGINS OF 'ETHOLOGY' AND 'COMPARATIVE PSYCHOLOGY'

By JULIAN JAYNES

Department of Psychology, Princeton University, Princeton, New Jersey

Animal behaviour is a field of study shared academically by several sciences. In recent decades, it has come to be known not without some confusion as comparative psychology in psychology departments, and as ethology in biology departments. The result has sometimes been competition, sometimes amalgamation, sometimes an antipathy eroding truth into loyalty, and sometimes, fortunately, a division of labour benefiting all. Because there has been confusion about the meaning of these terms, it seems timely to attempt a clarification by inquiring into their historical origins.

The Cuvier–Geoffroy-Saint-Hilaire Debates

Both terms came out of the intellectual milieu of early nineteenth-century France. It was an era dominated in biology by the indefatigable Baron Cuvier, the great apostle of the immutability of species, geological catastrophes which allowed God to re-create living beings several times, and therefore of comparative anatomy which then studied the static interrelationships of these created beings. His influence as head of the Académie des Sciences and the most famous scientist of his time was huge, suffocating, and literally keeping those thinking along different lines out of high scientific positions. Among these was the meek Lamarck and then the brilliant early evolutionist, Étienne Geoffroy-Saint-Hilaire, once Cuvier's collaborator, whose central life-thought was the unity of plan of composition throughout all animal species (É. Geoffroy-Saint-Hilaire 1818; see also Cahn 1962). Cuvier's emphasis was always on laboratory-discovered facts. The emphasis of Geoffroy-Saint-Hilaire was on trends as they are found in nature. The opposition between the two grew into the famous debates at the Académie des Sciences around 1830 in which the naturalistic evolutionary point of view came out second best. Cuvier smothered the tender, unsupported suggestions of the younger man with mountains of data. Geoffroy-Saint-Hilaire was right in principle, but wrong in his facts, Cuvier was right in his facts, but wrong in principle.

Debates exacerbate their issues rather than decide them. And the polarization of points of view in biology thus begun lasted the rest of the century. The bitterness was still rankling in mid-century when the Cuvier side emphasizing laboratory analysis founded comparative psychology, and the Geoffroy-Saint-Hilaire side emphasizing naturalistic observation founded ethology. And it is interesting that both terms, while never exactly defined, have kept their nineteenth-century connotations to our own times. I shall describe these foundings in turn, then what happened to both these terms in the rest of the century, and then briefly suggest the career of each in the twentieth century.

The Ambiguous Founding of Ethology

Ethology, as the study of the characters of animals in their natural habitats, was founded terminologically by Isidore Geoffroy-Saint-Hilaire, the son of the forementioned, in 1859. But this is complicated by an earlier founding with a very different meaning. The word comes from the Greek *ethos*, which in various Greek eras with various lengths of 'e' has an assortment of meanings (Liddell & Scott 1961). Perhaps its best single translation is 'character', both in the sense of something that is characteristic of persons or animals and in the sense of moral character, particularly as the result of habit. By a Greek, Achilles might be called a man of great ethos or great character. And it is from this latter sense that the word ethics derives, and the first usage of the word ethology.

In the seventeenth century, an ethologist was an actor or mimic who portrayed human characters on the stage (see the *Oxford English Dictionary*). In the eighteenth century, an ethologist was one who studied ethology or the science of ethics. This usage was codified in England into a new science by John Stuart Mill in the second volume of his *Logic* in 1843. He wrote: 'If we employ the name Psychology for the science of the elementary laws of mind, Ethology will serve for the ulterior science which determined the kind of character produced in conformity to those general laws, by any set of circumstances, physical and moral. According to this definition, Ethology is the science which corresponds to the act of education, the widest sense of the term, including the formation of national or collective character, as well as individual' (Mill 1843, pp 176–177).

In spite of Mill's efforts, probably because he was interested in so many things, ethology as the science of building character was a long time leaving his printed page. Its greatest flowering, incidentally, was at the University of California around 1900, where courses in ethology were taught, and a journal of ethology was at least proposed. The most prominent name of these Millean ethologists was Bailey (1899a, b, c) whose titles in my reference list witness his emphasis of the term. By this time American dictionaries like *Webster's* were carrying ethology as defined in Mill's sense.

While Mill's usage crossed the Atlantic easily, it did not cross the linguistic barriers into France. And it was in ignorance of this English meaning that Isidore Geoffroy-Saint-Hilaire rather casually recreated ethology as part of a large classification of biology in a very interesting discussion of the life sciences in 1859 (Geoffroy-Saint-Hilaire 1854–1862). By it he meant the study of animals, not as corpses reeking with formaldehyde in the Cuvierian tradition, but as living things in their natural habitat. And by it he meant to continue his father's emphasis in the great debate 30 years earlier.

While this is not precisely what comparative psychology was going to mean, the two terms immediately came into conflict, and ethology began to lose currency even as it was struggling to begin. But the reasons were not intellectual so much as political, and can only be understood by the manner in which comparative psychology came into being.

Flourens Founds Comparative Psychology

Comparative psychology was founded somewhat differently, and, as a term, had a more immediately successful fate. Cuvier's protégé, Pierre Flourens, in the early part of the nineteenth century, had become famous with his studies on brain structure in relation to behaviour (Flourens 1842). Precise extirpation of parts of the brain, he argues, was preferable to 'nature's experiments' or the random lesions of disease or accident in animals or men which had been the main source of evidence previously. Removing the cerebral lobes of a pigeon and showing that it thereby lost its 'faculties' of willing, perception, and intelligence, was the most widely talked of French experiment since Trembley's discovery of regeneration in hydra in 1742. Such a pigeon with the cerebral lobes removed would remain still until it died of starvation, would not fly unless thrown into the air, nor move unless stimulated. He then cleared up a great deal of the vagueness about the nervous system, dividing it on the basis of his empirical evidence into the cerebral hemispheres, the cerebellum, the corpora quadrigemina, the medulla, the spinal cord, and the nerves—six units in all, each with a single unitary function, yet all acting together in a common way, since the removal of one of the parts reduces the energy of every other. I have mentioned Flouren's work to this extent to point out his Cuvierian emphasis on experimental analysis, and a prejudice against 'nature's experiments' or naturalistic observation. Most of this work was first published in 1824 and 1825. Thereafter, his experimental work was at a minimum and his honours at a maximum. In 1828 he was elected to the Académie, and in 1833, because of Cuvier's dying request, he was made Secrétaire Perpétuel of the Académie des Sciences.

Few scientists have been able to survive high position. Certainly not Flourens. His scientific work became ceremonious and empty, and he retained his reputation more by momentum out of the past than by any mastery of experimental fact. He began that disagreeable habit of cursorily re-writing old books, attaching a new chapter here and there. And in all this he paid only mincing attention to the rise of evolutionary theory in the rest of Europe. When Darwin published the *Origin of Species* in 1859, the largest body of evidence anyone had ever brought together to make this early nineteenth-century idea plausible, Flourens, senile with dignity, as the leader of French science, led the attack on it in a very bad book published in 1864. And there followed in the same year an even worse book that I regret to report founded comparative psychology in name (Flourens 1864). It was partly a rewrite of earlier work (Flourens 1861), but he added among other things a new first chapter and, probably, to counteract the non-Cuvier connotations of ethology founded 6 years earlier, re-titled the book *Psychologie Comparée*. While it is possible that the term may have been used earlier in a trivial way, this is the first attempt to found comparative psychology as a new science. In the first chapter, Flourens is quite conscious of this. Comparative psychology is to combine human psychology as it is represented in Descartes, i.e. from a mechanistic neurological standpoint, and animal psychology as it has been represented by Réaumur, Leroy, and Cuvier.

Comparative Psychology After Flourens

It is impossible to know when a new name for something is needed. But how quickly it is taken up, if at all, is certainly an indication of that need. And immediately the phrase, comparative psychology, was spoken of everywhere. In the 1870s, the decade in which Romanes (1876), Spalding (1872), Lubbock (1882), McCook (1879) and Schneider (1880) were doing experiments in the area, there were no less than five texts with comparative psychology as their titles. In France there was one by Henri Joly (1877), a somewhat philosophically oriented one which distinguished between need, desire, tendency, and instinct; and another by Tissot (1878), which in a similar fashion pays no heed to evolution, and makes a sharp division between animal and man. In Italy in the same year, there were two such texts, one by Vignoli (1877) which was somewhat more Darwinian, stressing the continuity of consciousness, intelligence, will, imagery, and communication with animal senses and instincts, and the other by Espinas (1877a) who, as if to balance the matter, warned against anthropomorphism, maintaining that we can only comprehend an intelligence, of whatever kind it may be, when we can find its analogue in our own intellectual life. This was also published in French in the same year under a slightly different title (Espinas 1877b).

In America, the President of the University of Wisconsin, John Bascom, wrote his *Com-*

parative Psychology or the Growth and Grades of Intelligence (1878), whose title suggests its contents and who was one of the first to oppose the 'lapsed intelligence' theory of instinct, championing Spalding's observations. And the article by Herbert Spencer (1875) using the term as its title, another anonymous one (Anon 1876) which also introduced the concept of 'environment', and Romanes' use of comparative psychology in his important books (1883, 1884), firmly established the term in the scientific world.

The history of comparative psychology from here, as it stuffed itself into apparatus throughout academia, particularly in America, is beyond the scope of the present paper. But it might be noted here that all through this history, through an expanding experimental movement in the latter part of the nineteenth century, its flowering in the first decade of this century, and its decadence under the dry paradigms of behaviourism, it always maintained its early laboratory bias that very often became a failure to appreciate the importance of naturalistic observation.

Ethology Refounded by Giard

The fortunes of ethology were of a different sort. Biology in the nineteenth century, faced with the successes of physics, was in panic lest it be unscientific in exactly the same way psychology was to be a half century later. It tried to make itself precise by leaving the fields and the woods and the beaches and tucking into dissecting benches all over Europe and America. Zoology and comparative anatomy became convertible terms. When a zoologist saw a new creature, he was burning to cut it up and get it under the microscope. Larger questions were forgotten. Ethology was a protest against this ridiculous situation. But its founder was no Flourens. Isidore Geoffroy-Saint-Hilaire was only the enthustiastic and passionate supporter of his more famous father, and occupied no such high academic position from which to moon over the tides of science. Then, too, English and American dictionaries were already following the influential Mill, defining ethology as something else.

Indeed, the term would probably have dropped out of sight, had it not been that a small adamant group of French biologists still wished for a term that would take them out of the Cuvierian atmosphere altogether. The ecological group which is perhaps least susceptible to laboratory simulation of its environment are the organisms of the seashore, whose patterns of behaviour are inextricably woven into the patterns of tide and climate. It was thus reasonable that the protest against overemphasis on laboratory methods should come from students of beach animals.

This position became very articulate in the person of Alfred Giard, an untiring and prolific worker in all biological fields, particularly with marine species. During his life he established several marine biological stations, the major one being at Wimereux near Boulogne, from which came fifty volumes of research during his lifetime In 1888 at the Sorbonne, a special Chair was established for him which gave him the title of Professor in the Evolution of Organic Beings. In the 1870s he began using ethology more and more as a classification of studies that related the organism to its immediate habitat, studies such as those on convergent evolution, on mimicry in butterflies, on the effects of dehydration on the development of wasps, studies on the 'enemies' of bees, studies of parasites, of pearl formation, as well as anything which Ernst Haeckel was at the same time calling oecology (presently ecology), defined in 1857 as the relationship of the organism to its environment (see Haeckel 1898). In 1875, Giard was quite clear on his emphasis: 'It seems to me that for some years we have neglected ethological research too much and given exclusive importance to anatomy and physiology properly speaking; it would perhaps be time to come back a little to what we might call exterior physiology, the study of the customs of animals and their mutual relationships' (Giard 1875, as quoted by Bohn 1910, p. 32; my translation). And in the titles of these myriad papers, he is quite careful to distinguish ethology in this sense from comparative psychology which he reserves for his studies of the movements of individual animals, their senses, habits of orientation, or their preference behaviour.

One reason why he so stressed ethology was that he made himself the great French apologist for Lamarck whose views of course were based on the relationship of the animal to its habitat (Giard 1904). While not absolutely denying natural selection, he regarded Lamarckian factors in evolution as the primary ones, namely heat, climate, light, electricity, water salinity, air humidity, agitation and circulation of water, nutrition, and so on, indeed all the factors that affect the behaviour of an animal in its ethological relationship to its habitat. And to prove the Lamarckian hypothesis, he made several studies that he felt showed the direct influence of environment on heredity, such as one on the influence of habitat on pigments in studies of protective mimicry, particularly in the sea mollusc, *Lamellaria perspicus* (Giard, as cited in Bohn 1910).

Since ethology had extant then two different meanings and was also being confused with Haeckel's 'oecology', there was a threefold confusion surrounding the term which diluted the force of Giard's protest. Nor did Haeckel help when he coined still another term in 1874, referring to '. . . the many and various relations of plants and animals to each other and to their environment, which are treated in *bionomy* (the *oecology* or *ethology* of organisms)' (Haeckel 1910, p. 74). This confusion, together with Giard's Lamarckism, that was finally being buried by Weissman's brilliant arguments, deafened biology to his criticisms, prevented his ethology from becoming a scientific movement, and indeed made the men and ideas associated with it the cast-outs and derogations of a new generation.

Ethology Since Giard

At the turn of the century, a few kept the term and its emphasis on naturalistic observation alive into the twentieth century. George Bohn, Giard's student, called himself an ethologist, reviled psychophysics, soft-pedalled the Lamarckian aspects of Giard, and mixed his invertebrate ethology with a strong dose of Loeb, calling the result 'ethological psychophysiology' (Bohn 1906). In each of his chief books (Bohn 1909, 1911) he devoted a chapter to 'La méthode éthologique'. Oskar Heinroth (1911) also maintained the distinction between ethology and comparative psychology in Giard's sense.

William Morton Wheeler, from the rostrum of Harvard in the 1920s, for precisely the same reasons as Geoffroy-Saint-Hilaire (from whom he obtained the term), Giard, and Bohn, espoused the study of ethology with all the strength, vigour, and ineffectiveness of his biophilosophical type of mind. Wheeler was, of course, interested particularly in the social life of ants, and this again was something which must be studied in their natural habitat (Wheeler 1903). He was very adamant about the matter and felt that the biology of his time, in turning to genetics and cell biology, was turning the wrong way. Ethology, or the study of animal behaviour in its habitat, was the 'stolon' of biology, and when biology 'mistook the stolon for the bud', it was lost (Wheeler 1939). But partly because ethology had its ethical connotation in America, partly because naturalistic observations since Agassiz had been associated with anti-Darwinian theory, and partly because entomologists tend to be parochial and not influence the rest of biology, and partly, too, it must be said, because Wheeler, a thorny, sarcastic, impatient man, was detested by students, his brilliant arguments never got off the page into the enthusiasm of disciples.

In the 1930s there are even fewer references to the term. Its most articulate continuation at this time is in Paul Pelseneer (1935) who had picked up the term from Bohn. He insisted that ethology, 'the study of the entire life of an individual and its behaviour in its natural environment', must be (a) quantitative, (b) comparative both between species and between different ecological systems, and (c) phylogenetic. Pelseneer particularly criticized colleagues who used descriptive qualitative terms in behaviour work, as well as those studying an animal in artificial surroundings.

The Situation After World War II

In the late 1940s, ethology as a term comes into a wider, if sometimes confusing, use. This rise in its frequency is due to the need of those studying animal behaviour in natural surroundings to distinguish themselves in Europe from the phenomenological psychology that stemmed from Husserl, and in America from the tortuous and ungenerative legacy of behaviourism as evidenced in learning theory. This was particularly true of a group of students of bird behaviour. Since Whitman (1919) and Craig (1918) in America, Selous (1901), Huxley (1923), and Howard (1920) in England at the beginning of the century, there had been a continuous development of concepts and observations up to Lorenz (1935) and Tinbergen (1940) in the 1930s. While none of these had previously used the term 'ethology' in any distinguishing sense, it came to be used more and more as a designative association for their work. G. P. Baerends, who was associated with Tinbergen as this began to happen, has told me that none of them knew where the term came from or any of its earlier history. But since the emphasis of this group was on the study of animals in their natural habitat, the use of the term was what it always had been (unlike some later erroneous designations, such as Lashley's calling ethology 'the science of racial characteristics' (Lashley 1957, p. x). Indeed, the situation was partly a repetition of what had happened in the nineteenth century. But instead of ethology as a protest against the excessive laboratoriness of the rest of biology, it was this time against the artificial laboratory situations of comparative psychology itself.

There followed a period of partisanship in some quarters between comparative psychologists in psychology departments and ethologists in zoology departments that in the long run had a beneficial effect in exposing and correcting the theoretical excesses on both sides. Certainly by the 1960s, most of this division of loyalties had diminished, and both psychologists and zoologists were getting back to the cooperative venture. To those indeed who still retain some feelings of prejudice one way or another between ethology and comparative psychology, I hope that I have suggested here that the origins of their feelings are in a history that stretches back to a polarization of thought in the early nineteenth century. The unknown tyranny of the past is the source of all unreason.

Summary

The connotations of the terms comparative psychology and ethology are traced to the Cuvier–Geoffroy-Saint-Hilaire debates of the early nineteenth century. Their founding as 'sciences' as well as their subsequent histories are shown to reflect continuously this polarization of thought between laboratory analysis and naturalistic observation.

REFERENCES

Anonymous (1876). Comparative psychology. *Pop. Sci. Mon.*, **8**, 257–269.

Bailey, T. P. (1899a). *Ethology: Standpoint, Method, Tentative Results*. Berkeley: Univ. of California Press.

Bailey, T. P. (1899b). Bibliographical references in ethology. *Univ. Calif. Lib. Bull.*, **13**. Berkeley: Univ. of California Press.

Bailey, T. P. (1899c). Ethological psychology. *Psychol. Rev.*, **6**, 649–651.

Bascom, J. (1878). *Comparative Psychology or the Growth and Grades of Intelligence*. New York: Putnam.

Bohn, G. (1906). Attitudes et mouvements des Annélides, essai de psychophysiologie éthologique. *Annls Sci. nat.*

Bohn, G. (1909). *La Naissance de l'Intelligence*. Paris: Flammarion.

Bohn, G. (1910). *Alfred Giard et son oeuvre*. Paris: Mercure de France.

Bohn, G. (1911). *La Nouvelle Psychologie Animale*. Paris: Alcon.

Cahn, T. (1962). *La vie et l'oeuvre d'Étienne Geoffroy-Saint-Hilaire*. Paris: Presses Universitaires de France.

Craig, W. (1918). Appetites and aversions as constituents of instincts. *Biol. Bull.*, **34**, 91–107.

Espinas, A. (1877a). *Psicologia Comparata*. Rome: Borgano.

Espinas, A. (1877b). *Des Sociétés Animales Étude de Psychologie Comparée*. Paris: Baillière.

Flourens, P. (1841). *Analyse Raisonnée des Travaux de Georges Cuvier, Précedée du son Éloge Historique*. Paris: Chez Paulin.

Flourens, P. (1842). *Recherches expérimentales sur les propriétés et les fonctions du systeme nerveux dans les animaux vertébratés*. Paris: Baillière.

Flourens, P. (1861). *De la raison, du génie, et de la folie*. Paris: Carnier frères.

Flourens, P. (1864). *Psychologie Comparée*. Paris: Carnier frères.

Geoffroy-Saint-Hilaire, E. (1818). *Philosophie Anatomique*. Paris: Baillière.

Geoffroy-Saint-Hilaire, I. (1847). *Vie, Travaux et Doctrine Scientifiqued'Etienne Geoffroy-Saint-Hilaire*. Paris: Librairie de la Société Géologique de France.

Geoffroy-Saint-Hilaire, I. (1854–1862). *Histoire Naturelle Générale*, 3 vols. Paris: Masson.

Giard, A. M. (1904). *Controverses Transformistes*. Paris: C. Nand.

Haeckel, E. (1898). *Natürliche Schöpfungs-Geschichte*. Berlin: Reimer.

Haeckel, E. (1910). *The Evolution of Man* (trans. Joseph McCabe). London: Watts.

Heinroth, O. (1911). *Beiträge zur Biologie, namentlich Ethologie und Psychologie der Anatiden*. Berlin: Verh. V. Int. Orn. congr.

Howard, E. (1920). *Territory in Bird Life*. London: John Murray.

Huxley, J. S. (1923). Courtship activities of the red-throated diver (*Colynbus stellatus* Pontopp.); together with a discussion on the evolution of courtship in birds. *J. Linn. Soc.*, **35**, 253–293.

Joly, H. (1877). *Psychologie Comparée, l'Homme et l'Animal*. Paris: Heurand Phil.

Lashley, K. A. (1957). Introduction. In *Instinctive Behavior* (ed. by C. H. Schiller). New York: International Universities Press.

Liddell, H. G. & Scott, R. (1961). *A Greek-English Lexicon*. Oxford: Clarendon Press.

Lorenz, K. (1935). Der Kumpan in der Umwelt des Vogels. *J. Orn., Lpz.*, **83**, 137–213; 289–413.

Lubbock, J. (1882). *Ants, Bees, and Wasps*. London: Kegan, Paul & Trench.

McCook, H. C. (1879). *Natural History of the Agricultural Ant of Texas*. Philadelphia Acad. of Nat. Sci.

Mill, J. S. (1843). 'Psychology and ethology', Ch. III, from *A System of Logic*. Reprinted in Wayne Dennis, *Readings in the History of Psychology* (1948). New York: Appleton-Century-Crofts.

Pelseneer, P. (1935). *Essai d'Ethologie Zoologique d'aprés l'étude des Mollusques*. Bruxelles: Palais des Académies.

Romanes, G. J. (1876). Plasticity of instinct. *Pop. Sci. Mon.*, **8**, 449–453.

Romanes, G. J. (1883). *Animal Intelligence*. New York: Appleton.

Romanes, G. J. (1884). *Mental Evolution in Animals*. New York: Appleton.

Schneider, G. H. (1880). *Der thierische Wille*. Leipzig.

Selous, E. (1901). *Bird Watching*. London: Constable & Co.

Spalding, D. A. (1872). On instinct. *Nature*, **6**, 485–486.

Spencer, H. (1875). Comparative psychology. *Anthrop. Journal*, **5**, 301–316.

Tinbergen, N. (1940). Die Übersprungbewegung. *Z. Tierpsychol.*, **4**, 1–40.

Tissot, J. (1878). *Psychologie Comparée*. Paris: A. Maresq aîné.

Vignoli, T. (1877). *Di Psicologia Comparate*. Milano: Dumolard.

Wheeler, W. (1903). Ethological observations on the American ant. *J. Psychol. Neurol., Lpz.*, **2**, 31–64.

Wheeler, W. (1939). The dry-rot of an academic biology. In *Essays in Philosophical Biology*. Cambridge: Harvard Univ. Press.

Whitman, C. O. (1919). *The Behavior of Pigeons* (ed. H. Carr). Publ. No. 257, pp 1–161. Washington, D.C.: Carnegie Institute.

(*Received 7 September* 1968; *revised 7 February* 1969; *Ms. number:* A755)

Psychological Review
1969, Vol. 76, No. 4, 337–350

SCALA NATURAE:

WHY THERE IS NO THEORY IN COMPARATIVE PSYCHOLOGY [1]

WILLIAM HODOS [2]   AND   C. B. G. CAMPBELL

Walter Reed Army Institute of Research   *Center for Neural Sciences, Indiana University*
Washington, D. C.

The concept that all living animals can be arranged along a continuous "phylogenetic scale" with man at the top is inconsistent with contemporary views of animal evolution. Nevertheless, this arbitrary hierarchy continues to influence researchers in the field of animal behavior who seek to make inferences about the evolutionary development of a particular type of behavior. Comparative psychologists have failed to distinguish between data obtained from living representatives of a common evolutionary lineage and data from animals which represent divergent lineages. Only the former can provide a foundation for inferences about the phylogenetic development of behavior patterns. The latter can provide information only about general mechanisms of adaptation and survival, which are not necessarily relevant to any specific evolutionary lineage. The widespread failure of comparative psychologists to take into account the zoological model of animal evolution when selecting animals for study and when interpreting behavioral similarities and differences has greatly hampered the development of generalizations with any predictive value.

Nearly two decades have passed since Beach (1950) presented his classic paper "The Snark was a Boojum" in which he deplored the decline of comparative psychology as a result of "excessive concentration upon a single species," namely, the albino rat. His paper appears to have stimulated a renewed interest in an animal psychology which is more broadly comparative than the rat learning studies which were prevalent in the 1940s and 1950s. Rhesus monkeys and White Carneaux pigeons have now been added to the animal psychologist's standard menagerie. Occasional studies of behavior in teleost fish, reptiles, and carnivores have also appeared in psychological journals and some attempts at comparison across species have been made. In addition, several text-

books and collections of readings in comparative psychology recently have been published. However, much of the current research in comparative psychology seems to be based on comparisons between animals that have been selected for study according to rather arbitrary considerations and appears to be without any goal other than the comparison of animals for the sake of comparison. This rather tenuous approach to research has apparently been brought about by the absence of any broad theoretical foundation for the field. Such a theoretical foundation, though partly or even totally incorrect, would at least have the virtue of encouraging a systematic study of animal behavior rather than the current haphazard manner of operation.

The purpose of this paper is to point out some of the factors which have hindered theoretical development in comparative psychology and to suggest some ways of remedying the situation. Many of the concepts that will be discussed are not novel; indeed, they would be regarded as rather elementary by students of such fields as systematic biology, paleontology, physical anthropology,

[1] The authors wish to express their gratitude to their colleagues and students for their helpful comments on this paper and to J. Z. Young and the Oxford University Press for their permission to reproduce the phylogenetic trees shown in Figures 1–4.

[2] Requests for reprints should be sent to William Hodos, Department of Experimental Psychology, Walter Reed Army Institute of Research, Walter Reed Army Medical Center, Washington, D. C. 20012.

9

etc. However, even a casual examination of the recent literature in the behavioral and neural sciences leads one to the conclusion that many experimenters are greatly misinformed about these fundamental concepts. As a result, a number of unjustified conclusions about behavioral and neural evolution have been drawn from the data of comparative studies.

THE SCALA NATURAE

In attempting to find order in an apparently chaotic universe, Aristotle (1910, 1912a, 1912b; Ross, 1949) attempted various organizational schemes for classifying animals. These classifications were based on such characteristics as number of legs, whether or not the organism appeared to possess blood, whether they were oviparous or viviparous in their reproductive mechanisms, etc. Aristotle also proposed that the various categories of animals might be arranged on a graded scale of complexity or perfection, with man at the top. Although Aristotle did not advocate any such ranking of the animals within each category, later scholars expanded his suggestions so that there came to be general acceptance of the concept that all animals could be ranked on a unitary, graded, continuous dimension known as the *scala naturae* or Great Chain of Being (Lovejoy, 1936; Wightman, 1950). The lowest position on the *scala naturae* was occupied by sponges and other creatures considered to be essentially formless. At the intermediate levels were insects, fish, amphibians, reptiles, birds, and various mammals. At the top of the scale was man. Furthermore, as Lovejoy (1936) points out in his extensive treatment of the history of this subject, the *scala naturae* eventually became involved in theological formulations which considered that God was perfect and all other creatures were merely progressively less perfect copies. Thus, angels were somewhat imperfect copies, man more imperfect, apes still more imperfect, and so on, down the scale to the "formless" sponges.

The attractiveness of the notion of a *scala naturae* is attested to by its persistence throughout the centuries and its influence on contemporary scientific thought. The recent literature in the life sciences dealing with comparisons between different groups of animals abounds with references to a hierarchy called the "phylogenetic scale," which appears to be the modern counterpart of the *scala naturae*. According to their relative positions on this scale, animals are designated as "subprimate" or "submammalian" or "higher animals" or "lower animals." However, there seems to be no compilation of the phylogenetic scale to which one could refer to answer such questions as "Is a porpoise a higher animal than a cat?" Nevertheless, in a recent textbook, Waters (1960) characterizes comparative psychology as "the study of behavior wherever exhibited along the phylogenetic scale . . . [p. 14]." Likewise, Ratner and Denny (1964), in a discussion of the evolution of behavior, state that "As one climbs the scale from fish to primates the principle seems best stated as follows: The higher the phyletic level, the greater the multiple determination of behavior [p. 680]." The meaning of such terms as "phyletic level" is usually not specified but the implication seems to be that an organism's phyletic level is determined by its proximity to man on the *scala naturae*. Apparently, these writers and numerous others have confused the *scala naturae* with another organizational arrangement of animals, one based on probable lines of evolutionary descent: the phylogenetic tree. However, as Simpson (1958a) has pointed out, the phylogenetic tree is a geneology. It is based on the data of paleontology and comparative morphology and represents the current state of knowledge about the course of evolution of the various animal species.[3] Like any other historical survey, it is subject to change with the acquisition of new data and by itself gives no indication of the relative status of the individuals listed with respect to any gradational arrangement. On the other hand, the *scala naturae* or phylogenetic scale is a hierarchical classification. While such a hierarchy can provide interesting information about relative performance and relative degrees of structural differentiation, it tells us nothing about evolutionary development since it is unrelated to specific evolutionary lineages. Thus, to say

[3] The term "phylogenetic tree" is used here in a generic sense since such trees, constructed by various evolutionary theorists, would differ in some details.

that amphibians represent a higher degree of evolutionary development than teleost fish is practically without meaning since they have each followed independent courses of evolution. Moreover, one can find characteristics in which teleosts exceed amphibians as well as vice versa. For example, the central nervous system of teleost fishes in many ways exhibits a greater degree of differentiation and specialization than does that of amphibians (Ariëns Kappers, Huber, & Crosby, 1960). Indeed the general absence of amphibians from recent comparative studies of learning or intelligence such as those of Bitterman (1965a, 1965b) suggests that their behavior patterns may be relatively inflexible. The difficulties encountered in the training of these organisms are discussed by McGill (1960) and van Bergeijk (1967).

An important feature of the *scale naturae* is the concept of a smooth continuity between living animal forms rather than the discontinuities implicit in the theory of evolution as a result of the divergence of evolutionary lines and the extinction of many intermediate forms. This continuity, which Lovejoy (1936) calls the "principle of unilinear gradation," has also had a profound influence on contemporary research design and theorization in the comparative life sciences. For example, in a paper on the evolution of learning, Harlow (1958) speculates that

simple as well as complex learning problems might be arranged into an orderly classification in terms of difficulty, and that the capabilities of animals on these tasks would correspond roughly to their positions on the phylogenetic scale [p. 283].

A survey of the literature reviews and research reports of the past 10 years might lead one to the conclusion that meaningful statements could be made about the evolution of some morphological, physiological, or behavioral characteristic by comparing goldfish, frog, pigeon, cat, and man. As Simpson (1958a) puts it,

some such sequence as dogfish-frog-cat-man is frequently taught as "evolutionary," *i.e.,* historical. In fact the anatomical differences among these organisms are in large part ecologically and behaviorally determined, are divergent and not sequential, and do not in any useful sense form a historical series [p. 11].

Another characteristic of the *scala naturae,*

which seems to be implicit in discussions of a phylogenetic scale, is the notion that man is the inevitable goal of the evolutionary process and that once he has evolved, the phylogenetic process ends. These ideas have been succinctly expressed in the following lines by Emerson:

Striving to be man, the worm
Mounts through all the spires of form.

While this view of the animal kingdom may have a certain amount of face validity, it too runs contrary to the currently accepted data on the course of evolutionary history which indicate that primates represent only one of the many lines of vertebrates which have evolved and survive today.

THE PHYLOGENETIC TREE

Figure 1 presents a phylogenetic tree showing the approximate times of origin and probable lineages of the various classes of living vertebrates and some related groups of animals (Young, 1962). The animals represented across the top form an approximation of the *scala naturae* or phylogenetic scale. Note that the sequence of animals from left to right is completely arbitrary. A very different sequence would result from merely having some evolutionary lines branch to the left instead of the right. This would in no way alter the schematic representation of evolutionary lineages.

Several additional features of this phylogenetic tree should be noted. First, the evolutionary line of vertebrates leading to mammals, which begins in the Cambrian period, passes only through lobe-finned fishes (crossopterygians), amphibians, and reptiles. Second, the line of fishes which gave rise to amphibians evolved fairly early in fish evolution and followed a course of development quite separate from that of other fishes. The teleost fishes, so often used as a basis for evolutionary comparison with "higher vertebrates," are descendents of a line of development which is collateral to that giving rise to tetrapods. Therefore, no teleost fish ever was an ancestor of any amphibian, reptile, bird, or mammal. Likewise, birds represent another line of specialization from the reptiles and cannot be regarded as ancestral to mammals.

A similar situation exists in the phylo-

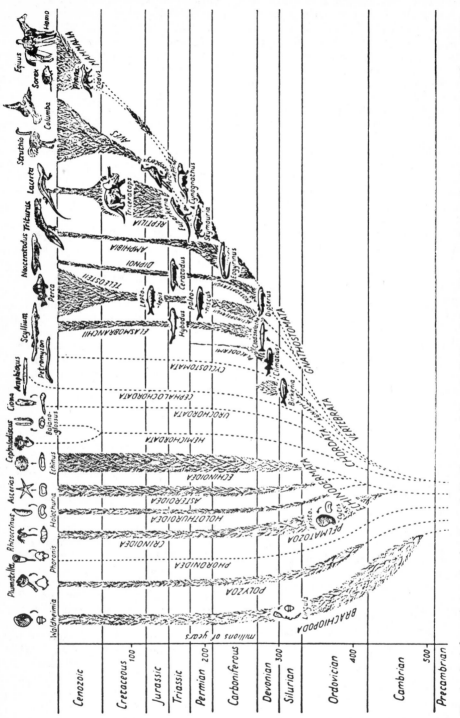

Fig. 1. A phylogenetic tree showing the probable times of origin and affinities of the vertebrates and some related groups of animals (Young, 1962).

genesis of mammals. As may be seen in Figure 2, which represents a phylogenetic tree of mammals (Young, 1962), primates evolved as a specialized branch of the insectivore line (i.e., shrews, moles, hedgehogs, etc.). Carnivores and rodents, which are frequently compared with primates, have followed independent courses of development from the primate line and from each other since the late Cretaceous or early Paleocene periods. Rats were never ancestral to cats nor were cats ancestral to primates; rather, each represents a different evolutionary lineage. Therefore, from the point of view of the phylogenesis of primate characteristics, the rat-cat-monkey comparison is meaningless.

Figure 3 represents a phylogenetic tree of primates (Young, 1962). The earliest primates, the prosimians, appear to have developed as a specialization of the line of the insectivores. The living prosimians (tarsiers, lorises, and lemurs) retain some insectivore characteristics (LeGros Clark, 1959). A comparison could therefore be made between living insectivores, prosimians, cercopithecid (Old World) monkeys, pongids (great apes), and hominids (men) which would give some clue to patterns of

evolution in the human lineage. Such a comparison was recently made by Diamond (1967) as an attempt to infer the course of evolution of neocortex in man.

Although primates are more closely related to each other than to other mammalian orders, there is still considerable variation and specialization within the primate order. Scott (1967) has recently warned that

Subhuman primates are not small human beings with fur coats and (sometimes) long tails. Rather, they are a group which has diversified in many ways, so that they are as different from each other as are bears, dogs and racoons in the order Carnivora. The fact that an animal is a primate therefore does not automatically mean that its behavior has special relevance to human behavior [p. 72].[4]

Evolutionary Inferences from the Study of Living Animals

Even though one may select animals for study that are descendants of a common evo-

[4] The term "subhuman" connotes relative position on the *scala naturae* or phylogenetic scale. A term more in keeping with the conceptual framework of the phylogenetic tree would be "nonhuman." Similar implications are carried in the term "subprimate" which should be replaced by "nonprimate" and "submammalian" which should be replaced by "nonmammalian."

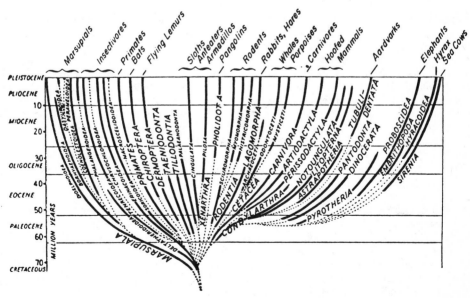

Fig. 2. A phylogenetic tree showing the probable times of origin and affinities of the orders of mammals (Young, 1962). (Common names have been added at the top.)

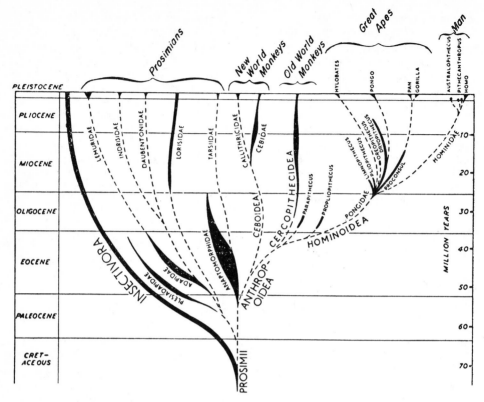

Fig. 3. A phylogenetic tree showing the probable times of origin and affinities of the primates (Young, 1962). (Common names have been added at the top.)

lutionary lineage, the question remains as to what can be learned about evolution, behavioral or otherwise, from the study of living animals. The rationale for such a study is based on the assumption that the living animals that have been selected are sufficiently similar to the ancestral forms that some inferences about the ancestral forms can be drawn. Our knowledge of ancestral vertebrates is based on fossilized skeletons. Soft tissues, including the central nervous system, do not usually fossilize; nor does behavior. Therefore, a living animal species which appears to be skeletally very similar to fossil ancestors, may in fact have undergone some change in its soft tissues or behavior. Thus, conclusions about evolution, even though they are based on the study of living animals selected because they are descendents of a continuous evolutionary lineage, do retain some degree of uncertainty. However, for the study of behavioral evolution, there are no alternatives. The behavior of ancestral organisms can only be

inferred from the behavior of living organisms which appear to be structurally similar and which inhabit similar environments. A method based on these assumptions has worked with reasonably good success in the study of morphological evolution and there seems to be good reason to believe that it will serve psychologists as well as it has served morphologists (Mayr, 1958; Simpson, 1958a).

Two general approaches can be used to collect data which are meaningful for the study of behavioral evolution. The first is the historical or "phylogenetic" approach similar to that used in comparative anatomy. In this instance, an attempt is made to infer changes in behavioral characteristics or patterns through time by comparing living animals which form a quasi-evolutionary series within a common lineage. An important consideration in such comparisons is the fact that the animals which have been chosen to represent ancestral groups are not the actual ancestors, but merely descendents of them. They are suitable for phylogenetic comparisons because they possess many characteristics which are primitive; that is, unchanged from ancestral forms (Simpson, 1961). The primitive behavior pattern of a group can often be inferred by comparing the behaviors of the living members of the group and looking for elements of the behavior pattern common to all. However, the greater the degree of diversity and specialization within a group, the greater the need for studying more variants. Furthermore, these elements should be sought in related groups and in living representatives of ancestral groups.

In using the "phylogenetic" method, the student of behavior has the same problems which face morphologists in the study of evolution. Some attempt must be made to determine which characteristics of the behavior are primitive, that is, derived from the behavior of the ancestors of the species, and which are specializations of the species studied. However, Simpson (1961) has cautioned that the concepts of primitive and specialized are meaningful only when related to a particular taxon, lineage, or phylogeny. Therefore, a behavioral characteristic which is found as a specialization in one animal group may be a primitive trait in another.[5]

In the case of living animals, the assumption is usually made that the more primitive characteristics a given species has, the more likely it is to resemble the ancestral form. However, the behaviorist has no behavioral fossil record to corroborate his decisions. He must decide on the basis of the properties of the behavior itself. Moreover, Klopfer and Hailman (1967), in their discussion of behavioral phylogenesis, conclude that

there is no good reason to assume that the most complex form has been evolved from the simpler one, since there are many cases of secondary simplification of morphological structures among animals. Also, one cannot infer direction of evolution from the relative abundance of variants; one cannot know a priori, whether the variation represents the end of an evolutionary process of adaptation (the commonest variant being the most advanced one) or merely the beginning (the commonest variant being the most primitive) [p. 187].

[5] See LeGros Clark (1959) and Simpson (1961) for a fuller discussion of the concepts of specialized and primitive.

A case in point is the study by Doty, Jones, and Doty (1967). These investigators compared learning set performance in four species of carnivores. They found that domestic cats (which rank with domestic dogs as the "standard" carnivores) acquired the learning set more slowly than did weasels, skunks, or ferrets. While these data are of considerable interest, there is, unfortunately, no way of concluding from the behavior itself whether the inferior learning set performance of the domestic cats represents a primitive state, comparable to that which presumably existed in ancestral carnivores or whether it represents a more recent secondary simplification of an older, more complex form of behavior.

One possible means of resolving this problem would seem to be to fall back on the assertion that behavior is subject to the same evolutionary principles as any other characteristic of the organism. As Nissen (1958) has argued

it seems just as logical and possible that an adaptive behavior should give selective value to a related structural character as that an adaptive anatomic feature should lend selective advantage to behavior which incorporates or exploits that structure [p. 186].

We might further assume that an animal which is morphologically primitive will be behaviorally primitive and one which has developed morphological specializations will have also developed appropriate behavioral specializations. This assumption seems justified in view of the strong emphasis which paleontologists have placed on the relations between form and function in survival (Colbert, 1958; Simpson, 1958b).

Attempts to set up quasi-evolutionary series of living animals for the purpose of determining trends in behavioral or nervous system evolution have usually been unsatisfactory because the animals chosen for the series were highly specialized species of widely divergent lineages. For example, von Békésy (1960) traced the course of evolution of the organ of Corti from bird to alligator to duckbill to man. Unfortunately, specific conclusions about the evolution of the organ of Corti are unjustified from this group of animals since birds are not ancestral to alligators or to mammals. Moreover, there are virtually no paleontological data on the monotremes, and their relationship to the other mammalian orders is obscure (Romer, 1966). Similarly, Bishop (1958), in a discussion of the evolution of the cerebral cortex, chose the brain of a snake to represent the reptile group from which mammals evolved. Snakes are among the most specialized of the living reptiles (Goin & Goin, 1962) and first appear in the fossil record in the Cretaceous period, 100 million years after the origin of the reptilian group which gave rise to the mammals (Romer, 1966).

Quasi-evolutionary series also often suffer from being too restrictive; that is, they attempt to represent all of vertebrate evolution with four or five species and sometimes even fewer. Bishop (1958), for example, based his evolutionary conclusions on three brains, one of which was the unlikely composite of a cat and a monkey.

Aside from the uncertainties inherent in using living animals to approximate actual evolutionary sequences and the necessity of choosing species which retain the most primitive traits, another problem arises. In some instances no living representatives of truly ancestral groups exist. Students of evolutionary patterns within the placental mammals, including the primates, however, are fortunate in that relatively unchanged direct descendants of the ancestral insectivores that gave rise to other placental mammals are living today. All of the living insectivores have diverged from ancestral insectivores to some degree, but the Erinaceidae (hedgehogs) are the most primitive and retain a relatively primitive eutherian status (Anderson & Jones, 1967). Study of this group of animals in some detail will probably be very profitable. Marsupials and placentals presumably had a common ancestry (Romer, 1966) and comparative studies of the primitive members of these two groups might allow some inferences to be made about the earliest mammals. Although monotremes were probably never ancestral to marsupials or placentals (Romer, 1966), they do retain many more reptilian characteristics than do the latter groups of mammals. The study of monotremes may therefore provide some insight into the behavioral characteristics of the therapsid reptiles from which all mammals evolved.

Comparative studies of behavioral or neural evolution of fishes have a particular advantage in that there are over 25,000 species of living fishes (Herald, 1961), a number of which closely resemble ancestral forms. Furthermore, fishes have undergone a considerable degree of evolution and occupy a great variety of ecological niches. In contrast, the living amphibians are relatively poor in number of species and diversity of terrain occupied and are generally regarded as a decadent class containing many relict groups (Darlington, 1957; Goin & Goin, 1962).

The crocodilians are living descendents of the archosaurian reptiles which also gave rise to birds (Romer, 1966) and appear to have remained relatively unchanged. Although the avian and crocodilian lineages are divergent, comparisons of the behavior and central nervous systems of these groups might be useful in view of their common archosaurian heritage.

There are unfortunately no surviving representatives of the reptile groups which gave rise to the mammals. These therapsid reptiles disappeared from the fossil record in the Jurassic period and since their lineage branched off from the stem reptiles very early, none of the living reptiles can be considered to be very closely related to mammals. Although turtles seem to be relatively unchanged since the Triassic period, they are highly specialized. *Sphenodon,* a surviving rhynchocephalian, also seems to be little changed since the Mesozoic, and the crocodilians mentioned previously are only slightly modified following their origin from thecodonts in the Triassic period (Romer, 1966). Comparative studies on the more primitive reptiles might allow some inferences about the behavioral repertoire of the ancestral reptiles from which the mammalian lineage is also derived. However, this would be a "weak inference" in the terminology of Klopfer and Hailman (1967) since it would rest on the assumption that the most frequently observed characteristics are primitive.

In his discussion of the evolution of intelligence, Bitterman (1965a, 1965b) compares the performance of teleost fish, turtles, pigeons, rats, and monkeys on probability and discrimination reversal learning tasks and characterizes their performance as "fishlike" or "ratlike." However, these comparisons do not permit generalizations to be made about the evolution of intelligence or any other characteristic of these organisms since they are not representative of a common evolutionary lineage. Figure 4 is a diagrammatic representation of two vertebrate phylogenetic trees. The left tree shows the approximate evolutionary relationships among the various animals studied by Bitterman in the visual reversal problem and the right tree shows the evolutionary relationships among the animals in the visual probability problem. The squares indicate the animals whose behavior was characterized by Bitterman as "ratlike" and the triangles indicate the animals whose behavior was characterized as "fishlike." Assuming for the moment that these animals are sufficiently similar to ancestral forms that some specific evolutionary generalizations could be made from them, one might conclude that the "ratlike" pattern in visual probability learning is limited to mammals. However, since no rat was ever an ancestor of any monkey, it is not clear whether the rat and monkey independently evolved the "ratlike" pattern or whether it was inherited from a common reptilian ancestor. The absence of this pattern in turtles would not support either possibility since turtles are so far from the line (or lines) of reptiles that were ancestral to mammals. In the case of the visual reversal learning data, the "ratlike" performance pattern is present in pigeons, rats, and monkeys, but absent in turtles. Again, no firm conclusions can be drawn. On the one hand, the assumption might be made that the "ratlike" pattern evolved independently in birds and mammals, since turtles, which share a remote common ancestry with birds and mammals in the stem reptiles (Romer, 1966), possess the presumably primitive "fishlike" pattern. On the other hand, the absence of the "ratlike" pattern in turtles may represent a secondary simplification of behavior. Still a third possibility must be considered in the analysis of Bitterman's data; that is, whether the "fishlike" pattern is a primitive characteristic at all. In the absence of data on the distribution of the "fishlike" pattern in am-

phibians and nonteleost fish, it is not possible to determine whether this pattern was independently acquired by teleosts and turtles or inherited from a common ancestor.

Similar problems attend Harlow's (1959) interpretation of evolutionary trends in learning set performance in primates. Harlow compares data from New World monkeys, Old World monkeys, chimpanzees, and humans. Old World monkeys and chimpanzees, although specialized in their own ways, are reasonable enough representatives of human ancestors (Romer, 1966) that meaningful conclusions about the phylogenesis of man's behavior may be drawn. However, the New World monkeys appear to have evolved from New World prosimians which are not closely related to the Old World prosimians from which are derived Old World monkeys, apes, and men. Consequently, New World monkeys should not be used as representatives of man's ancestors (Campbell, 1966; Romer, 1966). A more appropriate representative would have been one or more species of the Old World prosimians.

The comparative studies of Bitterman, Harlow, and others discussed in this paper have been selected to illustrate some of the complexities involved in the interpretation of evolutionary relationships, not as a critique of their research. Unless comparative psychologists are prepared to deal with the details and intricacies of the evolutionary history of vertebrates, meaningful descriptive statements or theoretical formulations of specific behavioral phylogenies will not be forthcoming.

ANALYSIS OF ADAPTATION

A second and equally important approach to the study of behavioral evolution is through the analysis of adaptation. This method is based on the study of living animals, selected because they possess differing degrees of specialization (adaptation) with respect to some particular characteristic such as development of sense organs or central nervous system, the amount of postnatal care given to offspring, complexity of courtship patterns, etc. Such animals need not be descendants of a common evolutionary lineage and consequently any conclusions drawn

17

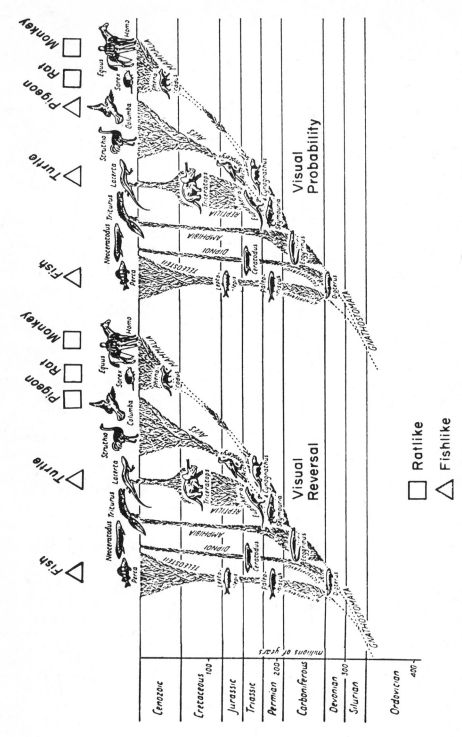

Fig. 4. Data from the table presented by Bitterman (1965a) plotted on segments of the phylogenetic tree shown in Figure 1 to indicate their relationship to approximate lineages. (The characterization of the behavior as "ratlike" or "fishlike" is Bitterman's notation.)

from such comparisons will be applicable only to general principles of adaptation and survival. They will give no direct clues to specific sequential patterns of evolutionary development in specific lineages. For example, Weiskrantz's (1961) description of the differential effect of lesions in the visual system in frogs, birds, rats, cats, dogs, monkeys, and man does not provide us with a picture of the sequential evolutionary history of the visual system and its function in the line of vertebrates leading to man; however, it is very useful in understanding the general relationship between the development of certain structural adaptations and their function in behavior. The same may be said of Woolsey's (1958) comparative studies of the sensory-motor cortex in rat, rabbit, cat, and monkey. They are extremely useful in relating structure and function, but are of no value in describing the sequence of evolutionary development in this system since each of these animals reached its respective degree of cortical development quite independently of any of the others.

Commenting on problems of the analysis of morphological evolution, Davis (1954) observed that most studies of comparative anatomy were concerned with determining the particular course of evolution rather than the reasons that one course was followed and not another. In his view, comparative studies should also be aimed at the mechanisms of adaptation. Similarly in comparative psychology, the study of analogous behavior in animals of divergent groups may be very useful in formulating generalizations about behavioral adaptation to specific problems of survival. Such generalizations might have broad applicability to a number of lineages of the phylogenetic tree and would greatly aid in the interpretation of data obtained through the phylogenetic approach.

Thus, the phylogenetic and adaptation approaches are not mutually exclusive. Data obtained through one approach can be used to augment conclusions based on the other. However, the experimenter must be clear as to which method of comparison he is using if he is to avoid the interpretive pitfalls described above.

CRITIQUE OF THE PHYLOGENETIC MODEL

King and Nichols (1960) object to the use of a phylogenetic model as a basis for the study of comparative psychology for three reasons: First, one apparently cannot predict behavior from one phylogenetic level to another. Second, the experimenter is required to make inferences about the behavior of extinct forms. Third, some taxonomic groups are differentiated only by characteristics which appear to be relatively unrelated to behavior. They suggest instead that comparative psychology develop its own system of classification based on behavior. However, such a classification would simply be a behavioral hierarchy and since it would not necessarily be related to evolutionary lineages, it would be nearly useless in understanding the evolution of behavior. Unless comparisons are made between organisms of a common evolutionary lineage, the relationship between the evolution of structure and the evolution of behavior will never become discernible. The apparent failure of the zoological model of evolution to lead to meaningful predictions of relative behavioral performance has been due to the fact that many comparative psychologists, neuroanatomists, physiologists, etc., have applied the inappropriate phylogenetic scale model rather than the appropriate phylogenetic tree model. Furthermore, they have generally failed to recognize the important taxonomic principle that there are diverse sources of similarity (both morphological and behavioral) among various organisms. Only one of these sources is inheritance from common ancestors and is usually referred to as "homology." On the other hand, similarities may also be due to the independent evolution of similar characteristics by more or less closely related forms. This similarity, not due to inheritance from a common ancestor, is referred to as "homoplasy." Homoplasy is a generic term which includes such forms of similarity as parallelism, convergence, analogy, mimicry, etc.[6] When nonhomologous characters serve similar *functions,* whether or not they are similar in appearance, they are referred to as "analogous." Thus, the hands of a racoon and a man are homologous as anterior pentadactyl appendages and homoplastic in their particular appearance as hands. They are not homologous as hands since they were evolved independently of each other. Finally, they are analogous in their functions as prehensile organs.

[6] For a more extensive discussion of homoplasy and homology, see Simpson (1961).

19

There would then seem to be little point in looking for parallels between a hierarchy of behavioral complexity and the phylogenetic tree unless the behaviors were homologous. Behaviors that are convergent or analogous may provide insights into general mechanisms of survival and adaptation, but will not shed any light on the specific behavioral history of any particular group of organisms.

Another deterrent to theoretical development in comparative psychology has been the typological approach to behavior. As Mayr (1968) has described it, "When the learning psychologist speaks of The Rat or The Monkey, or the racist speaks of The Negro, this is typological thinking [p. 597]." The typological approach carries with it the implication that the particular species being investigated is a generalized representative of the entire order or class when in fact that species may be highly specialized and not at all representative. Simpson (1958a, 1958b) has also discussed this point. Bitterman (1965a, 1965b) has regrettably used typological designations of "ratlike" and "fishlike" as a shorthand characterization of the behavior of the teleosts, reptiles, birds, and mammals which he has studied in probability learning and reversal learning problems. Unfortunately, this typology implies that the "fishlike" behavior of the particular fishes which Bitterman studied is representative of most fishes or possibly all fishes. Considering the diversity of specialization in teleost fishes, one would not be surprised to find several or even many species which had evolved the capacity for behavior analogous to that which Bitterman has called "ratlike."

CONCLUSIONS

Beach (1950) has suggested that any experiments in which a nonhuman species is compared with another nonhuman species or with humans should be considered as being within the realm of comparative psychology. His main point is that the term comparative psychology should be reserved for experiments in which organisms of different species are *compared*. We would like to expand this definition by further suggesting that any experiments carried out with nonhuman subjects, in which no attempt is made to compare these subjects to other species of animals or humans, be regarded as simply animal psychology. In other words, the term comparative psychology should be reserved for experiments in which interspecies comparisons are made.

Schneirla (1949) has stated that

The general problem of the animal psychologist is the nature of behavioral capacities on all levels of accomplishment. He must contrive to understand how each animal type functions as a whole in meeting its surrounding conditions: what its capacities are like and how they are organized . . . [p. 245].

This would seem to be a reasonable goal for animal and comparative psychologists alike. The difference between the two would be the emphasis of the latter on the similarities and differences between various taxonomic groups of organisms. However, Ratner and Denny (1964) warn that "capricious comparisons" will add little to our understanding of systematic differences and similarities among species. This is not to say that questions such as "Do pigeons acquire learning sets faster than rats?" are without meaning if there is a specific reason for comparing those particular organisms and the suggestion is not made that the outcomes of the comparisons necessarily imply anything about the evolution of these behaviors. However, our opinion is that if comparative psychology is ever to develop a theoretical model capable of predicting behavior, experimenters will have to specify their independent variable more precisely than "species difference." Similarly, an experimenter who reports differences in visual acuity in several species that have varying degrees of differentiation of the visual cortex might be criticized on the grounds that these animals also vary in the near point of accommodation which could be a confounding variable. This example illustrates the point that comparative psychologists have the same problems as other experimenters in determining that their chosen independent variable is indeed the only relevant variable operating.

What then can we hope for as attainable goals for comparative psychology? First, as Schneirla (1949) has suggested, would be a description of the behavioral capacities of organisms throughout the animal kingdom. A second would be the search for systematic trends in behavior which hopefully would vary reliably with other taxonomic indexes, since form and function in nature are inextricably interrelated. A third would be an attempt to reconstruct the historical development of behavior as best as can be done from the data of paleontology and the study of living organisms which resemble, as closely as possible, ancestral forms of particular evolutionary lines. A fourth goal would be the analysis of the general mechanisms of adaptation and survival. These goals can best be attained by ridding ourselves of concepts like the phylogenetic scale, higher and lower animals, nonrepresentative behavioral typologies, and other notions which have had the effect of oversimplifying an extremely complex field of research.

REFERENCES

ANDERSON, S., & JONES, J. K. *Recent mammals of the world.* New York: Ronald, 1967.

ARIËNS KAPPERS, C. U., HUBER, G. C., & CROSBY, E. C. *The comparative anatomy of the nervous system of vertebrates, including man.* New York: Hafner, 1936. (Republished: 1960.)

ARISTOTLE. *Historia animalium.* (Trans. by D. W. Thompson) Oxford: Clarendon, 1910.

ARISTOTLE. *De partibus animalium.* (Trans. by W. Ogle) Oxford: Clarendon, 1912. (a)

ARISTOTLE. *De generatione animalium.* (Trans. by A. Platt) Oxford: Clarendon, 1912. (b)

BEACH, F. A. The snark was a boojum. *American Psychologist,* 1950, 5, 115–124.

BISHOP, G. H. The place of cortex in a reticular system. In H. H. Jasper et al. (Eds.), *Reticular formation of the brain.* Boston: Little, Brown, 1958.

BITTERMAN, M. E. The evolution of intelligence. *Scientific American,* 1965, 212, 92–100. (a)

BITTERMAN, M. E. Phyletic differences in learning. *American Psychologist,* 1965, 20, 396–410. (b)

CAMPBELL, B. G. *Human evolution.* Chicago: Aldine, 1966.

COLBERT, E. H. Morphology and behavior. In A. Roe & G. G. Simpson (Eds.), *Behavior and evolution.* New Haven: Yale University Press, 1958.

DARLINGTON, P. J. *Zoogeography: The geographical distribution of animals.* New York: Wiley, 1957.

DAVIS, D. D. Primate evolution from the viewpoint of comparative anatomy. *Human Biology,* 1954, 26, 211–219.

DIAMOND, I. T. The sensory neocortex. In W. D. Neff (Ed.), *Contributions to sensory physiology.* Vol. 2. New York: Academic Press, 1967.

DOTY, B. A., JONES, C. N., & DOTY, L. A. Learning set formation by mink, ferrets, skunks and cats. *Science,* 1967, 155, 1579–1580.

GOIN, C. J., & GOIN, O. B. *Introduction to herpetology.* San Francisco: Freeman, 1962.

HARLOW, H. F. The evolution of learning. In A. Roe & G. G. Simpson (Eds.), *Behavior and evolution.* New Haven: Yale University Press, 1958.

HARLOW, H. F. Learning set and error factor theory. In S. Koch (Ed.), *Psychology: A study of a science.* Vol. 2. New Haven: Yale University Press, 1959.

HERALD, E. S. *Living fishes of the world.* New York: Doubleday, 1961.

KING, J. H., & NICHOLS, J. W. Problems of classification. In R. H. Waters, D. A. Rethlingshafter, & W. E. Caldwell (Eds.), *Principles of comparative psychology.* New York: McGraw-Hill, 1960.

KLOPFER, P. H., & HAILMAN, J. P. *An introduction to animal behavior: Ethology's first century.* Englewood Cliffs, N. J.: Prentice-Hall, 1967

LeGROS CLARK, W. E. *The antecedents of man.* Edinburgh: Edinburgh University Press, 1959.

LOVEJOY, A. O. *The great chain of being.* Cambridge: Harvard University Press, 1936.

MAYR, E. Behavior and systematics. In A. Roe & G. G. Simpson (Eds.), *Behavior and evolution.* New Haven: Yale University Press, 1958.

MAYR, E. The role of systematics in biology. *Science,* 1968, 159, 595–599.

McGILL, T. E. Response of the leopard frog to electric shock in an escape-learning situation. *Journal of Comparative and Physiological Psychology,* 1960, 53, 443–445.

NISSEN, H. W. Axes of behavioral comparison. In A. Roe & G. G. Simpson (Eds.), *Behavior and evolution.* New Haven: Yale University Press, 1958.

RATNER, S. C., & DENNY, M. R. *Comparative psychology.* Homewood, Ill.: Dorsey, 1964.

ROE, A., & SIMPSON, G. G. (Eds.). *Behavior and evolution.* New Haven: Yale University Press, 1958.

ROMER, A. S. *Vertebrate paleontology.* Chicago: University of Chicago Press, 1966.

ROSS, W. D. *Aristotle.* London: Methuen, 1949.

SCHNEIRLA, T. C. Levels in the psychological capacities of animals. In R. W. Sellars, V. H. McGill, & M. Farber (Eds.), *Philosophy for the future.* New York: Macmillan, 1949.

SCOTT, J. P. Comparative psychology and ethology. *Annual Review of Psychology,* 1967, 18, 65–86.

SIMPSON, G. G. The study of evolution: Methods and present status of theory. In A. Roe & G. G. Simpson (Eds.), *Behavior and evolution.* New Haven: Yale University Press, 1958. (a)

SIMPSON, G. G. Behavior and evolution. In A. Roe & G. G. Simpson (Eds.), *Behavior and evolution.* New Haven: Yale University Press, 1958. (b)

SIMPSON, G. G. *Principles of animal taxonomy.* New York: Columbia University Press, 1961.

VAN BERGEIJK, W. Anticipatory feeding behavior in the bullfrog (*Rana catesbeiana*). *Animal Behaviour,* 1967, 15, 231–238.

VON BÉKÉSY, G. Experimental models of the cochlea with and without nerve supply. In

G. L. Rasmussen & W. F. Windle (Eds.), *Neural mechanisms of the auditory and vestibular systems.* Springfield, Ill.: Charles C Thomas, 1960.

WATERS, R. H. The nature of comparative psychology. In R. H. Waters, D. A. Rethlingshafter, & W. E. Caldwell (Eds.), *Principles of comparative psychology.* New York: McGraw-Hill, 1960.

WEISKRANTZ, L. Encephalization and the scotoma. In W. H. Thorpe & O. L. Zangwill (Eds.), *Current problems in animal behaviour.* Cambridge: Cambridge University Press, 1961.

WIGHTMAN, W. P. D. *The growth of scientific ideas.* Edinburgh: Oliver & Boyd, 1950.

WOOLSEY, C. N. Organization of somatic sensory and motor areas of the cerebral cortex. In H. F. Harlow & C. N. Woolsey (Eds.), *Biological and biochemical bases of behavior.* Madison: University of Wisconsin Press, 1958.

YOUNG, J. Z. *The life of vertebrates.* Oxford: Oxford University Press, 1962.

(Received July 12, 1968)

Reprinted from AMERICAN PSYCHOLOGIST, Vol. 26, No. 2, February 1971
Printed in U. S. A.

REFLECTIONS ON THE FALL OF COMPARATIVE PSYCHOLOGY:
IS THERE A MESSAGE FOR US ALL? [1]

ROBERT B. LOCKARD [2]

University of Washington

WHAT we once knew as comparative psychology has been overrun by a scientific revolution. In the wake of that revolution lies the debris of what was once a traditional branch of psychology, now a confused scatter of views of nature, problems, and methods. The confusion persists for the same reason the revolution occurred; psychologists understood one view of behavior, but not another, and it was the other that won out. The gulf between these two grand views

[1] The preparation of this article was made possible by a fellowship from the National Institutes of Health which enabled the author to spend a sabbatical year with the Department of Zoology at the University of California at Davis.

[2] Requests for reprints should be sent to Robert B. Lockard, Department of Psychology, University of Washington, Seattle, Washington 98105.

was so wide that most psychologists misunderstood what was happening at the time and remain dazed by it all, unable to say where we are now, what the best modern synthesis is, and where the frontiers are. We could simply accept the demise of comparative psychology without understanding it, much as one accepts the death of an old friend without inquiry into the pathological details, were it irrelevant to the whole of psychology. The relevance, however, is clearly there. It is direct and unambiguous for any branch of psychology that uses animals or connects with animal research as a scientific substratum. It is suggestive and thought provoking for the other areas of psychology that aspire to be more than a collection of empirical findings—to be based on a natural science of behavior with durable foundations. But the relevance is not easily extracted as a few principles ringing with self-evident truth; rather, it unfolds slowly as one examines the rise and fall of comparative psychology, how its premises and traditions crumbled, and why a vigorous scientific movement of separate origin has so many implications for psychology.

Development of Comparative Psychology

Charles Darwin was the father of comparative psychology. It was not the *Origin of Species* (Darwin, 1859) which launched it; this was a highly technical work about a theory of species diversity. It was not about behavior and not about man, and it had little effect on people with those interests. It was Darwin's later work, *The Descent of Man* (Darwin, 1871), which launched comparative psychology and determined its future as well. Until Darwin, animals had been separate, special creations, and man even more separate and more special. Darwin made animals relevant to man by arguing that the animal mind and the human mind are quite similar, differing only in degree. His central argument was that man had evolved from animals, was related to them, and that the animal mind and the human mind were merely points on a continuum, differing quantitatively but not qualitatively. Darwin (1871) wrote, "My object in this chapter is to shew that there is no fundamental difference between man and the higher animals in their mental faculties [p. 99]." This was the hypothesis of mental continuity. It was novel; it was staggering; and it was discussed at great length. Darwin argued that animals, if carefully examined, show intelligence, problem-solving abilities, and other mental traits to a degree just below that of humans. He came very close to naming the exact research topics later pursued by comparative psychology. He discussed insight into mechanical problems requiring unusual behavior to attain the goal (1871, p. 111), associations of the mind (p. 112) and the capacity for progressive improvement in tasks (p. 122), the intelligence of "the common rat" (pp. 122–123), animal insight and uniting former images and ideas to create brilliant and novel results (p. 113), solving the problem of obtaining objects out of reach beyond the bars of the cage (p. 116), and monkeys using sticks to solve problems connected with boxes (p. 123). He even discussed two cases of aversive conditioning: that of a fish, where the painful consequences of a response came to prevent its repetition "so strongly was the idea of a violent shock associated in his feeble mind with the attempt [p. 115]," and "with monkeys, as we shall presently see, a painful or

merely a disagreeable impression, from an action once performed, is sometimes sufficient to prevent the animal from repeating it [p. 115]." Darwin even mentioned concept formation (p. 126).

Darwin provided both the hypothesis of mental continuity and the specific kinds of near-experiments needed. Romanes (1881, 1883, 1887), a friend and supporter of Darwin, pursued the same direction and topics. As Waters (1942) wrote in Moss's *Comparative Psychology*, "The most characteristic aspect of the period immediately following Darwin, however, was probably the vigorous search for and claim to have found higher mental traits in animals [pp. 20–21]." Clearly, the period from Darwin to around 1900 was so; and the next two decades or so were characterized by Boring (1950, p. 629) as efforts to find the "missing link" between the mind of man and common mammals, for the hypothesis of mental continuity needed support, and one of the great issues was whether or not animals could retain mental images. This was the era of maze learning, obstruction boxes, the delayed response, multiple-choice methods, and the temporal maze. As late as 1936, a new edition of Washburn's exploration of the nature of animal consciousness, *The Animal Mind,* was published; and Katz (1937), in *Animals and Men: Studies on Comparative Psychology*, wrote, "Psychology may be defined in various ways, but no definition can be satisfactory which does not include its connections with the phenomena of consciousness [p. 25]."

Watsonian behaviorism eventually had influences that exterminated the anecdotal method, abolished the animal mind and consciousness, took instinct out of the realm of the credible, and brought in a mixture of rigor and dogmatic environmentalism. New elements did enter; one was the topic of motivation, which was intellectually tied to learning and which showed up in comparative psychology as food deprivation, running-wheel activity, and fluid preferences. Another new element was physiological psychology, whose history traces to the dissecting-table tradition of Cuvier, who was a believer in the fixity of species and whose dogmatic school was thoroughly opposed to Darwin. The Cuvier tradition was compatible with behaviorism, with S-R theory, and the telephone-switchboard theories of behavior; it sought explanations in pathways and connections, in structures and proximal causes. It was a fragment of biology—being only anatomy and physiology, lacking the dynamic processes of biology: adaptation, natural selection, ecological significance, and evolution. Its close union with comparative psychology allowed the attitude that the field was very biological at a time when biology had already shifted its thinking from morphological statics to the dynamic processes (cf. Jaynes, 1969).

What is significant to abstract from this hasty sketch is that on the surface there seemed to be steady progress in rigor, methods, and so on; but underneath, the traditional topics remained the same—animal intelligence, associations of the mind, improvement in tasks, detour problems, and the other issues concerned with learning and mental continuity. The whole enterprise of comparative psychology worked itself into an extremely narrow position, scientifically speaking, by ignoring all but a tiny fraction of the behavior of animals and incorporating an elaborate set of premises about animal behavior into a dogmatic tradition.

If we as experimental psychologists are missing an opportunity to make significant contributions to natural science—if we are failing to assume leadership in an area of behavior investigation where we might be useful and effective—if these things are true, and I believe that they are, then we have no one but ourselves to blame [Beach, 1950, p. 124].

Some of the premises that would have been widely accepted in the 1950s are as follows.

1. There is a phylogenetic scale, a sort of linear arrangement from simple to complex, from unintelligent to intelligent, from amoeba to man.

2. Convenient animals such as chickens, rats, cats, dogs, and monkeys can be arranged in order along the scale.

3. The comparative method is essentially a scaling problem of arranging animals of differing degrees of intelligence on the phylogenetic scale.

4. Because of the scale, animals lower in the scale are increasingly simpler but not different in kind. A white rat is a simple version of a human.

5. Learning is the key to animal behavior because most behavior is acquired. Hunger, thirst, sex, respiration, and a thing or two more may be built in as initial tendencies, but these few things are merely the unconditioned responses on which behavior is built.

6. Because so little is built into animals, genetics and evolution are irrelevant to psychology.

7. Most animals are pretty much alike. Species differences are few and are probably accounted for by sensory differences and different experiences.

8. There are laws of behavior that are best formulated within the framework, "Such-and-such a treatment has such-and-such an effect."

9. Animal behavior can be studied best in the laboratory because of the controlled conditions. Laboratory conditions simplify behavior.

10. The best variables to study the effects of are physical variables.

These are interesting premises; they form a coherent view of the natural world, a framework within which to do research and relate it to human beings. While these assumptions functioned within psychology mainly as beliefs beyond disconfirmation, it was not so in other branches of science; other sets of presumptions were formed, and by following these out we can arrive at a new perspective from which to view the above list of premises.

Behavioral Biology

The other view of behavior—the one that won out over comparative psychology—is widely misunderstood as consisting of ethology and as having a short history and a shaky foundation. These misconceptions vanish when one sees that modern behavioral biology is an outgrowth of the whole revolution in biology which traces to Darwin's (1859) *Origin of Species*. Darwin has been called "the Newton of biology." "He rendered evolution inescapable as a fact, comprehensible as a process, all-embracing as a concept [Huxley, 1960, pp. 1–2]." From Malthus, Darwin knew that animals reproduce in greater numbers than would sustain a constant population. Since populations are largely constant, a large proportion of the offspring must fail to survive to maturity. Since animals are demonstrably in competition for the resources of the environment, there will be an active "struggle for existence." Darwin was well aware of the variation within animal populations, and rightly believed these variations to be inherited while freely stating that "The laws governing inheritance are for the most part unknown [Darwin, 1859, p. 36]." In a variable population, the ontogenetic elimination of some individuals and the successful survival of others must be related to how the different individuals fit the environment. The sum of all factors responsible for survival in a given environment is embodied in the phrase "favorable variations." These, being heritable, are passed on to the next generation, where the process is repeated. The preservation of favorable variations by reproduction and the elimination of unfavorable variations Darwin called "natural selection." He thus showed that a natural, inevitable, comprehensible process brought about evolution by the gradual accumulation of favorable characters, slowly changing the characteristics of a population toward superior adaptation. More modern phraseology would sum up the short-term process of natural selection as differential reproduction of variants, and the longer-term process as selection pressure with respect to a character. The theory of natural selection doomed the doctrine of the fixity and special creation of separate species, showed that the seemingly mysterious order inherent in the taxonomy of Linnaeus actually had its basis in relationships, made the fossil record interpretable, and rendered understandable the success of plant and animal breeders as a special case of selection.

Especially in Germany, zoologists developed to precision what became known as the comparative method and made great advances in comparative morphology and comparative embryology. Paleontology and systematics flourished. About 1900, Mendel was rediscovered, modern genetics was launched, and soon the only missing element of Darwin's great synthesis—the mechanism of inheritance—had a well-understood factual basis. Population genetics developed in the 1930s and combined with the up-dated theoretical structure then called "neo-Darwinism" to produce a powerful quantitative synthesis. A true milestone was reached in R. A. Fisher's (1930) *The Genetical Theory of Natural Selection.* Meanwhile, ecology was coming of age, and the barriers between what had been separate disciplines began to drop; the morphologist, working with preserved museum specimens, could not understand properly various anatomical features, some of them strikingly bizarre, without a knowledge of the ecology of the animal, and therefore the selection pressures responsible for the adaptation. What became known as "the modern synthesis" was in the making. It was signaled by Dobzhansky's *Genetics and the Origin of Species* in 1937; then Mayr's *Systematics and the Origin of Species* was published in 1942; and Huxley's *Evolution: The Modern Synthesis* appeared in 1942.

What is so enormously important about these developments is that an interlocking, a modern synthesis, of diverse areas of scientific knowledge had developed. The formerly separate areas of biology began to unify into an understandable whole, and at the heart of the synthesis was evolution. It showed the reality basis for taxonomy. It explained the marvelously precise adaptations animals have to their environments. It explained the fossil record. It explained zoo-geography. It gave a basis for understanding ecological complexities in plant and animal communities. And on and on; the list of accomplishments is very, very long. But —and this is an important but—behavior was largely left out of the modern synthesis. One reason was that, in 1940, behavior belonged to psychology. Another reason was that the modern synthesis applied only when a character had a heritable basis. The climate of opinion at the time was that behavior was the product of experience, not natural selection, and was therefore somehow outside the realm of the modern synthesis.

But this was the mainstream of thought, the popular opinion; behind the scenes were the beginnings of the advances that were to grow to prominence in time. Darwin (1871) provided the first cues in his statement that "the greater number of the more complex instincts appear to have been gained . . . through the natural selection of variations of simpler instinctive actions [p. 102]." The next clear anticipation of the modern view was by the American zoologist Whitman, who wrote in 1898 that "instincts and organs are to be studied from the common viewpoint of phyletic descent [p. 328]." Heinroth (1910) and Craig (1912) were important pioneers. But a true movement actually began with the publications of Lorenz (1931, 1932, 1935, 1937, 1941, 1950, 1957, 1965) and Tinbergen (1936, 1937). Details of the development are given in Beer (1963, 1964). For roughly a decade after the publication of the first book in the field (Tinbergen, 1951), the word "ethology" was used and connoted a European movement within zoology concerned with objective and biological approaches to the study of animal behavior, often instinctive behavior in relation to important aspects of the habitat. What is sometimes not appreciated is how much the field has expanded and changed in character in the last decade. In the United States, it linked up with genetics and ecology, and with developmental biology and physiological ecology here and elsewhere. Ethology has come close to losing its name; it is sometimes now called "the biology of behavior" because its intellectual foundations are as broad as biology itself. Today the field is routinely treated in textbooks of ecology (e.g., Smith, 1966), is part of the academic curriculum of most departments of zoology, and plays important roles in many branches of biology, even systematics: "In modern taxonomic publications we find more and more references to characters which are not purely morphological, such as ecological requirements, migratory status, pairing habits . . . and so on [Mayr, 1963, p. 20]."

Scientifically speaking, only two pieces of information were needed to bring behavior into the modern synthesis of the new biology: the fact that behavior has a genetic basis, thus making it heritable and therefore subject to natural selection; and the fact that behavior, or rather, particular behaviors, are adaptive—that they bear intimate relationships to particulars of the environment such that some kind of advantage results. The genetic basis of hundreds and hundreds of particular behaviors has been demonstrated beyond doubt, and the adaptive significance of particular behaviors has been demonstrated in hundreds of cases.

Against this background, a view of animal behavior totally different from the view of comparative psychology has developed. An animal has a plurality of behaviors—lots of separate behaviors. Each of these behaviors has a history of natural selection and some sort of genetic basis—sometimes simple, sometimes complex—as far as we know, about the same story as the genetic basis of morphological characters. Generation after generation, natural selection works on the phenotypic expression of these behaviors, preserving by reproduction those that are adaptive and eliminating those that are maladaptive. The statistical properties of the gene pool change gradually with time, the behaviors change toward highly efficient and detailed functions, and the net result at some point in time —like the present—is that any animal species alive today has evolved some considerable number of particular behaviors, each one highly adapted to specific features of its habitat. Pick any animal species at random, study its behavior in its normal habitat throughout its life cycle, and you will discover an intricate set of behaviors, many of them of almost incredible matching relationships to demands of the environment, like a lock and key. Study further and you will find that the social organization of the species has a genetic basis and is an evolved adaptation to particulars of the environment. You may also find that natural selection has produced special learning abilities such that some ecologically relevant task is learned at a much faster rate than an arbitrary task, or natural stimuli are much more effective than artificial stimuli. Julian Huxley summed up this view when he said "animals are bundles of adaptations." Ledyard Stebbins added that they are bundles of coadapted, interlocking adaptations (see Lorenz, 1965).

Since each animal species evolved unique and separate adaptations to its own niche, and each niche is unique, it would at first seem that a science of behavior could not proceed beyond catalogs describing all the independent behaviors of all species. Generalizations about seemingly valid categories of behavior such as parental care or hoarding or social organization are unlikely to prove fruitful because each kind of behavior evolved independently a number of times. Thus, what we may perceive as a meaningful and natural category is actually a mere collection of unlike phenomena, unlike because they work in different ways at the basic levels while appearing similar superficially. For example, the wings of arthropods, pterosaurs, birds, bats, and flying fish evolved independently and now show a variety of embryological origins and morphological structures. It has not been scientifically advantageous, nor is it now defensible, to group together "flying animals," and it now seems equally inappropriate to group together behaviors that seem similar or to assume that the same basic process underlies the various behaviors that might be so grouped. Although there is a great deal of truth in this principle which might be called "the principle of independent evolution of behaviors," it is still the case that the one great theoretical principle that unites all of behavior is evolution; and from this come two very important principles modifying the above one.

The first is the principle of phylogenetic relatedness: Behavioral homologies increase in frequency and detail among different animal species as proximity to a common ancestral species increases. Since evolution proceeds by small modifications, species with a common ancestor have many similar behaviors because they were derived from a common set of behaviors. As time goes on and each species becomes increasingly adapted to its peculiar habitat and more remotely related to each other, the proportion of uniquely evolved behaviors will increase over the proportion forming the common core, eventually predominating. Thus, one finds many homologous (truly similar because of common ancestry) behaviors among the species in a genus, detectable trends and similarities among the genera in a family, and a few similarities among the families of an order. However, at about the level of orders, the common ancestry is so remote that generalizations become few and often weak. For example, few general statements hold for all the orders of mammals.

The principle of phylogenetic relatedness is the basis of the comparative method, discussed by Tinbergen (1959, 1960), Lorenz (1950, 1957), Hinde and Tinbergen (1958), and Morris (1957). The two key assumptions are that similarities between related forms are the result of phyletic closeness, while differences between related forms are the result of specialized adaptations to their differing modes of existence. Thus, the anatomical similarities of the anthropoid apes are due to common ancestry; but the very different feeding habits, social behaviors, and the like are divergent adaptations to their ecological specializations. The gibbons, for example, diverged in the direction of the upper-canopy monkeys; the gorilla, toward a terrestrial browser; and hominids, toward socially cooperative carnivores.

The second important principle emerging from modern work is the principle of ecological convergence: Similar behaviors among unrelated forms result from similar selection pressures. This principle is the basis for what might be called the ecological method, discussed or informatively used by Brown (1964), Crook (1964), Ford (1960), Hamilton (1964), Hinde (1956), MacArthur and

Pianka (1966), Orians (1961, 1962), Lack (1968), and Smith (1968). The emphasis here is on attaining understanding and generalizations about the ecological factors that promote the evolution of analogously similar behaviors—those that are admittedly unrelated and probably have different basic underlying mechanisms, but that have the same functions or external appearances. For example, territoriality seems to evolve in certain situations (Brown, 1964); it is not a trait of any particular group of animals whose relatedness accounts for it, but rather related to seasonally abundant food, the actual defensibility of an area, and other factors. In the realm of social organization, polygamy seems to have evolved independently in certain ecological situations, monogamy in different ones (Crook, 1962; Orians, 1969; Selander, 1965). Perhaps the great power of the ecological method will prove to be the ability to provide generalizations allowing a prediction of behavior from knowledge of ecology. It can also, however, account for differences. The classical work of Cullen (1957), for example, showed how nearly 60 different behaviors of a gull, the Kittiwake, matched the properties of the nesting habitat, narrow ledges on cliff faces. In various other behaviors, the Kittiwake is similar to ground-nesting gulls, but the behaviors associated with its nest and young differ adaptively from those of other gulls.

Against this brief background, let us return to the list of premises attributed here to the comparative psychology of some years back, and examine how these become viewed in the light of modern knowledge:

1. There is no phylogenetic scale. True, if the series of extinct ancestors of any living species could be brought to life and arranged in temporal order, the evolution of any character could be traced. But all ancestors of all living forms are dead. The living species of today form no scale at all, except for partial reconstructions made with great caution and competence within a related group, as Lorenz (1941) did with ducks. The living species of today are not preserved ancestral forms; they are highly evolved derivatives of ancestral forms that underwent adaptive radiation and ecological specialization. They are contemporaneous with man, as highly evolved in their own way as man is in his. The ancient "scale naturae" idea is pleasingly simple, but simply wrong (cf. Hodos & Campbell, 1969).

2. Comparisons between chicks, rats, cats, and the other familiar fauna adapted to the laboratory have been based on naive views of phylogeny and have been uninformative. The underlying assumption has been that of a phylogenetic scale, or that the same processes underlie behaviors of unrelated animals. Laboratory comparisons of two animal species unrelated by descent and dissimilar ecologically would seem to have limited scientific utility. On the other hand, animal species studied within the context of either the comparative method or the ecological method can be soundly based and informative.

3. The century-old linkage between comparative psychology and animal intelligence is disconnected. What we used to call intelligence and tested as problem-solving ability now appears to be an aggregate of special abilities, each one evolved as a response to ecological factors posing problems. Thus, "intelligent" animals are intelligent in quite different ways more successfully understood in relation to ecological demands than to phyletic position. Broad-niche opportunistic birds like the common crow are thus more "intelligent" than narrow-niche mammals like the mountain beaver (*Aplodontia rufa*); wasps (*Ammophila sp.*) superior in delayed-response problems than Norway rats; and pocket-gophers better than horses and other open-range animals are at maze problems. Strangely enough, since the animal intelligence problem was only a part of the large problem of a science of mental faculties in animals, the modern view raises rather than dashes hopes for rewarding discoveries and analysis of animal mental faculties. It turns attention away from the view that animals are incomplete humans and toward the view that animals should actually have a great many, quite different mental faculties evolved as adaptations to many very different ecological requirements.

4. White rats are not simple versions of humans. Studies purporting to show similarities between the two have four interpretations: (*a*) Some truly homologous property, perhaps widespread in mammals, was demonstrated. (*b*) Unknown ecological factors happened to produce analogous properties in these two—and perhaps no more—mammals which have superficial resemblances, but which differ in fundamental ways not explored. (*c*) Coarse analyses often produce results that fail to discriminate between things that are actually quite different. (*d*) The general climate of opinion and the eagerness to find similarities have led to casual interpretation and an easy task of persuasion of a credulous audience. One currently has no way of knowing which interpretation to give a study, and it matters a great deal from a scientific point of view. Rodents and primates either nearly or completely fail to share a common ancestor; the fossil record leaves the matter unclear. Their remoteness (100 million years or so) of relationship makes

them irrelevant to each other for all comparative purposes. The place of rodents in psychology is for the study of rodent behavior, not human behavior. Animal behavior research can illuminate human behavior in the context of the comparative method or the ecological method; but research on animals unrelated to humans by one of these two methods has no scientific relevance in its results.

5. Learning is not the key to animal behavior because most behavior is not acquired. The overwhelming majority of animals (96%) are invertebrates; of these, most are insects. Perhaps many writers mean "vertebrates" when they write "animals" or "organisms" (which include plants); but this includes fish, amphibians, reptiles, and birds as well as mammals. The role of learning in these classes is not at all clear; it is a very different thing to demonstrate that an amphibian can learn something than to place the burden of explanation of its behavior on learning. Current thinking seems to be that learning is not unimportant, but conceptualizations of its roles have been clouded on the one hand by perpetuation of a learning versus endogenous factors formulation and on the other hand by overenthusiastic environmentalism and sometimes nativism. But partisan views are waning, and the near future may see significant advances in the understanding of the role of learning. The old concept of an animal as having some degree of intelligence and thus able to learn nearly anything in accord with its endowment is giving way to the view that natural selection has probably produced rather specific learning mechanisms that correspond to ecological demands. There are certain aspects or particular details of an animal's ecology such that it is more adaptative to evolve a particular learning ability than to evolve an endogenous response. For example, Cullen (1957) concluded that the Kittiwake cannot learn the identity of its own young, whereas ground-nesting gulls readily do so. The young of the Kittiwake do not wander about on the narrow cliff ledges, so there has been no selection pressure for this particular learning; whereas the young of ground-nesting gulls wander about and become intermingled, and gulls able to recognize and feed their own young would contribute a greater share of their genes to future generations than would gulls feeding some other gull's young. In short, learning abilities may evolve as discrete entities related to environmental particulars where they convey a reproductive advantage.

6. Because so much is built into animals, genetics and evolution are of the utmost importance to any science of behavior. It is on this point that environmental psychologists once balked and re-sponded with incredulity. But not without reason; the literature prior to about 1950 suggested a sort of vague but loose connection between genetics and behavior, and a good strong case awaited such work as Spieth (1952), Bastock (1956), Caspari (1958), Hirsch (1959), the text by Fuller and Thompson (1960), Dilger (1962), the text edited by Hirsch (1967), and the review of strain differences in Robinson (1965). The climate of opinion has changed, and the very existence of a new discipline, behavior genetics, shows this. The early work such as Tryon's (1940) left the impression that behavior is sometimes influenced by genes because the criterion behavior was an invented psychological abstraction like intelligence, emotionality, or general activity. Work such as Dilger (1962), Eibl-Eibesfeldt (1963), and Leyhausen (1956, 1965) suggests that what natural selection produces are genetic mechanisms that produce elements of courtship, parts of nestbuilding, components of predation—smaller units of behavior than maze brightness or emotionality. Ewer (1968) summarized the current view for mammals in stating

What is built in is the minimum required to ensure that the correct end result is attained, together with an innate responsiveness to the latter, so that once attained it is "recognized." This permits individual learning to perfect the pattern in relation to the detailed circumstances of the situation. The second principle is that this result can be achieved on the basis of innately determined individual movements [p. 326].

7. Animals are quite different from species to species; each has its own autecology and its own set of adaptations. The former emphasis upon similarity among species was an outgrowth of the mental continuity hypothesis; animals were viewed as qualitatively alike. As qualitative differences began to be demonstrated several decades ago, these findings were in disharmony with prevailing psychological views and were regarded as almost subversive. Now views have done nearly a complete turn; a researcher extrapolating from studied to unstudied species is viewed with suspicion. Certainly, the old view that the same hidden but lawful processes resided in all animals is untenable both in the face of empirical findings and because of the independent origins of behaviors. However, the old view would seem to be severly modified, not demolished, by the recent advances in understanding. Life on Earth presumably had a single origin, so certain general processes may indeed be shared by animals; such is nearly the case with DNA, certain genetic mechanisms, and cellular construction. It is completely unclear to what extent analogous uniformities might hold for behavior. Second, Earth imposes certain overall constraints and uniformities such that one would expect Earth

fauna to resemble itself more than fauna from another planet. Third, there are similarities among related animals due to common descent and among unrelated animals due to similar selection pressures, as discussed earlier. So there are recognized processes producing similarities and recognized processes producing differences, and one task for the animal behaviorists of the future is to add to our knowledge of these and work toward a predictive theory of similarities and differences.

8. The prospects for laws of behavior have changed completely. Because of the independent evolution of behaviors, laws based on specified treatments having specified effects wrongly presume homologous underlying processes and are therefore unlikely to have scientific merit except for restricted cases of related taxa. Thus, valid statements about animals in general or behavior in general obeying some treatment-effect paradigm should remain few. However, the methodology associated with the comparative method should allow an increasing number of valid statements as the kingdom name, animals, is progressively replaced by taxon designations closer and closer to species name. For example, a number of valid statements can be made about heteromyid rodents (e.g., Eisenberg, 1963), a greater number about kangaroo rats (genus *Dipodomys*). The other direction in which the pursuit of laws of behavior now seems valid is by way of the ecological method. It allows, for example, theoretical formulations such as "Monogamy should be relatively rare among mammals but should be the predominant mating pattern among birds [Orians, 1969, p. 596]." This sort of formulation now seems likely to predominate the future search for laws of behavior (see also Hirsch, 1967, pp. 307–321).

9. The laboratory has limited usefulness and subtle disadvantages in the study of animal behavior; a new role for the laboratory is emerging. The numerous behavioral adaptations of animals and how these fit particulars of the habitat in which they evolved have a much higher probability of detection in the field. There, events will happen that the investigator would never have dreamed of, unsuspected relationships are revealed, and new hypotheses are born. Often the hypotheses can be tested in the field by standard research methods; but sometimes the problem can be analyzed only so far, and it must be moved into the laboratory. However, since animals match their environments but mismatch the laboratory, severe distortions of behavior are common. To eliminate such artifacts, the environmental conditions are made as suited to the species as possible, and then the phenomena under study are carefully checked for fidelity with

respect to field conditions. If and when this important check shows detailed correspondence, analysis can proceed. The key laboratory findings can then be validated by replication under field conditions. This procedure allows problems to originate in the real world, avoiding the expenditure of effort on laboratory-born problems which may be irrelevant. It allows a happy marriage of field and laboratory procedures, exploiting the best of each. And it allows the investigator to see how his animal functions in its world, not his. Much of the history of comparative psychology consisted of inventing clever procedures and imposing them upon animals; today, the interest is not in what an animal can be made to do, but in how it normally functions (cf. Breland & Breland, 1966, pp. 62–69).

10. The best variables to study are probably biological variables. It is unlikely that much behavior is adapted to or controlled in a simple way by physical variables, although examples can be found. It is much more likely that biological stimuli are the most intimately connected with behavior. For example, among gulls the kinds of stimuli with clearly associated behaviors are bill dimensions and color, egg properties, nest site properties, predators, etc. Behaviors associated with physical variables like light intensity are now known in many cases to be related not because of the intrinsic properties of the stimulus, but because of its ecological correlates. For example, certain insect activities are "controlled" by light intensity; however, what is crucial to the success of these activities is humidity. Light correlates with humidity, and somehow the behavior became attached to a correlate.

Implications for Psychology

Comparative psychology. At the level of a curriculum, students and faculty should strive for modernization of comparative psychology courses. Outmoded ideas and concepts should be frankly treated as such. Students committed to the area should be encouraged to seek training in genetics, developmental biology, evolution, ecology, and other biological areas. Students in biological disciplines should be advised to train in the areas of experimental expertise in which psychologists excel—experimental design, laboratory methodology, and the like. Joint psychological-biological training programs would seem ideally suited to the educational needs of future animal behaviorists.

At the professional level, it is not clear that comparative psychology still exists as a field or that any effort should be made to continue it. The modern phrase is animal behavior, and it has the advantage of disconnecting current work from the past of comparative psychology. Looking farther ahead, psychologists may or may not be able to retrain themselves so as to handle animal behavior well. Unfortunately, the field resembles paleontology in that researchers must be competent in a variety of disciplines. There is a current trend toward localization of expertise in animal behavior in zoology departments, but this may not persist because of a tendency to regard the area as "tender-minded" or on the fringes of science. Psychology may therefore again find itself the dominant influence in the area.

Animal laboratories. The rat lab so characteristic of psychology departments needs careful reconsideration. If rodents are irrelevant to humans phylogenetically and ecologically, why do we assign them such a key role? If psychology includes all of animal behavior, why not maintain colonies of a variety of species? If our focus is on humans, why not maintain a kind of animal relevant to humans? Tradition here has become so strong that we feel comfortable about perpetuating rats when, in fact, we fumble for credible scientific justifications for doing so.

Animal learning. Because of the past intermixing of this area with comparative psychology, much of this article refers to animal learning directly and need not be repeated. However, the numerous implications remain, and the problems confronting animal learning as an area are less likely to be seen than in comparative psychology because animal learning is more remote from biology. If comparative psychology failed because of its premises, its overdone environmentalism, and its scientific apartheid policy, animal learning could be next. Breland and Breland (1961) sounded the alarm; the response has been slow.

Developmental psychology. The dedication to environmentalism is not over, and there is a dangerously wide gulf in some quarters between developmental psychology and developmental biology. Some research traditions show a tendency to discover that developmental pathways are not rigidly fixed, but can be altered by environment. The discussion sometimes sounds like a commercial for the point of view that nothing is really built in, but is the product of experience. The problem here is not the finding, but the interpretational context. In developmental biology, it is widely understood that natural selection need only produce a developmental program which produces the adaptive phenotype in the normal environment. Environments are mainly dependable, and additional pathway buffers need not be evolved to protect the developmental pathway against all possible environmental novelties. When the environment is predictably unpredictable—as in the case of cuckoos hatched by foster parents—the developmental pathway is protected against early experience—the cuckoos fledge, fly off, sing like a cuckoo, and display like a cuckoo, and mate with another cuckoo despite their early environment. In still other situations, dual developmental pathways have evolved such that an early switch makes the phenotype adaptive. The water buttercup, for example, occurs in areas with unpredictable flooding patterns. When it grows submerged, the aquatic phenotype is produced; when on land, the very different terrestrial phenotype occurs. Thus, there already exists an overall conceptual framework for environmental interactions, and advertisements for the point of view that "the environment is important" seem scientifically irrelevant to the task of attaining a dispassionate and deep understanding of development.

Human psychology. Humans are animals, perhaps very special animals, but animals nonetheless. Just as the other fauna of this planet are the products of organic evolution and are now being understood in the framework, humans evolved and deserve understanding in this context. But the promise that research in animal behavior will illuminate human behavior is over a century old, and remains unfulfilled. We have no animal-based science of human behavior despite the assemblage of suspect analogies. If anything, we have had a human-based methodology of animal behavior, and the thrust of this article is that history sent us down the wrong road. Many psychologists seem pessimistic about the prospects for a human behavioral science with animal foundations and are moving toward frankly empirical foundations or toward fundamentals unrelated to the biology of the species. As it becomes more widely appreciated that the relevance of comparative psychology was largely illusory, the patience and credulity of the human psychologist could reach a low ebb. Of the many implications of this, one of the more amusing is a reversal of the past prestige hierarchy in which rat-runners become seen as misguided and unscientific.

But what a shame it would be to react so late, when what amounts to no less than a modern synthesis of behavior is taking shape. Help is on the way! We can now see the relevance of animals in the comparative method and in the ecological method; the animals that are behaviorally relevant are those related to man by common ancestry, or those with similarities due to similar selection pressures. Apes are relevant by relatedness, wolves for ecological reasons.

It is not true, however, that an easy road to comprehending the fundamental aspects of human behavior now exists. It seems like a difficult road. There are too few ape species, each too specialized, for easy use of the comparative method; and too few ecologically analogous species for easy use of the ecological method. The task is not hopeless, but it will require competence of the most sophisticated kind for its doing. If we want realistic foundations for human behavioral science, we will have to raise our own experts in these methods, experts who can develop the modest formulations of today into very powerful methods. They cannot do this from studying books, or apes, or rats; they must study related groups of animals to refine the comparative method, and ecologically analogous adaptations to develop the ecological method. For this reason, animals of all sorts suddenly become relevant to psychology, relevant for the sharpening of scientific tools, not for casual and direct extrapolations to human behavior. Psychologists are bright and adaptable; if they crossed their experimental sophistication with evolutionary biology, a vigorous and fertile hybrid should result (cf. Beach, 1950).

The general lesson in this case history is clear: Comparative psychology developed a culture of traditions in a prescientific era and clung to them as they became discredited. Other areas show similarities. Perhaps the time has come to unify with the natural sciences, to delete untenable premises, and to recognize that we cannot continue to study the behavior of what evolution has produced while denying the relevance of evolution.

Old ideas give way slowly; for they are more than abstract logical forms and categories. They are habits, predispositions, deeply engrained attitudes of aversion and preference. Moreover, the conviction persists—though history shows it to be a hallucination—that all the questions that the human mind has asked are questions that can be answered in terms of the alternatives that the questions themselves present. But in fact intellectual progress usually occurs through sheer abandonment of questions together with both the alternatives they assume—an abandonment that results from their decreasing vitality and a change of urgent interest. We do not solve them: we get over them. Old questions are solved by disappearing, evaporating, while new questions corresponding to the changed attitude of endeavor and preference take their place. Doubtless the greatest dissolvent in contemporary thought of old questions, the greatest precipitant of new methods, new intentions, new problems, is the one effected by the scientific revolution that found its climax in the "Origin of Species" [Dewey, 1965, p. 19, orig. publ. 1909].

REFERENCES

BASTOCK, M. A. A gene mutation which changes a behavior pattern. *Evolution,* 1956, **10,** 421–439.

BEACH, F. A. The snark was a boojum. *American Psychologist,* 1950, **5,** 115–124.

BEER, C. G. Ethology—The zoologist's approach to behavior. Pt. I. *Tuatara,* 1963, **11,** 170–177.

BEER, C. G. Ethology—The zoologist's approach to behavior. Pt. II. *Tuatara,* 1964, **12,** 16–39.

BORING, E. G. *A history of experimental psychology.* New York: Appleton-Century-Crofts, 1950.

BRELAND, K., & BRELAND, M. The misbehavior of organisms. *American Psychologist,* 1961, **16,** 681–684.

BRELAND, K., & BRELAND, M. *Animal behavior.* New York: Macmillan, 1966.

BROWN, J. L. The evolution of diversity in avian territorial systems. *Wilson Bulletin,* 1964, **76,** 160–169.

CASPARI, E. Genetic basis of behavior. In A. Roe & G. G. Simpson (Eds.), *Behavior and evolution.* New Haven: Yale University Press, 1958.

CRAIG, W. Observations on doves learning to drink. *Journal of Animal Behavior,* 1912, **2,** 273–279.

CROOK, J. H. The adaptive significance of pair formation types in weaver birds. *Zoological Society of London,* 1962, **8,** 57–70.

CROOK, J. H. The evolution of social organization and visual communication in the weaver birds (Ploceinae). *Behaviour,* 1964, No. 10, 1–178.

CULLEN, E. Adaptations in the Kittiwake to cliff-nesting. *Ibis,* 1957, **99,** 275–302.

DARWIN, C. R. *On the origin of species.* London: Murray, 1859. (References from Mentor edition, New American Library, New York, 1958.)

DARWIN, C. R. *The descent of man.* London: Murray, 1871. (References from 1914 edition.)

DEWEY, J. The influence of Darwinism on philosophy. In J. Dewey (Ed.), *The influence of Darwin on philosophy.* Bloomington: Indiana University, 1965. (Originally published in *Popular Science Monthly,* 1909.)

DILGER, W. C. The behavior of lovebirds. *Scientific American,* 1962, **206,** 88–98.

DOBZHANSKY, T. *Genetics and the origin of species.* New York: Columbia University Press, 1937.

EIBL-EIBESFELDT, I. The interactions of unlearned behaviour patterns and learning in mammals. In J. F. Delafresnaye (Ed.), *Brain mechanisms and learning.* C.I.O.M.S. Symposium, Blackwell, Oxford, England, 1963.

EISENBERG, J. F. The behavior of heteromyid rodents. *University of California Publications in Zoology,* 1963, **69,** 1–114.

EWER, R. F. *Ethology of mammals.* New York: Plenum Press, 1968.

FISHER, R. A. *The genetical theory of natural selection.* Oxford: Clarendon Press, 1930.

FORD, E. B. *Ecological genetics.* New York: Wiley, 1960.

FULLER, J. L., & THOMPSON, W. R. *Behavior genetics.* New York: Wiley, 1960.

HAMILTON, W. D. The genetical evolution of social behavior. *Journal of Theoretical Biology,* 1964, **7,** 1–52.

HEINROTH, O. Beitrage zur Biologie, namentlich Ethologie und Physiologie der Anatiden. *Verh. 5 Int. Orn. Kong.,* 1910, 589–702.

HINDE, R. A. The biological significance of the territories of birds. *Ibis,* 1956, **98,** 340–369.

HINDE, R. A., & TINBERGEN, N. The comparative study of species-specific behavior. In A. Roe & G. G. Simpson (Eds.), *Behavior and evolution.* New Haven: Yale University Press, 1958.

HIRSCH, J. Studies of experimental behavior genetics: II. Individual differences in geotaxis as a function of chromosome variations in synthesized *Drosophila* populations. *Journal of Comparative and Physiological Psychology,* 1959, **52,** 304–308.

HIRSCH, J. (Ed.) *Behavior-genetic analysis.* New York: McGraw-Hill, 1967.

HIRSCH, J. Behavior-genetic analysis and the study of man. In, American Association for the Advancement of Science Symposium, *Science and the concept of race.* New York: Columbia University Press, 1968.

HODOS, W., & CAMPBELL, C. B. G. Scala naturae: Why there is no theory in comparative psychology. *Psychological Review,* 1969, **76**, 337–350.

HUXLEY, J. S. *Evolution, the modern synthesis.* London: Allen & Unwin, 1942.

HUXLEY, J. S. The emergence of Darwinism. In S. Tax (Ed.), *Evolution after Darwin.* Vol. I. *The evolution of life.* Chicago: University of Chicago Press, 1960.

JAYNES, J. The historical origins of 'ethology' and 'comparative psychology.' *Animal Behaviour,* 1969, **17**, 601–606.

KATZ, D. *Animals and men—Studies in comparative psychology.* London: Longmans, Green, 1937.

LACK, D. *Ecological adaptations for breeding in birds.* London: Methuen, 1968.

LEYHAUSEN, P. Verhaltensstudien an Katzen. *Zeitschrift für Tierpsychologie,* 1956, Beiheft 2, 1–120.

LEYHAUSEN, P. Über die Funktion der relativen Stimmungshierarchie (dargestellt am Beispiel der phylogenetischen und ontogenerischen Entwicklung des Beutesfangs von Raubtieren). *Zeitschrift für Tierpsychologie,* 1965, **22**, 412–494.

LORENZ, K. Beitrage zur Ethologie der sozialer Corviden. *Journal of Ornithology,* 1931, **79**, 67–127.

LORENZ, K. Betrachtungen über das Erkennen der arteigenen Triebhandlungen der Vogel. *Journal of Ornithology,* 1932, **80**, 50–98.

LORENZ, K. Der Kumpan in der Umwelt des Vogels. *Journal of Ornithology,* 1935, **83**, 137–214, 289–413.

LORENZ, K. Über den Begriff der Instinkthandlung. *Folia Biotheoretica,* 1937, **2**, 17–50.

LORENZ, K. Vergleichende Bewegungsstudien an Anatinen. *Journal of Ornithology,* 1941, **89**, 194–294. (Supplement)

LORENZ, K. The comparative method in studying innate behaviour patterns. *Symposium of the Society for Experimental Biology,* 1950, **4**, 221–268.

LORENZ, K. The nature of instinct. In C. E. Schiller (Ed.), *Instinctive behavior.* New York: International Universities Press, 1957.

LORENZ, K. *Evolution and modification of behavior.* Chicago: University of Chicago Press, 1965.

MACARTHUR, R. H., & PIANKA, E. R. On optimal use of a patchy environment. *American Naturalist,* 1966, **100**, 603–609.

MAYR, E. *Systematics and the origin of species.* New York: Columbia University Press, 1942.

MAYR, E. *Animal species and evolution.* Cambridge: Harvard University Press, 1963.

MORRIS, D. The feather postures of birds and the problem of the origin of social signals. *Behaviour,* 1957, **9**, 75–113.

MOSS, F. A. *Comparative psychology.* New York: Prentice-Hall, 1942.

ORIANS, G. H. The ecology of blackbird (*Agelaius*) social systems. *Ecological Monographs,* 1961, **31**, 285–382.

ORIANS, G. H. Natural selection and ecological theory. *American Naturalist,* 1962, **96**, 257–264.

ORIANS, G. H. On the evolution of mating systems in birds and mammals. *The American Naturalist,* 1969, **103**, 589–603.

ROBINSON, R. *Genetics of the Norway rat.* New York: Pergamon, 1965.

ROMANES, G. J. *Animal intelligence.* London: Kegan Paul, 1881.

ROMANES, G. J. *Mental evolution in animals.* London: Kegan Paul, 1883.

ROMANES, G. J. *Mental evolution in man.* London: Kegan Paul, 1887.

SELANDER, R. K. On mating systems and sexual selection. *The American Naturalist,* 1965, **99**, 129–141.

SMITH, C. C. The adaptive nature of social organization in the genus of tree squirrels *Tamiasciurus. Ecological Monographs,* 1968, **38**, 31–63.

SMITH, R. L. *Ecology and field biology.* New York: Harper & Row, 1966.

SPIETH, H. T. Mating behavior within the genus Drosophila (Diptera). *Bulletin of the American Museum of Natural History,* 1952, **99**, 395–474.

TINBERGEN, N. *L. a. argentatus Pontopp. Beitrage Fortpflanzungsbiologie Vogel,* 1936, **12**, 89–96.

TINBERGEN, N. Über das Verhalten kampfender Kohlmeisen (*Parus m. major L.*). *Ardea,* 1937, **26**, 222–223.

TINBERGEN, N. *The study of instinct.* Oxford: Clarendon Press, 1951.

TINBERGEN, N. Comparative studies of the behaviour of gulls (*Laridae*): A progress report. *Behaviour,* 1959, **15**, 1–70.

TINBERGEN, N. Behaviour, systematics, and natural selection. In S. Tax (Ed.), *Evolution after Darwin.* Vol. I. *The evolution of life.* Chicago: University of Chicago Press, 1960.

TRYON, R. C. Genetic differences in maze-learning ability in rats. *Yearbook of the National Society for the Study of Education,* 1940, **39**, 111–119.

WASHBURN, M. F. *The animal mind.* New York: Macmillan, 1936.

WATERS, R. H. The historical background of comparative psychology. In F. A. Moss (Ed.), *Comparative psychology.* New York: Prentice-Hall, 1942.

WHITMAN, C. O. Animal behavior. In, *Biological lectures, Marine Biology Laboratory.* Woods Hole, Mass., 1898.

Reprinted from PSYCHOLOGICAL REVIEW, Vol. 72, No. 1, January 1965
Printed in U. S. A.

(4)

CONTEMPORARY INSTINCT THEORY AND THE FIXED ACTION PATTERN [1]

HOWARD MOLTZ [2]

Brooklyn College

The observable properties of the Fixed Action Pattern (FAP) as well as the processes assumed by the contemporary instinct theorist to underlie the structure and organization of this allegedly unique response class are described. An attempt is then made to assess the significance of the FAP for psychology. Finally, a critical evaluation of the FAP, in the light of a review of relevant empirical evidence, is presented. On the basis of this evaluation it is concluded that the empirical properties of the FAP do not require the assumptions of genetic encoding and central itemization—assumptions the instinct theorist considers indispensable—but instead can be interpreted in a manner broadly consonant with an epigenetic approach.

Despite the many vicissitudes which the concept of instinct has undergone during the course of its long and multifaceted history, its essential approach to the analysis of behavior has remained virtually unchanged: the postulation of some form of invariant genotypically fixed response nucleus around which the more flexible and plastic components of a behavior repertoire allegedly develop. Holding forth the seemingly attractive promise that such a nucleus would constitute for understanding the structure and organization of a species' repertoire, it is not surprising that the concept of instinct has managed to remain viable

despite repeated attempts to exorcise it from the body of science. The purpose of the present paper is to discuss and critically evaluate its most recent bid for redemption—a bid embodied in the form of a new theory of instinct.

This theory, formulated by several European ethologists of whom the most notable are Lorenz and Tinbergen, has as its core the concept of the Instinctive Movement or the Fixed Action Pattern (FAP). Based primarily, although by no means exclusively, on naturalistic observations of free-ranging species, the concept of the FAP has come to occupy a position of such central importance in contemporary instinct theory that one can hardly discuss the current state of that theory without describing the observable characteristics of FAPs as well as the neurophysiological events which have been assumed to underlie their structure and organization. Accordingly, our first task shall be to delineate briefly those empirical and theoretical properties which have been assumed to render the FAP a distinct class of response events. (Detailed accounts and illustrations of a wide variety of FAPs are to be found in

[1] The present paper was written while the author was in receipt of Research Grant M3855 from the National Institutes of Health, United States Public Health Service.

[2] Anyone familiar with the writings of Schneirla will recognize the profound and pervasive influence they have had on my thinking about problems of behavioral development in general and about the genesis of species-typic responses in particular. It is a pleasure to acknowledge what is indeed a deep indebtedness. Equally worthy of mention are the critical and penetrating insights offered by Evelyn Raskin—insights from which the present paper profited immeasurably.

Eibl-Eibesfeldt and Kramer, 1958, in Hinde, 1959, and in Moltz, 1962.) We shall then attempt, in the light of a review of the relevant empirical evidence, to assess the significance of the FAP as well as to evaluate the theory into which it has been incorporated. This evaluation will draw upon such valuable appraisals of instinct theory as those of Hebb (1953), Hinde (1954, 1959), Lehrman (1953, 1956), and Schneirla (1956, 1957).

Before beginning, however, two points should be made explicit. First, because the contemporary instinct theorist often refers to himself as an "ethologist" and because he often speaks of ethology as having derived from the study of the FAP, there has been a tendency on the part of American and European psychologists alike to regard all ethologists as instinct theorists. Nothing indeed could be further from the truth. Many investigators call themselves "ethologists" simply to indicate that they are zoologists engaged in the comparative study of animal behavior; they would strongly object to being classified as instinct theorists and sorely disappointed if their contributions came to be regarded as relevant only to instinct theory. For a detailed review of the general "orienting attitudes" of ethology and for a discussion of its history in mediating research, see Hinde (1959).

Secondly, the impression should not be gained that all those who have contributed to the nexus of ideas and concepts referred to herein as "contemporary instinct theory" have remained fixed in their beliefs. There have been apostasies to be sure, most notably that of Tinbergen himself (1955; see also Hinde & Tinbergen, 1958) who has repudiated some of his earlier theoretical formulations. That no mention is made of this in what follows is due simply to the fact that our task is not to examine the views of any individual theorist nor to discuss the way in which his views might have changed, but rather to evaluate a particular approach to the understanding of species-typic behavior—an approach which continues to have a profound influence on the current thinking of those concerned with developmental problems.

EMPIRICAL PROPERTIES OF THE FAP

Although there is widespread agreement that FAPs comprise a unique class of responses, there is little agreement among ethologists in general or even among instinct theorists themselves concerning the criteria requisite for class inclusion. However, each of the four properties which we shall discuss below in attempting to delineate the empirical character of the FAP has been considered a distinguishing and primary feature and each has in turn posed rather important theoretical issues.

Stereotypy of the FAP

A reasonably precise distinction is often made by ethologists and instinct theorists alike between appetitive behavior and consummatory acts. "Appetitive behavior" is the term used to designate the labile initial components of a behavior sequence, while "consummatory act" is the term used to designate the rigid and terminal components (Thorpe, 1954, 1956).

Those movements or movement patterns designated as FAPs are classified as consummatory acts since they usually comprise the terminal aspects of a response sequence and since they are rigidly stereotyped and constant in form. Their most salient characteristic seems to be their stereotypy; indeed, in this respect, they have been compared with morphological traits, for, like such traits, FAPs are expressed in a highly invariant manner within a taxonomic group (Lorenz, 1956).

As an example of this invariance we may consider an aspect of the reproductive behavior of the three-spined stickleback. Aeration of the stickleback nest, which is apparently necessary to maintain the oxygen concentration of the surrounding water at a level appropriate for egg development, is accomplished through a movement called "fanning." This consists of using the pectoral fins to exert a forward pressure on the water and simultaneously using the tail and caudal fin to exert a backward pressure equal in intensity to the forward pressure. The sequence of movements performed by these structures is the same on each occasion that fanning is exhibited (Baerends, 1957). Indeed, even under circumstances which apparently force the fish to adopt an atypical position in relation to the substrate, the patterning or coordination of the component response elements remains invariant.

Independence from Immediate External Control

If a movement pattern is to be classified as an FAP, the temporal sequence of muscular contractions comprising the pattern must be independent of afferent regulation. Such independence is evidenced by the fact that the movement will often continue to completion irrespective of changes in external conditions. This property serves to distinguish the FAP from movements termed "taxes" which once elicited continue to be directed by events external to the animal and cease to occur once the external stimulus is removed. The egg-retrieving pattern of the graylag goose, described

in detail by Lorenz and Tinbergen (1938), illustrates the difference between the taxis and the FAP.

A brooding graylag goose, observing that an egg has rolled out of its nest, reacts in a characteristic manner. It slowly rises from the nest and approaches the displaced egg. Upon reaching it, the neck is extended downward and forward so that the undersurface of the bill comes to rest against the far side of the egg. Two distinct movements are then employed which serve to roll the displaced egg in the direction of the nest—a sagittal movement that keeps the egg rolling in the bird's median plane, and a lateral or side-to-side movement that keeps it from deviating too far either to the right or left.

The sagittal movement has been classified as an FAP since its form remains constant despite the irregularities of the terrain over which the egg is rolled and despite differences in the shape of those objects that have been experimentally substituted for the egg. Furthermore, if the egg rolls away from the bill, as occasionally happens in the natural situation, the goose will often continue to perform this movement in the same manner as when the egg was present, indicating that the movement is apparently no longer under extrinsic control.

The lateral movement is classified as a taxis, since it is both evoked and continuously directed by contact of the egg with the undersurface of the bill. Thus, if the egg deviates slightly from the bird's median plane, a compensatory movement either to the right or to the left immediately restores it to its path. If an object that is unlikely to deviate (e.g., a cylinder or light wooden cube) is substituted for the displaced egg, few or no lateral movements are performed; finally, if the egg happens to roll completely free of the bill, the lateral movement, unlike the sagittal, ceases.

Although the example just given illustrates quite clearly the distinction between the taxis and the FAP, it is difficult in many cases to determine whether a particular movement is directed by external events or is simply released by such events (Baerends & Baerends-van Roon, 1950). Furthermore, the taxis and the FAP frequently occur either simultaneously or in close succession, such interlocking making differentiation additionally difficult (Lorenz, 1937).

At this point it is appropriate to emphasize what has thus far been implicit in our discussion, namely, that the FAP does not possess the characteristics of a chain reaction. Although it may involve a relatively complex pattern of muscle contractions, the FAP cannot be fractionated into successive response links with different external stimulus factors responsible for their evocation. Each component of an FAP, in other words, can be elicited only by the same stimulus or stimulus complex as that which elicits the entire FAP.

Spontaneity

A third property of the FAP is its spontaneity, a term used here to denote fluctuations in threshold that are independent of changes in external conditions. The general rule observed to apply to such fluctuations is that an organism's readiness to perform a particular FAP and the intensity with which that performance occurs are a positive function of the time elapsing since the movement was last evoked. Van Iersel (1953) demonstrated that when a male stickleback is prevented from fanning for several minutes, a significant increase in the intensity of this activity will occur after the fish is allowed to return to its

nest. This is not due to changes in such extrinsic conditions as the accumulation of carbon dioxide and other gases released by the eggs in the fish's absence, since the same result was obtained when the experiment was repeated with the nest kept completely covered.

Fatigue has also been ruled out as a factor contributing to the fluctuations in the occurrence and intensity of FAPs. If one keeps a cichlid fish in close confinement with conspecifics so that stimuli evoking fighting are continuously present, the thresholds of such agonistic movements as lateral tail beating, spreading the gill membranes, and erecting the median fins are raised (Lorenz, 1956). Neither general fatigue nor fatigue of specific effectors can account for this finding, inasmuch as the fish will at the same time perform other activities involving the same effectors and apparently requiring just as much effort.

The most dramatic bit of evidence regarding the spontaneity of the FAP is its tendency under certain circumstances to occur *in vacuo*. That is, when prevented from occurring for a considerable period by the withdrawal of the external stimulus normally responsible for its "release," an FAP will sometimes be performed in the absence of that stimulus.

For example, van Iersel (1953) reports that fanning is occasionally exhibited in perfect detail by the stickleback in the absence of a nest. Similarly, Lorenz has called attention to the fact that the complex motor pattern involved in the weaver bird's weaving strands for its nest is sometimes performed in the absence of plant fibers that normally serve as the functional object.

Although vacuum activities are performed infrequently and performed under conditions atypical for the species, the tendency for less extreme variations in elicitability to occur as a function of the time elapsing since previous performance is as already indicated considered to be characteristic of all FAPs. Moreover, this characteristic is often emphasized in the attempt to distinguish it from reflexes or reflex-like movements (Eibl-Eibesfeldt & Kramer, 1958; Lorenz & Tinbergen, 1938; Thorpe, 1954).

Independence from Individual Learning

A fourth criterion for membership in the class of FAPs is the exclusion of the possibility that the movement or movement pattern has been specifically learned prior to its first occurrence. Lorenz (1956), for example, maintains that even wide fluctuations in environmental conditions during ontogeny will in no way alter the FAP provided the health of the organism is not impaired.

The isolation technique is frequently regarded as the critical method for assessing the influence of learning (Eibl-Eibesfeldt, 1961). In its simplest form, this technique consists of removing an animal at the time of birth or hatching from members of its own species and then determining whether a given response is subsequently performed in a manner identical to that shown by animals reared with conspecifics. Thus, Tinbergen (1942) and Cullen (1960) report that male sticklebacks reared in isolation performed a typical zigzag courting dance before they had ever seen another stickleback; in fact it was performed on the first occasion that they were introduced to a cardboard model of a gravid female.

The appearance of many movements designated as FAPs very early in ontogeny is also considered evidence that they could not have been learned in

any ordinary sense of that term. Thus, the side-to-side head movement of the human infant is present at birth (Prechtl, 1958), and the gaping response of the thrush is present at hatching (Tinbergen & Kuenen, 1939).

Additional evidence that the FAP is dependent neither on individual learning or practice, comes from observations that the FAP occurs even when certain structures involved in the movement are absent. For example, in one species of surface-feeding ducks, courtship involves a preening movement by which the drake exposes and wriggles a brilliantly colored tertiary feather. Lorenz (1955) reports the case of a drake that had, for unknown reasons, failed to develop this feather but which nonetheless persisted in performing the preening movement. Similarly, FAPs can appear in ontogeny long before they possess functional utility and hence long before a (presumably) necessary condition for learning is present. For example, a young gosling in an aggressive encounter holds its adversary in exactly the same position in space and uses exactly the same beating movement as the adult goose despite the fact that its wings are not large enough to touch its opponent (Lorenz, 1956).

This last example reveals the narrow conception of learning held by most instinct theorists. They reason that, if no source of reinforcement can be identified in connection with a particular response, then the response is perforce not learned (Eibl-Eibesfeldt & Kramer, 1958; Lorenz, 1955). But, despite their tendency to equate the absence of reinforcement with the absence of learning, they have admittedly pointed to many aspects of animal behavior which appear to be nonlearned. They have not, however, thereby demonstrated the reality of behavior elements that are uninfluenced during ontogeny by extrinsic stimulus conditions, or by what may be more simply labeled experience. Subsequently, we shall have occasion to argue that learning and experience are not equivalent agents in the determination of behavior.

THEORETICAL PROPERTIES OF THE FAP

In our delineation of the empirical characteristics of the FAP, it thus far has been treated solely as a descriptive concept. Now, however, we must turn to an analysis of some of the mechanisms or processes which have been inferred by instinct theorists to underlie the development and organization of the FAP and which in turn explain its empirical properties.

Genetic Encoding

Instinct theorists contend that an organism inherits FAPs just as it inherits morphological structures (Eibl-Eibesfeldt & Kramer, 1958). Although this position does not imply that instinct theorists believe that FAPs develop independently of a specific embryogenic environment, it does imply that the elements of the genic constitution participate in or contribute to the FAP in a functionally congruent manner.

Indeed, Lorenz and others (e.g., Thorpe, 1961) have been quite explicit in maintaining that each FAP is genetically encoded, and that such encoding is expressed in the organization of neural centers which serve to control and coordinate the sequence of muscle actions involved in performance. Bullock (1961) has stated the instinct theorists' position on this point quite precisely:

It seems at present highly likely that for many complex behavioral actions the nervous system contains not only genetically determined circuits but also genetically determined physiological properties of their components so that the complete act is represented in coded form and awaits only an adequate trigger, either internal or external [p. 55].

The recent work of Miller (1957), Andersson (1953), and Harris, Michael, and Scott (1958) has, of course, demonstrated the close association between neural loci and specific responses. But instinct theorists go much further, for they speak of the FAP as being not only centrally integrated but centrally blueprinted—a blueprint that is directly provided for in the growth process itself. And they contend that it is by virtue of the intrinsically established blueprint that the FAP—as a temporally patterned system of response elements—can appear without having been ontogenetically organized. Indeed, since such systems are considered to be genetically specified down to the smallest detail, it is understandable that the influence of experiential events in determining their configuration and phenotypic expression is held to be not only unnecessary but ineffective (Lorenz, 1937, 1956). And it is equally understandable, granting once more the specific encoding, that they should speak of FAPs as constituting the nucleus of an animal's response repertoire—a nucleus which, although overlaid with acquired elements during ontogeny, nevertheless retains its distinctive character in the behavior of the adult organism.

Action Specific Energy

As already pointed out, instinct theorists have been particularly impressed with the spontaneity of the FAP, often regarding it as that property which renders the FAP a unique behavioral event. To Lorenz, this spontaneity suggested that each FAP possesses its own source of energy which accumulates in that locus of the central nervous system responsible for its coordination. This accumulation is assumed to occur while the particular movement is quiescent and to be expended when the movement is discharged. Tinbergen (1951) has also proposed an essentially similar reservoir-model of motivation involving a hierarchically organized system of neural centers responsible for the activation of a chain of functionally related activities (e.g., those involved in reproduction).

Of particular theoretical interest with respect to the reservoir-type model of motivation is the assumption by the instinct theorist that motor impulses are endogenously produced in a specific center and that the basic pattern of production not only occurs independently of afferent inflow but is in fact refractory to modulation by such inflow. In maintaining that the spontaneity of the FAP is a manifestation of such a purely central automaticity, the instinct theorist points to cardiac and respiratory activities, as well as other basic functions, and considers evidence regarding their spontaneity as providing clues for understanding the neurological basis of complex behavioral spontaneity.

In this connection, the studies of Adrian (1931), von Holst (1934), Maynard (1955) and others are frequently cited. Adrian and Buytendijk (1931), for example, concluded that respiratory activity is endogenously generated after finding that potential changes recorded from the isolated brain stem of the goldfish exhibit the same frequency as that of normal breathing movements. Maynard (1955) found that when the factors which influence heart beat in the lobster are held constant, a complex periodic pattern of impulses is still generated by the cardiac ganglion.

It obviously requires a long inductive leap to go from the comparatively simple functioning of an isolated segment of the nervous system to the temporally organized behavior of the intact animal. But it is precisely this leap that the instinct theorist has taken.

Significance of the FAP

Before attempting to analyze the psychological implications of the FAP, two sources of misunderstanding, each of which has led to some confusion concerning the significance of the FAP, must be clarified. In the first place, it should be apparent that the FAP is not to be identified with response patterns which have been traditionally regarded as instinctive and which have usually been given such global designations as maternal behavior, filial behavior, migratory behavior, etc. What must be emphasized is that each of these labels refers to a myriad of functionally related activities of which only a few might be both empirically and conceptually identical to the FAP. To the author's knowledge, no contemporary instinct theorist ever considered maternal behavior, for example, to be innate in the same sense that the FAP is considered to be innate. Certainly, it is irrelevant to criticize either the reality or the significance of the FAP by showing that patterns like maternal behavior, or any pattern of such heterogeneous composition, is experientially organized and consequently could be neither genetically encoded nor endogenously generated.

Secondly, assessment of the FAP must be twofold, since its value as an empirical concept is independent of the validity of those hypothetical mechanisms assumed by instinct theorists to underlie its structure and organization. In discussing significance, we must, therefore, clearly distinguish between the empirical and theoretical roles which the FAP plays.

Significance of the FAP as an Empirical Concept

As a class of response events, FAPs appear to be important empirically in at least three respects: taxonomically, evolutionally, and genetically.

Consider first their taxonomic value. A behavior pattern that possesses the phenotypic properties of the FAP would seem ideally suited to serve as a classificatory device. The particular virtues of stereotypy and resistance to ontogenetic modification should make it possible for the FAP to provide taxonomic information both of a diagnostic and of an associative nature (Mayr, 1958).

Consistent with this claim is the fact that the taxonomist no longer relies exclusively on morphological data; indeed, when structural and behavioral evidence lead to conflicting classificatory decisions, he is often inclined to give greater weight to the latter. And, relevantly enough, many of the responses thus employed appear to be phenotypically akin to FAPs, if not phenotypically identical with them. Crane (1941, 1957), for example, used certain display movements to classify species of fiddler crabs—species that are so structurally alike that a hand lens and a trained eye are required to differentiate them anatomically. Similarly, Hinde (1955), Lorenz (1958), and Tinbergen (1959) have used motor patterns involved in aggression and courtship to elucidate relationships among some closely related avian taxa.

Secondly, the FAP can be used as an instrument in studying behavioral evolution. The morphologist interested in reconstructing phylogenetic histories has many available traits with which to work—traits that are quantitatively delineable, ontogenetically stable, and interspecifically differentiable. The student of behavior who is devoted to the same pursuit is far less fortunate, since response traits suitable for evolutionary analysis are rare. Again the FAP should prove valuable. The readiness with which it can be discriminated from other components of a species' repertoire, the degree to which it resists ontogenetic modification, and the manner in which it is distributed among related taxa (neither too conservatively nor too divergently) make it ideally suited as an object of phylogenetic study.

Reports already in the literature support this evaluation. Hinde and Tinbergen (1958), and Tinbergen (1954), for example, have offered stimulating evolutionary analyses of certain display movements in birds and Baerends and Baerends-van Roon (1950) have been able to carry out a parallel study for cichlid fishes. Similar analyses have also been performed on many elements of invertebrate behavior that appear empirically akin to FAPs: Crane (1941) on the courtship response of fiddler crabs; Evans (1953) on the wing movements of wasps; and Blest (1960) on the settling behavior of moths, to mention only a few.

A third empirical consequence arising from the discovery of the FAP is its utility in the study of gene-behavior relationships. As Fuller and Thompson (1960) have stressed, selection of appropriate phenotypic measures is one of the most pressing and significant problems for the psychologist interested in behavior genetics. Here also FAPs, because of their environmental stability, their stereotypy, their particulate and quantitatively delineable character, provide highly satisfactory analytic units for psychogenetic research. Several attempts (e.g., Dilger, 1959, 1962; Hinde, 1956; Ramsay, 1961) have already been made to employ them in just this capacity.

Significance of the FAP as a Theoretical Concept

In its role as a theoretical concept, what possible contributions does the FAP make toward increasing our understanding of behavior? To answer this question, let us accept provisionally the theoretical inferences which the instinct theorist has drawn and examine some of their implications.

It will be recalled that FAPs are conceived to constitute the nucleus of an animal's response repertoire—a nucleus that is encoded in the genome and that subsequently interlocks with all acquired elements of behavior. Although the relationship between these nuclear elements and the more complex learned patterns of behavior has not as yet been elaborated for any species, the instinct theorist nonetheless has contended that analysis of a repertoire into component elements—an essential first step in understanding the behavior of any species—must proceed from the genetically given to the individually acquired. It is considered literally impossible to understand learning, for example, without first understanding the innate substructure upon which it is based and by which it is in turn affected (Lorenz, 1960; Tinbergen & Perdeck, 1951).

One implication then of the theoretical inferences that have been drawn from the FAP is a policy for conducting research: the nuclear elements of a response repertoire must first be distinguished, their properties analyzed, and their influence on all other components investigated. After completion of these tasks, ontogenetic research should then be undertaken but only in relation to those response systems designated as acquired. Obviously, there would be no need to study the cumulative effects of organismic-environmental interactions on innate responses; genetically encoded and centrally blueprinted, their organization should not be influenced to any significant extent by experiential events.

Another consequence of the FAP as a theoretical concept derives from its alleged capacity to provide an index of certain neurophysiological events. It will be recalled that each FAP is considered to be centrally preformed in the sense that a genotypically fixed isomorphism is assumed to exist between its phenotypic properties and the anatomical and physiological characteristics of its neural coordinating center. On this basis, instinct theorists have concluded that it should be possible to make relatively detailed inferences about the nature of such centers from observations carried out at the molar level (Lorenz, 1960).

The opportunity to proceed from the molar to the molecular in so direct and specific a fashion would undoubtedly be of inestimable value in studying neural processes. A temporally integrated response pattern, isomorphic with a localized encapsulated brain region, would provide an instrument, hitherto unavailable, for rendering molar properties into physiological mechanisms. Indeed, even if we were convinced that the translation would not be simple, the very assumption of an isomorphic relationship of the kind postulated by the instinct theorist has profound empirical consequences—consequences quite different from those which would result if we were to assume that FAPs, like most other temporally integrated responses, are probably determined by a complex of functionally heterogeneous neural processes which occur in anatomically diverse brain regions and which do not correspond either topologically or topographically to the behavioral events they underlie. Thus, expecting functional congruency between the molar and molecular levels makes us prone to homologize all response elements having analogous functional characteristics. As Lehrman (1953) has pointed out, this results in an approach that is essentially anticomparative insofar as phenotypic resemblances tend to be abstracted from diverse phyletic levels and translated into identical physiological mechanisms without regard for differences in species capacities.

There is a third theoretical consequence, still more far reaching in its implications for psychology than the two we have discussed thus far. If the FAP is a temporally integrated behavioral entity which is uniquely organized and with characteristic properties specifically derived from this organization, then laws singularly applicable to the FAP would be necessary to accommodate the fact of its existence. Such a prescription obviously results in a search for novel functional relationships, and this is what the instinct theorist has evidently tried to do. On the one hand, he has attempted to show that responses identified as FAPs cannot be subsumed either by the laws of learning or by the laws of reflex action. On the other hand, he has made an effort to study what he considers to be innately determined perceptory mechanisms—mechanisms which, upon being activated by specific environmental stimuli, presumably function to release the FAP (e.g., Lorenz, 1960, 1961; Tinbergen & Perdeck, 1951).

CRITICAL EVALUATION OF THE FAP

Critics of instinct theory do not deny the reality of the FAP, nor do they belittle the importance of studying the FAP in understanding vertebrate behavior. The questions which have been asked revolve first about the theoretical constructs used to explain the FAP: do the empirical properties of the FAP demand the kind of hypothetical neurophysiological events deduced by the instinct theorist or can these same properties be subsumed under what might be called an epigenetic approach? A corollary to this question is whether these species-typic responses require the formulation of special developmental laws or can they be integrated within a single developmental theory that embraces acquired responses as well?

We have already noted that the empirical properties of the FAP have been interpreted to support conclusions concerning genetic encoding and central itemization. At the outset, it must be emphasized that there is no evidence, either genetic or embryologic, which in principle contraindicates the possible validity of this interpretation. Nor is behavioral evidence available which would establish conclusively that responses designated as FAPs cannot be innate in the very sense in which the instinct theorist has used that term. It is, however, meaningful to inquire whether the empirical features of the FAP can in fact be explained without recourse to propositions involving the idea of genetic preformism.

Since most FAPs have not been subjected to experimental study, they cannot, by and large, be used to exemplify the manner in which ontogenetic processes can function in determining the structure and organization of species-type behavior. Our analysis, therefore, will frequently draw on research involving responses which are only crudely analogous to the FAP. As a consequence, the evidence and arguments presented cannot rule out the possibility that the instinct theorist may be correct; but it does provide us with a reasonable and perhaps more cogent alternative for conceptualizing the FAP.

Alternative Routes to Stereotypy

Let us begin by trying to understand how a temporally integrated response exhibited in a virtually identical manner by all members of a taxon could arise even if the response itself were not genetically encoded. Of the number of possible alternative sources for such stereotypy, the most obvious lies in the environment itself.

Involved in the biotic province of any species are certain environmental constancies which may function to produce parallel responses in all normal members (Hebb, 1953; Lehrman, 1953). As Lehrman in particular has pointed out, this homogenization can occur either as a consequence of such constancies channeling ontogeny in congruent directions so that only certain developmental possibilities are realized or of their providing each individual with identical avenues for response expression so that, even when alternate forms of the same response are present in the repertoire, only one is likely to be manifest.

Thus Harker (1953) reports that the highly stereotyped diurnal activity rhythm exhibited by the adult mayfly does not occur unless the individual organism has been subjected to at least one 24-hour light-dark cycle prior to the termination of the larval period (see also Brown, 1959). Thorpe and Jones (1937) showed that the recurrent selection of the flour moth by the parasitic ichneumon fly, *Nemeritis canescens,* for the purpose of oviposition is significantly changed in Nemeritis offspring when they are reared on a different host. Apparently, host

selection by an adult is in part a consequence of exposure to the specific chemical and nutritional milieu which Nemeritis experiences while in a preimaginal stage. And finally, Van der Kloot and Williams (1953a, 1953b) have pointed to characteristically invariant environmental factors which influence the cocoon-construction of Cecropia silkworms. Of special interest here is the fact that, when the caterpillar of this lepidopteran species is deprived of the usual physical support (an upright twig crotch) on which to spin its finely tapered cocoon, it will use spinning movements which are quite atypical, resulting in a cocoon markedly distinct from the normal.

The anatomical and functional properties of peripheral structures also provide a possible explanation of behavioral stereotypy, for such structures can function directly to render specific response patterns invariant. Perhaps the clearest exemplification of the detailed interrelationships which can exist between response elements and associated peripheral mechanisms is provided by the work of Davis (1957) on the spotted and brown towhees. These birds forage for food by using a scratching movement which is performed in a highly stereotyped but essentially different manner in each species. Scratching by the brown towhee occurs with a backward thrust that is noticeably less powerful than that manifested by the spotted towhee and incorporates a pronounced lateral component that its congeneric counterpart does not exhibit. Davis has argued convincingly that interspecific differences in the expression of the scratching movement are directly determined by characteristic differences in the osteology and myology of the hindlimbs.

In the present context, it is important to emphasize that functionally similar stereotyped responses need not be governed by the same causal events, as illustrated by two instances of invariant behavior occurring at widely different levels of the phyletic scale. The jellyfish, for example, exhibits certain characteristic feeding movements which appear to be a direct consequence of the functional properties of its medusoid nerve-net system and the spatial arrangements of its tentacles and manubrium (Maier & Schneirla, 1935). The great tit (Paris major) also exhibits certain species-typic feeding movements but, in contrast to the jellyfish, these movements develop over many ontogenetic pathways and involve more complex interrelationships between intrinsic and extrinsic factors.

Thus, as Schneirla has repeatedly emphasized (e.g., 1946, 1956), stereotypy can arise from causes which operate directly and are immediately apparent or from causes which are considerably more subtle and involve the operation of disparate ontogenetic mechanisms. Our discussion of environmental constancies and structural equipment as conceivable sources of stereotypy does not mean, therefore, that one or the other of these factors is involved in all instances of behavioral rigidification or that their mode of influence is always the same. Not only may there be additional modes of origin but it is also impossible to generalize with respect to the manner in which any one of them operates to homogenize different response patterns at different phyletic levels.

Innateness and the Distinction between Learning and Experience

Let us turn now to consider another characteristic of the FAP—independence from individual learning—and attempt first to see what this criterion means and then to determine whether

independence as such necessarily entails the assumption of innateness.

As we have already pointed out, the instinct theorist seems to conceive of learning in a way that is entirely too restrictive. When a conventional reinforcing agent does not seem to be involved, he is likely to assume that learning could not have occurred. In view of the controversial status of the reinforcement issue in learning theory itself, the absence of reward can hardly be considered as *prima facie* evidence for the absence of learning. But even if we broaden the classificatory criteria for distinguishing the learned from the nonlearned and even if we were to grant that these criteria may change as our understanding of the learning process expands (Beach, 1955; Verplanck, 1955), it still seems reasonable to designate as nonlearned those responses whose development cannot be explained in terms of any extant learning paradigm. Viewed in this way, the FAP can be classified—at least provisionally—as a nonlearned response.

The question which remains to be answered is whether genetic encoding becomes the only plausible way to conceptualize the manner in which nonlearned behavioral elements can arise in ontogeny. The answer is clearly in the negative, for we know that experiential interactions not presently included within the scope of learning can influence the structure and organization of behavior in specific and important ways (Schneirla, 1956, 1957; Schneirla & Rosenblatt, 1961).

Schneirla has used the term "experience" to denote a wide range of stimulative involvements which determine trace effects varying in complexity from specific physicochemical changes in somatic tissue to general functional integrations in the central nervous system. As he goes on to point out, the manifestations of such effects, in turn, can represent very different levels of behavioral organization. Thus, compare host selection in certain arthropods as influenced by the composition of the medium on which the larvae are fed (Thorpe & Jones, 1937) with the influence of early patterned light stimulation on form discrimination and interocular transfer in vertebrates (Chow & Nissen, 1955; Riesen, 1951, 1958, 1960). Again, contrast the reciprocal stimulative associations ("trophallaxis") apparently essential for the organization of certain insect colonies (Schneirla, 1946) with the development of avoidance responses in mammals as effected by isolation from conspecifics (Melzack & Scott, 1957).

Each of the cases just cited entails ontogenetic processes which, currently at least, are not describable as learning but which nonetheless depend on some type of interaction between the organism and its sensory environment. To clarify the distinction involved here, let us consider one example in detail. Recent studies (Hebb, 1946; McBride & Hebb, 1948; Melzack, 1952; Riesen, 1961) of the genesis of emotional behavior in vertebrates indicate that intense fear can be elicited by strange, although innocuous, visual stimuli. What is necessary for this development is commerce with a structured sensory environment—commerce in which the very fact of exposure seems sufficient to establish the visually familiar. It is evident that the animal does not have to *learn* to discriminate the familiar from the unfamiliar nor does it have to undergo avoidance conditioning before it comes to fear stimuli which differ markedly from those already encountered. Once early contact delimits the perceptually typical, presentation of an incongruous stimulus combination is all that is necessary to evoke an emotional response.

Admittedly, the term experience is difficult to define precisely, but some such term is evidently needed to designate instances, such as those just cited, in which involvement with the ontogenetic milieu operates to structure behavior through channels which do not appear to depend on learning as currently conceived.

We have already mentioned the isolation technique as a means for assessing the influence of learning. What about its value in assessing the influence of experience? There is no doubt that, if proper control conditions are employed, the isolation technique can provide evidence as to the importance of social interaction as a developmental variable. When Cullen (1960), for example, showed that male sticklebacks reared in isolation performed the typical zigzag "courting" dance on the first occasion that they were presented with a model of a gravid female, she thereby demonstrated that, whatever else is necessary for the ontogenesis of the dance, experience with conspecifics is not. But to say that the zigzag dance does not develop out of the interaction with species members is obviously not equivalent to asserting that the "whole 'blueprint' of a specifically structured receptor and effector apparatus is contained in the genoma [Lorenz, 1961, p. 183]." This unwarranted deductive leap—one which the instinct theorist often makes on the basis of an isolation experiment—results from the failure to realize that an animal removed from the company of species members is not necessarily removed from other nonsocial environmental effects which in themselves might be sufficient for the organization of the observed behavior pattern.

Indeed, with respect to the genesis

of certain response patterns, the isolation and normal situations may not be significantly different in that they may both provide conditions guaranteeing the occurrence of exactly the same critical experiential involvements. As Lehrman (1953) has put it, "The important question is not 'Is the animal isolated?' but *From what* is the animal isolated? [p. 343]." For example, there is compelling evidence (Birch, 1956; Schneirla & Rosenblatt, 1960; Steinberg & Bindra, 1962) that, in the rat and cat, certain self-stimulative processes, particularly those involved in licking the posterior parts of the body and ingesting vaginal fluids, are implicated in the development of maternal behavior. Separation from conspecifics could hardly be expected to inhibit the occurrence of such processes any more than the presence of conspecifics would be expected to facilitate their expression.

We do not wish to impugn the value of the isolation technique nor to deny the importance of determining whether or not social interactions is critical for the organization of species-typic responses. We merely wish to point to the obvious fact that social interaction is not the only channel through which extrinsic stimulative effects can participate in the genesis of nonlearned behavior and consequently that the isolation experiment cannot be considered decisive in relation to the question of whether a particular response element is genetically encoded or experientially organized.

Independence from Immediate Afferent Control and Neurogenesis

It will be recalled that freedom of the FAP from immediate afferent control has been adduced to support two theoretical propositions: that the component response elements of the FAP are centrally coordinated by virtue of genetically organized neural circuits, and that the threshold fluctuations characteristic of the FAP arise solely from the accumulation and discharge of endogenously generated motivational impulses.

The problem of how the nervous system becomes structured to support the orderly relations among the constituent parts of a movement pattern is not to be confused with the problem of how central coordinative mechanisms, whether maturationally organized or experientially established, participate in energizing such patterns. The two problems are obviously distinct and warrant separate consideration. We shall treat the first of these in the present section.

To begin with, it should be emphasized that no contemporary student of behavior would maintain (contrary to the contention of Lorenz, 1960) that the embryonic growth process simply leaves an equipotential homogeneous network out of which every neuronal linkage must subsequently be forged by training or experience. At the very least, all would agree that the basic architecture of the nervous system is determined by intrinsic developmental forces—in other words, that the location of nuclear centers and the topographical arrangement of fiber tracts become established during embryogeny in species-typic fashion (Sperry, 1951, 1958). But for the instinct theorist, the role inherited structures play in the organization of the FAP is highly specific—there are coordinating structures in the brain and spinal cord containing genetically patterned circuits which determine the FAP down to its smallest detail. For the critics, in contrast, the intrinsic contribution is very much less determinate and, with the possible exception of mechanisms underlying certain simple reflex reactions, does not include neuronal anlagen sufficient in themselves to provide for the expression of any temporally integrated response. Rather, the growth process, in establishing the general structural and functional plan of the nervous system, is conceived to provide a substrate against which neural configurations subserving coordinated behavior gradually become refined and elaborated through environmental interactions—a substrate, in other words, that essentially determines the directions and limits of a response repertoire but not its details.

With this distinction in mind, we can now turn to the theoretical issue raised by evidence of independence from immediate afferent control. When a response is released but not guided by extrinsic stimuli, it is reasonable to assume that an organized central system has been activated and that the properties of this system influence the phenotypic character of the observed behavior. It is quite likely that such systems underlie the FAP, for, in addition to the presumptive evidence supplied by field observations, there are experimental results which support the same conclusion. Thus Hess (1949) and Hess and Brugger (1943) have demonstrated that, in the cat, punctate electrical stimulation of diencephalic loci can evoke discrete behavioral items normally involved in eating, sleeping, and fighting. More recently, von Holst and St. Paul (1960, 1962) have been able to produce a broad range of movements by stimulating a variety of localized points in the brain stem of domestic fowl. The movements elicited were species-typic and functionally identical with those exhibited in caring for the young, in pecking, and in flight from enemies.

The instinct theorist considers data of the kind just cited to indicate the existence of endogenously predetermined neuronal systems sufficiently organized to integrate the component elements of the FAP into an orderly spatial and temporal amalgam. However, no really critical evidence has as yet been adduced in support of this possibility.

First, the fact that punctate stimulation can effect the discharge of an integrated response is in itself not decisive with respect to determining the nature of antecedent neurogenic events. Miller (1957, 1958, 1960), for example, was able to elicit a previously learned bar-pressing response in satiated rats by stimulating ventromedial nuclei in the hypothalamus. In this case, it is obvious that extrinsic induction rather than intrinsic self-differentiation was the primary organizing agent underlying the observed behavior. Secondly, the research we have cited involving the "release" of responses which have at least some of the phenotypic properties of the FAP, has employed only adult animals and consequently cannot rule out the possibility that the underlying neuronal configurations, instead of being genetically blueprinted, required experientially instigated refinement before achieving the degree of functional specificity necessary to support response expression.

Finally, as both Gloor (1954) and Lehrman (1953, 1956) have emphasized, the instinct theorist has tended to overinterpret the work of Hess and his associates. The diencephalic areas they stimulated did not exhibit the characteristics of self-contained encapsulated units awaiting only adequate releasing stimuli before discharging their responses. Rather, the effects of stimulation depended partly on the nature of concurrent afferent inflow, the form of the response as well as its latency of release being modified accordingly. This, of course, does not corroborate the view that

47

autogenous differentiation is sufficient to provide for the coordination of the FAP. Indeed, whatever the extent of their genetically induced organization, it is possible that these areas must be continuously directed by information coming from cortical and somatic sources in order to support temporally integrated behavior. Whether the same interpretation can also be offered in relation to the work of von Holst and St. Paul remains to be determined.

Response Elicitability and Action-Specific Energy

That a temporally integrated behavioral pattern like the FAP should seem to exhibit an activity-specific rhythm of exhaustion and recovery has posed challenging problems for all students of behavior. As already indicated, this rhythmicity has led the instinct theorist to propose a reservoir model of motivation and, in addition, to conjecture that the underlying process must be central in origin and neurologically akin to the evidently endogenous activity shown by the cardiac ganglion of the lobster and the brain stem of the goldfish.

One can never be certain, however, even when working with isolated nerve-cell preparations, that the environment is not partly responsible for the pattern of excitation that is present (Adrian, 1950). All that one can be sure of is that a particular neural rhythm is not the result of a corresponding afferent rhythm. However, there is a great deal of evidence which, although not absolutely conclusive, nonetheless makes it reasonable to infer that the invertebrate as well as the vertebrate nervous system is continuously active, generating patterned impulse-sequences that arise neither from phasic nor from nonphasic sensory input (Bullock, 1961; Prechtl,

1956). But to grant the validity of this inference is not tantamount to consenting to the instinct theorist's attempt to relate such endogenously determined impulse sequences to fluctuations in the elicitability of the FAP. There are simply no neurological data which convincingly support the idea that the motivational dynamics of the FAP, or of any other temporally integrated movement pattern for that matter, are controlled and regulated by the automatic production of response-specific impulses.

To illustrate the inductive gap which in fact exists here, consider the type of evidence to which the instinct theorist has repeatedly appealed. Weiss (1941) implanted a piece of spinal cord and a limb bud onto the back of an amblystoma embryo and found that movement occurred as soon as efferent fibers made contact with the limb despite the fact that afferent connections had not yet been established. Although this result does provide dramatic evidence of neural automaticity, it certainly does not show that the source of energy for a response pattern as complex as the FAP is neurologically akin to the innervation of a limb bud nor even that coordinated locomotion can arise independently of sensory input. In relation to the question of coordination, it should be emphasized that the movements Weiss observed were only spasmodic or paroxysmal, hence, differing markedly from the smooth ambulatory rhythm normally evinced by the adult amblystoma. Significantly enough, studies by Gray and Lissman (1940, 1946a, 1946b) have demonstrated that peripheral excitation is absolutely essential for the typical locomotory pattern of the amphibian and, by implication, for all other vertebrates as well (also see Gray, 1950).

Of course, the status of the reservoir model of motivation does not rest solely on the neurological speculations advanced by the instinct theorist. The behavioral implications of the model are considerably more important and it is upon them that a definitive evaluation must be based.

The reservoir model makes reduction in elicitability contingent upon response expression since it holds that the discharge of action-specific energy can occur only through the performance or execution of the response. On this basis, it seems appropriate to ask whether reduction in elicitability necessarily requires response performance and, correlatively, whether a behavioral model involving the accumulation and release of action specific energy is generally applicable.

Prechtl (1953) found that the gaping response of young chaffinches can be elicited by visual, acoustic, and vibratory stimuli. He then discovered that the exhaustion of gaping by repeated presentation of one stimulus left the nestling relatively unaffected in its readiness to gape to the other stimuli. Hinde (1954, 1960a, 1960b) has also reported similar results in relation to other responses having the functional characteristics of the FAP, and has emphasized that, for such responses at least, stimulus-specific satiation rather than the discharge of response-specific energy appears to be the mechanism effecting reduction in elicitability.

The reservoir model must also be considered inadequate because it fails to incorporate the fact that FAP availability can change as a function of other types of afferent relationships which are perhaps even more subtle. A relevant case here is the incubation behavior of the black-headed gull (Beer, 1961, 1962; Moynihan, 1953). In settling on a clutch of eggs, these birds perform a sequence of movements which include lowering the chest, waggling the tail from side to side, and rapidly quivering the body. Of particular significance as Beer has pointed out, is the fact that the frequency with which this sequence occurs is related not to energy consumption, but in part at least, to thermal effects consequent upon settling. More specifically, if the pattern of sensory stimulation received from the eggs fails to satisfy the temperature requirements of the brood patch, and probably the requirements of other structures as well, then the bird will begin again and repeat the entire settling sequence. In fact, it can be made to do this many times simply by decreasing the normal clutch number or by causing the eggs to become disarranged.

In addition to stimulus effects of the kind we have just discussed, brief mention might also be made of the role played by the absolute level of afferent input. Hebb (1955) has drawn attention to the significance of the brain-stem reticular system, proposing that its innervation by peripheral inflow induces a general arousal state which influences all behavior regardless of the specific control mechanisms involved. The reticular formation, functioning in the capacity of a nonspecific activator, could then produce widespread threshold changes. If this in fact proves to be so in relation to the FAP, then the reservoir model would have to accommodate not only the influence of specific stimulus factors but the influence of general ones as well.

It seems clear from the evidence cited thus far that reduction in the elicitability of an FAP is not necessarily contingent on its performance. On this basis, it is reasonable to conclude that the reservoir model, involving as it does the concept of response-effected energy discharge, does not offer a framework comprehensive enough to integrate all instances of threshold change in the FAP.

An Epigenetic Approach to the FAP

The above analysis indicates that the theoretical position of the instinct theorist is not in fact demanded by the empirical properties of the FAP. Indeed, we are able to show that each of these properties can reasonably be interpreted in a manner broadly consonant with what may be called an epigenetic approach. In conclusion it would be well to attempt a general characterization of the major features of this approach.

An epigenetic approach holds that all response systems are synthesized during ontogeny and that this synthesis involves the integrative influence of both intraorganic processes and extrinsic stimulative conditions. It considers gene effects to be contingent on environmental conditions and regards the genotype as capable of entering into different classes of relationships depending on the prevailing environmental context. In the epigeneticist's view, the environment is not benignly supportive, but actively implicated in determining the very structure and organization of each response system.

Contrast this view with the template conception of the instinct theorist which maintains that FAPs result from the virtually passive translation of genetic factors into phenotypic traits through the medium of tissue growth and tissue differentiation. Each FAP, in other words, is represented in the genome by functionally congruent genic agents which become transmuted into underlying neural coordinating centers as long as conditions consonant with viability prevail.

According to an epigenetic concep-tion of development, however, there is no adaptively organized response—species-typic or otherwise—that exhibits the genetic parallelism of which the instinct theorist speaks. Rather, the behavioral significance of genetic entities, and consequently of organic traits, is conceived to derive, in part as least, from the particular environmental context with which they become intermeshed during ontogeny. It is this coalescence of the endogenous and the extrinsic which, in an epigenetic view, makes each integrated response an emergent and which thus renders it gravely misleading to conceptualize maturational elements as functioning isomorphically in behavioral development.

REFERENCES

Adrian, E. D. The control of nerve-cell activity. *Symposia of the Society for Experimental Biology,* 1950, 4, 85–91.

Adrian, E. D., & Buytendijk, F. J. J. Potential changes in the isolated brain of the goldfish. *Journal of Physiology,* 1931, 71, 121–130.

Adrian, E. D. Potential changes in the isolated nervous system of Dytiscus marginalis. *Journal of Physiology,* 1931, 72, 132–151.

Andersson, B. The effect of injections of hypertonic NaCl-solutions into different parts of the hypothalamus in goats. *Acta Physiologica Scandinavica,* 1953, 28, 188–201.

Baerends, G. P. The ethological analysis of fish behavior. In M. E. Brown (Ed.), *The physiology of fishes.* Vol. 2. New York: Academic Press, 1957. Pp. 229–269.

Baerends, G. P., & Baerends-von Roon, J. M. An introduction to the study of the ethology of cichlid fishes. *Behaviour,* Supplement I, 1950.

Beach, F. A. The descent of instinct. *Psychological Review,* 1955, 62, 401–410.

Beer, C. G. Incubation and nest-building behaviour of black-headed gulls. I: Incubation behaviour in the incubation period. *Behaviour,* 1961, 18, 62–106.

Beer, C. G. Incubation and nest-building behaviour of black-headed gulls. II: Incubation behaviour in the laying period. *Behaviour*, 1962, 19, 283–304.

BIRCH, H. G. Sources of order in the maternal behavior of animals. *American Journal of Orthopsychiatry*, 1956, 26, 279–284.

BLEST, A. D. The evolution, ontogeny and quantitative control of the settling movements of some new world saturniid moths, with some comments on distance communication by honey-bees. *Behaviour*, 1960, 16, 188–253.

BROWN, F. A., JR. The rhythmic nature of animals and plants. *American Scientist*, 1959, 47, 147–168.

BULLOCK, T. H. The origins of patterned nervous discharge,. *Behaviour*, 1961, 17, 48–59.

CHOW, K. L., & NISSEN, H. W. Interocular transfer of learning in visually naive and experienced infant chimpanzees. *Journal of Comparative and Physiological Psychology*, 1955, 48, 229–237.

CRANE, J. Eastern Pacific Expeditions of the New York Zoological Society. XXVI. Crabs of the genus *Uca* from the West Coast of Central America. *Zoologica*, 1941, 26, 145–208.

CRANE, J. Basic patterns of display in fiddler crabs (*Ocypodidae*, Genus Uca). *Zoologica*, 1957, 42, 69–82.

CULLEN, E. Experiment on the effect of social isolation on reproductive behaviour in the three-spined stickleback. *Animal Behaviour*, 1960, 8, 235. (Abstract)

DAVIS, J. Comparative foraging behaviour of the spotted and brown towhees. *Auk*, 1957, 74, 129–166.

DILGER, W. Nest material carrying behavior of F_1 hybrids between *Agapornis fischeri* and *A. roseicollis*. *Anatomical Record*, 1959, 134, 554.

DILGER, W. C. Behavior and genetics. In E. C. Bliss (Ed.), *Roots of behavior*. New York: Harper, 1962. Pp. 35–47.

EIBL-EIBESFELDT, I. The interactions of unlearned behaviour patterns and learning in mammals. In J. F. Delafresnaye (Ed.), *Brain mechanisms and learning*. Oxford: Blackwell Scientific Publications, 1961. Pp. 52–73.

EIBL-EIBESFELDT, I., & KRAMER, S. Ethology, the comparative study of animal behavior. *Quarterly Review of Biology*, 1958, 33, 181–211.

EVANS, H. E. Comparative ethology and the systematics of spider wasps. *Systematic Zoology*, 1953, 3, 155–172.

FULLER, J. L., & THOMPSON, W. R. *Behavior genetics*. New York: Wiley, 1960.

GLOOR, P. Autonomic functions of the diencephalon. A summary of the experimental work of Prof. W. R. Hess. *Archives of Neurological Psychiatry*, 1954, 71, 773–790.

GRAY, J. The role of peripheral sense organs during locomotion in vertebrates. *Symposia of the Society of Experimental Biology*, 1950, 4, 112–126.

GRAY, J., & LISSMAN, H. W. The effect of de-afferentation upon the locomotor activity of amphibian limbs. *Journal of Experimental Biology*, 1940, 17, 227–236.

GRAY, J., & LISSMAN, H. W. Further observations on the effect of de-afferentation on the locomotory activity of amphibian limbs. *Journal of Experimental Biology*, 1946, 23, 121–132. (a)

GRAY, J., & LISSMAN, H. W. Coordination of limb movements in the amphibia. *Journal of Experimental Biology*, 1946, 23, 133–142 (b)

HARKER, J. E. Diurnal rhythms in the animal kingdom. *Biological Reviews and Biological Proceedings of the Cambridge Philosophical Society*, 1958, 33, 1–52.

HARRIS, G. W., MICHAEL, R. P., & SCOTT, P. P. Neurological site of action of stilbesterol in eliciting sexual behavior. In, *Neurological basis of behavior*. Boston: Little, Brown, 1958. Pp. 236–254.

HEBB, D. O. On the nature of fear. *Psychological Review*, 1946, 53, 250–275.

HEBB, D. O. Heredity and environment in mammalian behaviour. *British Journal of Animal Behaviour*, 1953, 1, 43–47.

HEBB, D. O. Drives and the C.N.S. (Conceptual nervous system). *Psychological Review*, 1955, 62, 243–254.

HESS, W. R. Das Zwischenhirn: Syndrome, Lokalizationem, Funktionem. Basel: Benno Schwabe, 1949.

HESS, W. R., & BRUGGER, M. Das subkortikale Zentrum der Affektiven Abwehrreaktion. *Helvetica physiologica et pharmacologica acta*, 1943, 1, 33–52.

HINDE, R. A. Changes in responsiveness to a constant stimulus. *British Journal of Animal Behaviour*, 1954, 2, 41–55.

HINDE, R. A. A comparative study of the behaviour of certain finches. *Ibis*, 1955, 97, 706–745, 98, 1–23.

HINDE, R. A. The behaviour of certain cardueline F_1 interspecies hybrids. *Behaviour*, 1956, 9, 202–213.

HINDE, R. A. Some recent trends in ethology. In S. Koch (Ed.), *Psychology: A study of a science*. Vol. 2. New York: McGraw-Hill, 1959. Pp. 561–610.

HINDE, R. A. Concepts of drive. In M. Brazier (Ed.), *The central nervous system and behavior.* New York: Josiah Macy Foundation, 1960. Pp. 277–305. (a)

HINDE, R. A. Motivation. *Ibis,* 1960, **101,** 353–357. (b)

HINDE, R. A., & TINBERGEN, N. The comparative study of species-specific behavior. In A. Roe & G. Simpson (Eds.), *Behavior and evolution.* New Haven: Yale Univer. Press, 1958. Pp. 251–268.

HOLST, E., VON. Studien über Reflexe and Rhythmen beim Goldfisch (*Carassius auratus*). *Zeitschrift für vergleichende Physiologie,* 1934, 20, 582–599.

HOLST, E. VON, & ST. PAUL, U. Von Wirkungsgefuge der Triebe. *Naturwissenschaften,* 1960, **18,** 409–422.

HOLST, E. VON, & ST. PAUL, U. Electrically controlled behavior. *Scientific American,* 1962, **206,** 50–59.

IERSEL, J. J. A., VAN. An analysis of the parental behaviour of the male three-spined stickleback. *Behaviour,* Suppl. III, 1953.

LEHRMAN, D. S. A critique of Konrad Lorenz's theory of instinctive behavior. *Quarterly Review of Biology,* 1953, **28,** 337–363.

LEHRMAN, D. S. On the organization of maternal behavior and the problem of instinct. In, *L'instinct dans le comportement des animaux et de l'homme.* Paris: Masson et Cie, 1956. Pp. 475–514.

LORENZ, K. Uber die Bildung Instinktbegriffes. *Die Naturwissenschaften,* 1937, **25,** 289–300, 307–318, 324–331. Translated in C. Schiller (Ed.), *Instinctive behavior.* New York: International Universities Press, 1957. Pp. 129–175.

LORENZ, K. Morphology and behavior patterns in closely allied species. In B. Schaffner (Ed.), *Group processes.* New York: Josiah Macy Foundation, 1955. Pp. 75–163.

LORENZ, K. The objectivistic theory of instinct. In, *L'instinct dans le comportement des animaux et de l'homme.* Paris: Masson et Cie, 1956. Pp. 51–64.

LORENZ, K. The evolution of behavior. *Scientific American,* 1958, 199, 67–78.

LORENZ, K. Prinzipien der Vergleichenden Verhaltensforschung. *Fortschritte der Zoologie,* 1960, 12, 265–294. Translated by E. Klinghammer, University of Chicago.

LORENZ, K. Phylogenetische Anpassung und Adaptive Modifikation des Verhaltens. *Zeitschrift für Tierpsychologie,* 1961, 18, 139–187.

LORENZ, K., & TINBERGEN, N. Taxis und Instinkthandlung in der Eirollberwegung der Graugans. *Zeitschrift für Tierpsychologie,* 1938, 2, 1–29. Translated in C. Schiller (Ed.), *Instinctive behavior.* New York: International Universities Press, 1961. Pp. 176–208.

MAIER, N. R. F., & SCHNEIRLA, T. C. *Principles of animal psychology.* New York: McGraw-Hill, 1935.

MAYNARD, D. M. Activity in a crustacean ganglion. II: Pattern and interaction in burst formation. *Biological Bulletin,* 1955, 109, 420–436.

MAYR, E. Behavior and systematics. In A. Roe & G. Simpson (Eds.), *Behavior and evolution.* New Haven: Yale Univer. Press, 1958. Pp. 341–362.

McBRIDE, A. F., & HEBB, D. O. Behavior of the captive bottle-nose dolphin Tursiops truncatus. *Journal of Comparative and Physiological Psychology,* 1948, **41,** 111–123.

MELZACK, R. Irrational fears in the dog. *Canadian Journal of Psychology,* 1952, 6, 141–147.

MELZACK, R., & SCOTT, T. H. The effects of early experience on the response to pain. *Journal of Comparative and Physiological Psychology,* 1957, 50, 155–161.

MILLER, N. E. Experiments on motivation: studies concerning psychological, physiological and pharmacological techniques. *Science,* 1957, **126,** 1271–1278.

MILLER, N. E. Central stimulation and other new approaches to motivation and reward. *American Psychologist,* 1958, 13, 100–108.

MILLER, N. E. Motivational effects of brain stimulation and drugs. *Federation Proceedings,* 1960, **19,** 846–854.

MOLTZ, H. The fixed action pattern: emperical properties and theoretical implications. In J. Wortis (Ed.), *Recent advances in biological psychiatry.* Vol. 4. New York: Plenum Press, 1962. Pp. 69–85.

MOYNIHAN, M. Some displacement activities of the Black-headed Gull. *Behavior,* 1953, **5,** 58–80.

PRECHTL, H. F. R. Zur Physiologie der Angeborenen Auslösenden Mechanismen. I. Quantitative Undersuchungen über die sperrbewegung junger Singvogel. *Behaviour,* 1953, **5,** 32–50.

PRECHTL, H. F. R. Neurophysiologische Mechanismen des formstarren Verhaltens. *Behaviour,* 1956, **9,** 243–319.

PRECHTL, H. F. R. The directed head turning response and allied movements of the human baby. *Behaviour,* 1958, **13**, 212–242.

RAMSAY, A. O. Behaviour of some hybrids in the mallard group. *Animal Behaviour,* 1961, **9**, 105–106.

RIESEN, A. H. Post-partum development of behavior. *Chicago Medical School Quarterly,* 1951, **13**, 17–24.

RIESEN, A. H. Plasticity of behavior: Psychological series. In H. F. Harlow & C. N. Woolsey (Ed.), *Biological and biochemical bases of behavior.* Madison: Univer. Wisconsin Press, 1958. Pp. 425–450.

RIESEN, A. H. Receptor functions. In P. H. Mussen (Ed.), *Handbook of research: Methods in childhood development.* New York: Wiley, 1960.

RIESEN, A. H. Stimulation as a requirement for growth and function in behavioral development. In D. W. Fiske & S. R. Maddi (Eds.), *Functions of varied experience.* Homewood, Ill.: Dorsey Press, 1961. Pp. 57–80.

SCHNEIRLA, T. C. Problems in the biopsychology of social organization. *Journal of Abnormal and Social Psychology,* 1946, **41**, 385–402.

SCHNEIRLA, T. C. Interrelationships of the "innate" and the "acquired" in instinctive behavior. In, *L'instinct dans le comportement des animaux et de l'homme.* Paris: Masson et Cie, 1956. Pp. 387–439.

SCHNEIRLA, T. C. The concept of development in comparative psychology. In D. B. Harris (Ed.), *The concept of development: An issue in the study of human behavior.* Minneapolis: Univer. Minnesota Press, 1957. Pp. 78–108.

SCHNEIRLA, T. C., & ROSENBLATT, J. Behavioral organization and genesis of the social bond in insects and mammals. *American Journal of Orthopsychiatry,* 1961, **31**, 223–253.

SPERRY, R. W. Mechanisms of neural maturation. In S. S. Stevens (Ed.), *Handbook of experimental psychology.* New York: Wiley, 1951.

SPERRY, R. W. Physiological plasticity and brain circuit theory. In H. F. Harlow & C. N. Woolsey (Ed.), *Biological and biochemical bases of behavior.* Madison: Univer. Wisconsin Press, 1958.

STEINBERG, JUNE, & BINDRA, D. Effects of pregnancy and salt-intake on genital licking. *Journal of Comparative and Physiological Psychology,* 1962, **55**, 103–106.

THORPE, W. H. Comparative psychology. *Annual Review of Psychology,* 1961, **12**, 27–50.

THORPE, W. H. *Learning and instinct in animals.* Cambridge: Harvard Univer. Press, 1956.

THORPE, W. H. Some concepts of ethology. *Nature, London,* 1954, **174**, 101–106.

THORPE, W. H., & JONES, F. G. W. Olfactory conditioning in a parasitic insect and its relation to the problem of host selection. *Proceedings of the Royal Society of London, Series B,* 1937, **124**, 56–81.

TINBERGEN, N. An objectivistic study of the innate behaviour of animals. *Bibliotheca biotheoretica, Leiden,* 1942, **1**, 39–98.

TINBERGEN, N. *The study of instinct.* Oxford: Oxford Univer. Press, 1951.

TINBERGEN, N. The origin and evolution of courtship and threat display. In A. C. Hardy, J. S. Huxley, & E. B. Ford (Eds.), *Evolution as a process.* London: Allen & Unwin, 1954.

TINBERGEN, N. Some aspects of ethology, the biological study of animal behaviour. *British Association for the Advancement of Science,* 1955, **12**, 17–19.

TINBERGEN, N. Comparative studies of the behaviour of gulls (Laridae): A progress report. *Behaviour,* 1959, **15**, 1–70.

TINBERGEN, N., & KUENEN, D. J. Uber die auslosenden und die richtunggebenden Reizsituationen der Sperrbewegung von jungen Drosseln. *Zietschrift für Tierpsychologie,* 1939, **3**, 37–60. Translated in C. Schiller (Ed.), *Instinctive behavior.* New York: International Universities Press, 1961. Pp. 209–238.

TINBERGEN, N., & PERDECK, A. C. On the stimulus situation releasing the begging response of the newly hatched herring gull chick (*Larus argentatus argentatus*). *Behaviour,* 1951, **3**, 1–39.

VAN DER KLOOT, G., & WILLIAMS, C. M. Cocoon construction of the cecropia silkworm. I: The role of the external environment. *Behaviour,* 1953, **5**, 141–156. (a)

VAN DER KLOOT, G., & WILLIAMS, C. H. Cocoon construction of the cecropia silkworm. II: The role of the internal environment. *Behaviour,* 1953, **5**, 157–174. (b)

VERPLANCK, W. S. Since learned behavior is innate, and vice versa, what now? *Psychological Review,* 1955, **62**, 139-144.

WEISS, P. Self-differentiation of the basic patterns of coordination. *Comparative Psychology Monographs,* 1941, **17**, 1–96.

(Received November 1, 1963)

PART 2 Behavior Genetics

Behavior genetics is a relatively new branch of the science of animal behavior. As the name implies, the concern is with the effects of genotype on behavior. But it should be noted at once that the behavior geneticist is not studying "instinct," as classically defined. Instead he is concerned with the role that genetic differences play in the determination of *behavioral differences* within a population. An example may clarify this distinction. Suppose that all females of a given bird species build identical nests, in identical ways, at a precise time of the year. This would suggest a challenging series of studies for those interested in the development of such an extremely stable behavioral sequence. But, since there are no behavioral differences to work with, the techniques of behavior genetics could not be used. On the other hand, if a variety of nests is built, in different ways, and at different times of the year, the raw material for behavior-genetic investigations exists. By appropriate breeding experiments, the behavior geneticist could study the effects of genotype on the behavioral differences in nest building.

The behavior geneticist, then, requires variation in the traits he studies. Traits, whether morphological, physiological, or behavioral, vary within a population in two major ways. First, they may vary *qualitatively*, that is, in a discontinuous fashion. This means that the organisms can be placed in mutually exclusive categories on the basis of the trait. Examples are red and white flowers, straight and curled *Drosophila* wings, normal and frizzled chicken feathers. Such qualitatively varying traits were studied by Mendel as he established the principles of genetics.

Second, traits may be said to vary *quantitatively*, or continuously, over a broad range within a population. Height and weight offer good examples. Such traits usually can be shown to result from the interaction of many genes with each other and with the environment. A branch of genetics, known as "quantitative genetics," studies such traits, primarily through the use of complex statistical procedures. Because most behavioral traits vary quantitatively rather than qualitatively, the techniques of quantitative genetics are used frequently in behavior genetics.

In most experiments it is possible to specify two classes of variables: independent and dependent. An independent variable is systematically changed by the experimenter; it is varied *independently* of the other variables in the experiment. (These "other variables," ideally, are controlled. They are held as constant as possible for all groups throughout the course of the experiment.) A dependent variable is that which is under investigation, that which is being measured. Most hypotheses state that changes in an independent variable will result in changes in a dependent variable. Thus most experiments can be entitled "The Effects of_____(Independent Variables) on_____(Dependent Variable)." In experiments in behavior genetics, genotype is usually the independent variable, and some measurable aspect of behavior is the dependent variable. Obviously, if genotype is to be used as an independent variable, the experimenter must be able to manipulate and vary it while holding other variables constant.

The two most frequently used methods of manipulating genotype are selective breeding and the use of inbred strains. In a typical selection experiment, males and females with high values of the trait in question are mated. At the same time, other males and females with low scores are mated. Genetic effects on behavior are demonstrated if discrete populations result from several generations of selective breeding.

A different experimental design is used if the population consists of inbred strains. Inbreeding is defined as the mating of close relatives, usually brothers and sisters. The objective of inbreeding is not to arrive at a particular value for a particular trait as in selective breeding, but rather to establish the highest possible degree of *homozygosity* in the population. Chromosomes usually occur in pairs, so that each gene has a "partner" at the corresponding locus of the homologous chromosome. "Homozygosity" simply means that the members of each pair of genes are identical; if gene

A occurs on one chromosome, its partner must also be gene A. Inbreeding produces genetically similar animals, so that all like-sexed members of an inbred strain have the same, or nearly the same, genotype. The members of the strain may then be described as genetically *homogeneous.*

Part 2 begins with a position paper by Jerry Hirsch. Hirsch has conducted extensive research in behavior genetics and has given considerable thought to the role of the behavior-genetic approach in a broad range of problems. The paper reviews a bit of the history of behavior genetics and concludes with a discussion of the application of behavior-genetic analysis to the study of man. The possibility that a rigid caste system based on genetic endowment may develop as human environments become more similar is considered.

Behavior is a product of the evolutionary process. Furthermore, what an animal does, its behavior, can be critical in the determination of its survival to reproductive age. Therefore, behavior-genetic research is important in the study of evolution, and vice versa. In Reading 6, Aubrey Manning, Secretary-General of the International Ethological Conference, considers how "behavior evolves in relation to the behavioral results of genetic changes," while in the next paper Lee Ehrman reports studies showing that differences in behavioral patterns can lessen the probability of interbreeding between incipient species. Reading 8, by W. C. Rothenbuhler, presents one of the best-documented cases of the single-gene control of behavior. But, with the two preceding readings in mind, the results pose certain problems concerning the evolution and biological adaptiveness of the mode of inheritance discovered by Rothenbuhler. Why are these important behaviors controlled by recessive genes?

Since inbred strains of mice have been particularly important in behavior-genetic experiments, the next three selections deal with these animals. In Reading 9, G. E. McClearn provides a succinct review of such work in several different areas. The next paper deals with memory processes in mice. Here R. E. Wimer and his colleagues clearly demonstrate that conclusions from behavior-genetic experiments are specific to the populations studied and to the testing procedures used. These limitations to the behavior-genetic approach are not always recognized by those concerned with such items as racial differences in human potential.

The first six readings in Part 2 amply demonstrate that genotype has profound effects on a surprising variety of behaviors. But equally surprising is the difficulty in demonstrating genetic control for certain behaviors previously assumed to be inherited. An example is given in Reading 11 where R. L. Collins presents evidence indicating that laterality (hand or paw preference) is probably *not* a genetically determined trait.

Reprinted from AMERICAN PSYCHOLOGIST, Vol. 22, No. 2, February, 1967
Printed in U. S. A.

(5)

BEHAVIOR-GENETIC, OR "EXPERIMENTAL," ANALYSIS:

THE CHALLENGE OF SCIENCE VERSUS THE LURE OF TECHNOLOGY [1]

JERRY HIRSCH

University of Illinois

MY assignment today is to introduce or reintroduce the general experimental psychologist to heredity. The program committee's invitation indicated that they envisioned my "presentation as tutorial." They said that it "could be thought of as instructional in nature." Therefore the emphasis will be more on fundamental concepts than on the most recent experiment.

Throughout my career in psychology, Division 3 —Experimental—has always been looked upon as the ivory tower, our sanctum sanctorum of pure science. Whatever the other divisions might do and think, this one was devoted to truth and purity—to knowledge in its most fundamental and most general form. Therefore I propose to examine some concepts, beliefs and approaches to behavior study with respect to their influence on the development of a science of behavior.

I shall distinguish between science and technology. By science I mean the search for knowledge and understanding—both the understanding of something that is complex in terms of its simpler components and the understanding of a given phenomenon in terms of the relations between it and our other knowledge about the world. By technology I mean the application of whatever is presumed to be already known to the accomplishment of immediate goals. According to my former teacher in Berkeley, California, the distinguished chemist Joel Hildebrand (1963) "the duty of a university is to examine the discrepancies between actual phenomena and the currently accepted explanations for them [p. 11]." It is in this academic and contemplative spirit, which Hildebrand attributes to a university, that I am using "understanding." The other approach, which emphasizes prediction and control, is much less inclined to question traditional assumptions so long as practical goals appear attainable: Given the so-called laws of learning (i.e., some correlation between performance and temporal sequences of practice conditions) let us get on with the task of teaching and education, let us administer behavior therapy, let us modify deviant behavior, and so on. In the hierarchy or pyramid of sciences the latter approach stays on its own level and minds its own business.

The approach committed to understanding is the one I call "behavior-genetic analysis" (see Hirsch, 1967, Ch. 20). It attempts to relate the phenomena of behavior to the knowledge that exists at other levels of biosocial organization and in other branches of science. Precisely because we have paid attention to our place in the pyramid of sciences many formerly insoluble problems now appear in an entirely different perspective. Many of them now appear to be what the old logical positivists used to call pseudoquestions. I am thinking of such problems as the heredity-environment question, the race differences or racial superiority-inferiority question, the individual-differences question, the mind-body problem, plus a series of other more specialized problems.

A FALSE START

Because of the stubborn and persistent opposition to the study of heredity and behavior, far too much effort has been spent proving the trivial points that this or that behavior shows a genetic component or a genotype-environment interaction, or in chasing single genes in order to have a more clear-cut case. Behavior geneticists have been so preoccupied with the defeat of environmentalist opposition that they have had little time for the more important task of a critical analysis of their own work.[2]

In the rest of my discussion today I shall assume that the battle to overcome ignorance and the behavioristic opposition to according heredity its proper place in the behavioral sciences has been won effectively and decisively. Of course, I do not really believe that our arguments have convinced

[1] Invited address presented to Division 3, American Psychological Association, New York, September 4, 1966. This work was prepared with the support of Mental Health Training Grant No. 1 TO1 MH 10715-01 BLS for Research Training in the Biosocial Sciences. Limitations of time and space do not permit me to cover everything mentioned in the preconvention extended abstract (Hirsch, 1966, but see Hirsch, 1967) or to consider an important related topic (see Gray, 1966).

[2] See Bernhard's (1967) unfortunate account of the recent Rockefeller University fiasco. The present discussion criticizes behavior-genetic studies and its last section proposes a rational alternative.

the people who opposed them. The historians of science show that, in fact, very few people are ever converted from one point of view to a radically new one. In his very fine study on *The Structure of Scientific Revolutions* T. S. Kuhn (1964) tells us that

Copernicanism made few converts for almost a century after Copernicus's death. Newton's work was not generally accepted, particularly on the Continent, for more than half a century after the *Principia* appeared. Priestley never accepted the oxygen theory, nor Lord Kelvin the electro-magnetic theory, and so on. The difficulties of conversion have often been noted by scientists themselves. Darwin, in a particularly perceptive passage at the end of his *Origin of Species,* wrote: "Although I am fully convinced of the truth of the views given in this volume . . . . I by no means expect to convince experienced naturalists whose minds are stocked with a multitude of facts all viewed, during a long course of years, from a point of view directly opposite to mind. . . . [B]ut I look with confidence to the future,—to young rising naturalists, who will be able to view both sides of the question with impartiality." And Max Planck, surveying his own career in his *Scientific Autobiography,* sadly remarked that "a new scientific truth does not triumph by convincing its opponents and making them see the light, but rather because its opponents eventually die, and a new generation grows up that is familiar with it" [pp. 149–150].

Maybe I should say that my discussion today is addressed to the younger generation.

It is widely acknowledged today that John Broadus Watson supplied the pattern assumed by so much of present day thinking in psychology—in 1957 the American Psychological Association presented the citation:

To Dr. John B. Watson, whose work has been one of the vital determinants of the form and substance of modern psychology. He initiated a revolution in psychological thought, and his writings have been the point of departure of continuing lines of fruitful research [Skinner, 1959, p. 198].

Since it is now incontrovertibly clear that our behavioristic heritage (excessively anti-intellectual) did much to steer us off the advancing stream of science, it becomes important that we understand Watson's fallacious reasoning. Watson appears to have reached his intellectual high water mark just prior to the first world war when he wrote *Behavior: An Introduction to Comparative Psychology* (1914). He was at least superficially familiar with the latest developments in the science of that time and this shows in his book. None of his later works reflect the same broad intellectual curiosity. Johannsen's demonstration—that variation (*a*) *within* pure lines is of environmental origin and not inherited and (*b*) *between* pure lines shows independence of environment and is inherited—became a milestone of genetics being the first clear

separation of nonheritable from heritable variation. In the section of Watson's book entitled "Continuous Variation Due to Direct Action of Environment upon the Developing Organism" (p. 159) he alleges "It is now generally admitted that continuous variation is due to the direct action of the environment upon the body or soma of the developing organism." He reports Johannsen's experiment correctly, calls to our attention that "as was first shown by Quetelet, the distribution of such [= continuous] variations around the racial [!] average follows the law of chance distribution." Watson then goes on to explain that

The effect of environment upon the production of variation in the soma can be seen quite clearly in the . . . investigations of Stockard, Fuld, and Cunningham. Stockard has shown that while the eggs of the fish (*Fundulus*) under ordinary conditions produce normal two-eyed fish, the addition of magnesium salts to the water causes them to develop into cyclopean monsters.

His next section is entitled "The Non-Inheritance of Continuous Variation." Here Watson points out

The belief that continuous variations of the type considered are inherited was shared by all investigators up to recent times. The whole Darwinian theory of evolution is based upon this concept. In 1903 a crucial test by W. Johannsen.

He then recapitulates his account of Johannsen's experiment and comes to the conclusion that "The results of this experimental work . . . prove conclusively that the vast majority of the variations of organisms are not inherited"—a fantastic *non sequitur*. The very observations that, to biology, meant noninheritance of environmental influences and that variation could be analyzed intelligibly into both genetic and environmental components, provided psychology, through Watson's *mis*interpretation, with the procrustean frame which was to trap us in typological thinking for another half century. (Of course, if the whole Darwinian theory of evolution hinges upon the inheritance of continuous variations and Watson had really shown them to be nonheritable, then that would have buried Darwin's theory of evolution!)

Later in the same chapter Watson accepts a theory of the environmental determination of mutations and flirts with the Lamarckian ideas about the inheritance of acquired adaptive characters—though he does acknowledge that the evidence for Lamarckian inheritance is still not solid. So much for Watson and his unfortunate influence.

Griffin's remark about "Biologists . . . becoming aware that behavior is much too important to be left to the psychologists [in Etkin, 1959, p. 225]" and Lindzey's (1965) complaint about the "array of psychological journals so you can publish anything [p. 334]" are both signs that our scientific household might be in serious need of extensive rearrangements. To the ones just cited we can surely add Harlow's (1962) farewell message as editor of the *Journal of Comparative and Physiological Psychology*—that masterpiece of irony entitled "Fundamental Principles for Preparing Psychology Journal Articles." By the way, there is nothing new or unusual about a state of affairs in which a science is in need of a change. Mendel's work received no recognition in his lifetime *not* because no one important had ever heard of it, but because an eminent member of the contemporary German biological establishment, a physiologist and typological thinker strongly prejudiced against *non*-physiologists, von Nageli, refused to concede its merit (Iltis, 1966, pp. 198–199).

A Reorientation

In order to gain some perspective in our attempts to understand the uncompromisingly rigid stand taken toward heredity in the behavioral sciences, it is important for us to grasp certain concepts that are now seen to be fundamental. First and foremost we must appreciate the distinction between typological thinking and population thinking, as Ernst Mayr (1959) says "No two ways of looking at nature could be more different [p. 2]." The typological mode of thought is the older one. It is pre-Mendelian and pre-Darwinian. It has been ubiquitous in the behavioral sciences and ironically, it has been the dominant outlook throughout the majority of the more successful sciences like physics, chemistry, physiology, and anatomy as well as in medicine. To typologists individual events only have meaning and importance insofar as they are representative of some class of events. Within such a class individual differences can only be error.

Misguided by "opinion leaders" like Clark Hull (Woodger's disciple) and later converts to mathematical theory, psychology entered a cul-de-sac that genetics had prudently avoided. There we were hobbled by a philosophy of physics we had uncritically accepted as a philosophy of all science. As Toulmin (1966) shows: "Woodger's proposed axiomatization of genetics could have been—if his professional colleagues had taken serious notice of it—a major obstacle to progress [p. 133]" in that science. An important task for our immediate future is to cast off the hand-me-down philosophy, overgeneralized from physics, and to develop one appropriate for biosocial science.

Paradoxically it has been my common experience that many people as well as most genetics textbooks assimilate genetics itself to the typological frame of reference, which both biology and psychology have inherited from philosophy, physics, and physiology. They simply never succeed in breaking the old mental set: There are typologically conceived traits and typologically conceived genes, and wherever you can establish a correlation between the two you have a reductionistic causal explanation. Furthermore, their frame of reference does not allow for anything else.

Population thinking, on the other hand, is based upon a detailed appreciation both of the Mendelian mechanism and of various other complexities in the reproductive process. It involves much more than an awareness that man and his favorite laboratory animals possess diploid genes. It views the same facts and relations as the typologist sees, but with a much broader historical perspective. In doing so it has provided deeper insight into many troublesome problems. Yes, both ourselves and our pet animals are diploid genetically. Yes, genes are a necessary condition for the development of traits. And it certainly is true that a strong correlation between genes and a trait *can* lead to a reductionistic causal explanation. The population thinker, however, first considers the entire genome at once and he immediately perceives the absolute uniqueness of each individual genotype.

Because of recurrent mutation, because of the recombination of genes and chromosomes that occurs every generation both at meiosis and at fertilization, and because of population equilibria, there is always a spectrum of genotypes throughout a population—what we call individual differences. At the level of the phenotype every genotype has a *norm of reaction:* Under varying environmental conditions the same genotype can produce different phenotypes. In fact, sometimes environmental influence will be so strong that it can force one genotype into developing a mimic of the phenotype of an entirely different genotype—called a phenocopy. Moreover the expression of each individual gene depends upon the genetic background in which it is placed. Because of the foregoing conditions and because of others as well, the same phenotype can occur for quite different genetic reasons. Therefore, in most cases any facile assumption that an allele of a given gene is *the* cause of one expression of a given trait is much too simplistic. To be concrete: It is one thing to find a gene like the one associated with the phenylketonuria condition in man; but it would be folly to claim that the bad allele of this gene produces mental deficiency and its good allele produces mental sufficiency. We know very well that mental deficiency can occur in other ways—without the presence of the phenylketonuria condition. Furthermore, high phenylpyruvic acid in the urine is not invariably accompanied by mental deficiency. The expression of any gene depends upon both the prevailing genetic background and the prevailing environmental conditions.

Now you may begin to see why today, rather than use such labels as psychogenetics, genetics *of* behavior, behavior genetics, or behavioral genetics, I attempt to speak only of behavior-genetic analysis. As a matter of fact, I began my own experimental work by asking the question: How far can we carry genetic analysis *of* a behavior? We went to the fruit fly, an animal that had been very well analyzed genetically, in the hope that we could take advantage of the great body of genetical knowledge and techniques that had accumulated in the study of this organism.

While it certainly is true that I started out to study the genetics *of* a behavior, in the course of much thinking and experimenting over more than a decade I have come to realize that it is impossible to study the genetics *of* a behavior. We can study the behavior of *an* organism, the genetics of *a* population, and individual differences in the expression of some behavior by the members of *that* population. Therefore, we now speak of behavior-genetic analyses, understanding by that expression simultaneously the experimental analysis of well-defined behaviors into their sensory and response components, the reliable and valid measurement of individual differences in the behaviors and in their component responses, *then* subsequent breeding analysis or, for man, pedigree analysis by the methods of genetics over a specified set of generations in the history of a given population under known ecological conditions. We know full well that both the behavioral and the genetical properties can and will vary over time, over ecological conditions, and among populations. Furthermore, there will be no simple isomorphism between the two.

The Tryon Effect

Now I should like to examine some specific problems from the point of view just outlined. One of the best known and most widely referenced experiments in the behavior genetics literature is the Tryon selective breeding study of maze learning in rats, begun in 1925 and continued until 1940. Many aspects of Tryon's simple experiment have been replicated in the same and different behaviors in the same and different species. One of his replicable results has stood in the field as an enigma for over 26 years. It has even been embalmed like a classic and labeled the "Tryon effect" in the literature (Scott & Fuller, 1965, p. 264). Tryon bred rats selectively on the basis of their error scores in learning a multiple T maze. Three times between the eleventh and twenty-second generations of selection the reproductively isolated bright and dull strains were test-crossed to produce F_1 and F_2 progeny. According to Mendelian theory, because of segregation in the F_2, its variance should be detectably larger than that of the F_1. All three times this expected result failed to appear. It is this failure to obtain a jump or increase in variance from the F_1 to the F_2 generation that has been called the "Tryon effect." It has happened often, though not invariably, in behavior-genetic studies.

Tryon (1940, p. 116) puzzled over possible explanations for his findings and, long before the advent of the computer, he developed ingenious Monte Carlo methods for generating models with dice. Quite correctly, he believed that he was dealing with a polygenic situation—in those days called multiple-factor determination. In 1951 Calvin Hall, Tryon's first student, suggested that lack of sufficient inbreeding in the selected lines might account for the Tryon effect, and of course he was correct! But that is only one aspect, and not the most important. In 1958 Ernst Caspari suggested that behavior may be showing properties that are different from morphology. Possibly behavioral heterosis is expressed in increased variability while morphological heterosis shows greater uniformity. Quite wisely, he qualified his remarks by indicating the need for more evidence. In 1960, in the text that established the field, Fuller and Thompson made use of both the Hall and the Caspari interpretations. In 1962, I too described the results of a selection and hybridization study (of phototaxis in *Drosophila*) in the following terms (Hirsch, 1962):

Our first attempt at analysis for phototaxis seemed successful. The F_1 hybrid was no more variable than the selected strains. . . . Furthermore, the F_2 was more variable than the F_1. . . . we immediately attempted to replicate this important result. Our replication foundered on the same shoals as much of the previous mammalian work. The F_1 hybrid was as variable as the F_2 [p. 16].

In what threatens to become an extensive literature on behavior genetics there are no discussions explaining why these experiments were doomed to failure from the outset. Typological thinking had blinded us all to the nature of the biological situation in Tryon's study and in many of the others. We were thinking of *the* rat and hoping to map its chromosomes in the same reductionistic way that brains were supposed to have been mapped against behavior in physiological studies.

Now if we stop thinking about the archetypal rat, however, and focus our attention on a species

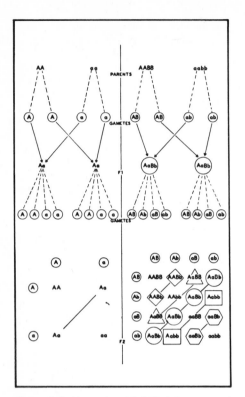

FIG. 1. Left side: mating of individuals homozygous for different alleles of one gene and production of uniformly heterozygous F_1 offspring, intermating of the F_1 with segregation of the different alleles to separate gametes and recombination of gametes at fertilization to produce three F_2 genotypes in the 1:2:1 ratio. Right side: mating of individuals homozygous for different alleles of two genes and production of F_1 offspring uniformly heterozygous for both genes, intermating of the F_1 and segregation of alleles plus recombination of segregating alleles from different loci to produce the F_1 gamete array followed by recombination of gametes at fertilization to produce nine F_2 genotypes in the 4:2:2:2:2:1:1:1:1 ratio. In the genotype matrix on the right, similar genotypes are connected by a line and enclosed in the same type of geometric form.

population of unique organisms having a karyotype of 21 pairs of chromosomes, the flaw in the reasoning about these studies will become embarrasingly obvious. If, for simplicity, we treat the chromosomes as major indivisible genes, a little Mendelian algebra (see Figure 1) will show the nature of the experiment that breeds F_1 and F_2 generations by hybridizing two strains having different sets of chromosomes (assuming that the strains being crossed are perfectly homozygous for different forms of each chromosome).

The number of different kinds of gametes ($=$ ova or sperm) that can be produced is a number equal to 2 (for the two chromosomes in each pair) raised

to a power equal to the number of chromosome pairs in the set. Since the rat has 21 chromosome pairs, it can produce $2^{21}(= 2,097,152)$ or over 2 million kinds of gametes. For the rat the matrix of genotypes analogous to the illustrations shown in the figure would have to contain $4^{21}(= 4,386,-046,511,104)$ or over 4 trillion cells. Such a matrix would contain $3^{21}(= 4,782,969)$ or about $4\frac{3}{4}$ million different genotypes. Of these, slightly over 2 million appear only once, in the main diagonal of the 4-trillion-celled matrix, if and only if the theoretical distribution of proportions is realized *exactly*. Otherwise, unless the matrix is replicated many times, some of them will not appear at all. Naturally, any experiment, intended to sample the spectrum of possible genotypes, must be planned so that there is a statistically sufficient number of replications of the appropriate genotype matrix. In other words these experiments never had the slightest chance of making the measurements for which they were intended.

Reductionistic Naïveté

One of the most prestigious and ostensibly fruitful approaches to the study of relations between biology and behavior has been the physiological approach. That approach exemplifies the typological mode of thought in many of its details. The organism is viewed as a machine and the behavior is explained in terms of the functioning of, and the interrelations among, the parts of the machine. A small number of subjects are assumed to be representative of an entire species or even of some higher taxonomic category.

With the advent of behavior-genetic studies some new perspectives have been attained. The existence of the Tryon strains, sometimes inappropriately labeled bright and dull rats, suggested to certain workers that an analysis of chemical and physiological differences between these strains might yield a reductionistic explanation of their differences in behavior. Work with the acetylcholine-cholinesterase-cholinacetylase system revealed a significant correlation between brain cholinesterase level and behavior. For ever so many years studies kept appearing in the literature describing various biochemical or physiological aspects of the same correlation. When the appropriate hybridization control experiments were belatedly performed, however, the presumed reductionistic explanation simply vanished (Rosenzweig, Krech, & Bennett, 1960, p. 484). The correlation between behavior and chemistry was exploded by the independent assortment of chromosomes and their genes in the production of the F_2 hybrid. Exactly the same thing happened in the F_2 with a correlation other workers had found between alcohol dehydrogenase level in the liver and a behavioral measure of alcohol preference among inbred strains of mice (McClearn, 1965, p. 802). Other studies also illustrate the extreme complexity of the relations between different levels of biosocial organization (Hirsch, 1963, p. 1438).

While it is certainly true that we have learned about many relationships between behavior and the other levels of biosocial organization, much still remains to be learned about both the generality and the relative importance of these relationships. The moral of this part of the story seems to be that many of the physiological-behavioral correlations may have to be reexamined from the perspective of a *non*typological point of view—with the power of the appropriately designed behavior-genetic analysis. Remember that it was the eminent physiologist Jacques Loeb, the man under whom Watson (see 1936, p. 273) avoided doing his doctoral dissertation, who long ago urged psychology to "accept the consequences of Mendel's theory, according to which the animal is . . . an aggregate of independent hereditary qualities [1964, pp. 52–53]."

Correlational Naïveté

I shall now consider another problem, which, though it may appear unrelated at first, will later be seen to fit right into the pattern of the foregoing discussion. When I was a student of statistics, in our discussions we often partitioned psychology on the basis of two different approaches to nature. Our dichotomy correlated fairly well with the distinction between the laboratory manipulations of the experimentalists and the field observations of others.

There were those who manipulated an independent variable and measured changes in some other variable that were predicted to be correlated with, and therefore dependent upon, their independent variable. The nonexperimentalists observed two or more variables and reported their correlations. The former employed the analysis of variance statistics while the latter employed the statistics of correlation, regression, and factor analysis. As experimentalists we tended to be somewhat skeptical, even intolerant, of the second approach, because we knew that correlation does not mean causation. Without getting involved in a discussion of causality, I should like to reexamine the question of correlations from the point of view of behavior-genetic analysis. Remember that correlations are the basic data of entire fields like personality. Professor Mosteller once asked me whether genetics did not have more to offer than the ubiquity of diversity. I think it will be seen that the approach which analyzes the problems of psychology from this more general point of view might very well have something more to offer the various fields of the discipline.

Gardner Lindzey (1964) in his presidential address to Division 8, Personality and Social Psychology, has made a strong plea that we give more serious consideration to the correlations between physique and behavior that people like William Sheldon have so long been emphasizing. There is still another genetic relationship which now proves to be of exceptional importance in this context. The Hardy-Weinberg equilibrium is a well-known condition which tells us that, when mating in a population occurs at random, the proportions of the different alleles of a given gene remain constant over the generations. The Hardy-Weinberg rela-

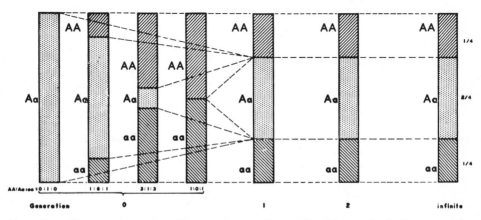

Fig. 2. Four different populations whose allele proportions p_A and q_a are 1/2 each in generation 0. Attainment of the Hardy-Weinberg equilibrium in one generation of random mating (after Stern, 1960, p. 156).

tion applies to every individual gene regardless of its number of alleles, and this is true for any number of genes.

If we think of two alleles at a locus, say *A* and *a,* existing in proportions *p* and *q*, respectively, the Hardy-Weinberg equilibrium is given by the binomial expansion familiar from elementary algebra: $(p + q)^2 = p^2 + 2pq + q^2$. The relative frequencies of the three genotypes corresponding to the three possible combinations of the two alleles— two homozygotes, *AA* and *aa,* and one heterozygote, *Aa*—are given by the terms in the expansion, p^2, q^2, and $2pq$, respectively. It is these proportions that remain at a constant equilibrium under random mating, as illustrated in Figure 2.

While this relationship is well known, what has not been generally appreciated is the outcome when several loci are considered simultaneously. If we now confine our attention to independent hereditary factors, let us say entire chromosomes, then it follows that *independent* quantities are uncorrelated. Of course, in practice, since we do not know beforehand which factors are independent and which are not, we measure correlations and infer the dependence or independence of the factors from the presence or absence of a correlation.

In diploid organisms many correlations are going to be found that will *mis*lead us into inferring dependence where there is actually biological independence!—a state of affairs that appears never to have been realized by the very people who most consistently use correlations. How can this be? It occurs for a reason that is essentially

simple but unfortunately may not appear simple the first time it is considered.

We have already shown that under random mating the distribution of the alleles of each gene attains an equilibrium, that the equilibrium values are reached immediately and that they are maintained indefinitely. Where two genes are independent, all the possible combinations of their separate alleles should show a chance distribution when mating is at random in a large population. While this is true in theory, in fact it often does not work out this way. Populations do not suddenly come into existence as large groups. They grow pretty much the way Malthus claimed they do. They start out from a small number of *founders* that arrive in a given region. Figure 3 illustrates what happens when the joint distribution of the alleles of two (or more) genes are considered simultaneously.

The concept of random mating is a very useful assumption from the point of view of a mathematical model. However, we should note what it means: that every conceivable kind of a heterosexual union occurs *equally* often and produces an *equal* number of progeny, that this implies incest both between members of the same generation and across generations, that inbreeding occurs as frequently as outbreeding, that matings between distant individuals occur as often as between close individuals no matter how distance may be defined—geographically, socially, economically, in terms of education, etc. Clearly, this assumption, that is so convenient for a mathematical model,

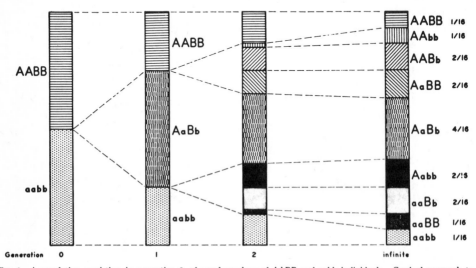

FIG. 3. A population consisting, in generation 0, of equal numbers of AABB and aabb individuals. Gradual approach to equilibrium over successive generations of random mating (after Stern, 1960, p. 170).

represents a condition we have no reason to believe ever has prevailed or is ever likely to prevail, especially in human populations. Since random mating is the exception rather than the rule, statistically significant but biosocially *un*important correlations between functionally independent traits may be maintained indefinitely. Many of the trait correlations that distinguish racial, ethnic, and national groups can be of just this fortuitous nature, maintained by reproductive isolation and nonrandom idiosyncratic systems of mating. I consider this a most important result. Its full implications are going to take us a very long time to unravel.

THE STUDY OF MAN [3]

Next, I want to consider behavior-genetic analyses in man—an important subject and one in which interest is growing rapidly. By and large behavior-genetic analyses in man have amounted to a series of rounds in the heredity-environment controversy. A spectrum of behavior traits has provided the battlegrounds for numerous repetitions of this sterile controversy.

In their summary of behavior genetics through 1960 Fuller and Thompson observe that

The distinction between human and animal behavior genetics is more than a matter of the species studied or the techniques which are feasible in the two fields. The primary objectives of the workers in the two areas are different. Animal experimenters use genetics as a device to study the nature of the variables which determine behavior. In getting such information, traits and subjects are selected for study because of experimental convenience, not because wheel running, maze learning, and audiogenic seizures in rodents are socially or economically important. In contrast, workers in human behavior genetics have concentrated on problems of social significance and accumulated a great body of observations on intelligence (particularly mental defect), psychoses, and other psychiatric problems. The desire to put the newly discovered science of genetics at the service of human welfare led some early twentieth-century scientists to make excessive claims for the importance of heredity in the origin of social maladjustment. The antiheredity movement was equally one-sided in the opposite direction. Though the battle between hereditarians and environmentalists no longer rages conspicuously, the concern with applied problems still persists among most human geneticists who deal with psychological characters [p. 95].

I am now going to argue for the importance of a pure science approach to behavior-genetic analysis

in man as well as in animals. Near the end of the same book Fuller and Thompson observe that

Possibly the most significant contribution of behavior genetics is its documentation of the fact that two individuals of superficially similar phenotypes may be quite different genotypically and respond in completely different fashion when treated alike [p. 38].

While Fuller and Thompson's observation may be self-evident to evolutionary biologists who fully appreciate the population concept, it remains incomprehensible to the majority of behavioral scientists (students of learning, especially) still trapped by what Ernst Mayr calls the typological mode of thought. It certainly suggests that behavior measurement offers an approach with extremely high resolving power for the analysis of human diversity.

A pure science approach to behavior-genetic analysis in man has as its objective the discovery and understanding of natural units. In animal ethology, there is a face validity to according natural-unit status to such behaviors as nesting, courtship, and predation—activities that have obviously been molded by the prolonged interaction of the species genome and the forces of natural selection. Man too is an animal whose characteristics have evolved through natural selection. But, as we now study his behavior in civilization, there is no comparable face validity permitting us to apply the label "natural" to most of the units we observe.

In contemporary behavioral science, far more attention is paid to man's social roles than to his biological properties. In industrial psychology, for example, tests are devised to select individuals who will most skillfully perform those tasks for which they are needed by industry. Because of the speed of cultural evolution, man cannot possibly have been subjected to intense natural selection for his technological skills—though man must employ the capacities he has evolved in the exercise of skills. The great challenge now before the behavioral sciences lies in the behavior-genetic analysis of man's biological properties and the elucidation of their modus operandi in a sociotechnological context.

A review of the world's literature on the relationship between heredity and tested intelligence by Erlenmeyer-Kimling and Jarvik (1963) has revealed the remarkable fact that, for the distributions of correlational measures collected over the past half century, a most consistent pattern exists. The value of the intelligence correlation between relatives increases as the degree of biological relationship becomes closer. This story supports, though

[3] The ideas in this section were first presented in September 1964 to Symposium No. 27 of the Wenner-Gren Foundation for Anthropological Research at Burg-Wartenstein, Austria. They are discussed in J. H. Spuhler (in press) and in *Behavior-Genetic Analysis* (Hirsch, 1967, Ch. 20).

certainly does not prove, the suggestion that behavior may provide one of our most sensitive measures of the human diversity we now know exists.

Clearly, data like those in the review merely demonstrate the heritability of a trait. That tested intelligence or most other human characteristics will show some measurable heritability, however, is knowledge that should no longer evoke surprise. Since heritabilities are population, situation, and generation specific, studies that merely estimate their magnitude contribute knowledge of little general significance at this time.

The great challenge referred to a moment ago lies in the identification and behavior-genetic analysis of the phenotypic dimensions of human variation. In my opinion, they will not be identified through the exclusive study of complex behaviors, because we would expect them to be relatively simple, numerous, and largely uncorrelated. Estimates place the number of human genes at well in excess of 10,000. Over several generations and across a world population of more than 3 billion individuals, by the nature of the genome, very many of these genes must be assorting independently. It is therefore very unlikely that we shall learn much about their primary influences on behavior by omnibus tests of intelligence or personality. The trouble with broad spectrum tests is that they measure too much. While they may be useful instruments of classification to serve the practical needs of society, because of their omnibus nature and their focus on social categories, we should not expect them to be very precise measures of biological differences, which, because of the mosaic nature of the genome, should prove to be relatively fine grained.

Intelligence testing classifies individuals on the basis of their test performance (*a*) Idiots score below 20, (*b*) imbeciles 20–49, (*c*) morons 50–69, (*d*) borderline deficients 70–79, (*e*) dullards 80–89, (*f*) normals 90–140, and (*g*) geniuses over 140. Since there are practically an unlimited number of ways of obtaining any score, lumping together all individuals who fall in the same category on cultural tests undoubtedly obscures many biological differences. When heritabilities are calculated, heredity and environment are interpreted as "accounting for" the estimated proportions of the variation over the range of test scores.

Forty-two years ago H. J. Muller, the second Nobel laureate in genetics, studied "Mental Traits and Heredity" (1925) in a pair of female monozygotic twins reared apart. His comments on those observations are still relevant:

The responses of the twins to all these tests—except the intelligence tests—are so decisively different almost throughout, that this one case is enough to show that the scores obtained in such tests indicate little or nothing of the genetic basis of the psychic make-up . . . it is necessary to institute an intensive search for ways of identifying more truly genetic psychic characters . . . despite the diverse reactions to almost all the non-intellectual tests used . . . there are really many other mental characteristics in which the twins would agree closely could we but find appropriate means of measuring them. Thus . . . the twins both seem possessed of similar energy and even tension, in their daily activity, with a tendency to "overdo" to the point of breakdown; both have similar mental alertness and interest in the practical problems about them, but not in remote or more purely intellectual abstractions and puzzles; both are personally very agreeable (as indicated by their popularity); both display similar attitudes throughout in taking the tests, even to such detail as lack of squeamishness in blackening the fingers for the fingerprints, and in being pricked for the blood tests—but turning away before the needle struck. The tastes of both in books and people appear very similar. It would seem, then, that operations of the human mind have many aspects not yet reached by psychological testing, and that some of these are more closely dependent upon the genetic composition than those now being studied [pp. 532–533].

Thus, there is reason to question the validity of prevaling testing procedures for the measurement of biologically significant properties both when heritability is present and when it is absent.

Another factor that worked against our discovering the socially relevant biological dimensions of behavioral variation has been our preoccupation with typological reifications like learning, perception, and motivation—recently Frank Beach (1965) has deplored the faculty-psychology organization of our textbooks. The classical approach has been to measure the performance of groups of subjects on specified tasks, average their scores, and infer the nature of some "process" from properties of an average curve. The subjects are obtained through schools, hospitals, industry, military installations, etc. Rarely are observations made on their kin. So, two conditions essential for uncovering the culturally significant biological dimensions of human variation are hardly ever satisfied in most behavioral science research: careful analysis of human differences and tracing through kinships whatever segregation such differences show.

Both theory and observation point to the need for a radically different approach to behavior study. Theoretically, it is implied by our modern picture both of the mosaic organization of the individual genome and of the heterogenic nature of human populations. The complex of characteristics that constitutes the total phenotype of each unique member of a population is the developmental result of thousands of genes, most of which, due to crossing over, undoubtedly assort independently.

Empirically, individual differences have been measured in the phenotypic expression of many traits and, for some, observations have been made on the similarities and differences both within and between families. On seven variables related to autonomic nervous function (vasomotor persistence, salivary output, heart period, standing palmar conductance, volar skin conductance, respiration period, and pulse pressure) measured in children from three relationship categories (monozygotic twins, siblings, and unrelated individuals) Jost and Sontag (1944) found that score similarity increased with genetic similarity. Fivefold within family threshold differences have been found (von Skramlik, 1943) with taste stimuli that showed identical thresholds in monozygotic twins (Rümler, 1943). With somewhat more complex measurements, the fine structure of auditory curves was found to exhibit high intrapair concordance among monozygotic twins, intrafamilial similarities, and significant differences among unrelated subjects (von Békésy & Rosenblith, 1950).

Individual differences in memory span have been measured among adult Caucasian men (Wechsler, 1952) as well as among Chinese boys and girls (Cheng, 1935). When attention span (immediately after oral presentation of a series of digits, demonstration by written reproduction of the number of digits remembered, and introspective report that this performance did not involve mental grouping of the digits) and memory span (again, oral presentation and written reproduction, but with mental grouping permitted) were studied in the same individuals, both measures yielded well-dispersed arrays having a rather low correlation and very little overlap. The importance of the mental grouping operation is shown by the almost uniformly higher scores for memory span than for attention span (Oberly, 1928). With practice some intelligent subjects can improve their memory span by learning to group items. Practice does not, however, seem to affect their attention span, which apparently sets a limit to the number of items they can combine into a group (Martin & Fernberger, 1929).

It is not at all uncommon to find that only some individuals in a diagnostic category receive extreme scores on specific trait measures. In 1914, Binet and Simon noticed the incapacity of some mental defectives to discriminate points on the skin and they incorporated a test of this in their early intelligence measures (O'Connor & Hermelin, 1963). Birch and Mathews (1951) found poor auditory discrimination for tones above 6 KC in many, but not all, mental defectives. O'Connor (1957) found the incidence of color blindness in imbecile males to be higher than that in males of the general population. Berkson, Hermelin, and O'Connor (1961) found that the blocking of the EEG alpha rhythm, following the presentation of a bright light, lasted longer in some mental defectives than in normals. Siegel, Roach, and Pomeroy (1964) found that, following ethanol loading, some alcoholics showed significantly different plasma amino acid patterns from normals.

Many interesting family correlations can also be obtained. The relative paucity of available data can more likely be attributed to lack of interest in family studies on the part of behavioral scientists rather than to its nonexistence. Lennox, Gibbs, and Gibbs (1940) found that, although only 10% of normal subjects showed occasional EEG abnormalities, some 60% of the relatives of known epileptics had abnormal rhythms. Lidz, Cornelison, Terry, and Fleck (1958) reported marked distortions in communicating among many of the nonhospitalized parents of schizophrenic patients. McConaghy (1959), using an objective test for irrelevant thinking, found that at least one of the nonhospitalized parents of each of 10 schizophrenic inpatients showed significant thought disorders. Of the 20 "normal" parents, 12, or 60%, scored within the range of responding characteristic of their offspring; whereas of 65 normal controls, only 6 individuals, or 9%, scored in the range characteristic of the schizophrenics.

The most radical change in behavior study now being recommended involves a shift of focus away from insubstantial abstractions like learning, perception, and motivation to concern with consanguinity relations among the subjects we observe and to the study of the simplest possible units of intellectual functioning among individuals of known ancestry.

In closing I should like to point out certain trends that are now developing. As the social, ethnic, and economic barriers to education are removed throughout the world, and as the quality of education approaches a more uniformly high level of effectiveness, heredity may be expected to make an ever larger contribution to individual differences in intellectual functioning and consequently to success in our increasingly complex civilization. Universally compulsory education, improved methods of ability assessment and career counseling, and prolongation of the years of schooling further into the reproductive period of life can only increase the degree of positive assortative mating in our population. From a geneticist's point of view our attempt to create the great society might prove to be the greatest selective breeding experiment ever undertaken.

Some might fear that this trend can only serve further to stratify society into a rigid caste system and that this time the barriers will be more enduring, because they will now be built on a firmer foundation. On the other hand, it may be noted that at least two conditions should prevent this from happening:

1. There is undoubtedly a significant contribution made to intellectual functioning by the unique organization of each individual's total genotype and by its idiosyncratic environmental encounters. Furthermore, mutation, recombination, and meiotic assortment, plus our inability to transmit more than a small part of individual experience as cultural heritage guarantee new variation every generation to produce the filial regression observed by Galton and to contribute to the social mobility discussed by Burt (1961).

2. The ever-increasing complexity of the social, political and technological differentiation of society creates many new niches (and abolishes some old ones) to be filled by each generation's freshly generated heterogeneity.

REFERENCES

BEACH, F. A. Review of S. C. Ratner & M. R. Denny, *Comparative psychology: Research in animal behavior.* *Contemporary Psychology,* 1965, **10,** 345–346.

BÉKÉSY, G. VON, & ROSENBLITH, A. The mechanical properties of the ear. In S. S. Stevens (Ed.), *Handbook of experimental psychology,* New York: Wiley, 1950. Pp. 1075–1115.

BERKSON, G., HERMELIN, B., & O'CONNOR, N. Physiological responses of normals and institutionalized mental defectives to repeated stimuli. *Journal of Mental Deficiency Research,* 1961, **5,** 30–39.

BERNHARD, R. Genetics and human intelligence: Rockefeller University Conference portrays a field promising much and delivering little. *Scientific Research, McGraw-Hill's News Magazine for Scientists,* 1967, **2,** 30–34.

BIRCH, J. W., & MATHEWS, J. The hearing of mental defectives: Its measurement and characteristics. *American Journal of Mental Deficiency,* 1951, **55,** 384–393.

BURT, C. Intelligence and social mobility. *British Journal of Statistical Psychology,* 1961, **14,** 3–24.

CASPARI, E. W. Genetic basis of behavior. In A. Roe & G. G. Simpson (Eds.), *Behavior and evolution.* New Haven: Yale University Press, 1958.

CHENG, P. L. [A preliminary study of range of perception]. *Journal of Testing* (in Chinese), 1935, **2**(2), 1–31. *Psychological Abstracts,* 1936, **10,** No. 5217.

ERLENMEYER-KIMLING, L., & JARVIK, L. F. Genetics and intelligence: A review. *Science,* 1963, **142,** 1477–1478.

ETKIN, W. Review of A. Roe & G. G. Simpson (Eds.), *Behavior and evolution. Contemporary Psychology,* 1959, **4,** 225.

FULLER, J. L., & THOMPSON, W. R. *Behavior genetics.* New York: Wiley, 1960.

GRAY, P. H. Historical notes on the aerial predator reaction and the Tinbergen hypothesis. *Journal of the History of the Behavioral Sciences,* 1966, **2,** 330–334.

HALL, C. S. The genetics of behavior. In S. S. Stevens (Ed.), *Handbook of experimental psychology.* New York: Wiley, 1951.

HARLOW, H. F. Fundamental principles for preparing psychology journal articles. *Journal of Comparative and Physiological Psychology,* 1962, **55,** 893–896.

HILDEBRAND, J. L. To tell or to hear some new thing. *American Scientist,* 1963, **51,** 1–11.

HIRSCH, J. Individual differences in behavior and their genetic basis. In E. L. Bliss (Ed.), *Roots of behavior: Genetics, instinct, and socialization in animal behavior.* New York: Hoeber-Harper, 1962.

HIRSCH, J. Behavior genetics and individuality understood: behaviorism's counterfactual dogma blinded the behavioral sciences to the significance of meiosis. *Science,* 1963, **142,** 1436–1442.

HIRSCH, J. Behavior-genetic, or "experimental," analysis: The challenge of science versus the lure of technology. *Proceedings of the 74th Annual Convention of the American Psychological Association,* 1966, **2,** 7–8.

HIRSCH, J. (Ed.) *Behavior-genetic analysis.* New York: McGraw-Hill, 1967.

ILTIS, H. *Gregor Johann Mendel, Leben, Werk und Wirking.* (Orig. publ. 1924) Trans. by E. Paul & C. Paul, *Life of Mendel.* Reprinted: London: Allen & Unwin, 1966.

JOST, H., & SONTAG, L. W. The genetic factor in autonomic nervous-system function. *Psychosomatic Medicine,* 1944, **6,** 308–310. (Reprinted: in, C. Kluckhohn & H. A. Murray (Eds.), *Personality in nature, society, and culture.* (2nd ed.) New York: Knopf, 1953. Pp. 73–79.)

KUHN, T. S. *The structure of scientific revolutions.* Chicago: University of Chicago Press, 1964.

LENNOX, W. G., GIBBS, E. L., & GIBBS, F. A. Inheritance of cerebral dysrhythmia and epilepsy. *Archives of Neurolology and Psychiatry,* 1940, **44,** 1155.

LIDZ, T., CORNELISON, A., TERRY, D., & FLECK, S. Intrafamilial environment of the schizophrenic patient: VI. The transmission of irrationality. *Archives of Neurology and Psychiatry,* 1958, **79,** 305.

LINDZEY, G. Morphology and behavior. Presidential address presented at Division 8, American Psychological Association, Chicago, September 1964. (To appear in J. H. Spuhler (Ed.), *Behavioral consequences of genetic differences in man.* Chicago: Aldine, in press.)

LINDZEY, G. Discussion. In S. G. Vandenberg (Ed.), *Methods and goals in human behavior genetics.* New York: Academic Press, 1965. P. 334.

LOEB, J. The significance of tropisms for psychology. (Orig. publ. 1909) Reprinted in, *The mechanistic conception of life.* Cambridge: Harvard University Press, 1964.

MARTIN, P. R., & FERNBERGER, S. W. Improvement in memory span. *American Journal of Psychology,* 1929, **41,** 91–94.

MAYR, E. Darwin and the evolutionary theory in biology. In B. J. Meggers (Ed.), *Evolution and anthropology: A centennial appraisal.* Washington, D. C.: Anthropological Society of Washington, 1959. Pp. 1–10.

McCLEARN, G. E. Genotype and mouse behavior. In S. J. Geerts (Ed.), *Genetics today, Proceedings of the XI International Congress of Genetics.* New York: Pergamon Press, 1965. Pp. 795–805.

McConaghy, N. The use of an object sorting test in elucidating the hereditary factor in schizophrenia. *Journal of Neurology, Neurosurgery and Psychiatry,* 1959, 22, 243.

Muller, H. J. Mental traits and heredity. *Journal of Heredity,* 1925, 16, 433–448.

Oberly, H. S. A comparison of the spans of "attention" and memory. *American Journal of Psychology,* 1928, 40, 295–302.

O'Connor, N. Imbecility and color blindness. *American Journal of Mental Deficiency,* 1957, 62, 83–87.

O'Connor, N., & Hermelin, B. *Speech and thought in severe subnormality.* (Experimental study) London: Pergamon Press, 1963.

Rosenzweig, M. R., Krech, D., & Bennett, E. L. A search for relations between brain chemistry and behavior. *Psychological Bulletin,* 1960, 57, 476–492.

Rümler, P. *Die Leislungen des Geschmacksinnes bei,* Zwillingen, Inaugural Dissertation, Iena, 1943. Cited by H. Piéron, *La psychologie différentielle.* (2nd ed.) Paris: Presses Universitaires de France, 1962. P. 97.

Scott, J. P., & Fuller, J. L. *Genetics and the social behavior of the dog.* Chicago: University of Chicago Press, 1965.

Siegel, F. L., Roach, M. K., & Pomeroy, L. R. Plasma amino acid patterns in alcoholism: The effects of ethanol loading. *Proceedings of the National Academy of Science,* 1964, 51, 605–611.

Skramlik, E. von. Verbungsforschungen auf dem Gebiete des Geschmacksinnes. *Ienaische Zeitschr. für Medizin und Naturwissenschaft,* 1943, 50. Cited by H. Piéron, *La psychologie différentielle.* (2nd ed.) Paris: Presses Universitaires de France, 1962. P. 97.

Skinner, B. F. John Broadus Watson, behaviorist. *Science,* 1959, 129, 197–198.

Spuhler, J. H. (Ed.) *Genetic diversity and human behavior. A comprehensive overview of the field of behavioral genetics and its applications.* Chicago: Aldine Publishing Company, Wenner-Gren Foundation, 1967, 291 pp.

Stern, C. *Principles of human genetics.* (2nd ed.) San Francisco: W. H. Freeman, 1960.

Toulmin, S. Review of C. G. Hempel, *Aspects of scientific explanation and other essays in the philosophy of science. Scientific American,* 1966, 214, 129–133.

Tryon, R. C. Genetic differences in maze learning in rats. In, *National Society for the Study of Education, the thirty-ninth yearbook.* Bloomington, Ill.: Public School Publishing Co., 1940. Pp. 111–119.

Watson, J. B. *Behavior: An introduction to comparative psychology.* New York: Holt, 1914.

Watson, J. B. In C. Murchison (Ed.), *A history of psychology in autobiography* III. Worcester: Clark University Press, 1936. Pp. 271–281.

Wechsler, D. *The range of human capacities.* (Rev. ed.) Baltimore: Williams & Wilkins, 1952.

Reprinted from
GENETICS TODAY
Proceedings of the XI International Congress of Genetics
The Hague, The Netherlands, September, 1963
PERGAMON PRESS
OXFORD · LONDON · EDINBURGH · NEW YORK
PARIS · FRANKFURT
1964

EVOLUTIONARY CHANGES AND BEHAVIOUR GENETICS

AUBREY MANNING

Department of Zoology, University of Edinburgh, Scotland

In this paper I shall try to consider the evidence we have on the manner in which behaviour evolves in relation to the behavioural results of genetic changes. I shall confine my attention to instinctive behaviour. Only in this context can we speak meaningfully of the inheritance and evolution of behaviour patterns themselves. The evolution of the cerebral cortex through the vertebrate series has resulted in greatly increased behavioural potentialities and flexibility, but it has been roughly paralleled by a reduction in the repertoire of inherited behaviour. At present we can only talk about the evolution of learning abilities in the most general terms, but we can do more for instinctive patterns. These are usually rigid and easily recognized and altogether bear comparison with morphological features.

We are faced with formidable problems of analysis at present. So many different things can affect the performance of a behaviour pattern. To put it naïvely, we must consider all the chain of mechanisms between sense organs and muscles, with genes operating at every link in the chain. Even if we can classify behaviour into sensible units, we are usually unable to do more than express the effects of genetic changes in purely behavioural terms and mechanism eludes us. Nevertheless, there is a consistency in these effects which does give us a meaningful insight into the way behaviour evolves.

Considering first the more directly genetical evidence, work has proceeded in three main ways:

(1) The comparison of behaviour between animals whose genotypes differ, as near as possible, only at a single locus.

(2) The comparison of inbred lines.

(3) The production of behaviourally divergent lines by deliberate selection.

All the evidence leads to the same conclusion. The basic form of instinctive behaviour patterns is very stable, but almost any genetic change produces effects of a quantitative type and alters the frequency with which the patterns are performed.

For example, in her study on the effects of the mutant *yellow* on the sexual behaviour of *Drosophila melanogaster*, Bastock (1956) showed that it reduced the frequency with which males performed certain patterns, but their form was identical with that of normal flies. By selection for speed of mating—also in *D. melanogaster*—Manning (1961, 1963) was able to alter the behaviour of males in a similar manner. Ewing (1961) describes quantitative differences in behaviour between lines of *D. melanogaster* selected for body-size criteria. The changes are subtle and certainly not due merely to the mechanical effects of changed size. Inbred lines of guinea pigs (Goy and Jakway, 1960; Jakway, 1960) and mice (McGill, 1962) differ quantitatively in a number of measures of latency and performance frequency of elements of sexual behaviour. By selection, Wood-Gush (1960) was able to alter the levels of sexual responses in domestic cockerels.

In all these examples changes to the genotype have changed thresholds of performance somewhere within the system. In few cases can we say much more than this, but sometimes analysis has proceeded a bit further and gives some clues on the action of genes. The Maudsley reactive and non-reactive strains of rats which show large differences in their emotional responses to a new and rather frightening environment, have proved to differ in their thyroid activity (Feuer and Broadhurst, 1962). Here the genes may operate, at least partially, to affect behaviour through the endocrine balance. Wood-Gush, Goy and Jakway, on the other hand, did not find that hormone levels are responsible for the differences between their lines, although these lines showed differing responsiveness to exogenous hormones.

I must now turn from this brief sample of the more directly genetical work and examine the nature of micro-evolutionary changes. The evidence comes from the comparative behaviour studies of ethologists. These mostly concern birds, fish and arthropods and it is sexual behaviour which has attracted most attention because of its conspicuous nature and relatively rapid evolution.

Some of the commonest features of micro-evolution are easily related to what we know of the effects of genetic changes. Thus, closely related species generally show the same instinctive repertoire, but differ in the frequency with which the elements are performed.

Drosophila offers many good examples. Brown (1962, 1963) describes the repertoire of courtship patterns common to the *obscura* group. The males' "rowing" movement with the legs is common in *miranda*, moderately so in *obscura*, but is extremely rare, though still occasionally seen in *pseudoobscura* and *persimilis*. In the *melanogaster* group, the sibling pair *melanogaster* and *simulans* differ markedly in frequency of the "scissoring" wing movement in the males' display (Manning, 1959). Scissoring is not normally seen in *melanogaster* but can be evoked in certain circumstances.

Differences between performance frequencies suggest effects on behavioural thresholds and some micro-evolutionary changes demonstrate this most vividly. The herring-gull (*Larus argentatus*) and the lesser black-backed gull (*L. fuscus*) have virtually identical alarm calls, but the latter species requires stronger stimuli to produce them; walking into a mixed colony will often cause the herring-gulls to call, but not their relatives (Goethe, 1954). Blest (1957) describes a similar case from the defence displays of Saturnioid moths. The aposematic species display at a light touch, the more cryptic species only after vigorous prodding.

Sometimes a species may apparently lack a pattern which is found among its close relatives, the *Drosophila* examples given above are a case in point. Nevertheless, it is very unlikely that behaviour patterns can disappear so easily. Their threshold may be so raised that they never normally appear, but the requisite neural mechanisms will still be there. In general, hybrids show the same behaviour patterns as the parent species but at intermediate frequencies. Hinde's (1956) work with Cardueline finch hybrids and that of Clark, Aronson and Gordon (1954) with Xiphophorin fish show this, and indicate that multiple loci are involved in determining pattern frequency. Sometimes, as in Hörmann-Heck's (1957) work with cricket (*Gryllus*) hybrids, species differences in frequency appear to be due to a single locus. Most of the observations on hybrids tell us nothing about the actual neural organization of the patterns or its inheritance. Certainly the development of an instinctive pattern must depend upon numerous genes. Hybridization is normally possible only between close relatives who possess very similar behaviour repertoires. A fine analysis of a pattern into its smallest separately "viable" units, such as one might expect to pick up in F_2 hybrids, is difficult. Bits of a behaviour pattern or malformed behaviour patterns are not so easily recognized as their morphological equivalents.

Changes to the sequence with which behaviour patterns are performed may well be another result of threshold changes, but we know too little about the organization of sequences to be confident. However it is interesting that whilst patterns themselves are so stable, sequence control does appear to be sensitive to genetic changes. The courtship displays of ducks, for example, consist of a number of easily recognized patterns (Lorenz, 1941). These patterns are similar from species to species but as well as showing different performance frequencies, species may differ in the sequence of patterns they perform. Species X may have A–B–C as its commonest pattern sequence; species Y, A–C–B. The work of Ramsay (1961) and van der Wall (unpublished, quoted by Hess, 1962) shows that species hybrids usually perform the patterns quite normally but often in odd sequences. Sometimes F_1 and F_2 hybrids perform sequences never seen in either parent species. Clearly the breakdown of the naturally evolved genotype upsets sequence control before the control of the individual patterns. Apart from the duck family, sequence changes have played some part in the behavioural radiation of *Drosophila*. Within the *melanogaster* group, some species normally perform a courtship sequence we may denote as A–B–C–D, others, using homologous patterns, have the order A–C–D–B.

So far I have been considering species differences in relation to threshold changes. Some of the other common types of evolutionary divergence are less obviously related to them.

(i) Species may differ in the speed with which homologous movements are performed.

This is seen in the defence displays of moths (Blest, 1957), the threat displays of gulls (Tinbergen, 1959), and probably the wing vibration displays of *Drosophila* species.

(ii) Species may differ in the relative "emphasis" given to the various parts of a homologous pattern. Most of the gulls have a "long-call" pattern in which the head is moved upwards and backwards on an extended neck whilst calling. The degree to which the head is thrown back during the call varies between species; it is least marked in the western gull (*Larus occidentalis*) and most emphasised in the common gull (*L. canus*), (Tinbergen, 1959). The *obscura* group of *Drosophila* vary in the degree to which the trailing-edge of the males' wing is drooped during the wing-vibration display. In *D. obscura* this drooping is most marked and there are detectable differences in this respect between *D. pseudoobscura* and *D. persimilis*, whose displays have often been regarded as identical (Brown, 1962 and *in press*). In fiddler-crabs of the genus *Uca*, the males show a rhythmic waving of an enlarged claw during courtship. Species vary in the relative emphasis given to "up-down" and "side-to-side" components of the wave, and also in the degree to which they raise and lower the whole body on the walking legs in time with the wave (Crane, 1957).

The form of a pattern in hybrids tends to be intermediate between the parental types. Hinde's (1956) finch hybrids sometimes had distinct but quite serviceable display patterns, half-way between those of the parents. However the work of Dilger (1959) on the F_1 hybrids between two species of parrot (*Agapornis*) shows how the intermediate between the two very distinct parental patterns for gathering nest material produces a very inadaptive result.

(iii) Species may differ in the relative importance of the various sensory modalities involved in the perception of displays. Within the *melanogaster* group, *Drosophila auraria* will not mate in the absence of light, *D. simulans* and *D. rufa* show reduced mating, but *D. melanogaster* is unaffected (Spieth and Hsu, 1950). Part of this variation probably relates to the degree by which the different females are stimulated by visual aspects of their males' courtship. Klopfer (1959) found some variation in the responsiveness of newly hatched ducklings to sound or visual stimuli from an object to which they were being imprinted. Ducklings of the surface-nesting species were most responsive to visual stimuli but those of the hole-nesting woodduck (*Aix sponsa*) would respond to sound alone. Subsequently Klopfer and Gottlieb (1962) have discovered that responsiveness to sound and visual stimuli varies even within a single brood of the mallard (*Anas platyrhynchos*). They suggest that this behavioural polymorphism reflects a genetic polymorphism and have begun a selective breeding programme.

The above are but three of many possible types of behavioural change; Blest (1961) considers them all more fully. At first sight they appear very heterogeneous, but even if we know next to nothing about the mechanisms involved, there seems no reason to suppose that gene action is fundamentally different in each categoiy. It is reasonable to suggest that all these changes have been produced by the accumulation of small threshold changes. For example, the change of emphasis within a pattern could result from threshold changes on the motor side of a mechanism such that particular muscle groups came into action earlier, or later, for a shorter time or a longer one, and so on. In this way small quantitative changes could summate to produce the great diversity of variants on a common "ancestral" pattern which we see in most groups. Again, changes to the importance of one stimulus modality with respect to another could be produced by threshold changes on the sensory side of the organization, perhaps accompanied by changes to the sense organs themselves.

There is no doubt that all natural populations show considerable variability for genes which affect behaviour and that this variability has been the raw material upon which selection has operated. In general I think the correspondence between gene effects and micro-evolutionary changes in behaviour is a good one, which is as it should be.

The relationship between behaviour and evolution is not all in one direction. Changes to behaviour, perhaps themselves the result of genetic changes, may in turn affect the course of evolution. For example, genetic differences between populations may alter their preferences for particular conditions of light, temperature or humidity and thus influence their choice of habitat. This may lead to changes in the degree to which they are isolated ecologically from one another.

Genetic changes also affect the sexual isolation between populations. This is an important and well-worked field but I have space to discuss only one aspect of it. This is the repercussions which the gradual "quantitative" evolution of behaviour have had on the development of sexual isolation. The shifts of performance frequency which will so commonly be the initial behavioural result of genetic divergence, are probably inadequate to prevent hybridization unless backed up by some more positive identification mark. This is often provided by colour patterns in birds, reptiles and fish, whilst among insects changes in scent are often important. Within the subgenus *Sophophora* of *Drosophila* where hybrids are very rare, sexual isolation is usually based on the female's ability to identify the scent of her own males and much less on her "sampling" their courtship displays. This is not to deny, of course, that selection will operate to make females most responsive to courtship of their own male's type, but they can identify males before courtship has proceeded far. It is not surprising that in the two cases where we have behavioural data on the effects of selection for increased sexual isolation between strains or species (Koopman, 1950; Pearce, 1962) it is discrimination which has been altered and not the courtship patterns.

A comparable example of behavioural differences being supported by chemical ones is provided by Hunsaker's (1962) work with lizards of the genus *Sceloporus*. He has shown that a species-specific pattern of head-bobbing is one of the factors which cause females to approach conspecific males but this selection is reinforced by chemical discrimination.

If most types of behavioural change accompanying the divergence of populations are too imprecise for reliable identification, those occurring in species with acoustical signals may be better. Quite small quantitative changes to the motor patterns which make up the mating calls of birds, frogs and crickets, can result in detectable sound differences. In crickets, for example, changes to pulse length, to the interval between pulses and to the amplitude of pulses within a series, all these and more have been developed to avoid interspecific confusion (Alexander, 1962). Sympatric species tend to be more different in their calling songs than allopatric ones. Blair (1955) has demonstrated a similar divergence of sexual call notes in the two sibling frog species, *Microhyla olivacea* and *M. carolinensis*. Samples taken from those parts of their range where only one species lives sound very similar, but where the two occur together in the same breeding ponds their calls are distinct. The three species of *Phylloscopus* warblers which often inhabit the same areas in Europe have similar alarm notes and courtship displays, but markedly different songs.

Sometimes it appears that isolation is based solely upon the response of females to the calls of their own males. Blair (1955) says that other isolating mechanisms between the *Microhyla* species are weak, and Perdeck (1958) found a similar situation in two sibling grasshopper species. However sound differences may also be backed up by chemical differences between species in some crickets (Alexander, 1962), just as plumage differences often reinforce song differences among birds.

My argument has been that the early stages of behavioural divergence, as opposed to any associated morphological or chemical changes, are often only quantitative and indistinct. I feel therefore that it behoves us to be cautious when suggesting that the evolution of elaborate courtship displays within a group has been dictated by the need for sexual isolation between overlapping species. The genus *Drosophila*, where there is the likelihood that several species will gather to mate on a common food source, is a case in point. Here we have an elaborate courtship evolved, but their quite close relatives the Tachinids and Anthomyids include a large number of species which similarly associate on food yet the males have no courtship at all. They mount and attempt to copulate with any fly of roughly the right size and females apparently distinguish their own males on contact and repel others. Sexual isolation, based presumably on scent differences, is as effective here as in *Drosophila*, and as we have seen it is doubtful whether female *Drosophila* discriminate against foreign males on the basis of their courtship displays.

It is, of course, unrealistic to separate completely the purely behavioural aspects of courtship from scent, colour or any of the other specially evolved releasers involved in reproduction. One function of the behaviour patterns may be to display conspicuously some patch of colour or to expose some scent gland and thereby enhance discrimination based on these structures. Clearly the advantages of sexual isolation have often been a factor in the evolution of courtship, but so have the need for behavioural synchrony, the appeasement of conflicting tendencies and perhaps sexual selection.

So far I have been considering the evolution of instinctive behaviour solely in the conventional terms of selection operating on small, undirected mutations. Certainly much of the adaptiveness of behaviour has been attained in this way but I want, in conclusion, to consider another source of adaptiveness, that of genetic assimilation (Waddington, 1961). The starting point is the organism's ability to make an adaptive response to an environmental stimulus. If this stimulus is consistent between generations and the response has survival value, selection will favour a more rapid and complete response. Eventually the threshold may be so lowered that the response occurs even in the absence of any exogenous stimulus. In behavioural terms, this means that patterns which were originally learnt become inherited. If selection is consistent the speed of learning will increase and the response itself will become more precisely adaptive. Eventually the response becomes encoded within the nervous system of the developing individual who requires only the correct environment to produce it fully perfected at the first exposure. These ideas are discussed by Ewer (1956) who suggests that imprinting responses, where, for example, a parent figure or a food plant are learnt extremely rapidly and perhaps at a single exposure, may represent an intermediate stage in the evolution of completely inherited behaviour.

Waddington (1961) has most elegantly demonstrated experimentally the genetic assimilation of acquired morphological and physiological characters. To do the same for behaviour is difficult, but a start has been made using as the acquired response the type of "larval conditioning" which Thorpe (1939) first showed that *Drosophila* make to contaminants in their culture medium (Moray and Connolly, 1963). Clearly genetic assimilation and the selection of random mutations are not completely distinct processes. Both must have played a part in the evolution of instinctive behaviour. I believe that once the arthropod level of organization and learning ability has been reached, assimilation may well be important for the incorporation of novel motor patterns into the instinctive repertoire which are subsequently modified in a more quantitative way.

The study of behaviour genetics is only just beginning, but already we can report some progress. If we must remain vague on mechanism, yet we can certainly consider the details of behaviour's evolution in genetical terms. Further work will be of value, not only for its elucidation of evolutionary mechanisms, but for information on the organization of behaviour within the nervous system which we get by investigating how genes affect it.

REFERENCES

ALEXANDER, R. D. (1962) Evolutionary change in cricket acoustical communication. *Evolution* **16**, 443-467.
BASTOCK, M. (1956) A gene mutation which changes a behavior pattern. *Evolution* **10**, 421-439.

BLAIR, W. F. (1955) Mating call and stage of speciation in the *Microhyla olivacea—M. carolinensis* complex. *Evolution* **9**, 469-480.

BLEST, A. D. (1957) The evolution of protective displays in the Saturnioidea and Sphingidae (Lepidoptera). *Behaviour* **11**, 257-309.

BLEST, A. D. (1961) The concept of ritualization. In Thorpe, W. H. and Zangwill, O. L. *(Eds.) Current Problems in Animal Behaviour*. Cambridge, pp. 102-124.

BROWN, R. G. B. (1962) A comparative study of mating behaviour in the *Drosophila obscura* group. D. Phil. Thesis, Univ. of Oxford.

BROWN, R. G. B. (1963). *In press. Behaviour.*

CLARK, E., ARONSON, L. R. and GORDON, M. (1954) Mating behaviour patterns in two sympatric species of Xiphophorin fishes: their inheritance and significance in sexual isolation. *Bull. Amer. Mus. Nat. Hist., N.Y.* **103**, 135-226.

CRANE, J. (1957) Basic patterns of display in fiddler crabs (Ocypodidae, genus *Uca*). *Zoologica* **42**, 69-82.

DILGER, W. C. (1959) Nest material carrying behaviour of F_1 hybrids between *Agapornis fischeri* and *A. roseicollis. Anat. Rec.* **134**, 554.

EWER, R. F. (1956) Imprinting in animal behaviour. *Nature* **177**, 227-228.

EWING, A. W. (1961) Body size and courtship behaviour in *Drosophila melanogaster. Anim. Behav.* **9**, 93-99.

FEUER, G. and BROADHURST, P. L. (1962) Thyroid function in rats selectively bred for emotional elimination. II. Differences in thyroid activity. *J. Endocrinol.* **24**, 253-262.

GOETHE, F. (1954) Vergleichende Beobachtungen über das Verhalten der Silvermowe *(Larus a. argentatus)* und der Heringsmowe *(Larus f. fuscus). Proc. XI Int. Orn. Congr.* 557-582.

GOY, R. W. and JAKWAY, J. S. (1960) The inheritance of patterns in sexual behaviour in female guinea pigs. *Anim. Behav.* **7**, 142-149.

HINDE, R. A. (1956) The behaviour of certain Cardueline F_1 inter-species hybrids. *Behaviour* **9**, 202-213.

HESS, E. H. (1962) Ethology. In Brown, R., Salanter, E., Hess, E. H. and Mandler, G. *New Directions in Psychology*. Holt, Rinehart, Winston, New York, pp. 159-266.

HÖRMANN-HECK, S. VON (1957) Untersuchungen über den Erbgang einiger Verhaltensweisen bei Grillen-bastarden *(Gryllus campestris* L. x *Gryllus bimaculatus* De Geer). *Z. Tierpsychol.* **14**, 137-183.

HUNSAKER, D. (1962) Ethological isolating mechanisms in the *Sceloporus torquatus* group of lizards. *Evolution* **16**, 62-74.

JAKWAY, J. S. (1960) The inheritance of patterns of mating in the male guinea pig. *Anim. Behav.* **7**, 150-162.

KLOPFER, P. H. (1959) An analysis of learning in young Anatidae. *Ecology* **40**, 90-102.

KLOPFER, P. H. and GOTTLIEB, G. (1962) Learning ability and behavioural polymorphism within individual clutches of wild ducklings. *Z. Tierpsychol.* **19**, 183-190.

KOOPMAN, K. F. (1950) Natural selection for reproductive isolation between *Drosophila pseudoobscura* and *Drosophila persimilis. Evolution* **4**, 135-148.

LORENZ, K. (1941) Vergleichende Bewegungstudien an Anatinen. *J. Orn.* **89**, 194-294.

MANNING, A. (1959) The sexual behaviour of two sibling *Drosophila* species. *Behaviour* **15**, 123-145.

MANNING, A. (1961) The effects of artificial selection for mating speed in *Drosophila melanogaster. Anim. Behav.* **9**, 82-92.

MANNING, A. (1963) Selection for mating speed in *Drosophila melanogaster* based on the behaviour of one sex. *Anim. Behav.* **11**, 19, 341-350.

McGILL, T. E. (1962) Sexual behaviour in three inbred strains of mice. *Behaviour* **19**, 341-350.

MORAY, N. and CONNOLLY, K. (1963) A possible case of genetic assimilation of behaviour. *Nature* **199**, 358-360.

PEARCE, S. (1962) Evolution of mating behaviour in *Drosophila* under artificial selection. M/S. of paper read to *Brit. Ass. Adv. Sci.* 1962.

PERDECK, A. C. (1958) The isolating value of specific song patterns in two sibling species of grasshoppers *(Chorthippus brunneus* Thunb. and *C. biggutulus* L.). *Behaviour* **12**, 1-75.

RAMSAY, A. O. (1961) Behaviour of some hybrids in the mallard group. *Anim. Behav.* **9**, 104-105.

SPIETH, H. T. and HSU, T. C. (1950) The influence of light on the mating behavior of seven species of the *Drosophila melanogaster* group. *Evolution* **4**, 316-325.

THORPE, W. H. (1939) Further experiments on pre-imaginal conditioning in insects. *Proc. Roy. Soc.* B. **127**, 424-433.

TINBERGEN, N. (1959) Comparative studies of the behaviour of gulls. *(Laridae)*: a progress report. *Behaviour* **15**, 1-70.

WADDINGTON, C. H. (1961) Genetic assimilation. *Adv. Genet.* **10**, 257-293.

WOOD-GUSH, D. G. M. (1960) A study of sex drive of two strains of cockerels through three generations. *Anim. Behav.* **8**, 43-53.

AM. ZOOLOGIST, 4:147-153 (1964).

COURTSHIP AND MATING BEHAVIOR AS A REPRODUCTIVE ISOLATING MECHANISM IN *DROSOPHILA*

LEE EHRMAN

The Rockefeller Institute, New York

Species of sexually reproducing organisms are genetically closed systems. They are closed systems because they do not exchange genes or do so rarely enough so that the species differences are not swamped. Races are, on the contrary, genetically open systems. They do exchange genes by peripheral gene flow, unless they are isolated by extrinsic causes such as spatial separation. The biological meaning of the closure of a genetic system is simple but important—it is evolutionary independence. Consider these four species—man, chimpanzee, gorilla, orangutan. No mutation and no gene combination arising in any one of them, no matter how favorable, can benefit any of the others. It cannot do so for the simple reason that no gene can be transferred from the gene pool of one species to that of another. On the contrary, races composing a species are not independent in their evolution; a favorable genetic change arising in one race is, at least potentially, capable of becoming a genetic characteristic of the species as a whole.

Species are genetically closed systems because the gene exchange between them is impeded or prevented by reproductive isolating mechanisms. The term "isolating mechanism" was proposed by Dobzhansky in 1937 as a common name for all genetically conditioned barriers to gene exchange between sexually reproducing populations. According to Mayr (1963), isolating mechanisms are ". . . perhaps the most important set of attributes a species has. . . ." It is a remarkable fact that isolating mechanisms are physiologically and ecologically a most heterogenous collection of phenomena. It is another remarkable fact that the

isolating mechanisms which maintain the genetic separateness of species are quite different not only in different groups of organisms but even between different pairs of species in the same genus.

Several classifications of the reproductive isolating mechanisms have been proposed. That of Mayr is a simple and convenient one. The two major groups are the premating barriers which prevent the formation of hybrid zygotes, and the postmating barriers which impede the survival or reproduction of these zygotes.

Three of the premating mechanisms are:

1) Potential mates do not meet (seasonal and habitat isolation).
2) Potential mates meet but do not mate (ethological or sexual isolation).
3) Copulation attempted but no transfer of gametes takes place (mechanical isolation).

Four of the postmating barriers are:

4) Gametes transferred but no fertilization, and hence no zygote formation takes place (gamete mortality).
5) Death of the zygotes (hybrid inviability).
6) The F_1 zygotes are viable but partly or completely sterile (hybrid sterility).
7) F_1 hybrids are fertile but the fitness of the F_2 or backcross hybrid is reduced (hybrid breakdown).

Since our primary interest today centers on the relations between genes and behavior, ethological isolation, sometimes also termed sexual or psychological isolation, should be discussed here in more detail. The phenomenon observed is usually that the mutual attraction between conspecific females and males is greater than the attraction between males and females of different species. Successful analysis of this form of isolation requires

The work reported here has been carried out under Contract No. AT-(30-1)-3096, U. S. Atomic Energy Commission.

a detailed description of the courtship rituals and the mating behavior in the pure species concerned. Species of the genus *Drosophila* offer abundant and favorable material for such analysis; their courtship and mating can be observed easily at any season of the year and under reasonably precisely controlled laboratory conditions.

My favorite materials are the incipient species of the *Drosophila paulistorum* complex or superspecies. As the name "incipient species" implies, these forms are very closely related and can be regarded either as very similar sibling species or as very distinct races standing on the brink of full species separation. This close relationship is, of course, very favorable for analytical purposes. What we wish to study is speciation in the process and the closeness permits a genetic analysis to be carried further than would be possible with full species.

The six incipient species of *Drosophila paulistorum* inhabit a part of the Neotropical zoogeographic region, from Guatemala and Trinidad in the north to southern Brazil in the south. Each incipient species has a distribution area of its own, but these are in part overlapping, so that in some places two, three, or even four incipient species live together, sympatrically, and apparently without producing any hybrids.

Thanks to the work of many authors, especially H. T. Spieth (1952) the sexual behavior in *Drosophila* is fairly well known. Sexual recognition is a trial and error affair among drosophilids. Males will generally attempt to court females of any *Drosophila* species, even distantly related ones.

At least four distinct elements can be distinguished in the courtship process in *Drosophila paulistorum*. The first element or stage is that of circling. The male approaches a female, attracts her attention, and may limit her movements by running around her. He never completes a full circle however, turns around, reversing the direction of his movement about every 330°.

Next he begins a tapping action—an important aspect of the courtship in this species (Fig. 1A). The male lightly touches the legs or the abdomen of the female with his own legs. At first, only one leg of each fly is involved. Since many taps may be necessary before it is established that the male has located a female of his own species, the male continues to circle between contacts. Here, the question of the female's receptivity is settled (this is probably mediated by samples taken by the great number of chemoreceptive hairs on the body of both insects); she will either remain still so that circling is no longer necessary, and then spread her wings to receive the male between them; or she will vigorously kick the courting male and do her best to depart.

Licking and wing vibrating occur next (Fig. 1B), both as a prelude to mounting. As Spieth (1952) has described it, the male "goes to the rear of the female and assumes a slightly crouched position with the tip of his abdomen slightly curled. Having positioned himself, he extends one wing 70° to 90° and vibrates it periodically, twisting his body on the longitudinal axis as he vibrates, taps (uppercuts), and occasionally licks or attempts to lick the female." In licking, the male proboscis contacts the female genitalia—and this is a reliable sign that the male is about to rush in for the mount. In *D. paulistorum* wing vibrations are not so important a part of courtship as in some of the other species. The one wing that is vibrated is used for leverage as the male raises himself on the body of the female.

Mounting and insertion seem to be accomplished simultaneously. A portion of the male reproductive organ is used in a clasping manner and, after mounting, the male secures his position on the female by placing his forelegs on top of her slightly-spread wings. This additional support is imperative because copulation lasts a fairly long time in this species (an average of 17 minutes and 12 seconds). During the copulatory period, the female may turn about or walk around; and she may even

A

B

C

FIG. 1. These "stills" were taken from a 16 mm color film prepared by Mr. Richard F. Carter of the Rockefeller Institute and by the author; the project was supported by a grant from The Society of the Sigma Xi. This study of courtship behavior in *Drosophila paulistorum* was shown, in part, when this paper was delivered.

A. Tapping (the male is the smaller, active individual with the rumpled wings)—an initial stage in courtship.

B. Licking—often seen just before mounting.

C. The formation of a chain wherein one re-

find herself having to fend off other males (Fig. 2).

When copulation is nearly over, the female attempts to dislodge the male by vigorously kicking and swinging her body from side to side. The male loses his hold on her wings when she snaps them together, and seconds later he falls off backwards. Thereafter, the female repels all sexually excited males by raising the tip of her abdomen, rendering her vaginal orifice inaccessible.

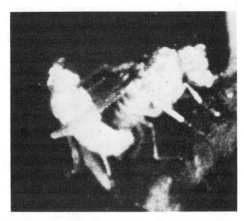

FIG. 2. Photograph of the full mount during which time the female may move about freely and even feed.

Notice that throughout this entire procedure, it is the female that at all stages, is "discriminatingly passive" while the male is "indiscriminately eager" (Bateman, 1948). *D. paulistorum* males are very active and will court almost anything: a dead fly, a mired fly, lumps of food, and often other males. It is not unusual to observe the formation of a chain initiated by a male courting a female, and in turn being himself courted by another male who is being approached by yet another male. These chains, of course, are of short duration (Fig. 1C).

jecting female (with extruded ovipositor) is being courted by a male who is in turn being courted by a male, etc., for a total of one female and three males—these chains are necessarily of short duration but do emphasize the fact that *D. paulistorum* males will certainly court the other males. See text for detailed explanation.

Now that the normal courtship and mating behavior of the species-complex has been recorded, we are ready to consider the evolution of this superspecies *Drosophila paulistorum* (Dobzhansky et al., 1964).

One of the first of the many interesting evolutionary phenomena exhibited by the *D. paulistorum* complex of seven known races or incipient species to be analyzed genetically was the complete hybrid male sterility discovered when crosses between the races were successful. The male sterility was found to be genic in nature (Ehrman, 1960a), and to be expressed via the genotype of hybrid mothers. This kind of hybrid sterility, unique in the genetic literature, operates in the following manner. Suppose that we cross two races, A and B, one or both of them having one or more chromosomes marked with suitable mutant genes. The distribution in the progeny of the chromosomes of different racial origin can then be followed by inspection of the external morphology of the flies. The interracial hybrid males are sterile, but the females are fertile and can be backcrossed to either A or to B males. After several backcrosses, flies are obtained which carry all but one of the chromosomes from race A, or all but one from race B. Females of this sort are, of course, fertile and can again be backcrossed to males of the recurrent race. Half of this progeny, of either sex, will carry all chromosomes of the same race, and half will contain one race-foreign chromosome. (Crossingover is suppressed in these hybrids.) Now, the striking fact is that males of both kinds are completely sterile. The sterility of the males identical in chromosomal constitution with males of one of the "pure" races can only mean that the sterility is in this case determined not by the chromosomal constitution of the individual itself but by that of his mother. The presence of at least one race-foreign chromosome in the developing egg cell before meiosis somehow modifies the cytoplasm or some other property of the egg, and makes a male individual developing from this egg sterile.

Once the above facts were established, the question logically arose whether the ethological isolation observed in races of *D. paulistorum* has the same peculiar genetic basis as the sterility of the hybrid males, that is, a genic-maternal effect. The ethological isolation is in all probability the mechanism which keeps the gene pools of these races separate in nature where the races share the same territory. Indeed, race hybrids have never been found in nature, and the cytological study of their chromosomes by Dobzhansky and Pavlovsky (1962) shows that genetically effective hybridization of the races is rare, if it occurs at all.

The genetic basis of the ethological (sexual) isolation was studied by Ehrman (1961). The method used was in principle the same as that applied for the analysis of the hybrid sterility, i.e., making crosses and backcrosses of strains of different races having some of their chromosomes marked with suitable mutant genes. It was here that the knowledge of the courtship and mating behavior of *D. paulistorum* became important.

Hybrid males of *D. paulistorum* transfer no sperm into the body of the female with which they copulate. F_1 hybrid males produce no motile spermatozoa, because a restitution nucleus is formed presumably after the first meiotic division, and then all the gametic material degenerates. Backcross hybrid males are even more profoundly sterile, since they frequently have no testes at all, or only one testis, or no gonial cells within the abnormally *thick* testicular sheath. Yet these males are normal in external morphology and have normal genitalia and internal reproductive organs other than testes. Their patterns of courtship and mating behavior are also normal. Since dissections of the female reproductive tract for the storage of transferred sperm (as is usually done in analyses of this sort where fertile males are involved) would be out of the question here; the entire analysis of the genetic architecture of sexual isolation as a reproductive isolating mechanism was made by using the simple but informative, direct-observation technique.

One may conclude from these direct-observation studies that the sexual isolation, which makes matings between the females and males of the *D. paulistorum* races much less likely to occur than matings within the races, is due to polygenes in every one of the three pairs of chromosomes which the species possesses. These polygenes control the sexual preferences of their carriers. Their effects seem to be simply additive. A female of hybrid origin which carries a majority of the chromosomal material derived from a given race is most likely to accept a male of that race. And conversely, a hybrid male is most likely to be accepted by females whose chromosomal constitution is closest to his. The source of the cytoplasm or the genetic constitution of the mother do not seem to matter. This is clearly not at all comparable with the genetic basis of the hybrid sterility, where the properties of an egg are determined, as far as the sterility of the backcross males is concerned, by the genotype present in it before meiosis, and not by that formed following fertilization.

We may surmise that this peculiar chromosomal-cytoplasmic mechanism of sterility arose first in the evolutionary history of these races, and that it arose in allopatric races becoming adapted to different environments in their respective geographic areas. Sexual isolation might then be built by natural selection, as a much less wasteful and more efficient reinforcement of the bar to gene exchange between the races. When this sexual isolation became strong or complete, the races became able to coexist sympatrically, as they have been found to do in some localities in the northern part of the South American continent (Dobzhansky et al, 1964) where as many as four races have been found to live in the same places.

How effective can sexual isolation be, what with omnipresent variations in environmental influences and the undeniable susceptibility of behavior patterns to these influences? Consider the case of the rare hybrids obtained in the laboratory between the races of *Drosophila paulistorum* inhabiting northern and southern Brazil, respectively. These hybrid individuals are most difficult to obtain and possess a genetic constitution discordant enough so that the hybrid females repel the courtship of all males, and will mate with none; their sterile hybrid brothers will court and will be rejected by almost all females, including their own hybrid siblings. There is no question of gene flow through the hybrid males, because they are absolutely sterile. Their sisters, however, are potentially fertile. This has been verified not only by dissection of their internal and external reproductive apparatus, but more conclusively by a direct experiment. Some etherized hybrid females are exposed to many mature, unanesthetized males; the males approach, mount and inseminate the females in question; the hybrid females subsequently recover and deposit fertilized eggs which develop normally (Ehrman, 1960b).

More recently, Carmody et al. (1962) investigated a possible correlation between the occurrence of hybrid sterility and sexual isolation within the *D. paulistorum* complex. In this massive study, more than sixteen thousand females from all of the then known *D. paulistorum* races were dissected and their sperm-storing organs checked. Each *Drosophila paulistorum* female, hybrid or not, has three sperm-storing organs. The "male choice" experimental method was used to test mating preferences of different strains comprising the races. Briefly, this involves groups of ten virgin females of each of two races (a total of twenty females), aged for three to four days after hatching, marked for recognition by clipping a very small part of one of the wings of one of two types of females, and then confined with males of one of the two races for twenty-four to forty-eight hours, i.e., A ♂♂ × A ♀♀ + B ♀♀ or B ♂♂ × B ♀♀ + A ♀♀. All the females are then dissected in a physiological saline, and their sperm receptacles are examined for the presence or absence of sperm.

Strains of the same race but of different geographic origin often show significant preferences for homogamic matings, but strains of different races show such preferences to a much greater extent. On the average, sexual isolation is lower in interracial matings involving the transitional race, the bridge to fertile hybrids between all the other races. The degree of sexual isolation shows only a weak positive correlation with the fertility or sterility of the hybrids between the strains crossed.

More study is needed to unravel the interrelations of the sexual isolation and hybrid sterility. As indicated above, sexual isolation is most effective in limiting or preventing the appearance of interracial hybrids with reduced reproductive fitness. A problem of considerable interest is whether isolating mechanisms which decrease the chances of production of hybrid offspring are stronger between sympatric than between allopatric populations of the *same* pairs of races or subspecies or incipient species. When two or more Mendelian populations of sexually reproducing and cross-fertilizing organisms share the same territory, these populations are exposed to the risk of hybridization and gene exchange. If such a gene exchange leads to production of adaptively inferior genotypes, natural selection may favor genetic constitutions which hinder or prevent hybridization. On the other hand, the gene exchange and introgression may weaken the reproductive isolation, and may eventually lead to fusion of the previously separate populations. Experiments were made to test whether the sexual isolation between sympatric strains of a given pair of races is, on the average, greater or smaller than that between allopatric strains of the same races. They showed (Dobzhansky et al., 1964) that natural selection had encouraged the spread and maintenance, in sympatric populations of incipient species, of those genes which limit or prevent the reproductive wastage resulting from gene flow between these populations.

However, one may suppose as Muller (1942) does that reproductive isolation arises as an incidental by-product of genetic divergence. When populations become adapted to different environments they are likely to become different in progressively more and more genes. Reproductive isolation then might arise because the action of many genes is pleiotropic. Some gene differences selected for different reasons, or resulting from random genetic drift, may thus have isolating side-effects.

That selection can indeed produce, or at least strengthen, reproductive isolation has been demonstrated experimentally by Koopman (1950) and by Knight, Robertson, and Waddington (1956). Koopman set up experimental populations in laboratory population cages consisting of two species, *D. pseudoobscura* and *D. persimilis*. Each species was homozygous for a different recessive mutant gene with easily visible external effects. The pure species and the hybrids were thus made easily distinguishable. In every generation the adult flies were taken from the cages, etherized, classified, and counted. The hybrids were then discarded and new population cages were started with nonhybrid progenies. By these means Koopman was selecting the progenies of intraspecific, and excluding those of interspecific, matings. In a surprisingly small number of generations he obtained strains of *D. pseudoobscura* and *D. persimilis* which showed a more nearly complete sexual isolation than did the original strains. The results of Knight, Robertson, and Waddington are, in a way, even more dramatic, since they obtained by selection a significant, though of course incomplete, sexual isolation of strains of *D. melanogaster* which originally showed no such isolation.

The incipient species of *D. paulistorum* seem to furnish a good illustration of the two processes postulated above. It is not easy to imagine the sterility of male hybrids between these incipient species conferring any adaptive advantage upon them. But once this sterility has arisen as *a by-*

product of *their genetic divergence,* it is probable that natural selection would favor genetic constitutions which make the sterile hybrids rare. The sexual isolation between the incipient species may be a reproductive barrier contrived as such by the action of *natural selection.*

Dobzhansky and Spassky (1959) first suggested that *Drosophila paulistorum* is a cluster of species in *statu nascendi,* a borderline case of uncompleted speciation. This suggestion is borne out by the work since then. *Drosophila paulistorum* is a superspecies composed of six races or incipient species. The interest of the situation lies precisely in that these six may be considered about equally legitimately as very distinct races or as very closely related species. Each race inhabits a geographic area different from the others, but the areas of some of the races overlap. Where two or more "races" share a common territory they apparently do not interbreed, and thus behave like full-fledged species. The Transitional race and transitional strains yield, however, fertile hybrids with some other races. The possibility of gene flow between the incipient species is, therefore not excluded, although it is questionable whether it is actually taking place.

Last year, in his Vice Presidential address on *Genes and the Study of Behavior,* Caspari (1963) cautioned ". . . the analysis of F_1 species hybrids cannot give us, in principle, information about genetic units. This will only be possible through further crosses, F_2 and backcrosses." The step-by-step, often tedious analysis of the *D. paulistorum* situation, as presented here today, certainly indicates how correct he was. Understanding of the genetic basis of the sexual isolation among these races would have been impossible without a systematic study of the backcross individuals, in conjunction with a survey of the courtship and mating behavior in the F_1 hybrids and in the "pure" races. Surely "the genetic basis of behavioral characters is important, because it is the genes which are the basic units transmitted and reshuffled in the evolutionary process and which are arranged by selective forces into adaptive action patterns." (Caspari, 1963.)

REFERENCES

Bateman, A. J. 1948. Intra-sexual selection in *Drosophila.* Heredity 2:349-368.

Carmody, G., A. Diaz Collazo, Th. Dobzhansky, L. Ehrman, J. S. Jaffrey, S. Kimball, S. Obrebski, S. Silagi, J. T. Tidwell, and R. Ullrich. 1962. Mating preferences and sexual isolation within and between the incipient species of *Drosophila paulistorum.* Am. Midl. Nat. 68:67-82.

Caspari, E. 1963. Genes and the study of behavior. Am. Zoologist 3:97-100.

Dobzhansky, Th. 1937. Genetics and the origin of species. First edition. Columbia Univer. Press, New York.

Dobzhansky, Th., L. Ehrman, O. Pavlovsky, and B. Spassky. 1964. The superspecies *Drosophila paulistorum.* Proc. Natl. Acad. Sci. 51:3-9.

Dobzhansky, Th., and O. Pavlovsky. 1962. A comparative study of the chromosomes in the incipient species of the *Drosophila paulistorum* complex. Chromosoma 13:196-218.

Dobzhansky, Th., and B. Spassky. 1959. *Drosophila paulistorum,* a cluster of species in *statu nascendi.* Proc. Natl. Acad. Sci. 45:419-428.

Ehrman, L. 1960a. The genetics of hybrid sterility in *Drosophila paulistorum.* Evolution 14:212-223.

———. 1960b. A genetic constitution frustrating the sexual drive in *Drosophila paulistorum.* Science 131:1381-1382.

———. 1961. The genetics of sexual isolation in *Drosophila paulistorum.* Genetics 46:1025-1038.

Knight, G. R., A. Robertson, and C. H. Waddington. 1956. Selection for sexual isolation within a species. Evolution 10:14-22.

Koopman, K. F. 1950. Natural selection for reproductive isolation between *Drosophila pseudoobscura* and *Drosophila persimilis.* Evolution 4: 135-148.

Mayr, E. 1963. Animal species and evolution. Harvard Univer. Press, Cambridge, Mass.

Muller, H. J. 1942. Isolating mechanisms, evolution, and temperature. Biol. Symp. 6:71-125.

Spieth, H. T. 1952. Mating behavior within the genus *Drosophila* (Diptera). Bull. Am. Mus. Nat. Hist. 99:395-474.

BEHAVIOR GENETICS OF NEST CLEANING IN HONEY BEES. IV. RESPONSES OF F_1 AND BACKCROSS GENERATIONS TO DISEASE-KILLED BROOD

Walter C. Rothenbuhler

Department of Zoology and Entomology, The Ohio State University

INTRODUCTION

The honey bee is in one striking way different from most animals. Much of the animal kingdom lives a more or less solitary existence (except for a minimal amount of social life involved in mating activity and reproduction), whereas the honey bee lives in colonies of up to 60,000 individuals. Honey-bee colonies are much more than aggregations, flocks, or herds, for the individuals within one are so dependent upon one another that no individual, nor even a group of a few hundred individuals, can survive and perpetuate the species in nature.

Some further facts of bee biology are basic to this paper. The nest is the center of colony life, and is composed of a number of wax combs arranged vertically in a suitable cavity such as a hollow tree. In modern apiculture, hives, instead of hollow trees, provide the cavities, and combs are contained inside wood frames which permits their removal from the nest, their examination, and rearrangement. Brood is reared and food is stored in these combs which are used over and over again, year after year.

The drone and the queen (male and fe-male) are the reproductively important members of the colony. Drones develop from unfertilized eggs, and are consequently haploid in origin and in transmission of genetic factors. Queens arise from fertilized eggs, which makes them diploid in origin and similar to any diploid animal in transmission of genetic factors. The third kind of bee in the colony, the worker bee, is a reproductively undeveloped female which arises from a fertilized egg, the same as the queen.

Colony behavior is almost exclusively the behavior of worker bees. It is the worker bees that secrete wax and build comb, nurse the brood, keep the colony warm or cool as the need may be, defend the colony, keep the combs and hive interior clean, and go to the field to gather nectar, pollen, water, and propolis. Such colony labor is further divided among worker bees on the basis of their age. Normally the younger workers engage in duties inside the hive whereas older workers carry out the field activities. By this time, it is perhaps apparent that a social insect such as the honey bee displays a far greater variety of behavior than could be expected of insects living a solitary life. More information on life history, behavior, and social organization of honey bees may be found in Butler, 1954; Von Frisch, 1950; Grout, 1963; Lindauer, 1961; Michener and Michener, 1951; Ribbands, 1953; Root, 1962; as well as in a host of other sources.

The stock-in-trade of the behavior geneticist, however, is variation in behavior, and the honey bee has it. Different races and strains of bees vary, for instance, in the number of times their colonies swarm, in the number of times they sting, and in the amount of pollen stored. They even engage in different dances in reporting the same food source to the colony (Boch,

The data contained in this paper were obtained while the author was a staff member of the Department of Zoology and Entomology, Iowa State University, Ames, Iowa. In addition to support from the Iowa Agricultural Experiment Station, this investigation was supported in part by Research Grant E599(C7) from the National Institute of Allergy and Infectious Diseases, Public Health Service, made to Iowa State University, and is presently supported by Research Grant HD00368-01 from The National Institute of Child Health and Human Development, Public Health Service, made to The Ohio State University.

The author's deep appreciation is expressed to Mrs. Christina Barthel (nee Garwood), technician, and Mr. Victor C. Thompson, research associate, for their competent assistance with these experiments.

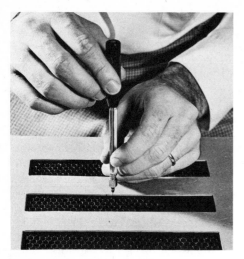

FIG. 1. Inoculation of larval food with spores of *Bacillus larvae* by use of microsyringe.

1957; and others). There is a great deal of behavioral variation in bees but a great lack of careful, quantitative investigation of this variation. More study in this field would be rewarding.

Our studies have been concerned primarily with two differences in behavior. The first one is response to immature individuals which have died, in the cells of the brood comb, of the disease American foulbrood; and the second one, studied to a lesser extent, is response to the beekeeper —more specifically, stinging behavior.

NEST-CLEANING BEHAVIOR

Description and nature of investigation

The adults of certain colonies of bees remove foulbrood-killed larvae and pupae from the combs very quickly, whereas the adults of other colonies allow these dead individuals to remain in the combs for days, or weeks, or indefinitely. Such larvae and pupae, dead of American foulbrood, allowed to remain in the brood nest are a source of the pathogen, *Bacillus larvae*, and lead to new infections. This hygienic behavior, by which dead larvae and pupae are quickly removed, is one mechanism of resistance to the disease (Rothenbuhler and Thompson, 1955).

Differences in response to American foulbrood-killed brood were discovered more than 20 years ago by O. W. Park (1936) at Iowa State College, and by Alan Woodrow and E. C. Holst (1942) of the United States Department of Agriculture at Laramie, Wyoming, as they were investigating the mechanisms of resistance to disease. The research reported here was undertaken as part of our investigation of resistance to American foulbrood, but it has grown into a new effort on behavior genetics of bees (Rothenbuhler, 1958, 1960, 1964; Jones and Rothenbuhler, 1964; Thompson, 1964).

Hygienic behavior may be studied by techniques indicated in Figures 1, 2, and 3. A sample of eggs from a suitable mated queen is obtained in a comb, and is placed for hatching and rearing in the colony whose behavior is to be studied. At the appropriate larval age, the larval food surrounding each larva is inoculated, by means of a microsyringe, with spores of the pathogen dispersed in water. Control (or check) larvae are inoculated with water

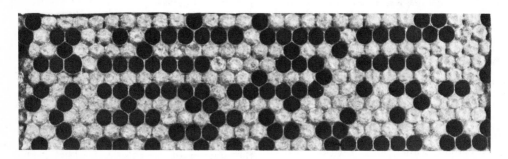

FIG. 2. Comb of brood, reared in a Brown, hygienic colony, about two days before brood emergence, showing that many individuals are missing from the spore-inoculated rows. All brood remaining in this comb was found to be alive.

FIG. 3. Comb of brood, reared in a Van Scoy, non-hygienic colony, showing that most of the brood seems to be present. When uncapped in the laboratory, many individuals in the spore-inoculated rows were dead of American foulbrood.

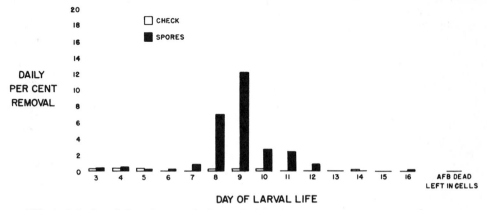

FIG. 4. Behavior of three Brown colonies resulted in the removal of all American foulbrood-killed (AFB) individuals before the end of the experiment.

only, or are uninoculated, as the situation requires.

Figure 2 is a picture of a comb photographed at the end of an experiment. It shows spore-inoculated rows of brood from which many individuals have been removed as contrasted with the check rows of brood. This brood was reared in a colony showing hygienic behavior. Figure 3 is a picture of brood reared in a colony which did not show hygienic behavior. Nearly all individuals seem to be present, but when these cells were manually uncapped, large numbers of larvae were found to be dead of American foulbrood in the spore-inoculated rows.

Experimental results

Figures 4, 5, and 6 show graphs of the data from an experiment involving colonies from our Brown resistant line, our Van Scoy susceptible line, and the F_1 generation re-

sulting from a cross of the two. All tests were made concurrently.

Figure 4 shows the pooled daily percentage removals of check and spore-treated larvae from three Brown-line colonies. On the first day of larval life, not shown in the graph, the larvae were inoculated. On the second day of larval life the larvae were counted and this was the base count for the subsequent calculations. On the horizontal axis it can be seen that, by the third day, a small percentage of the base count of checks was removed, and also a small percentage of the spore-inoculated base count. It may be pointed out here that capping of the cells occurs between the 4th and 6th days, and the larval stage ends by about the 8th day. There was a substantial amount of removal of spore-inoculated larvae on the 8th, 9th, 10th, and 11th days, and no substantial removal of checks. Very little removal occurred on the last days of

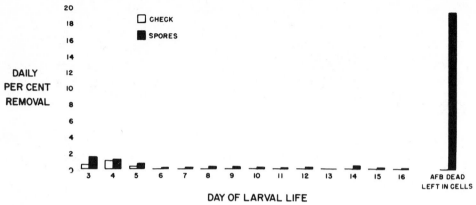

FIG. 5. Behavior of four Van Scoy colonies left most foulbrood-killed individuals in the comb until the end of the experiment on the 16th day.

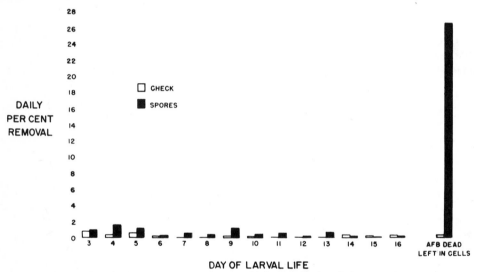

FIG. 6. Behavior of five F_1 colonies resembled the behavior of the Van Scoys.

the experiment. On the 16th day, at the end of the experiment, all cells were uncapped manually and no individuals dead of American foulbrood were found remaining in the combs. This graph is based upon 622 spore-fed larvae and 322 water-fed larvae.

Figure 5, presenting the pooled performance of four Van Scoy susceptible-line colonies, shows a contrast. Practically no removal of brood occurred throughout the experiment, and at the end, when the cells were uncapped, many of the spore-inoculated larvae were found dead of American foulbrood and remaining in the comb.

This graph is based upon 753 spore-fed larvae and 383 water-fed checks.

The pooled performance of five F_1 colonies, presented in Figure 6, was very close to the Van Scoy susceptible-line performance. Here again a large number of larvae were involved—837 spore-fed, and 459 water-fed. These results indicate that the gene or genes for hygienic behavior were recessive. How many loci are involved is now a prominent question.

To get an answer, 29 backcrosses of the F_1 generation were made. For the preceding test, F_1 workers had been reared, but they do not normally reproduce. F_1 queens were necessary for reproduction. From such F_1 queens, drones were obtained. These drones, having developed from unfertilized eggs were gametes—gametes with wings, in fact, and the capability of producing 6 to 10 million more genetically identical gametes in the form of sperms. Such a gamete, from an F_1 individual, when mated by artificial insemination to an inbred queen of the parental line, will produce a colony of bees of similar genotype. Twenty-nine such drones or gametes from two queens of the F_1 generation were mated to 29 queens of the Brown line which were expected to be homozygous for the recessive genes for hygienic behavior. If $\frac{1}{2}$ of the 29 colonies developed from the backcrosses were hygienic, one would conclude that one locus only was involved in the difference in hygienic behavior between the two lines. If only $\frac{1}{4}$ were hygienic, 2 loci would be involved; if $\frac{1}{8}$, three loci. It was necessary, of course, to run controls along with the backcrosses, so 7 colonies from the hygienic Brown line were tested, along with 7 colonies of the non-hygienic Van Scoy parental line. Also 8 backcrosses were made to the Van Scoy line.

Figure 7 presents graphs of the hygienic behavior of the seven hygienic-line control colonies and a graph of the pooled results. The pooled data in the upper left corner involve a total of 1383 spore-fed larvae and 698 water-fed checks. The same pattern seen previously in the Brown line is obvious. Not a single dead individual remained beyond the 12th day. An unexpectedly high number of check larvae were removed. There is no reason to think that these were dead; in fact it is likely that they were living larvae that for some reason were removed, and consequently they present a problem for the future. The individual responses of the seven colonies are plotted in the seven other graphs which show great uniformity with respect to the main point—that Browns remove foulbrood quickly.

Figure 8 shows seven cases of Van Scoy non-hygienic behavior, with the pooled results again, in the upper left. This too resembles the non-hygienic behavior already seen. Here it is seen that there was only a slight amount of removal of either spore or check larvae. In the end, about 14% of spore-fed larvae were left dead in the cells of the comb. Less than .5% of the check larvae were dead and left. A glance at the seven individual-colony results shows that all colonies left foulbrood-killed brood in the comb. Some colonies removed more spore-fed larvae than others, but this removal was erratic as to when it occurred.

The 29 backcrosses to the Brown line broke up into 4 groups, each of which is presented in a separate figure. Figure 9 presents a group of 6 colonies that showed complete hygienic behavior. Five of the 6 showed behavior nearly identical to the Brown line. M 1423 was about 2 days later in removal than expected, but no dead larvae remained. Six colonies constitute about $\frac{1}{4}$ of 29, which suggests that 2 loci are involved.

None of the other 23 colonies showed hygienic behavior, but Figure 10 presents some results that were unexpected. Nine colonies left uncapped dead larvae in the combs. In fact the caps on cells containing dead brood had been removed in every case except for 1 cell in the M 1428 colony and about half such cells in the M 1444 colony. This result was in contrast to the remaining 14 colonies, all of which retained dead brood in capped cells.

There is some variation in the colonies of Figure 10. M 1416, in the upper left, removed to a considerable extent. Perhaps it belongs in the hygienic group, but it did not show complete hygienic behavior. The next seven cases seem to be more surely uncappers and non-removers. M 1444, in the lower right, was not completely uncapped at the end of the experiment but seems to belong in this group, nevertheless.

In addition to the indication of two loci from the proportion of hygienic colonies, the $\frac{1}{4}$ that uncapped suggests that one locus pertains to uncapping. If there is one locus for uncapping in a two-locus situation, the other one should be a locus for removing. This idea can be tested by examining the 14 remaining colonies to see whether or not they will remove dead larvae following human uncapping.

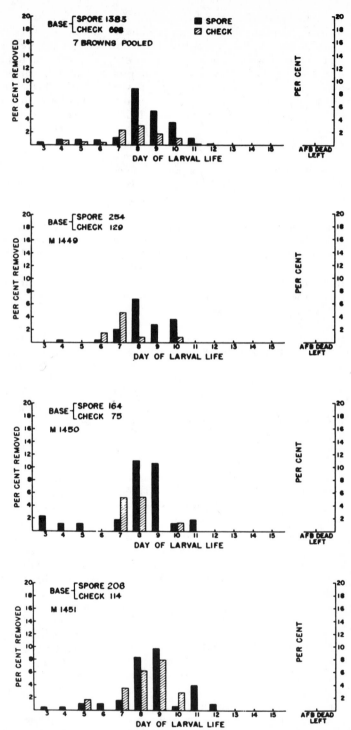

FIG. 7. Responses of seven, Brown-line, control colonies to the indicated numbers of spore-inoculated and check-treated larvae. Data from the seven different matings have been pooled in the upper left graph.

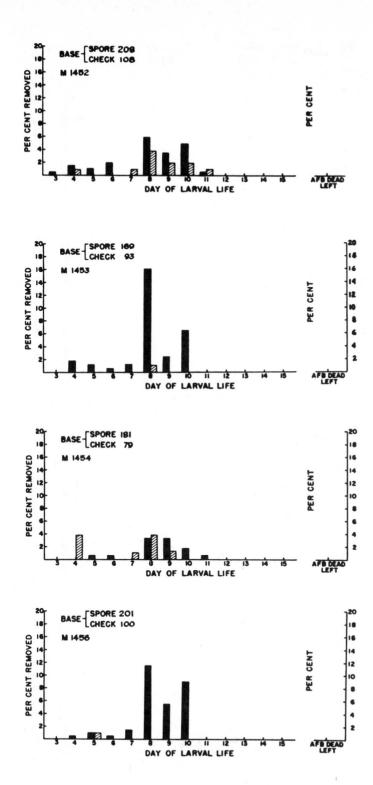

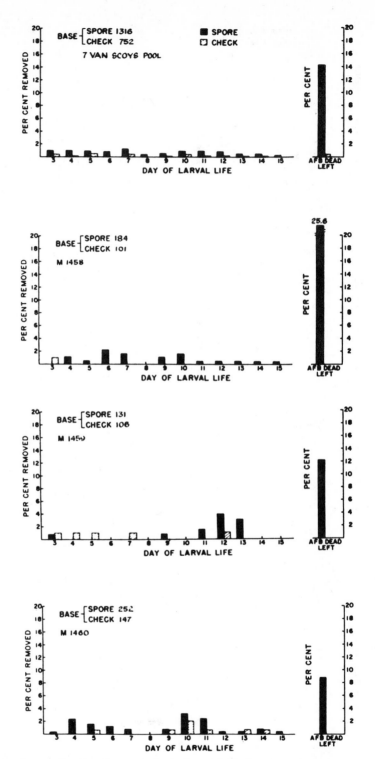

FIG. 8. Responses of seven, Van Scoy-line, control colonies to the indicated numbers of spore-inoculated and check-treated larvae. Data from the seven matings have been pooled in the upper left graph.

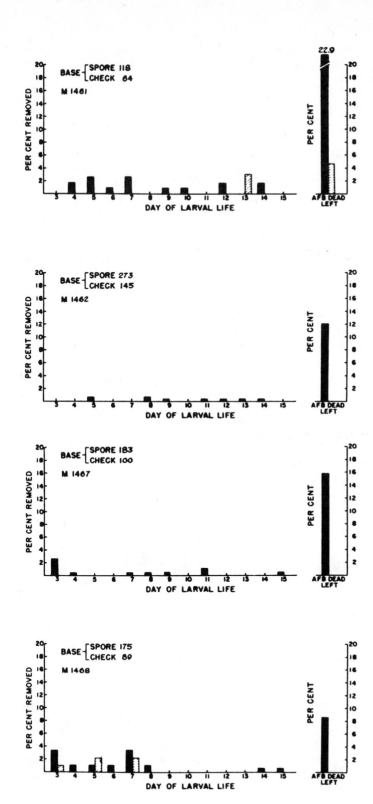

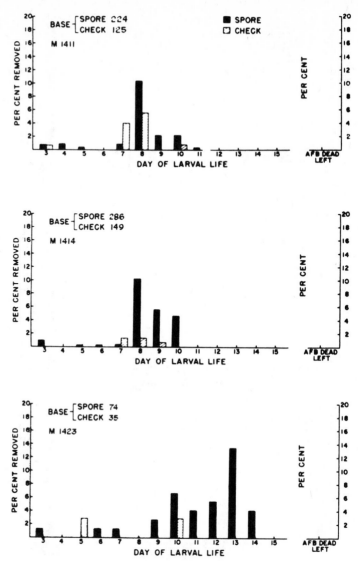

FIG. 9. Hygienic responses of 6 of 29 colonies developed in each case from a backcross of one drone from an F_1 queen to a Brown-line queen.

Figure 11 shows a group of 6 colonies that showed very little hygienic behavior during the course of the experiment and retained a lot of dead brood. When the combs containing foulbrood-killed individuals were uncapped by us, reassigned to different colonies, and placed in them for testing, the colonies removed a large percentage of the dead brood in 2 days. As can be seen in Table 1, M 1412, M 1415, and M 1431 removed more than 90% in two days. The other three ranged from 53 to 75%. All of these colonies removed more on the second day of the removal test than on the first, indicating perhaps, that worker bees were being increasingly attracted to the job.

The last group of 8 colonies (Fig. 12) showed very little hygienic behavior during the course of the experiment, and re-

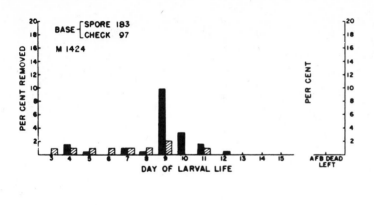

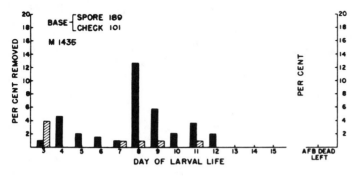

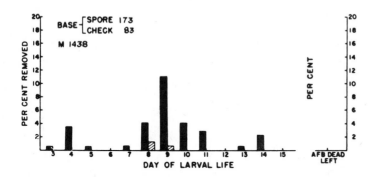

moved fewer uncapped individuals than the preceding group during the second test (Table 2). Matings 1429, 1432, and 1434 did not remove a single dead individual, and M 1443 removed 3% in 2 days time. The other colonies ranged from 15 to 47% total removal.

Although this group of 14 colonies is not as discretely separated into removers and non-removers as the whole group of 29 was separated into uncappers and non-uncappers, for the time being the 14 are

TABLE 1. *Percentage of dead individuals removed from uncapped comb on each day based on number present at beginning of day, and percentage of total sample removed.*

M. No.	Dead individuals	Per cent removed		
		1st day	2nd day	Total
1412	47	70	71	91
1415	38	63	79	92
1430	30	13	46	53
1431	38	50	89	95
1436	16	25	67	75
1441	29	24	55	66

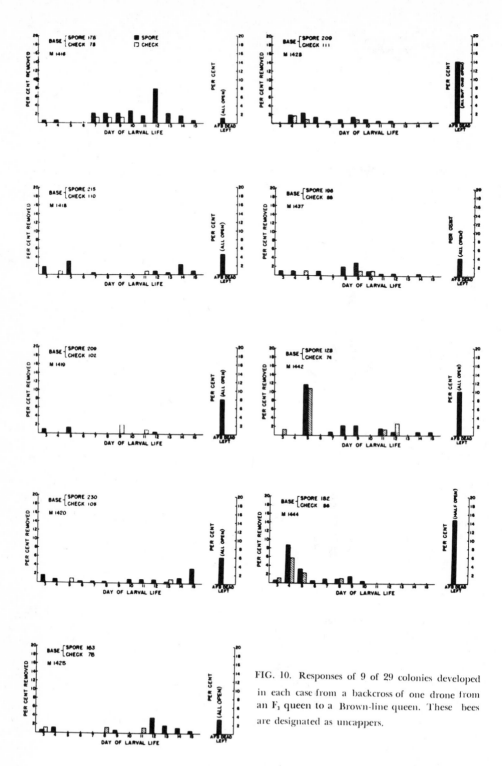

FIG. 10. Responses of 9 of 29 colonies developed in each case from a backcross of one drone from an F_1 queen to a Brown-line queen. These bees are designated as uncappers.

TABLE 2. *Percentage of dead individuals removed from uncapped comb on each day based on number present at beginning of day, and percentage of total sample removed.*

M. No.	Dead individuals	Per cent removed		
		1st day	2nd day	Total
1413	33	9	33	39
1417	38	29	26	47
1429	18	0	0	0
1432	21	0	0	0
1433	22	0	23	23
1434	41	0	0	0
1440	32	6	10	16
1443	39	3	0	3

interpreted as falling into two groups. This seems to be the simplest possible explanation and justifiable in the light of inadequate knowledge about the environmental factors that affect removal rate.

The backcrosses of sons of F_1 queens to the Van Scoy-line queens present something of a problem. None of these colonies was expected to show hygienic behavior because Van Scoy queens were expected to be homozygous for dominant genes for non-hygienic behavior. As Figure 13 shows, M 1409 showed a typical pattern of hygienic behavior. This result is beyond explanation at present. No F_1 colony has ever displayed complete hygienic behavior and in this case the backcross of an F_1 to the Van Scoy line does so. We cannot disregard this result, regardless of how much we would like to, but we are basing the genetic hypothesis on the other data.

Hypothesis

From the foregoing, the hypothesis presented in Figure 14 has·been developed. Hygienic behavior (in the upper left corner) depends upon homozygosity for two recessive genes—one a gene (designated u) for uncapping of cells containing dead larvae, the other a gene (designated r) for removal of dead larvae. A cross between the two opposite homozygous types would result in an F_1 which is non-hygienic. An F_1 queen would produce four kinds of drones or gametes which, backcrossed to the parental type showing hygienic behavior, would result in four kinds of backcross colonies in a 1:1:1:1 ratio. In this case a 6:9:6:8 ratio was obtained.

One of the most attractive features of this hypothesis is the ease with which it can be tested. One can predict how each of these classes should behave in further breeding. Queens and drones from the hygienic group should breed true for hygienic behavior. The uncapping group should breed true for uncapping, and the removing group for removing. For the time being, however, most effort is going into studies of the environmental factors that may conceivably affect the colony's response to dead brood. For these investigations, the parental lines have been and are being used. It is equally important to test the F_1 generation for its stability and variability under various environmental conditions.

TABLE 3. *Frequency distribution of four groups of colonies according to the total number of times the beekeeper was stung while engaged in the same operations with each under similar conditions. Fourteen visits were made to each colony.*

Type of colony	Total number of stings																
	0	1	2	3	4	5	6	7	8	11	15	19	20	21	23	26	31
Seven Van Scoy colonies—None hygienic	6	1															
Seven Brown colonies—All hygienic									1	1		1	1	1		1	1
Twenty-nine colonies from backcrosses of F_1 to Brown line—Six hygienic	9	9	2	3	1	2	1	1				1					
The six hygienic colonies from above backcrosses	2	3					1										

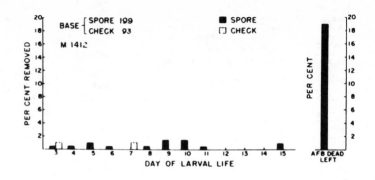

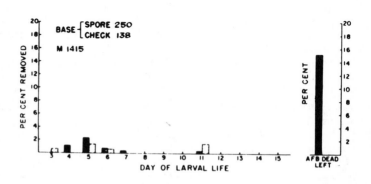

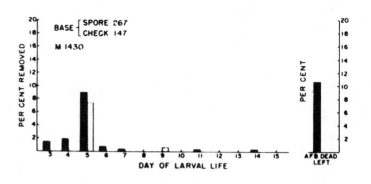

FIG. 11. Responses of 6 of the 29 backcross colonies. This group did not uncap, but did remove following human uncapping.

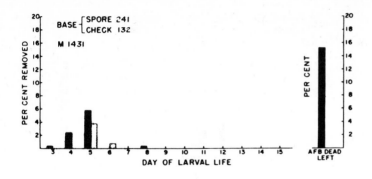

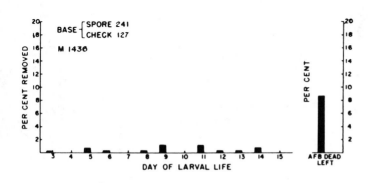

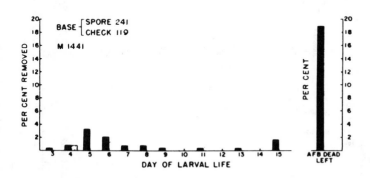

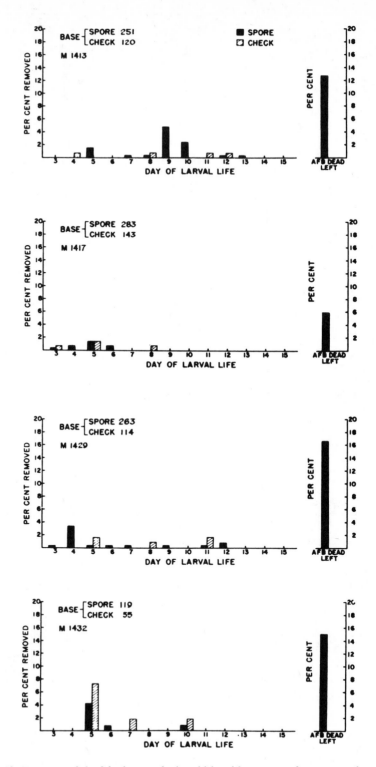

FIG. 12. Responses of the 8 backcross colonies which neither uncapped nor removed.

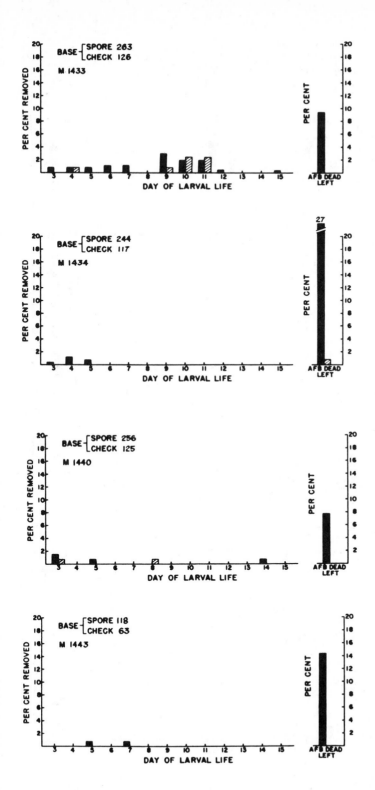

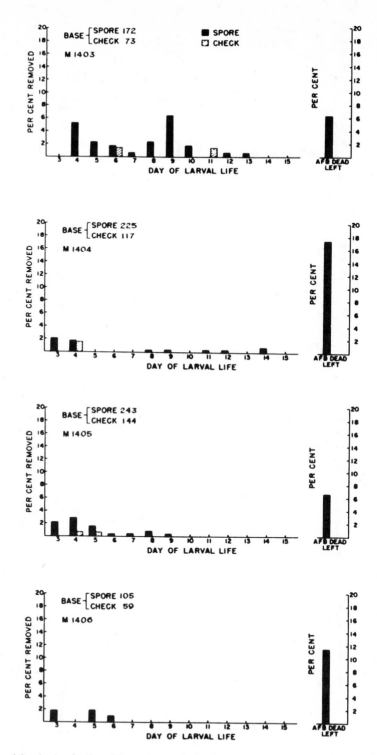

FIG. 13. Responses of 8 colonies developed in each case by backcrossing one drone from an F_1 queen to a queen from the Van Scoy line.

100

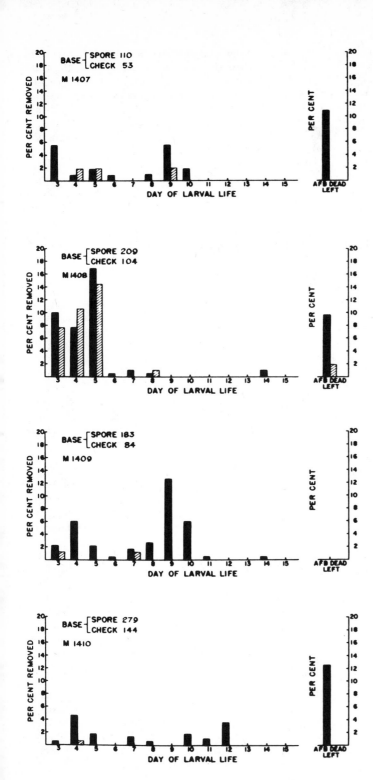

In the hygienic behavior experiment, observations on several other characteristics were made. One of the most obvious was stinging behavior. Table 3 presents the data. In the course of 98 visits to the 7 Van Scoy colonies, we were stung only once. In the course of 98 similar visits on the same days to the 7 Brown colonies, we were stung 143 times. The fact that this was an obvious characteristic needs no emphasis, and it may be said that sophisticated quantitative measurements were not really necessary to alert us that we had a real, line difference.

It has been thought by most people that disease-resistant bees are always cross, and logically explained further that keeping the brood nest free of dead larvae and defending the colony against the beekeeper is a manifestation of the same general characteristic—a high level of vigor in the bees.

If hygienic behavior and stinging behavior are due to the same underlying characteristic, namely vigor, the hygienic colonies among the backcrosses ought to be stingers. This was not so. There were 2 hygienic colonies that never stung, 3 stung once each, and one stung 7 times. The colony that stung equally as much as the parental, hygienic line was non-hygienic. The stinging behavior of all 29 of the backcross colonies indicates that more than one or two loci are involved in this behavior difference.

In these experiments, colony behavior characteristics which appeared together in the parental lines have separated in the backcross colonies. We are accustomed to this result among individuals, but here it is happening among colonies made up of many individuals. This can occur only when the individuals making up the colony are genetically similar, and they can be genetically similar only when the mother of the colony is highly inbred and has been mated to a single haploid drone. With the exception of the sex locus, the mother makes identical (or nearly identical) genetic contributions to every worker bee, and the father's contribution is expected to be genetically identical in every case. This *inbred queen - single drone* technique promises to be useful in the analysis of colony behavior characteristics (Rothenbuhler, 1960).

SUMMARY

Two lines of honey bees differ greatly in the response of their colonies to brood killed by the disease American foulbrood and in the number of times they sting the beekeeper during a colony inspection. The Brown line removed dead larvae quickly (hygienic behavior), and in one experiment in which counts were made, stung the beekeeper about 1.5 times per colony visit. The Van Scoy line left dead larvae in the brood nest throughout the course of the experiment and stung the beekeeper about 0.01 times per colony visit.

The F_1 generation allowed dead larvae to remain in the brood nest as did the Van Scoy line. No observations were recorded on the stinging behavior of the F_1.

A technique of mating single drones from F_1 queens to inbred queens of the original lines was employed to secure colonies with genetically similar worker bees in each for colony tests. Colonies resulting from such backcrosses to the Brown line were of four types: (1) uncappers of cells and removers of dead brood contained therein, (2) uncappers only, (3) removers only after human uncapping, (4) neither uncappers nor removers.

From these results a two-locus hypothesis has been developed. It states that uncapping of a cell containing dead brood is dependent upon homozygosity for a single recessive gene (designated u), and removing is dependent upon homozygosity for a single recessive gene (designated r). The hypothesis can be tested by breeding and

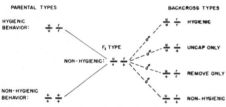

FIG. 14. Genetic hypothesis offered in explanation of different responses to AFB-killed brood observed in 63 colonies of bees.

investigating further generations within each phenotypic class, but before this is done, information is needed on the effect of certain environmental factors. Such information is being collected presently.

The same backcrosses that were tested for hygienic behavior indicated that stinging behavior is dependent upon more than one or two loci. Stinging behavior and hygienic behavior assorted independently in the backcross colonies. This result shows that the two behaviors depend upon different genetic bases.

REFERENCES

Boch, R. 1957. Rassenmassige Unterschiede in den Tänzen der Honigbiene (*Apis mellifica* L.). Z. vergleich. Physiol. 39:289-320.

Butler, Colin G. 1954. The world of the honeybee. Collins, St. James Place, London.

Frisch, K. von. 1950. Bees, their vision, chemical senses, and language. Cornell University Press, Ithaca, New York.

Grout, Roy A. (ed.). 1963. The hive and the honey bee. Dadant & Sons, Hamilton, Illinois.

Jones, Ronald L., and Walter C. Rothenbuhler. 1964. Behavior genetics of nest cleaning in honey bees. II. Responses of two inbred lines to various amounts of cyanide-killed brood. Animal Behaviour (in press).

Lindauer, Martin. 1961. Communication among social bees. Harvard University Press, Cambridge, Massachusetts.

Michener, Charles D., and Mary H. Michener. 1951. American social insects. D. Van Nostrand Company, Inc., New York, N. Y.

Park, O. W. 1936. Disease resistance and American foulbrood. Am. Bee J. 74:12-14.

Ribbands, C. R. 1953. The behaviour and social life of honeybees. Bee Research Association Ltd., London.

Root, J. A. (ed.). 1962. The ABC and XYZ of bee culture. The A. I. Root Company, Medina, Ohio.

Rothenbuhler, Walter C. 1958. Genetics of a behavior difference in honey bees. Proc. 10th Inter Cong. of Genetics, Vol. II:242.

———. 1960. A technique for studying genetics of colony behavior in honey bees. Am. Bee J. 100: 176-198.

———. 1964. Behavior genetics of nest cleaning in honey bees. I. Responses of four inbred lines to disease-killed brood. Animal Behaviour (in press).

Rothenbuhler, Walter C., and Victor C. Thompson. 1955. Resistance to American foulbrood in honey bees. I. Differential survival of larvae of different genetic lines. J. Econ. Entomol. 49:470-475.

Thompson, Victor C. 1964. Behavior genetics of nest cleaning in honey bees. III. Effect of age of adult bees on their response to disease-killed brood. J. Apic. Res. (in press).

Woodrow, A. W., and E. C. Holst. 1942. The mechanism of colony resistance to American foulbrood. J. of Econ. Entomol. 35:327-330.

Reprinted from
GENETICS TODAY
Proceedings of the XI International Congress of Genetics
The Hague, The Netherlands, September, 1963
PERGAMON PRESS
OXFORD · LONDON · EDINBURGH · NEW YORK
PARIS · FRANKFURT
1964

(9)

GENOTYPE AND MOUSE BEHAVIOUR*

GERALD E. McCLEARN

University of California, Berkeley, U.S.A.

IT was inevitable that the laboratory mouse would be extensively used in the rapidly developing field of behavioural genetics. By virtue of its long history of employment in more orthodox genetics, a number of inbred mouse strains were immediately available for examination for behavioural differences. Furthermore, the accumulated knowledge of genetic determination of physiological and anatomical characteristics in these strains offered prospects of hypotheses concerning behavioural causation, the established linkage groups gave promise of future possibilities of cytological analysis, some mutant alleles with obvious behavioural effects were known, and so on. In addition, the knowledge that the mouse continues to be a prime genetics research animal assures that these bounties will become greater and greater in the future.

For reasons perhaps less valid, the mouse also recommended itself from the behavioural point of view. Although *Mus musculus* had never been widely employed in behavioural research, it has a close apparent resemblance to that most popular of all psychological research animals, the rat. It may have been thought that the refined behavioural measurement techniques established for use with the rat could be readily modified for mouse investigations. Such an assumption has proved to be only partially correct, but the mouse has by now been sufficiently well studied in its own right that the necessity for borrowing rat techniques has diminished strikingly. In any event, the mouse now seems to be well entrenched as a standard research tool in behavioural genetics, and the purpose of this paper is to review the data available to date. The literature is already too extensive for an exhaustive review in the space available, so I shall select for discussion studies which in my opinion are representative of the current status of the field.

Because it is defined in terms of the kind of phenotype investigated, behavioural genetics cuts across other subdivisions of the field of genetics: quantitative, physiological, developmental, and evolutionary. Following a description of the kinds of behavioural phenotypes that have been studied in the mouse, results pertaining to these specific topics will be discussed.

BEHAVIOURAL PHENOTYPES OF THE MOUSE

Much of the research on mouse behavioural genetics has involved the comparison of inbred strains. With this approach a wide variety of behavioural phenotypes has been investigated, including maze-learning ability, locomotor activity, sexual behaviour, food-

* The original researches of the author described in this paper were supported by grants from the National Science Foundation.

drive, alcohol preference, emotionality, aggressiveness, and audiogenic seizures. Figures 1, 2, and 3 give distributions of several strains on three of these traits as examples of results obtained.

In Fig. 1, distributions are given for six inbred strains measured for locomotor activity in a novel situation (McClearn, 1959). The animals were placed on a floor which was marked off into small squares and which had a series of barriers erected at regular intervals.

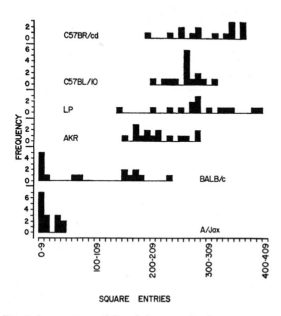

FIG. 1. Locomotor activity of six mouse strains.

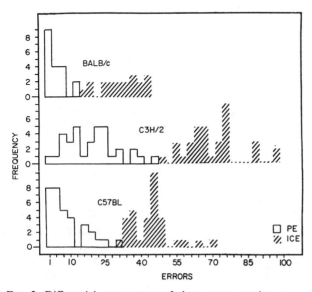

FIG. 2. Differential error scores of three mouse strains on an elevated maze problem.

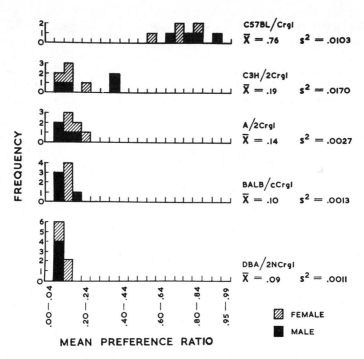

Fɪɢ. 3. Mean alcohol preference ratios of five inbred strains.

The activity was measured by counting the number of squares traversed in a 5 min period. The strain differences on this measure are extreme, with animals from the more active strains crossing squares nearly once per second on the average, and animals from the least active strain crossing barely four times a minute. Differences in variance are also evident, suggesting that the strains differ in susceptibility to uncontrolled environmental variation.

Figure 2 shows error scores for three inbred strains tested for learning performance on an 8 cul-de-sac elevated maze (McClearn, 1958). Initial entries (ICE) and repeated or perseverative entries (PE) into culs-de-sac were recorded separately and the distributions for both types of error are shown. It may be seen that the C3H/2 animals made more mean errors of both kinds than did the BALB/c or C57BL animals. Indeed, on the initial error measure, the most error prone BALB/c mouse performed better than the least error prone C3H/2 mouse.

Figure 3 shows, for five strains, the average per cent of total daily fluid intake consumed from a 10% ethyl alcohol solution when both the solution and water were available for a two week period (McClearn and Rodgers, 1961). C57BL animals consumed substantial amounts of ethanol, whereas animals of the other strains drank very little of the ethanol solution.

Other behaviour traits for which large strain differences have been described include tendency to hoard food (Smith and Powell, 1955), aggression against other mice (Ginsburg and Allee, 1942; Scott, 1942), and emotionality, as measured by the tendency to defecate in an open, brightly-illuminated chamber (Lindzey, 1951; Lindzey et al., 1960; Thompson, 1956), among others.

106

With respect to activity large strain differences have been described by numerous investigators using a wide variety of measurement techniques. In addition to the barrier field (McClearn, 1959; Thompson, 1953) already described, these have included the time required to exit from one compartment into another (Bruell, 1962; McClearn, 1959); the time spent in the centre of an open area as opposed to the time spent adjacent to a wall (Fredericson, 1953; McClearn, 1959; Smith and Powell, 1955); the time required to climb down a pole from a platform (Bruell, 1962); the number of barriers hurdled in a given period of time (McClearn, 1959); the number of revolutions in a revolving wheel (Bruell, 1962), and locomotion in a Y-shaped enclosed maze (Thompson, 1956). It is interesting to note that in all of these measures, various of the C57 strains and substrains have proved to be very active and various A substrains have proved to be inactive.

Such uniformity of results with different techniques is not always obtained, and, indeed, is not to be expected on *a priori* grounds. A general rubric such as "activity" or "learning" or "emotionality" may include an immense number of subtraits with different genetic determinants, in whole or in part, for each. C3H/2 mice, for example, have been shown to be markedly inferior to BALB/c mice on an elevated maze pattern (McClearn, 1958), and also on a visual discrimination problem requiring the animals to choose consistently between a black alley and a white alley, and a tactual discrimination problem requiring choice between a rough floored and a smooth floored alley (McClearn, 1961). In all of these studies, the animals were tested while hungry and they received a food reward for the correct response. In another experiment, Royce and Covington (1960) required animals to climb over a barrier when a sound stimulus was presented in order to avoid an electrical shock to the feet. In this situation, C3H mice were significantly superior to BALB/c mice, with the latter requiring nearly twice as many trials to establish a conditioned response. Furthermore, C3H mice were found to be inferior to A and DBA animals in maze learning for food reward (Lindzey and Winston, 1962; Winston, 1963), but superior in learning to escape from water. Although different substrains were used by these investigators, the results taken together indicate that C3H animals perform better to escape noxious stimulation than to obtain a positive reward. Further research on the comparative motivational dynamics of these strains should prove fruitful.

The phenotypes discussed to this point have been measured on quantitative scales, and are very probably determined polygenically. Major genes may also have important behavioural consequences. The gross effects of the various neurological mutants, for example, are too well known to require any elaboration at this point.

It is easy to imagine somewhat less dramatic behavioural effects of other mutant conditions. There might be an impairment of visual stimulus processing capacity of albino animals, for example, but very little is in fact known about such effects at the present time. Efforts to improve knowledge in this area are being made, however, and promising results can be reported. Denenberg *et. al.* (1963) have described an experiment in which inbred strains with forced heterozygosity at certain loci were compared on a series of behavioural tests. *Pintail*, *hairless*, *pale-ear*, and *short-ear* mutants, and their respective normal controls were observed for defecation in a novel environment, activity in an open field, learning to swim to an escape platform to get out of water, shock-escape learning and extinction trial performance after shock-escape learning. The shock-escape situation required the animal to run the length of an electrified grid to reach a non-electrified escape platform. After a series of trials, the animal was placed in the apparatus with the shock-current off, and the distance run toward the escape platform was noted. This constituted the "extinction" trial.

Neither *pale-ear* nor *short-ear* animals differed from their control animals on any test. *Hairless* animals were found to be significantly less active than controls in the open field, and were notably poorer swimmers in the swimming task, but did not differ on other measures. There was some evidence that *pintail* animals did not run as far down the alley as did their controls in the shock-escape extinction trial. The authors point out the possibility of linked genes determining the described behavioural effect rather than the named mutant loci, since in neither case had the mutation occurred in an already highly inbred strain. The strain in which *hairless* was segregating was in process of inbreeding, and *pintail* was being successively backcrossed onto a C57BL/6J background. Nevertheless, the relevant genetic material has been located within quite narrow limits.

A somewhat different approach has been taken by v. Abeelen (1963). Whereas the other investigations described have typically been concerned with measuring only one or a few responses, selected *a priori*, v. Abeelen placed animals in standard situations and made frequency counts for a large number of response categories. *Yellow, pink-eyed dilution*, and *jerker* animals were compared with their controls. It was found that animals homozygous for the *pink-eyed dilution* allele made a particular type of visual orientation response and a paw-lifting response less often than controls. *Jerker* animals were found to be affected in exploratory activity more than in fighting, feeding and sexual behaviour.

These studies have demonstrated that effects on behaviour other than gross abnormalities may be determined by relatively little chromosomal material. Important developments await the pursuit of further studies of this nature and the subsequent application of the many techniques available for the study of major genes.

QUANTITATIVE ASPECTS OF MOUSE BEHAVIOURAL GENETICS

The quantitative nature of most behaviour traits studied in the mouse has led naturally to attempts to apply biometrical techniques of analysis. By virtue of the fact that the initial evidence of genotypic determination generally has been obtained from inbred strain comparisons, most studies on quantitative analysis have employed F_1, F_2, and backcross generations derived from inbred strains, rather than using parent-offspring regression, sib and half-sib analyses, or examination of response to selection pressure.

Using similar testing situations, Fuller and Thompson (1960) and McClearn (1961) attempted to assess the degree of genetic determination of barrier field activity. Although one study used C57BR/a and the other C57BL as the highly active parent, and different substrains of the A strain were employed as the inactive parent, the results were in good accord, with between 1/3 and 2/3 of the F2 phenotypic variance being attributed to genetic factors, depending upon the source of the estimate of the environmental variance component. Rather lower estimates of degree of genetic determination are provided by the data of Bruell (1962) who tested generations derived from C57BL and A strains on various other activity tests. These latter results are not necessarily conflicting, of course. Different measuring techniques were employed, and different facets or subcharacters of the behavioural domain called "activity" were probably being examined.

One very interesting outcome of these studies has been that F_1 variance is sometimes greater than parent strain variance (Bruell, 1962; McClearn, 1961). This finding, quite at odds with the typical result with morphological or physiological characters, is nonetheless consistent with some other comparisons of behavioural variance of F_1 and parent strains in other species (see Caspari, 1958, for review). These data have apparent implications for the theoretical issue of developmental buffering, or canalization, or homeostasis of heterozygotes as compared with homozygotes, and also have relevance to the practical problem of behavioural assay.

In the first explicit investigation on this problem, Mordkoff and Fuller (1959) compared the locomotor activity of two inbred strains, their F_1, and an outcrossed group. One of the inbred strains (C57BL/6) showed the greatest variance, and the other inbred strain (DBA/2) showed the least variance of all groups tested. The F_1 variance was numerically greater than the DBA/2 variance, but not significantly so. One difficulty of this study was the correlation between means and variances. One way of coping with such a problem is obviously to contrive a situation in which the means of the compared groups are roughly of the same value. This was accomplished by Schlesinger and Mordkoff (1963) for the same strains used in the previous study, but with a different activity testing situation. Under these circumstances the F_1 variance was strikingly lower than that of either parent strain.

In many circumstances, the principal object is analysis of extreme crosses and this tactic is not feasible. Scalar transformations might be useful in such cases. A special type of scaling problem, perhaps more frequent in the behavioural than in other characters, might sometimes be encountered. Not only may there be a "floor" to the measuring scale by virtue of the impossibility of getting, say, negative activity scores, there may also be a "ceiling", perhaps a bit less clearly defined than the floor, but imposing nonetheless an upper bound on the performance capabilities of the organism—a physiological limit. By the same sort of reasoning that justifies a logarithmic transformation on the basis of

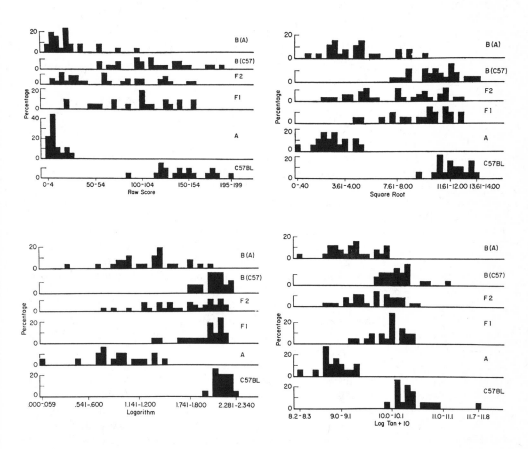

FIG. 4. Distributions of locomotor activity scores for two inbred strains and derived generations. The same data are shown on original measurement scale (raw score), and on three transformed scales (square root, logarithmic, and log tangent).

constant percentage increments with increase in the number of "plus" alleles, it might be suggested that situations such as that just described involve increasing phenotypic increments to a point, after which decreasing phenotypic increments occur. Such a situation would therefore require a transformation which stretched both ends of the scale. The effects of a transformation of this kind are compared with those of more conventional transformations in Fig. 4. The data are from a study on the barrier field type of activity (McClearn, 1961). The excessive variance of the F_1 on the raw data scale is immediately apparent, as is the inequality of parent strain variances. The square root transformation brings the parent strain variances to similar values, but leaves the F_1 variance excessively large. The logarithmic transformation is rather too strong, and results in unequal parent strain variances. The log tangent transformation, performed by assigning the value of 1° to the lowest score obtained and 89° to the highest score obtained, interpolating intermediate scores linearly, and determining the log tan values, provides the most satisfactory results. Parent strain and F_1 variances are roughly equated and, in addition, the Matherian A, B, and C criteria for scalar adequacy are more closely satisfied by this transformation than by the others.

Although this is not an appropriate place for a discussion of the merits of scalar transformations, it might be suggested that in other situations, both behavioural and non-behavioural, a transformation of the kind described might be useful.

PHYSIOLOGICAL ASPECTS OF MOUSE BEHAVIOURAL GENETICS

The physiological, biochemical and anatomical intermediates between genotypic differences and behavioural phenotypic differences are being studied with increasing vigour. This field of study is treated in detail in Dr. Fuller's paper in this symposium. I shall, therefore, mention only a few supplementary points.

One important advantage to the use of genetically specified material, such as inbred strains, in behavioural research is that data collected by various investigators on various traits may give rise to hypotheses about physiological mechanisms underlying the behaviour. Amin et al. (1957), for example, found the strain order on a measure of thyroid activity to be (from highest to lowest): C57BL/6, C57BR/cd, BALB/c, and A/Jax. When this outcome is compared with the activity results cited earlier, the hypothesis that thyroid activity is an important determinant of locomotor activity immediately presents itself.

Similarly, following a report by Caspari (1960) on differences in brain serotonin between C57BL/10J and BALB/cJ mice, Maas (1963) studied the relationship of serotonin to measures of emotionality in these strains. More recently, Pryor et al. (1963) have extended these observations and have found an inverse relationship between brain serotonin and rated emotionality across six strains: A, C57BL, C3H/2, DBA/2, RIII, and BALB/c.

This approach to an understanding of the physiological substratum of behaviour is a most valuable one. An important precaution in interpretation of this type of result must be noted, however. This point can be illustrated by a recent series of experiments on possible determinants of alcohol preference in mice.

Rodgers et al. (1963), with small samples, found an apparent association between alcohol preference and alcohol dehydrogenase. Subsequent work with larger samples substantiated the finding that C57BL animals had much higher levels of liver alchohol dehydrogenase activity than did DBA/2 mice. In an unpublished study of an F_2 generation derived from C57BL and DBA/2 strains, however, the correlation between alcohol preference and alcohol dehydrogenase activity was essentially zero, suggesting strongly that, in this population at least, alcohol dehydrogenase is not an important determinant of alcohol intake.

It is clear that further genetic research is required to eliminate the possibility that associations of characteristics in inbred strains are fortuitous.

DEVELOPMENTAL ASPECTS OF MOUSE BEHAVIOURAL GENETICS

In studying developmental processes, two general approaches have been taken. The descriptive approach has simply recorded a behavioural phenotype value at different ages for different strains. The second approach has been to administer environmental stress at certain developmental periods, searching for strain differences in the subsequent effect.

An example of the former type of study is given by the finding of Kakihana and McClearn (1963) that the alcohol consumption of young BALB/c mice is moderately high, but drops rather rapidly to the typical low adult values at about 9 weeks of age. Such a shift in alcohol intake has not been noted in the other strains studied.

To illustrate the second sort of study, the results of Lindzey and collaborators (1963) may be cited. Animals of the C57BL, C3H, DBA, and JK strains were subjected to 2 min of severe auditory stress daily from the fourth through the seventh days of life. Later, at 30 and 100 days of age, the animals were compared with controls on emotional defecation in an open field test. In general, mice exposed to this noxious stimulation were more "emotional" and "timid" as adults. There was strong interaction of genotype and treatment, however. The C57BL strain was identified as being most susceptible to the effects of noxious infantile stimulation. In another study, Winston (1963) examined the effects of similar infantile trauma on the adult learning of mice. C3H, A, and DBA strains were investigated. When tested on an enclosed maze as adults, the A strain animals were found to be more adversely affected than were the DBA animals. C3H mice appeared to be entirely unaffected.

These results establish the point that developmental patterns of behaviour may differ among strains and that different genotypes may differ in susceptibility to traumatic environmental events occurring during development.

EVOLUTIONARY ASPECTS OF MOUSE BEHAVIOURAL GENETICS

A thorough treatment of evolution and behaviour is given by Dr. Manning at this symposium. I shall make only a few remarks specifically relating to *Mus musculus*. Insofar as they have selective value, all of the traits discussed to this point might be related to evolutionary processes. One constellation of behaviour patterns, those related to reproductive success, would seem to be particularly relevant, however.

McGill (1962) has studied in detail the male sexual behaviour of three inbred strains of mice. The C57BL mating pattern was found to be rapid, with quick intromission and ejaculation. The DBA males had difficulty gaining intromission, but ejaculation occurred rapidly. BALB/c males required the longest time, with more than one hour between initial intromission and ejaculation. It is difficult to believe that these differences would not lead to different reproductive prospects in a natural situation.

Levine (1958, 1963) has examined reproductive success directly by placing an ST female mouse in a mating cage with an ST and a DBA male mouse, both of which had previously been proven fertile. The coat colour of these strains permits easy identification of paternity, and examination of the litters showed that, in most circumstances, the ST male sired more offspring than did the DBA male. Studies on the relative contribution of different behavioural components, such as female choice, male aggressiveness, and copulatory pattern, will be most valuable.

In the next, and final, example, a suggestion of the relevant behaviour mechanism has been provided. Calhoun (1956) placed small groups of C57BL/10 and of DBA/2 animals separately in large compartments permitting observation under semi-natural conditions. The C57BL/10 mice succeeded much better than the DBA/2 mice in maintaining themselves reproductively. Observation suggested that the difficulty of the DBA/2 population was in the relatively unrestrained aggression of the dominant male, directed not only against other males, but also against females, including pregnant ones.

CONCLUSION

In conclusion, I hope that the foregoing has provided a representative picture of mouse behavioural genetics. In some areas only beginnings have been made, but enough has been done to indicate the promise of future research.

The mouse has contributed substantially to the evidence that is motivating the current retreat from the extreme environmentalism that characterized psychology and other behavioural sciences for several decades. The hope might be expressed that the body of information is now sufficiently extensive as to offer a whole new set of phenotypes for the service of the parent discipline of genetics.

REFERENCES

ABEELEN, J. H. F. v. (1963) Behavioral effects of single genes in mice: an investigation with the use of ethological methods. *Proc. XI Internat. Congr. Genetics*, The Hague, Vol. I, 250.

AMIN, A., CHAI, C. K. and REINEKE, E. P. (1957) Differences in thyroid activity of several strains of mice and Fl hybrids. *Amer. J. Physiol.* 191, 34-36.

BRUELL, J. H. (1962) Dominance and segregation in the inheritance of quantitative behavior in mice. In E. L. Bliss (Ed.), *Roots of Behavior*. Harper, New York, 48-67.

CALHOUN, J. B. (1956) A comparative study of the social behavior of two inbred strains of house mice. *Ecol. Monogr.* 26, 81-103.

CASPARI, E. (1958) In A. Roe and G. G. Simpson (Eds.), *Behavior and Evolution*. Yale University Press, New Haven, 103-127.

CASPARI, E., Paper presented at the American Psychological Association Annual Convention, Chicago, September 1960.

DENENBERG, V. H., ROSS, S. and BLUMENFIELD, M. (1963) Behavioral differences between mutant and nonmutant mice. *J. Comp. Physiol. Psychol.* 56, 290-293.

FREDERICSON, E. (1953) The wall-seeking tendency in three inbred mouse strains *(Mus musculus)*. *J. Genet. Psychol.* 82, 143-146.

FULLER, J. L. and THOMPSON, W. R. (1960) *Behavior Genetics*. Wiley, New York.

GINSBURG, B. and ALLEE, W. C. (1942) Some effects of conditioning on social dominance and subordination in inbred strains of mice. *Physiol. Zool.* 15, 485-506.

KAKIHANA, RYOKO and McCLEARN, G. E. (1963) Development of alcohol preference in BALB/c mice. *Nature* No. 4892, 511-512.

LEVINE, L. (1958) Studies on sexual selection in mice. I. Reproductive competition between albino and black-agouti males. *Amer. Naturalist* 92, 21-26.

LEVINE, L. (1963) Factors affecting mating competition in mice. *Proc. XI Internat. Congr, Genetics*. The Hague, Vol. I, 249-250.

LINDZEY, G. (1951) Emotionality and audiogenic seizure susceptibility in five inbred strains of mice. *J. Comp. Physiol. Psychol.* 44, 389-393.

LINDZEY, G., LYKKEN, D. T. and WINSTON, H. D. (1960) Infantile trauma, genetic factors, and adult temperament. *J. Abnorm. Soc. Psychol.* 61, 7-14.

LINDZEY, G. and WINSTON, H. (1962) Maze learning and effects of pretraining in inbred strains of mice. *J. Comp. Physiol. Psychol.* 55, 748-752.

LINDZEY, G., WINSTON, H. D. and MANOSEVITZ, M. (1963) Early experience, genotype, and temperament in *Mus musculus*. *J. Comp. Physiol. Psychol.* 56, 622-629.

MAAS, J. W. (1963) Neurochemical differences between two strains of mice. *Nature*, No. 4864, 255-257.

MCCLEARN, G. E. (1958) Performance differences among mouse strains in a learning situation. *Amer. Psychol.* 13, 405 (abstract).

MCCLEARN, G. E. (1959) The genetics of mouse behavior in novel situations. *J. Comp. Physiol. Psychol.* 52, 62-67.

MCCLEARN, G. E. (1961) The generality of mouse strain differences in learning. *Amer. Psychol.* 16, 558 (abstract).

MCCLEARN, G. E. (1961) Genotype and mouse activity. *J. Comp. Physiol. Psychol.* 674-676.

McClearn, G. E. and Rodgers, D. A. (1961) Genetic factors in alcohol preference of laboratory mice. *J. Comp. Physiol. Psychol.* **54**, 116-119.

McGill, T. E. (1962) Sexual behavior in three inbred strains of mice. *Behaviour* **19**, 341-350.

Mordkoff, A. M. and Fuller, J. L. (1959) Variability in activity within inbred and crossbred mice. *J. Hered.* 6-8.

Pryor, G. T., Schlesinger, K. and Calhoun, W. H. (1963) Brain serotonin related to a measure of emotionality in mice. Personal communication.

Rodgers, D. A., McClearn, G. E. Bennett, E. L. and Hebert, Marie (1963) Alcohol preference as a function of its caloric utility in mice. *J. Comp. Physiol. Psychol.* **56**, 666-672.

Royce, J. R. and Covington, M. (1960) Genetic differences in the avoidance conditioning of mice. *J. Comp. Physiol. Psychol.* **53**, 197-200.

Schlesinger, K. and Mordkoff, A. (1963) Variability in activity and oxygen consumption in two inbred strains of mice and their F1 hybrids. *J. Hered.*, in press.

Scott, J. P. (1942) Genetic differences in the social behavior of inbred strains of mice. *J. Hered.* **33**, 11-15.

Smith, W. I. and Powell, Elizabeth K. (1955) The role of emotionality in hoarding. *Behaviour* **8**, 57-62.

Thompson, W. R. (1953) The inheritance of behaviour: Behavioural differences in fifteen mouse strains. *Canad. J. Psychol.* **7**, 145-155.

Thompson, W. R. (1956) The inheritance of behavior: Activity differences in five inbred mouse strains. *J. Hered.* **47**, 147-148.

Winston, H. D. (1963) Influence of genotype and infantile trauma on adult learning in the mouse. *J. Comp. Physiol. Psychol.* **56**, 630-635.

Journal of Comparative and Physiological Psychology
1968, Vol. 65, No. 1, 126–131

DIFFERENCES IN MEMORY PROCESSES BETWEEN INBRED MOUSE STRAINS C57BL/6J AND DBA/2J[1]

RICHARD E. WIMER, LAWRENCE SYMINGTON, HERTHA FARMER, and PHILIP SCHWARTZKROIN

The Jackson Laboratory, Bar Harbor, Maine

2 experiments on differences between strains of house mice in characteristics related to processes of memory trace formation are reported. In Experiment 1, performances on active shock-escape and passive shock-avoidance tasks were observed under massed and distributed practice conditions; on both tasks strain DBA/2J mice were superior when learning trials were massed, while strain C57BL/6J mice were superior when trials were distributed. In Experiment 2, immediate posttrial etherization facilitated learning of both tasks for strain DBA/2J mice, but had no effect on strain C57BL/6J.

[1] This investigation was supported in part by Public Health Service Research Grants MH 01775 and MH 11327, by Public Health Service Graduate Training Grant No. CRT 5013 from the National Cancer Institute, and by National Science Foundation Science Education Grants GE2888, GE646, and GE113. The invaluable assistance of William Mace is gratefully acknowledged. This investigation was reported in part at the 1966 meetings of the American Psychological Association, New York City.

Recent evidence indicates that substantial differences in processes of learning and memory may exist among diverse genetic stocks of animals within the same species. Specifically, what has been established clearly so far is that different animal stocks may vary in (a) optimal temporal distribution of practice trials for learning (McGaugh, Jennings, & Thomson, 1962)

113

and in (b) how and when they are affected by posttrial treatment with agents (ECS or a drug) thought to affect memory (Breen & McGaugh, 1961; McGaugh, Thomson, Westbrook, & Hudspeth, 1962; McGaugh, Westbrook, & Thomson, 1962; Ross, 1964; Stratton & Petrinovich, 1963; Thomson, McGaugh, Smith, Hudspeth, & Westbrook, 1961). These studies raise many broad questions concerning (a) the scope of individual differences in optimal distribution of practice and in the processes of memory trace formation, (b) the possibility of relating these two phenomena, and (c) the nature of their biological bases.

The present experiments are devoted to the establishment of a genetically associated difference in optimal distribution of practice for two learning tasks for mice and the search for correlated differences in the consolidative process as indicated by differential effects of posttrial etherization upon memory.

METHOD

Subjects

The house mouse (*Mus musculus*) was selected over other species for study because of the greater number of genetically varying animal stocks this species affords. The Jackson Laboratory alone maintains 25 production and research mouse strains, 6 F₁ hybrids derived from them, and has over 100 mutant stocks available for special purposes (Green, 1964; Lane, 1966), and many more stocks are available elsewhere (Jay, 1963). On the basis of a preliminary survey of small numbers of animals from nine inbred mouse strains, DBA/2J and C57BL/6J were selected for thorough investigation. All mice used were males about 6 wk. old at time of testing.

Apparatus

The apparatus used was a modification of one devised by Maatsch (1959). A translucent box with a grid floor and a plastic shelf was constructed of ¼-in. sheet plastic, with outside dimensions of 7 × 6¾ × 6¾ in. The grid floor, mounted 1 in. above the base, consisted of ³⁄₃₂-in. stainless-steel rods separated by ¼ in. measured between centers. The box was covered with a removable plastic lid. Other pieces of equipment were a Grason-Stadler shock generator and a Meylan electric timer measuring in .01-min. intervals.

For the active task, a shelf 1½ in. wide running completely around the inside walls of the apparatus was mounted 2⅝ in. above the grid floor. For the passive task, a shelf 1 in. wide and 5⅜ in. long was inserted along one wall only, 1 in. above the floor; this shelf could be rotated about a pivot point at one end so that it lay virtually flat against one of the walls of the box when in a vertical position.

General Procedures

Active shock-escape learning. Learning trials were preceded by a familiarization period in the apparatus, during which S was placed for .50 min. on the shock-escape shelf followed by .50 min. on the grid floor. Immediately following familiarization, the first training trial was begun by activating the shock generator while S was on the grid and measuring latency until S escaped to the shelf. The shock generator was set initially to deliver .10 ma. at 340 v. ac. Whenever S froze or was relatively inactive, current level was momentarily increased by a factor of 10. If S failed to escape to the shelf by .50 min., the current was increased to .13 ma. This was followed by additional current level increases to .16 ma. and .20 ma. at successive .50-min. intervals if S was still on the grid. Animals remaining on the grid more than 2 min. on the first trial were discarded. The same shock level adjustment procedure was followed on the second and third trials, with the exception that maximum shock level was not raised above the maximum necessary to produce shock escape on the preceding trial. A final current level of .1 ma. on the fourth trial was reached with all but a few Ss. On all trials following the first, each S was placed directly on the grid floor and the shock was turned on with a delay period of less than .02 min. Training was continued for six trials.

The learning measure on each trial was time in .01-min. units to escape from grid floor to shelf. An S's learning score, which summarized performance on the critical learning trials and was amenable to simple statistical analysis and graphic presentation, was the sum of the learning measures for Trials 3, 4, 5, and 6. (Trial 2 was not included because of very high variability.)

Passive shock-avoidance learning. The S was placed on the narrow shock-avoidance platform and latency of descent to the grid floor, i.e., placing all four paws on the grid floor, was measured. When S descended, the latency timer was stopped and the shock-avoidance shelf was rotated into its vertical position. Shock was then delivered through the grid floor for .07 min. at an intensity of .10 ma. at 340 v. ac. Training was continued for six training trials, or until S remained on the shock-avoidance shelf for the full session length of 2.0 min.; Ss attaining criterion prior to the sixth trial were discontinued and given credit for 2.0 min. on remaining allotted trials. The learning score was the sum of the learning measures for Trials 2–6. (The Trial 2 score, not used for the active task, had to be used here because an occasional S reached criterion on this trial.)

EXPERIMENT 1

The purpose of this experiment was to establish a strain difference in optimal temporal distribution of practice trials. Learning performances of the two strains were studied under highly massed and distributed conditions for both the active and the passive tasks.

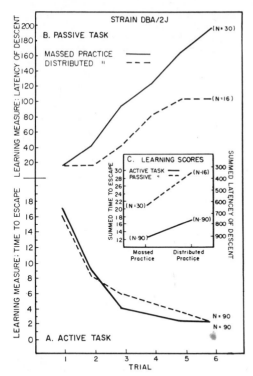

FIG. 1. Learning measures and learning scores for active and passive tasks under conditions of massed or distributed practice for strain DBA/2J.

Method

Under the active condition, 360 Ss of the strains DBA/2J and C57BL/6J were tested with an intertrial interval of 5–40 sec. (massed) or 24 hr. or more (distributed). For the passive task, 92 Ss were used. The intertrial interval was either approximately 2 min. or 24 hr. or more.

Results

The learning measures for each strain considered separately are presented in Figures 1 and 2, together with the corresponding learning scores (latencies combined across trials). Analyses of variance for the learning scores were carried out separately for the active and the passive task. For the active task, mice of strain DBA/2J performed better under the conditions of massed practice ($F = 16.0$, $df = 1/178$, $p \leqslant .001$), while mice of strain C57BL/6J performed better under the distributed condition ($F = 8.8$, $df = 1/176$, $p \leqslant .01$). Results for the passive task were similar: strain DBA/2J performed better under the massed-practice condition ($F =$

13.1, $df = 1/44$, $p \leqslant .001$) while mice of strain C57BL/6J performed better under the distributed condition ($F = 16.7$, $df = 1/44$, $p \leqslant .001$). Note that scales for time to escape shock on the active task and time to descend from the platform on the passive task are plotted in opposite directions for graphs of learning scores, so that points for high levels of performance for both tasks are low on the ordinate and points for low levels of performance for both tasks are high. Thus graphs of learning scores of strains with similar optimal distribution of practice characteristics for active and passive tasks will show lines with similar slopes for the two tasks.

EXPERIMENT 2

Results of Experiment 1 indicate that there is a substantial strain difference in optimal distribution of practice for learning. Experiment 2 was devoted to a search for evidence that this difference in optimal distribution between strains DBA/2J and C57BL/6J is based upon a difference in some aspect of the processes of memory trace formation. One source of such evidence is the establishment of differences between them in direction, magnitude, and time course of effect on memory produced by agents which facilitate or impede the processes of memory trace formation. Post-trial etherization is one of several treatments which has been reported to produce forgetting in both rats (Pearlman, 1966; Pearlman, Sharpless, & Jarvik, 1961) and mice (Abt, Essman, & Jarvik, 1961; Essman & Jarvik, 1961). It was selected for use in the present study because of (a) established efficacy with mice, and because (b) duration of ether administration can be adjusted easily to assure approximately comparable levels of anesthesia for various strains.

Method

Mice of strains DBA/2J and C57BL/6J learned either the active or the passive task under one of three different ether treatments. The Ss of the immediate-ether groups were etherized immediately following a trial; Ss in the delayed-ether groups were put in holding cartons for 2 or 4 hr. and then etherized; a third group of Ss received no ether. Etherization was achieved by placing S in a bell jar containing cotton saturated with ether and allowing it to remain there until righting response was lost and breathing became very deep and irregular (about .58 min.). Then S was

115

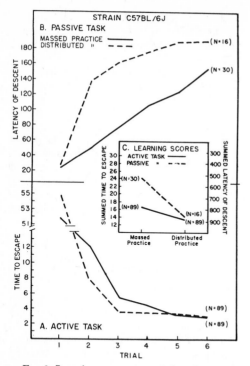

FIG. 2. Learning measures and learning scores for active and passive tasks under conditions of massed or distributed practice for strain C57BL/6J.

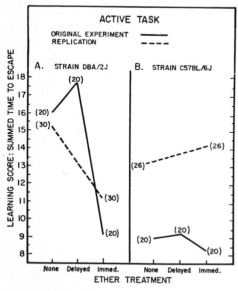

FIG. 3. Summed latency in hundredths of a minute for Trials 3–6 to escape from shock grid to platform. (Numbers in parentheses are sample sizes.)

removed and observed until the righting response returned.

For the active task, there was an interval of 24 hr. or more between trials, and the delayed-ether interval was always 2 hr. There were 20 Ss from each strain in each treatment group. For the passive task, there was some indication of either a longer time course of memory trace formation or a proactive effect of etherization; so replications of the experiment were carried out with an altered ether-delay interval of 4 hr. (R2), or with a changed intertrial interval of 72 hr. or more (R3), as well as with the 2-hr.-ether-delay and 24-hr.-intertrial interval (R1) used for the active task. About 40 Ss from each strain were used in each replication.

Results

Active task. Comparisons of the three ether treatments for strains DBA/2J and C57BL/6J on the active task are presented in Figure 3. Analysis of variance for strain DBA/2J indicated a substantial treatment difference ($F = 4.8$, $df = 2/57$, $p \leqslant .05$) which subsequent t tests showed to be due to significantly lower learning scores of the group receiving immediate posttrial etherization compared to that of the no-ether and delayed-ether groups, which did not differ from each other. Analysis of variance of the learning scores for strain C57BL/6J indicated no difference among the treatment groups ($F = .25$, $df = 2/57$, $p > .05$).

Because several previous studies had shown decreased learning to result from posttrial etherization, it was decided that the study should be repeated. A different E, using only the immediate-etherization and no-ether procedures of the original experiment, tested approximately 60 mice each of the two strains. Results for this replication are also shown in Figure 3. Again, posttrial etherization had a facilitative effect on the performance of strain DBA/2J ($F = 7.2$, $df = 1/58$, $p \leqslant .01$), but no effect on the performance of strain C57BL/6J ($F = .26$, $df = 1/50$, $p > .05$).

Passive task. For the passive task, R1 in Figure 4 shows results for the same ether-delay time and the same intertrial interval as that used for the active task. Analysis of variance of the R1 results for DBA/2J indicated a significant ether treatment effect ($F = 5.27$, $df = 2/33$, $p \leqslant .05$) which subsequent t tests showed to be due largely to superior performance of the immediate etherization group to

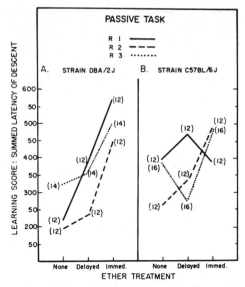

PASSIVE TASK

R 1 ————
R 2 – – –
R 3 ·········

A. STRAIN DBA/2J   B. STRAIN C57BL/6J

LEARNING SCORE : SUMMED LATENCY OF DESCENT

None Delayed Immed.   None Delayed Immed.
ETHER TREATMENT

Fig. 4. Summed time to descend from shelf to grid floor in hundredths of a minute for Trials 2–6. (Numbers in parentheses are sample sizes.)

that of the no-ether group ($p \leqslant .01$). However, the crucial delayed-etherization control group was intermediate in performance and not quite significantly different from either of the other two groups. Results for strain C57BL/6J indicated no significant ether treatment effects ($F = .38$, $df = 2/33$, $p > .05$). As in strain DBA/2J, however, there was an indication that delayed etherization might have a facilitative effect on retention. It was the possibility of longer time course of memory trace formation on a passive task which led to replication R2. The possibility that ether was having a general facilitative effect on the next day's performance was tested in replication R3. The results of the three experiments did not differ significantly for either strain, and were combined for analysis of variance. When this was done, it was clear that etherization treatments had substantial effects on the performance of Ss of strain DBA/2J ($F = 9.98$, $df = 2/105$, $p \leqslant .001$), but not on Ss of strain C57BL/6J ($F = 1.78$, $df = 2/111$, $p > .05$). Subsequent t tests for strain DBA/2J show performance of the immediate-etherization group to be superior to that of both the delayed-etherization and no-ether groups, which did not differ from each other.

Contrary to expectation, then, the results indicate that immediate posttrial etherization has no effect on retention in strain C57BL/6J and actually facilitates retention in strain DBA/2J for both the active shock escape and the passive shock-avoidance tasks.

DISCUSSION

The objective of the present experiments was to establish genetically associated differences in learning performance for mice under different temporal distributions of practice trials, and to identify some possibly related difference in processes involved in memory trace formation.

The results of Experiment 1 clearly show that different inbred strains of house mice can vary substantially in optimal distribution of practice for learning. Indeed, such differences among mice may be common, for a survey of nine inbred strains resulted in identification of at least two which are quite different. Results for the active and passive tasks were consistent, indicating that differences in optimal distribution of practice may be broad trait-like characteristics involving many different tasks. However, there is already evidence that different strain characterizations for optimal distribution of practice can be obtained, possibly because of the relative contributions of such factors as fatigue, stress, and conflict. Thus, Bovet, Bovet-Nitti, and Oliverio (1966), studying shuttling with a temporally complex practice schedule consisting of varying intervals of time between successive long sets of massed trials, found DBA performance superior under their distributed condition. Unfortunately, detailed comparison of our study with that of Bovet et al. (1966) cannot be performed because of the complexity of their task and practice conditions.

In view of the literature on the effects of ether on memory showing increased forgetting or no effect (Bures & Buresova, 1963; Ransmeier & Gerard, 1962), the present finding of substantially improved retention in strain DBA/2J on both active and passive tasks came as a distinct surprise. Though it produces a reduction both in amplitude and in frequency of electrical activity of the nervous system, which some have thought likely to interfere with processes of memory trace formation (Pearlman et al., 1961), there are also possible mechanisms for a facilitative effect of etherization. Briefly, they are (a) increased ease of alteration in neuronal membrane structure, (b) rise in brain glucose, and (c) altered release of brain transmitter substances such as norepinephrine and acetylcholine (Wimer, 1968). It seems not unreasonable to us to assume that altered activity of transmitter substances is the initial process on which the enduring changes in form or function in nervous system which are learning are based, and that the third consequence of etherization is highly likely to be involved in its observed effects on memory.

Our observed strain difference in the ether facilitation effect, as well as the discrepancy between our findings and those of Es who have found that ether produces forgetting, are probably due at least in part to biological differences between the stocks of animals used. Thus, ether might have diverse effects upon different stocks depending upon, say, their varying characteristic levels of transmitter activity. There have been reports (e.g., Bennett, Crossland, Krech, & Rosenzweig, 1960; Kurokawa, Machiyama, & Kato, 1963; Roderick, 1960; Sudak & Maas, 1964) demonstrating differences between brains of different stocks in the availability of transmitter substances and related enzymes. Though this literature is still small, there is a strong impression that extensive biochemical diversity between various stocks of animals exists, and that many discrepancies between them, in result from various treatments, may be expected. Some have been noted or suggested for various stocks already (e.g., Prien, Wayner, & Kahan, 1963).

Since our findings involve only two inbred strains—which must be considered as two large sets of genetically identical individuals—some aspects of the results must be regarded with caution. Both the consistency between results for the active and the passive task and the apparent relation between (a) strain characteristics of optimal distribution of practice trials and (b) effects of posttrial etherization on retention may be based on fortuitous associa-tion by fixation of genetically independently controlled systems (Falconer, 1960). Given that the two strains differ in two characteristics, a relation must be apparent, though the basic processes the phenomena represent may be unrelated save in the trivial sense that they exist within the same organisms.

REFERENCES

ABT, J. P., ESSMAN, W. B., & JARVIK, M. E. Ether-induced retrograde amnesia for one-trial conditioning in mice. *Science*, 1961, **133**, 1477–1478.

BENNETT, E. L., CROSSLAND, J., KRECH, D., & ROSENZWEIG, M. R. Strain differences in acetylcholine concentration in the brain of the rat. *Nature*, 1960, **187**, 787–788.

BOVET, D., BOVET-NITTI, F., & OLIVERIO, A. Short and long term memory in two inbred strains of mice. *Life Sci.*, 1966, **5**, 415–420.

BREEN, R. A., & McGAUGH, J. L. Facilitation of maze learning with posttrial injections of picrotoxin. *J. comp. physiol. Psychol.*, 1961, **54**, 498–501.

BURES, J., & BURESOVA, O. Cortical spreading depression as a memory disturbing factor. *J. comp. physiol. Psychol.*, 1963, **56**, 268–272.

ESSMAN, W. B., & JARVIK, M. E. Impairment of retention for a conditioned response by ether anesthesia in mice. *Psychopharmacologia*, 1961, **2**, 172–176.

FALCONER, D. S. *Introduction to quantitative genetics.* New York: Ronald Press, 1960.

GREEN, E. L. *Handbook of genetically standardized Jax mice.* The Jackson Laboratory, Bar Harbor, Maine, 1964.

JAY, G. E. Genetic strains and stocks. In W. J. Burdette (Ed.), *Methodology in mammalian genetics.* San Francisco: Holden-Day, 1963. Pp. 83–123.

KUROKAWA, M., MACHIYAMA, Y., & KATO, M. Distribution of acetylcholine in the brain during various states of activity. *J. Neurochem.*, 1963, **10**, 341–348.

LANE, P. *Lists of mutant genes and mutant-bearing stocks of the mouse.* Production Department, The Jackson Laboratory, Bar Harbor, Maine, June 1, 1966. (Mimeo)

MAATSCH, J. L. Learning and fixation after a single shock trial. *J. comp. physiol. Psychol.*, 1959, **52**, 408–410.

McGAUGH, J. L., JENNINGS, R. D., & THOMSON, C. W. Effect of distribution of practice on the maze learning of descendants of the Tryon maze bright and maze dull strains. *Psychol. Rep.*, 1962, **10**, 147–150.

McGAUGH, J. L., THOMSON, C. W., WESTBROOK, W. H., & HUDSPETH, W. J. A further study of learning facilitation with strychnine sulphate. *Psychopharmacologia*, 1962, **3**, 352–360.

McGAUGH, J. L., WESTBROOK, W. H., & THOMSON, C. W. Facilitation of maze learning with posttrial injections of 5-7-diphenyl-1-3-diazadamantan-6-ol (1757 I.S.). *J. comp. physiol. Psychol.*, 1962, **55**, 710–713.

PEARLMAN, C. A., JR. Similar retrograde amnesic effects of ether and spreading cortical depression. *J. comp. physiol. Psychol.*, 1966, **61**, 306–308.

PEARLMAN, C. A., SHARPLESS, S. K., & JARVIK, M. E. Retrograde amnesia produced by anesthetic and convulsant agents. *J. comp. physiol. Psychol.*, 1961, **54**, 109–112.

PRIEN, R. F., WAYNER, M. J., JR., & KAHAN, S. Lack of facilitation in maze learning by picrotoxin and strychnine sulphate. *Amer. J. Physiol.*, 1963, **204**, 488–492.

RANSMEIER, R. E., & GERARD, R. W. Effects of temperature and metabolic factors on rodent memory and EEG. *Amer. J. Physiol.*, 1962, **203**, 782–788.

RODERICK, T. H. Selection for cholinesterase activity in the cerebral cortex of the rat. *Genetics*, 1960, **45**, 1123–1140.

ROSS, R. B. Effects of strychnine sulphate on maze learning in rats. *Nature* (London), 1964, **201**, 109–110.

STRATTON, L. O., & PETRINOVICH, L. Post-trial injections of an anti-cholinesterase drug and maze learning in two strains of rats. *Psychopharmacologia*, 1963, **5**, 47–54.

SUDAK, H. S., & MAAS, J. W. Central nervous system serotonin and norepinephrine localization in emotional and non-emotional strains of mice. *Nature*, 1964, **203**, 1254–1256.

THOMSON, C. W., McGAUGH, J. L., SMITH, C. E., HUDSPETH, W. J., & WESTBROOK, W. H. Strain differences in the retroactive effects of electroconvulsive shock on maze learning. *Canad. J. Psychol.*, 1961, **15**, 69–74.

WIMER, R. Bases of a facilitative effect upon retention resulting from posttrial etherization. *J. comp. physiol. Psychol.*, 1968, **65**, in press.

(Received January 30, 1967)

On the Inheritance of Handedness

I. Laterality in inbred mice

ROBERT L. COLLINS

Reprinted from the Journal of Heredity, Vol. 59, No. 1, January-February, 1968
(Copyright 1968 by the American Genetic Association)

RIGHT and left handedness are alternative expressions of a fundamental behavioral asymmetry. Although hereditary theories of the origin of human hand preference have occurred periodically in the scientific and popular literature[8], a well-defined relationship between lateral preference and genetic variation has not been successfully established[5, 6]. Part of the difficulty in evaluating the hereditary hypothesis is due to the evident modifiability of hand preference through formal and informal training during early human development and the subsequent entanglement of these environmental effects with the presumed genetic influences[4]. However, it may be possible to evaluate the hereditary hypothesis in detail if lateral preference were demonstrated and studied in laboratory animals whose genetic constitution is controlled, and whose environment presumably does not differentially favor the use of either hand. To this end laterality was studied using highly inbred strains of mice and two hybrid crosses. The results show that an enduring hand preference can be observed in mice and that this preference cannot be attributed to hereditary differences.

Materials and Methods

To define handedness the following criteria were used: a) one hand must be used significantly more frequently than the other in a free-use task; b) this lateral preference should be enduring upon retest;

The author is associate staff scientist, The Jackson Laboratory, Bar Harbor, Maine 04609. Supported by research grants MH 11327 and MH 1775 from the National Institutes of Health. The principles of laboratory animal care as set forth by the National Society for Medical Research are observed in this Laboratory.

and c) lateral preference should be consistent with lateral superiority measured in a forced-use task. A total of 370 mice from highly inbred strains was tested for paw preference. Specific strain comparisons were made between 114 male C57BL/6J and 101 male DBA/2J mice. The remaining groups included A/J, A/HeJ, C3H/HeJ, C57BL/10J and DBA/1J mice. Hybrid male mice from crosses between C3H/HeJ and DBA/1J and between C57BL/6J and DBA/2J were studied. Mice initially were tested between 2.5 to 3 months of age. Mice were deprived of food for 24 hours prior to testing. Individuals were placed in plastic chambers 11.4 cm high by 6.4 cm deep by 3.8 cm. On the front wall of each cubicle a 9 mm glass feeding tube, equally accessible from the right or left, was attached 5.7 cm from the floor. Maple flavored rolled wheat (Maypo) was placed within the feeding tube so that a subject could withdraw food by using a single paw (Figure 1). Fifty reaches were observed and serially recorded for each mouse. Scores were defined as the number of right paw entries (RPE's) in 50 observations. Low RPE's reflected the predominant use of the left paw, and high RPE's, the right paw. Mice were classified as dextral or sinistral by considering each subject a "coin", which could land either R or L. A subject who scored above 25 RPE's was designated R, and L was assigned to one who scored below 25 RPE's. In the infrequent case of a tie score, the "biological coin" was considered to have landed on "edge" and was not counted; only four such cases were observed during initial testing.

The consistency of an individual's paw preference over time was determined in three ways. Within the initial testing session, data were divided into two blocks of 25 reaches, and the number of RPE's in each block was compared for 100 randomly chosen mice. To determine short-term consistency, 15 mice were tested 4 times at 4-day intervals. An additional 60 mice were tested 4 times at monthly intervals to evaluate long-term consistency. Pearson product moment correlations were computed for each comparison using RPE scores. Tetrachoric correlations were used to assess the stability of the laterality classifications.

Later in the study an attempt was made to determine whether the preferred paw in food reaching was also the superior paw on a forced-use task. Grip strength was tested in 29 A/J and 32 A/HeJ males. Tape was first placed over one paw. A mouse was then picked up by the tail and allowed to grasp a 6.4 × 6.4 mm mesh wire screen attached to a Grass FT-10 force displacement transducer connected to a Grass polygraph. The mouse was pulled upward until he released the wire screen, and the maximum force displacement was measured in g of grip strength. Each mouse was tested 20 to 30 times on the first day. On the second day mice were tested with the opposite paw under the same conditions. Order of testing was balanced with respect to preferred and non-preferred paws, and all procedures were performed double-blind. Data were analyzed by comparing the daily average of the five highest grip strengths for the preferred and non-preferred paws between and within subjects.

Results

If paw preference were a heritable characteristic, laterality differences between strains would provide a convenient basis for further genetic investigation. Figure 2A illustrates the frequency distribution of RPE scores for 114 C57BL/6J mice. Modes occurred at 3–5 and 39–44 RPE's. The proportion of right paw reaches was 0.489; left was 0.511. The binomial distribution of expected frequencies according to these proportions is superimposed upon the observed distribution as a dashed line. These frequencies yield the expected distribution of RPE performance under the hypothesis that mice exhibit no lateral preference. The chi-square test between observed and expected frequencies was 2.42×10^3 (P <0.0001, df = 113). Figure 2B presents the same information for 101 DBA/2J mice. Modes occurred at 3–5 and 41–44 RPE's. The proportion of right paw entries was 0.494, and left, 0.506; $\chi^2 = 2.17 \times 10^3$ (P <0.0001, df = 100). Individuals in both highly inbred strains used one paw more frequently to retrieve food even though the likelihoods of observing a right or a left reach were approximately equal across subjects. According to the procedure for assigning laterality classifications, the proportions of right paw preferent mice for C57BL/6J and DBA/2J strains were 0.51 and 0.50, respectively. Considered in this manner, almost exactly one-half of the mice within both highly inbred strains were dextrals and one half, sinistrals.

Table I summarizes the paw preference data for all experimental groups. A bimodal distribution of paw preference scores was evident for the seven inbred strains and the two hybrid crosses. Since both right and left preferent subjects were observed within each of nine sets of genetically uniform mice, the heritability of paw preference for each group must be close to zero. No association of lateral preferences could be detected in intra-litter comparisons.

Figure 2C illustrates the frequency distributions of RPE's for 370 inbred and 221 hybrid mice. Both distributions are clearly bimodal. Maxima were observed at 3–5 and 42–44 RPE's for inbreds, and at 6–8 and 42–44 RPE's for hybrids. However, the distributions are slightly asymmetrical in opposite directions. Omitting the region of ambilaterality

FIGURE 1—A mouse retrieving a food flake from the feeding tube using the left paw. The photograph was taken near the end of the behavioral sequence. The feeding tube is equidistant from the two walls of the chamber.

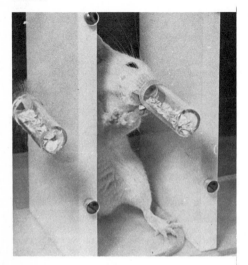

between 21 and 29 RPE's, the percentages of hybrid mice in the left paw preferent region were higher than those for the inbred subjects in 6 of 7 cases. The converse relationship was observed in the right preferent region. Analysis of these distributions indicated that there were statistically different

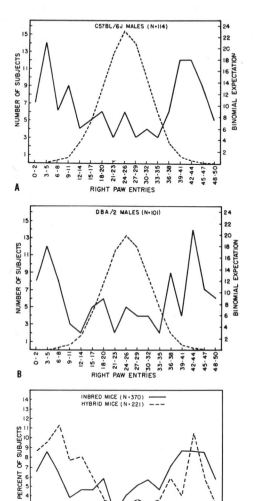

FIGURE 2—*A* shows the frequency distribution of lateral preference scores for C57BL/6J in mice in terms of the number of right paw entries into the feeding tube in 50 observations. The abscissa is divided into 17 blocks of 3 right-paw entries. The binomial distribution of expected frequencies according to the proportions given in the text is superimposed as a dashed line upon the observed distribution. *B*—frequency distribution of lateral preference scores for DBA/2J mice. Expected frequencies are superimposed as a dashed line. *C*—mean frequency distributions of lateral preference scores for inbred and hybrid mice.

($\chi^2 = 42.8$, P <0.001, df $= 16$). For all inbred and hybrid mice, the proportions of dextrals were 0.543 and 0.409, respectively. These values differ statistically ($\chi^2 = 11.4$, P <0.001, df $= 1$).

Table II summarizes the correlations for the consistency of paw preference scores as well as the stability of the laterality classifications during repeated testing. Within the initial test session, approximately 20 percent of the subjects produced identical RPE scores in the first and second blocks of 25 observations. During the second block, 35 percent of the subjects increased the use of the preferred paw slightly, while 45 percent decreased its use. All 100 mice maintained the same laterality classification in both halves of the initial test. During 4-day retesting there were small variations in the RPE number for some mice. However, the smallest inter-test correlation, observed between tests 1 and 4, was 0.92 and all 16 subjects maintained the same laterality classifications throughout short-term retesting. Thirty C57BL/6J and thirty DBA/2J mice

Table I. Summary of paw preference data

Strain	Number of subjects	Proportion of right paw entries	Proportion of dextral mice
C57BL/6J	114	0.489	0.51
DBA/2J	101	0.494	0.50
A/J	40	0.562	0.67
A/HeJ	35	0.570	0.51
DBA/1J	42	0.570	0.61
C3H/HeJ	33	0.518	0.58
C57BL/10J	5	0.552	0.60
Total inbred mice	370	0.519	0.543
C3H/HeJ × DBA/1J	64	0.423	0.36
C57BL/6J × DBA/2J	157	0.438	0.43
Total hybrid mice	221	0.434	0.409

were tested monthly for four months. A small but steady increase in the proportion of mice occupying the two extreme RPE class intervals was observed for C57BL/6J mice; this trend was absent in the DBA/2J subjects. During these retests four C57BL/6J and eight DBA/2J mice exhibited a single fluctuation in their laterality classifications. The classifications for 80 percent of the subjects remained invariant during four months of retesting. All 26 intercorrelations listed in Table II are statistically significant (P <0.01 that ρ or $\rho_t = 0$).

The average grip strength across both paws for A/J mice was 69.1 g, and for A/HeJ, 63.0 g (P <0.05, $F = 5.17$, df $= 1/57$). Grip strength for mice tested on the first day with the preferred paw was 68.1 g, while that for mice tested with the non-preferred paw was 64.0 g. The 4.1 g difference in this between subjects comparison did not reach a conventional level of statistical significance (P $\simeq 0.08$, $F = 3.26$, df $= 1/57$). There was no interaction of strain and preference. In the within subjects comparison, the average grip strength for 61 mice tested on the preferred side was 64.9 g, while the mean for the opposite paw was 61.2 g. This 3.7 g difference was statistically significant using a two-tailed test (P <0.025, $t = 2.33$, df $= 60$).

Discussion

Three criteria for the demonstration of functional laterality in mice were supported by these data. Mice used one paw significantly more often than the other to retrieve food; lateral preference was consistent over time; and grip strength was correlated to paw preference within subjects.

Since both dextral and sinistral mice were observed within each of nine genetically uniform populations, it would appear that individual genetic differences are not required to explain laterality differences. In fact, equal representation of the two classes as observed in the two most intensively studied strains produces the maximum possible

Table II. Intercorrelation matrix of paw preference scores. and laterality classifications for mice retested at intervals: of four days ($n = 16$) and one month ($n = 60$).

	1	2	Four day retest 3	4
1	0.92*	0.92†	0.92	0.93
	1.00*	1.00‡	1.00	1.00
2	0.88	—	0.93	0.95
	0.98	—	1.00	1.00
3	0.82	0.93	—	0.97
	0.96	1.00	—	1.00
4	0.75	0.91	0.94	—
	0.85	0.97	0.97	—
		Monthly retest		

* Within session split-block correlation ($n = 100$).
† Product moment correlation of the number of right paw entries in 50 observations.
‡ Tetrachoric correlation of laterality classifications.

phenotypic variance. This is somewhat surprising considering that the two strains have minimal genetic variance.

The sole experimental result indicating a possible genetic effect upon lateral variation was that the proportion of dextral mice in the two hybrid crosses was smaller than that for the inbred strains. Replication of this finding would suggest that a directional bias in the distribution of lateral asymmetries may be associated with heterozygosity at one or more loci. Accordingly, while these data do not support a conclusion that lateral preference in mice is determined genetically, it cannot be denied that the probability of alternative phenotypic forms may be influenced by genotypic differences. This hypothesis could be tested by studying laterality in additional classical cross generations. For example, using methods of genetic analysis outlined elsewhere[1], the phenotypic distributions of the segregating generations between C57BL/6J and DBA/2J might be congruent to expectations based upon a single or multiple locus difference. However, in view of the ambiguity that would exist between a genotype and either alternative phenotypic form, lateral preference would remain largely unresponsive to selection pressure and the expected realized heritability for each form would be essentially zero. It is of interest to note that in an early study, Peterson reported no change in the frequencies of right and left paw preferent rats through more than seven generations of selection[7]. A similar finding was re-

ported for the heritability of foliar asymmetries in *Cocos nucifera*[3].

In light of the extensive evidence showing genetic effects upon diverse behavioral characters, it is striking that this basic behavioral difference would be so recalcitrant to genetic analysis and manipulation if it were in fact determined by hereditary differences. Indeed, there would seem to be little advantage in having genes determine which hand was preferred. Phenotypic variation arising from environmental sources would insure the continued survival of a species if it were subject to selection pressure for lateral uniformity. In addition, an environmental regulation may confer to each new generation a greater plasticity for adaptation than could be granted genetically. Genetic variation may simply provide the ability to develop functional asymmetries without specifying the alternative phenotypic form, just as genetic variation might favor acquisition of language without specifying the vocabulary and grammar.

On the basis of these experimental results using mice, a mathematical reanalysis of the published data concerning the inheritance of human lateral preference was performed[2]. The results provided no support for a view that human hand preference is determined by individual genetic differences. Thus, *Mus musculus* may not be unique among species in that the lateral preference of its members remains largely unspecified by their genotypes.

Summary

Paw preference was tested experimentally in 591 mice from 7 highly inbred strains and 2 hybrid crosses. Consistency of preference over time and grip strength were assessed. Mice exhibited reliable functional laterality and their individual preferences were enduring. Both right and left paw preferent mice were observed within each of the nine genetically uniform groups. One-half the subjects in C57BL/6J and DBA/2J strains were dextral, and one half, sinistral. This indicates that maximal variation in lateralization may exist in populations possessing minimal genetic variance, and suggests that hand preference is not determined by hereditary factors.

Literature Cited

1. COLLINS, R. L. A general nonparametric theory of genetic analysis: I. Application to the classical cross. *Genetics* 56:551. 1967.
2. ———. On the inheritance of handedness. II. Reanalysis of human data. (In preparation). 1968.
3. DAVIS, T. A. The non-inheritance of asymmetry in *Cocos nucifera*. *J. Genetics* 58:42–47. 1962.
4. FALEK, A. Handedness: a family study. *Amer. J. Hum. Genet.* 11:56–62. 1959.
5. FULLER, J. L. and W. R. THOMPSON. Behavior Genetics. John Wiley & Sons, New York. 1960.
6. McKUSICK, V. A. Mendelian Inheritance in Man. The Johns Hopkins Press, Baltimore. 1966.
7. PETERSON, G. M. Mechanisms of handedness in the rat. *Comp. Psychol. Monogr.* No. 46. 1934.
8. UHRBROCK, R. S. Laterality of Function Bibliography (2813 references). American Documentation Inst. Washington, D.C. 1963.

PART 3 Neural and Hormonal Control of Behavior

The readings in Part 2 presented many examples of the effects of genotype on behavior. An important question related to the material in that section is "How does genotype affect behavior?" The answers to this question are largely unknown and probably immensely complex. Nevertheless, it is possible to make some general statements about the intermediate steps whereby genes affect behavior. First, it is generally agreed that genes control the production of enzymes and enzyme systems. Enzymes in turn mediate the complex metabolic activities necessary for the growth and differentiation of cells. Tissues and organs are thus formed. The resulting morphology and physiology are the substrates on which behavior ultimately depends. These substrates are, of course, not immutable, and we shall cover many examples of environmental and behavioral effects on physiology and anatomy.

Most important for the study of the physiology of behavior are the nervous system and the endocrine system. Therefore, the readings that follow are concerned primarily with brain function and the influence of hormones on the brain and on behavior.

If a stimulus is repeatedly presented, an organism will usually habituate, that is, stop responding or reduce the level of response to the stimulus. Habituation is obviously of great importance in the life of an animal. It is also a good behavioral end-point for studies of the nervous system. Reading 12, from the laboratory of Holger Ursin in Norway, describes an investigation of the neural control of habituation of the important "orienting response" in the cat. The useful technique of chronically implanted electrodes is illustrated in this selection.

If one compares photographs of a predator's response to prey, a "stalking-attack" such as a lion pulling down a deer, with photographs of the same animal in an aggressive mood toward a member of its own species, it becomes apparent that the postures and facial expressions are quite different in the two situations. It has been shown that these two types of attack can be elicited from different sites in the hypothalamus. In Reading 13, Hutchinson and Renfrew, using implanted electrodes, successfully elicit stalking-attack and eating behavior from the same site. Findings such as theirs are important in the development of theories of motivation and emotion.

In the two readings just described, implanted electrodes were activated by the experimenter to elicit behavior from the animal. It has been known for a number of years that, if an electrode is properly located, an animal will perform a task such as bar pressing in order to activate the electrode and stimulate its own brain. Activity in this area of research has been equaled or exceeded by work concerned with "biological clocks" in plants and animals. Many of these clocks exhibit circadian (about-a-day) rhythms. Both areas of research are nicely illustrated in Reading 14 where Terman and Terman demonstrate a circadian rhythm in rate of self-stimulation in rats.

The next few papers deal with hormone-behavior interactions. It has been known that hormones affect both morphology and behavior. Reading 15 presents a relatively unusual example of such effects. Here Lindzey, Thiessen, and Tucker show that territorial marking in male gerbils is under hormonal control.

In Part 2, several examples of genotypic effects on behavior were presented. These were followed by a report indicating that laterality, in spite of several hypotheses about how it is inherited, is probably not genetically determined. This finding illustrates the danger of making seemingly logical assumptions in the absence of data. In Reading 16, Jay Rosenblatt presents another such example. His research indicates that, previous assumptions to the contrary, maternal behavior in the rat has no hormonal basis.

For several years D. S. Lehrman has been involved in research elucidating the intricate relationships among hormones, behavior, and external stimulation in ring doves. Reading 17 is an example of work from Lehrman's laboratory illustrating how both behavior and external stimuli can alter hormone secretions.

One of the ways in which hormones can affect behavior is by direct action on particular parts of the nervous system. Reading 18 by Julian Davidson provides a carefully controlled example of such an effect. Davidson's work shows that in the adult rat certain neurons in the brain are sensitive to the presence of testosterone. Implants of testosterone in other parts of the brain are ineffective in activating castrated males; that is, the adult brain is organized.

What determines the organization of the nervous system? An hypothesis directed at a partial answer to this question was formulated in the 1950s by the late W. C. Young. On the basis of his work on the effects of hormonal manipulation in the developing organism, Young hypothesized that early hormones function to organize the nervous system. In the adult, the same hormones activate the previously organized mechanisms. In Reading 19, Levine and Mullins review the literature on the effects of hormone treatments early in life on later behavior. Reading 20 by Bronson and Desjardins reports a specific example of research in this area. They show that neonatal hormone injections can modify the aggressiveness of the animal in adulthood.

In the final reading in Part 3, Essman illustrates how differences in the external environment can produce differences both in the internal environment and in behavior.

Neuropsychologia, 1969, Vol. 7, pp. 313 to 318. Pergamon Press. Printed in England

HABITUATION OF THE ORIENTING RESPONSE ELICITED BY STIMULATION OF THE CAUDATE NUCLEUS IN THE CAT

Holger Ursin, Håkan Sundberg and Steven Menaker

Institute of Physiology, University of Bergen, Norway

(*Received* 6 *January* 1969)

Abstract—High frequency (100/sec) electrical stimulation of eight points in the head of the caudate nucleus in six unanesthetized, freely moving cats yielded an orienting response from all points. The behavior observed was indistinguishable from the orienting response elicited by novel, acoustic stimulation and by electrical stimulation of the amygdala, parts of cortex, and the mesencephalic reticular formation.

The cats habituated to the caudate stimulation just as cats habituate to non-signal, peripheral sensory events. The same has previously been found for stimulation of amygdala and cortex, while no habituation is observed to stimulation of the mesencephalic reticular formation.

As early as 1875 Danilewski [1] reported that electrical stimulation of the caudate nucleus resulted in slowing of breathing and a cessation of spontaneous movements. Later research [2, 3] also describes inhibitory functions for this nucleus.

Kaada [4] described *two* general types of inhibitory phenomena elicited by electrical stimulation, a *short lasting arrest* with no loss of muscle tone, and a *long lasting inhibition* with loss of muscle tone. In later work, Kaada and collaborators found that the short lasting arrest observed during anesthesia is a part of the orienting response. When these "arrest" zones are stimulated in freely moving cats, the whole orienting response is seen; there is initial arrest of ongoing activity followed by orienting movements, behavioral arousal and electroencephalographic desynchronization [5–7].

The present report deals with two questions: Is the behavior response elicited by electrical stimulation of the caudate nucleus of a broad inhibitory nature, or is the response identical to the orienting responses we have observed from the stimulation of other structures? If orienting responses are elicited, are they subject to habituation in the same way as those elicited by stimulation of the other arrest areas [8], or do associated inhibitory phenomena interfere with gradual disappearance of the orienting response?

MATERIALS AND METHODS

A total of 8 electrodes in 6 cats constitute the material. Electrodes were implanted during anesthesia by the ordinary stereotaxic procedure. Electrodes were 0.18 mm thin platinum wires covered by Teflon except for 1 mm at the tip, protruding into the brain tissue through a stainless steel catheter of 0·6 mm bore. This shielding served as ground for the unipolar stimulation.

The animal was stimulated while freely moving in an observation chamber ($45 \times 55 \times 145$ cm) surrounded by a one-way mirror on one side, and conventional mirrors on the other three sides. The cats were stimulated by a radio-controlled stimulator [9]. A "stimoceiver" carried by the cat weighed 14 g including battery. The stimoceivers were found to work reliably, producing constant current rectangular pulses. Pulse width, frequency and amplitude could be controlled from the radio transmitter. The frequency used was 100/sec of 1 msec duration. The observation chamber, two observers, and the radio transmitter were placed inside an electrically shielded and sound-attenuated room.

The intensity of the orienting response was evaluated by a scoring method described previously. Briefly, it consisted of four categories of behavior (see Table 1, modified from Roeloffs *et al.* [10]). The level of arousal was evaluated just before stimulus onset, and a second score was given for the behavior during and immediately after the stimulation. The difference between these two scores has been used as an indicator for the arousal effect of stimulation.

Table 1. Scoring schedule

Points	Head	Eye-lids	Ears	Posture
6				Running
5	Searching			Walking
4	Turning	Open		Standing
3	Lifted	Half open	Moving	Sitting
2	Quiet	Membrana nict. contracted	Quiet	Lying on belly
1	Laid down	Closed		Curled up or lying on side

The cats had not been used for other experiments before the operation. At least 48 hours after screening the effects from the various electrode sites, avoiding unnecessary stimulation, habituation sessions were run for all electrode sites yielding clear-cut orienting responses. Stimulation intensity was chosen separately for each site as the lowest intensity giving a pre- and post-stimulatory difference of at least 3 points in the behavior score. Intertrial intervals varied from 30 sec to several minutes, a stimulus was never given unless the cat was quiet (behavior score less than 9). Habituation was said to occur when the cat, for three trials in a row, did not show more than 0.5 in the difference between the pre-and post-stimulation score. Dishabituation was then produced by introducing other arousal stimuli, and the number of trials necessary to produce rehabituation was tested for most electrodes. At the end of the experiment the animals were killed, the brains perfused and the electrode sites identified histologically in Nissl-stained material.

RESULTS

Caudate orienting responses

Electrical stimulation of the caudate nucleus elicited highly predictable changes in behavior. Any ongoing activity was stopped immediately at the stimulus onset, once threshold had been reached ("arrest"). Then the eyes were opened, the ears were moved forward, and the head was lifted and turned to the side opposite of that stimulated. This head movement was often slow, stepwise, and oscillating, and was referred to as "searching" in the scoring categories. The cat often sat up and moved around at higher intensities. The time course depended on the stimulation intensity. The response was adequately described by the scoring categories shown in Table 1, and is indistinguishable from the response ("orienting response") seen when a cat is subjected to any novel stimulus.

Other responses

One additional electrode, situated dorsally in the left caudate nucleus, yielded no observable orienting response. During stimulation, simple motor movements such as turning around the body axis, chewing, and mouth opening were observed. Following stimulation, the cat seemed alerted but no clearcut orienting response was observed. In addition to orienting responses at low current intensity for other sites, a stronger stimulation sometimes led to after-discharges and, occasionally, to full fledged tonic-clonic fits.

Habituation to stimulation of the caudate nucleus

Repeated stimulation of the caudate nucleus invariably led to gradual disappearance of the orienting behavior (Fig. 1). A declining slope followed the waxing and waning pattern described as occurring with external stimuli and with electrical stimulation of the amygdala and the cortex [8].

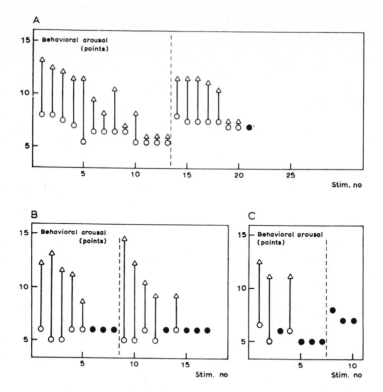

FIG. 1. Habituation to electrical stimulation of three points (A, B and C) in the caudate nucleus. Open circle: level of arousal before stimulation; open triangle: maximum intensity of orienting response during or immediately following the stimulation; filled circle: no orienting behavior to stimulation. Dishabituation indicated by stippled line. A drop in base line was sometimes observed (A), but this was not a necessary condition for habituation to occur (B). When very few trials were necessary to reach habituation, dishabituation sometimes was difficult to obtain without prolonging the inter-trial interval, or using very intense dishabituating stimuli (C).

The number of trials (Fig. 2) required for habituation of the caudate sites was very close to that required for the amygdala sites, and slightly lower than the level observed for cortical stimulation sites [8].

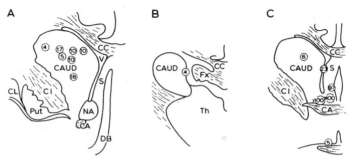

FIG. 2. Frontal sections. Localization of points stimulated indicated by circles, the number inside the circle indicates number of stimulus presentations necessary to reach habituation. A and B, present material; C previously published material [8]. CA, anterior commisure; CAUD, caudate nucleus; CC, corpus callosum; CI, internal capsule; CL, claustrum; DB, diagonal band; Fx, fornix; NA, accumbens; Put, putamen; S, septum; Th, thalamus; V, ventricle.

Dishabituation

When the habituation criteria had been reached the response to stimulation of the caudate nucleus returned again when arousal was produced by some other stimulus, such as knocking on the observation cage. This phenomenon, "dishabituation", is also illustrated in Fig. 1. When habituation then was again produced by repeating the stimulation, fewer trials were required than for the original habituation. Changing the stimulus parameters also had the same effect. The dishabituating effect did not seem to depend on the kind of stimulus used. These findings are similar to the findings for cortical and amygdala stimulation.

Localization

The placement of the electrode sites is shown in Fig. 2. No differential localization of function within the caudate nucleus was observed in the present material.

Interference with ongoing eating

Stimulation of caudate sites in 3 cats during eating showed no evidence of facilitation or inhibition of food intake except for the arrest associated with the orienting response. Consequently, this incidental inhibition of eating disappeared as habituation to the caudate stimulation took place. The same type of interference, limited to arrest and response-competition with the orienting response, was seen in four cats where caudate stimulation was given during performance of a learned food-approach response in a Wisconsin General Test Apparatus.

DISCUSSION

Several authors have pointed out that the behavioral effects observed with stimulation of the caudate nucleus depend on the frequency used [2, 11]. Low frequency stimulation in this area, as in many other areas of the brain, elicits a variety of "inhibitory" and sleep-like phenomena that will not be discussed here. In this paper, we are only concerned with the effects of high frequency stimulation of the caudate.

Contralateral head-turning and circling have been described by most reports on the effects of caudate nucleus stimulation in the freely moving cat. In fact, LAURSEN [12] claimed that these were the only "motor" responses of caudate origin. LAURSEN further stated that the cats looked as if they were searching for something, and he interpreted this response as a complex behavioral manifestation rather than a stereotyped movement. It is our conclusion that this response, observed by most authors with high frequency stimulation, is the same behavior that we have called the orienting response. This has also been suggested by GALEANO et al. [13]. This response is similar to that elicited by stimulation of the amygdala, the cortex or the mesencephalic reticular formation. In our experience, it is also indistinguishable from the orienting response observed when a novel sound is presented to a cat. It is impossible for us to tell from the observed behavior whether a given orienting response is being elicited by external stimulation or brain stimulation.

In none of the electrode sites studied was there any evidence of "inhibitory" phenomena such as eye closure, lying down, or other evidence of sleep or "de-arousal". The only "inhibitory" phenomena observed were the arrest response that is a part of the orienting response, and the habituation to the stimulation. In other words, there was no additional "inhibition" to the caudate response as compared to the orienting response elicited by external sound or electrical stimulation in the amygdala or over the lateral or supra-sylvian gyrus [8].

The gradual decrease of the orienting responses to caudate stimulation is considered to be habituation since the response re-occurred when arousal was produced by some other stimulus. This phenomenon is called "dishabituation", and is commonly regarded as a necessary condition for concluding that habituation was present [14]. It should be kept in mind that the present habituation concept is limited to decrements in the orienting response, and is not used indiscriminately for any or all response decrements [15]. The presence of dishabituation is a strong argument against interpretations of the response decrement as being due to such artifactual things as polarization of the electrode or damage to the nervous tissue by electrolytical effects.

The orienting response elicited by brain stimulation and showing the habituation phenomenon, should not, in our opinion, be interpreted as a motor response elicited from "arousal areas". The orienting response is the fixed action pattern of any cat to any novel stimulus. Any experience the brain is not "set" to expect will elicit this response. Therefore, it is to be expected that this response will be elicited by stimulation of many different types of functional systems within the brain. There is, therefore, no serious discrepancy between the demonstration of organization within the caudate nucleus discussed by DIVAC [16] and our lack of finding any localization.

The experience elicited by caudate stimulation seems to be treated in the same way as adequate sensory stimulation since the response shows the habituation phenomenon. In other words, the brain may identify such stimulations as "non-signals" and stops reacting to them. By contrast, stimulation of the mesencephalic reticular formation does not habituate [8]. In this latter case, therefore, it is most likely that one is dealing with an arousal motor. Still a third way of producing arousal by stimulation of the brain is to interfere with the systems involved in motivational and emotional responses. This has been suggested as a separate arousal system by ROUTTENBERG [17], and is probably the way arousal and orienting behavior is elicited when the electrodes are close to the pericommisural parts of the septal region (Fig. 2C).

REFERENCES

1. DANILEWSKY, B., JR. Experimentelle Beiträge zur Physiologie des Gehirns. *Pflügers Arch. ges. Physiol.* **11**, 128–138, 1875.
2. BUCHWALD, N. A., WYERS, E. J., LAUPRECHT, C. W. and HEUSER, G. The "caudate-spindle". IV. A behavioral index of caudate-induced inhibition. *Electroenceph. clin. Neurophysiol.* **13**, 531–537, 1961.
3. METTLER, F. A., ADES, H. W., LIPMAN, E. and CULLER, E. A. The extrapyramidal system. An experimental demonstration of function. *A.M.A. Archs. Neurol. Psychiat.* **41**, 984–995, 1939.
4. KAADA, B. R. Somato-motor, autonomic and electrocorticographic responses of "rhinencephalic" and other structures in primates, cat and dog. *Acta physiol. scand.* **24** (suppl. 83), 1–285, 1951.
5. FANGEL, C. and KAADA, B. R. Behavior "attention" and fear induced by cortical stimulation in the cat. *Electroenceph. clin. Neurophysiol.* **12**, 575–588, 1960.
6. KAADA, B. R. and JOHANNESSEN, N. B. Generalized electrocortical activation by cortical stimulation in the cat. *Electroenceph. clin. Neurophysiol.* **12**, 567–573, 1960.
7. URSIN, H. and KAADA, B. R. Functional localization within the amygdaloid complex in the cat. *Electroenceph. clin. Neurophysiol.* **12**, 1–20, 1960.
8. URSIN, H., WESTER, K. and URSIN, R. Habituation to electrical stimulation of the brain in unanesthetized cats. *Electroenceph. clin. Neurophysiol.* **23**, 41–49, 1967.
9. DELGADO, J. M. R. Aggressive behavior evoked by radio stimulation in monkey colonies. *Am. Zool.* **6**, 669–681, 1966.
10. ROELOFS, G. A., VAN DEN HOOFDAKKER, R. H. and PRECHTL, H. F. R. Sleep effects of subliminal brain stimulation in cats. *Expl Neurol.* **8**, 84–92, 1963.

11. McLennan, H., Emmons, P. R. and Plummer, P. M. Some behavioral effects of stimulation of the caudate nucleus in unrestrained cats. *Can. J. Physiol. Pharmacol.* **42**, 329–339, 1964.
12. Laursen, A. M. Movements evoked from the region of the caudate nucleus in cats. *Acta physiol. scand.* **54**, 175–184, 1962.
13. Galeano, C., Roig, J. A. and Sommer-Smith, J. A. Conditioning of subcortical telencephalic stimulation effects. *Electroenceph. clin. Neurophysiol.* **17**, 281–293, 1964.
14. Sokolov, Y. N. *Perception and the Conditioned Reflex.* Pergamon Press, Oxford, 1963.
15. Thompson, R. F. and Spencer, W. A. Habituation: A model phenomenon for the study of neuronal substrates of behavior. *Psychol. Rev.* **73**, 16–43, 1966.
16. Divac, I. Functions of the caudate nucleus. *Acta biol. exp.*, (*Vars.*) **28**, 107–120, 1968.
17. Routtenberg, A. The two-arousal hypothesis: Reticular formation and limbic system. *Psychol. Rev.* **75**, 51–80, 1968.

Journal of Comparative and Physiological Psychology
1966, Vol. 61, No. 3, 360–367

STALKING ATTACK AND EATING BEHAVIORS ELICITED FROM THE SAME SITES IN THE HYPOTHALAMUS[1]

R. R. HUTCHINSON and J. W. RENFREW

Anna State Hospital, Illinois

Electrical stimulation of the lateral hypothalamus in cats produced stalking attack against rats. Lower intensity stimulation of each of these same brain sites produced eating behavior. Other experiments showed the eating to be normal ingestive behavior. It is suggested that the area of the lateral hypothalamus from which stalking or predatory attack is elicited is responsible for the mediation of food acquisition responses, attack being one form of such behavior.

It has recently been shown that electrical stimulation of the hypothalamus in cats can produce "stalking attack" against rats (Wasman & Flynn, 1962). This type of attack behavior is quite different in features of topography and collateral sympathetic manifestation from the classic "affective" attack behavior described by Hess and Brugger (1943), Hess (1954), and Wasman and Flynn (1962). During a stalking attack episode, a cat moves about the test space quickly and quietly. Its back is arched while the cat sniffs at

[1] Supported by Grant 4925 from the National Institute of Mental Health, Grant 17-118 from the Psychiatric Training and Research Fund, and the Mental Health Fund of the Illinois Department of Mental Health. We thank N. H. Azrin, D. F. Hake, and W. Gale for their help.

the floor. Approaching a rat, the cat will lunge and seize it by the back of the neck with its teeth while holding the rat to the floor with one paw. The behavior is not accompanied by the hissing, snarling, or growling typically associated with the classic affective attack pattern.

These two types of attack have been shown to be elicitable from different areas of the hypothalamus. Affective attack has been elicited from a narrow lamina of the hypothalamus in and immediately adjacent to the ventro-medial nucleus (Nakao, 1958) and in the area of the fornix (Hess & Brugger, 1943; Wasman & Flynn, 1962). Stalking attack, on the other hand, has been elicited most typically from more lateral placements in the hypothalamus (Roberts & Kiess, 1964; Wasman & Flynn, 1962). This area corresponds closely to the area where other investigators have produced eating behavior (Brugger, 1943; Delgado & Anand, 1953; Hess, 1954; Robinson & Mishkin, 1962; Wyrwicka, 1964). Thus, it appears that there are areas of the lateral hypothalamus which mediate predatory attack behavior and other areas, closely adjacent to or overlapping the former, which mediate eating. An alternative possibility, however, is that stalking attack is a form of food-getting behavior. If this were the case, it should be possible to elicit either attack or eating from the same sites in the brain. This study investigated the possibility of such an anatomic and behavioral relationship.

METHOD

Subjects

The Ss were 10 adult male cats not previously used in laboratory research. They were individually placed in the test chamber with a rat during a 30-min. observation period. No cat was used in the experiment if it displayed any attack against the rat.

The Ss were implanted with two to six monopolar electrodes aimed at the lateral hypothalamus and adjacent structures. Electrodes were 26-gauge, Formvar insulated, stainless steel wires which were straightened and ground to a point and were free of insulation for 1 mm. at the sharpened end. Electrodes were anchored to the skull by dental acrylic and connected to pins of a 12-contact socket. The indifferent electrode was a 36-gauge stainless steel wire placed below the scalp in contact with the surrounding musculature. A 7-day postoperative recovery period was allowed before testing.

Apparatus and Procedure

The observation chamber was a plywood and Plexiglas cubicle 43 × 32 × 39 in. One side and the top were made of clear Plexiglas. The cubicle was placed inside a soundproof chamber, one side of which had a large one-way mirror for unrestricted observation of Ss. A cable and swivel arrangement allowed Ss freedom of movement within the chamber.

Stimulation consisted of trains of balanced biphasic pulse pairs occurring 60 times per second. Each pulse pair was composed of individual pulses of 1-msec. duration separated by .3 msec. The stimulus voltage impressed across S was calibrated using the differential input of a Tektronix 502 oscilloscope. Current calibration was accomplished by connecting the same oscilloscope across a 1,000-ohm resistor connected in series with S. Stimulation was monitored continuously on a Tektronix 360 stimulus indicator unit connected across the 1,000-ohm resistor. Voltages employed in this study ranged as high as 2 v. and current intensities as high as 670 μa.

Stimulus trains varied in length from 1–45 sec.; 4 min. was allowed between stimulation tests in order that response thresholds would remain constant.

As a precaution against the possibility that eating or attack behaviors might be the result of food deprivation, all Ss were fed their entire daily food ration 1 hr. before the experimental test sessions. In addition, food or a rat was placed in the test chamber 20 min. before any tests for elicited eating or attack were conducted on each day. If any eating occurred, as it did only infrequently, then no tests were conducted until an additional 20-min. period of no eating had elapsed. If, during a series of stimulations, any eating episode was observed which did not immediately follow the onset of the stimulus, but began "spontaneously" between stimulation trials, tests were discontinued until no further eating behavior was observed for 20 min. Attack was never observed at any time during any test session except during stimulation.

When all testing was completed, histological determination of electrode placement was undertaken. The Ss were anesthetized and perfused with saline followed by 10% formalin. Brains were frozen, serially sectioned, examined, photographed "wet" and unstained at three different magnifications on Polaroid film, and compared with a stereotactic atlas (Jasper & Ajmone-Marsan, 1954).

RESULTS

Experiment 1

Each of the 37 implanted electrodes in the 10 Ss was systematically tested at various stimulus intensities while S was in the presence of a male Sprague-Dawley 150-day-old albino rat. Stalking attack against rats was elicited from 18 of the electrodes. When stimulated, Ss would crouch close to the cage floor, creep up to the rat, and grasp the head or neck in its jaws while pinning the rat to the floor with one paw. The attack was silent and accompanied by pupillary dilation, piloerection restricted to the tail region, and increased respiration. When stimulation was terminated, the attack ceased immediately. If stimulation was prolonged up to 45 sec., then stimulus adaptation became very noticeable and by 60 sec. was in most cases complete. At lower stimulus intensities, S would approach after longer latencies but would only sniff or lick the rat. Some Ss tended to stalk in a circular pattern in a direction contralateral to the side on which the activated electrode was located.

Ascending thresholds for attack behavior were determined for each electrode by progressively increased current intensity in steps of from 10–50 μa. Attack threshold for any given electrode, determined within a single session, was taken as the minimal stimulus intensity which produced attack during each of two consecutive 30-sec. stimulus trials. An attack was defined as any tooth contact with the rat. Table 1 depicts the thresholds for each of the 18 positive electrodes.

Experiment 2

Each of the 37 electrodes in the 10 *S*s was also tested in the absence of a rat but in the presence of a bowl of horsemeat at stimulus intensities from zero up through and including the intensities used previously to elicit attack behavior. Eating behavior was elicited from each of the 18 placements from which stalking attack behavior could be elicited and from none of the remaining 19 placements.

When stimulated in the presence of food, *S* would approach the dish after 15–20 sec. and eat for the duration of the stimulus. Thresholds for eating, determined in exactly the same manner as those for attack, are presented in Table 1.

It was observed that a period of decreased likelihood of responding followed stimulation and that successive instances

of stimulation resulted in progressively higher eating thresholds until it was impossible to elicit eating for a period of 2–10 min. even at higher intensities: the greater the intensity, duration, and frequency of the stimulus, the more prolonged and complete was this cessation of eating.

At the higher intensities employed, behavior typically ceased during the initial stimulation episode after 45–60 sec. even though the stimulus continued.

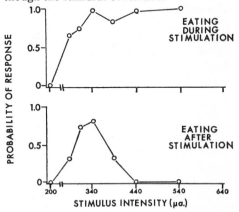

FIG. 1. Probability of food ingestion during and immediately after stimulation of the hypothalamus. (Each point represents the average of seven determinations.)

TABLE 1

THRESHOLDS (IN MICROAMPERES) FOR ELICITATION OF ATTACK AND EATING BEHAVIORS, AND ATLAS COORDINATES (IN MILLIMETERS) FOR POSITIVE ELECTRODES

| *S* | Electrode number | Attack during stimulation | Eating | | Coordinates | | |
			During stimulation	After stimulation	A-P	Horizontal	Lateral
20	7	540	270		15.0	−3.9	3.2
20	5	400	200		13.0	−4.0	3.0
8	1	540	560		13.0	−4.0	3.1
19	7	540	500		12.0	−3.0	3.0
18	6	440	340		12.0	−4.0	2.8
14	6	540	270		12.0	−4.1	2.6
18	1	420	270	340	11.5	−3.5	2.7
22	5	640	500		11.5	−4.0	3.1
18	4	580	400	400	11.5	−4.4	2.6
13	7	540	340	440	11.5	−5.0	3.0
13	1	480	260	260	11.5	−5.0	2.5
6	3	400	340	360	11.0	−3.5	2.0
14	3	270	200	240	10.5	−4.8	1.9
14	4	400	200	240	10.5	−5.7	2.6
18	3	340	340	340	10.0	−3.9	3.1
8	7	270	170	260	10.0	−5.3	3.0
9	3	340	300	500	10.0	−5.7	2.8
13	5	540	340		9.0	−5.6	2.6

Poststimulation eating was obtained in eight of the 10 Ss, with 10 of the 18 placements. For several seconds to (in one case) 5 min. after the stimulation was turned off, S continued mastication and ingestion with no interruption for other behaviors. Poststimulation eating was most pronounced at the low intensities of stimulation immediately above thresholds for stimulus-bound eating. Figure 1 shows that with one placement maximum probability of poststimulation eating rose rapidly and achieved the maximum near that point where eating probability during stimulation approached 1.0. As the intensities of stimulation were further increased, poststimulation eating became progressively less probable until, at even higher intensities, no eating whatever occurred. Results for the remaining nine placements were similar to those displayed in Figure 1.

The duration of these poststimulation eating episodes varied as a function of stimulus intensity in the same manner as their probabilities of occurrence. That is, the longest episodes followed stimulus intensities where stimulus-bound eating first achieved maximal probability; poststimulation eating durations decreased rapidly to zero at higher stimulus intensities. In fact, as the intensity of stimulation was raised beyond the point where any poststimulation eating was observed, Ss would not only cease eating abruptly but would actually eject from their mouths after stimulation food which had been taken up during stimulation. Whether these latter findings point to some unique stimulus adaptation processes or represent the display of an active inhibitory process triggered by the stimulation is not understood at this time.

With 16 of the 18 electrodes, eating was elicited at intensities below those necessary to elicit stalking attack behavior. For one S (S 18, Pin 3) attack was elicited at as low a stimulus intensity as was eating behavior. Another S (S 8, Pin 1), which had a lower threshold for attack than for eating, was not tested for eating until several months after the threshold for attack had been determined. Since all thresholds increased by 10–50% of initial values in all Ss over a period of several months, it is probable that the eating threshold would have been lower if tested earlier.

When stimulated in the presence of food at the higher stimulus intensities, all Ss displayed stalking behavior toward the food dish. At these intensities, ingestion was interrupted for stalking about the cage.

The complete anatomic correspondence between the stimulation points which produced eating and those that produced stalking attack provided strong evidence that the two behaviors are in some way related. Perhaps the attack is a particular form of food approach behavior appropriate to the available food object, i.e., the rat. Alternatively, the eating might represent a form of less intense attack behavior directed against whatever environmental object was present, in this case the dish of food. A third, though less probable, explanation is that the stimulation simply produced biting and chewing motor movements toward any environmental objects present.

Experiment 3

To see if the elicited eating behavior paralleled normal appetitive behavior in its directedness toward only palatable food-like substances, three Ss were tested for choices between a bowl of horsemeat and a bowl of moist earth at the lowest stimulus intensities which had, with each electrode, produced eating behavior at a probability of 1.0 in those tests where only food had been present. When stimulated, each S went to and consumed only the food on 10 consecutive trials, even when the food and earth preparations were rearranged within the chamber to ensure that S would contact the earth before the food. The S might occasionally approach the earth first, sniff at it, and then move to and consume the food; on no occasion was any oral contact made with the dirt. This demonstrates that the eating behavior was not simply an elicitation of chewing and ingestional motor movements toward any objects present but was normal appetitive behavior.

To help us to decide whether at higher intensities the behavior became simply disorganized chewing and ingestion movements, three Ss were now tested at the higher intensities of stimulation which had produced reliable attack behavior during initial testing. The positions of the food and earth were frequently reversed within the chamber to ensure equal probability of random contact. Each S displayed the same pattern of behavior. Two Ss contacted and ingested only the food on 16 consecutive trials even though one of the Ss approached and sniffed at the dish of earth first on nine of the 16 trials. The other S actually licked or chewed at the earth on nine of the first 12 trials, then displayed a 100% preference for the food on the remaining 48 trials. This result shows that the high intensities of stimulation produced eating behavior which was specifically directed at a palatable substance and was not simply disorganized chewing movements toward any stimulus object.

In the present experiment the durations of eating episodes produced by these higher stimulus intensities were much shorter than were those produced at lower stimulus intensities. The Ss tended to seize small bites and continue stalking around the chamber. These observations correspond to those made in Experiment 1 as well as to those interpreted by other investigators (Roberts & Kiess, 1964; Wasman & Flynn, 1962) as convincing evidence that stalking attack behavior bore no direct relation to appetitive behavior.

As was shown in Experiment 2, however, lower stimulus intensities do produce well-organized, sustained eating episodes. The present experiment shows that ingestive preference for palatable food substances is present at those low stimulus intensities and is maintained even at the higher intensities of stimulation. These data then indicate that a direct relation does indeed exist between eating and stalking attack.

Experiment 4

Although Experiment 3 demonstrated that the approach to and ingestion of food represented normal eating behavior, additional experiments were conducted to see if a preference might exist for a rat as the food object as compared to a dish of food.

Two Ss were tested for their choice between a rat and a bowl of horsemeat at the minimal intensities of stimulation which had produced high probability eating during original testing. Each S chose the food on seven or more consecutive trials. Occasionally, S might approach a rat, sniff, and then perhaps even lick the rat before proceeding to the food and continuing to eat for the remainder of stimulation.

This result agrees with the finding that eating was elicited at stimulus values below those necessary to elicit attack behavior when both food and rat were tested individually. That both Ss chose food supports the interpretation that the stimulation produced a state similar to hunger and that no preference for a rat as a food object existed.

Since cats had consistently attacked rats when a sufficient stimulus intensity was used during earlier tests, it might be that the higher levels of stimulation would produce a change in the directional nature of the elicited behavior from food toward a suitable object of attack. The two Ss tested at lower stimulus intensities were now tested for a choice between a rat and a bowl of horsemeat at intensities which had previously produced reliable stalking attack behavior. Rats were restrained on some trials with a vest and leash arrangement to ensure their location in a specific part of the chamber and prevent the rat from escaping S and thereby fortuitously increasing the probability of contact with the dish of horsemeat.

Whether Ss displayed stalking attack toward a rat or stalked and consumed food depended entirely upon which object was contacted first. When the rat and food dish were arranged so that the rat was closest to S, the rat was attacked on more than six consecutive trials by both Ss. Conversely, if the bowl of food was placed closest to S, it was eaten on 10 or more consecutive trials. Both attack behaviors and eating tended to be interrupted frequently by further prowling behavior. That no preference was displayed between a rat and other food agents offers further evidence in support of the conclusion that the attack behavior displayed against rats is not independent of food acquisition behaviors.

Anatomical Findings

When all testing was completed, histological verification of electrode placements was undertaken. Table 1 shows that 17 of the electrodes which produced attack and eating behavior were located in the lateral hypothalamus in a narrow lamina, approximately 1.2 mm. wide, extending from the optic chiasm caudally to the posterior tip of the posterior hypothalamic nucleus. The eighteenth positive electrode was located in the preoptic area. Figure 2 illustrates one of the 18 positive electrode placements (S22-5). The placements reported in Table 1 correspond to and elaborate upon those reported to produce stalking attack (Roberts & Kiess, 1964; Wasman & Flynn, 1962) and eating behavior (Brugger, 1943; Delgado & Anand, 1953; Hess, 1954; Robinson & Mishkin, 1962). A summary of the anatomic locations of the electrode tips for both positive and negative placements is provided in Figure 3. The present study found several more anterior positive placements than those typically reported by other workers. In this study, however, the more posterior placements (from A-P 10.0 to A-P 11.0) produced the lowest thresholds for both attack and eating. Furthermore, it may be noted that poststimulation eating effects were elicited only from the more posterior placements.

Various behaviors were elicited by stimulation through the 19 electrodes which did not yield the eating and stalking attack behavior. During stimulation of four of these (S6-1, S6-6, S9-1, and S11-4) *S*s manifested escape behaviors in which *S* would run rapidly about the chamber, sometimes hissing, and jump toward ceiling and walls, most commonly in an upward direction. Stimulation of four other electrodes (S8-8, S8-3, S14-1, and S11-6) resulted primarily in affective attack behavior, in which *S*s typically hissed and snarled prior to directed attack against a rat. Stimulation of two of these electrodes (S8-8 and S14-1) also yielded some escape behavior. Tests of two electrodes (S22-4 and S19-1) resulted in some of the components of behaviors that were elicited from the 18 which produced eating and stalking attack; *S*s sniffed and turned or circled in the chamber but did not make any contact with either food or a rat. Stimulation of one electrode (S9-7) resulted in ingestion of food, but no test for stalking attack was performed. For eight of the other electrodes tested, stimulation produced such responses as alerting, vocalization, eye blinks, circling, pupillary dilation, or increased respiration. These electrodes were: S20-1 (A 16.0, H-4.0, L 4.0), S20-3 (A 14.5, H-below brain, L 3.5), S20-6 (A 14.5, H-below brain, L 3.5), S11-3, S11-7 (A 13.5, H-below brain, L 4.2), S20-4 (A 13.5, H-below brain, L 4.5), S6-7, and S9-6.[2]

DISCUSSION

The perfect anatomic correspondence found between placements which produced eating and those which produced stalking attack, with eating consistently elicited at lower intensities than attack behavior, indicates that the area of the lateral hypothalamus wherein stimulation will produce stalking or predatory-like attack behavior is, in fact, principally responsible for the mediation of appetitive behavior. It is suggested that the attack behavior elicited from this area represents a particular topographic form of food acquisition behavior determined by the food object available.

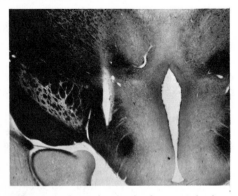

FIG. 2. A photomicrograph of an unstained section of the hypothalamus and immediately adjacent structures from one *S* employed in the present study. (The electrode tract shown was one of the 18 placements which produced both eating and stalking attack behaviors.)

[2] Atlas coordinates given for those electrode placements not presented in Figure 3.

Ackerman, Andersson, Fabricius, and Svensson (1960) have reported the interesting result that stimulation of the lateral hypothalamus in the pigeon produces searching and pecking behavior at the floor of the test chamber. These observations seem relevant in light of the data gathered in this study, since both have found that stimulation in the lateral hypothalamus can produce unique topographic patterns of food acquisition behavior adequate to the particular food agents present.

If the attack behavior represents food acquisition, it might be expected that the attack would have been followed by ingestion of the rat carcass. This, however, was never observed during any of the tests. Several factors contributed to this result. In Experiments 2, 3, and 4 it was seen that the response topography of stalking and attack behaviors elicited at the higher stimulus intensities was incompatible with the topography of eating. A more important factor was that the total time period necessary for the display of a completed attack episode was 40–60 sec. Since adaptation to the electrical stimulus was almost

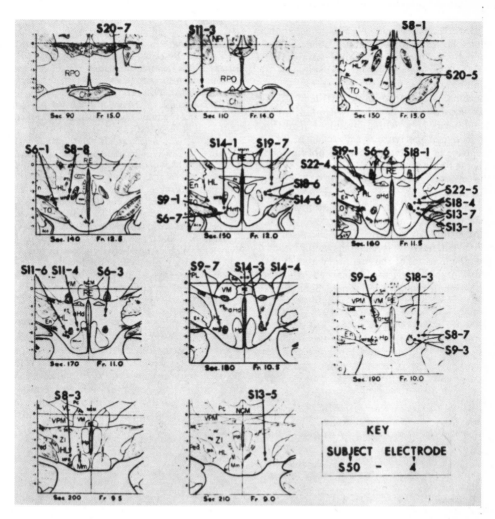

Fig. 3. Partial sections from the Jasper and Ajmone-Marsan Atlas of the cat brain, showing positive and negative placements found in this study. (Positive placements have been depicted on the right and negative placements on the left, irrespective of the side in which they were actually implanted.)

complete in 60 sec., no display of an ensuing period of ingestion was possible.

The necessity for higher intensities of stimulation to elicit attack behavior, from all points, indicates that the attack behavior was not simply a spread-of-current effect from the area within the lateral hypothalamus which mediates eating behavior to another portion within the lateral area uniquely involved with attack behavior. Rather, it appears that the lateral hypothalamus, which is responsible for food acquisition and ingestion behavior, may direct signals, most probably via fibers of passage, to some further removed areas wherein stalking attack behavior is mediated.

Roberts and Kiess (1964) have shown that lateral area stimulation intense enough to produce stalking attack can motivate a cat to learn the response of running to the side of a Y maze which contains a rat. Similarly, Miller (1958) has shown that low level stimulation of the lateral area which produces ingestion of food can motivate a rat to learn a new response of pushing a panel to obtain food. These findings offer indirect support for the present results which show that both the behaviors of ingestion and attack can be elicited from the same anatomic sites, and that stalking attack represents food acquisition. An inference from these studies taken collectively is that the actual topographic features of the predatory attack display might constitute a learned response rather than reflexive unlearned behavior.

REFERENCES

AKERMAN, B., ANDERSSON, B., FABRICIUS, E., & SVENSSON, L. Observations on central regulation of body temperature and of food and water intake in the pigeon (*Columba livia*). *Acta physiol. Scand.*, 1960, **50**, 328–336.

BRUGGER, M. Fresstrieb als hypothalamisches symptom. *Helv. physiol. pharmacol. Acta*, 1943, **1**, 183–198.

DELGADO, J. M. R., & ANAND, B. K. Increase in food intake induced by electrical stimulation of the lateral hypothalamus. *Amer. J. Physiol.*, 1953, **172**, 162–168.

HESS, W. R. *Functional organization of the diencephalon.* New York: Grune & Stratton, 1954.

HESS, W. R., & BRUGGER, M. Das subcorticale zentrum der affektiven abwehrreaktion. *Helv. physiol. pharmacol. Acta*, 1943, **1**, 33–52.

JASPER, H. H., & AJMONE-MARSAN, C. *A stereotaxic atlas of the diencephalon of the cat.* Ottawa: National Research Council of Canada, 1954.

MILLER, N. E. Central stimulation and other new approaches to motivation and reward. *Amer. Psychologist*, 1958, **13**, 100–108.

NAKAO, H. Emotional behavior produced by hypothalamic stimulation. *Amer. J. Physiol.*, 1958, **194**, 411–418.

ROBERTS, W. W., & KIESS, H. D. Motivational properties of hypothalamic aggression in cats. *J. comp. physiol. Psychol.*, 1964, **58**, 187–192.

ROBINSON, B. W., & MISHKIN, M. Alimentary responses evoked from forebrain structures in *Macaca mulatta. Science*, 1962, **136**, 260–262.

WASMAN, M., & FLYNN, J. P. Directed attack elicited from hypothalamus. *Arch. Neurol.*, 1962, **6**, 220–227.

WYRWICKA, W. Electrical activity of the hypothalamus during alimentary conditioning. *EEG clin. Neurophysiol.*, 1964, **17**, 164–176.

(Received May 27, 1965)

Circadian Rhythm of Brain Self-Stimulation Behavior

Michael Terman and Jiuan S. Terman

Abstract. *Under constant conditions of light, sound, temperature, and humidity, rats exhibited circadian rhythmicity in rate of bar-pressing with hypothalamic and septal reinforcing brain stimulation. Variations in reinforcer magnitude affected absolute levels of operant response emission but not the frequency of the circadian rhythm. In long sessions, the time of peak responding deviated systematically from a strict 24-hour period. Such data show marked similarity to free-running rhythms of motor activity.*

Oscillation is a temporal property that unites and interrelates biological systems. Studies of behavioral oscillation have concentrated on stabilimetric activity or locomotor response chains. Both of these measures reflect complex and unspecified behavioral repertoires, and various subsets of such behavior samples may dominate an activity count at different times. Overall rates of behavior output do not change as much as the relative dominance of particular topographical units (*1*). Isolation and measurement of a narrowly defined, highly probable response unit would likely lead to a more refined analysis of cyclic behavior patterns and their associated physiological oscillation mechanisms. A popular way to insure the high probability of a response is to reinforce it, rather than to rely on its "spontaneous" emission. For our experiments, we selected the relatively stereotyped operant bar-press as the unit for measurement. To maintain responding for long periods, we used brain stimulation as the reinforcer, eliminating (or minimizing) the rapid satiation effects found with traditional nutritive reinforcers. We report a circadian periodicity in operant response rate during long-term self-stimulation sessions, with the use of a variety of stimulation parameters, electrode loci, and reinforcement schedules. The cyclic response patterns show many of the same

characteristics as locomotor activity as well as hormonal, neural, and cellular rhythms, and may reflect common biological oscillation mechanisms (*2*).

Male albino laboratory rats (Charles River, CD strain) were implanted with septal or hypothalamic bipolar electrodes (Plastic Products, MS 303), or both, and were allowed to self-stimulate in continuous sessions for as long as 1 month. Placements were verified by subsequent histological analysis. Bar-pressing was reinforced by 0.5-second trains of constant-current bidirectional rectangular pulses, 0.2 msec in duration, equally spaced in time. A single peak-current level and electrode locus were chosen for a given session. The experimental compartment was enclosed in a controlled environment chamber (Sherer-Gillett, CEL 44) with dry food and water continuously available. An incandescent lamp illuminated the chamber, maintaining a constant luminance of 10 ft lam (10.7 mlam) on the wall at the level of the bar. External noise was attenuated by the multilayered enclosure, and temperature was set at 70°F (21°C) with 50 percent relative humidity (*3*).

When an animal starts a self-stimulation session, it usually responds at a high rate without resting. Subsequent deceleration in response rate occurs, but its onset depends on stimulation intensity. At high intensities the initial

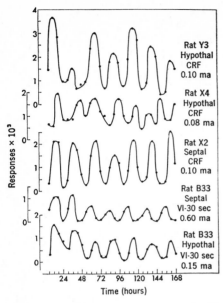

Fig. 1. Week-long response records (6-hour blocks) sampled from continuous sessions of intracranial self-stimulation.

response spurt may last as long as 2 days without rest periods of more than a few minutes. Only later does the animal periodically slow its responding and take long enough rests to exhibit a circadian rhythm. Initial response deceleration, occurring after about 8 hours of self-stimulation (sometimes thought to parallel a food "satiation" effect) has previously been reported only for septal placements (4). We observed the effect for both hypothalamic and septal loci with low and medium stimulation intensities; at high intensities the initial response deceleration was greatly delayed.

Figure 1 includes continuous week-long samples of response output from several animals under a selection of locus, intensity, and schedule conditions. Responses were tallied in 6-hour blocks, and smooth curves were fitted by eye. The records show wide differences in peak rates under the various reinforcement conditions (ranging from approximately 500 to 3700 responses in a 6-hour block), as well as in day-to-

day regularity in response output by individual animals. For example, rat X2, in the septal condition under continuous reinforcement (CRF) at 0.10 ma, showed relatively stable oscillations, with peaks generally exceeding 2000 bar-presses, declining to less than 400 bar-presses in quiet periods. By contrast, rat Y3, in the hypothalamic CRF condition at 0.10 ma, showed great daily fluctuations in peak response output (ranging from about 1500 to 3700 bar-presses), with no clear trend across days.

Regardless of the amplitude characteristics of the individual records, these animals all exhibited orderly cycles of high and low rates of bar-pressing, approximating a 24-hour period (5). The most orderly records show successive peaks following each other in every fourth 6-hour block, with rest periods symmetrically interspersed. Responses may be intermittently reinforced (see Fig. 1, rat B33) without obscuring the cyclic pattern, and the locus of reinforcing brain stimulation is not critical. Similar records of locomotor activity are often said to reflect an endogenous circadian timing mechanism (6).

Our data suggest that learned behaviors, maintained exclusively by the reinforcement contingency (7), may be subject to similar temporal control. Many studies of locomotor activity (6, 8) index the time of discrete onset of activity, disregarding amplitude characteristics of the rhythm, although subtle gradations in daily activity output have been noted (9). For brain self-stimulation, we find a continual behavior stream with no discrete activity onset, and the analysis concentrates on rhythmic oscillations in amplitude, which parallel measures of physiological variables (10).

The rate of response is proportional to reinforcer magnitude, within limits, for both brain stimulation (11) and conventional ingested reinforcers (12). However, this phenomenon has been demonstrated only in short sessions and has not accounted for daily oscillations in responsiveness. By manipulating stimulation intensity in long-term sessions, we have found that reinforcer magnitude and oscillation factors jointly determine momentary response rate. Results for rat X2 in the hypothalamic CRF condition are plotted as a family of curves in Fig. 2. Four intensities were presented in irregular orders (to minimize possible series effects) for periods ranging from 1 week to 1 month. The uppermost curve represents responding at 0.30 ma—a very high intensity for this animal. Over the 3 days sampled, response totals ranged from about 18,000 to 38,000 in 6-hour blocks, with the distinct circadian pattern also noted for this rat under septal reinforcement (Fig. 1). The curves for lower intensity values indicate propor-

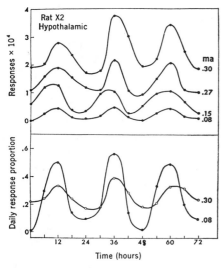

Fig. 2. Three-day samples of response records for rat X2, with various intensities of hypothalamic stimulation. The upper panel shows selected records of total responses (6-hour blocks), and the lower panel plots response proportions for the highest and lowest intensity presented, for successive days. The curves have been superimposed on the abscissa in order to emphasize the similarity in phase characteristics.

tional declines in the baseline level of response. Aschoff (13) has suggested that an important parameter of circadian rhythms is the "level around which the system oscillates," which, in our situation, was controlled by stimulation intensity. The circadian pattern of responding seemed unaffected by changes in response baseline due to reinforcer magnitude. Under all conditions, successive peaks followed each other at about 24-hour intervals.

The lower panel of Fig. 2 shows a transformation of the absolute response totals for the lowest and highest intensities to a proportional measure, correcting for the amplitude difference. Responding in successive 6-hour blocks is expressed as a proportion of daily (24-hour) response output. Both curves show circadian periodicity, but the oscillation is more pronounced under the condition of low intensity (0.08 ma) stimulation. This effect contrasts with the absolute response records in the upper panel of Fig. 2, which show greater amplitude variation under the condition of high intensity (0.30 ma) stimulation, and thus a more dramatic circadian pattern. When the animal rested in the low-intensity condition, its response rate dropped to nearly zero for extended periods, while in the high-intensity condition it still emitted about 20,000 responses in a 6-hour "quiet" period. The extremely low response levels obtained with low-intensity reinforcement resulted in the more discrete dips and peaks in the response proportion function. However, the rate of temporal oscillation was neither accelerated nor decelerated by changes in reinforcer magnitude or baseline response levels.

One ubiquitous characteristic of free-running circadian rhythms is the consistent small deviation from an exact 24-hour period, in the absence of external pacing stimuli (13, 14). Thus, the

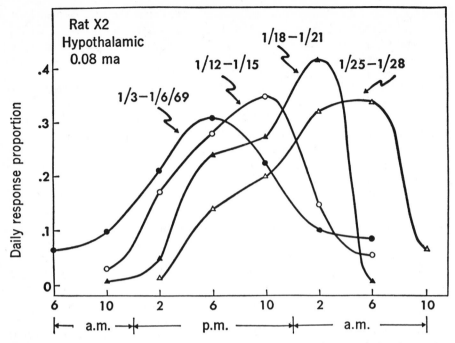

Fig. 3. Averaged daily response proportions (4-hour blocks) for sampled 3-day periods in the course of a month's testing with low-intensity hypothalamic stimulation, for rat X2.

time of peak activity is found to shift later when the circadian period exceeds 24 hours, or earlier when the period is less than 24 hours. Since the deviation from 24 hours is small, long sessions are required to demonstrate the peak shift empirically. Figure 3 summarizes such a record for rat X2 in the hypothalamic CRF condition at 0.08 ma. Four curves are superimposed on the abscissa (Eastern Standard Time), with 3-day samples from the month-long session averaged in terms of daily response proportions (correcting for day-to-day variations in baseline response output). From 3 to 6 January 1969, peak response rate occurred at about 6 p.m.; when the behavior pattern was sampled 1 week later, the peak had shifted to the next 4-hour block, centered at 10 p.m. Subsequent samples revealed a continuing shift to later peak periods, reaching 6 a.m. near the end of Janu-

ary. The transition from peak activity to low activity appeared to become more abrupt as the month progressed. The data show that, on the average, peak response rate occurred about 20 minutes later each day; in 2.5 months, we would predict that the animal would "lose" about one objective day. A computer analysis of these data showed that the least-squares fit to a 24.3-hour trial period yields a ratio of 0.076 between the standard error of the amplitude and the amplitude itself (15). Such data support the conclusion that the operant behavior rhythm is not synchronized by an external clock corresponding to the 24-hour day. This result agrees with Aschoff's rule, which predicts that a nocturnal animal in constant light will show a circadian rhythm greater than 24 hours.

The present experiment demonstrates that the technique of intracranial self-stimulation can be profitably used to refine behavioral activity analyses. Indeed, Prescott (16) has shown that one index of general activity correlates positively with self-stimulation rate. Perhaps an oscillating temporal factor, related to physiological arousal states (17), modulates reinforcement strength. Our self-stimulation records may reflect rhythms in hypothalamic or limbic neural activity. Not only does the hypothalamus mediate strong positive reinforcement effects, but also its control over pituitary secretions (for example, adrenocorticotrophic hormone) is thought to underlie changes in general motor activity (18).

MICHAEL TERMAN
JIUAN S. TERMAN

Department of Psychology,
Northeastern University,
Boston, Massachusetts 02115

References and Notes

1. D. Bindra, *Psychol. Rev.* **68**, 205 (1961); R. C. Bolles, *J. Comp. Physiol. Psychol.* **56**, 456 (1963).
2. *Biological Clocks* [*Cold Spring Harbor Symp. Quant. Biol.* **25**, whole issue (1960)] (The Biology Laboratory, Cold Spring Harbor, New York, 1961); J. Aschoff, Ed., *Circadian Clocks* (North-Holland, Amsterdam, 1965).
3. Rat B33 was run on the variable interval (V I) 30-second schedule in an earlier experiment in which a 60-hz sine brain-stimulation waveform was used (peak-to-peak current was specified). This animal received a liquid diet of diluted Carnation condensed milk, and food intake was monitored by a photocell circuit at the drinking tube. It is interesting to note that feeding occurred only during the animal's active bar-pressing period; during quiet periods, the animal mainly groomed and slept.
4. J. Olds, *J. Comp. Physiol. Psychol.* **51**, 675 (1958).
5. In contrast, it would be possible to measure a circadian rhythm of pausing, specified by the extent of zero slope on the cumulative response record. Emphasis on rhythms of "not-responding" may relate closely to physiological cycles of sleep and arousal. See A. Hobson, *Science* **165**, 932 (1969).
6. C. P. Richter, *Biological Clocks in Medicine and Psychiatry* (Thomas, Springfield, Ill., 1965); K. S. Rawson, in *Photoperiodism and Related Phenomena in Plants and Animals,* R. B. Withrow, Ed. (AAAS, Washington, D.C., 1959), p. 792.
7. When stimulation was inadvertently terminated (for example, when electrode leads broke) responding rapidly dropped to near zero levels.
8. P. J. DeCoursey, *Cold Spring Harbor Symp. Quant. Biol.* **25**, 49 (1960).
9. W. B. Quay, *Photochem. Photobiol.* **4**, 425 (1965).
10. F. Halberg, *Annu. Rev. Physiol.* **31**, 675 (1969).
11. R. W. Reynolds, *J. Comp. Physiol. Psychol.* **51**, 193 (1958); R. E. Keesey, *ibid.* **55**, 671 (1962); J. S. Terman, M. Terman, J. W. Kling, *Physiol. Behav.* **5**, 183 (1970).
12. N. Guttman, *J. Exp. Psychol.* **46**, 213 (1953); G. Collier and L. Myers, *ibid.* **61**, 57 (1961).
13. J. Aschoff, *Cold Spring Harbor Symp. Quant. Biol.* **25**, 11 (1960).
14. R. J. Wurtman, *Science* **156**, 104 (1967).
15. F. Halberg provided the computer analysis.
16. R. G. W. Prescott, *J. Comp. Physiol. Psychol.* **64**, 346 (1967).
17. G. Moruzzi and H. W. Magoun, *Electroencephalogr. Clin. Neurophysiol.* **1**, 455 (1949).
18. F. Halberg, E. Halberg, C. P. Barnum, J. J. Bittner, in *Photoperiodism and Related Phenomena in Plants and Animals,* R. B. Withrow, Ed. (AAAS, Washington, D.C., 1959), p. 803.
19. Supported by PHS grants MH-16218-01 and FR-07085-03 Sub. No. 9. This research was performed while the authors were at Brown University. We thank J. W. Kling for his advice and encouragement.

20 March 1970

Development and Hormonal Control
of Territorial Marking in the Male
Mongolian Gerbil (*Meriones unguiculatus*)

GARDNER LINDZEY
D. D. THIESSEN
ANN TUCKER

Department of Psychology
University of Texas
Austin, Texas

LINDZEY, GARDNER, THIESSEN, D. D., and TUCKER, ANN (1968). *Development and Hormonal Control of Territorial Marking in the Male Mongolian Gerbil* (Meriones unguiculatus). DEVELOPMENTAL PSYCHOBIOLOGY, 1(2): 97–99. Male Mongolian gerbils were either castrated or sham operated at 30 days of age. Assessment of territorial marking was carried out every 6 days beginning at 52 days of age and extending to 100 days of age. After each marking test, 10 intact males received 640 μg testosterone propionate subcutaneously; 10 other intact animals and 10 castrates received oil injections. The ventral sebaceous scent gland, used by the gerbil to deposit sebum on objects during the marking response, was measured after each test. Behavioral marking and the scent gland were entirely absent in castrates. Relative to controls, marking in hormone-treated animals began earlier and reached higher frequencies. Gland development was also responsive to the hormone, but lagged behind marking activity.

castration   development   gerbil   gland size   territorial marking   testosterone propionate

THE MONGOLIAN GERBIL (*Meriones unguiculatus*) is rapidly becoming an important subject of research. It is hearty, thrives well on ordinary Purina Laboratory Chow, has little odor, and requires no water other than that derived from the metabolism of foods. Behaviorally, the animals have much to recommend them. They are docile, highly curious, learn well, and show some unusual species-common behaviors. In our laboratory, all animals tested appear deficient in visual cliff behavior, but are not blind (Thiessen, Friend, & Lindzey, in press), and a certain proportion of those tested convulse when placed in a strange environment. The latter effect appears to be regulated by a dominant gene. Further, as this paper shows, gerbils mark territories with a ventral scent gland.

The species *unguiculatus* is of the genus *Meriones*, subfamily *Gerbilinae*, family *Cricatidae*, and order *Rodentia* (Schwentker, 1963). Its close relatives include the Cotton rat of the Eastern United States, the Golden and Chinese hamster, the Deer mouse and the Desert rat of North Africa. As an adult, the gerbil weighs from approximately 70 to 90 g.

The behavioral marking response, discussed in this paper, is particularly interesting. Both males and females rub a midventral sebaceous gland over low-lying, prominent objects, leaving a sebum which is oily to the touch and musky in odor. The frequency of marking is about twice as great in the male, as in the

Received for publication 15 February 1968.

Developmental Psychobiology, 1(2): 97–99 (1968)

female, corresponding roughly to the sex difference in gland size. The response is highly discrete, involving a rapid approach to an object, a sniffing of the object, a mounting and press or skimming of the ventral sebaceous gland against the surface followed by a rapid forward dismount. The complete marking response is accomplished in about 1 sec.

The sebaceous gland is a highly organized, fusiform pad which is orange in color. In a well-developed male, it measures approximately 3.0 cm in length, 0.7 cm in width, and 0.2 cm in depth. It is easily seen by parting the ventral hairs enfolding the gland. Marking behavior disappears and the sebaceous gland atrophies following castration of the male, but are easily reinstated with injections of testosterone propionate (Thiessen *et al.*, in press). It seems likely that this marking behavior involves territorial signaling, since a male becomes more hesitant in a field recently occupied by another gerbil of either sex. This paper describes the ontogeny of marking in the male, and associates the development of the gland and the behavior with the presence or absence of androgen.

METHOD

Marking behavior and general activity were assessed in a grey, wooden field measuring 1 square meter and lined off into 16 squares of equal size. A roughened Plexiglas peg, measuring 2.6 cm in length, 1.2 cm in width and 0.7 cm in height, was positioned at each of the 9 lined intersections. The field was surrounded by grey wooden walls 46 cm high. On each wall was mounted one 15 w light bulb, shielded at the top, and focused into the interior of the field.

Thirty male gerbils were included in the experiment. At 30 days of age, at least 40 days before maturity, 10 males were castrated under general anesthesia and the additional 20 males received a sham operation. Beginning at 52 days of age, all animals were tested individually for 5 min in the marking field. A test consisted of placing a gerbil in one square of the field and recording the number of peg marks and line crossings during a 5-min period. A mark was recorded whenever an animal skimmed a peg, flattening its abdomen over the surface. A line crossing was recorded whenever an animal stepped over a line with all four feet. The entire apparatus was thoroughly cleaned after each test with a 70% alcohol solution. Testing was carried out during the midpart of the light half of a 12-hr, light–dark cycle, in a darkened room, with only the apparatus lights providing illumination. Immediately after each test, the animal was weighed and the sebaceous gland exposed with a hair depilatory (Sergex) and then measured in cm (length × width). After the gland measurement, each animal was injected subcutaneously with 0.05 ml of testosterone propionate (640 mg/injection), of the vehicle alone (safflower oil). The oil vehicle allowed slow assimilation of the hormone. Ten castrate and 10 intact gerbils received the vehicle only, and 10 intact gerbils received testosterone propionate. Testing, measurement, and injections were continued once every 6 days until the animals were 100 days of age.

RESULTS

Figure 1 illustrates the development of marking, and Figure 2 shows the differential development of gland size. Analyses of variance revealed highly significant variations between groups ($F = 4.61$ and 23.60, respectively; $df = 2$ and 27; $p < .05$ and $p < .01$). Most of the between group variation is accounted for by the castrate animals, but all groups differ among themselves (Ducan Multiple Range Test: $p < .05$) after group separation is apparent on day 6 for marking and day 7 for gland size. The mean body weight for the castrate animals exceeded that of the intact and sham animals ($p < .05$), and no differences in activity appeared among the three groups.

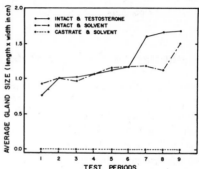

Fig. 2. Development and hormonal control of ventral sebaceous gland size in the Mongolian gerbil. Measurements began at 52 and ended at 100 days of age. Sebaceous pad measurement expressed in cm and converted to a single index of length × width.

DISCUSSION

The development of marking and the concomitant size of the ventral sebaceous gland are clearly related to the androgen status of the male. Marking generally begins around 80 to 90 days of age, but the onset may be either accelerated by large doses of testosterone propionate, or virtually eliminated by pre-pubertal castration. By 100 days of age, when intact gerbils approach their highest marking frequency, gerbils receiving large doses of hormone show significantly greater marking activity. The response of the gland to testosterone propionate is evident and even shows a critical period for hormone-sensitivity (unusual for testosterone-dependent tissues), in that hormone treatment is not effective until the animals are 94 days of age. Marking is evidently more sensitive to the hormone level than is gland size, suggesting, perhaps, a central nervous system effect. This notion is presently being explored by implanting crystalline testosterone into the hypothalamus of castrate males in an attempt to elicit marking behavior independent of a change in the sebaceous gland.

NOTES

This work was supported by Grant MH-1407-01 and Research Development Award MH-11, 174-01 to Delbert D. Thiessen from the National Institute of Mental Health, U.S. Public Health Service. Wayne Kamin kindly helped on all aspects of the problem.

Mailing address: D. D. Thiessen, Department of Psychology, University of Texas, Austin, Texas 78712, U.S.A.

REFERENCES

SCHWENTKER, V. (1963). Veterinarian, 6: 5–9.
THIESSEN, D. D., FRIEND, H. C., and LINDZEY, G. (In press). Science.

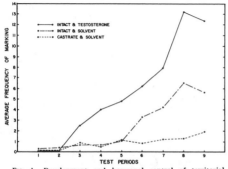

Fig. 1. Development and hormonal control of territorial marking in the Mongolian gerbil. Testing began at 52 and ended at 100 days of age. Frequency of marking recorded for 5-min periods.

Reprinted from Science, June 16, 1967, Vol. 156, No. 3781, pages 1512-1514

Nonhormonal Basis of Maternal Behavior in the Rat

Abstract. *Rats were tested for induction of maternal behavior by exposing them to young pups continuously for 10 to 15 days. Nonpregnant intact, ovariectomized, and hypophysectomized females were studied, as well as intact and castrated males. Nearly all the animals exhibited the four main items of maternal behavior and there were only minor differences in the latencies for the onset of maternal behavior among the various groups. It is concluded that all rats have a basic level of maternal responsiveness which is independent of hormonal stimulation.*

From the earliest studies, maternal behavior in the rat has been considered to be dependent upon hormones. It appears during a particular phase of the endocrine reproductive cycle (namely, postparturition), and its onset is closely associated with the onset of lactation, which is known to be under hormonal control. After parturition nearly all females show maternal behavior upon being exposed to pups, but in the single study in which a large number of animals were tested, even after 4 days of continuous exposure, maternal behavior appeared in only 30 percent of nonpregnant females (1).

In several mammalian species [mouse (2), hamster (3), wolf (4), monkey (5), and human beings] young elicit maternal behavior in nonpregnant females, as well as at the usual time after parturition. This is particularly striking in the mouse. Maternal behavior appears in nonpregnant mice and, since hypophysectomy does not prevent it, it is clearly not based upon hormones (2).

We exposed nonpregnant female rats to pups for 10 to 15 days and tested daily for the appearance of maternal behavior. Lengthening the period of exposure to pups proved highly successful in eliciting maternal behavior, and the study was extended to include males, gonadectomized females and males, and hypophysectomized females.

Three groups of nulliparous females of the Charles River strain, 80 to 120 days old, were used: intact ($N = 14$), ovariectomized ($N = 12$), and hypophysectomized ($N = 11$). The hypophysectomized females, which were obtained commercially, were examined by means of daily vaginal smears to confirm the absence of estrous cycling. The operations were performed approximately 2 weeks before the start of testing. In addition two groups of males of the same strain and age-range were used: intact ($N = 13$) and castrated ($N = 12$). Each animal was housed in a large rectangular cage, 45.7 by 50.8 by 41.9 cm, with transparent plexiglass walls, a grid floor, wall feeder, water bottle, and two bins containing hay and coarse wood shavings for nesting material. After 3 days of habituation to the cages, five pups, 5 to 10 days old, were placed at the front of each cage. Measures of latency for the onset of

Table 1. Percentage of animals displaying each of the four items of maternal behavior. Number in each group is in parentheses.

Group	Re-trieve	Crouch	Lick	Build nest
Females				
Intact (14)	93	100	100	100*
Ovariec-tomized (12)	92	83	100	92
Hypophysec-tomized (11)	100	100	100	100
Males				
Intact (13)	77	77	85	46
Castrated (12)	83	75	83	67

*Observations made inadveretntly on only 10 of the 14 females of this group.

maternal behavior were taken from this time. Retrieving was observed for 30 minutes starting when the pups were first introduced, then observations of crouching over the young (as in nursing), licking, nest-building, and other items of behavior were observed over the next 2 hours for 1-minute periods at 20-minute intervals. These pups remained with the female until the next morning at which time nests were scored, the pups were removed and weighed, and a fresh litter of five pups of the same age-range was placed in the cage and testing was repeated, now with a 15-minute retrieving test. Testing was done for 10 days if an animal displayed maternal behavior on 3 separate days, and for 15 days otherwise (6).

Group percentages for the appearance of the four main items of maternal behavior (Table 1) and group latencies for the onset of these items (Table 2) were used to evaluate the effects of pup stimulation on the appearance of maternal behavior. The percentage of nonpregnant females displaying each of the items of maternal behavior was nearly 100 percent, which represents an increase over the 30 percent found when only 4 days of exposure was used (1). There was no indication that the ovaries were involved in the induction of maternal behavior. First, induction of maternal behavior had no effect on estrous cycling. The average interval between estrous vaginal smears was 4.7 days (out of a total of 127 female days) among 11 of the 14 females induced to show maternal behavior, as compared to 4.8 days for a group of five control females that subsequently lived in the same cages as the experimental females but were not exposed to pups and therefore, of course, did not exhibit maternal behavior. Second, the ovariectomized females showed maternal behavior with the same high percentages as the intact females. It can be said, in fact, that the induction of maternal behavior in the nonpregnant females was not dependent upon any hormones since all of the hypophysectomized females also showed all four items of maternal behavior.

Males also were induced to show maternal behavior by exposure to pups and although smaller percentages displayed the different items of maternal behavior, only with respect to nest-building did the males differ significantly from the females ($z = 2.14$ to 3.48, $P < .05$ to $.01$). The two groups of males themselves did not differ (nest-building: $z = 1.50$, $P > .10$).

The average latencies for the onset of the various items of maternal behavior in the nonpregnant females were all longer than 5 days. This explains why Wiesner and Sheard (1), who used only 4 days of exposure to pups, failed to find a significant proportion of the females becoming maternal. Latencies for retrieving, crouching, and licking were not affected by ovariectomy but removal of the pituitary caused a significant reduction in latencies for the onset of crouching and licking (median test; crouching: chi-square test $= 6.82$, df $= 1$, $P < .01$; licking: chi-square test $= 9.1$, df $= 1$, $P < .01$). Among the hypophysectomized females nest-building was precipitated in 10 of the 11 animals before they were exposed to young, and among the ovariectomized females 6 of the 11 animals were affected similarly. This effect of hypophysectomy on nest-building has already been reported but the effect of ovariectomy on nest-building is at odds with previous reports (1). There were, therefore, significant differences in latencies for the onset of nest-building among the three groups (Kruskal-Wallis one-way analysis of variance: $H = 17.64$, df $= 2$, $P < .001$).

There were no significant differences in latencies between the two

Table 2. Latency for the onset of each of the four items of maternal behavior, mean day ± standard deviation.

Group	No.*	Retrieve	No.	Crouch	No.	Lick	No.	Build nest
				Females				
Intact	13	6.77 ± 2.81	14	6.36 ± 2.34	14	6.50 ± 0.30	10	5.90 ± 2.07
Ovariectomized	11	7.09 ± 2.97	10	5.20 ± 1.66	12	6.12 ± 2.47	11	3.45 ± 2.11
Hypophysectomized	11	6.18 ± 3.71	11	4.27 ± 2.26	11	3.33 ± 0.52	11	1.64 ± 2.02
				Males				
Castrated	10	6.80 ± 4.02	9	6.00 ± 3.02	11	4.50 ± 2.87	6	2.33 ± 3.59
Intact	10	7.40 ± 4.80	10	5.70 ± 7.55	10	4.55 ± 2.75		

* Positive cases only.

groups of males nor between the males and the three groups of females. Too few intact males built nests consistently to establish a reliable average latency and the few castrated males that built nests consistently represent too small a sample and were too variable to compare with the hypophysectomized females.

After the onset of maternal behavior the various items continued to appear with regularity in all groups of females but the males were somewhat less regular than the females. The maintenance ratio (the ratio of positive tests to tests after onset) for each of the maternal items ranged from .63 to .95 in the females and from .34 to .88 in the males.

Our results show that there is a basic maternal responsiveness in rats which is not dependent upon hormones or sex for its arousal. Further, there are no marked changes in ovarian and pituitary activity during the induction of maternal behavior. It requires however an average of 6 days of exposure to pups to elicit maternal behavior in nonpregnant females while the postparturient female responds immediately to her pups when they are born. From this we conclude that hormonal changes during pregnancy and parturition cause an increase in maternal responsiveness over the basic level found in the nonpregnant female. We have already found such an increase in maternal responsiveness when pregnant females were delivered by Caesarean section at progressively later stages of pregnancy (for example, 10, 13, 16, 19 days). Tested in the same manner as the animals of the present study, these females showed latencies for the onset of maternal behavior that were shorter than those of the nulliparous intact females of the present study, and more significantly, were progressively shorter as pregnancy advanced (8). It is likely, therefore, that hormonal stimulation during pregnancy and parturition, acting on the basic maternal responsiveness of the nulliparous female, is an additional factor which contributes to the rapid appearance of maternal behavior at parturition (9).

J. S. ROSENBLATT

Institute of Animal Behavior, Rutgers University, Newark, New Jersey

References and Notes

1. B. P. Wiesner and N. M. Sheard, *Maternal Behaviour in the Rat* (Oliver and Boyd, Edinburgh, 1933); J. S. Rosenblatt and D. S. Lehrman, in *Maternal Behavior in Mammals*, H. L. Rheingold, Ed. (Wiley, New York, 1963).
2. C. P. Leblond, *J. Genet. Psychol.* 57, 327 (1940); ——— and W. O. Nelson, *Amer. J. Physiol.* 120, 167 (1937); E. Beniest-Noirot, *Monogr. Francaise Psychol.* 1 (1958); E. Noirot, *Anim. Behav.* 12, 52 (1964).
3. T. E. Rowell, *Anim. Behav.* 9, 11 (1964).
4. B. E. Ginsburg, in *Sex and Behavior*, F. A. Beach, Ed. (Wiley, New York, 1965).
5. T. E. Rowell, R. A. Hinde, Y. Spencer-Booth, *Anim. Behav.* 12, 219 (1964).

6. The patterning of maternal items in nonpregnant females, which very likely differs from that of lactating mothers, was not studied and therefore comparisons between the nonpregnant and lactating mother are not an issue here.

7. C. P. Richter, *Cold Spring Harbor Symp. Quant. Biol.* **5**, 258 (1937); C. P. Stone and W. A. Mason, *J. Comp. Physiol. Psychol.* **48**, 456 (1955).

8. D. F. Lott and J. S. Rosenblatt, in *Determinants of Infant Behavior*, B. M. Foss, Ed. (Methuen, London, in press), vol. 4.

9. After the present study was completed we discovered independent confirmation of our results in studies by J. Cosnier [*Compt. Rend. Soc. Biol.* **157**, 1611 (1963)] and J. Cosnier and C. Couturier [*ibid.* **160**, 789 (1966)] who used exposures of newborn for 2 hours a day to induce maternal behavior in intact and ovariectomized nonpregnant females. The latencies that they observed appear to be similar to the ones found by our method.

10. Research supported by NIMH research grants MH-03398 and 08604. Preliminary studies were done with Dr. D. F. Lott. We thank A. Trattner for assistance and Dr. D. S. Lehrman for suggestions. Publication No. 48 from the Institute of Animal Behavior, Rutgers University, Newark.

31 March 1967

REPRINT NO. 697 from *Animal Behaviour*, **15**, 4, October, 1967

Anim. Behav., 1967, **15**, 433–437

EXTEROCEPTIVE STIMULATION OF THE REPRODUCTIVE SYSTEM OF THE FEMALE RING DOVE (*STREPTOPELIA RISORIA*) BY THE MATE AND BY THE COLONY MILIEU*

BY DALE LOTT, SUSAN D. SCHOLZ & D. S. LEHRMAN†

Institute of Animal Behavior, Rutgers University, Newark, New Jersey 07102

It was pointed out many years ago by F. H. A. Marshall (1936, 1942) that external stimuli from the ecological and social environment play a significant and essential role in the regulation of the reproductive cycles of many species of animals. More recently, it has become clear that such stimuli affect the reproductive cycle through their ability to stimulate changes in pituitary activity through the hypothalamic control of the pituitary gland (Harris, 1964; Lehrman, 1959; Marshall, 1959).

In the ring dove, it is evident that ovarian development culminating in ovulation normally occurs only in the presence of the male (Lehrman, Brody & Wortis, 1961). As in the domestic pigeon (Matthews, 1939), ovarian development in female ring doves may be induced by non-contact stimulation from males, perceived through a glass barrier. This effect on the female's reproductive system of the presence of the male is very much reduced if the male has been castrated (Erickson & Lehrman, 1964). It thus appears that the gonad-stimulating effect of the male occurs not merely because of his presence but because of his performance of behaviour patterns induced by secretions from his own testis. This is further indicated by the fact that castrated males injected with testosterone propionate are more stimulating to the reproductive system of females who perceive them through a glass plate than are untreated castrated males (Erickson, 1965).

Lott & Brody (1966) have shown that a female ring dove will usually lay eggs if she is kept in a cage (in the colony room) equipped with a mirror, so that she sees herself instead of a male mate. If she is kept in a sound-isolated cage with such a mirror, she will rarely lay eggs *unless* she can hear from a loudspeaker the sound picked up by a microphone in the colony room.

These experiments show that under some circumstances (e.g. when there are sounds from the

*Contribution No. 41 from the Institute of Animal Behavior, Rutgers University.

†We gratefully acknowledge the assistance of the United States Public Health Service, through a training grant (GM-1135), a research grant (MH-02271) and a research career award to D.S.L.

colony) stimulation from the male mate is effective in inducing ovarian development. Under other circumstances (e.g. in the presence of a non-courting ring dove), stimulation from the colony may be similarly effective. However, since the wild ancestor of the ring dove (*Streptopelia roseogrisea*, the rosy-gray dove of Africa) breeds in loosely-organized colonies, it is important for a full understanding of the function of socially-stimulated endocrine development in this species to ask whether, in the normal situation (female associating with a male mate and with stimulation from the colony milieu), stimuli from the mate and stimuli from birds of the surrounding colony co-operate to produce a level of reproductive development greater than that which would be produced by either of these sources of stimulation alone.

The purpose of the experiment reported here is to investigate the effect on the reproductive development of female ring doves of auditory stimulation from the colony with and without stimulation from the courting male.

Method

Subjects

The subjects were seventy-two female ring doves (*Streptopelia risoria*), hatched in the laboratory. In addition, seventy-two male doves, also hatched in the laboratory, served as stimulus objects. All these birds were descendants of a heterogeneous stock originally procured from J. W. Steinbeck of Concord, California, and occasionally replenished by him.

Housing and Maintenance Conditions

Breeding cages were of wood, each 33 in. wide, 18 in. deep and 14 in. high with wire-mesh front doors. They were provided with dispensers for water, food and a grit-and-mineral mixture, and with a glass bowl $4\frac{1}{4}$ in. in diameter, in which the birds built their nests. These cages were illuminated by strips of fluorescent lights mounted on a wall 5 ft 6 in. in front of the doors. Stock cages were 35-in. cubical cages built with wooden frames and wire-mesh sides.

Isolation cages were hanging double-width rat cages $16\frac{1}{2}$ in. wide, $9\frac{1}{2}$ in. deep and 7in. high, mounted in racks. These cages provided visual isolation.

Water, food and grit were continuously available in all cages. Nesting material when present consisted of pine needles or hay placed on the floor in a corner of the cage.

Breeding cages, stock cages and isolation cages were kept in separate rooms. Lights in all rooms were clock-controlled, being turned on at 6.00 a.m. and off at 8.00 p.m. EST. Temperature in all rooms was 72° to 74°F, except for brief and irregularly distributed periods of malfunctioning of the temperature control apparatus

Experience Prior to Testing

All the subjects had had previous breeding experience consisting of the successful production of at least one brood of young. (For detailed definition of this experience see Lehrman & Wortis, 1967.) Subsequent to their breeding experience, the females had been used in various experiments in which their presence had served as a source of stimulation for male subjects who were subsequently autopsied. These females were thus surplus females and were returned to the stock cages in all-female flocks of seven to ten birds, from which they were taken for the start of this experiment. The intact males had similarly been used in previous experiments in which they served as stimulus objects for female subjects. The castrated males had been castrated 6 to 18 months before the beginning of this experiment and had similarly been used as stimulus objects in experiments with female subjects.

In short, the subjects, both male and female, were birds with previous breeding experience. They had been used in previous experiments in ways which we deemed not to impair their usefulness for the present purpose.

Experimental Procedures

Preparation of subjects. Each bird was placed in a visual-isolation cage 3 weeks before it was due to be used in the experiment.

When a castrate male was selected for the experiment, he was removed from the stock cage and placed, with a female taken from a stock cage, into a breeding cage divided in half by a glass partition covered with a sheet of cardboard. The male and female were on opposite sides of this partition. They were left in the cage for 10 min after which the cardboard was removed, so that the birds could see each other through the glass plate. They were observed continuously for 30 min. If the male performed any bowing-coo or nest-call during this observation period, it was assumed that he was not completely castrated, and he was discarded. Males which did not show courtship behaviour were then examined internally through an exploratory laparotomy on each side under a dissecting microscope for any traces of testicular tissue. If no such tissue was found, the male and female were both placed in isolation cages.

Intact males were treated in exactly the same way, their testes being touched with a probe through the exploratory laparotomy to duplicate the handling to which the castrated birds had been subjected.

Sound-isolation chambers. The experiment was carried out in twelve sound-isolation chambers constructed by Industrial Acoustics, Inc. These were steel chambers, the inside dimensions of which were the same as those of the breeding cages in our colony rooms, and which were so constructed as to attenuate sounds in the range of the ring dove's voice by 26 to 30 dB. Birds kept in these chambers were thus effectively auditorily isolated from each other. Each chamber was divided in half by a partition of glass from the floor to 8 in. above the floor, the remaining $5\frac{1}{2}$ in. being $\frac{1}{4}$ in. wire mesh (to allow air circulation over the glass partition). The chambers were supplied with air circulation and with lighting controls which provided the same day-length as in all of our bird rooms. In addition, each chamber had mounted in the centre of the angle between the ceiling and the rear wall a small loudspeaker; provision was made for making a connection to the loudspeaker through a jack outside the chamber, without interfering with the sound-reducing properties of the chamber. For this experiment, a male and female were placed on opposite sides of the glass plate in the chamber. Food and water were available on both sides of the glass plate; a nest bowl and a supply of nesting material were placed on the female's side of the partition.

A microphone was placed in a breeding cage in a colony room containing forty-eight such cages, on a different floor of the laboratory from that on which the sound-isolation chambers were located. The output of the microphone was amplified and fed into a control box in the room containing the sound-isolation chambers. This box was connected to each of the loudspeakers in the twelve sound-isolation chambers, and the experimenter could, by operating switches on its control panel, feed the sound picked up in the colony room to any or all of the sound-isolation chambers. At the beginning of the experiment, the experimenter set the sound level in one of the sound-isolation chambers until it sounded to him approximately the same as the sound level in the colony room, which would be heard by a bird in one of the breeding cages in the colony room. This match is of course only approximate, but a sound-level meter and level controls on the control panel enabled us to make sure that the sound level in all of the sound-isolation chambers was exactly the same.*

Experimental design. The subjects (females) divided into four groups, were treated as follows:

(a) Sound-castrate: Placed into the chamber with a castrate male and with sound from the colony room continuously fed into the chamber.

(b) Sound-intact: With an intact male and with sound continuously fed into the chamber.

(c) No sound-castrate: Placed into the chamber with a castrate male and without exposure to the colony sound.

(d) No sound-intact: With an intact male and no exposure to the colony sounds.

All birds, when introduced into the sound-isolation chambers for the experiment, had been in standard (visual) isolation cages for 3 weeks.

The experiment was carried out in six successive replications. At each replication, N = 3 for each of the four groups. For the experiment as a whole, therefore, N = 18 for each of the four groups.

The groups were rotated from chamber to chamber on successive replications, so that each chamber was used for each of the four groups. In each replication the male was in the left half of the chamber (from which the air supply came) in half of the cases, the female in the other half, and this male-female distribution was changed in each chamber in successive replications.

In short, female subjects were exposed to normal or castrate males which they could experience through a glass partition, with or without sound from the colony room, and precautions were taken to prevent either of the two experimental variables from being confounded with the location of the test chamber or the position in the chamber.

Observations. Exactly 7 days after their introduction into the chamber, the females were removed for autopsy. The data consist of an assessment of the degree of ovarian development achieved by each bird. In the case of birds which had not ovulated at the time of autopsy, the oviduct weight is an adequate ordinal indicator of ovarian activity. However, since the oviduct gives up weight in the form of egg albumen after the ovary has released the ovum, oviduct weight is not a satisfactory measure of ovarian development once ovulation has occurred. Where ovulation had occurred, we used the following scale to indicate ovarian development beyond that represented by the highest oviduct weight achieved by a non-ovulated bird: 1—egg high in oviduct; 2—egg in cloaca, soft shell; 3—egg in cloaca, hard shell; 4—egg in nest; 5—egg in nest and egg high in oviduct; 6—egg in nest and egg in cloaca, soft shell; 7—egg in nest and egg in cloaca, hard shell; 8—two eggs in nest.†

Statistical treatment. Since the scores arrived at by the two procedures described above are not commensurate with each other, the ovarian status indicators for all birds in all four groups were converted to ranks 1 to 72, No. 1 being the bird with the lowest oviduct weight. All statistical comparisons were then made using the ranks as data.

Statistical comparisons among the basic groups (N = 18) were made by the Mann-Whitney U test. When larger, combined groups were being compared (N = 36), we used the median test, employing chi-square (Siegel, 1956).

Results

The results are set out in Table I. When the two main variables are each considered separately across all groups, it is apparent that the

*The sound level was measured later, using equipment which was not available at the time the experiment was carried out. The background noise (mostly from air movement in the chamber) was approximately 68 dB on the C scale of a General Radio Corp. Type 1565-A sound-level meter; a discrete bowing-coo raised the level by 8-10 dB.

†We are indebted to Mr Charles Barbiere for assistance in the collection of data.

Table I. Median Rank of Ovarian Development (Median Oviduct Weight in Mg)
N = 18 per group

	With castrate male	P	With intact male	For combined groups
With colony sound	40·5 (1079·5)	<0·025	55·5 *	46 (1811)
P	<0·05		<0·05	<0·05
No colony sound	15·5 (310)	<0·001	44·5 (1432)	28 (711·5)
For combined groups	24 (568)	<0·01	49·5 (5001·5)	

*Egg high in oviduct; see text for explanation.

ovarian development of the female is significantly affected by the presence of the testes in the stimulus males (median test: $\chi^2 = 8\cdot0$, $P<0\cdot01$) and is also significantly affected by the presence of the ambient sounds from the colony (median test: $\chi^2 = 3\cdot97$, $P<0\cdot05$). This confirms the conclusions reported, under somewhat different experimental conditions, by Erickson & Lehrman (1964) and by Lott & Brody (1966).

Of more immediate interest are the comparisons of the separate groups. Here it can be seen that the difference between the effect of the intact male and of the castrate male is significant whether or not the ambient colony sounds are present, and that the difference in ovarian development of females with and without the ambient colony sounds is significant whether the females are with castrate or intact males. In effect, this means that the rate and degree of ovarian development in the normal colony situation are an additive or synergistic effect, both of stimulation from the bird's mate and of stimulation from the colony milieu surrounding the pair.

Our analysis is based primarily upon four comparisons between groups (the P's in the body of Table I, between primary groups). If these four comparisons are made separately within each of the six replications (N = 3 per group for each comparison), 21 of the 24 resulting comparisons are in the same direction as those reported in Table I for the combined data from all replications.

Our females who could hear the colony sounds but saw no male courtship behaviour (rank 40·5), and those who could see and hear a courting male, but not the colony sound (rank 44·5) were stimulated to approximately the same degree (U = 145·4, N = 18/18, $P>0\cdot05$).

Discussion

So far, we have demonstrated the effect of auditory stimulation upon ovarian development in the ring dove only when the auditory stimulation occurred concurrently with the visual presence of another dove, either an intact or castrate male (our present experiment; Erickson & Lehrman, 1964), or the female's mirror-image (Lott & Brody, 1967). Lott & Brody report that female doves who hear the colony sounds, but without seeing another bird or themselves in the mirror, do not lay eggs. The question of whether the colony sounds can stimulate ovarian development in the absence of visual stimulation from another dove should, however, still be considered open; we intend to investigate this using the criterion of oviduct development, which may show some effects short of the actual production of eggs.

Auditory stimulation has been shown to be effective in stimulating ovarian development in the budgerigar (*Melopsittacus undulatus*), a bird which breeds in close flocks (Ficken *et al.*, 1960; Brockway, 1962). In addition, Warren & Hinde (1961) have shown that a singing male canary stimulates ovarian development in the female, although their experimental situation does not permit a confident distinction between auditory and visual stimulation from the courting male.

Darling (1938) suggested that social stimulation from other members of the colony stimulates gonadal development in colony-breeding birds, and that larger colonies would consequently have more closely synchronized breeding times than smaller colonies. Although this synchronization is an observed fact, ecological evidence is by no means unanimous in ascribing it to the 'Fraser Darling Effect', rather than to a tendency for birds whose cycles are already, for other reasons, synchronized to find each other and breed together (Coulson & White, 1956). The experiment reported in the present paper does show that stimulation from the surrounding colony is capable of producing acceleration of reproductive development over and above that induced by day-length and by interaction with the mate.

Summary

Female ring doves were exposed for 7 days to stimulation (through a glass partition) from intact or castrate males, either with or without ambient sounds from the breeding colony. Intact males induced more ovarian development than did castrate males, and more ovarian development was induced with sounds from the colony milieu than without, whether the female was with the intact or with the castrate male.

It is concluded that, in the normal colony situation, stimuli from the mate and those from the surrounding colony environment combine in inducing ovarian development in female doves.

REFERENCES

Brockway, Barbara F. (1962). Investigations of the auditory stimuli for laying in budgerigars (*Melopsittacus undulatus*). *Am. Zoologist*, **2**, 508–509.

Coulson, J. C. & White, E. (1956). A study of colonies of the Kittiwake *Rissa tridactyla*. *Ibis*, **98**, 63–79.

Darling, F. F. (1938). *Bird Flocks and the Breeding Cycle*. Cambridge: Cambridge University Press.

Erickson, C. J. & Lehrman, D. S. (1964). Effect of castration of male ring doves upon ovarian activity of females. *J. comp. physiol. Psychol.*, **58**, 164–166.

Erickson, C. J. (1965). A study of the courtship behaviour of male ring doves and its relationship to ovarian activity of females. Unpublished Ph.D. thesis. Rutgers University.

Ficken, R. W., van Tienhoven, A., Ficken, Millicent S., & Sibley, F. C. (1960). Effects of visual and vocal stimuli on breeding in the budgerigar (*Melopsittacus undulatus*). *Anim. Behav.*, **8**, 104–106.

Harris, G. W. (1964). Sex hormones, brain development, and brain function. *Endocrinology*, **75**, 627–648.

Lehrman, D. S. (1959). Hormonal responses to external stimuli in birds. *Ibis*, **101**, 478–496.

Lehrman, D. S., Brody, P. N. & Wortis, Rochelle P. (1961). The presence of the mate and of nesting material as stimuli for the development of incubation behavior and for gonadotropin secretion in the ring dove (*Streptopelia risoria*). *Endocrinology*, **68**, 507–516.

Lehrman, D. S. & Wortis, Rochelle, P. (1967). Breeding experience and breeding efficiency in the ring dove. *Anim. Behav.*, **15**, 223–228.

Lott, D. S. & Brody, P. N. (1966). Support of ovulation in the ring dove by auditory and visual stimuli. *J. comp. physiol. Psychol.*, **62**, 311–313.

Marshall, A. J. (1959). Internal and environmental control of breeding. *Ibis*, **101**, 456–478.

Marshall, F. H. A. (1936). Sexual periodicity and the causes which determine it. *Phil. Trans. R. Soc.*, **226B**, 423–456.

Marshall, F. H. A. (1942). Exteroceptive factors in sexual periodicity. *Biol. Rev.*, **17**, 68–90.

Matthews, L. H. (1939). Visual stimulation and ovulation in pigeons. *Proc. R. Soc.*, **126B**, 557–560.

Siegel, S. (1956). *Non-parametric Statistics for the Behavioral Sciences*. New York: McGraw-Hill.

Warren, Rosalyn P. & Hinde, R. A. (1961). Does the male stimulate estrogen secretion in female canaries? *Science*, **133**, 1354–1355.

(*Received* 17 *October* 1966; *revised* 24 *January* 1967; *Ms. number:* A512)

Activation of the Male Rat's Sexual Behavior by Intracerebral Implantation of Androgen

JULIAN M. DAVIDSON

Department of Physiology, Stanford University School of Medicine, Stanford, California

ABSTRACT. The hypothesis that sexual behavior in the male results from the direct action of testosterone on specific brain regions was tested, using intracerebral implantation of crystalline testosterone propionate in castrate male rats. Following establishment of a criterion for the loss of sex behavior in castrates, it was determined that the minimum effective dose of subcutaneously administered testosterone for stimulation of the accessory sex glands was less than that required for restoration of sex behavior. It was found that intracerebral implantation of testosterone could result in reappearance of the complete pattern of male sexual behavior in the absence of any histologically demonstrable stimulation of the seminal vesicles or prostate. These results never followed the implantation of cholesterol, showing that they were not due to lesion production by the implant. Although occasional responses were found following implants in other areas of the brain, all the most effective implants were in the hypothalamic-preoptic region, with the most consistent behavioral reactivation resulting from medial preoptic implants. It is concluded that sexual behavior in the male may be virtually completely independent of androgen-sensitive peripheral mechanisms, and that it is dependent upon activation by testosterone of structures lying within the hypothalamic-preoptic region of the brain. (*Endocrinology* **79**: 783, 1966)

Received April 7, 1966.

The preliminary experiments in this study were carried out in 1963 while the author was a USPHS postdoctoral fellow in the laboratory of Frank A. Beach at the University of California, Berkeley, and were supported by USPHS Grant MH 0400 to Dr. Beach. Subsequent work in 1964–65 was supported by USPHS Grant HD 00778 to the author.

THE CAPACITY to display sexual behavior is dependent, in both sexes, on the present or prior exposure of the animal to gonadal hormones (1, 2). Several possibilities exist as to the locus at which these hormones act to elicit sexual behavior. Thus, (a) their action may be to stimulate specific centers in the brain responsible for the organization of this behavior, or (b) it may be more general, affecting widespread regions of the central nervous system, or (c) it may be extracerebral, possibly affecting organs supplying afferent input to the brain.

Evidence has been presented to the effect that estrogens act on specific hypothalamic centers to activate the mating pattern in female cats (3) and rats (4). In the male it would appear *a priori* to be less likely that sexual behavior is the result of the direct effect of testosterone on a discrete cerebral center, since successful mating in this sex depends upon a highly co-ordinated series of activities rather than a relatively simple reflex lordosis as in the female. In laboratory rodents, the male's behavior is particularly complex, and involves an intricate pattern of mounts, intromissions and ejaculations. Hypothalamic lesions have been shown to inhibit sexual behavior in male guinea pigs (5) and rats (6, 7) and the effects of the lesions were not reversible by testosterone treatment (5, 6). These experiments, although suggesting that hypothalamic structures may be essential for sexual behavior in the male, do not constitute direct evidence that the action of testosterone on the hypothalamus is a causal factor in activation of this behavior. More relevant, perhaps, is a brief report which appeared in 1956 (8) on manifestations of "exaggerated sexual responses" in a small proportion of normal male rats receiving intracerebral injections of a soluble testosterone salt.

This study deals with the question of whether or not the action of testosterone on specific brain structures is sufficient to elicit the full pattern of normal sexual behavior in male rats which have ceased to display this behavior by virtue of long-term castration. The method used is the stereotaxic implantation of small quantities of crystalline testosterone propionate in specific brain regions. Since any effects of the implanted testosterone could be due either to direct effects on brain tissue or to release of the hormone into the systemic circulation, it was necessary to establish a criterion which would permit elimination of the second alternative. Such a criterion was found to be the absence of any histologically demonstrable stimulation of the prostate and seminal vesicles. The results of this study were presented in part at the 22nd International Congress of Physiological Sciences (9).

Materials and Methods

Sexually mature Long-Evans rats[1] were supplied with illumination from 12 AM to 12 PM each day and tests of sexual behavior were conducted during the dark phase of the daily cycle. Stimulus females were prepared by injecting 0.1 mg estradiol benzoate 48–72 hr before the onset of testing. Only females showing highly estrous responses were used. Tests were conducted in glass-fronted semicircular cages 16 in. high, 30 in. wide and 18 in. deep. After the male had been in the cage for 3 min, the female was introduced through a trap door leading from a special compartment. All mounts, intromissions and ejaculatory patterns[2] were recorded on an Esterline Angus event recorder.

Each test was continued until (a) occurrence of the first intromission after the ejaculatory pattern, or (b) 25 min after the first intromission (in the event that no ejaculatory pattern occurred in that time), or (c) 15 min after commencement of testing (in the event that no intromission occurred in that time). If no intromissions had occurred after approximately $7\frac{1}{2}$ min of testing, females were switched to provide an additional stimulus.

The following behavioral indices were measured or calculated for all tests:
Intromission latency. Time from onset of test (introduction of female) to first intromission.
Intromission frequency. Number of intromissions before first ejaculatory pattern.
Ejaculation latency. Time from first intromission to ejaculatory pattern.
Mount frequency. Number of mounts (with pelvic thrusts) before ejaculatory pattern.
Post-ejaculatory interval. Time from occurrence of ejaculatory pattern to first intromission of next series.

Following trans-scrotal castration, tests were conducted weekly or biweekly until a criterion for the loss of sexual behavior was satisfied (see Results). Subsequently, males were either subcutaneously administered testosterone propionate in oil, or crystalline testosterone propionate was implanted intracerebrally. Testing was resumed 1–4 days later, and was continued twice weekly thereafter for 1–3 weeks, with 3- or 4-

---

[1] Simonsen Laboratories, Gilroy, Calif.
[2] The term "ejaculatory pattern" is used to describe the overt behavior (*e.g.*, long intromission and slow dismounting, followed by a period of sexual inactivity) which accompanies seminal emission in the intact male, denoting the successful completion of a sequence of sexual behavior (10).

day intervals between tests. Normal body weight increases were found in almost all cases following implantation.

Intracerebral implantation was performed stereotaxically with the aid of deGroot's atlas (11). In most experiments implants were prepared, as described previously (12), by tamping a pellet of crystalline testosterone propionate or cholesterol into one end of a length of 20-gauge stainless steel tubing. The pellets were ejected into specific brain locations after fixation of the tube to the skull with dental cement. The crystalline material was protected during implantation by a thin film of sucrose which covered the tip, and its weight (approximately 200 μg) was determined by differential weighing on a Mettler M5 microbalance. In experiments in which a lesser surface area of exposure of brain to the hormone was desired, molten testosterone propionate was drawn into the end of the 20-gauge tubing and the outside of the tube was cleaned with solvents so that testosterone remained only at the end and flush with it. The precise rate of absorption from these crystalline depots of testosterone is unknown. It may, however, be presumed that absorption is very slow, since identically prepared implants (pellets or fused) in the median eminence result in testicular atrophy one month following implantation and the crystalline material can usually be observed, at this time period, as a compact mass at the tip of the implant tube.

On cessation of the experiment, seminal vesicles and ventral prostates were fixed in Bouin's solution, paraffin-embedded and stained with hematoxylin and eosin for histological study. Where required, brains were removed, fixed in formalin, frozen, serially sectioned and stained, to determine the location of the implants.

Results

Criterion for loss of sexual behavior. Failure of the ejaculatory pattern on one behavioral test does not imply irreversible loss of this behavior in castrate rats (10). Before attempting the restoration of sexual behavior it was therefore necessary to establish a criterion on which to base a judgment that the spontaneous reappearance of sexual behavior in animals fulfilling this criterion was reasonably improbable. The absence of ejaculatory patterns on three consecutive weekly tests (*i.e.*, 3 "negative tests") appeared to be a suitable criterion. Forty rats were tested for additional periods of 13 to 70 days following three such negative tests. Fig. 1 shows the results. Of 265 tests in these 40 animals, only eight tests (3%) were "positive" for completion of the mating pattern. In no case did a rat show more than one positive test during the whole period of testing. Accordingly, this criterion was met before behavioral restoration was attempted by systemic or intracerebral steroid administration, except in a few cases in which the absence of any intromissions on any of five successive daily tests was substituted.

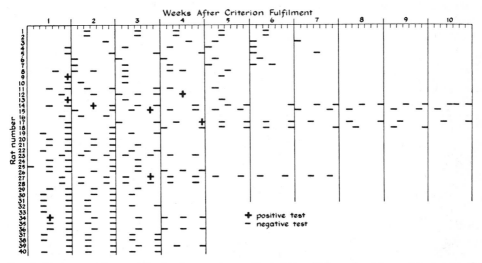

FIG. 1. Mating tests in rats following 3 successive weekly tests in which no ejaculatory pattern occurred ("criterion fulfillment"). Tests scored positive or negative according to whether ejaculatory patterns occurred or not.

Differential sensitivity to testosterone of morphological and behavioral responses. To compare the minimum effective dose of androgen necessary to restore the ejaculatory pattern with that required to produce histologically demonstrable stimulation of the accessory sex glands, castrates were injected with testosterone propionate in doses of 25, 50, 75 or 100 μg daily for periods of seven or 21 days. Biweekly behavioral tests were conducted in all cases at three- or four-day intervals throughout the period of injections. In seven of the rats, seminal vesicle biopsies were performed after one week's treatment, and injections were then continued for two further weeks.

In 14 castrate control rats sacrificed 21 to 83 days after castration, the follicular epithelium of both seminal vesicles and ventral prostate was invariably squamous. Histological stimulation of these glands was considered to be present only if cuboidal or columnar epithelium was clearly present in a large proportion of follicles. Since the evaluation was qualitative and subjective, all cases in which stimulation appeared to be borderline were regarded as not stimulated. Virtually complete correlation was found between seminal vesicle and prostate stimulation.

Table 1 shows that, with the seven-day injection period, one half of the animals tested manifested accessory sex gland stimulation at the 25 μg dose level; histological stimulation was almost always present at higher dose levels. When injections were continued for 21 days, all animals showed accessory stimulation at all dose levels.

Behavioral restoration (the occurrence of at least one ejaculatory pattern) was obtained with higher dose levels than were necessary in order to stimulate the accessory sex glands, and this was true for all doses and durations of treatment. Restoration of behavior in 100% of animals tested was achieved only with the 100 μg dose level. In no case was behavioral restoration noted in the absence of accessory stimulation. Accessory stimulation in the absence of behavioral restoration was, however, noted in a total of 21 cases. Its occurrence did not appear related to the amount of time elapsing between castration and the onset of injections, which varied in this group from 29 to 151 days.

Testosterone implantation. In *preliminary* experiments testosterone pellets weighing 227 ± 28[3] μg were implanted in 18 rats in locations intended for the midbasal diencephalic region, but histological study of the brains for verification of implant locations was not performed. On autopsy, four of these showed histological stimulation of the ventral prostate (2 cases) or of both prostates and seminal vesicles. In the remaining 14 rats no signs of accessory sex gland stimulation could be observed. Three to seven tests were performed in the first one

---

[3] Mean $\pm$ standard error of the mean.

TABLE 1. Effects of various subcutaneous doses of testosterone propionate on the histology of the ventral prostates and seminal vesicles and on sexual behavior in castrate rats

Dose (μg/day)	Duration of treatment (days)	No. of rats tested	% of rats responding		Cases of:	
			Accessory sex glands	Sexual behavior (ejaculatory pattern)	Stimulation without behavior	Behavior without stimulation
25	7	10	50	10	4	0
25	21	4	100	50	2	0
50	7	15	87	47	6	0
50	21	7	100	29	5	0
75	7	8	100	75	2	0
75	21	4	100	50	2	0
100	21	4	100	100	0	0
Total: Accessory stimulation without behavior					21	
Total: Behavior without accessory stimulation						0

to two postoperative weeks at three to four-day intervals. Eight of these animals displayed ejaculatory patterns on at least one of the postoperative tests and four did so on more than one test. Despite the absence of seminal emission, the behavioral pattern was indistinguishable from that occurring in the intact rat. Fig. 2 shows a comparison of the performance of these rats with that of 40 unimplanted animals (discussed above) and of 15 with cholesterol implants. The results suggested that the implantation of testosterone in at least some forebrain areas could result in the reappearance of the full pattern of male sexual behavior, although no conclusions would be drawn with regard to the precise area involved.

In 67 rats, testosterone pellets weighing 220 ± 4^3 μg were implanted in various brain areas, the locations of which were later verified histologically. Five postoperative behavioral tests were performed. In six of these rats, microscopic examination of the accessory sex glands removed at autopsy showed signs of stimulation. Only one of these six ejaculated on any of the tests, and it was removed from further consideration. Thirty-nine rats displayed the complete sequence of mating behavior culminating in an ejaculatory pattern on at least one postoperative test, in the presence of com-

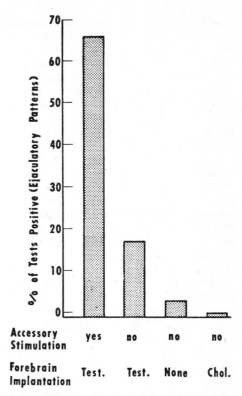

FIG. 2. Percentages of mating tests on which ejaculatory patterns occurred after intracerebral testosterone implantation in preliminary experiments, compared with effects of cholesterol implantation or no treatment.

TABLE 2. Behavioral responses of rats with large testosterone implants (pellet ejected) or cholesterol in various brain regions. Each rat was tested five times following implantation. Tests on which ejaculatory patterns occurred were designated positive.

	No. of rats tested	No. of positive tests						% of tests positive
		0	1	2	3	4	5	
			(figures below are no. of rats)					
Testosterone implants:								
Hypothalamus*	16	3	4	1	4	3	1	44
Medial preoptic†	8			3	4		1	57
Supraoptic and lateral preoptic areas	6	6						0
Thalamus	8	5	2	1				10
Cortex-corpus callosum	7	5	1	1				9
Hippocampus	9	4	3	2				16
Other:	12							20
Posterior colliculus			1	1				
Midbrain		1	2	1				
Zona incerta		1		1				
Caudate-putamen		2	1	1				
Cholesterol implants:								
Hypothalamus (6), Preoptic (6) Thalamus (3)	15	15						0

* Includes area caudal to posterior hypothalamic nucleus but anterior to habenulo-peduncular tract.
† 1.25 mm or less from the midline.

pletely atrophied accessory sex glands. Mean postoperative latency to first positive test was 7.7 days; the range was two to 20 days. The reactivation of behavioral patterns was particularly striking since, in a number of animals, no mounts (without intromission) were observed on the three pre-implantation tests, *i.e.*, there was no evidence of any of the constituents of sexual behavior in these rats.

Table 2 shows the frequencies of positive tests resulting from implants in different anatomical locations. Although the occurrence of at least one positive test in the series of five performed was found following implants in many different areas of the brain, the frequency of positive tests was much greater for animals with implants in the hypothalamic and medial preoptic than for any other region. Fifty per cent of the hypothalamic and 62% of the medial pre-optic rats showed positive responses on more than half the tests performed (*i.e.*, 3 or more positive tests/rat), while none of the animals in any of the other groups responded positively on more than two of the five postoperative tests.

Since one positive test (complete behavioral pattern) in a series is occasionally seen in untreated castrates following "criterion fulfillment" (Fig. 1), the anatomical diagrams (Fig. 3, 4) portray separately animals showing one positive test, and those showing more than one. Behavioral restoration resulted most consistently from implants in a relatively circumscribed area of the medial preoptic region at or close to the plane of juncture of the anterior commissure (Fig. 3B). All of eight animals with implants in this region showed more than one positive test, while no positive tests resulted from implants in the adjacent or immediately anterior areas (Fig. 3A, 3B). The results of hypothalamic implantation were somewhat more variable, and the effective area was more widespread. As shown in Fig. 3C, 3D and 3E, points yielding more than one positive test were dotted throughout this area, and were interspersed with others yielding one or no positive tests.

Cholesterol implants were placed in 15 rats, in the hypothalamic-preoptic region (n = 12), and in the thalamus. The locations of all of these implants are shown in Fig. 3.

Fig. 3A–E. Intracerebral distribution of large testosterone implants (pellets ejected from 20-gauge tubing) at frontal planes extending from anterior preoptic to posterior hypothalamic regions. Implant locations on each diagram include points projected from an anterior posterior distance of 0.5 mm. O: No positive tests; ◪: one positive test; ●: more than one positive test; ☆: cholesterol implant. DBB: diagonal band of Broca; MS: medial septum; LS: lateral septum; CPU: caudate-putamen; POA: preoptic area; MFB: medial forebrain bundle; GP: globus pallidus; SC: suprachiasmatic nucleus (n.); CA: anterior commissure: CI: internal capsule; RE: n. reuniens; AHA: anterior hypothalamic area; LHA: lateral hypothalamic area; VMH: ventro-medial hypothalamic n.; PVH: paraventricular n.; HPC: hippocampus; VE: n. ventralis; VM: n. ventralis pars medialis; ARH: arcuate n.; PMV: premammillary n.; MM: medial mammillary n.; ML: lateral mammillary n. Adapted from deGroot's atlas (11).

None of the 75 postoperative tests performed on these animals was positive.

In order to reduce the surface area of brain exposed to testosterone, thereby decreasing the opportunity for diffusion of testosterone from the implant to distant sites in the brain, smaller implants were used. In these, the hormone was fused to the implantation tube in such a way that the testosterone-brain interface was limited to the bore of the tube. With this procedure, only hypothalamic and preoptic implantation resulted in behavioral restoration, but the percentage of implants in these areas which yielded positive results and the percentage of positive tests were considerably less than in the case of the larger implants (Table 3). However, decreasing the size of the implant did not result in a more precise localization of responsive regions within the hypothalamic-preoptic area, since, as shown in Fig. 4, positive tests were occasionally found to follow posterior hypothalamic and lateral preoptic implantation.

Analysis of restored behavior. Detailed analysis of the behavior records from testosterone-implanted rats showed considerable variability in the latencies and frequencies of the recorded behavior. On many tests in animals with implants in the hypothalamic-preoptic regions, behavioral scores were

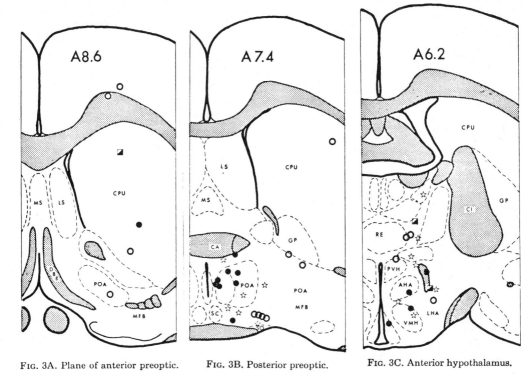

FIG. 3A. Plane of anterior preoptic.   FIG. 3B. Posterior preoptic.   FIG. 3C. Anterior hypothalamus.

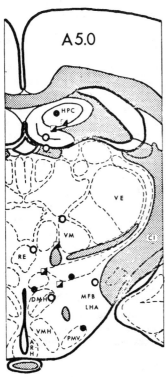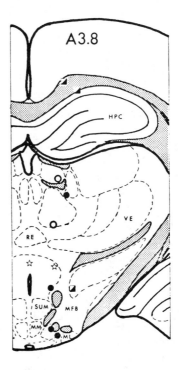

FIG. 3D. Medial hypothalamus.   FIG. 3E. Posterior hypothalamus.

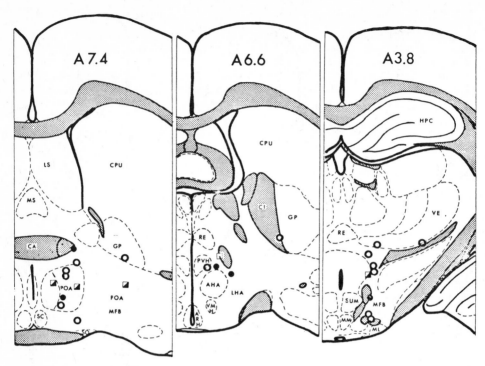

FIG. 4. Intracerebral distribution of small testosterone implants (hormone fused to 20-gauge tubing) at frontal planes passing through posterior preoptic region (*left*); anterior hypothalamus (*center*); and posterior hypothalamus (*right*). See legend to Fig. 3 for abbreviations and other comments.

similar to precastration values in the same animals. On other tests in these groups, and more often in animals with implants in other areas of the brain, the behavior tended to resemble that of long-term castrates with maintenance of sexual behavior (10) in which intromission and ejaculation latencies, intromission and mount frequencies and post-ejaculatory intervals are increased. Fig. 5 shows intromission latencies in rats with implants in the hypothalamic, preoptic and other regions of the brain as well as the values obtained from the same animals on precastration tests. The mean latency was highest in "other" rats, 336 ± 67 seconds, and the difference between this group and the preoptic animals (mean 141 ± 43 sec) was significant at the 5% level (*t* test). The great inter-test variability reduces the significance of the mean differences between groups, but it is clear that low intromission latencies were found

most often in rats from both the hypothalamic and preoptic groups, and that the resemblance between the distributions of values from pre-castration and post-implantation tests was much greater than in the case of "other" animals. Similar variability was noted in other behavioral parameters, and no significant differences were found between the mean intromission frequencies, mount frequencies, ejaculation latencies or post-ejaculatory intervals in the three groups. Similarly, the pre-castration scores for these parameters did not differ significantly from the post-implantation scores.

The mean latencies in days from implantation to occurrence of the first positive test for implantation in different brain areas were as follows: medial preoptic area 5.9 ± 1.0 (range 3–11); hypothalamus 6.7 ± 1.2 (range 3–20); other areas 9.3 ± 1.1 (range 2–16).

The comparative latency to first ejaculatory pattern for rats injected with testosterone (see above) was 6.5 ± 0.8. It should be noted that the accuracy of these latency estimates is limited by the fact that tests were conducted only every three or four days. The differences between the latencies of the various groups are not statistically significant.

Discussion

The validity of any attempt to restore sexual behavior after castration by the local action of intracerebrally implanted crystalline material depends upon the demonstration that the observed results are not secondary to 1) the production of lesions or nonspecific irritation at the site of

TABLE 3. Behavioral responses following small testosterone implants (hormone fused to bore of tube). See Table 2 for further details.

	No. of rats tested	No. of positive tests						% of tests positive
		0	1	2	3	4	5	
			(figures below are no. of rats)					
Hypothalamus*	12	7	2	2		1		17
Medial preoptic*	9	5	2		2			17
Anterior and lateral preoptic	3	2	1					7
Other Areas:	8							0
Basal ganglia	2	2						
Thalamus	2	2						
Anterior midbrain	2	2						
N. accumbens	2	2						

* As defined in Table 2.

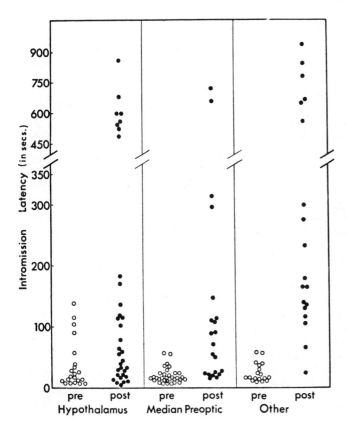

FIG. 5. Intromission latencies in seconds on individual mating tests in animals with large testosterone implants in the hypothalamus, preoptic and other brain regions. Abbreviations: pre, tests before castration; post, tests after implantation of testosterone.

implant, 2) "leakage" of the material into the systemic circulation in sufficient quantities to produce the behavior regardless of any local action, or 3) the spontaneous reappearance of behavior in the castrate. These requirements were adequately satisfied in the excellent study of Harris and Michael (3), who showed that intracerebral estrogen implants restore receptivity in the castrate female cat.

In the present investigation on male rats, the complete absence of any behavioral restoration in cholesterol-implanted animals shows that the observed effects of testosterone implantation were not due to destruction or nonspecific stimulation of the brain by the tube and or the crystalline material. Since the minimum effective dose of testosterone to restore behavior was shown here to be higher than that required for histological stimulation of the accessory sex glands, behavioral restoration in the face of completely atrophied seminal vesicles and prostates cannot be explained by release of the hormone from the implant into the systemic circulation. The extreme rarity of ejaculatory patterns in unimplanted rats tested after having fulfilled the criterion of three negative weekly tests, and the fact that this never occurred on more than one test in these animals despite repeated testing, eliminates, too, the factor of spontaneous behavioral restoration as playing a significant role in the results. It may therefore be concluded that the restoration of the full pattern of sexual behavior in the male rat may be achieved by the exposure of brain tissue to testosterone propionate, and that this restoration results from the direct action of the hormone on the brain.

Occasional "positive" tests (*i.e.*, those in which the complete mating pattern occurred) resulted from implants in several different brain areas. However, implants in the hypothalamic-preoptic region were clearly more effective than all others, both with regard to frequency of positive tests and (to a somewhat lesser extent) with regard to quality of the restored behavior. The fact that intromission latency was well above preoperative levels in almost all the relatively few positive tests in rats with extrahypothalamic implants is an indication that sex "drive" or "motivation" was

decreased in these animals below their preoperative performance. It was also below that of animals with implants in the hypothalamic-preoptic regions. The latter groups displayed intromission latencies within their preoperative ranges on many of the postoperative tests.

The relatively large extent of the "effective" area constitutes evidence contrary to the concept of a discrete and neuroanatomically well-defined androgen-sensitive sexual behavior "center" in the male. It is of interest that a generally similar intracerebral distribution of estrogen implants effective in restoring female sexual behavior has been described by Michael[1] (13). This widespread distribution may have resulted either from diffusion of hormone to sites distant from the implant, or from the existence of widespread cerebral structures capable of responding to androgen by activating the behavioral pattern. In Michael's studies, autoradiographic evidence was presented which ran counter to the former alternative (14). The present study provides no information as to the actual mobility of the implanted hormone. However, since the best and most consistent results were obtained with implants in the preoptic-hypothalamic region, it is conceivable that the occasional effectiveness of extrahypothalamic implants was due to diffusion of testosterone to this region. The additional possibility that the effectiveness of hypothalamic-preoptic implants was due to diffusion to a smaller "center" within this region (such as the medial preoptic region) was tested by implanting small-surface area, fused implants. If the hypothesis were correct, these implants should have been quite effective but only within a smaller region. They were in fact relatively ineffective at any location, including the medial preoptic, but some positive tests resulted from implants throughout the whole extent of the preoptic-hypothalamic region although none resulted from implants outside it.

------

[1] The resemblance between the anatomical distribution of "effective" implants in this study and Michael's is particularly striking in the plane of the anterior commissure and optic chiasm [compare Fig. 4 (center) with Fig. 3 in ref. 13].

Unlike Michael's conclusions based on estrogen implants in female cats (13), Lisk favors a more discrete estrogen-sensitive sexual behavior center in the anterior hypothalamus of the female rat (4). Although the implants in the present study were relatively large compared to those used by Lisk, testosterone is much less potent than estradiol, and in none of the rats in this study could "leakage" into the systemic circulation be implicated in behavioral restoration. As discussed above, the use of smaller implants reduced the probability of obtaining behavioral activation, but did not increase the anatomical discreteness of the effective area. It appears then that a relatively large area of brain tissue needs to be exposed to the action of the hormone for behavioral activation to occur with reasonable probability. The data are consistent with the following hypothesis: A "network" of testosterone-sensitive neurons exists in the hypothalamic-medial preoptic region of the male rat. Exposure of any significant portion of this "network" to the direct action of the hormone will restore sexual responsiveness to the castrate male. Certain portions of the "network" (e.g., the medial preoptic) appear more responsive than others in terms of the probability of achieving behavioral restoration following testosterone implantation. This may be due to a greater density in these areas of "network" cells or fibers.

Complete behavioral restoration (i.e., all 5 postoperative tests positive) resulted in only two cases. Furthermore, analysis of the behavior of animals with hypothalamic-preoptic implants showed that the restored behavior was not completely normal in many cases. It appears, therefore, that the crystalline testosterone depots were not necessarily capable of the complete restoration of normal male rat behavior. Presumably, the implants could not duplicate precisely the pattern of delivery of testosterone to the brain areas involved which occurs in physiological conditions, especially if a relatively widespread area of brain has to be perfused. On the other hand, the observed discrepancies in behavior might have resulted from the absence of sensory feedback from peripheral receptors, such as the penile papillae, which require androgen stimulation for their maintenance (15). However, since these behavioral discrepancies were often relatively minor or absent, one must conclude that no androgen-dependent extracerebral mechanism appears essential for normal sexual behavior in the male rat.

Acknowledgments

I am most grateful to Dr. F. A. Beach for help in the initial stages of this project, and to Linda Coates, Thornton Ege and Darlene DeManincor for able technical assistance. The testosterone was kindly supplied by Schering Corporation.

References

1. Beach, F. A., Hormones and Behavior, Cooper Square Publisher, Inc., New York, 1961, p. 368.
2. Young, W. C., In Young, W. C. (ed.), Sex and Internal Secretions, vol. II, Williams and Wilkins, Baltimore, 1961, p. 1609.
3. Harris, G. W., and R. P. Michael, J Physiol (London) 171: 275, 1964.
4. Lisk, R. D., Amer J Physiol 203: 493, 1962.
5. Brookhart, J. M., and F. L. Dey, Amer J Physiol 133: 551, 1941.
6. Soulairac, M. L., Ann Endocr (Paris) 24: No. 3 (suppl.), 1963.
7. Phoenix, C. H., J Comp Physiol Psychol 54: 72, 1961.
8. Fisher, A. E., Science 124: 228, 1956.
9. Davidson, J. M., Abstracts of papers, 23rd Intern. Congr. Physiol. Sci., 1965, p. 647 (Abstract).
10. ———, Anim Behav 14: 266, 1966.
11. de Groot, J., Trans Roy Neth Acad Sci 52: No. 4, 1959.
12. Davidson, J. M., and S. Feldman, Endocrinology 72: 936, 1963.
13. Michael, R. P., Brit Med Bull 21: 87, 1965.
14. ———, In Martini, L., and A. Pecile (eds), Hormonal Steroids, vol. 2, Academic Press, New York, 1965, p. 469.
15. Beach, F. A., and G. Levinson, J Exp Zool 114: 159, 1950.

Hormonal Influences on Brain Organization in Infant Rats

Hormones present during critical periods of development may exert a direct action on the central nervous system.

Seymour Levine and Richard F. Mullins, Jr.

Dr. Levine is associate professor in the department of psychiatry, Stanford University, Stanford, California. Mr. Mullins is a graduate student in the department of psychology, Stanford University.

Biological systems are unified and interdependent. The internal and external milieus are equally important interacting systems on which the very nature of the organism's function—whether it be on the cellular or the behavioral level—depends. There now exists an abundance of information which emphasizes the importance of environmental events during sensitive periods in ontogeny as determinants of adult physiological and behavioral processes (1). Although we have somewhat arbitrarily separated behavioral and physiological phenomena, the fact remains that behavioral phenomena can and must be viewed in biological perspective. Behavior is as adaptive a process as is the production of glucocorticoids under certain physiological conditions, and the two phenomena can produce equally maladaptive effects. In this article we describe some of the effects of altering the environment of the newborn animal, and we present a model which attempts to account in part for some of the observed results.

In brief, we propose that the presence of hormones (sex, thyroid, or adrenal) during critical periods of development exerts a direct action on the central nervous system, producing profound and permanent changes in the subsequent psychophysiological processes of the organism.

Gonadal Hormones

In the past 10 years many studies have been made of the effects of varying the amounts or kinds of gonadal hormones present in newborn animals. The early research in this area dealt mostly with transplantation of gonads; the more recent work has involved either prenatal or postnatal injections of hormones. Since several recent reviews have dealt with the effects of prenatal injections (2, 3), our discussion concerns only studies of animals injected after birth.

Clark (4) reported that castration of male and female rats 1 or 2 days after birth abolished the normal sex differences in pituitary gonadotropin. Thus, castrated males exhibited a concentration of gonadotropin in the pituitary which was significantly higher than that of normal males and did not differ from that of females. Pfeiffer (5) transplanted gonads of the newborn male rat to litter-mate females, and vice versa. There were numerous other treatments in this monumental study. The principal conclusions were that all rats at birth are physiologically female, but are capable of differentiation into males if testes are present. Testicular transplants into the newborn intact or castrate female led to acyclicity (associated with persistent vaginal cornification) and other permanent changes in reproductive function. In the castrate female these transplants also resulted in overt morphological change. When ovaries were transplanted into the newborn intact male, there was no observable effect. This is in contrast to observations in more recent work (6–8) where injection of estrogen into intact newborn male rats did disturb male reproductive function. In this instance the differences were possibly attributable to dose level, since the transplanted ovary may not produce sufficient estrogen to block the action of the endogenous androgens in the intact newborn male. However, in the adult male rat which has been castrated at birth, ovarian transplants develop corpora lutea in a cyclic manner, as in the normal female. More recent work (9) has confirmed these observations on the effects of castration of the newborn male. Although Pfeiffer believed it was the pituitary that became sexually differentiated, the evidence (see 10) indicates that these effects are probably mediated by the hypothalamus and higher central-nervous-system structures.

From 1943 to 1958 this area of research lay dormant, but recently many studies have been reported. There is one major difference between the procedures used in the early work and those used in the more recent studies. Most of the earlier investigators used large multiple doses of hormones, whereas in the later work single injections have been given. Selye (11), in 1940, reported that 1 milligram of androgen given daily to female rats from birth through age 30 days markedly impaired ovarian function. Wilson et al. (12) treated female rats postnatally with testosterone propionate, the injections beginning the day after birth and continuing 3 times a week for 4 weeks. The total doses ranged from 3 to 36 milligrams. This treatment resulted in a loss of spontaneous mating behavior (13), acyclicity, sterility, and a lack of

a behavioral or uterine response to exogenous estrogen in the mature animal. These data are similar to those of later investigators (6, 14, 15) and indicate that postnatal administration of androgen during critical periods markedly and irreversibly affects subsequent reproductive and behavioral functions. Injections given when the rat is more than a week old are superfluous.

There are procedures which suppress ovulation but do not produce a lack of sexual receptivity. Barraclough and Gorski (16) report that administration of 10 micrograms of testosterone propionate to newborn female rats blocks ovulation and produces constant vaginal estrus, but that these females are constantly sexually receptive. Similar results have been obtained by Mullins and Levine (17) with androgen, but these workers found that the degree of sexual receptivity varied inversely with the size of the neonatal dose (Fig. 1). Moreover, although the females were constantly receptive, the sexual behavior was aberrant. Lordosis was maintained for long periods and these females were extremely passive and inactive.

In 1943, two reports were published which bear on the problem of the specificity of hormone treatment (18). In these studies it was found that continuous treatment of female rats with estrogen in doses varying from 0.037 milligram to 2.3 milligrams, when started at 1.5 or at 10 days of age, resulted in acyclicity, lack of spontaneous sexual behavior (mating), impaired ovarian function, and failure to respond to administration of exogenous estrogen by changes in the uterus or by "estrous behavior" (after administration of exogenous estrogen the usual copulatory reflex following manual stimulation on the back and pudendal regions could not be elicited).

More recent studies tend to support this earlier work. However, instead of large multiple doses of hormone, single injections of hormones at various dos-

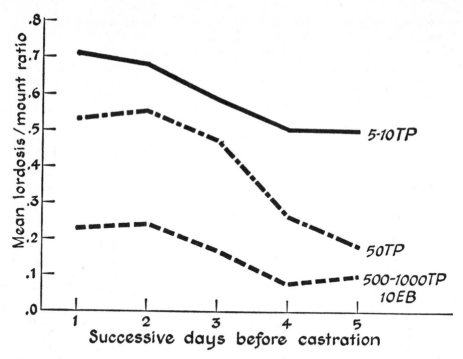

Fig. 1. Mean lordosis-to-mount ratio for female rats given 5, 10, 50, 500, or 1000 micrograms of testosterone propionate (*TP*) or 10 micrograms of estradiol benzoate (*EB*) either 96 or 120 hours after birth. Tests with a sexually vigorous male took place when the animals were 90 days old.

ages have been used. Harris and Levine (*6*) report that a single dose of estrogen administered to females 96 hours after birth resulted in permanent ovarian disfunction, similar in some ways to that produced by androgen. However, the effect of this neonatal estrogen on adult female sexual behavior was to abolish sexual receptivity; this effect was observed at all dose levels from 10 micrograms upward (*7*). By contrast, androgen administered to newborn females has paradoxical effects on sexual receptivity which are dependent on dose level. Although both hormones abolish ovulation, estrogen produces irregular vaginal cyclicity with long periods of estrus (*19*), whereas androgen produces constant vaginal cornification. Thus, it is apparent that the organization of sexual behavior is differentially affected by administration of androgen or estrogen to the newborn female.

Male rats given estrogen in infancy also show marked defects in sexual behavior. These males show a great deal of mounting behavior (although these mounts are often directed to the head or side of the female), they rarely achieve intromission, and they never ejaculate. It is difficult to attribute these effects to an alteration in the central nervous system, since a single injection of estrogen when the rat is 4 days old results in marked atrophy of the reproductive system (Fig. 2) and failure of the os penis to develop. On the basis of sexual behavior alone, no conclusion can be drawn about the central-nervous-system effects of administration of estrogen to the newborn male. Castration of the newborn male rat, however, does markedly alter sexual behavior. Adult males that were castrated in early infancy exhibit complete female sexual behavior if they are given injections

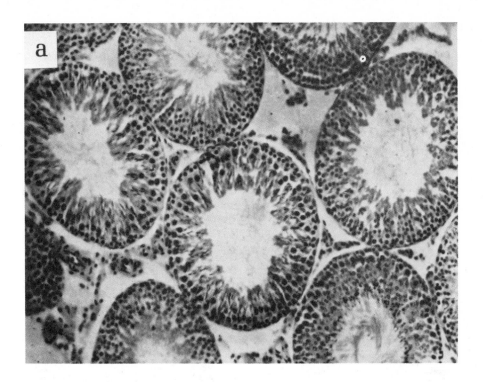

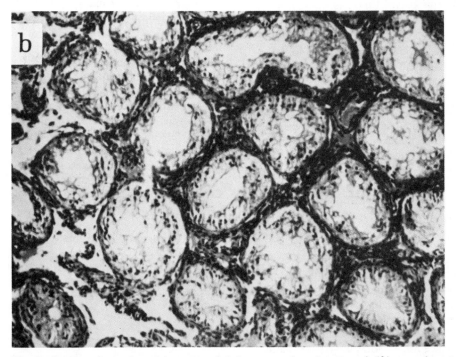

Fig. 2. Sections from the adult testes of (a) a normal male rat and (b) a male rat given a large dose of estrogen when it was 5 days old; b shows degeneration of the seminiferous tubules.

of estrogen and progesterone at low dosages (3, 20), or if they receive a transplanted ovary (9). Males castrated in adulthood show no such behavior after these procedures.

There are data which do indicate that sexual differentiation in the male rat is affected by administration of estrogen to the newborn animal. Throughout the psychological literature there are numerous reports of behavioral differences between males and females. Differences in activity (21), avoidance conditioning (22, 23), and ulcer formation (24) have been reported. The fact that these differences are not solely a function of the gonadal hormones in the circulation is apparent from the work of Anderson (25), who reported striking differences between males and females in defecation and ambulation behavior and also in timidity in open-field tests, although the experimental animals, of both sexes, had been castrated long before the open-field testing. An experiment was recently performed (26) to determine the effects of administration of sex hormones to the newborn rat on male-female differences in open-field behavior. Untreated female rats are usually more active than males in this test situation. Estrogen was more effective than androgen in reducing this sex difference, but the total amount of open-field activity was reduced in all animals.

It has been suggested (3, 9) that gonadal hormones exert a dual influence on the central nervous system—inductive or organizational during development and excitatory or activational in the adult. The studies discussed in this article show that the presence of either androgen or estrogen in the newborn rat causes the sexually undifferentiated brain to be organized so that the acyclic, male pattern of hormone release occurs in the adult. In the absence of gonadal hormones, the basic female (cyclic) hormone-release pattern becomes established. Both of these patterns of hormone release are part of a "hormonostat" whereby the concentration of sex steroids being produced "feeds back" and influences the central nervous system, which, in turn, controls the rate of steroid production or release, or both. Although the altering of steroid concentrations in the newborn permanently alters the functioning of this hormonostat, studies with hormone replacement in adulthood have shown that it is not a deficit in the amount of sex hormones which causes the aberrant neuroendocrine function and behavior that are observed in adult animals given hormones in infancy. A probable explanation is that this procedure alters the sensitivity of the controlling brain mechanisms with regard to both the type and the temporal sequence of hormones to which they will respond.

In order to obtain the effects on sexual behavior and physiology that have been discussed, the experimental procedure must be carried out during a certain period of development, often referred to as a "critical period." In the rat, the critical period for affecting sexual development occurs in part after birth. Several experiments (3, 6, 14) have shown that the presence of androgen in small amounts (as little as 5 micrograms) in female rats during the first 5 days of postnatal life results in modification of the gonadotropin-releasing mechanism in the central nervous system from a cyclic to an acyclic one. Conversely, absence of androgen in the male rat during the first 48 hours after birth results in establishment of the release mechanism in its basic, cyclic, form. The presence of estrogen in either the intact female or the castrated male during this early period also disrupts the development of normal sexual function.

Although 5 to 6 days after birth is considered the critical period for affecting sexual development, there can be variation of as much as 3 days in this period, depending upon individual differences among the animals and the amount of hormone given. Another important determinant of these effects is the length of time the hormone is or is not present in the newborn animal within the critical period (Fig. 3). Studies now in progress (27) indicate that testosterone alone, which is metabolized in about 8 hours in the 1-day-old rat, does not produce the androgen sterilization in female rats that is seen when testosterone propionate, a longer-acting preparation, is used. Work with guinea pigs has shown that intrauterine injections of testosterone propionate must be given for a number of days in order for masculinization of female offspring to occur.

Thyroid Hormone

The number of studies dealing with early thyroid deficiency or excess has been growing. Absence of thyroid hormone in the developing organism has significant consequences for more physiological and behavioral functions than does the absence of androgen (28, 29). If thyroidectomy is performed immediately after birth in the rat, cretinism develops. Growth is normal for the first 2 weeks of life, but then it levels off at the animal's normal 3-week size. Opening of the eyes and vagina is retarded, and maturation of many reflex behaviors, such as the righting response, is delayed. In the central nervous system, myelination is retarded, and there is less-than-normal branching and connecting of cell processes in the cortex. Protein synthesis is also impaired in the nervous system, and electroencephalogram patterns are abnormal. Behaviorally, such animals are lethargic and show reduced capacity for learning and remembering. Thus, the absence of thyroid hormone does not affect any specific class of behaviors but alters the animals' basic ways of interacting with the total environment.

Control of thyroid hormone secretion is partially accomplished by means of a feedback mechanism similar to the "hormonostat" discussed for the gonads (30). There is recent evidence (31) that administration of thyroid hormone, thyroxin, to a newborn rat will cause permanent hypothyroidism in the animal. It is not known whether this is a result of damage to the thyroid itself or of an alteration in the central-nervous-system control mechanisms, but disruption of the hormonostat is indicated by the fact that pituitary and blood concentrations of thyroid-stimulating hormone are consistently low even though there is a deficit of thyroxin. As is the case in animals subjected to thyroidectomy shortly after birth, there is an impairment in both body growth and thyroid goiter response in these rats which received thyroxin in infancy.

Many of these deficits can be wholly or partially corrected if thyroid hormone replacement is begun within a certain critical period (15 days) following birth. However, once the critical first days of life have passed, many of the effects of hypothyroidism are irreversible and cannot be corrected by thyroid hormone replacement in adulthood (29). However, some of the behavioral deficits produced by thyroidectomy in adulthood can be corrected with hormone replacement (32).

Adrenal Hormones

We have discussed the effects that the alteration of hormone concentrations in the newborn animal has on the neuroendocrine regulation of gonadotropins and thyrotropin in the adult. There is also evidence that the central-nervous-system regulation of ACTH concentrations in adult rats may be a function of environmental events occurring during critical periods in infancy. Although there is little direct evidence that variation in the concentration of adrenal steroids in the newborn animal can cause permanent alteration in brain mechanisms, in light of the known effects of other hormones given during infancy, this possibility warrants serious consideration.

A number of studies have shown that adult animals given various forms of stimulation during a critical period in infancy differ markedly from nonstimulated animals in the temporal pattern of their steroid response to acute noxious stimulation and the magnitude of their steroid response to novel stimulation or novel experiences. Much of this research has been reviewed elsewhere (33), and only a brief summary is given here.

Animals that were stimulated in infancy by being picked up daily, placed in another cage for 3 minutes, and then returned to the nest show a more rapid and greater steroid response to a brief but intensive electric shock in adulthood than is shown by animals not handled in this way (34). (The word "handling," as used throughout this article, refers to this procedure.) Animals that have not been handled respond more slowly to the stress, but in such animals the response to stress tends to persist over a much longer period (35). However, a recent experiment (36) has shown that, at 0, 5, and 15 minutes after the end of a 3-minute period of free activity in an open field, rats that had been handled in infancy secreted significantly *less* adrenal steroids than rats not handled

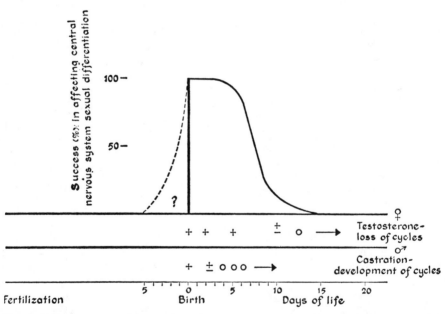

Fig. 3. Diagram summarizing various data concerning the critical period during which the central nervous system of the rat becomes sexually differentiated. The upper line of symbols (+, effective; ±, possibly effective; 0, ineffectual) shows the days after birth when administration of testosterone to the female rat evokes masculinization of the nervous system. The lower line of symbols shows the days when castration of the newborn male rat allows retention of a female type nervous system. The curve shows success in affecting central-nervous-system sexual differentiation. [From Harris (9)]

in infancy (Fig. 4). The handled rats do show a response to the novel situation, but a less extreme one. It has also been shown (22) that rats handled in infancy explore more freely and defecate less in a novel environment than their nonhandled controls do.

On the basis of these experiments the hypothesis has been developed that one of the major consequences of handling in infancy may be the endowment of the organism with the capacity to make responses more appropriate to the demands of the environment, including

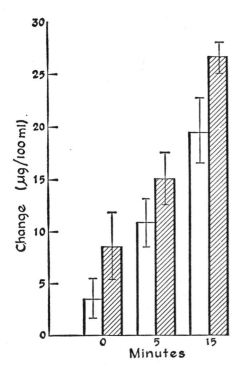

Fig. 4. Mean change in plasma concentrations of corticosteroids at 0-, 5-, and 15-minute intervals after a 3-minute period of open-field testing in adulthood for rats which had either been handled (open columns) or not handled (hatched columns) in infancy. The values for change were derived by subtracting the values obtained for steroid concentrations after the open-field testing from the mean value for base-line control subjects. The small bars represent the standard error of the mean.

appropriate responses to stress. If "adaptiveness" includes the ability to respond according to the demands of the environment, then animals handled in infancy can be said to be more adaptable since they can respond with a moderate steroid output to a novel situation and with a near-maximum output to a physically threatening one, while animals not handled in infancy can only give a near-maximum response to any change in the environment.

The question which now arises concerns the nature of the physiological processes in the newborn animal whereby handling in infancy can permanently affect the adrenal system so that the adult animal can respond more appropriately. There are differences in the development of the hypothalamo-pituitary-adrenal system in handled and nonhandled rats which may help to provide an answer. The ability of the infant rat to respond to cold with a significant depletion of adrenal ascorbic acid appears several days earlier in the animal that has been handled (37). Recently in our laboratory (38) it has been shown that, in handled animals as young as 3 days old, a significant increase in adrenal steroids occurs following electric shock, while no such increase is seen in nonhandled animals younger than about 9 days old (Fig. 5). In addition, handled animals show a greater steroid response to ACTH injected either 6 or 9 days after birth (Fig. 6). Thus there are changes in the adrenal steroid levels in the handled rat at a time during development when the central-nervous-system mechanisms that control physiological functions in the adult are not yet permanently established.

A Possible Central-Nervous-System Mechanism

In proposing models which partially explain the fact that animals handled during the critical period are able to make more appropriate responses to the environment than nonhandled animals, one can approach the problem either in terms of the animal's ability to make the necessary discriminations among stimuli on the input side or in terms of its ability to make differential responses on the output side. There is no evidence available concerning the effects of early handling on the animal's ability to discriminate among stimuli, but there is a model which might explain the effects of early handling in terms of the responses available to the organism.

It has been postulated that control of adrenal cortical function in adult organisms is partially accomplished by means of a homeostatic feedback mechanism or hormonostat (39). In such a system, the concentration of corticosteroids in the blood is monitored in the central nervous system and compared with a controlling set point. If the concentration of circulating steroids is higher than this set point, ACTH secretion and, consequently, adrenal output diminish. If the concentration is below this set point, then ACTH is released and more steroids are produced.

In this hormonostat, moreover, the set point is not fixed at a given level; it can vary to some extent, depending upon the demands of the environment and the inner states of the organism. The sensitivity of the hormonostat is determined by the number of values this set point can have between its minimum value, which corresponds to the concentration of steroids when the animal is resting, and its maximum value, which corresponds to the concentration under conditions of extreme stress. Thus it may be that handling, by

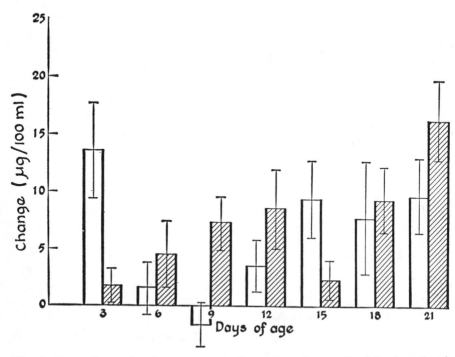

Fig. 5. Mean change in plasma concentrations of corticosteroids following electric shock (0.1 milliampere) in previously handled (open columns) and nonhandled (hatched columns) infant rats, at various ages. The small bars represent the standard error.

causing variation in the concentration of adrenal steroids in the infant animal, modifies the set point during a critical time in development so that it can vary in a graded manner in the adult, with several possible values between the minimum and the maximum. This could explain why handled rats are able to respond to novel but not physically threatening stimuli, such as the open field, with a moderate increase in adrenal steroids, and to shock with a large and rapid increase. In the nonhandled newborn rat there is less variation in adrenal steroid concentration during the critical period, and the set point develops fewer possible values. In these animals the hormonostat tends to operate either at "resting" level, if there is no change in the environment, or at levels close to maximum if there is any change at all, whether or not the change is physiologically threatening.

Recent work in our laboratory suggests that the variation in concentration of steroids that is seen in the handled animal may come about not only as a result of the handling of the infant but also as a result of disturbance of the mother during the handling process. The resulting variation in the mother's steroids could be communicated to the young, possibly through the milk. This idea is supported by findings which in-

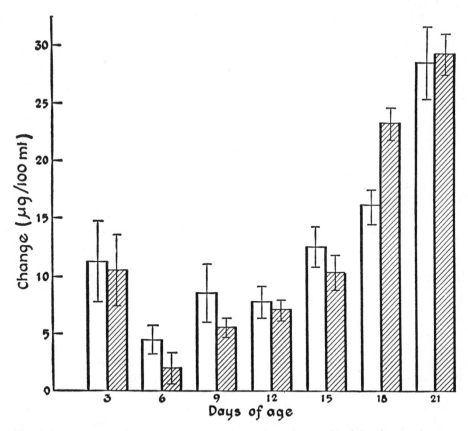

Fig. 6. Mean change in plasma concentrations of corticosteroids following an intravenous injection of ACTH (10 milliunits per 100 grams) in previously handled (open columns) and nonhandled (hatched columns) rats, at various ages. The small bars represent the standard error.

dicate that the circulatory portal system between the median eminence of the hypothalamus and the pituitary is not developed before the animal is 5 days old (40), and that feedback mechanisms of the type found in the adult thus would not be operating in the newborn animal.

Although there is no direct evidence that the more varied steroid output of the adrenal system in the handled animals causes the permanent changes in the central-nervous-system mechanisms that have been hypothesized, it seems reasonable to assume that adrenal steroids in the newborn animal play an important role in determining the sensitivity of the brain areas which control adrenal functioning in the adult.

Implicit in the foregoing discussion is the notion that there are specific time periods in development during which particular types of stimulation will have profound and irreversible effects upon the physiology and behavior of the adult organism. Here again is the idea of a critical period before or after which stimulation will have little or no effect. Although there has been controversy concerning this hypothesis (41), data do exist which indicate that handling during the first 5 days of life is critical for subsequent physiological changes in both developing and adult organisms. Levine and Lewis (42) handled infant rats on days 2 to 5, 6 to 9, 10 to 13, or 2 to 13 after birth; control animals were not disturbed. When the animals were 14 days old, studies were made to determine whether adrenal ascorbic acid was depleted following exposure to cold. The groups handled on days 2 to 5 or 2 to 13 exhibited significant depletion of adrenal ascorbic acid, but the other groups did not. Bell, Reisner, and Linn (35) handled rats on days 2 to 5, 6 to 9, and 10 to 13, and they also used undisturbed controls. When the rats were 46 days old, half the animals in each group received electroconvulsive shock. Twenty-four hours later blood samples were obtained from all the animals, and the glucose concentration was measured. Those rats which had been handled on days 2 to 5 showed no significant increase in glucose levels following shock; the blood sugar concentrations of the shocked animals in the other groups were significantly higher than those of their controls.

These results appear somewhat paradoxical, but it should be noted that, whereas in the Levine and Lewis study (42) the depletion in adrenal ascorbic acid was measured 90 minutes after the onset of stress, in the experiment of Bell and his co-workers (35) the blood glucose concentrations were determined after an interval of 24 hours. In addition to demonstrating that there is a critical period for handling of newborn animals, these data also indicate a difference between the time course of the stress response in adult animals that were handled during the critical period and those that were not.

Thus we have an instance where the same treatment of the newborn has an effect for two different stresses, two physiological measures, and two test ages. Much more evidence concerning critical periods has been reported, but it is by no means as clear as that just presented. Denenberg (43) has pointed out that the intensity of the infantile experience may be an important determinant of the critical period. He has demonstrated (44) that rats handled from days 1 to 3, 3 to 5, and 1 to 5 of life did not differ from controls in avoidance learning (no physiological measures were taken), whereas animals shocked on those days did differ from the controls (45). More recently, in our laboratory we have found that a single exposure to extreme cold within the first 12 hours after birth improves avoidance conditioning in adulthood. In contrast, a single handling experience during the same period is without effect. Inasmuch as we are hypothesizing that the effects of handling in infancy are attributable to an increase in adrenal steroids and the action of these steroids on the central nervous system during a critical period in development, it seems reasonable to assume that the intensity of the stimuli to which the newborn animal is exposed is an important determinant of the magnitude and duration of its steroid response.

Unfortunately, the evidence for a critical period for early stimulation which affects later adrenal response and central-nervous-system organization is not nearly as definitive as the evidence which has been presented for the effects of gonadal hormones in the newborn on sexual differentiation of brain mechanisms. However, it seems reasonable to postulate at this time that changes in the central nervous system occur when stimulation is applied during critical periods of development.

Discussion

All the experimental evidence presented here supports the view that alterations in the hormonal status of the newborn animal have profound and permanent effects on the animal's subsequent biological functioning. More specifically, we hypothesize that hormones in the newborn are partially responsible for the organization of some of the central-nervous-system control mechanisms which will control the activation of these hormones in the adult. For the three hormone systems discussed above, the effects of varying hormone concentrations in newborn animals have differed slightly.

In the gonadal system, we have postulated that the action of steroids in the newborn animal alters the patterns, and probably also the amounts, of hormone secretion in the adult. In addition, the steroids present in the infant also determine to what hormones the brain

centers controlling sex behavior in the adult will be responsive. If testosterone is removed from the male rat immediately after birth, through castration, the animal will show complete female receptive behavior in response to administration of estrogen or progesterone in adulthood. This is not the case in animals which are castrated after the first 5 days of life. Similarly, administration of testosterone or estrogen, in large doses, to female rats during the first 120 hours after birth renders them incapable of responding normally to female sex hormones in adulthood. Paradoxically, females given estrogen in infancy sometimes show complete male sex behavior patterns in response to testosterone in adulthood, while adult animals not given estrogen in infancy only show mounting behavior when given the same amount of testosterone.

It has been found that administration of thyroid hormone to the newborn rat permanently suppresses thyroid function. It may be that the set point for the thyroid hormonostat is set so low by the early treatment that very small amounts of thyroid hormone are able to shut down the thyrotropin-releasing mechanisms in the brain. For the adrenal system, we have proposed that the increased variation of concentrations of adrenal steroids in the infant animal following handling allows the controlling set point of the brain hormonostat to elicit, in the adult, graded adrenal responses appropriate to the demands of the environment. The smaller amount of variation in the nonhandled animals means that, in the adult, the adrenal system will respond in a more "all-or-none" manner, and that any change in the environmental demands on the animal will elicit a near-maximum response.

Another indication that hormones may have different actions at different stages of development comes from evidence that endocrine systems are active during the first few days after birth, cease functioning for a week or more, and then assume adult functioning. With regard to the production of male sex hormone, two distinct generations of Leydig cells have been described in rat testes (46), one occurring in the fetus and infant and the other appearing at puberty. In the rat, a change in concentration of corticosteroids can be elicited in the first 3 to 4 days after birth by an injection of ACTH, but a response of the same magnitude cannot be obtained again until the rat is about 15 days old (Fig. 6). In the two cases, there is a similar ontogenetic pattern of hormone activity, with two active periods of endocrine function separated by a period of little hormone secretion. Further evidence regarding a unique role for hormones in newborn animals is given by the data on critical periods. Unless handling is begun shortly after birth, sex hormone treatment within 4 to 5 days of birth, and thyroid replacement in thyroid-deficient animals within 2 weeks of birth, irreversible changes in physiology and behavior occur.

Perhaps most indicative and exciting for future research are the interrelationships which have been found among the endocrine systems. It has been shown that manipulation, in infancy, of either the adrenal, gonadal, or thyroid systems can affect the functioning of another of these systems.

The common biochemical derivation of the adrenal and gonadal steroids may in part explain some of the interactions which have been found. Male rats given estrogen in infancy show a greater adrenal-steroid response to the stress of ether anesthesia than do injected controls (27). Injection of sex hormones into newborn animals also affects later emotional behavior (26) and thyroid function (6). Simply injecting female rats with saline right after birth reduces the amount of male mounting observed when they are given testosterone after

castration in adulthood, as shown by recent work in our laboratory. Conversely, handling in infancy advances the onset of puberty in rats, an event which is partially controlled by the sex and thyroid hormones (47), and also affects thyroid response to cold (48). Further, it has been shown that both emotional and physical stress can markedly alter thyroid function (49). These results are only the beginning of what will eventually be a long list of interactions among the neuroendocrine systems at all stages of development.

It appears that the effects of variations of both the external and the internal environment are mediated through basic, but as yet undetermined, biochemical processes. The elucidation of these processes should bring us much closer to an understanding of the intimate relationship between physiology and behavior.

References and Notes

1. R. A. Hinde, in Lessons from Animal Behavior for the Clinician, S. A. Barnett, Ed. (National Spastics Society, London, 1962); J. P. Scott, Science 138, 949 (1962).
2. W. C. Young, in Sex and Internal Secretions, W. C. Young, Ed. (Williams and Wilkins, Baltimore, ed. 3, 1961), vol. 2, 1173–1239.
3. ———. R. W. Goy, C. H. Phoenix, Science 143, 212 (1964).
4. H. M. Clark, Anat. Record 61, 193 (1934).
5. C. A. Pfeiffer, Amer. J. Anat. 58, 195 (1936).
6. G. W. Harris and S. Levine, J. Physiol. London 181, 379 (1965).
7. S. Levine and R. Mullins, Jr., Science 144, 185 (1964); R. E. Whalen and R. D. Nadler, ibid. 141, 273 (1963).
8. R. E. Whalen, J. Comp. Physiol. Psychol. 57, 175 (1964).
9. G. W. Harris, Endocrinology 75, 627 (1964).
10. ——— and D. Jacobsohn, Proc. Roy. Soc. London Ser. B 159, 263 (1952).
11. H. Selye, Endocrinology 27, 657 (1940).
12. J. G. Wilson, W. C. Young, J. B. Hamilton, Yale J. Biol. Med. 13, 189 (1940).
13. In most of the studies in this area, mating has been used as a criterion, for sex behavior. However, the conclusion that mating has occurred is usually based on observation either of sperm or a plug in the vagina at some unspecified time after the male and female are placed together, and not on direct observation of sexual behavior.
14. C. A. Barraclough, Endocrinology 68, 62 (1961).
15. S. J. Segal and D. C. Johnson, Arch. Anat. Microscop. Morphol. Exp. 48, 261 (1959).
16. C. A. Barraclough and R. A. Gorski, Anat. Record 139, 205 (1961).

17. R. F. Mullins, Jr., and S. Levine, "Sexual behavior in female rats injected with testosterone 120 hours after birth," presented at Midwestern Psychological Assoc. Meeting, 1964.
18. J. G. Wilson, *Anat. Record* 86, 341 (1943); ――― and H. C. Wilson, *Endocrinology* 33, 353 (1943).
19. R. A. Gorski, *Amer. J. Physiol.* 205, 842 (1963).
20. H. H. Feder and R. E. Whalen, *Science* 147, 306 (1965).
21. C. P. Richter, *Endocrinology* 17, 445 (1933).
22. S. Levine and P. L. Broadhurst, *J. Comp. Physiol. Psychol.* 56, 423 (1963).
23. C. Y. Nakamuara and N. H. Anderson, *ibid.* 55, 740 (1962).
24. W. L. Sawrey and D. H. Long, *ibid.* 55, 603 (1962).
25. E. E. Anderson, *J. Genet. Psychol.* 56, 149 (1940); *ibid.*, p. 159; *ibid.*, p. 169.
26. J. Gray, S. Levine, P. W. Broadhurst, *Animal Behavior* 13, 33 (1965).
27. S. Levine and R. F. Mullins, Jr., unpublished data.
28. J. T. Eayrs, *Animal Behavior* 7, 1 (1959).
29. J. T. Eayrs, *British Med. Bull.* 16, 122 (1960).
30. S. Reichlin, in *Thyrotropin*, S. C. Werner, Ed. (Thomas, Springfield, Ill., 1963).
31. J. L. Bakke and N. Lawrence, in "6th Pan American Congress of Endocrinology," *Excerpta Med. Intern. Congr. Ser. No. 99* (1965), p. E60.
32. J. T. Eayrs and S. Levine, *J. Endocrinol.* 25, 505 (1963).
33. V. H. Denenberg, in *The Behaviour of Domestic Animals*, E. Hafez, Ed. (Williams and Wilkins, Baltimore, 1962), pp. 109–138; G. Newton and S. Levine, Eds., *Early Experience* (Thomas, Springfield, Ill., in press).
34. S. Levine, *Science* 135, 795 (1962).
35. R. W. Bell, G. Reisner, T. Linn, *ibid.* 133, 1428 (1961).
36. S. Levine, G. Haltmeyer, V. Denenberg, unpublished data.
37. S. Levine, M. Alpert, G. W. Lewis, *J. Comp. Physiol. Psychol.* 51, 774 (1958).
38. S. Levine, in "6th Pan American Congress of Endocrinology," *Excerpta Med. Intern. Congr. Ser. No. 99* (1965), p. E103.
39. F. E. Yates and J. Urquhart, *Physiol. Rev.* 42, 359 (1962); S. Schapiro, E. Geller, S. Eiduson, *Proc. Soc. Exp. Biol. Med.* 109, 937 (1962).
40. R. S. Glydon, *J. Anat.* 91, 237 (1957).
41. T. C. Schneirla and J. S. Rosenblatt, *Science* 139, 1110 (1963); J. P. Scott, *ibid.*, p. 1115.
42. S. Levine and G. W. Lewis, *ibid.* 129, 42 (1959).
43. V. H. Denenberg, *Psychol. Rev.* 71, 335 (1964).
44. ―――, *J. Comp. Physiol. Psychol.* 55, 813 (1962).
45. ――― and N. J. Kline, *Can. J. Psychol.* 18, 1 (1964).
46. M. Niemi and M. Ikonen, *Endocrinology* 72, 443 (1963).
47. J. H. Morton, V. H. Denenberg, N. X. Zarrow, *ibid.*, p. 439.
48. V. Denenberg, B. Eliftheriou, L. Grota, unpublished data.
49. J. G. Gibson, *J. Psychosomatic Res.* 6, 93 (1962).
50. This study was supported by NIH research grant MH 07435; NSF research grant GB 2570; the Leslie Fund, Chicago; research career development award 5-K3-19, 9 16-02 (to S.L.); and NIH predoctoral fellowship 5 F1 MH-22, 091 (to R.M.). We thank Drs. David Hamburg and Joan Danellis for their critical reading of the manuscript and Dr. R. B. Clayton for invaluable suggestions concerning some of the concepts discussed.

Aggression in Adult Mice: Modification by Neonatal Injections of Gonadal Hormones

Abstract. *Incidence of spontaneous aggression in adult male mice given a single injection of estradiol benzoate (0.4 milligram) when they were 3 days old was less than that of controls injected with oil. Aggressiveness was increased among adult females injected with either estradiol or testosterone propionate (1 milligram) at the same age. The increased aggressiveness noted among females given androgen was further documented during subsequent mating tests, when these females often attacked, wounded, and, in one case, killed naive males.*

The sexual differentiation of particular behavioral or neuroendocrine control systems may be influenced by the presence of gonadal hormones during infancy in rodents (*1*). For example, neonatal administration of androgens to females results in an acyclic, male-like secretion of gonadotropin during adulthood rather than in the cyclic pattern characteristic of normal adult females (2). Similarly, sexual behavior of female rats may be masculinized to a degree if they are given neonatal injections of androgen, or that of males may be feminized if they are castrated during infancy, provided that appropriate gonadal hormones are administered during adulthood (1, 3). Estrogens, depending upon the time and dose of their injection, may mimic some of these effects of androgens (4). We hypothesized that aggressive behavior could also be modified following treatment with androgens or estrogens during infancy. Our results demonstrate that aggressiveness was increased in adult female mice if they were given either androgen

or estrogen as neonates; aggressiveness in adult males was partially suppressed if they were injected with estrogen during infancy.

Complete litters of 3-day-old C57BL/6J mice of both sexes were injected subcutaneously with 0.05 ml of corn oil containing either 1 mg of testosterone propionate, 0.4 mg of estradiol benzoate, or nothing. Mice were weaned at 21 to 25 days of age and housed singly until tested for aggressiveness at 80 to 90 days of age. Spontaneous aggression (5) was measured in test chambers (12 by 12 by 6 inches) with removable partitions in the middle. Single mice of the same sex and treatment were placed on either side of the partition. It was removed 20 minutes later and the mice were observed until a fight was initiated, or for a maximum of 15 minutes (Table 1). The same pair of mice was tested once daily for three consecutive days, after which vaginal smears were obtained for five consecutive days from all females. All males and 12 females from each group were then autopsied to verify the expected effects of neonatal injections on reproductive tract morphology. Ovaries, uteri, and testes were weighed and examined histologically. Seminal vesicles were homogenized in water and analyzed for fructose (6).

The remaining females from each of the three groups received subcutaneous injections of progesterone (0.3 mg per mouse per day) for 8 days to induce estrous cycles (7). On the afternoon of the 8th day, they were paired with naive males in the females' home cages. Our purpose in this secondary experiment was to verify the lack of mating in females treated neonatally with testosterone or estradiol and to follow a suggestion by Barraclough that changes in aggressiveness might be more obvious in such a situation (8). Incidence of fighting was recorded for the first hour after pairing, and all pairs were in-

Table 1. Number of pairs (of same sex) in which fighting occurred at least once during three encounters and total number of fights occurring during all three encounters.

Neonatal treatment	Fighting at least once (No.)	Fights in three encounters (No.)
Males		
Oil	23/24	51/72
Testosterone	18/19	46/57
Estradiol	10/20	20/60
Females		
Oil	1/24	1/72
Testosterone	5/18	10/54
Estradiol	4/14	5/42

Table 2. Number of male-female pairs in which severe fighting occurred within the first hour after pairing and number in which wounding of one member occurred within 18 hours. Females had been previously tested in the primary experiment (Table 1), after which they were given progesterone daily for 8 days and then paired with naive males.

Neonatal treatment of females	Fighting (1st hour)	Wounding (18 hours)
Oil	0/20	0/20
Testosterone	12/23	5/23*
Estradiol	4/14	0/14

* One pair in which female was wounded, three pairs in which male was wounded, and one pair in which male was killed.

178

spected for wounding and presence of vaginal plugs on the following three mornings. Males used in this experiment were about 100 days old, intact, and sexually and experimentally inexperienced; each male had been housed with four or five others since weaning.

The results of the primary experiment, in which mice were given the opportunity to fight only members of the same sex and treatment group, are presented in Table 1. Spontaneous fighting occurred at least once during three encounters in all but one pair of males in each of the two groups that received injections of either oil or testosterone during infancy. Neonatal injections of estradiol reduced the incidence of fighting in adult males to 50 percent ($P<.01$). Only 4 percent of the control females fought, whereas fighting among pairs that had received neonatal injections of either testosterone or estradiol increased to 28 and 29 percent, respectively ($P < .05$ in both cases).

The secondary experiment, in which females were injected with progesterone for 8 days and then paired with normal males, revealed marked aggressiveness on the part of females injected neonatally with testosterone (Table 2); fighting among such pairs was often vicious and usually initiated by the females. Females treated with estradiol also fought with males, but both the incidence and severity of fights were lower. No fighting was noted among pairs in which the female had been injected only with oil in infancy. No vaginal plugs were found in any females receiving steroid neonatally, but 55 percent of the females injected with oil had plugs during the 3 days after pairing.

The effects of neonatal injections of estradiol or testosterone on vaginal cycles and reproductive tracts were similar to previous findings (2, 4) and will be reported here only to an extent necessary for correlation with the behavioral data. Neonatal injections of

Table 3. Body weight, relative (paired) organ weights, and fructose concentrations in seminal vesicles of males treated neonatally with oil, testosterone, or estradiol; body and relative uterine weights of similarly treated females (mean ± standard error).

Neonatal treatment	Males					Females		
	No.	Body wt. (g)	Testes (mg/g body wt.)	Seminal vesicle (mg/g body wt.)	Seminal vesicle fructose (µg)	No.	Body wt. (g)	Uterus (mg/g body wt.)
Oil	48	27.8 ± 0.4	7.53 ± 0.52	2.42 ± 0.27	174.0 ± 6.3	12	22.6 ± 0.7	3.19 ± 0.31
Testosterone	37	27.3 ± 0.5	5.93 ± 0.20*	1.98 ± 0.08*	137.0 ± 5.4*	12	28.2 ± 1.0*	5.23 ± 0.67*
Estradiol	40	24.4 ± 0.4*	4.61 ± 0.41*	1.07 ± 0.15*	48.2 ± 4.7*	12	23.1 ± 0.8	2.37 ± 0.38

* Significantly different from oil controls, as determined by analysis of variance, with a probability of at least $P < .05$.

estradiol in males resulted in decreased body and reproductive organ weights and relative aspermia. Injections of testosterone in infancy also decreased weights of male organs but to a lesser extent than that caused by estradiol (Table 3). All vaginal smears obtained from all females injected neonatally with either steroid contained approximately 80 percent cornified cells and 20 percent leukocytes, and ovaries of such females were polyfollicular and devoid of corpora lutea. Body and uterine weights were increased among females injected neonatally with testosterone.

Androgen is a necessary prerequisite for attack behavior in inexperienced male mice (9), whereas estrogen administered during adulthood has no effect on aggressiveness of males (10). The reduction in spontaneous aggression shown by males injected with estrogen in our study was correlated with large changes in their reproductive tracts, and secretion of testicular androgen was probably considerably reduced. Weights of reproductive organs were also lower in males given neonatal injections of androgen, but they were as aggressive as control males. These facts suggest that those males injected with androgen neonatally probably had sufficient androgen in their circulation during adulthood to permit a high degree of aggressive behavior, whereas those that received estrogen did not. The amount of fructose in seminal vesicles, a good correlate of androgen titers (6), was reduced by 72 percent among males given estradiol in infancy compared to that in controls given oil (Table 3). The comparable figure for males receiving testosterone neonatally was only 21 percent and, hence, the postulate appears reasonably good on this basis.

The low incidence of spontaneous aggression found among control females agrees well with observations of other workers using mice (11). Androgen will not increase aggressiveness in either immature or mature gonadectomized females (12). However, neonatal injections of testosterone, and to a lesser extent estradiol, increase aggressiveness in females after maturity. These effects were significant in both experiments although more dramatic in the uncontrolled secondary experiment where some previously tested females were paired with naive males in the females' home cages after receiving progesterone to induce estrous cycles. Under such conditions mating did not occur, and the females usually attacked and sometimes wounded males. Wounding was sufficiently severe to cause death in one case. The reasons for the dramatic effects observed in this experiment are not readily obvious because of its uncontrolled nature and the data are presented only as an extreme example of a phenomenon observed in the primary experiment. Two investigators have reported that "masculine or aggressive responses" interfered with normal female sexual behavior when rats were treated with estrogen or testosterone in infancy (13) but not to the extent shown in the present study with mice.

A reasonable hypothesis to explain the increased aggressiveness of females treated neonatally with gonadal hormones is the alteration of a neural mechanism whose sexual differentiation is normally regulated by androgen in infancy. Such a concept parallels the conclusions of many studies dealing with either sex behavior or the hypothalamic control of gonadotropin secretion, and some degree of experimental mimicking of androgen by estrogen is well documented in this respect. It does not seem reasonable at this time, however, to suspect the hypothalamus at the expense of other neural structures because the number of brain areas known to function in aggression is relatively large (14). Furthermore, as evidenced by changes in body weight in both sexes, the effects of early administration of steroids may be widespread.

F. H. Bronson
Claude Desjardins

Jackson Laboratory,
Bar Harbor, Maine 04609

References and Notes

1. S. Levine and R. F. Mullins, *Science* **152**, 1585 (1966).
2. C. A. Barraclough, *Endocrinology* **68**, 62 (1961); R. A. Gorski, *J. Reprod. Fertil. Suppl.* **1**, 67 (1966).
3. R. E. Whalen and D. A. Edwards, *Anat. Rec.* **157**, 173 (1967).
4. G. W. Harris and S. Levine, *J. Physiol. London* **181**, 379 (1965).
5. J. P. Scott, *Amer. Zool.* **6**, 683 (1966).
6. J. S. Davis and J. E. Gander, *Anal. Biochem.* **19**, 72 (1967).
7. C. A. Barraclough, *Fed. Proc.* **15**, 9 (1956).
8. ——, personal communication.
9. E. A. Beeman, *Physiol. Zool.* **20**, 373 (1947); E. B. Sigg, C. Day, C. Colombo, *Endocrinology* **78**, 679 (1966).
10. J. E. Gustafson and G. Winokur, *J. Neuropsychiat.* **1**, 182 (1960).
11. E. Fredericson, *J. Comp. Physiol. Psychol.* **45**, 89 (1952).
12. J. V. Levy, *Proc. West Virginia Acad. Sci.* **26**, 14 (1954); J. Tollman and J. A. King, *Brit. J. Anim. Behav.* **6**, 147 (1956).
13. H. H. Feder, *Anat. Rec.* **157**, 79 (1967); A. A. Gerall, *ibid.*, p. 97.
14. J. M. R. Delgado, *Amer. Zool.* **6**, 669 (1966).
15. This investigation was supported in part by PHS grants FR-05545-05 and HD-00767.

Journal of Comparative and Physiological Psychology
1968, Vol. 66, No. 1, 244–246

DIFFERENCES IN LOCOMOTOR ACTIVITY AND BRAIN-SEROTONIN METABOLISM IN DIFFERENTIALLY HOUSED MICE[1]

WALTER B. ESSMAN

Queens College of the City University of New York

Male CF-1 mice were isolated or group housed from weaning (21 days) until 45 days of age. At 45 days of age, isolated animals showed higher levels of locomotor activity, elevated brain-serotonin levels, and an increased rate of brain-serotonin turnover, with a lower brain-serotonin turnover time than did mice housed under aggregated conditions. These differences suggest that the behavioral pattern which develops in mice as a result of housing under isolated conditions may be related to the altered pattern of brain-serotonin metabolism which emerges with isolation

Several studies have indicated that differential housing in mice leads to a variety of behavioral differences as well as differences in the physiological response of the animal to pharmacological conditions. Among such behavioral differences are increased excitability and aggressiveness in isolated as compared

with group-housed mice (Allee, 1942; Scott, 1947; Welch & Welch, 1965; Yen, Stanger, & Milliman, 1959). Welch and Welch (1965) have accounted for behavioral differences resulting from differential housing on the basis of elevated brain norepinephrine levels in individually housed mice. It has also been shown that Swiss-Webster mice, isolated for 3 wk. postweaning, showed greater locomotor activity levels than aggregated animals by the fourth postweaning day (Essman, 1966). Also, CF-1

[1] This study was supported in part by Grants MH-08698-03 and MH-13191-01 from the United States Public Health Service.

strain mice, isolated from weaning through adulthood, tended to show higher locomotor activity levels than did aggregates. Whereas brain norepinephrine was somewhat higher in aggregated animals maintained under these conditions for a prolonged period of time, concentrations of the amine were negatively correlated with locomotor activity in isolated animals (Essman & Smith, 1967). With 4 wk. of isolation or grouping, male albino mice were shown to have comparable concentrations of brain serotonin, but greater concentrations of the major serotonin metabolite, 5-hydroxyindoleacetic acid (Garattini, Giacaloni, & Valzelli, 1967). There is a major discrepancy between these findings, which indicated an increase in serotonin turnover time in isolated compared with group-housed (ten per cage) mice, and our findings (Essman & Smith, 1967), which showed an increase in turnover time in aggregated (five per cage) mice. The differences in the two studies were the strain of mice used, the number of mice in the group-housed condition, the age at which differential housing was introduced, and the duration of differential housing. The purpose of the present study was to determine the extent to which differential housing would lead to differences in locomotor activity and brain-serotonin metabolism under conditions wherein such differential housing was introduced at weaning and maintained for 3 wk.

Method

All male CF-1 strain mice, from litters matched for age and size, were randomly assigned to one of two differential housing conditions at weaning (21 days of age). Sixteen mice were isolated, i.e., individually housed in transparent plastic cages (18 × 25 cm.), and provided with Sanicel bedding and ad-lib food and water. For 20 Ss, aggregation housing conditions involved housing five mice in an identical cage. At 23 days of age Ss were tested for locomotor activity. Each S was individually placed in a Lucite box (16 × 26 × 12.5 cm.) with a floor consisting of four aluminum plates (7 × 11 cm.), separated by a space of 5 mm., each mounted on a Lucite rod. The plates were wired through an external power supply requiring approximately 35 μa. to activate the input to an external six-digit counter panel. When S completed the circuit by maintaining momentary contact between any two adjacent plates, a single count was registered on the counter. The activity boxes were located on individual shelves in an insulated chamber, maintained at 26° C., with a low ambient level of illumination. All activity testing was done between 9:30 and 11:30 A.M. and the testing sequence for individual Ss was determined from a table of random numbers. A total cumulative record for the 15-min. testing session was recorded for each S.

From 23–45 days of age Ss were maintained under the respective housing conditions; each S

was transferred to an identical clean cage two times each week. At 45 days of age activity testing was again carried out and a total cumulative activity record for the 15-min. testing session was again obtained.

Procedures for the estimation of brain-serotonin metabolism were carried out 1 hr. after the completion of the activity testing. These involved the application of steady-state kinetics (Tozer, Neff, & Brodie, 1966) to determine the turnover of brain serotonin under conditions wherein synthesis rate equals degradation rate. Use of a monoamine oxidase inhibitor to increase brain serotonin and decrease 5-hydroxyindoleacetic acid provided for conditions wherein the rate of 5-hydroxyindoleacetic acid decrease equaled the synthesis rate (Garattini et al., 1967). All Ss were given an ip injection of tranylcypromine (20 mg/kg) and then killed by cervical section at various times following injection. In addition, nine Ss, housed under identical isolated conditions, and five Ss, housed under identical aggregated conditions, were individually included for assay at this time. The whole brain was removed from the skull and was frozen with 5 sec. in a beaker containing Freon 21. The cerebellum and olfactory bulbs were removed and discarded, and the brains were bisected through the midline and each hemisphere was independently weighed and then stored at −30° C. The tissue samples were individually homogenized and separately extracted for assay of serotonin, according to a modification of the method of Bogdanski, Pletscher, Brodie, and Udenfriend (1956); and 5-hydroxyindoleacetic acid was determined, utilizing the method of Udenfriend, Weissbach, and Clark (1955). Steady-state kinetic measurements of serotonin turnover were determined from rate constants of 5-hydroxyindoleacetic acid loss from the brain tissue, calculated according to the method of Tozer et al. (1966).

TABLE 1
Locomotor Activity Counts for Differentially Housed Mice

Experimental condition	n	At 23 days of age		At 45 days of age	
		M	SD	M	SD
Isolated	16	234.75	64.87	153.26	76.00
Aggregated	20	215.05	76.25	85.78	55.00

Results

Locomotor activity data for the isolated and aggregated Ss are summarized in Table 1. The raw activity data were logarithmically transformed and a t test of the mean log differences was performed. At 23 days of age, 2 days following the initiation of differential housing, no significant differences between the activity of isolated and aggregated Ss emerged ($t = .83$, $df = 34$, $p > .40$), whereas after 24 days of differential housing, the locomotor activity level of the isolated Ss was significantly higher than that shown by the aggregated animals ($t = 2.78$, $df = 34$, $p < .01$).

The data for brain-serotonin metabolism in the differentially housed Ss are summarized in Table 2. Differences in brain-serotonin concentration were statistically significant ($t = 2.58$, $df = 48$, $p < .02$), with the isolated Ss showing appreciably higher brain-serotonin levels than were observed for the aggregated Ss. The concentration of 5-hydroxyindoleacetic acid was also significantly higher in the brains of isolated Ss ($t = 3.05$, $df = 48$, $p < .01$). The turnover time for brain serotonin, although somewhat longer among isolated Ss, did not differ significantly as a function of differential housing. Brain-serotonin turnover rate of isolated Ss was greater by approximately 31%. The chemical values obtained from 14 Ss which were differentially housed, but not tested for locomotor activity, were equivalent to those obtained from activity-tested Ss.

DISCUSSION

The data from this experiment indicate that male CF-1 mice that were isolated for a period of 24 days beginning at weaning showed locomotor activity levels which were significantly higher than those shown by mice of the same age and strain, housed five to a group for the same period of time. This finding is consistent

TABLE 2
BRAIN SEROTONIN METABOLISM FOR DIFFERENTIALLY HOUSED MICE

Experimental condition	*n*	Concentration (μg/gm)				Serotonin turnover	
		Serotonin		5-Hydroxy-indoleacetic acid		Rate (μg/gm/hr)	Time (in min.)
		M	SD	M	SD		
Isolated	25	1.02	.35	.56	.10	.64	96
Aggregated	25	.69	.15	.38	.07	.49	85

with previous observations reported for Swiss-Webster mice (Essman, 1966). For the present study, some basis upon which such activity differences emerge as a result of differential housing may be found in the observed differences in the serotonin metabolism. These results are partially consistent with other data (Essman & Smith, 1967) indicating that CF-1 mice, differentially housed at weaning, showed differences in serotonin metabolism, in that there was a greater turnover rate in isolated as compared with aggregated mice. The findings also agree

with those of Garattini et al. (1967), in which 4 wk. of differential housing led to increased brain-serotonin turnover time in isolated male albino mice. It is interesting to note that in their study, levels of brain serotonin did not differ as a result of differential housing and those concentrations reported for isolation- as well as group-housed mice were quite comparable with those obtained in the present study for the aggregated Ss. This observation might well indicate that the differences in brain-serotonin concentration emerged with differential housing only when such conditions were introduced at an early age; the data from the present study indicate that 21 days of age is early enough to result in the differences in brain serotonin reported.

The present data tend to suggest that brain-serotonin concentration is elevated as a result of isolation introduced at weaning, since the data for the aggregated Ss appeared consistent with previous data (Essman, 1967), in which mice of the same age and strain, housed ten per cage, showed comparable levels of brain serotonin.

Differences in locomotor activity, which emerged with differential housing, appear to be associated with differences in the concentration and metabolism of serotonin in the brain. It is, however, difficult to formulate a definite causal relationship between these observations inasmuch as increased locomotor activity as a result of isolation might account for the observed differences in serotonin metabolism, or differences in serotonin metabolism as a result of isolation might account for increased locomotor activity. It is also possible that the observed biochemical differences may not be directly related to isolation or to the increased locomotor activity levels which develop in isolated mice. A further consideration of brain-serotonin metabolism is suggested in relation to other behaviors, i.e., aggressiveness, dominance, fighting, and locomotor activity, which emerge with differential housing.

REFERENCES

ALLEE, W. C. Group organization among vertebrates. *Science*, 1942, **95**, 289–293.

BOGDANSKI, D. F., PLETSCHER, A., BRODIE, B. B., & UDENFRIEND, S. Identification and assay of serotonin in brain. *J. Pharmacol. exp. Ther.*, 1956, **117**, 82–88.

ESSMAN, W. B. The development of activity in isolated and aggregated mice. *Anim. Behav.*, 1966, **14**, 406–409.

ESSMAN, W. B. Changes in memory consolidation with alterations in neural RNA. *Neuropsychopharmacology: Proceedings V International Congress C.I.N.P.*, 1967, **129**, 108–113.

ESSMAN. W. B., & SMITH, G. E. Behavioral and neurochemical differences between differentially housed mice. *Amer. Zool.*, 1967, **7,** 792.

GARATTINI, S., GIACALONI, E., & VALZELLI, L. Isolation, aggressiveness and brain 5-hydroxytryptamine turnover. *J. pharm. Pharmacol.*, 1967, **19,** 338–339.

SCOTT, J. P. "Emotional" behavior of fighting mice caused by conflict between weak stimulatory and weak inhibitory training. *J. comp. physiol. Psychol.*, 1947, **40,** 275–282.

TOZER, T. N., NEFF, N. H., & BRODIE, B. B. Application of steady state kinetics to the synthesis rate and turnover time of serotonin in brain of normal and reserpine-treated rats. *J. Pharmacol. exp. Ther.*, 1966, **153,** 177–182.

UDENFRIEND, S., WEISSBACH, H., & CLARK, C. T. The estimation of 5-hydroxytryptamine (serotonin) in biochemical tissue. *J. biol. Chem.*, 1955, **215,** 337.

WELCH, B. L., & WELCH, A. S. Effect of grouping on the level of brain norepinepherine in white Swiss mice. *Life Sciences*, 1965, **4,** 1011–1018.

YEN, C. Y., STANGER, R. L., & MILLIMAN, N. Ataractic suppression of isolation-induced aggressive behavior. *Arch. int. Pharmacodyn.*, 1959, **123,** 179–185.

(Received August 14, 1967)

PART 4 The Development of Behavior

Part 3 covered material that might be described as part of the "biological background" of animal behavior. We covered several examples showing that hormone treatment early in life can affect the development of an organism and have important consequences for its adult behavior. Part 4 deals specifically with the study of behavioral development. However, the independent variables used in the experiments that follow are primarily *experiential* rather than physiological. This area of research has been under intensive investigation in recent years. Major insights into problems of behavioral determination have resulted from these studies and more are to be expected in the future.

In order to study the effects of differential early experience on behavior, we need base-line data on the normal development of the animal. Examples of such data are presented in Reading 22, in which C. L. Scudder and his colleagues compare the development of several groups of mice. You will note that the authors relate developmental differences to differences in the natural history of the genotypes. Would the authors of Reading 2 object to the comparisons made in this paper?

Once the normal developmental sequence of a species is known, it is possible to perform experimental investigations by adding or withholding certain early experiences. In Reading 23, John Fuller summarizes a series of such experiments performed over a number of years at The Jackson Laboratory in Bar Harbor, Maine. Fuller is a behavior geneticist and thus is always interested in the effects of genotypic differences on behavior. The experiments he describes generally involved two or more different breeds of dogs, especially beagles and terriers. Once again, as in Reading 10, important genotype–environment interactions are revealed.

A more complex example of such interactions is given in the next paper. Many different experiments have demonstrated that stressing a pregnant animal can affect the later behavior of her offspring. In Reading 24, DeFries, Weir, and Hegmann show that the magnitude of the effect depends both on the genotype of the mother and on the genotype of the fetus. Such complex interactions make life difficult for the experimenter, but they should be kept clearly in mind when interpreting experimental results, particularly when extrapolations to human behavior are made.

In the introduction to Part 1, and in certain readings in that section, the nature–nurture controversy was reviewed. Two of the favorite behavioral patterns discussed during that controversy were the development of pecking in domestic chickens and the development of bird-song. Reading 25 is a modern analysis of the former. Note particularly the thoughtful discussion of the term *innate* that Dawkins provides at the end of this paper.

Bird-song was an excellent choice for those wishing to take part in the nature–nurture argument because, by judicious selection of species, one could "prove" that bird-song is completely innate, or completely learned, or partially innate and partially learned. Present investigators find such controversies fruitless. Instead, the song of each individual species is viewed as the result of a complex developmental process that must be painstakingly analyzed by careful experiments. Reading 26 by Peter Marler and Miwako Tamura is a good example of modern work in the area.

The next study deals with the effects of early handling on later behavior. It has been known for some time that the simple act of removing a rat pup from its home cage for a brief period each day from birth until weaning affects its adult morphology and behavior. This is surprising enough, but in Reading 27 Denenberg and Rosenberg report that such treatment can affect the weaning weight and activity of the *grandpups* of the handled subjects. The effect is called *nongenetic transmission of information.* Consider the importance of this finding if it can be demonstrated for other species and for other kinds of early experience. How does this differ from Lamarckism?

Denenberg has made many other contributions in the general area of behavioral development. The next reading is also from his laboratory and deals with the rat's "instinctive response" of killing mice.

The next four papers concern imprinting and the concept of critical (or sensitive) periods in development. Much of this work has been done with birds, and we begin with a paper by Eric Fabricius that provides a general review of this literature. But imprinting is not restricted to birds, or even to developing organisms, as Klopfer and Klopfer show in Reading 30, which deals with maternal imprinting in goats. Their paper is particularly interesting because they include a bit of speculation concerning the physiological basis of the phenomenon. Are there alternative possibilities?

As originally proposed, imprinting had several characteristics, one of which was that the effect was irreversible. Salzen and Meyer provide a test of this hypothesis in Reading 31.

Imprinting has been defined as rapid learning during a sensitive period. For many birds this sensitive period occurs during the first couple of days after hatching. Is a bird of this age capable of any other kind of learning? In the next selection, Bateson and Reese report a series of experiments concerned with the relationships among imprinting, the sensitive period, and operant conditioning.

The last three papers of this section deal with monkeys. The old saying has it that "birds of a feather flock together." In reading 33, Pratt and Sackett present the fascinating finding that monkeys reared under particular circumstances prefer social interaction with similarly reared monkeys even when the animals are strangers to one another. Of course we must not conclude that all monkey behavior patterns are a product of early experience. For example, in the next reading, Sackett reports the responses of monkeys reared in isolation from birth to nine months to different visual input. The responses of these animals to colored slides of infant monkeys or of threatening adults support the hypothesis that certain adult social responses can occur without experience in this species.

The final selection is one of a famous series from the laboratory of Harry F. Harlow. These experiments deal with the effects of different kinds of deprivation on later behavior in Rhesus monkeys. In this reading, Arling and Harlow describe the maternal behavior of females who were raised in isolation from other monkeys.

BEHAVIOURAL DEVELOPMENTAL STUDIES ON FOUR GENERA AND SEVERAL STRAINS OF MICE*

By C. L. SCUDDER, A. G. KARCZMAR & L. LOCKETT

Institute for the Study of Mind, Drugs and Behavior, Department of Pharmacology and Therapeutics, Loyola University, Stritch School of Medicine, Hines, Illinois

The present study deals with neonatal behaviour of several strains and genera of mice. The development and behaviour of pups of several inbred strains have been recorded over one month's period (Williams & Scott, 1953; King, 1958; and Fox, 1965). These studies as well as the more general discussion of behavioural development by Fox (1964a) and Hafez (1964) established the design of the experiments reported here, particularly with regard to characteristics which differentiate closely related strains and genera. Additionally, several tests of the young and of the nursing mother previously not described in the literature were employed in order to formulate definitive values indicative of the emerging behavioural profiles of the adult.

Developmental studies on relatively few genera of mammals, e.g. sheep, dog, and mouse, have led to a classification of development into stages such as neonate, juvenile and adolescent, defined by behavioural and developmental traits (Fox, 1964b; Williams & Scott, 1953; and Scott, 1962). The separation of development into stages, in the course of which physical and behavioural changes occurred in parallel, may not represent a basic mammalian design. These traits may fluctuate independently of one another, even among closely related genera, in relation to the social and ecological status of the animal. This study was intended to clarify the interaction between development on one hand and social and ecological factors on the other.

Method

Subjects

The present experiments deal with *Microtus ochrogaster*, *Peromyscus maniculatus Bairdii*, *Onychomys leucogaster*, and with three strains of *Mus*, the laboratory strains *Mus musculus CF-I* and *C57BL/6J*, and a wild strain from Columbia, Missouri identified as *Mus musculus 'Mo.'*.

Microtus, *Onychomys*, and *Mus musculus 'Mo.'* mice were live-trapped by collectors, *Microtus* and *Mus* in the field in the vicinity of Columbia, Mo., and *Onychomys* in the arid area near Tucson, Arizona.† The trapping period lasted some 2 weeks; as soon as trapped,

the males were isolated from females. *Peromyscus maniculatus Bairdii* and the inbred *Mus* strain *C57BL/6J* were obtained from Roscoe B. Jackson Memorial Laboratory. *CF-I* mice were purchased from Carworth Farm.

All the mice were shipped to this laboratory by Air Express. Upon arrival, the mice were paired off and treated routinely for parasites. Following this two weeks post-reception period, they were placed, still mated, in an environment room under controlled conditions of temperature (75 ± 5°F) and humidity. They were housed, two per cage, in transparent plastic 12 in. × 7 in. × 5 in. cages, with sawdust on the cage floor. Regular laboratory mouse pellets were provided in hampers, water was supplied *ad libitum*. The cages were cleaned weekly. Each cage was checked twice a day for new litters. When a litter was dropped, the male was removed and the mother and pups were set aside.

In the case of *Onychomys*, which does not breed readily in captivity, the experiments described below were carried out with mothers and pups of the first generation obtained in captivity. In the case of *Microtus*, *Peromyscus*, and the three strains of *Mus*, further breeding was carried out. Following a maturation period of 21 days, during which the young mice were kept with their mothers, siblings were mated. When the litters were dropped, the experiments described were carried out; thus, in the case of these five strains, the second generation pups, bred in captivity, and their mothers constituted the experimental material..

Experimental Procedure and Design

A total of eight litters of each genus or strain were studied each day until the pups were 20 days of age. Daily measurements were made also on litters which, because of cannibalism, did not survive the 20-day period.

The following eight tests were carried out on each litter, beginning with the first day of life, in the sequence as indicated. (1) *Defence of young*. The young were removed with a soft rubber forceps. The response of the mother was evaluated as follows: 0, for lack of attention; 1, for nosing and pushing; 2, for mild biting; and 3, for savage attack. (2) The litter was *weighed* as a group. (3) The appearance of dorsal and ventral *pigmentation* and *fur*, and of upper and lower *teeth* was noted under a dissecting microscope. (4) Each pup was placed on its belly; its capacity to *support its weight* on its legs alone

*This work was supported in part by Illinois Mental Health Grant No. 17-176.

†We are indebted to Dr D. M. Cameron, Jr., Dept. of Zoology, University of California, Davis, California, for taxonomic identification of these strains from the skulls and pelts which we provided.

188

and to walk was recorded. (5) Each pup was placed on its back and the *righting reflex* was scored depending on whether a torso twist, awkward righting, or an immediate (rapid) righting reflex was exhibited. (6) *The balancing wheel*. This was a revolving drum, covered with fine 20-gauge screen, $3\frac{1}{2}$ in. wide, and with a $2\frac{1}{2}$ in. radius. The pups were placed parallel to the direction of motion, at a point directly above the axle, and rotated downward tail first at the rate of one revolution per min. During the first days of life, the pups fell off the drum onto a cotton padding after a few revolutions; the time from the start of the rotation till that moment was recorded. As the mice became increasingly capable of clinging to the drum and of moving on its screen, some of them became 'hoppy' and left the screen immediately upon being placed on it. The day on which this occurred was designated as 'too active' (cf. Fig. 4); subsequent daily tests with this particular mouse were discontinued, and the average time spent on the wheel was calculated for the remaining animals of the strain. (7) It was noted in the course of the above test whether the *eyes* were open or closed. (8) After the above measurements were completed, the litter was placed back in the home cage 10 in. away from the mother; the time that elapsed until the mother nosed one of the infants was recorded as a measurement of *'maternal interest'*.

Results

Litter Size

The average number of young in the litters studied is shown in Table I. The three strains of *Mus*, particularly the laboratory strain *CF-1*, bred more than the other three genera. There was a three-fold difference in litter size between *CF-I* mouse and *Onychomys*.

Table I. The Average Number of Young per Litter of Six Mice Strains

Genus of Strain	No. of young
Onychomys leucogaster	3·2
Peromyscus maniculatus Bairdii	3·8
Microtus ochrogaster	4·2
Mus musculus C57BL/6J	5·1
Mus musculus 'Mo.'	6·3
Mus musculus CF-I	9·5

Growth

As a rule growth curves of mice reflect two breaks (cf. Fig. 1). The first probably occurs at the onset of paucity of mother's milk; the second, which usually correlates with the opening of the eyes, occurs when young mice make a transition from milk to solid food (McDowell et al., 1930).

Microtus ochrogaster young were born almost twice as heavy as either of the strains of *Mus* (Fig. 1). Their growth continued at an increasing-

ly rapid rate, with only a brief change in rate at 11 days. Their eyes opened at 9 days, and ingestion of solid food began at this time. The young often remained attached firmly to the mother's breast for some time after the eyes opened; a period of weaning was not sharply defined. Since the growth rate of *Microtus* was steep (Fig. 1) as compared with that of other genera, it may be suggested that the former have adequate milk or food at all times and that the transition to solid food is not traumatic.

Peromyscus pups were born somewhat heavier than those of *Mus*. Their growth curve resembled that described in the literature for *Mus*; a break in the curve occurred during the first week, perhaps due to an inadequate supply of milk; a second break was noted at 12 days, shortly after their eyes opened, when the young became capable of an independent existence (Fig. 1). The early appearance of the second break corresponded to the maturation of the eyes. Growth was levelling off by the eighteenth day at a level slightly above that for *Mus*.

Onychomys young were born heavier and were considerably heavier after 20 days of growth than the pups of *Mus* (Fig. 1). The initial break in the curve occurred at about 5 days and may be attributed to an inadequate supply of milk. The second break occurred at 9 to 12 days; it did not correlate well with the approximate onset of vision which occurred in *Onychomys* at 2 weeks or later. It may be that the aggressive traits emerging early in the young of this strain (cf. below) interfered with nursing.

The three strains of *Mus* grew less rapidly and attained less weight by 20 days than the other genera (Fig. 1). They did not differ much in their final weight, although the wild type (*Mus. m.* 'Mo.') was less heavy at birth than the other two strains (Fig. 1).

Maternal Interest

The maternal interest shown by *Microtus* mothers was high and consant during the time of rapid growth of the young (1 to 11 days; Fig. 2). *Microtus* mothers seemed almost fearless in their home cages and readily approached a novel object such as a pencil or finger stuck in their cage. The mother showed immediate concern for her young when they were returned to her; the retrieval was immediate and fearless. Incidental to this study it has been observed that a *Microtus* mother will retrieve the father and attempt to drag him back to the nest. The male, when allowed to remain with the family, has been observed in this laboratory to be solicitous of the young and to retrieve them back to the nest. Intense maternal interest continued until the early maturation and weaning of *Microtus* young at 11 days. Thereafter, the mother's interest became inconsistent, and the young were treated progressively more like adult *Microtus*.

Peromyscus mothers were not immediately attentive to their young (days 1 to 3) but, like *Onychomys* and most *Mus* (cf. below), they

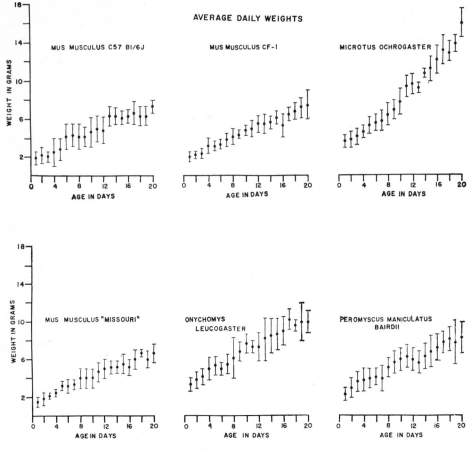

Fig. 1. Average daily weight gains of six strains of mice. Abscissa: age in days; ordinates: weight in grams. Standard error of each point indicated in the graph.

exhibited increasing maternal interest subsequently. Their increased maternal interest on the 3rd day may be related to increased milk production and a variety of neuronal and hormonal events. Thereafter, the mothers fluctuated in their response to the young and often engaged in somersaulting, persistent jumping, or digging in one spot without exhibiting immediate interest for the young when they were returned to the cage. Weaning began after the second week.

Initially, *Onychomys* mothers did not attend the litter too closely and the maternal interest fluctuated during the first week (Fig. 2). They became very attentive to the pups during the second week and not as erratic as the wild *Mus* (*Mus musculus 'Mo.'*) or *Peromyscus*. Subsequently, they became more indifferent to the young, the low in maternal interest occurring

on the 16th day, but actual weaning was late and the mothers exhibited interest even on the 20th day.

Maternal interest of the three strains of *Mus* varied considerably. All three showed an initial 3 to 4 days' period of increasing interest; low initial interest and its marked subsequent increase were conspicuous in the case of *Mus musculus 'Mo.'* (Fig. 2). The wild *Mus*, however, always remained somewhat slow in attending to the young, whereas the other two strains came to their young quickly and were not ignoring them even near the 20th day when the former had begun to show signs of indifference. Besides this relative indifference to their pups, *Mus musculus 'Mo.'* exhibited also more cannibalism than any of the mice studied.

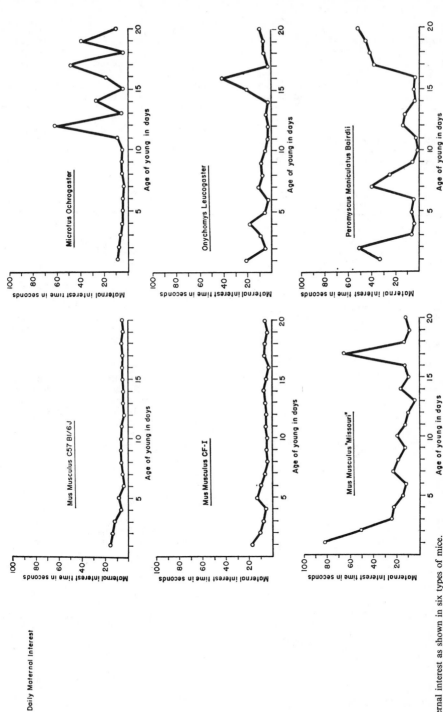

Daily Maternal Interest

Fig. 2. Maternal interest as shown in six types of mice. Abscissa: average time (in sec) elapsed till the mothers contacted the pups placed in the home cage; cf. also Methods. Ordinates: age of young in days. Note that the maternal interest is expressed as inversely proportional to the times elapsed,

Defence of Young

The three strains of *Mus* were not highly aggressive in response to the interference with their young (Fig. 3). In fact, among the genera studied, *Mus* was the least aggressive toward humans in the nest situation. This seemed due to indifference of two laboratory strains and to the timidity of the wild form. In the case of the other three genera, defence of the young tended to increase during the first week, just as maternal interest, and was at its peak after the neonate was 7 to 8 days old. *Peromyscus*, although slow to show 'maternal interest', defended its young within the first week of life (Fig. 3). This moderate aggression toward the disturbing human persisted after the young matured, and may not be correlated with the nest situation. *Microtus* defended the young until they began to forage for themselves; its defence of the young slackened thereafter (Fig. 3). The most highly protective animal was *Onychomys* (Fig. 3). Even the young would snap after their eyes had opened. The similarity of the behaviour of a litter of *Onychomys* to that of a litter of kittens was often noted in this laboratory (see also Clark, 1962).

It should be emphasized that the aggression described here was directed toward humans disturbing the young. In reference to other mice, *Mus musculus* was found to be by far the most aggressive of the genera studied (Scudder *et al.*, in preparation); there may be a relationship between this fact and the high incidence of cannibalism among *Mus*.

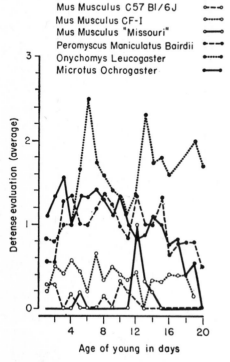

Fig. 3. An evaluation of the defence of the young shown by mothers of six strains of mice. Abscissa: defence index (0–3, cf. Methods); ordinate: age of young in days.

Wheel Balance Data

Data obtained during the first few days of life measured the ability of the very young pups to cling to the screen; once this ability was present, the mice could exhibit the preference for either climbing up or jumping off the wheel. Figure 4 shows, therefore, both the ability of the mice to cling to the screen, as well as the day on which some of the mice ceased staying on the wheel ('too active day', Fig. 4; cf. also Methods); the wheel data are concerned, therefore, with physical and behavioural development.

Microtus, although rapidly maturing, never clung to the screen (Fig. 4). Being relatively heavy it fell off quickly until it acquired sufficient motor coordination; thereafter it made no attempt to remain on the wheel. On the other hand, *Peromyscus* and the somewhat heavier *Onychomys* both developed the ability to stay on the wheel for more than 30 sec on the 11th to 14th day (Fig. 4).

Subsequently, *Peromyscus* mice clung to the wheel for long time periods, even though their eyes opened on the 11th day, till they became hoppy 4 days later. On the other hand, some *Onychomys* jumped off the drum soon after their eyes had opened on the 15th day, and they never clung to the wheel for any time length (Fig. 4).

Mus presented an entirely different picture. Their ability and tendency to cling to the screen and creep up the wheel was apparent well before their eyes were open. Subsequently, neither of the two laboratory strains, *CF-I* and *C57BL/6J*, exhibited a pronounced 'hoppy' stage; they remained on the wheel for a long time. On the other hand, *Mus m. 'Mo.'* became 'hoppy' by the 17th day (Fig. 4).

Development

The rates of development of the various traits are illustrated in Fig. 5. The length of development of the various mice varied from that of *Microtus* which matured quickly with a brief childhood through *Peromyscus* and *Onychomys* to the three strains of *Mus*. While *Microtus* pups were capable of independent existence at about 10 days of age, the young *Mus* remained helpless for a long time (Fig. 5).

Generally, the upper fur and pigment appeared before the lower; lower teeth erupted before upper dentation (Fig. 5). In *Microtus*, the teeth erupted very early compared with the other genera. Also the torso twist, righting, and walking occurred early in *Microtus* although the pups were heavier than those of other genera. *Onychomys* young were quite inactive and helpless at first; they did not attempt to right themselves until the 11th day.

The day when the eyes of the young opened was important; they showed at that time an interest in solid food and responded at a distance to other animals and to visual disturbances. Eyes opened on the 9th day for *Microtus*, 11th for *Peromyscus*, 14th for *Mus m. 'Mo.'*, 15th for *Onychomys*, 16th for *C57BL/6J* and *CF-I* (Fig. 5). Soon after the eyes opened, all the

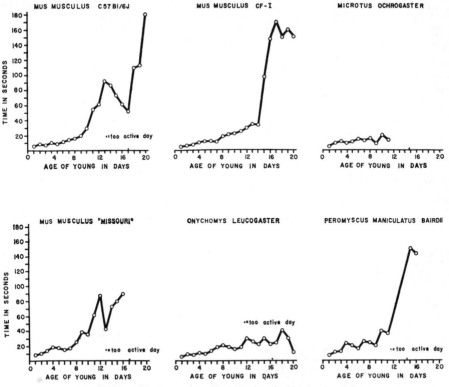

Fig. 4. The average times spent on the balancing wheel by six mice strains. Abscissa: time elapsed (in sec) from the start of rotation until the mice fell off or left the wheel (cf. Methods). The day on which some of the mice jumped off the wheel is indicated by a point near ordinates ('too active day', cf. Methods).

young tended to become jumpy and hyperactive. This hyperactive stage of the juveniles may be correlated not only with the opening of the eyes, but also with thyroid activity (McKeever, 1964). The *CF-I* never showed as pronounced a 'hoppy' stage as other *Mus*. In both *Peromyscus* and the wild *Mus*, this timidity, jumpiness, and hyper-reflexia appeared slightly before the eyes were behaviourally functional.

Discussion

Growth, maternal interest in the pups, defence of the young, development, and behaviour in a wheel balancing situation were measured in the course of this study in four different genera of rodents including three strains of *Mus*. A summary of these data is shown in Table II. The sequence of development of this wide variety of traits was similar for all the strains studied (Fig. 5), and their order of occurrence did not fluctuate independently of one another. Thus, it seems justified to refer to a particular event, such as opening of the eyes, as a criterion for differentiating a neonate from a juvenile. This conclusion, reached on the basis of an investigation of several ecologically different but genetically related strains and genera, is similar to that of Scott (1962) and Fox (1964b), based

on a study of relatively few, genetically distant, genera.

It was recognized that the daily handling of the pups affected their responses (Delger, 1964; Lieberman, 1963; Lindzey, *et al.* 1963; and King & Eleftheriou, 1959); it was felt however, that this factor was constant for all genera and that it might even have accentuated the inter-strain differences.

Growth

The weight growth curves for some of the strains were similar to those reported in the literature (McDowell *et al.*, 1930; and Enzmann, 1933). Under uniform conditions, growth curves for *Mus musculus* have been found to show a break after the first week and at 14 days of age, due to paucity of mother's milk and to the beginning of a more adult diet, respectively. In the experiments reported here, no attempt was made to cull the young; infant mortality accounted for the large standard error.

There was no clear-cut correlation between growth rate and rate of development (Table II). Although *Microtus* developed and grew fastest and was the largest mouse studied, *Onychomys*, the carnivore, was large and put on weight fast while developing relatively slowly, while *Pero-*

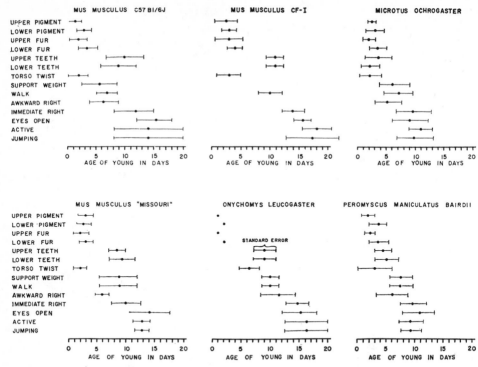

Fig. 5. Graphs showing the development of pups of six ice strains. The traits studied showed in the left hand column (cf. also Methods). The points indicate the average days of the first occurrence of the traits in question; horizontal lines show standard errors. In the case of *Onychomys ochregaster*, the appearance of the fur and of the pigmentation was confined to the day indicated in the graph; thus, there was no standard error with regard to the points in question.

myscus developed faster than *Onychomys* although it grew slowly and remained small. The three strains of *Mus* grew and matured slowly.

Maternal Interest and Defence of Young

'Maternal interest' was slight in the new-born wild *Mus* and increased as the young matured, and suckled from the mother; thus, milk production which increased during the first week, weight of young, and interest were correlated. The two laboratory strains of *Mus* have been selectively bred for their indifference to man; in these strains a new-born pup elicited immediate attention perhaps due in part to the decreased timidity of the mother. In this genus, which was the slowest to develop and mature, maternal interest persisted to the 20th day.

Onychomys and *Microtus* resembled *Mus* somewhat in that they showed marked interest during the first 10 to 15 days; however, the interest of *Microtus* mother began almost at birth of the pups and ended abruptly after the 12th day (Fig. 2).

Peromyscus mothers exhibited little early attention to their young; subsequently, their attention was variable and generally low (Fig. 2).

Because of the tendency of the mother to freeze under stress, the young were often left unattended (Scudder *et al.*, in preparation; Brant & Kavanau, 1965).

Maternal interest was generally correlated with development and ceased when the young opened their eyes and achieved some degree of coordination and independence. The exception to this might be *Mus* and *Onychomys*; in the case of the latter, continued interest of the mother may be related to training in prey hunting and trapping. In the herbivorous forms, e.g. *Microtus*, all maternal interest stops abruptly when the young assume independence.

Defence of Young

Onychomys was the most highly aggressive in defending its young. It has been noted that *Onychomys* can be trained to accept handling by humans and is benign (Bailey & Sperry, 1929). Similarly, *Microtus* exhibited aggression in relation to the home situation, although it does not seem aggressive otherwise (Clough, 1965). Goal-directed aggression associated with the defence of the young, and with obtaining of food is a different trait from the non-competitive aggression displayed by *Mus* (Scudder *et al.*,

Table II. An Abbreviated Chart of Development

The following represent approximations based on the 20-day period of the study.

Growth rate of young: *Microtus* > *Onychomys* > *Peromyscus* > *Mus musculus C57BL/6J* > *Mus musculus CF-I* > *Mus musculus 'Mo.'*

Maternal interest: *Mus musculus C57BL/6J* > *Mus musculus CF-I* > *Microtus* > *Onychomys* > *Peromyscus* > *Mus musculus 'Mo.'*

Defence of young: *Onychomys* > *Microtus* > *Peromyscus* > *Mus musculus CF-I* > *Mus musculus 'Mo.'* > *Mus musculus C57BL/6J*

Rate of development of eyes and neuromuscular co-ordination: *Microtus* > *Peromyscus* > *Onychomys* > *Mus musculus CF-I* > *Mus musculus 'Mo.'* > *Mus musculus C57BL/6J*

Tendency to cling to wheel: *Microtus* > *Onychomys* > *Peromyscus* > *Mus musculus 'Mo.'* > *Mus musculus C57BL/6J* > *Mus musculus CF-I*

---

in preparation). It appears that carnivorous *Onychomys* is behaviourally more like a cat than a rodent.

Peromyscus showed aggression not necessarily related to the nest. Its behaviour was emotional and stereotyped, biting occurred when it ran headlong into the investigator while performing repetitive jumps and wild dashes. The inbred laboratory *Mus* were indifferent to the investigator much of the time, and while exhibiting marked maternal interest, did not show aggressive defence of their young.

The Balancing Wheel

Peromyscus and *Mus* clung to the screen while *Onychomys* and *Microtus* rapidly escaped from it; both behaviours represent a reaction of the animal to the revolving drum and give the impression of an emotional, genus-specific problem solving response. *Mus* and *Peromyscus* are slightly hypothyroid and very timid (Fuller, 1964). The inbreeding of the laboratory *Mus* (*CF-I* and *C57BL/6J*) and of *Peromyscus* (Bruell, 1964a, 1964b, and 1966) could produce 'mild hypothyroidism' (Fuller, 1964) compared with the thyroid state of other strains and increase their innate timidity which in turn depresses their exploratory and escape behaviour. The two largest mice, *Microtus* and the easily tamed *Onychomys*, one a field form and the other a predator, are both relatively fearless animals (Scudder *et al.*, in preparation).

General Development

The slower development of *Mus*, compared with that of other genera, is meaningful in the light of the previously discussed data on maternal interest and defence of young. Among these rodents there is a beginning of a dichotomy similar to that seen in the development of precocious herbivorous and non-precocious carnivorous animals (Fox. 1964a). Carnivores (dog, cat) tend to have a long period of development during which the skills of hunting and prey trapping are learned. On the other hand, herbivores (sheep, guinea pig) may be born in a

relatively mature condition. The meadow vole, *Microtus*, and *Peromyscus* are two grassland forms (Harris, 1952; Getz, 1955) and they develop fast, as is typical for field animals. The teeth erupt early; and the young attach to the mother and are sheltered by her and defended (cf. Figs. 2 and 3). Their further development is rapid and they are equipped for a relatively independent life when they are weaned. In view of this fast maturation, the maternal interest and defence behaviour of these two strains seem unnecessary after 10 to 12 days of development (cf. Table II).

It is interesting that these two field mice, *Peromyscus* and *Microtus*, differ behaviourally. The former is timid and emotional as seen by its behaviour on the wheel, its tendency to freeze in stressful situations and to display stereotyped behaviour (Brant & Kavanau, 1965; and Scudder *et al.*, in preparation). *Microtus* is relatively fearless as indicated by its wheel behaviour and its behaviour with regard to its pups. On the other hand, *Onychomys*, a carnivore, matures slowly; and, while the mother shows a relatively low level of maternal interest, it shows the highest defence behaviour among the genera studied. With the longer period of socialization and learning in the nest, and with a highly protective mother, there is opportunity for development of a greater diversity of behavioural parameters; that is to say, *Onychomys* may acquire or learn some of the skills necessary for a successful predatory life during its prolonged pre-puberal period.

What can be said in this context about *Mus*, an omnivore? The pups of these three strains are the smallest and slowest to mature of all those investigated at present. Maternal interest is generally high (*CF-I*, *C57BL/6J*) and long lasting in the case of all three strains. Thus, *Mus* in many ways is neither a placid herbivorous animal like *Microtus*, nor a specialized predator like *Onychomys*, but an exploring, omnivorous, aggressive animal.

Mus is a particularly interesting and successful genus. The wild animal was found in this study to be jumpy and avoiding, and highly aggressive towards other mice of the same or related genera (Scudder, in preparation). Unlike *Peromyscus* strains, which have a genetically determined ecological preference (Harris, 1952; Wecker, 1963; Scudder *et al.*, in preparation) and which seldom migrate from the nesting site, *Mus* has radiated into many diverse environments; most striking is its invasion of the dwellings of man; it is more migratory and exploratory than *Peromyscus* (Caldwell & Gentry, 1965), and it evolves rapidly into behaviourally different strains (Denenberg, 1965; Fuller, 1965). The behaviour of the genus *Mus* suggests cleverness, variability, and adaptability. These qualities of the genus *Mus* (cf. McClearn, 1959) can be modulated and exploited by slow development, high degree of maternal interest, and highly exploratory behaviour, as compared with the other genera covered in this study.

Such wide behavioural and developmental differences between closely related genera must be the temporal correlates of differing chemistry and 'circuitry' of the brains of the animals in question. Indeed, their brain bioamines and related substances differ markedly (Scudder *et al.*, 1966), and, as could be expected, drug responses differ from strain to strain (Bourgault *et al.*, 1963). Comparative biochemical and pharmacological data may provide the necessary information needed to translate mammalian brain structure into function.

Summary

The present study deals with the development and behaviour of the young of several genera and strains of mice. The animals studied were *Microtus ochrogaster, Peromyscus maniculatus Bairdii, Onychomys leucogaster* and three strains of *Mus, Mus musculus* 'Mo.' (a wild type), *Mus musculus CF-I,* and *Mus musculus C57BL/6J.* The first 20 days of life were investigated in regard to changes in maternal defence, weight gain, the appearance of fur and teeth, the ability to walk and right themselves, the behaviour of the neonate on a balancing wheel apparatus, and the maternal interest shown by the mother when the litter was returned to her. The results are discussed with particular attention to the emerging behavioural profiles of the adults. The order of occurrence of various traits was relatively constant across the genera with a few exceptions. The differences between the herbivorous genera and *Onychomys* and the importance of a longer period of interaction within the nest for the carnivorous and omnivorous commensals were noted with regard to the behavioural profiles of the adults.

REFERENCES

Bailey, V. & Sperry, C. C. (1929). Life history and habits of the grasshopper mice, genus *Onycnomys. U.S. Dept. Agric. Tech. Bull.*, **145**, 1–19.

Bourgault, P. C., Karczmar, A. G. & Scudder, C. L. (1963). Comparison of C57Bl/6 and SC–1 strains of mice. *Life Sci.*, **8**, 533–553.

Brant, D. H. & Kavanau, J. P. (1965). Exploration and movement patterns in the canyon mouse *P. crinitus. Ecology*, **46**, 452–461.

Bronson, F. H. & Eleftheriou, B. E. (1962). Some effects of crowding in *Peromyscus* and *C57Bl/10J* mice. *Abstr. Am. Zoologist*, **2**, 395.

Bronson, F. H. & Eleftheriou, B. E. (1963). Adrenal responses to crowding in *Peromyscus* and *C57Bl/10J* mice. *Physiol. Zool.*, **36**, 161–166.

Bruell, J. H. (1964a). Heterotic inheritance of wheel running in mice. *J. comp. physiol. Psychol.*, **58**, 159–163.

Bruell, J. H. (1964b). Inheritance of behavioral and physiological characters in mice and the problem of heteroses. *Am. Zoologist*, **4**, 125–138.

Bruell, J. H. (1967). Mode of inheritance of response time in mice. *J. comp. Psychol.*, in press.

Caldwell, L. D. & Gentry, J. B. (1965). Interactions of *Peromyscus* and *Mus* in a one acre field enclosure. *Ecology*, **46**, 189–192.

Clark, L. D. (1962). A comparative view of aggressive behavior. *Am. J. Psychiat.*, **119**, 336–341.

Clough, G. D. (1965). Lemmings and population problems. *Am. Scientist*, **53**, 199–212.

Delger, W. (1964). The interaction between genetic and experiential influences in the development of species-typical behavior. *Am. Zoologist*, **4**, 155–160.

Denenberg, V. H. (1965). Behavioral differences in two closely related lines of mice. *J. gen. Psychol.*, **106**, 201–205.

Enzmann, E. V. (1933). Milk production curve of the albino mouse. *Anat. Rec.*, **56**, 345–357.

Fox, N. W. (1964a). A phylogenetic analysis of behavioral neuroontogeny in precocial and non-precocial mammals. *Can. J. comp. Med.*, **28**, 197–202.

Fox, M. W. (1964b). The ontogeny of behaviour and neurological responses in the dog. *Anim. Behav.*, **12**, 301–310.

Fox, M. W. (1965). Reflex ontogeny and behavioural development of the mouse. *Anim. Behav.*, **13**, 234–241.

Fuller, J. L. (1964). Physiological and population aspects of behavioral genetics. *Am. Zoologist*, **4**, 101–109.

Fuller, J. L. (1965). Conference on neurological mutant mice. *Biol. Sci.*, **15**, 802.

Getz, L. L. (1965). Humidities in vole runways. *Ecology*, **46**, 548–551.

Hafez, E. S. E. (1964). Some physiological and behavioral responses in the neonate. *Cornell Vet.*, **LIV**, 545–560.

Harris, V. T. (1952). An experimental study of habitat selection by prairie and forest races of the deer mouse, *Peromyscus maniculatus. Contr. Lab. vertebr. Biol. Univ. Mich.*, **56**, 1–53.

King, J. A. (1958). Maternal behavior and behavioral development in two subspecies of *Peromyscus maniculatus. J. mammal.*, **39**, 177–190.

King, J. A. & Eleftheriou, B. E. (1959). Effects of early handling upon adult behavior of two subspecies of deer mice *Peromyscus maniculatus. J. comp. physiol. Psychol.*, **52**, 82–88.

Lieberman, M. (1963). Early developmental stress and later behavior. *Science*, **141**, 824–825.

Lindzey, G., Winston, H. D. & Manosevitz, M. (1963). Early experience genotype and temperament in *Mus musculus. J. comp. physiol. Psychol.*, **56**, 622–629.

McClearn, G. E. (1959). The genetics of mouse behavior in novel situation. *J. comp. physiol. Psychol.*, **52**, 62–67.

McDowell, E. C., Gates, W. H. & McDowell, C. G. (1930). The influence of the quantity of nutrition upon the growth of the suckling mouse. *J. gen. Physiol.*, **13**, 529–546.

McKeever, S. (1964). Variation in the weight of the adrenal, pituitary and thyroid gland of the white footed mouse, *Peromyscus maniculatus. Am. J. Anat.*, **114**, 1–15.

Noirot, E. (1964a). Changes in responsiveness to young in the adult mouse; the effect of external stimuli. *J. comp. physiol. Psychol.*, **57**, 97–99.

Noirot, E. (1964b). Changes in responsiveness to young in the adult mouse; IV. The effect of an initial contact with a strong stimulus. *Anim. Behav.*, **12**, 442–445.

Scott, J. P. (1962). Critical periods in behavioural development. *Science*, **138**, 949–958.

Scudder, C. L., Karczmar, A. G., Everett, G. M., Gibson, J. E. & Rifkin, M. (1966). Brain catechol and serotonin levels in various strains and genera of mice and a possible interpretation for correlations of amine levels with electroshock latency and behavior. *Int. J. Neuropharm.*, **5**, 343–351.

Wecker, S. C. (1963). The role of early experience in habitat selections by the prairie deer mouse, *Peromyscus maniculatus Bairdii. Ecol. Monogr.*, **33**, 322–325.

Williams, E. & Scott, J. P. (1953). The development of social behavior patterns in the mouse in relation to natural periods. *Behaviour*, **6**, 35–64.

Experiential Deprivation and Later Behavior

Stress of emergence is postulated as the basis for behavioral deficits seen in dogs following isolation.

John L. Fuller

Deprivation of sensory and motor experience during early life has been blamed for a considerable portion of mental retardation and social inadequacy in man. A controversy exists between proponents of the developmental interpretation and proponents of the defect interpretation of such inadequacies (*1*). In animals the relationship between experiential deprivation and behavioral development has been widely studied and reviewed (*2–4*). Other experiments have dealt with the effects of an enriched environment (*5*). These two types of investigation are fundamentally similar except for reversal of the designation of experimental and control groups.

Techniques and duration of deprivation vary widely in experimental studies, as do the criteria by which the results of deprivation are evaluated. King (*6*) has called for more parametric studies in this area, but relatively few have been performed, possibly because of the potential magnitude and complexity of such investigations. By imposing different types of deprivation which are primarily either (i) sensory or (ii) motor or social, attempts have been made to determine which aspects of experience are most critical in behavioral development. Evidence exists that an organism is most vulnerable to deprivation or stimulation at certain ages (critical periods), though this interpretation has been questioned (*7*).

The interpretation of the deprivation experiment has been debated. Hunt (*2*) opposes strongly the idea that behavior is genetically programmed and unfolds along with morphological growth and differentiation. Lorenz (*4*) believes that the appearance of species-specific patterns in organisms deprived of ordinary prior experience is evidence for the intrinsic determination of much behavior. Despite funereal pronouncements, the nature-nurture issue seems still a lively corpse. Most present-day psychologists and biologists are middle-of-the-roaders in this matter; they speak of behavior as the outcome of an interaction or coaction of heredity and environment.

This article is largely concerned with the effects of experiential deprivation in dogs. In the 1950's, McGill University was a center for such studies; the subjects were Scottish terriers. Excessive exploratory activity, whirling, immaturity of emotional responses, and deficiencies of response to pain were recorded as outcomes of severe or moderate restriction (*8–10*). The deficits were interpreted in terms of Hebb's (*11*) theory of the need for a long period of "perceptual learning" for organization of the nervous system. Isolation is primarily passive withholding of essential information. Fisher (*12*) reported similar results and interpreted them similarly, but emphasized the reversibility of isolation effects to a great-

The author is a senior staff scientist at the Jackson Laboratory, Bar Harbor, Maine.

er extent than the McGill group did.

More recently the Hebbian interpretation of the effects of isolation has been challenged by Lessac (13), who proposes that the inappropriate behavior of dogs after isolation is due to destructive or interfering effects upon previously organized processes. He provides evidence that, following isolation, dogs often perform more poorly than they did before isolation.

A third view, defended in this article, also emphasizes the active rather than the passive role of experiential deprivation, but considers that behavioral deficits following isolation result more from competing emotional responses than from failure of behavioral organization during isolation or from loss of established patterns (14). Actually, this view is compatible with Lessac's view (13) that isolated animals become habituated to a very low average level of stimulation and respond to moderate stimulation as normally reared animals respond to violent stimulation.

Programmed Life Histories

The Jackson Laboratory program on experiential deprivation in dogs was initiated as a series of studies on the persistent effects of modified early experience. In all the experiments we have used the same basic isolation procedure. Puppies are removed from their mother at the age of 21 days, when they can for the first time survive independently without special handling. They are placed in cages about 60 centimeters square which permit feeding, watering, and removal of wastes without physical or visual contact with a human being. The cages are furnished with a one-way observation window, are kept constantly lighted at a low level of illumination, and are ventilated by a blower, which provides some masking of external sounds.

Upon the monotonous background we can impose procedures such as removal of the puppies from the cage for varying periods at selected ages, provision of playthings, provision of opportunities for visual exploration, or rearing with another puppy. The technique permits rather precise programming of all aspects of a subject's early life history.

In all experiments the effects of isolation have been evaluated by means of an arena test, and some subjects have been tested for discrimination learning in a modified Wisconsin general test apparatus. The arena test includes 7½ minutes of observation of the subject's responses to a human handler, to toys, and to another puppy of the same age. The arena is 3½ meters square and is surrounded by an opaque barrier 1 meter high. The floor is divided by painted lines into nine equal squares. The procedure has been essentially constant over the series of experiments, but the scoring system has been radically altered. I shall not describe our original scoring procedure, except to indicate that it yields measures of orientation and of contacts with a human handler, with toys, and with a companion puppy as well as counts of squares entered—a measure of locomotion (15). More recently we have developed the "code for observational description" (COFOD) technique, in which observers record a subject's behavior at regular intervals as a series of five-letter words, each word providing a "snapshot" of the subject at an instant in time (14).

Letter 1 of each COFOD word denotes the stimulus toward which the subject is responding; letter 2 describes the nature of the response. Location in the testing area is indicated by letter 3, and type and level of activity by letter 4. Letter 5 denotes any one of various miscellaneous indicators of emotional arousal. For example, HMAJT describes a dog "manipulating" (M = pawing or mouthing) the handler (H). The dog is in the arena (A) jumping (J) up and down and wagging its tail (T).

A useful feature of COFOD is a numerical transformation for letters 2 and 4. Response intensities are graded from orientation through approach, investigation, contact, and manipulation. Adding the numerical values of these letters for each test provides a response index (RI) which is a measure of the average intensity of responses directed toward identifiable stimuli. Response indexes can also be calculated for individual stimuli. Similarly, numerical equivalents of letter 4 increase with increase in level of activity, from lying down through sitting, standing, walking, running, and jumping. The sum of these numerical equivalents yields an activity index (AI). Practiced observers obtain rank order correlation coefficients of about .90 on ratings of RI and AI. Observing is easier and agreement is better when subjects make relatively stereotyped responses, but satisfactory records can be obtained from all subjects.

Varying "Dosages" of Experience

Experiential deprivation is not an all-or-nothing matter. One approach to quantification is to rear animals under different regimens which can be ranked in terms of complexity or some similar dimension. We chose, instead, to rear dogs under a regimen which provided experience, in varying proportions, of standardized restricted and free environments. Two questions were posed: (i) How much (or how little) free-environment experience suffices to stimulate and sustain normal behavioral development? (ii) Does the effectiveness of free-environment experience vary with the age of the subject? The second question is more difficult to answer than the first because one cannot alter the age at which free-environment experience is allowed without changing the duration of prior isolation.

In one experiment (16) ten beagles and ten wirehaired terriers were reared on five different schedules, which provided different degrees of experience, to the age of 16 weeks. During weeks 16 to 19 each animal was given 16 arena tests. Prior to week 16, all subjects had been kept in isolation cages from the time they were 3 weeks old, with interruptions as follows: groups 1, 2, and 4 were given one, two, or four arena tests per week during weeks 4 through 15; and group 2' was observed biweekly during weeks 10 through 15. Group K was continuously isolated during weeks 4 through 15. Since the rate of acquiring experience, the age at which it is acquired, the amount of experience acquired, and the age at time of observation all vary in this study [such variation is inevitable in developmental experiments (17)], comparisons must be made among specific sets of data.

For example, groups 1, 2, and 4, given different amounts of experience in the arena, can be compared at the same ages. Puppies whose isolation is broken only once a week played with a ball about half as much as puppies given two or four isolation breaks (Fig. 1, top left). The numbers of contacts between companions were essentially equal for the three groups (Fig. 1, bottom left). However, these contacts were less intense in the one-break-per-week group, as evidenced by the low towel-contact scores, which measure intra-pair competitions (Fig. 1, top right). The groups score in reverse order on locomotor activity (Fig. 1, bottom right). The age at which group differences appeared varied with the nature of the measurement.

The same puppies were also compared after being given comparable amounts of experience in the arena. The results were highly consistent for

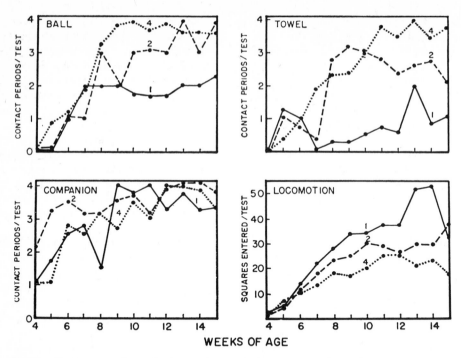

Fig. 1. Average number of observation periods, per test, in which contacts were made with a ball (top left), a companion puppy (bottom left), and a towel (top right) for dogs removed from isolation one, two, or four times per week from age 4 weeks through 15 weeks. (Bottom right) Average number of times per test that subjects crossed between nine squares marked on the arena floor. $N = 4$ per group.

most measures. Rate of change in behavior *per test* was at first more rapid in the groups given fewer tests per week—that is, in groups of puppies which were older when they were placed in the arena. Until a degree of biological maturity had been attained, the puppies appeared not to benefit from additional experience.

Still another mode of comparison is that between groups given experience at the same rate but at different ages. No differences were found in stimulus-contact scores for puppies tested biweekly from ages 4 through 9 weeks (group 2) and those tested similarly from ages 10 through 15 weeks (group 2'). Groups 4 and K, tested four times a week from age 4 weeks and 16 weeks, respectively, made, on comparable tests, about the same number of stimulus contacts, but

contacts of group K, whose training had been delayed, were less intense. Delayed onset of experience was clearly associated with increased locomotor scores for groups 2' and K, as compared with groups 1, 2, and 4.

An analysis of scores for the final week of arena tests allows comparison of the two breeds at the same age after the five groups (1, 2, 4, 2', and K) had been reared according to five different schedules of experience. Table 1 indicates that breed and schedule affected some, but not all, scores. In general, delaying experience (and restricting the amount) affected the intensity of contacts more than their number. Breed differences were demonstrated only on measures which were also modified by experiential programming, a fact which suggested that behavior most modifiable by variation in experience may also be particularly sensitive to genetic variation.

Experience did make a difference, but the amount of experience required to make the puppies behave essentially like ordinary laboratory-reared animals was on the order of 20 minutes per week. Group averages conceal conspicuous individual differences in the persistence of postisolation deficits. Since some animals reared under conditions of severe restriction performed so well, I began to suspect that the postisolation syndrome was not simply the result of withholding critical information during a biologically critical period. Experiments were designed therefore to modify conditions of emergence into the arena, and conditions of isolation.

Table 1. Significance levels for effect of schedules of experience (S) and breed (B), based on analysis of variance of scores for week 19. NS, no significance.

Measure	S	B
All contacts, handler	.05	NS
Strong contacts, handler	.01	.01
Contacts, pendulum	.05	NS
Contacts, ball	NS	NS
Contacts, companion	NS	NS
Contacts, towel (competition)	.05	.01
Arena squares entered	.01	.01

Emergence as a Stress

If isolation involves more than the withholding of information, what might this something else be? Behavioral organization could be deteriorating, as suggested by Lessac, but the schedules-of-experience results did not support this idea. On the contrary, there was even an indication of progressive behavioral organization during isolation. A third explanation emphasizes the contrast between the isolation cage and the arena and views the postisolation syndrome as dependent upon a prolonged "irrational fear" (18) of space

and novel environment. Such fear is not seen in normally reared puppies because the environment opens up gradually to a growing puppy as its motor and sensory capacities carry it out of the nest into the world. When the transition must be accomplished in an instant, adaptive mechanisms are overstrained. It follows that cushioning the shock of emergence should lessen the symptoms.

In several experiments we sought to reduce the stress of emergence by stroking and handling the puppies before or after testing in the arena and by administering chlorpromazine before the tests. The effect of stroking and handling by a human being is clear. Animals thus handled made more contacts, and more intense contacts, with humans and toys (and usually with other dogs) than did animals required to emerge unassisted from a transport cage into the arena (14). The case for a favorable effect of chlorpromazine is more complex. In two experiments we showed that administering the drug with food just prior to the first few arena tests reduced the incidence of bizarre behavior and made puppies reared in isolation appear much more like normally reared puppies. In particularly favorable cases (19), puppies removed from isolation while drugged played vigorously with toys, followed the experimenter about the arena, and approached him on call at the first opportunity. These animals had no more experience than other puppies reared in isolation, who froze or struggled, howled and defecated, and made no directed responses to stimuli which attract dogs reared as pets in home or laboratory. We concluded that the postisolation syndrome could not be explained as a simple experiential deficit. Simple approach and "manipulative" behavior, including species-specific social patterns, had developed in an extremely barren environment and appeared promptly when adequate eliciting stimuli were presented and when the suppressive effects of fear were attenuated by chlorpromazine.

In our first experiments of this series it appeared that chlorpromazine benefited only animals which simultaneously received extra handling from the experimenters. Little effect was noted in nonhandled animals required to move from a transport cage into the arena under their own power. An experiment was designed to test further the relationship between handling and drug administration. All subjects (16 beagle puppies) were allowed to emerge spontaneously into the arena. At the end of each arena test one member of each pair was handled for 5 minutes, the other was allowed 5 minutes in an open transport cage from which it could enter the arena freely. Half the pairs received chlorpromazine in spansule form (10 to 12 milligrams per kilogram) 30 to 60 minutes before each test commenced.

Figure 2 illustrates the most important finding. As the series of tests proceeded, handled puppies emerged sooner and spent more time in the arena; in these puppies no effect of chlorpromazine is discernible. In nonhandled puppies there is a strong chlorpromazine effect which reinforces rather than counteracts the effect of lack of handling. We tentatively explain the contradiction between this finding and results of the earlier study which showed favorable effects of the drug in terms of the difference in the tasks required of the puppies in the two experiments. With no handling, the tranquilized puppy simply stays in a familiar environment. In the first study, the moderate amount of handling was more reinforcing to the drugged than to the undrugged subject, but, in the second study, the larger amounts of handling were sufficient in themselves and the drug effect was superfluous.

Another way to cushion the shock of emergence into the arena is to modify the isolation environment in such a way that the transition from the cage to the arena is less abrupt. Puppies reared with toys and with a companion (paired isolates) behave very much like those raised under the most extreme conditions of deprivation (20). The behavior of puppies reared in cages with a window looking out onto a laboratory was intermediate between that of true isolates and that of puppies reared as pets. We concluded that space itself—the absence of the familiar cage walls—is more important in the etiology of the postisolation syndrome than lack of familiarity with specific stimuli used in the arena test.

Breed Variation in Vulnerability

Two breeds, beagles and wirehaired terriers, were used in several of our experiments. In the laboratory, beagles are characteristically less active and less aggressive than terriers. After emergence into the arena, beagles showed persistent depression of directed responses; terriers seemed to recover more rapidly. To test this somewhat subjective impression, puppies reared as pets and puppies reared in isolation, of both breeds, were compared in the standard arena test. Several modifications of the isolation environment were employed, but these had such small effects that, for the purpose of this article, it is legitimate to group all isolates.

Figure 3 shows the average activity indices for the four groups during the series of 20 tests. Terriers were consistently more active than beagles. From the third week of testing, terriers reared in isolation were more active ($P < .05$) than those reared as pets. Throughout the tests, beagles reared in isolation were less active than those reared as pets. Thus it appears that isolation magnifies the breed dif-

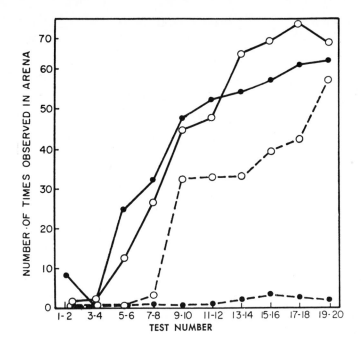

Fig. 2 The effect of posttest handling and administration of chlorpromazine upon emergence into the arena from a transport cage similar to the isolation cages. $N = 4$ per group. (Open circles, solid line) No drug, handled; (open circles, dashed line) no drug, not handled; (solid circles, solid line) drug, handled; (solid circles, dashed line) drug, not handled.

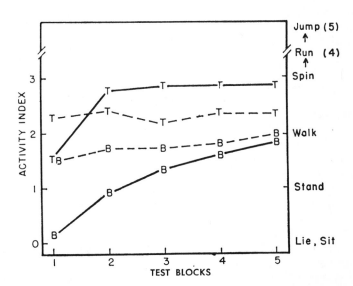

Fig. 3 Average activity indices for beagles (B) and wirehaired terriers (T): (solid lines) isolates $(N = 24)$; (dashed lines) pet-reared $(N = 8)$. Each block includes four tests given during 1 week (at age 16 to 20 weeks). Numbers in parentheses indicate degrees of activity.

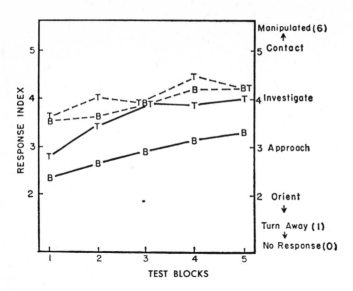

Fig. 4 Average response indices for beagles
(*B*) and terriers (*T*). Each block includes four tests given during
1 week (at age 16 to 20 weeks). Numbers in parentheses indicate degrees of activity.

ferences in activity seen in dogs reared
in standard fashion. The descriptive
terms at the right in Fig. 3 provide a
guide to the actual observations, but
it must be noted that a mean value of
2.0 does not indicate continuous walking but indicates a mix of standing,
walking, jumping, and so on, in
varied proportions.

Similarly, we may compare the response indices for the four groups
(Fig. 4). Here the curves for terriers
and beagles reared as pets do not differ. But, after isolation, terriers consistently responded more intensely than
beagles to the arena stimuli, and, from
the second week of testing, their responses were indistinguishable from
those of their pet-reared litter mates.
The beagles raised in isolation had not
come close to responding as freely as
their pet-reared litter mates by the end
of the experiment. By this measure,
too, isolation enhanced the difference
between the two breeds.

It is apparent, therefore, that genotype is one determinant of the direction, duration, and intensity of the isolation effect. If living in a more open
environment, typified by the arena, is
taken as a desideratum, beagles would
appear to be more vulnerable than terriers to the disruptive effects of isolation. One could, however, argue that
beagles are better adjusted to life in a
cell—perhaps the reason experimental
biologists favor them for laboratory
use. However, basing the argument
that terriers are better adapted to an
open environment upon the arena test
alone is risky. Under other circumstances beagles seem better adapted to
a free environment than terriers.
Groups of litter-mate terriers must
usually be split up in order to prevent gang attack upon subordinate
members; litter-mate beagles seldom
behave in this way (*21*). Observations
such as these provide strong support
for Hirsch's (*22*) assertion that "the
effects of experience are conditioned
by the genotype," but do not indicate
which genotype is more adaptive.
Clearly, investigators of experiential dep-

rivation should be careful in generalizing from species to species, since breeds within a species can differ so widely. The results should also make behavior geneticists cautious about generalizing behavioral phenotypes from situation to situation. Beagles and terriers raised in isolation will not show the same kinds of difference they would show if they were reared as pets, and analogies can probably be drawn for mice or men.

Learning Ability of Postisolates

The arena test is highly sensitive to the effects of isolation, but it makes minimal demands upon the learning ability of the puppy. The bulk of the evidence summarized by Hunt (2) indicates a decrement in measured intelligence following early experiential deprivation. Thompson's and Heron's (8) isolated Scottish terriers performed less well than controls on an orientation test and on a delayed-response test which required the animals to locate food on the basis of cues which were withdrawn before the response was initiated. Melzack's (9) isolated beagles were less efficient than controls in following reversals of a visual cue associated with food reward. On the other side, Harlow (23) states that learning ability of macaques is apparently little impaired by early experiential deprivation—perhaps not at all if sufficient time is allowed for recovery. Similar findings are reported by Angermeier, Phelps, and Reynolds (24). In our studies of postisolation learning ability we have used a modified version of the Wisconsin general test apparatus. Dishes containing a preferred food were covered by slides on which card holders were mounted. In the visual task, black and white cards were used as the discriminative stimuli: pushing against the correct card uncovered the food; pushing against the

incorrect slide did not. The position of the correct stimulus was varied in a complex predetermined order. For the spatial task, gray cards were placed on both slides. One side was consistently rewarded until ten consecutive correct responses had been made. The sides were then reversed. On both tasks, efficiency of learning was measured by the number of errors the dog made before attaining the criterion.

Individual variability in learning ability is great even among dogs of the same breed and rearing. It has proved more difficult to draw conclusions regarding effects of isolation upon learning than to draw conclusions regarding the effects upon social and manipulative behavior. The clearest finding is that 12 weeks of isolation do not necessarily impair reversal learning on the spatial task (25). Sixteen previously isolated dogs which had been observed for 5 weeks in the arena were trained. As each subject met criterion the position of the food was changed, and this procedure was continued until 12 complete series had been run. Six puppies reared as pets were tested in the same way.

On a spatial reversal problem the first trial of each new series is ordinarily nonreinforced. A well-trained subject may thereafter respond correctly, though typically some errors are made. In this study errors were scored from the second trial on. Figure 5 gives the result of the experiment. The values along the ordinate denote errors plus 1, in order that zero scores may be represented on a logarithmic scale. Mean values for errors show that the previously isolated dogs were consistently poorer learners than the pets. However, great variation was found within both groups, and the difference between the two groups reached statistical significance ($P < .05$, Mann-Whitney U test) only on series 2, the first reversal. Figure 5 also shows the errors made by the best and the poorest performers of each group. The values for the poorest performers among the pets were similar to those for the average performers among the isolates. On all but one series, however, the best performance for an isolate was equal to or better than the best for a pet.

Visual discrimination was measured in a separate group of 16 beagles, half of them reared in full isolation from week 4 through week 15 and half reared as "semi-pets" (with about one-third the handling provided in our standard pet-rearing procedure). As anticipated, visual discrimination (discrimination between black and white cards) proved to be more difficult than the spatial task—so difficult that one subject from each group failed to meet the criterion even once. The other subjects were tested on three series (two reversal series), the results of which are shown in Table 2. The data are much like those obtained on the spatial task; the dogs reared as pets showed superior performance only on the reversal problems. However, the differences do not reach conventional levels of significance (max $P = .104$ on the Mann-Whitney U test, one-tailed, for series 3). It would be unwise to conclude from these data that isolation had not impaired the capacity for discrimination reversal in some individuals, but the data show that the effect was not consistent.

Another group of eight beagles and eight terriers, all reared in isolation, was divided into two equal subgroups, given either spatial or discrimination reversal tests. No pet-reared controls were included in this experiment, as the major objective was a comparison of the two breeds after experiential deprivation. This set of animals performed less well than any other group we have trained. On the simpler spatial task (Table 3) one terrier failed to meet criterion and one beagle and one terrier developed phobic re-

actions and stopped working after a few series. On the visual task only one of the eight subjects met criterion on any reversal series. Though this experiment demonstrated that the breed difference in the effect of isolation upon performance in the arena test did not carry over into a learning task, the interpretation is clouded by the poor performance of all subjects, which suggests that testing conditions were not optimum. In retrospect, it appears that inclusion of a pet-reared group in this experiment might have helped to explain the results, but none was available at the time. Since then Ebel and Werboff (26) have shown that normally reared dogs perform as well as primates on the Wisconsin apparatus. It is thus probable that early isolation does have persistent detrimental effects on performance on the more complex visual reversal problem, but additional experiments are needed to resolve the question.

Table 2. Mean errors to criterion on successive black-white discrimination reversal tests.

Rearing	No. of subjects	Series		
		1	2	3
Semi-pets	7	60.1	86.0	86.6
Isolates	7	71.1	120.0	118.0

Table 3. Individual performances of beagles and terriers tested, after isolation, on spatial and visual reversal tests. Testing was discontinued when the subject failed to reach criterion within 300 trials or failed to approach the goal for 5 consecutive days.

Breed	No. of subjects	Series completed*
Spatial test		
Beagles	4	2, 12, 12, 12
Terriers	4	0, 3, 12, 12
Visual test		
Beagles	4	0, 0, 1, 2
Terriers	4	0, 1, 1, 1

* Maximum number of series, 12.

Theories and Generalizations

This series of studies has demonstrated marked individual differences in the disruption of behavior following early experiential deprivation. Isolation effects are modified by conditions of emergence into the arena, and differ for beagles and wirehaired terriers. Whether the effects are measured by problem-solving tests or by observation of the number and intensity of directed responses, it is found that a few subjects appear essentially unscathed by prior experiential deprivation. Isolation is necessary but not sufficient for the commonly observed reduction in directed responses and appearance of unusual behavior. A satisfactory theory must account for these findings.

As stated above, the major theories are the stimulus-deprivation theory of Thompson and Heron (8), based largely upon Hebb's (11) concept of a need for perceptual learning; the deterioration theory of Lessac (13); and the emergence-stress theory of Fuller and Clark (14). The predicted consequences of each of these models are shown in Fig. 6. I believe the emergence-stress theory provides the most satisfactory explanation of our data.

The deterioration theory is supported by evidence that young dogs that had been kept in isolation performed more poorly on several tests than they had before being isolated (13). Thus, isolation is more than simply the withholding of opportunity for perceptual learning. In our arena experiments the behavior patterns which were measured following isolation do not appear in young puppies prior to isolation; hence the fact that some dogs do not show these behavior patterns after isolation cannot be ascribed to deterioration. A more telling argument against the deterioration model is the fact that puppies removed from isolation at 16 weeks usually acquire social and ma-nipulative behavior in the arena *more* rapidly than 4-week-old puppies do (16). Instead of deterioration one finds evidence for continued perceptual and motor development under conditions of relatively severe restriction.

There are two major arguments against the model which postulates that stimulus deprivation causes failure of perceptual learning. One is the "instantaneous" appearance of simple orientation, approach, and manipulative behavior patterns in a few puppies when given their first arena test (14, 19). The other is the finding that experiential deprivation produces many poor learners but is compatible in other subjects with excellent learning (25). Neither argument is conclusive, and it is possible to express the deprivation theory in a form that accommodates the findings, but, in my view, at the sacrifice of the principle of parsimony. The persistent decrement in learning ability shown by the McGill isolates (8–10) might be considered evidence that something was fundamentally wrong with their neural organization. Learning was still impaired after overt emotional disturbance had subsided. These older animals had, however, a long history of failure on many tasks, and it is difficult to extricate the effects of their remote isolation experience from their more immediate experience of failure.

In the emergence-stress model, excessive arousal in an organism exposed to a myriad of unfamiliar stimuli is assumed to produce overload in the neural systems underlying many forms of behavior. One role of early experience is that of allowing the organism to become habituated to multitudinous stimuli, so that it can direct its responses to one or a few which are significant. Habituation plays a similar part in Harlow's (27) hypothesis of learning. Acquiring a complex discrimination, for example, always involves elimination of responses to nonpertinent fea-

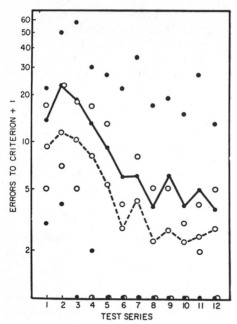

Fig. 5 (above). Average number of errors plus 1 before the subject attains criterion for the spatial task with reversal at each series. (Solid line, solid circles) Isolates ($N = 16$); (dashed line, open circles) dogs reared as pets ($N = 6$). In addition to the averages, the best and poorest performances in both groups are shown.

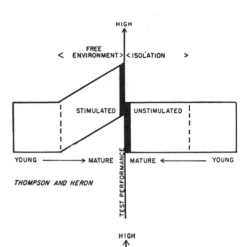

THOMPSON AND HERON

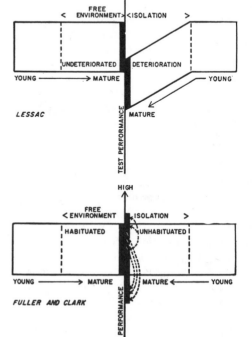

LESSAC

FULLER AND CLARK

Fig. 6 (right). Diagrammatic representation of three theories for the effects of experiential deprivation upon test performance. All are based upon interpretations of experiments with dogs. (Top) Unstimulated isolates fail to develop perceptual mechanisms; hence they rate lower on test performance than animals reared in a free environment. (Middle) Deterioration of established mechanisms occurs during isolation. This model yields a prediction similar to that of the stimulation, perceptual-learning model for postisolation group comparisons between subjects raised in isolation and subjects raised in a free environment. However, preisolation-postisolation changes within the two groups differ. A combination of the two models is logically admissible. (Bottom) Perceptual and motor development are assumed to proceed similarly in isolation and in a free environment. When confronted by a test situation, usually in an open space, unhabituated dogs reared in isolation are highly aroused and, in general, perform poorly. High arousal can facilitate some performances—for example, locomotor activity in some breeds of dogs.

tures of the environment. Lessac (*13*) also stresses the importance of habituation to particular levels of stimulus intensity. That part of his interpretation of postisolation behavior which emphasizes interference with adjustive patterns in overly aroused animals is compatible with the emergence-stress hypothesis. The difference lies in our nonacceptance of the concept of deterioration.

The difference between the 16-week isolate entering the arena for the first time and its litter mate who has visited the arena for extremely brief periods weekly is that the litter mate has received experience in small doses and has gradually become habituated to the entire complex. Its immaturity during early visits to the arena restricted sensory input to a manageable level, and overload did not occur at any stage.

Variation in vulnerability to postisolation disturbance of behavior could be primarily variation in the reaction to input overload. Habituation can occur later in life than is usual, but perhaps later habituation is less efficient. One would predict that, for a dog reared in isolation, the arena might serve as a fear-arousing stimulus in somewhat the way that an opening umbrella produced aversion in Mahut's (*28*) home-reared dogs. The behavioral effect of increased psychological arousal would vary with the complexity of the task, and it is conceivable that isolates might show superior performance on certain tasks. To accommodate breed differences, the emergence-stress model must assume inherited differences in the probability of substitutive responses—for example, "freezing" or spinning—on the part of dogs under stress. The emergence-stress model plays down the role of experience in guiding perceptual learning, though it does not deny the phenomenon. The theory also places more emphasis on intrinsic forces in behavioral development than accords with much current psychological thought.

The obverse of the arena test of dogs reared in isolation is the confinement of puppies reared in a free environment (*29*). Such puppies are disturbed and attempt to escape from a small cage, which isolates would prefer to a free environment. The emergence-stress model can be converted to a confinement-stress model for puppies habituated to a different world.

Does the theory proposed to explain the effects of isolation upon dogs bear upon the effects of experiential impoverishment upon children? The essential features of the emergence-stress model—exposure of an experientially deprived and neurologically well-developed organism to a complex alien environment—are to be found in many groups of children. It may be harder for children to become habituated to the new environment than it is for dogs, because of greater self-perception in the child. A 16-week-old dog is not embarrassed while acquiring ball-playing or social responses ordinarily acquired by 6-week-old puppies. A 16-year-old boy in a remedial-reading class is aware that the tasks set for him are appropriate for 6-year-olds. Such particularly human dimensions must be kept in mind in generalizing the emergence-stress model. Provided this is done, the hypothesis can be applied and tested with other species, including man. The search for an explanation of the lasting effects of early experiential deprivation is more than academic. Whether the effect of isolation is primarily deprivation, deterioration, or nonhabituation has implications for correction of the deficits produced. The emergence-stress model offers, perhaps, a little more hope for rehabilitation than the other two models do.

Summary

Our experiments on the effects of

experiential deprivation upon later behavior of dogs have dealt with four major areas. The programming of life histories has involved the scheduling of breaks in isolation and the introduction of specific stimuli to isolation cages. Biweekly breaks, of less than 10 minutes each, largely counteract the effects of isolation. An opportunity for the animal to look out of the isolation cage has some counteracting effect, but the presence of playthings or rearing with a companion does not.

Another series of experiments has centered on the circumstances of emergence from isolation. Special handling and administration of a tranquilizing drug at this time were effective in reducing the usual postisolation symptoms.

Genetic variation in reaction to early isolation has been observed in comparative experiments with beagles and wirehaired terriers. Genotype may modify the magnitude, the duration, and even the direction of effect. Behavioral phenotypes readily changed by varying the schedules of experience tend to be those for which the greatest differences are observed from breed to breed.

Observations of the effects of experiential deprivation upon problem solving (intelligence) are inconsistent. Some dogs raised in isolation perform very well, but many are poor performers. Deprivation does not necessarily, therefore, prevent normal development of intelligent behavior, but it appears to interfere with performance in vulnerable subjects.

The two major theories in the field have considered isolation effects to be primarily the result of deprivation of information necessary for perceptual development, or, alternatively, the result of deterioration of patterns of response through disuse. The series of studies described here suggests that major attention should be given to the circumstances of emergence from isolation and subsequent testing. Isolation may simply prevent organisms from becoming habituated to stimulus complexes, so that attending to pertinent components while disregarding others is made difficult. The stimulus overload would be particularly severe when the organism emerged from isolation. Genetic factors might play a major role in determining whether the response to the stress of emergence were withdrawal (beagle-type response) or hyperactivity (terrier-type response). Genetic and other factors affecting the persistence of the stress response could tilt the balance toward delayed but satisfactory behavioral adjustment or toward permanent retardation.

References and Notes

1. E. Zigler, *Science* 155, 292 (1967).
2. J. M. Hunt, *Intelligence and Experience* (Ronald, New York, 1961).
3. H. F. Harlow and M. Harlow, *Amer. Scientist* 54, 244 (1966).
4. K. Lorenz, *Evolution and Modification of Behavior* (Univ. of Chicago Press, Chicago, 1965).
5. M. R. Rosenzweig, D. Krech, E. L. Bennett, M. C. Diamond, *J. Comp. Physiol. Psychol.* 55, 429 (1962).
6. J. A. King, *Psychol. Bull.* 55, 46 (1958).
7. J. P. Scott, *Science* 138, 949 (1962); V. H. Denenberg, *Psychol. Rev.* 71, 335 (1964); T. C. Schneirla and J. S. Rosenblatt, *Science* 139, 1110 (1963).
8. W. R. Thompson and W. Heron, *J. Comp. Physiol. Psychol.* 47, 77 (1954).
9. R. Melzack, *ibid.*, p. 166.
10. —— and T. H. Scott, *ibid.* 50, 155 (1957); W. R. Thompson, R. Melzack, T. H. Scott, *Science* 123, 939 (1956).
11. D. O. Hebb, *The Organization of Behavior* (Wiley, New York, 1949).
12. A. E. Fisher, thesis, Pennsylvania State University (1955).
13. M. S. Lessac, thesis, University of Pennsylvania (1965).
14. J. L. Fuller and L. D. Clark, *J. Comp. Physiol. Psychol.* 61, 251 (1966).
15. J. L. Fuller, L. D. Clark, M. B. Waller, *Psychopharmacologia* 1, 393 (1960).
16. J. L. Fuller, in *Proc. World Congr. Psychiat. 3rd* (1961), vol. 3, p. 223; *Discovery* 25, No. 2, 18 (1964).
17. —— and M. B. Waller, in *Roots of Behavior*, E. L. Bliss, Ed. (Hoeber, New York, 1962).
18. D. O. Hebb and A. H. Riesen, *Bull. Can. Psychol. Ass.* 3, 49 (1943).
19. J. L. Fuller and L. D. Clark, *Canine Kaspar Hausers* (film shown to the American Society of Zoologists, Cleveland, 1963).
20. ——, *J. Comp. Physiol. Psychol.* 61, 258 (1966).
21. J. L. Fuller, *Ann. N.Y. Acad. Sci.* 56, 214 (1953).
22. J. Hirsch, *Science* 142, 1436 (1963).

23. H. F. Harlow, personal communication.
24. W. F. Angermeier, J. B. Phelps, H. H. Reynolds, *Psychonomic Sci.* **8**, 379 (1967).
25. J. L. Fuller, *ibid.* **4**, 273 (1966).
26. H. C. Ebel and J. Werboff, *Perceptual Motor Skills* **24**, 507 (1967).
27. H. F. Harlow, in *Behavior and Evolution*, A. Roe and G. G. Simpson, Eds. (Yale Univ. Press, New Haven, 1958).
28. H. Mahut, *Can. J. Psychol.* **12**, 35 (1958).
29. O. Elliott and J. P. Scott, *J. Genet. Psychol.* **99**, 3 (1961).
30. The research reported in this article has
been supported by the Rockefeller Foundation, the Ford Foundation, the Foundations Fund for Research in Psychiatry, and the U.S. Public Health Service (research grant MH-01775). Dr. Lincoln D. Clark (now at the College of Medicine, University of Utah) and Dr. Marcus B. Waller (now at the University of North Carolina) actively participated in many of the studies. Several research assistants have been associated with the program; in particular, Frank Clark and Jane Harris had major responsibilities for the experiments.

DIFFERENTIAL EFFECTS OF PRENATAL MATERNAL STRESS ON OFFSPRING BEHAVIOR IN MICE AS A FUNCTION OF GENOTYPE AND STRESS[1]

J. C. DeFRIES, MORTON W. WEIR, AND J. P. HEGMANN

University of Illinois

2 experiments concerning differential effects of prenatal stress on offspring behavior in mice are reported. In Experiment 1, inbred (BALB/cJ and C57BL/6J) females carrying either inbred or hybrid litters were subjected daily to physical stress throughout the latter half of pregnancy; from data regarding open-field activity of the resulting offspring, it was concluded that differential effects observed were a function of both fetal and maternal genotypes. In Experiment 2, adrenalin injections administered to females during Days 10 and 11 of pregnancy as the stress condition were not found to mimic those of physical prenatal stress.

When genetically distinct groups (usually two or more inbred strains) have been subjected to prenatal maternal stress, differential effects on offspring behavior have been observed (cf. Thompson & Olian, 1961; Weir & DeFries, 1964). This finding of a genotype-environment interaction indicates that the response to prenatal stress is a function of the genotype. In an attempt to assess the relative importance of the fetal and maternal genotypes in this response, DeFries (1964) administered physical stress to pregnant mice of two inbred strains (BALB/cCrgl and C57BL/Crgl) carrying either inbred or hybrid litters. Hybrid offspring were found to respond differently from inbreds which had mothers of the same strain, and hybrids from reciprocal crosses did not respond alike; thus, it was concluded that both the fetal and maternal genotypes were involved.

Two additional experiments are described in the present report. The primary objective of the physical stress experiment was to assess again the roles of the fetal and maternal genotypes in the response to physical prenatal stress. The experimental design, treatments, and test conditions were similar to those employed by DeFries (1964), but the substrains of mice were the same as those used by Weir and DeFries (1964). The primary objective of the chemical stress experiment was to assess the effects of a treatment over which more precise control was possible.

[1] This investigation was supported in part by Grant GM-12486 from the National Institute of General Medical Sciences. We thank Eugene A. Thomas for his assistance in the conduct of these experiments.

211

Using an experimental design similar to that of the physical stress experiment, maternal adrenalin injections were employed as the stress condition.

METHOD

Subjects

In both experiments, the two inbred parental strains (BALB/cJ and C57BL/6J) were mated so that offspring of both inbred strains and their reciprocal crosses would result. Upon mating (as evidenced by the presence of a vaginal plug), females were assigned at random to either the stress (treatment) or control group. In the physical stress experiment, 284 offspring were obtained. Subclass numbers of 8–31 in the 16 subclasses resulted when data were grouped according to strain of male parent, strain of female parent, treatment, and sex of offspring. In the chemical stress experiment, 174 offspring were obtained, with subclasses of 5–19 Ss.

Treatments

In the physical stress experiment, treatment was initiated 10 days after mating and consisted of daily exposure for 3 min. to each of three stress conditions throughout the remainder of pregnancy. Each morning, females were forced to swim in a laboratory sink with water temperature maintained at about 25° C.; 4 hr. later, groups of females were placed in a cage on an Eberbach reciprocating shaker which operated at about 170 cpm; 4 hr. later, groups of females were exposed to white noise at about 100-db. SPL at random intervals for 50% of the stress period.

In the chemical stress experiment, females were administered subcutaneous flank injections of .025 mg. of adrenalin chloride in .5 cc of Earle's solution during Days 10 and 11 of pregnancy. Control females received placebo injections of .5 cc of Earle's solution during this stage of pregnancy.

Offspring Testing

Beginning at 40 $\pm$ 3 days of age, offspring were tested for 3 min. on each of 2 successive days in a brightly lighted 36 × 36 in. white Plexiglas open field. Each S was placed in a clear Plexiglas cylinder in the corner of the field and then released at the start of the test period. Five light sources located 6 in. apart on each of two adjacent sides of the field were directed through infrared filters and holes (5-mm. diameter) located 15 mm. above the floor of the field. Photoconductive cells were located directly opposite from these light sources and activated counters when a light beam was broken. This formed a grid of light beams which effectively divided the field into 36 squares, 6 × 6 in. each. The total number of light beams interrupted during the two test periods was used as each S's activity score.

Statistical Analysis

Because of the presence of heterogeneous group variances, a square-root transformation of these activity scores was employed. The mathematical model assumed to represent these data included interactions and main effects due to strain of male parent, strain of female parent, treatment, and sex of offspring. Because of unequal and disproportionate subclass numbers, a least-squares analysis of variance was employed (Harvey, 1960).

RESULTS AND DISCUSSION

Physical Stress Experiment

Means and corresponding F ratios are presented in Tables 1 and 2, respectively. Large and highly significant ($p < .01$) main effects due to strain of male parent (M) and strain of female parent (F) were obtained. Offspring of BALB male parents had an average[2] transformed activity score of 10.52, whereas those of C57BL male parents had a mean of 15.11. Offspring of BALB and C57BL female parents, however, had average transformed activity scores of 9.52 and 16.10, respectively. This greater difference between the means when the data are grouped according to maternal strain suggests the presence of a general maternal effect on open-field activity. The highly significant interaction between strain of male and female parent (M × F) represents a comparison of inbred vs. hybrid progeny and is a direct test for heterosis. Inbred and hybrid progeny had mean transformed activity scores of 10.69 and 14.93, respectively.

The first-order interactions involving strain of male parent and treatment (M × T) and strain of female parent and treatment (F × T) are of primary interest. If the differential effects of prenatal stress were solely a function of the genotype of the mother, F × T should be significant, whereas M × T should not. However, if these differential effects were solely a function of the genotype of the fetus, these two interactions should be of equal magnitude. From Table 2 it may be seen that neither alternative is observed. Instead, M × T was highly significant, while F × T was nonsignificant. Experimental offspring of BALB male parents had reduced activity scores as compared to controls (10.00 vs. 11.02), whereas those of C57BL male parents had increased scores (15.82 vs. 14.40).

The highly significant M × T interaction, in the absence of an F × T interaction, suggests that both the fetal and maternal genotypes are involved in the differential response to prenatal physical stress. If mothers of the two inbred strains respond differently to physical stress (e.g., elaborate different amounts of some hormone) and if hybrid fetuses are affected differently from inbreds, the result could be an interaction between strain of male parent and

[2] Due to unequal subclass numbers, all values reported in the text of this paper which describe main effects and interactions are unweighted averages of individual subclass means.

TABLE 1

Mean Open-Field Activity Scores of Offspring from BALB/cJ and C57BL/6J Experimental and Control Mothers in Prenatal Stress Experiments

Parental strains		Physical stress experiment				Chemical stress experiment			
		Experimental		Control		Experimental		Control	
Male	Female	N	M	N	M	N	M	N	M
BALB	BALB	35	4.15	17	6.06	14	6.00	15	3.63
BALB	C57BL	44	15.86	34	16.00	20	14.91	23	12.92
C57BL	BALB	22	15.08	61	12.81	26	13.29	35	14.15
C57BL	C57BL	36	16.57	35	16.00	21	15.55	20	15.17

Note.—Average activity scores were obtained separately for males and females from transformed data, where each S's score is the square root of the total activity over the 2-day test period. Because of unequal numbers of males and females in each subclass, the values tabulated are unweighted means of these average transformed scores.

TABLE 2

Analyses of Variance of Open-Field Activity Data Obtained from Prenatal Stress Experiments

Effect	F ratios	
	Physical stress experiment[a]	Chemical stress experiment[b]
Strain of male parent (M)	118.1**	82.2**
Strain of female parent (F)	242.1**	88.6**
Treatment (T)	0.2	2.9
Sex of offspring (S)	1.1	0.0
M × F	100.5**	42.8**
M × T	8.3**	4.5*
F × T	0.0	0.1
M × F × T[c]	4.2*	0.5
Error mean square	10.8	12.6

[a] $df = 1/268$.
[b] $df = 1/158$.
[c] Other interactions were small and nonsignificant in both experiments.
* $p < .05$.
** $p < .01$.

treatment. The significant ($p < .05$) second-order interaction between strain of male parent, strain of female parent, and treatment (M × F × T) provides additional evidence that the fetal genotype was involved in this response.

Although the effects due to strain of male parent, strain of female parent, and their interaction account for a larger portion of the variance in open-field activity than main effects or interactions involving prenatal treatment, the direction of the treatment effect in each of the four mating groups in this experiment was identical to that found by DeFries (1964). These results suggest that the differential response to prenatal physical stress is a function of both the maternal and fetal genotypes.

Chemical Stress Experiment

As indicated in Tables 1 and 2, highly significant effects due to M, F, and their interaction were again found. In addition, a significant ($p < .05$) M × T interaction was observed; however, the magnitude of this interaction was less than that of the physical stress experiment, and the treatment effects were in opposite directions. These results suggest that the effects of maternal adrenalin injections on offspring open-field behavior do not mimic those of physical prenatal stress.

REFERENCES

DeFries, J. C. Prenatal maternal stress in mice: Differential effects on behavior. *J. Hered.*, 1964, **55**, 289–295.
Harvey, W. R. Least squares analysis of data with unequal subclass numbers. (No. ARS-20-8) Washington, D. C.: United States Department of Agriculture, 1960.
Thompson, W. R., & Olian, S. Some effects on offspring behavior of maternal adrenalin injection during pregnancy in three inbred mouse strains. *Psychol. Rep.*, 1961, **8**, 87–90.
Weir, M. W., & DeFries, J. C. Prenatal maternal influence on behavior in mice: Evidence of a genetic basis. *J. comp. physiol. Psychol.*, 1964, **58**, 412–417.

(Received March 11, 1966)

Department of Zoology, Oxford University, England

The ontogeny of a pecking preference in domestic chicks

By Richard Dawkins[1] [2]

With 3 figures

Received 30. 6. 1967

Introduction

Pecking in the domestic chick has been a favourite subject for students of behaviour ontogeny, and it has provided ammunition for both sides in the "nature or nurture" controversy (Spalding 1873, reprinted 1954; Breed 1911; Shepard and Breed 1913; Moseley 1925; Bird 1933; Cruze 1935; Padilla 1935; Kuo 1932; Lehrman 1953; Wood-Gush 1955; Schneirla 1956; Hess 1956; Fantz 1957, 1958). One reason for this popularity as a subject may have been that the young of this species receive rather little help in feeding from the parents, and develop an efficient feeding behaviour of their own within a few hours of hatching. Certainly my own interest in the ontogeny of this response is a largely functional one. Pecking preferences are regarded as part of the animal's equipment for survival, and their ontogeny as the process by which the genes, in interaction with their environment, achieve this equipment.

In an omnivorous animal, the most functionally interesting visual feeding preferences are those involving properties which a wide range of food objects are likely to have in common, and of these the most promising seemed to be solidity or three-dimensionality. Some work had been done before on the learned use of solidity cues by chicks (Benner 1938; Hess 1950, 1961), and it was known (Fantz 1958) that within the first two days of life, chicks reared in darkness gave more pecks in the first five minutes of sighted life to hemispheres than to comparable flat circles.

The first experiments to be described here also involve choice between a hemisphere, called S (for Solid), and a disc called F (for Flat). Chicks given various different previous treatments were given a choice between these two stimuli. In later experiments photographs of hemispheres and discs were used. Unless otherwise stated the chicks in all experiments were White Leghorns, 3 days or less in age, which had never been given food or water.

The solidity preference

Developmental changes

Chicks were placed individually in a small cardboard box with two stimuli stuck to one wall, 9 cm. above the floor and 3 cm. from each other. They were a hemisphere (S) and a flat

---

[1] Present address: Dept. of Zoology, University of California, Berkeley, 94 720, California, U.S.A.

[2] I wish to thank Professor N. Tinbergen F.R.S. who supervised this research, and also Drs. J. M. Cullen, M. Impekoven, M. H. Hansell and others for discussion and criticism. Mr. J. Adam largely made the automatic peck-counting apparatus. Miss C. Court drew the diagrams. Dr. E. Cullen translated the German summary. Messrs. Jennings of Garsington provided chicks free of charge. Financial support was received from the Science Research Council, and the Nature Conservancy.

214

circle (F) of equal diameter, 5 mm., both painted white. Each chick was watched and its pecks noted for a standard time, usually one minute only since it was found that isolated chicks, if they had not pecked within this period, were unlikely to peck after it. In any case the number of pecks was low; typically about 50 % of the chicks would not peck at all in the test period. At that time I did not appreciate the importance of familiarity of surroundings for the readiness of chicks to peck. Temperature was found to influence pecking rate, after which an attempt was made in subsequent tests to maintain the temperature in the testing box near the optimum of around 25 °C.

In assessing the results, the total numbers of pecks given by different chicks to the stimulus objects were never used as such, though they were sometimes used in ranked form: pecks are very often given in rapid bursts, and cannot be considered as independent data. The basic figure used for analysis is the number of chicks out of a group showing a preference, preference being defined either in terms of the first peck given by each chick, or the majority of each chick's pecks. These two measures of preference give very similar results.

Throughout this paper unless otherwise stated, significance levels for preferences were obtained as follows:

Maj. (majority of) pecks preferences — Wilcoxon matched pairs test; no. of pecks from each chick at one stimulus paired with no. from the same chick at the other stimulus. (For "chick" read "group of chicks" in the second part of the paper where chicks were tested together in groups.)

1st. peck preferences — Binomial test; no. of chicks giving 1st. peck to one stimulus versus no. of chicks giving 1st. peck to the other stimulus.

Statistical tests from SIEGEL, S. (1956): Nonparametric statistics for the behavioral sciences. McGraw-Hill, New York.

"S-preference" or "Solidity preference" means preference for S over F.

The chicks, which were males collected as day-olds from a local farm, were kept in normal light without food or water until testing, and were then subjected to the preference test described above, either on the day they were collected, called Day 1; or on Day 2 or on Day 3. In addition some were tested on more than one of these days. Most of the chicks had hatched the night before Day 1, but some were a little older. A different *batch* of chicks was collected and tested each week. Nine *batches* in all were tested.

A number of conclusions can be drawn from the results (Fig. 1):

(1) Most of the points on the graph lie above the 50 % mark, indicating that the

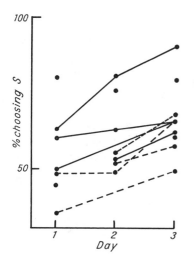

Fig. 1. Percentage numbers of chicks giving first pecks to Solid rather than Flat, at three different ages. Lines joining points signify that the chicks concerned came from the same weekly batch. Absence of a line attached to a point indicates that members of the batch concerned were tested on one day only. Continuous lines join points from chicks which had never, as individuals, been tested before. Dotted lines lead up to points from chicks which had had some experience, as individuals, of the testing situation

S-preference does indeed exist, as we should expect from FANTZ's finding. For most of the batches the preference was significant, in some cases very strongly so.

(2) The lines on the graph tend to slope upward from left to right, indicating that the strength of the *S-preference* increases over the 3 days. In order to show this conclusively it would be better to test chicks of different ages at the same time, but this would introduce difficulties owing to the great inter-batch variation (3).

(3) The gradients of the different lines are rather similar, or in other words the lines cross each other less than would be expected at random, suggesting that there is considerable batch-specific variation in absolute level of S-preference, but that each batch shows the same rate of increase in the preference. The effect may be represented in terms of a correlation between *earlier* and *later* points from the same batch, counting Day 2 points as "*earlier*" when compared with Day 3 ones, and as "*later*" when compared with Day 1 ones. The correlation, (Fig. 2) seems to be a strong positive one. It is not legitimate

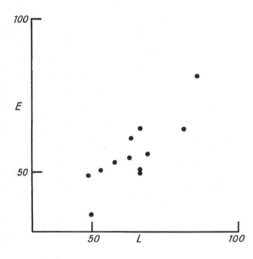

Fig. 2. Scatter diagram to show correlation between S-preference of chicks of the same batch in earlier (E) and later (L) tests. (See text for explanation of significance). S-preference is measured as percentage number of chicks giving first pecks to Solid rather than Flat

to take all the points on the scatter diagram in determining the significance of the correlation, because some Day 2 results are represented twice. However if this duplication is eliminated, the Spearman Rank Correlation Coefficient is still reasonably high at $+ 0.7$, and is significant ($P < 0.05$).

I call the batch-specific variation demonstrated by this correlation the "*Batch Effect*". It may or may not be genetic.

(4) In previously untested chicks there is a tendency for the total number of pecks given in the test period to increase over the three days, but in previously tested chicks there is a tendency for it to decrease. The difference between the two classes of chick is significant. Experience of the testing situation seems also to have a slight decreasing effect on Solidity preference, but it is not significant.

The waning in pecking tendency as a result of experience of the testing situation suggests a possible explanation of the ontogenetic increase in Solidity preference shown in Figure 1. This explanation will be discussed in the next section:

A possible explanation of the ontogenetic increase in S-preference

The explanation is based on the idea of waning or extinction mentioned above and depends on two conditions or assumptions.

A. The waning is stimulus-specific.

B. Chicks generalise from marks on the flat walls of their living boxes to the flat stimulus F rather than to the solid one, S.

In their cardboard living boxes the chicks spent much of their time pecking at grain-marks and other blemishes in the surface of the walls and floor. These marks have little in common except that they are seldom solid and are nearly always flush with the flat wall or floor. If waning is stimulus-specific then, and chicks can generalise between a wide variety of flat objects as against solid ones, we should expect that the longer chicks have had experience of these conditions before testing the more strongly should they have waned in their responsiveness to flat objects in general. Waning to solid objects should be less marked, since these are less common in the environment, and could easily be offset by the general ontogenetic increase in overall pecking tendency.

The stimulus-specificity of waning

An experiment was done to test the first condition directly. The testing method was the same as for the experiments described above. On the evening of Day 2, chicks were divided into 3 groups, 2 experimental groups containing 36 chicks each, and 1 extra control group of 12 chicks. (The latter control group was not crucial for the experiment). They were kept overnight in small cardboard boxes in the light, 6 to a box. The 12 control chicks were kept in ordinary plain cardboard boxes. One group of 36 experimental chicks, Group A, had 2 S stimuli stuck to the walls of each of their 6 boxes; the 6 boxes of the other group of 36, Group B, each had 2 F stimuli stuck to the walls. On the morning after, all were given the normal standard S-F preference test as described above.

Tab. 1. Nos. of chicks giving 1st. pecks and majority of pecks to Solid and Flat after unrewarded experience of them

	A: S-experience	B: F-experience	C: "no" experience
Chicks	36	36	12
Pecking	10	23	9
% Pecking	28 %	64 %	75 %
1st peck S	4	22	7
1st peck F	6	1	2
% 1st peck pref. S	40 %	96 %	78 %
Maj. S	5	23	7
Maj. F	5	0	1
% maj. pref. S	50 %	100 %	88 %

Significance of results:
B pecked more in total than A did $p < 0.03$ (Wilcoxon test, 2 tailed)
If either the four 1st peck numbers or the four Maj. peck numbers from groups A & B are used in a 2 x 2 X^2 contingency table, $p < 0.01$.

It is obvious (Tab. I) that the waning effect is highly stimulus-specific. We may surmise that the F pecking score of group A and the S pecking score of group B are roughly equivalent to those of normally reared chicks, and that the enormous differences in their pecking results are due to selective waning in responsiveness to the stimulus with which they had been reared. The results from the extra control group C are quite compatible with this, though the numbers are too small for direct comparison with A and B to be meaningful.

The first assumption or condition of the explanation outlined above is then confirmed.

"Flatness" generalisation

The second assumption or condition proposed above was that chicks would generalise in their selective waning from the flat walls and floor of their living environment to stimulus F rather than S. A prediction from this is that chicks reared in an environment where there are no flat walls should show a lower preference for S over F than "normally" reared controls, perhaps even reversed preference.

Experimental boxes were lined with *corrugated cardboard* all over the walls and floor so that chicks reared in these boxes had very little experience of flatness. Controls were reared in flat-walled boxes.

The experiment was repeated on several batches with minor differences in method which are not important: in all cases the experimental and control groups received the same treatment, except of course with respect to the experimental variable of box lining. Some of the batches were tested on more than one day. In these cases the data from the different days are given separately in the table. The testing method was the same as before in all cases.

Tab. 2. Nos. of chicks giving 1st. pecks to Solid and Flat after rearing with corrugated or flat cardboard

Rearing condition →		1st peck nos.				% 1st peck pref. S	
		Flat		Corrugated		Flat	Corrugated
Batch	Day	S	F	S	F		
E	2	15	13	17	11	54	61
E	3	24	14	17	16	64	52
F	1	19	11	14	10	64	58
F	2	17	4	14	4	81	78
F	3	20	2	13	4	91	76
I	3	28	7	24	16	80	60
J	3	31	5	18	10	86	64
K	2 & 3	4	1	3	3	80	50

The corrugated environment has not reversed the S over F preference, but in seven out of the eight experiments (Tab. 2) the corrugated-reared group gave a lower S-preference than the flat-reared controls. If the 1st. peck numbers themselves are considered rather than the percentage preferences calculated from them it will be seen that in 7 out of 8 cases more of the flat-reared chicks gave first pecks to S than of the corrugated-reared ones. Conversely in 5 out of 7 cases (one tie), more of the corrugated-reared chicks pecked first at F than of the flat-reared ones. Not surprisingly, the chicks which had had their S-pecks selectively reduced pecked less overall than those with reduced F-pecks. In two of the cases, significant results from within individual experiments support the overall conclusion that experience of the corrugated environment leads to a lower preference for S over F than experience of a flat one.

It seems then that selective waning of responsiveness to flat objects is a result of rearing in a flat-walled environment, and generalisation to the flat stimulus, F, may be a major cause of the normal ontogenetic increase in preference for S over F in unfed chicks.

I feel that this finding about the causation of the ontogenetic increase in S-preference is of little biological interest in itself, since it may well only apply to the artificial environment in which my chicks were reared. If it has any importance it is in showing two of the general ways in which adaptive feeding preferences may develop in nature. The extremely strong stimulus-specific waning in responsiveness shown in Table 1, and the powers of generalisation demonstrated in the experiments just described are likely to be of significance in the development of adaptive behaviour in general.

The solidity preference in dark-reared chicks

Having found a learning process which causes an increase in the solidity preference in light-reared chicks, and knowing also that this preference is often rather weak in first day chicks, we are naturally led to ask whether the preference is completely dependent on this process of flatness-specific waning. FANTZ's results from dark-reared chicks suggest that this is not the case and that the solidity preference develops in the absence of experience of this kind. It seemed worth-while to confirm FANTZ's findings using the method with which the above results were obtained, and also trying to limit the chicks' previous experience in light, even more than FANTZ did.

Sixteen chicks were hatched in a totally darkened room (i. e. to the dark-adapted human eye there was no visible light). They were kept in darkness until testing. The testing room was adjacent, also dark though not quite so perfectly as the rearing room. The two rooms were separated by a light-tight door, which was kept closed during testing. Each chick was tested once only. They were transferred one by one in darkness into the testing room, and placed in the normal preference-testing box described above, in front of the two stimuli, the normal S and F. Each test lasted fo 5 minutes, initiated by the light over the box being switched on. Eight chicks were tested on their first day, but their responsiveness was so low that I postponed testing the rest until the following day, on the basis of the result mentioned above showing an increase in responsiveness with time in untested chicks.

The behaviour of the chicks on their first experience of light was remarkable for its normality. Several of them jumped backwards as soon as the light was switched on, in an apparently startled manner, but they showed no overt signs of dazzle, and within a few seconds most were looking about them "attentively" giving the so-called "pleasure twitter" (COLLIAS and JOOS 1953). The only abnormal feature of their behaviour that I could see was the relatively great inaccuracy of their pecking. This would be expected from previous work (SHEPARD and BREED 1913; MOSELEY 1925; BIRD 1933; CRUZE 1935; PADILLA 1935). They were also somewhat unsteady on their feet but probably not much more so than normal chicks of the same age. No light-reared controls were kept, as the number of eggs available was limited.

Table 3. Choice of Solid and Flat by individual dark-reared chicks

Day	Chick	1st peck	No. pecks S	No. pecks F
1	1	F	2	1
	2	S	12	1
	3	–	0	0
	4	S	8	1
	5	–	0	0
	6	S	3	0
	7	–	0	0
	8	–	0	0
2	9	F	5	1
	10	S	10	0
	11	S	22	2
	12	S	41	14
	13	S	37	1
	14	S	5	0
	15	S	16	0
	16	S	11	0

Summary			
	S	F	p
1st pecks	10	2	< 0.02
Maj. of pecks	12	0	< 0.001

The preference for S over F (Tab. 3) is highly significant (P < 0.002 Wilcoxon, 1-tailed) if all the pecks are considered, and is significant (P < 0.02 Binomial test 1-tailed) if only first pecks are considered. FANTZ's result is thus confirmed. However of my 12 chicks which pecked, 5 pecked at other objects – small specks of dirt, their own feet, etc., before pecking at either S or F. Of the remaining 7 whose first peck was at either S or F, 5 pecked first at S and 2 at F. This difference is not significant. To be pedantic therefore, the solidity preference has not been conclusively demonstrated in chicks with no previous experience of pecking in the light. For the 5 chicks which pecked first at other objects before pecking at S or F, the number of such "stray" pecks was respectively 5, 1, 7, 2, and 10. It seems therefore almost safe to conclude that no previous experience of pecking in the light is necessary for the solidity preference to develop.

The Solidity preference in monocular chicks

A number of possible cues might be used by the chicks in discriminating S from F, for example stereoscopy, movement parallax, shadow casting, and surface shading (WOODWORTH and SCHLOSBERG 1954), and also rather less interesting ones such as apparent size when viewed from the side. Of these I was especially interested in surface shading (which will be discussed in the next section), but before beginning experiments on it, I did one experiment to test the importance of stereoscopy.

28 chicks were half-blindfolded by means of Elastoplast stuck over one eye, in 50 % of the cases the left eye and in 50% of the cases the right. Four stimuli were used instead of the usual 2 in an attempt at eliminating the effects of possible side preference which might have resulted from the sidedness of the blindfolding. The 2 Ss and Fs were arranged alternately in a horizontal row at the same height above the floor as in the normal 2-stimulus tests (9 cm.). The testing procedure was in other respects as usual. The two ways of arranging the stimuli, SFSF and FSFS were given equal numbers of times, the stimulus card being changed over every 5 tests. Twenty non-blindfolded control chicks were also tested. The experiment was carried out over 2 days, the second and third in the lives of the chicks, which were unfed and reared in the light in the usual way.

The half-blindfolded chicks showed a significant preference (Tab. 4) for S over F, and it was apparently no weaker than that of the controls. This shows that binocular vision is probably of little if any importance in this discrimination.

Tab. 4. Nos. of chicks giving 1st. pecks and majority of pecks to Solid and Flat when blindfolded in one eye

	Half – Blindfold	Control
Chicks	28	20
Pecking	13	12
1st peck S	10 ⎫	9 ⎫
1st peck F	3 ⎬ (p<0,05)	3 ⎬ n. s.
Maj. pecks S	10 ⎫	10 ⎫
Maj. pecks F	2 ⎬ (p<0,01)	2 ⎬ (p<0,001)

The ontogeny of the use of surface-shading cues of solidity

Introduction

Solid objects may be distinguished from flat in directed light by means of the differences in amount of light reflected from different surfaces. Since light tends to come mainly from above, solid objects usually appear lighter on top than underneath. This is one of the main ways in which solidity is identified by man in photographs or drawings (GREGORY 1966). A familiar illusion is the loss of solid appearance seen if photographs of solid objects are turned upside down (BENNER 1938; HESS 1961). It is presumably the use of this cue of solidity by predators that has led so many cryptic animals to adopt countershaded body coloration (COTT 1940; DE RUITER 1956).

HESS (1950, 1961) presented chicks with photographs of wheat grains taken in directed light. Normal and inverted prints of the same negative were presented simultaneously. Two groups of chicks were used, one reared normally with overhead lighting, and the other in a special cage with light coming from below. The pecking preferences of the chicks in a choice test between the two orientations of the photographs were measured weekly for the first 8 weeks of their lives. In the first week, both groups of chicks showed a slight but non-significant preference for the "correctly" oriented photograph, i. e. the one in which the grains of wheat were lighter on their upper surfaces than on their lower surfaces. During the following weeks the control chicks showed a gradual increase in this preference, while the experimentals slightly more slowly came to prefer the inverted photograph, and by the seventh week did so significantly. HESS suggests that there may be an innate predisposition to learn to prefer the correctly oriented photograph more easily than to learn to prefer the inverted one.

Since in HESS's photographs the grains cast very prominent shadows on the background, it is impossible to tell whether the cue being used in the discrimination is surface shading orientation or cast shadow orientation, or both. Furthermore the surface shading of HESS's photographs is not as prominent as it might be, and it could be that the chicks had difficulty in seeing it. The possibility therefore existed, and indeed was hinted at by HESS himself, that there is an unlearned preference for the surface shading qualities characteristic of solid objects. I decided to look into this further, in spite of FANTZ's (1958) conclusion that dark-reared chicks do not use surface shading cues of solidity. It seemed a very interesting case from the point of view of the ontogenetic origin of adaptedness (LORENZ 1961, 1965), since the environmental feature to which a preference for a "correctly" oriented photograph is presumably adapted, namely the prevailing direction of light in nature, is easily defined, and it is easy to control the animal's experience of it.

Methods

The chicks were placed, in groups of 6 unless otherwise stated, in a cubical testing compartment, 30 cm. square. Three of the walls were painted grey, and the fourth consisted of 6 layers of black netting, serving as a crude one-way screen, since the inside of the box was illuminated and the rest of the room was darker. In the wall opposite the netting screen, two 33 mm. square windows were cut, 3 mm. apart, with their tops 85 mm. above the floor. The stimulus objects appeared in the middle of these windows, mounted on small stiff cards. These cards were held in light frames, hinged at the top, so that when they were pecked they swung slightly backwards, thereby activating Bulgin microswitches, which had been made more sensitive by bending of their springs. These were connected up with a 48 V supply so that pecks were registered on counters. Most though not all of the pecks were counted. The data most commonly presented are the numbers of groups of 6 chicks which gave the majority of their pecks in a given time, 5 minutes unless otherwise stated, to each of the stimuli. Stimulus position was of course varied in successive trials, so that side bias could have no significant effect.

The stimuli were as follows:

GS (Grey Solid): A 5 mm. hemisphere, the same as S above but painted grey.

PS (Photo Solid): A photograph of a hemisphere taken in directed light.

    PSC (Photo Solid Correct): PS "correctly" oriented so that the lighter half was uppermost.

    PSI (Photo Solid Inverted): PS inverted so that the darker half was uppermost (Fig. 3).

PF (Photo Flat): A photograph of a flat disc.

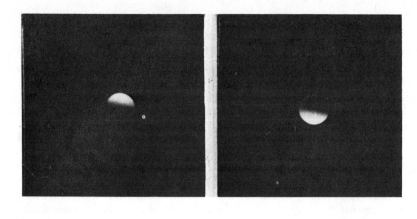

Fig. 3. PSC and PSI, respectively a correctly oriented and an inverted photograph of a solid hemisphere, taken in directed light. Scale: each small division = 1 mm.

The hemisphere and disc photographed were respectively half a ping-pong ball and a cardboard disc of the same diameter, both painted white. The background was a sheet of black cloth. In order to eliminate cast shadows both model objects were supported above the background. The final prints were made so that the stimulus objects were approximately the same size as the original S and F, 5 mm. The prints were glued on to stiff black cardboard rectangles and presented as described above.

Choice between photographs of a hemisphere and a disc

32 groups of 6 chicks were each tested once only for 2 minutes. In all tests the choice was between the hemisphere photograph PS, and the disc photograph PF, but in half the cases PS was "correctly" oriented (PSC) and in the other half it was inverted (PSI). The chicks were tested on Day 3. Before testing they had been kept under normal lighting conditions, and had not been fed or watered.

Tab. 5. Nos of groups of chicks giving majority of pecks to photographs of Solid (PS, correctly oriented or inverted) and Flat (PF)

	PS	PF	p
Orientation of PS			
PSC ("Correct")	14	1	<0.001
PSI (Inverted)	8	8	n. s.

There was a strong preference (Tab. 5) for PS over PF when PS was "correctly" oriented with the lighter side uppermost. When PS was inverted there was no preference between it and PF. A 2 × 2 test gives x^2 of 5.109 for 1 degree of freedom, with a 1-tailed P value of less than 0.05. We can conclude therefore that inverting the photograph PS has an effect in the expected direction on pecking. It seems probable therefore that chicks under 4 days old, and unfed, treat photographs of solid objects in the same kind of way as we do, responding only to correctly oriented ones as though they were solid.

Choice between a real hemisphere and photographs of a hemisphere and a disc

Since the correctly oriented photograph of a hemisphere PSC is so strongly preferred to a flat circle (and to PSI), a reasonable question to ask is whether it is still inferior to a real hemisphere as a stimulus.

The main technical difficulty was in deciding how to paint the real hemisphere so that it matched the photographs in brightness. A shade of grey was chosen so that, subjectively, it seemed to approach the photographs in brightness, but was still somewhat brighter. From previous work not described here, and also from CURTIUS (1954), it was known to be likely that if the chicks showed any brightness preference they would tend to choose the darker stimuli. Thus since the hypothesis being tested in these experiments was that the real Solid should be preferred to the photographs, it was arranged so that if a brightness preference were shown it should tend to favour the null hypothesis.

Three experiments, A, B and C were done, differing in minor details. In A, groups of 4 chicks were used instead of groups of 6, and were tested on Day 3. In B, the chicks were not from my usual supplier, and were of a different breed, Rhode Island Red X Light Sussex. They were tested on Days 1, 2, and 3. In C, the chicks were tested on Days 1 and 2. The chicks were reared in the light without food or water, as before.

In all three the same stimuli were used, GS, real hemisphere painted grey as explained above, PSC, a correctly oriented photograph of a hemisphere, and PF, a photograph of a disc. They were presented in all possible pair combinations.

The three experiments (Tab. 6) do not all give the same result, but they agree in confirming the preference already found for PSC over PF. Experi-

Tab. 6. Nos. of groups of chicks giving majority of pecks to real Solid (GS), and photographs of Solid (PSC) and Flat (PF)

Experiment	GS	PSC	p	PSC	PF	p	GS	PF	p
A	6	4	n. s.	8	2	<0.02	9	1	<0.02
B	28	7	<0.01	26	7	<0.01	33	1	<0.01
C	7	15	n. s.	17	4	<0.01	11	9	n. s.

ment B also shows a significant preference for GS over PSC (and also over PF), but experiment C shows no preference for GS over PSC, and even tends non-significantly in the other direction. I feel the most likely explanation for this discrepancy is batch-specific variation in tendency to attend to brightness (SUTHERLAND 1964). Both PS and PF, being slightly darker, should be preferred to GS if brightness alone were considered. If the batch of chicks used in Experiment C had a relatively strong tendency to attend to brightness the results actually obtained would be expected: a preference for PS over GS and an increased tendency to peck at PF as opposed to GS. The batch used in Experiment B on the other hand perhaps tended to ignore brightness and attend to some other cue, such as movements parallax. I would tentatively expect therefore that if there were no brightness differences between a real S and a photograph of one, the real one would always be preferred.

In any case, whether or not shading cues are the only ones used in the solidity discrimination in my tests, there can be no doubt that they are important, and that orientation of brightness gradients is very important to chicks just as it is to ourselves. These experiments were all done on chicks reared in the light, which had had the opportunity for experience with solid objects seen with overhead lighting. The next question is whether these shading cues are used by chicks without the opportunity for such experience.

Photograph preference tests using dark-reared chicks

The arrangements for dark-rearing were the same as for the experiment described above. The chicks were hatched in an incubator in one dark room, and transferred for testing into another.

The preference testing apparatus with the microswitches was used, but I was mainly interested in observing the first peck which each chick gave, since I wanted them to have had as little experience as possible. They were each tested alone for an indefinite period. Tests were discontinued if it was clear to me that the chick was very unlikely to peck. This is not difficult to judge: when a chick has begun its long series of distress calls characteristic of isolation (COLLIAS and JOOS 1953), it seldom breaks off to peck. 37 chicks were used, varying between 1, 2 and 3 days old at the time of testing. Only 19 pecked. The stimuli were PF, the photograph of a disc, and PSC, the correctly oriented photograph of a hemisphere.

No preference was shown (Tab. 7). It should be remembered that in the previous experiment on dark-reared chicks only 12 pecked, but this was enough

Tab. 7. Nos. of dark-reared chicks giving lst. pecks to photographs of Solid ("correctly" oriented PSC) and Flat

	PSC	PF
1st pecks	10	9

to show a strong preference for a real S over F, and also that all the 5 experiments done up till now, using these two photographs, gave strong evidence of a preference for PSC over PF. It seems therefore that FANTZ's conclusion (1958) that dark-reared chicks do not use shading cues in their solidity preference may indeed be true, though it would of course take many more experiments to be sure of this.

Discussion of results given so far on the use of shading cues

All chicks tested, whether reared in the light or in darkness prefer a real solid hemisphere S to a flat disc F. Light-reared chicks prefer a photograph of such a hemisphere to a photograph of a disc, but only if the photograph of the solid is oriented "correctly" so that it appears as a real solid object would appear lit from above, as in nature. If the photograph of the solid is inverted it receives significantly fewer pecks than if it is "correctly" oriented. Dark-reared chicks on the other hand do not prefer a "correctly" oriented photograph of a hemisphere to one of a disc.

One way in which these facts might be interpreted is in terms of learning. According to this theory chicks are hatched without any tendency to use shading cues of "solidity", but with the ability to use some other cue or cues, perhaps movement parallax. Within the few days of experience of overhead lighting that they have before testing, light-reared chicks come to learn the surface-shading properties of solid objects recognized by means of the other cue(s) which they can use from the moment of hatching. In other words this theory is that the same learning process observed by HESS over 7 weeks, under the circumstances of my experiments is shown to take place within a few days of hatching, and without food reinforcement. This was the theory which I thought the most plausible to account for my findings to date.

There is however another possibility. It could be that chicks are able to use shading cues of solidity without specific visual experience of solid objects in directed light, but that dark-reared chicks are unable to demonstrate this owing to the fact that light is necessary in order for their eyes to develop normally. Dark-reared chicks may in other words have some general defect in their vision, the result of light deprivation (WALK 1965), which prevents them from performing the rather subtle discrimination which may be necessary for the "photograph preference", but which does not drastically impair their performance in discriminating a real hemisphere from a disc.

A critical experiment to decide between these two possibilities is fortunately easy to do: if chicks are reared with light coming from *below* for two or three days, and then tested with a choice between PSC and PSI, a "correctly" oriented and an inverted photograph of a hemisphere, the two theories should predict opposite results. The "learning theory" predicts that they should prefer the inverted photograph, or at least that they definitely should not prefer the "correctly" oriented one. The "built in" theory on the other hand predicts with some certainty that they should show the usual strong preference for the "correctly" oriented photograph.

Experiment on chicks reared with underfloor lighting

The chicks were hatched in an incubator in a room which was kept completely dark from two days before the first chick hatched. Soon after hatching they were transferred in darkness into the next room, and placed in a cage with a wire netting floor, and with a black ceiling and black walls. Three 40 watt lights underneath the wire floor were then switched on. The chicks were tested in a partitioned-off corner of this cage, so that they never had any experience of overhead light from two days before hatching until after testing. They were tested on Day 2 or 3.

The stimuli, PSC and PSI were presented behind windows in an aluminium screen, similar to those of the automatic peck-counting apparatus. The screen was painted black like the walls and ceiling of the cage.

The chicks were tested singly and observed usually for 5 minutes each. Their first peck was noted, and also their pecks were counted during the 5 minute test period. Probably because their surroundings were familiar they pecked more than isolated chicks in previous experiments. Sometimes if a chick had not pecked within the 5 minute period, if I thought it might do so, I left it in the testing compartment for a little longer. In such cases of course I only used first pecks in the analysis, and the results from such chicks do not appear in the "majority of pecks" figures. Of the 31 chicks tested, 15 pecked within the 5 minute period, and 6 more gave their first peck a short time later.

The prediction of the "built in" theory was strongly and significantly fulfilled, and that of the learning theory disproved (Tab. 8). To this however

Tab. 8. Nos. of chicks reared with underfloor lighting which gave lst. pecks and majority of pecks to "correctly" oriented (PSC) and inverted (PSI) photographs of Solid (See Fig. 3)

	PSC (Correct)	PSI (Inverted)	p
1st pecks	18	3	< 0.002
Maj. of pecks	13	2	< 0.01

must be added the reservation that the eggs were kept in the incubator for 18 days with overhead lighting. Some kind of general effects of prehatching experience of light is to be expected (DIMOND 1966). It is just conceivable that the chicks might have learnt an association between gravity and the prevailing direction of light while they were in the egg. However it seems inconceivable that they could use this information to learn a preference for PSC over PSI, and in any case there is physiological evidence that the visual system of chick embryos does not normally begin to function until around the eighteenth day of incubation (PETERS, VONDERAHE and POWERS 1958).

General discussion

The use of deprivation experiments to determine whether a piece of behaviour should be called "innate" has been criticised (LEHRMAN 1953), partly on the grounds that it is impossible to deprive the developing animal of everything, and it is never obvious how much deprivation is needed to justify the use of the word "innate". On the other hand it is widely admitted that even if the word "innate" should not be used directly of behaviour itself, it can legitimately be used of an *abstract quality* of behaviour, individual difference (JENSEN 1961; DOBZHANSKY 1962; KONISHI 1966). It can be argued that the word "innate" could be used of other abstract qualities of behaviour such as complexity or information content (THORPE 1963), species specificity, or adaptiveness (LORENZ 1961, 1965). The latter functional approach to the interpretation of deprivation experiments is well exemplified by the last, and to me the most interesting of this series of experiments, that involving chicks reared with underfloor light. The argument is briefly that adaptiveness of behaviour implies the selective production, out of a wide range of possible behaviours, of those which "fit" with the environment in such a way as to favour the survival of the animal's genes, and that this in turn implies the possession by the animal of some kind of advance "information" about the part of the environment concerned (YOUNG 1957, 1964). Such "information" must have come from the environment by a process of selection; two such processes are known, reinforcement learning in the individual's own lifetime, and natural selection of its ancestors (PRINGLE 1951). If one defines clearly the particular feature of adaptiveness in which one is interested, it might in principle be possible to deprive the developing animal of the corresponding particular relevant features of the environment, and so determine the extent to which each of the two selective processes is involved.

In the present case, if we assume that a tendency to peck at solid objects rather than flat is advantageous, the preference for PSC, the correctly oriented photograph of a hemisphere, over PSI, the inverted one, relies for its correspondence with reality on the fact that in nature, light comes from above rather than from below. "Information" about this particular feature of the environment must have entered the chicks prior to the time when their preferences were tested. If this shorthand expression is found offensive, it can easily be restated: a selective agency, acting in the environmental condition of overhead light, has previously increased the chicks' relative tendency to peck at objects having the shading properties of solidity in overhead light. The simple deprivation experiment of rearing chicks in an environment in which the majority of light came from below provided a means of removing the possibility of one of the two types of selective process, learning, causing the development of this particular behavioural selectivity.

It is irrelevant to say that some kind of interaction with the environment was necessary in order for the preference to develop. (For example, chicks reared in darkness apparently do not differentiate PSC from PF.) Environmental interactions of many kinds including learning were no doubt indispensable for the development of pecking. However in this experiment, we are not concerned with the factors necessary for the development of pecking in general, nor with the factors necessary for the development of the PSC/PSI preference in common with all, or many other, preferences. We are concerned with the factors which might be expected to be specifically necessary for the development of a certain adaptive property of this preference in particular, and we have seen that in this case the relevant environmental factor, overhead light, was not necessary during the lifetime of the individual.

This case has been made rather too straightforwardly, and some objections must be raised. The technical one that the chicks might conceivably have learnt something about the prevailing direction of light while in the egg has already been mentioned, and more or less discounted as far-fetched as an explanation of the ontogeny of this relatively subtle pattern discrimination. More serious objections concern the unproved assumptions about survival value, which are necessary for the argument. There are two such assumptions, firstly that a preference for solidity is advantageous, and secondly that the survival value of the PSC/PSI preference has any relevance to solidity. (It is possible that PSC is preferred to PSI for an entirely different functional reason having no connection with the appearance of solid objects in overhead light.) I feel that both these unproved assumptions are probably justified, and that the interpretation of this experiment which I have given is a reasonable one.

Important though deprivation experiments inspired by such functional considerations may be, it is hard to see any advantage in using them as a device for the general rehabilitation of the word "innate" itself (LORENZ 1961, 1965). Though the functional approach to ontogeny may have ingeniously refuted cruder arguments against the use of the word, it has done nothing to allay the suspicion that the labelling of behaviour as "innate" may hinder research through appearing to explain, when really it only describes.

Furthermore it is a dangerously ambiguous word which may mean different things in different special cases. Probably the best solution to the problem of how to label behaviour shown to develop in spite of deprivations of various kinds, is to use descriptive operational expressions containing a brief reference to the kind of deprivation employed. For example if chicks show a certain pecking preference after being reared in darkness, it should be called a "dark-reared preference", rather than an "innate" peference. This term will then distinguish it from "diffuse-light-reared preferences", "underfloor-light-reared preferences"*, "unfed preferences", "isolation preferences", etc., all of which would be confused if given the common label "innate". It might be possible to plead that, with a proper understanding of the functional definition of "innateness" it should be clear which of the many possible deprivations is the relevant one in each particular case. Even if this were so, which is doubtful, it would still seem preferable to state, if only briefly, the precise operation performed in each deprivation experiment, and then allow the reader to form his own judgement whether he wishes to use the word "innate" for the case. The facts are no less interesting or important if they are stated simply and descriptively, than if they are condensed into the unclear conclusion that the behaviour is "innate". Let deprivation experiments inspired by an interest in the origin of adaptiveness continue to be performed. But let the conclusions drawn from them be operational and unambiguous.

In this concluding discussion, I have stressed the significance of the final underfloor lighting experiment, because its result seems to me particularly surprising and interesting. This does not mean of course that the type of behaviour development shown by this experiment is the only way, or even the most important way, in which chicks acquire adaptive preferences. Experiments described earlier showed that selective waning in responsiveness to inedible flat objects, and generalisation between flat objects probably play a part in the development of the Solidity preference. No doubt parallel processes are instrumental in the ontogeny of other preferences.

Other experiments using both food and radiant energy as reward in a Skinner Box showed that chick preferences can easily be modified by operant conditioning, for example the Solidity preference can be readily reversed. Obvious and predictable though facts of this kind are, their importance in the ontogeny of adaptive preferences should not be underestimated.

A number of vivid analogies have been put forward to characterise relevant aspects of the role of the genes in development. Thus LORENZ (1965) speaks of the "innate schoolmarm". The genetic information has been compared to a com-

---

*) I feel that the ugliness of phrases of this kind can be tolerated in the interests of brevity (FOWLER 1965: "Americanisms"). Alternatively they might be translated into German

puter programme (TINBERGEN 1965). YOUNG (1957) speaks of the organism making "predictions", and also (1957, 1964) of the organism containing a "representation" of the environment to which it is adapted, a concept which seems particularly appropriate when the adaptation concerned is one of selective responsiveness to an external stimulus situation.

In some cases the genes could be said to make detailed specific "predictions" about aspects of the environment of which the organism has had no previous experience. For example the chick's genes "predict" that light will tend to shine from above, and thus a selective responsiveness or preference for PSC rather than PSI develops even when the experimenter engineers that the prediction is incorrect, by rearing the animal in an environment with light coming from below.

In other cases the genes may "predict" nothing so detailed, and to pursue the computer-programming analogy mentioned above, some of the instructions are conditional upon data fed in from the environment, or such data may modify the programme. Thus the Solidity preference may be reversed if pecks at F are rewarded, or may be consolidated if persistent pecks at flat objects go unrewarded.

The extent to which each of these two general programming strategies is adopted by the organism will presumably depend on which is the most advantageous in particular cases. Two of the factors likely to have a bearing on this are firstly how early in life the character concerned is important for survival, and secondly the predictability of the ecologically relevant environment. As already mentioned, chicks must develop adaptive feeding preferences very early because they receive little parental help, but being omnivores the environment relevant to their feeding is probably in many respects unpredictable. It is therefore not surprising that their pecking preferences provide good examples of both types of programme/data relationship, and continue to be a promising subject for ontogenetic research.

Summary

1. Unfed domestic chicks, 3 days old or less, peck at a solid hemisphere (S) more than at a flat disc (F).

2. The strength of this "solidity preference", which shows batch-specific variations, increases over the first three days of life.

3. The total number of pecks given in the testing situation increases over the same period in experimentally naive chicks, but tends to decrease in chicks with previous experience of the testing situation.

4. This waning of pecking with experience is strongly stimulus-specific.

5. It is suggested that the normal ontogenetic increase in the strength of the solidity preference is caused by generalised waning of responsiveness to flat objects, as a result of unrewarded pecking at the flat walls of the living boxes. In support of this, chicks reared in boxes lined with corrugated cardboard have a weaker solidity preference than normally reared controls.

6. Chicks reared in complete darkness show the solidity preference on first exposure to the light.

7. Monocular chicks show a normal solidity preference.

8. Solidity can be recognised by man in flat pictures by means of surface shading cues: solid objects tend to be lighter on their upper surfaces owing to the prevailing direction of light. Young unfed chicks kept in normal light strongly prefer a photograph of a solid hemisphere taken in directed light to

one of a disc, provided that the former is correctly oriented (i. e. with lighter side uppermost).

9. A real solid hemisphere seems to be preferred to a photograph.

10. Chicks reared in darkness do not show any preference between photographs of a hemisphere and a disc. This is probably due to a general visual defect rather than to lack of specific learning, because:—

11. Young unfed chicks reared with light coming from *below* strongly prefer a normally oriented photograph of a solid hemisphere (i. e. with lighter side uppermost) to an inverted one. This suggests that chicks have an "inborn" ability to use surface shading cues of depth, in the sense of Lorenz's dichotomy between phylogenetic and ontogenetic sources of adaptation to particular environmental factors.

Literature cited

BENNER, J. (1938): Untersuchungen über die Raumwahrnehmung der Hühner. Z. Wiss. Zool. Abt. A. 151, 382–444 · BIRD, C. (1933): Maturation and practice: their effects upon the feeding reactions of chicks. J. Comp. Psychol. 16, 343–366 · BREED, F. S. (1911): The development of certain instincts and habits in chicks. Behav. Monogr. 1, 1—78 • COLLIAS, N., and M. JOOS (1953): The spectrographic analysis of sound signals of the domestic fowl. Behav. 5, 175–188 · COTT, H. B. (1940): Adaptive coloration in animals. Methuen, London · CRUZE, W. W. (1935): Maturation and learning in chicks. J. Comp. Psychol. 19, 371–408 · CURTIUS, A. (1954): Über angeborene Verhaltensweisen bei Vögeln, insbesondere bei Hühnerkücken. Z. Tierpsychol. 11, 94–109 · DIMOND, S. J. (1966): The influence of visual experience before hatching on the behaviour of the domestic chick. (Abstract). Anim. Behav. 14, 581 · DOBZHANSKY, T. (1962): Mankind evolving. Yale, Newhaven · FANTZ, R. L. (1957): Form preferences in newly hatched chicks. J. Comp. Physiol. Psychol. 50, 422–430 · FANTZ, R. L. (1958): Depth discrimination in dark-hatched chicks. Percept. & Motor Skills 8, 47–50 · FOWLER, H. W. (1965): Modern English usage. Oxford · GREGORY, R. L. (1966): Eye and brain. Weidenfeld and Nicolson, London · HESS, E. H. (1950): Development of the chick's response to light and shade cues of depth. J. Comp. Physiol. Psychol. 43, 112–122 · HESS, E. H. (1956): Space perception in the chick. Sci. Amer. 195 (2), 71–80 · HESS, E. H. (1961): Shadows and depth perception. Sci. Amer. 204 (3), 138–148 · JENSEN, D. (1961): Operationism and the question "Is this behaviour learned or innate?" Behav. 17, 1—8 • KONISHI, M. (1966): The attributes of instinct. Behav. 27, 316—328 • KUO, Z. Y. (1932): Ontogeny of embryonic behavior in Aves. 4. The influence of embryonic movements upon the behavior after hatching. J. Comp. Psychol. 14, 109–122 · LEHRMAN, D. S. (1953): A critique of Konrad Lorenz's theory of instinctive behavior. Q. Rev. Biol. 28, 337–363 · LORENZ, K. (1961): Phylogenetische Anpassung und adaptive Modifikation des Verhaltens. Z. Tierpsychol. 18, 139–187 · LORENZ, K. (1965): Evolution and modification of behavior. Methuen, London · MOSELEY, D. (1925): The accuracy of the pecking response in chicks. J. Comp. Psychol. 5, 75–97 · PADILLA, S. G. (1935): Further studies on the delayed pecking of chicks. J. Comp. Psychol. 20, 413–443 · PETERS, J. J., A. R. VONDERAHE and T. H. POWERS (1958): Electrical studies of functional development of the eye and optic lobes in the chick embryo. J. Exp. Zool. 139, 459–468 · PRINGLE, J. W. S. (1951): On the parallel between learning and evolution. Behav. 3, 90–110 · DE RUITER, L. (1956): Countershading in caterpillars. Arch. Néerl. Zool. 11, 285—341 • SCHNEIRLA, T. C. (1956): Interrelationships of the "innate" and the "acquired" in instinctive behaviour. In: L'instinct dans le comportement des animaux et de l'homme. Masson, Paris · SHEPARD, J. F., and F. S. BREED (1913): Maturation and use in the development of a instinct. J. Anim. Behav. 3, 274–285 · SPALDING, D. A. (1873, reprinted 1954): Instinct. With original observations on young animals. Anim. Behav. 2, 2–11 · SUTHERLAND, N. S. (1964): The learning of discriminations by animals. Endeavour 23, 148–152 · THORPE, W. H. (1963): Ethology and the coding problem in germ cell and brain. Z. Tierpsychol. 20, 529–555 · TINBERGEN, N. (1965): Animal behaviour. Time-Life, New York · WALK, R. D. (1965): The study of visual depth and distance perception in animals. In: Advances in the study of behavior (LEHRMAN, HINDE and SHAW eds.) Academic Press, New York · WOOD-GUSH, D. (1955): The behaviour of the domestic chicken: a review of the literature. Brit. J. Anim. Behav. 3, 81–110 · WOODWORTH, R. S., and H. SCHLOSBERG (1954): Experimental psychology. Methuen, London · YOUNG, J. Z. (1957): The life of mammals. Oxford · YOUNG, J. Z. (1964): A model of the brain. Oxford.

Culturally Transmitted Patterns of Vocal Behavior in Sparrows

Abstract. *Male white-crowned sparrows have song "dialects," acquired in about the first 100 days of life by learning from older males. In the laboratory an alien white-crowned sparrow dialect can be taught. Once the song is established further acoustical experience does not change the pattern. White-crowned sparrows do not copy recorded songs of other sparrow species presented under similar conditions.*

The white-crowned sparrow, *Zonotrichia leucophrys*, is a small song bird with an extensive breeding distribution in all but the southern and eastern parts of North America (*1*). Ornithologists have long remarked upon the geographical variability of its song. Physical analysis of field recordings of the several vocalizations of the Pacific Coast subspecies *Z. l. nuttalli* reveals that while most of the seven or so sounds which make up the adult repertoire vary little from one population to another, the song patterns of the male show striking variation (see *2*).

Each adult male has a single basic song pattern which, with minor variations of omission or repetition, is repeated throughout the season. Within a population small differences separate the songs of individual males but they all share certain salient characteristics of the song. In each discrete population there is one predominant pattern which differs in certain consistent respects from the patterns found in neighboring populations (Fig. 1). The term "dialect" seems appropriate for the properties of the song patterns that characterize each separate population of breeding birds. The detailed structure of syllables in the second part of the song is the most reliable indicator. Such dialects are known in other song birds (*3*).

The white-crowned sparrow is remarkable for the homogeneity of song patterns in one area. As a result the differences in song patterns between populations are ideal subjects for study of the developmental basis of behavior. If young male birds are taken from a given area, an accurate prediction can be made about several properties of the songs that would have developed if they had been left in their natural environment. Thus there is a firm frame of reference with which to compare vocal patterns developing under experimental conditions. Since 1959 we have raised some 88 white-crowned sparrows in various types of acoustical environments and observed the effects upon their vocal behavior. Here we report on the adult song patterns of 35 such experimental male birds. The several types of acoustical chamber in which they were raised will be described elsewhere.

In nature a young male white-crown hears abundant singing from its father and neighbors from 20 to about 100 days after fledging. Then the adults stop singing during the summer molt and during the fall. Singing is resumed again in late winter and early spring, when the young males of the previous year begin to participate. Young males captured between the ages of 30 and 100 days, and raised in pairs in divided acoustical chambers, developed song patterns in the following spring which matched the dialect of their home area closely. If males were taken as nestlings or fledglings when 3 to 14 days of age and kept as a group in a large soundproof room, the process of song

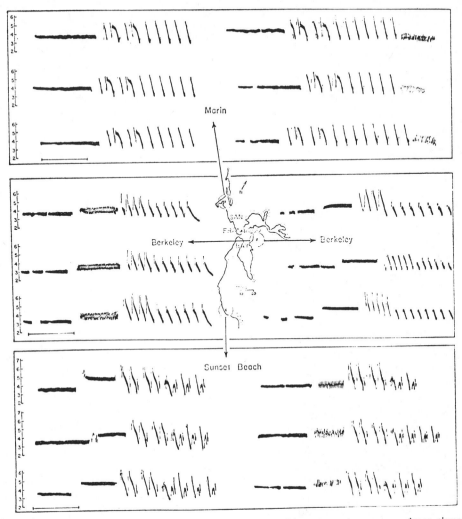

Fig. 1. Sound spectrograms of songs of 18 male white-crowned sparrows from three localities in the San Francisco Bay area. The detailed syllabic structure of the second part of the song varies little within an area but is consistently different between populations. The introductory or terminal whistles and vibrati show more individual variability. The time marker indicates 0.5 second and the vertical scale is marked in kilocycles per second.

development was very different. Figure 2 shows sound spectrograms of the songs of nine males taken from three different areas and raised as a group. The patterns lack the characteristics of the home dialect. Moreover, some birds from different areas have strikingly similar patterns (*A3, B2,* and *C4* in Fig. 2).

Males taken at the same age and individually isolated also developed songs which lacked the dialect characteristics (Fig. 3). Although the dialect properties are absent in such birds isolated in groups or individually, the songs do have some of the species-specific characterisites. The sustained tone in the introduction is generally,

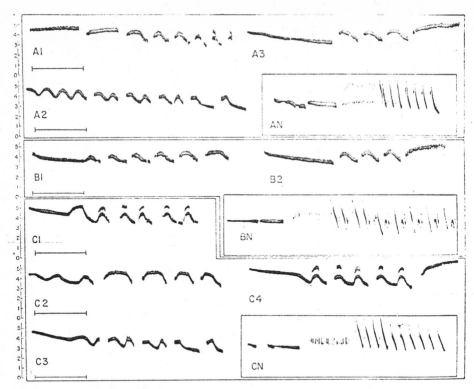

Fig. 2. Songs of nine males from three areas raised together in group isolation. *A1* to *A3*, Songs of individuals born at Inspiration Point, 3 km northeast of Berkeley. *B1* and *B2*, Songs of individuals born at Sunset Beach. *C1* to *C4*, Songs of individuals born in Berkeley. The inserts (*AN*, *BN*, and *CN*) show the home dialect of each group.

though not always, followed by a repetitive series of shorter sounds, with or without a sustained tone at the end. An ornithologist would identify such songs as utterances of a *Zonotrichia* species.

Males of different ages were exposed to recorded sounds played into the acoustical chambers through loudspeakers. One male given an alien dialect (8 minutes of singing per day) from the 3rd to 8th day after hatching, and individually isolated, showed no effects of the training. Thus the early experience as a nestling probably has little specific effect. One of the group-raised isolates was removed at about 1 year of age and given 10 weeks of daily training with an alien dialect in an open cage in the laboratory. His song

pattern was unaffected. In general, acoustical experience seems to have no effect on the song pattern after males reach adulthood. Birds taken as fledglings aged from 30 to 100 days were given an alien dialect for a 3-week period, some at about 100 days of age, some at 200, and some at 300 days of age. Only the training at the age of 100 days had a slight effect upon the adult song. The other groups developed accurate versions of the home dialect. Attention is thus focused on the effects of training between the ages of about 10 and 100 days. Two males were placed in individual isolation at 5 and 10 days of age, respectively, and were exposed alternately to the songs of a normal white-crowned sparrow and a bird of a different species. One male

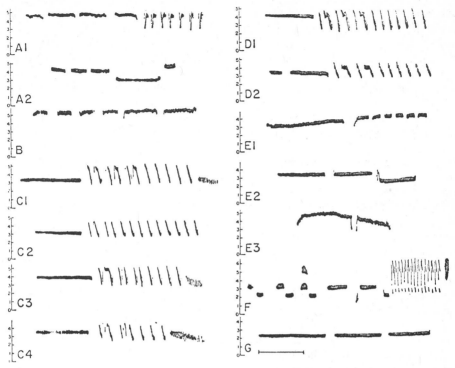

Fig. 3. Songs of 12 males raised under various experimental conditions. *A1* and *A2*, Birds raised in individual isolation. *B*, Male from Sunset Beach trained with Marin song (see Fig. 1) from the 3rd to the 8th day of age. *C1* to *C4*, Marin birds brought into the laboratory at the age of 30 to 100 days. *C1*, Untrained. *C2* to *C4*, Trained with Sunset Beach songs; *C2* at about 100 days of age, *C3* at 200 days, *C4* at 300 days. *D1*, Bird from Sunset Beach trained with Marin white-crowned sparrow song and a Harris's sparrow song (see *G*) from the age of 35 to 56 days. *D2*, Marin bird trained with Marin white-crowned sparrow song and a song-sparrow song (see *F*) from the age of 6 to 28 days. *E1* to *E3*, Two birds from Sunset Beach and one from Berkeley trained with song-sparrow song from the age of 7 to 28 days. *F*, A song-sparrow training song for *D2* and *E1* to *E3*. *G*, A Harris's sparrow training song for *D1*.

was exposed at 6 to 28 days, the other at 35 to 56 days. Both developed fair copies of the training song which was the home dialect for one and an alien dialect for the other. Although the rendering of the training song is not perfect, it establishes that the dialect patterns of the male song develop through learning from older birds in the first month or two of life. Experiments are in progress to determine whether longer training periods are necessary for perfect copying of the training pattern.

The training song of the white-crowned sparrow was alternated in one case with the song of a song sparrow, *Melospiza melodia*, a common bird in the areas where the white-crowns were taken, and in the other case with a song of a Harris's sparrow, *Zonotrichia querula*. Neither song seemed to have any effect on the adult patterns of the experimental birds. To pursue this issue further, three males were individually isolated at 5 days of age and trained with song-sparrow song alone from about the 9th to 30th days. The adult songs of these birds bore no resemblance to the training patterns and resembled those of naive birds (Fig. 3). There is thus a predisposition to learn white-crowned sparrow songs in preference to those of other species.

The songs of white-crowned sparrows raised in isolation have some normal characteristics. Recent work by Konishi (4) has shown that a young male must be able to hear his own voice if these properties are to appear. Deafening in youth by removal of the cochlea causes development of quite different songs, with a variable broken pattern and a sibilant tone, lacking the pure whistles of the intact, isolated birds. Furthermore, there is a resemblance between the songs of male white-crowned sparrows deafened in youth and those of another species, *Junco oreganus*, subjected to similar treatment. The songs of intact juncos and white-crowns are quite different. Konishi also finds that males which have been exposed to the dialect of their birthplace during the sensitive period need to hear themselves before the memory trace can be translated into motor activity. Males deafened after exposure to their home dialects during the sensitive period, but before they start to sing themselves, develop songs like those of a deafened naive bird. However, once the adult pattern of singing has become established then deafening has little or no effect upon it. Konishi infers that in the course of crystallization of the motor pattern some control mechanism other than auditory feedback takes over and becomes adequate to maintain its organization. There are thus several pathways impinging upon the development of song patterns in the white-crowned sparrow, including acoustical influences from the external environment, acoustical feedback from the bird's own vocalizations, and perhaps nonauditory feedback as well.

Cultural transmission is known to play a role in the development of several types of animal behavior (5). However, most examples consist of the reorientation through experience of motor patterns, the basic organization of which remains little changed. In the development of vocal behavior in the white-crowned sparrow and certain other species of song birds, we find a rare case of drastic reorganization of whole patterns of motor activity through cultural influence (6). The process of acquisition in the white-crowned sparrow is interesting in that, unlike that of some birds (7), it requires no social bond between the young bird and the emitter of the copied sound, such as is postulated as a prerequisite for speech learning in human children (8). The reinforcement process underlying the acquisition of sound patterns transmitted through a loudspeaker is obscure.

PETER MARLER
MIWAKO TAMURA
Department of Zoology,
University of California, Berkeley

References and Notes

1. R. C. Banks, *Univ. Calif. Berkeley Publ. Zool.* **70**, 1 (1964).
2. P. Marler and M. Tamura, *Condor* **64**, 368 (1962).
3. E. A. Armstrong, *A Study of Bird Song* (Oxford Univ. Press, London, 1963).
4. M. Konishi, in preparation.
5. W. Etkin, *Social Behavior and Organization Among Vertebrates* (Univ. of Chicago Press, Chicago, 1964).
6. W. Lanyon, in *Animal Sounds and Communication, AIBS Publ. No. 7*, W. Lanyon and W. Tavolga, Eds. (American Institute of Biological Sciences, Washington, D.C., 1960), p. 321; W. H. Thorpe, *Bird Song, The Biology of Vocal Communication and Expression in Birds* (Cambridge Univ. Press, London, 1961); G. Thielcke, *J. Ornithol.* **102**, 285 (1961); P. Marler, in *Acoustic Behaviour of Animals*, R. G. Busnel, Ed. (Elsevier, Amsterdam, 1964), p. 228.
7. J. Nicolai, *Z. Tierpsychol.* **160**, 93 (1959).
8. O. H. Mowrer, *J. Speech Hearing Disorders* **23**, 143 (1958).
9. M. Konishi, M. Kreith, and J. Mulligan cooperated generously in locating and raising the birds and conducting the experiments. W. Fish and J. Hartshorne gave invaluable aid in design and construction of soundproof boxes. We thank Dr. M. Konishi and Dr. Alden H. Miller for reading and criticizing this manuscript. The work was supported by a grant from the National Science Foundation.

14 September 1964

Nongenetic Transmission of Information

The handling of female rats in infancy has been shown to affect the activity and weaning weight of their grandchildren

by

VICTOR H. DENENBERG

and

KENNETH M. ROSENBERG

Department of Psychology, Purdue University, Lafayette, Indiana

WE have shown that one significant determinant of the rat's behaviour is the handling experience of the mother while she was an infant[1]. This experience was profound enough to modify her offspring's weaning weight and open field performance in adulthood. Thus the experience of one generation was visited on the next generation. Such a finding would appear to have broad implications for the evolution of behaviour. In this context a relevant question is: How far into the future can such effects extend? We have investigated this question by determining whether the experiences of female rats during their infancy would significantly affect the behaviour of their grandpups.

Again within an evolutionary framework, the habitat in which the animal is born and reared is known to affect profoundly his subsequent performance. We have shown that rats which are born and reared in a complex free environment between birth and weaning, or which are given free environment experience after weaning, differ along a number of behavioural dimensions from rats which are reared in standard cages during infancy and after weaning[2-5]. Thus for the laboratory rat, cages and free environments may be thought of as two different habitats. We investigated the effects of these habitats on the offspring's behaviour in this experiment.

The grandmothers' experience was as follows. At birth, litters of Purdue–Wistar rats were reduced to eight pups. Whole litters were randomly assigned to groups to be handled or not handled. Handling consisted of removing the pups from the maternity cage, leaving the mother in the cage, and placing each one into a tin can partially filled with shavings. The pups remained in the cans for 3 min and were then returned to their home cage. This procedure was followed once a day from day 1 until day 20. Non-handled controls were not disturbed between day 1 and 21, when all litters were weaned. The handled and non-handled females from these litters were the grandmothers of the animals used in this study. They were bred when about 100 days old. When pregnant, the females were assigned randomly to one of two housing conditions, to be described later.

The mothers' experiences were as follows. The females were placed either into stainless steel maternity cages (15 in. × 10 in. × 7·5 in.) or into free environment boxes. These boxes were triangular compartments formed by placing a diagonal insert into a 34 in.² box. Food was scattered on the floor, water was supplied by an externally mounted bottle, and "toys" (wooden block, can, ramp, running disk) were placed into each environment. At birth, litters were cut back to eight subjects consisting of four to six females.

When weaned on day 21, the females from each litter were randomly split into two groups, one going into a stainless steel laboratory cage (11 in. × 8·25 in. × 7·5 in.), and the other into a free environment. The free environments were the same as previously described except that the diagonal partition was removed. Two or three females were placed in each laboratory cage, while ten to twelve pups shared each free environment. On day 50 the females from the free environment were placed in the same type of laboratory cages as those described above.

These females were the parents of the animals used in this study. When approximately 150 days old, one female from each litter was bred to a randomly chosen colony male. All pregnant animals were placed in stainless steel maternity cages. At birth, litters were reduced to eight pups consisting, when possible, of four males and four females. No litter contained less than four pups. The pups remained undisturbed until they were 21 days old. At this time they were placed into a 32 in.² open field consisting of sixty-four squares. An activity count was recorded each time a pup made contact with a different square. Each pup was given one 3 min test, and after this was weighed.

Table 1 presents the experimental design, the mean activity score, the mean body weight, the number of pups and the number of litters for each of the eight treatment combinations. In the statistical analysis of these data the litter was used as the unit of measurement with a sub-classification for the sex of the pup. For example, the activity scores of all males within a litter were combined and a mean was obtained; the same procedure was applied to the females. These litter sex scores were subjected to a split plot unweighted means analysis of variance[6]. All F tests were based on 1/47 degrees of freedom.

Activity

The interaction of grandmother handling × mother preweaning housing was significant at the 0·01 level (F, 7·68): descendants of non-handled grandmothers were more active than descendants of handled grandmothers if their mothers had been reared in a maternity cage between birth and weaning. Exactly the opposite pattern was obtained if their mothers had been reared in a free environment during infancy. The grandmother handling × mother postweaning housing interaction was significant (F, 5·04; $P < 0·05$): the pattern was just the opposite to that described for the previous interaction. In addition, the preweaning housing × postweaning housing interaction was significant at the 0·05 level (F, 5·77). Offspring of mothers reared in two different environments during early life (that is, cage and free environment, or free environment and cage) were more active than the offspring of mothers which had been reared only in cages or only in free environments for the first 50 days of life.

The grandmother handling × sex interaction was significant at the 0·01 level (F, 21·44). Male weanlings were only slightly affected by the handling experience their grandmothers had received, while the females were markedly affected, with grandpups of handled females being significantly more active than grandpups of non-handled females. Finally, the preweaning housing × postweaning × sex

Table 1. SUMMARY OF MEANS FOR ALL EXPERIMENTAL CONDITIONS

Handling experience of grandmothers of experimental subjects	Preweaning housing of mothers of experimental subjects	Postweaning housing of mothers of experimental subjects	No. of litters	No. of subjects	Open-field activity Male	Female	Weaning weight (g) Male	Female
Non-handled	Maternity cage	Laboratory cage	17	123	17·00	15·02	50·00	47·05
		Free environment	17	133	23·60	20·70	48·43	46·26
	Free environment	Laboratory cage	11	82	13·08	9·31	51·45	50·32
		Free environment	11	85	15·48	11·58	45·63	44·29
Handled	Maternity cage	Laboratory cage	12	90	11·39	18·30	49·73	48·35
		Free environment	12	86	16·32	19·17	47·07	44·76
	Free environment	Laboratory cage	11	84	25·55	24·29	44·76	42·93
		Free environment	11	86	11·35	17·46	48·76	46·91

interaction was significant at the 0·05 level (F, 4·55).

Weaning Weight

The two main effects of grandmother handling and mother postweaning housing were both significant at the 0·05 level (Fs of 4·55 and 5·20, respectively), while the interaction of these two factors was significant at the 0·01 level (F, 8·49). All three of these effects were brought about by one cell: those weanlings whose grandmothers were not handled in infancy and whose mothers were reared in laboratory cages after weaning weighed significantly more than the other three groups making up this interaction. Such groups did not differ among themselves. In addition, the grandmother handling × preweaning housing × postweaning housing interaction was significant (F, 18·80; $P < 0·01$), and sex was significant (F, 87·99; $P < 0·01$) with male weanlings weighing more than females.

These data for activity and weaning weight reveal that handling females in infancy can have an effect two generations further on; that the nature of the mother's living quarters during her early life will affect her offspring, and that these variables act in a non-additive interactive manner. The interactive nature of the variables should be emphasized: if we had merely taken the female offspring of handled and non-handled grandmothers and maintained them in standard laboratory caging conditions from birth until adulthood (first and fifth groups listed in Table 1) most of the significant findings would have disappeared. Thus the occurrence of free environment experience some time during the mother's early ontogeny was necessary for the effects of the grandmother's handling experience to express itself in the grandpups.

Others have reported findings extending into the next generation. Ginsburg and Hovda[7] reduced the incidence of death from audiogenic seizures in *dba* mice by transplanting fertilized *dba* eggs into *C57Bl* foster mothers shortly after fertilization, and Ressler[8] has shown that the strain of foster grandparent rearing young mice will influence the operant response rate of the offspring of those mice. As far as we know, the present experiment is the first documentation that the experiences which an animal has in early life will influence her unborn descendants two generations away by nongenetic mechanisms.

The nature of the mechanisms underlying these effects is not known. Both handling and free environment experience has behavioural and biological effects on the stimulated organisms[2-5,9-12]. These effects could act through changes in grandmaternal or maternal behaviour or through physiological changes which would affect the developing foetus or modify the milk supply of the grandmother or mother.

This work was supported, in part, by grants from the National Institute of Child Health and Human Development and the National Institute of Mental Health, US Public Health Service.

Received September 6, 1967.

1 Denenberg, V. H., and Whimbey, A. E., *Science* 142, 1192 (1963).
2 Denenberg, V. H., and Morton. J. R. C., *J. Comp. Physiol. Psychol.*, 55, 242 (1962).
3 Denenberg, V. H., and Morton, J. R. C., *Anim. Behav.*, 12, 11 (1964).
4 Denenberg, V. H., Morton, J. R. C., and Haltmeyer. G. C., *Anim. Behav.*, 12, 205 (1964).
5 Whimbey, A. E., and Denenberg, V. H., *Multivar. Behav. Res.*, 1, 279 (1966).
6 Winer, B. J., *Statistical Principles in Experimental Design* (McGraw–Hill, New York, 1962).
7 Ginsburg, B. E., and Hovda, R. B., *Anat. Rec.*, 99, 621 (1947).
8 Ressler, R. H., *J. Comp. Physiol. Psychol.*, 61, 264 (1966).
9 Denenberg, V. H., Brumaghim, J. T., Haltmeyer, G. C., and Zarrow, M. X., *Endocrinology* (in the press, 1967).
10 Levine, S., Haltmeyer, G. C., Karas, G. G., and Denenberg, V. H., *Physiol. Behav.*, 2, 55 (1967).
11 Krech, D., Rosenzweig, M. R., and Bennett, E. L., *J. Comp. Physiol. Psychol.*, 53, 509 (1960).
12 Rosenzweig, M. R., *Amer. Psychol.*, 21, 321 (1966).

Killing of mice by rats prevented by early interaction between the two species[1]

VICTOR H. DENENBERG, RICHARD E. PASCHKE[2], AND M. X. ZARROW, *DEPARTMENTS OF PSYCHOLOGY AND BIOLOGICAL SCIENCES, PURDUE UNIVERSITY, Layfayette, Ind. 47907*

Forty control male rats were exposed to mice for the first time as adults; 18 (45%) killed one or two mice. Twenty experimental male rats lived with mice from 21 to 57 days of age and were later exposed to strange mice; no mice were killed. The implications of the findings for instinct theory and the "deprivation experiment" are discussed.

A common laboratory observation is that an adult rat is likely to attack and kill a mouse placed into a cage with the rat (Myer, 1964; Myer & Baenninger, 1966). This is a spontaneous event which occurs the first time that the rat sees the mouse. Since the killing response occurs in the absence of any prior experience with mice, and in the absence of any other form of prior experience with killing, this behavior meets the classical operational definition for an instinctive response (Eibl-Eibesfeldt, 1961; Lorenz, 1965). However, in a series of experiments in which we have raised rats and mice together from weaning, we have had virtually no incidence of rats killing mice (Denenberg, Hudgens, & Zarrow, 1964, 1966; Hudgens, Denenberg, & Zarrow, 1967). Because of

NOTES

1. This research was supported, in part, by Research Grant HD-02068 from the National Institute of Child Health and Human Development.
2. Supported by NIH Training Grant 1 T1 MH-10267.

the implications of our observations for classical instinct theory as well as for concepts concerning early socialization (Scott, 1962), we carried out an experiment to verify our findings in a controlled fashion.

Procedure. The experimental Ss were male Purdue-Wistar rats born and reared in a standard maternity cage until weaning in 21 days. At that time control rats were placed into groups of approximately 10 per cage where they remained until testing. They were never exposed to mice at any time until testing.

The experimental males were housed at weaning with C57BL/10 mice in social groups which consisted of two rats and two mice, or three rats and one mouse. When the animals were placed together at weaning observations were taken with respect to whether any of the rats killed any mice. At 57 days of age the mice were removed and the experimental rats were regrouped into units of 10 each in the same type of cages as the control males.

Starting at 90 days of age each rat was tested twice with a mouse. In each test one rat and one mouse were placed together into a plastic cage and were left for 24 h. Each rat was exposed to one black mouse (C57BL/10) and one white mouse (Rockland-Swiss albino). Half the rats were exposed to the black mouse first, the other half to the white mouse. Records were kept of the number of mice killed.

Results and Discussion. At 21 days of age one of 20 rats killed a mouse (5%). Another rat was substituted for this one; he did not kill at 21 days. At the 90-day test 18 of 40 (45%) control males killed one or two mice. Fourteen killed two mice; of the other four, one killed a white mouse and three killed black mice. Therefore, there was no difference in killing response to the black or white mouse. In contrast to this, none of the 20 experimental males killed any mice (p < 0.01).

The results demonstrate that the spontaneous "unlearned" response of mouse killing by the rat can be eliminated by early social interaction between the two species. Furthermore, this phenomenon will generalize to a very different subline within that species as shown by the fact that the experimental rats would not kill the white mice either, although their early social experience had only been with black mice. Finally, the data suggest that this change in behavior may be relatively permanent since the experimental rats were removed from the mice at 57 days of age and kept away from mice for 33 days before the tests for mouse killing began.

Our control rats met all the requirements of the classical deprivation experiment which has been specified as the sine qua non for the definition of an instinctive behavior (Lorenz, 1965). They killed mice. Our experimental animals were exposed to mice for 36 days during early development and then separated from them for 33 days before being tested. They did not kill mice. It is obvious, therefore, that the concept of instinct is insufficient to account for these data, and it is also apparent that the deprivation experiment is not a sufficient condition to define instinctive behavior. Indeed, the conditions under which we reared our control rats are essentially the same as those under which Eibl-Eibesfeldt (1961) reared his polecats. He, too, found that the killing response occurred. However, in order to understand an animal's behavior not only is it necessary to *subtract* experiences, as in the deprivation experiment, but it is also necessary to *add* experiences as we did with our experimental group. This was the procedure followed by Kuo (1930, 1938) in his studies of rat killing by cats.

It is only when a specific behavior pattern occurs in the same general form under a wide variety of environmental conditions that one can logically speak of that behavior as being instinctive (Ross & Denenberg, 1960). However, rather than use an instinct-learning classification, we feel that a more fruitful approach to an understanding of behavior is within a developmental framework in which the organism's behavior at any point in time is viewed as a function of the animal's accumulated experiences as well as his genetic background.

REFERENCES

DENENBERG, V. H., HUDGENS, G. A., & ZARROW, M. X. Mice reared with rats: Modification of behavior by early experience with another species. *Science*, 1964, 143, 380-381.

DENENBERG, V. H., HUDGENS, G. A., & ZARROW, M. X. Mice reared with rats: Effects of mother on adult behavior patterns. *Psychol. Rep.*, 1966, 18, 451-456.

EIBL-EIBESFELDT, I. The interaction of unlearned behavior patterns and learning in mammals, In J. F. Delafresnaye (Ed.), *Brain mechanisms and learning*. London: Blackwell, 1961. Pp. 53-74.

HUDGENS, G. A., DENENBERG, V. H., & ZARROW, M. X. Mice reared with rats: Relations between mothers' activity level and offspring's behavior. *J. comp. physiol. Psychol.*, 1967, 63, 304-308.

KUO, Z. Y. The genesis of the cat's response to the rat. *J. comp. Psychol.*, 1930, 11, 1-35.

KUO, Z. Y. Further study on the behavior of the cat toward the rat. *J. comp. Psychol.*, 1938, 25, 1-8.

LORENZ, K. *Evolution and modification of behavior*. Chicago: University of Chicago Press, 1938.

MYER, J. S. Stimulus control of mouse-killing rats. *J. comp. physiol. Psychol.*, 1964, 58, 112-117.

MYER, J. S., & BAENNINGER, R. Some effects of punishment and stress on mouse killing by rats. *J. comp. physiol. Psychol.*, 1966, 62, 292-297.

ROSS, S., & DENENBERG, V. H. Innate behavior: The organism in its environment. In R. H. Waters, D. A. Rethlingshafer, & W. E. Caldwell (Eds.), *Principles of comparative psychology*. New York: McGraw-Hill, 1960. Pp. 43-73.

SCOTT, J. P. Critical periods in behavioral development. *Science*, 1962, 138, 949-958.

 Division of Ethology, Department of Zoology, University of Stockholm

Crucial periods in the development of the following response in young nidifugous birds[1]

By Eric Fabricius

Eingegangen am 11. Juni 1963

Introduction

Spalding (1873) first showed that domestic chicks, as soon as they are able to walk, will follow any moving object, including human beings, and that they can be made to follow a human permanently if allowed to follow him from the first. He also described how such a chick could not be returned to the mother hen, but left her and ran to any person of whom it caught sight. Moreover, he pointed out that "a chicken that has not heard the call of the mother until eight or ten days old then hears it as if it heard it not". Although Spalding thus clearly recognised the crucial importance of early experience in the development of social responses in birds, it was not until Lorenz (1935, 1937) again drew attention to these phenomena that they were subjected to intense experimental work by a rapidly increasing number of behavior students. On the basis of observations made by Heinroth (1910) and himself, Lorenz showed that naive young goslings and ducklings follow the first moving object they encounter, and that they will thereafter follow only this very object or category of objects. In nature, the juvenile following response is thus fixed to the parent bird, but by allowing the inexperienced young bird to follow

---

[1] Dedicated to professor Konrad Lorenz on his 60th birthday.

another object from the first, it is possible to fix its following response to this object so rigidly that this substitute is preferred even to a conspecific parent bird. LORENZ also showed that this peculiar learning process, which he called "Imprinting", is confined to a short period in the life of the young bird. In the case of mallard ducklings, he supposed that this crucial period was restricted to some few hours after hatching.

The first following response and the sensitive period

The first following response in the inexperienced young bird evidently must be brought about by an innate releasing mechanism, reacting to certain unconditioned stimuli, or sign stimuli in the sense of TINBERGEN[2]). These sign stimuli are so few and simple, however, that the first release occurs with very little selectivity, and the imprinting process implies that they become supplemented by acquired conditioned stimuli which make the response more selective (FABRICIUS 1951).

Imprinting of the following response can thus be established only within the period during which it is possible to elicit this response in naive young birds by unconditioned stimuli. This has been called the sensitive period by FABRICIUS (1951), HINDE, THORPE and VINCE (1956), WEIDMANN (1958) and GUITON (1958). It has been shown, however, that this sensitive period is much longer than was originally supposed, and that it is probably not very sharply limited. Thus, FABRICIUS and BOYD (1954) could elicit a following response to a moving model in 1 of 7 naive mallard ducklings which had been kept in isolation for 10 days after hatching, and all these birds eventually developed a following response to siblings. In this work it was also found that up to a posthatch age of 65—72 hours, the proportion of ducklings in which a following response could be elicited was as high as 60%. A comparatively long sensitive period has also been demonstrated in domestic chicks, the figures given by different authors varying from 5 to 10 days (COLLIAS 1952, GUITON 1959, SALZEN and SLUCKIN 1959, JAMES 1960).

The unconditioned stimuli by which the first following response can be elicited during the sensitive period have been shown to be both visual and acoustic. Perception of movement seems to be the most effective visual stimulus. It had long been known that newly hatched young birds of several nidifugous species do follow living models, such as a walking man or even a moving human hand, and subsequently it has been shown that unarticulated moving models, such as balloons, boxes or duck decoys are also effective (RAMSAY 1951, RAMSAY and HESS 1954, FABRICIUS and BOYD 1954, HINDE, THORPE and VINCE 1956, JAYNES 1956, GUITON 1958 and others). Features of shape seem to be of comparatively little importance, although HESS (1959 a) reports that in domestic chicks a sphere was more effective than a stuffed hen. In chicks, some differences in the strength of the following response elicited by models of different colour have been demonstrated, blue being the most effective colour (HESS 1956, SHAEFFER and HESS 1959). However, these differences are apparently of much less importance than that between moving and stationary models. The size of models capable of eliciting the following response may also vary within wide limits, from a large moving hide (demonstrated in

[2]) This has recently been denied by MOLTZ (1960), who has attempted to explain the first occurrence of the following response in terms of classical conditioning. According to this hypothesis, any stimulus that is likely to command the attention of the animal at a time when its anxiety level is low would acquire reward value and would subsequently function to reinforce approach responses when anxiety is elicited. However, this theory seems to ignore the fact that actually the readiness for the following response is highest at the time when the anxiety level is low, or even before it is possible to elicit any anxiety (c. f. FABRICIUS 1951).

238

young coots and moorhens by HINDE, THORPE and VINCE 1956) or a walking man, down to a moving model with a diameter of about 4 centimeters (demonstrated in mallard ducklings by FABRICIUS and BOYD 1954). Some recent studies indicate that, at least in domestic chicks, the effective properties of the stimulus situation represented by the sight of a moving object could be rather simple. Thus, a flickering patch of light has been found to be an effective stimulus in eliciting approach in chicks (JAMES 1959, 1960, SMITH 1960, SMITH. and HOYES 1961). However, JAMES (1959) could not demonstrate any positive responses to a visual flicker in ducklings of two species (mallard and blue-winged teal), and he also found that different strains of domestic fowl varied in their responsiveness to this stimulus.

Concerning acoustic stimuli, it has been shown that almost any short and rapidly repeated low-pitched sounds are effective in releasing approach in ducklings of several species (FABRICIUS 1951, NICE 1953, FABRICIUS and BOYD 1954, RAMSAY and HESS 1954, COLLIAS and COLLIAS 1956, HESS 1957, WEIDMANN 1958, KLOPFER 1959 a, b and others). The same type of acoustic stimulation has also been found to be effective in domestic chicks (COLLIAS 1952, GUITON 1958, 1959). The properties of these acoustic stimuli have been analysed in some details by COLLIAS (1952) for domestic chicks and by COLLIAS and COLLIAS (1956) and KLOPFER (1959 a, b) for young Anatidae.

All investigators of the incidence of the following response in naive young birds agree that the readiness for this response undergoes certain characteristic changes during the neonatal period. Thus FABRICIUS (1951), in an experiment with young tufted ducks, found that the percentage of naive birds in which the following response could be elicited gradually declined after the first few hours after hatching, and similar results have been obtained in domestic chicks by COLLIAS (1952) and GUITON (1958), JAYNES (1957) and HESS (1959 a). Later investigations of mallard ducklings, however, using a larger number of birds of different post-hatch ages, have indicated that the picture is less simple in this species. The readiness for following appears to be comparatively low during the very first hours after hatching and then rises to a maximum, whereupon it gradually falls off again, finally approaching zero. This pattern has been found in mallard ducklings by FABRICIUS and BOYD (1954) and by WEIDMANN (1958). An increasing readiness for following during the first part of the post-hatch period has also been demonstrated in wild mallard ducklings by GOTTLIEB (1961), although he did not pursue the incidence of the following response in birds older than 30 hours. These observations also agree well with the findings of RAMSAY and HESS (1954) and HESS (1957, 1959 a, b), although their experiments were principally designed to study the effect of imprinting at different ages rather than to elucidate the incidence of the following response.

There is little doubt that one of the most important of the factors that limit the period during which the first following response can be elicited, and thus also the period when imprinting is possible, is the tendency, ever increasing with age, of the naive young birds to respond to moving objects by escape instead of by following them. This has been clearly demonstrated in young tufted ducks by FABRICIUS (1951), in mallard ducklings by FABRICIUS and BOYD (1954), RAMSAY and HESS (1954) and HESS (1957, 1959 a, b), in young moorhens and coots by HINDE, THORPE and VINCE (1956) and in domestic chicks by COLLIAS (1952), JAYNES (1957) and HESS (1959 b). However important the development of fear may be, there is also some evidence to indicate that it is not the only factor that puts an end to the period during which the first following response can be released, and that other factors as well, perhaps internally determined, could independently cause a decrease of the readiness for the following response (FABRICIUS 1951, WEIDMANN 1958, GUITON 1958, 1959, KAUFMANN and HINDE 1961). Apparently this question needs further study.

Imprinting and the critical period

As was first observed in young tufted ducks, the effectiveness of imprinting is not uniform throughout the whole sensitive period. Birds which had their experience of following near the end of the sensitive period followed hesitantly and with overt signs of fear in subsequent tests, showing an incomplete imprinting, whereas those trained at the beginning of this period followed closely and without fear, showing a more complete imprinting (FABRICIUS 1951). Similar observations have been made in mallard ducklings by WEIDMANN (1958).

These intimate relations of the effectiveness of imprinting to the age at first training have been subjected to a detailed and extensive analysis by HESS and his collaborators (RAMSAY and HESS 1954, HESS 1957, 1959 a ,b). It was shown that, at least under the experimental conditions of this work, a complete imprinting could only be established in mallard ducklings if the initial training took place at an age of 9—20 hours after hatching, and a distinct peak of maximum imprintability was demonstrated in the range from 13 to 16 hours. This period of maximum imprintability has been called the critical period or the critical age. On the other hand GOTTLIEB (1961 a) was not able to demonstrate a critical period for imprinting in mallard and Peking ducklings, but since he used only silent models or an apparently ineffective type of acoustic stimulus (ticking of a metronome) his findings do not disprove those of HESS, who used both visual and highly effective auditory stimuli. The visual stimuli used by HESS, moreover, seem to have been more effective in eliciting the following response since, in contrast to GOTTLIEB, he accomodated the movement of the model to the behavior of the ducklings (GOTTLIEB 1961 a). RAMSAY and HESS (1954) and HESS (1959 b) also demonstrated a similar short critical period in domestic chicks. The longer "critical periods" described for domestic chicks by JAYNES (1957) and JAMES (1960) apparently refer to what is here called the sensitive period, since they mainly concern the incidence of the following response in naive chicks. JAYNES, it is true, also studied the influence of initial training age on the strength of the following response in later tests, but as these retention tests did not involve checking of a possible preference for the initial model, his results are not directly comparable to those of HESS. However, he clearly demonstrated a distincly restricted period of maximum effect on the persistence of the following response, within the range of 24 to 54 hours at initial training.

The effect of imprinting is also dependent on other factors besides the age at first training during the critical period. It has been shown in young moorhens and coots (HINDE, THORPE and VINCE 1956) as well as in domestic chicks (JAYNES 1957, 1958 a) that massed practice lengthens the persistence of following. In mallard ducklings it was demonstrated by HESS (1957) that such practice, if occurring during the critical period, also produces a stronger preference for the initial model, thus affecting imprinting in the stricter sense. However, a detailed analysis showed that the most important factor is apparently not the time spent in following, but the distance travelled, or rather the effort expended by the young bird in following the model during the initial training. This has been expressed by Hess in his "law of effort", according to which "the strength of imprinting equals the logarithm of the effort expended by the animal to get to the imprinting object during the imprinting period" (Hess 1959 a). The importance of effort seems to explain why maximum imprintability is not present immediately after hatching, but is achieved some hours later, for maximum effort can not be expended until the young bird is physically capable of fast and persistent following. In domestic chicks Hess (1959 b) also showed that the motor ability is poor immediately after hatching, then rapidly rises during the period from 4 to 16 hours, thereby reaching a comparatively high level which is then maintained for a considerable length of time, rising only slowly with increasing age. Thus, the onset of the critical period is determined by the maturing motor ability. As to the end of the critical period, it seems to be determined, like the end of the sensitive period, largely by the development of fear responses. The importance of fear is strongly emphasized by Hess (l. c.), who points out that it is possible to predict in a series of animals, knowing only the time of onset of fear, the end of imprintability for that species, just as its onset can be predicted if the development of motor ability is known.

Although the onset and the end of the critical period are thus rather rigidly fixed by biological processes of growth and of maturation of certain responses, it has been found that there are several means by which the length of this period can be changed under experimental conditions. Thus, it was shown by Fabricius (1951), Collias and Collias (1956) and Klopfer (1959 a) that ducklings can be induced to follow an object when they will not do so on their own, by placing them in the company of others which show a strong following response to that object, and it has also been demonstrated that this "social facilitation" can produce imprinting in naive mallard ducklings up to a post-hatch age of 24—52 hours, and thus well beyond the critical period (Ramsay and Hess 1954, Hess 1957, 1959 a). When searching for an explanation for this kind of social facilitation, it should be remembered that the visual and acoustic perception of a fellow duckling apparently represents a more effective stimulus for eliciting the following response than the artificial stimuli used in the experiments referred to. The perception of a fellow duckling could thus elicit the following response in a reluctant duckling, thereby increasing the general tendency for this response; consequently an artificial model presented simultaneously or shortly thereafter would also be followed. Basically, this "social facilitation" would thus be a close parallel to the observation made by Hinde, Thorpe and Vince (1956) to the effect that "good" models often cause an increased responsiveness to "poor" models presented immediately afterwards, and to the finding of Guiton (1959) who stated that domestic chicks showed a stronger following response to models if they had been kept together in groups for a short time prior to testing. Reduction of fear by the presence of conspecific fellow birds could be another contributing factor.

In addition, it has been shown that it is possible to extend the critical period by the use of certain drugs. It was thus demonstrated by Hess (1957) that mallard ducklings given meprobamate or chlorpromazine at a post-hatch age of 12 hours could be imprinted fairly successfully at 24 to 26 hours, when the effect of the drug had worn off, although the period of maximum imprintability is normally terminated much earlier, at approximately 17 hours. These drugs were supposed to act by slowing down metabolism and thus stretching out the critical period. On the other hand, birds trained when actually under the influence of meprobamate could not be imprinted, apparently since meprobamate, as a muscle relaxant, interferes with the muscular effort which has been shown to be of such great importance for the establishment of imprinting. In this respect, chlorpromazine had a different effect, since training under the influence of this drug produced good imprinting, even if it took place at a post-hatch age of 24—26 hours and thus well beyond the normal critical period. This was explained by the assumption that chlorpromazine, which is not a muscle relaxant and thus does not interfere with the necessary effort, reduces emotionality and thus makes following and imprinting possible even in birds which have reached an age at which fear responses would normally prevent imprinting.

Finally, it has been shown that the strength and persistence of the following response can.be increased by the presence of unfamiliar or "frightening" stimuli. This seems to be a close parallel to the well known phenomenon that unfamiliar surroundings or the presence of frightening stimuli often cause the members of a bird flock or a fish school to approach each other more closely, forming a dense group (c. f. KEENLEYSIDE 1955). Particularly, this effect was obvious in an experiment with Peking ducklings made by MOLTZ, ROSENBLUM and HALIKAS (1959), who found that the greater the similarity between cues present during shock and those present during exposure to a moving familiar test object, the greater the strength at which the following of that object was maintained. However, it was not demonstrated that these conditions produced any preference for a particular test object, and thus their possible effect upon imprinting in the proper sense demands further study. This seems also to be the case with the effect of social deprivation demonstrated by GUITON (1958), who found that a long period of isolation could restore the capacity of following a moving model in domestic chicks which had already lost this capacity by being previously kept together in groups up to a post-hatch age of 74 hours.

In experimental work it has also proved possible to interfere with the critical period in the opposite way, by shortening it. In domestic chicks, prolonged exposure to siblings has thus been shown to reduce the tendency to follow subsequently encountered models (GUITON 1958, 1959) or to approach an intermittent light source (JAMES 1960 b). Since socialization with siblings leads to an earlier loss of the following response to artificial stimuli, it consequently shortens the critical period (and the sensitive period as well) in imprinting experiments. It was shown by GUITON (1959) that in chicks kept in groups from the time of hatching, this socialization already inhibits the following response to other objects at 72 hours, while fear is not sufficiently well developed to prevent a totally inexperienced chick from following strange objects until 96 hours. The most important reason for this "social inhibition" seems rather obvious. Since the following of the parent and the following of the siblings are apparently released primarily by the same comparatively broad and simple stimuli (FABRICIUS 1962), the perception of siblings must elicit the following response in a naive young bird, and if allowed to follow them for a sufficient length of time it becomes imprinted to them and thus prevented from following other objects.

Discussion

When discussing the development of the following response in young nidifugous birds, it is necessary, as has been stressed by GUITON (1958), to distinguish between f o l l o w i n g and i m p r i n t i n g. Whereas following can be defined as the approach by a young bird to a moving object, imprinting should properly describe a process involving the development of discrimination as a result of exposure to an object during a crucial period and demonstrable as the retention of a selective following response to that object beyond the crucial period. Actually, discrimination and preference resulting from a short early experience represent the very essence of imprinting, since the word imprinting was originally chosen as a metaphor, comparing this process with an image impressed on a piece of wax by a seal. Unless a selective responsiveness is demonstrated, the mere retention of the following response thus cannot be taken as evidence of imprinting, since a bird which would perhaps follow any moving object, including the training object, can by definition not be regarded as imprinted to that object. For the same reasons, demonstration of a period with maximum effect on the retention of the following response can not be taken as evidence of a critical period, unless an effect on discrimination is also demonstrated. This does not exclude, however, that the retention of the following response is also a result of early experience and constitutes one of the processes contributing to the imprinting phenomenon, as has been pointed out by WEIDMANN (1958).

Another important distinction, the neglect of which has also caused much confusion, is that between the sensitive period and the p e r i o d o f m a x i - m u m i m p r i n t a b i l i t y. As mentioned, the sensitive period can be defined as the period during which a young bird will follow a moving object it has not encountered before, or, more precisely, the period during which the first following response can be elicited. The period of maximum imprintability, on the other hand, is the period during which a following response elicited by certain stimuli produces a maximum of selective responsiveness to these stimuli and a maximum of intensity and retention of the following response elicited by them in subsequent tests. For this period, which is included in the sensitive period and constitutes only a short part of it, it seems appropriate to preserve the name c r i t i c a l p e r i o d, given to it by RAMSAY and HESS (1954). It has also been suggested by HESS (1959 a) that the imprinting processes occurring during the critical period are different in qualitiy from the processes occurring after that period, during the remaining part of the sensitive period.

The existence of these two periods offers some interesting biological problems. In a study of the incidence of the following response in mallard ducklings, BOYD and FABRICIUS (unpublished) could elicit following of moving non-calling models in 58% of naive birds within the range 10—20 hours after hatching, which approximately coincides with the critical period demonstrated by HESS and his collaborators. However, a significant decrease of the percentage of naive ducklings in which the following response could be elicited by a moving model was not found until after a post-hatch age of 40—50 hours. The biological significance of this maintenance of the following tendency at a high level far beyond the critical period probably lies in the fact that in nature the departure of young Anatidae from the nest does not always take place within that period. Accurate records are scarce, but COLLIAS and COLLIAS (1956) report that the departure of the young from a nest of the canvasback took place about 24˙hours after hatching, while a brood of young blue-winged teal did not leave their nest until about 36 hours old; according to my own observations young tufted ducks rarely leave their nests earlier than 24 hours after hatching. Since, as a consequence of the "law of effort", a strong imprinting can not possibly be developed until the young have followed their mother for some length of time, it is important that the responsiveness to unconditioned stimuli eliciting the following response is not lost until after the departure from the nest. Actually, it has been shown that the imprinting is not always completed in ducklings which have already followed their mother for a considerable length of time, since the following response of such birds can sometimes still be elicited by balloons or other artificial models (FABRICIUS and BOYD 1954). Basically similar observations have been made in domestic chicks by JAYNES (1958 b), who demonstrated, in an experiment on "generalization decrement", that an increasingly selective responsiveness to a particular model developed gradually in the course of several days, as a result of more practice with that model than with others. However, it remains to be explained why, under the conditions of the experimental work by HESS and his collaborators, maximum imprintability occurs within a period after which the imprinting is probably not yet completed under natural conditions.

Concerning the responsiveness to acoustic stimuli, this discrepancy seems to be even more marked. Thus, BOYD and FABRICIUS (1964, unpubl.), found that the percentage of naive mallard ducklings in which an approach response could be elicited by acoustic stimuli ("come, come" — calls) rapidly increased after a post-hatch age of 10—20 hours, reaching a maximum at 25—50 hours and then decreased again, although even at 240 hours it remained at a considerably higher level than the responsiveness to visual stimuli. In these experiments, the model was kept motionless while acoustic stimuli were presented, and since the decreasing tendency to follow moving non-calling models coincided with a marked increase of the percentage of ducklings showing fear reactions to moving objects, it seems possible that the reduction of stimuli eliciting fear was at least partly responsible for the higher level of responsiveness to acoustic stimuli exhibited under these conditions. Here the possibility of extending the critical period by the use of drugs that reduce emotionality, as demonstrated by HESS (1957), constitutes an interesting parallel.

When searching for an explanation of the fact that maximum responsiveness to acoustic stimuli seems to be reached at an age far beyond the critical period demonstrated by HESS, the conditions after the departure from the nest should again be considered. It is well known that dabbling ducks, such as the mallard, often nest at a considerable distance from the nearest water, to which the female then leads her young immediately after they have left the nest. During this dangerous and sometimes long journey, it is not uncommon that the ducklings have to penetrate through dense vegetation where they would soon be lost if they did not react to the acoustic stimuli emitted by the female, which ensure close following even under conditions where the effectiveness of visual stimuli is highly restricted. A high level of responsiveness to acoustic stimuli during the period shortly after the departure from the nest thus appears of vital importance for the young of the mallard and other ducks with similar nesting habits. It should be mentioned, however, that KLOPFER and GOTTLIEB (1962 a, b) could not find any relation between age and susceptibility to visual vs. auditory stimuli in Peking and mallard ducklings, but since birds older than 24 hours were not employed in their experiments, the high responsiveness to auditory stimuli found by BOYD and FABRICIUS in older ducklings, which would normally already have left the nest, is not contradicted by these results. In an additional experiment GOTTLIEB and KLOPFER (1962) also used somewhat older ducklings, up to a post-hatch age of 30—31 hours, but even here no close comparison is possible, since this experiment was only designed to examine the development of visual vs. acoustic imprinting, and no data are given on the incidence in naive ducklings of the following response elicited by these stimuli.

The duality of the sensitive period and the period of maximum imprintability was recognized by JAYNES (1957), who suggested that there are, in reality, two critical period curves, one for the ease of eliciting the relevant responses and another for the effect on imprinting at a later stage of development. Transferred to the terminology proposed in the present paper, the former curve refers to the sensitive period while the latter is, as mentioned, not comparable to the critical period demonstrated by HESS, since it does not refer to the development of a selective responsiveness. Thus, the finding of JAYNES (l. c.) seems to indicate the existence of a third crucial period, representing a maximum effect on the persistence and strength of the following response in later tests, disregarding discrimination and occurring at a considerably later age than the critical period proper. Since all the behavioral mechanisms which contribute to the development of the following response are dependent on different biological processes, each of which may have its own time pattern, it seems probable that future research, if extended to cover an increasing number of aspects of following and imprinting, will reveal the existence of even more periods which could be called "crucial", "sensitive" or "critical". As a consequence of the complex nature of these phenomena, it is often difficult to compare the results of different workers, since differences in the quality and strength of the stimuli used or in the method of testing may produce considerable differences in the determination of the periods in question. Another difficulty affecting the exact timing of crucial periods in neonatal birds is the discrepancy between developmental age and time of hatching. Here GOTTLIEB (1961 b), by chilling mallard eggs before placing them in an incubator and thus killing all embryos which had developed past the first cleavage stages, has been able to time the age of ducklings from the onset of incubation rather than from hatching. This method was found to reduce the variation in timing for the period of maximum effect of initial training on the retention and strength of the following response in later tests. It seems evident that developmental age provides a more accurate baseline for the determination of crucial neonatal periods than post-hatch age, at least in work designed to determine such periods within one or two days immediately after hatching. When considering longer periods, however, extending over several days, the comparatively small differences between developmental age and time of hatching will certainly be negligible, and this should also be the case if a sufficiently large number of birds is used. This is proved, for example, by the well defined critical periods based on post-hatch age which have been demonstrated by HESS and his collaborators.

Finally, it should be emphasized that evidently none of the periods discussed here is absolutely strictly limited. As has been recently pointed out by SCOTT (1962), it seems likely that the formation of a social attachment is a process that may take place throughout life, and that although it may take place more slowly outside of certain critical periods, the capacity for such an attachment is never completely lost.

Summary

In the neonatal life of young nidifugous birds, there are certain crucial periods determining the development of the following response. The s e n - s i t i v e   p e r i o d is the period during which it is possible to elicit the first following response in a naive young bird. The unconditioned stimuli eliciting this response are both visual (perception of movement) and acoustic (in ducklings and domestic chicks, perception of short and intermittent sounds). With increasing age the following tendency decreases, whereas there is an increasing tendency to respond to moving objects by escape, which apparently is one of the factors that limit the sensitive period.

Eliciting the following response initiates a learning process, called imprinting, which gradually results in a strong preference for the object first followed and in a persistence beyond the sensitive period of a following response to that object. Although some imprinting seems to be possible throughout the whole sensitive period, the length of which may exceed one week, there is a restricted subperiod of maximum imprintability within this period. The strongest and most complete imprinting can only be attained during this c r i t i c a l p e r i o d, the length of which rarely exceeds some few hours. The strength of the imprinting produced during the critical period is dependent on several factors, the most important of which seems to be the effort expended by the young bird in following.

Like the sensitive period, the critical period seems mainly to be limited by the development of fear responses, and the onset of both periods is apparently determined by the development of a motor ability sufficient to make the following response possible. Under experimental conditions, the length of these crucial periods can be changed by several factors, such as deprivation, social facilitation and the use of drugs reducing fear or slowing down metabolism.

In naive mallard ducklings, the following tendency is maintained at a fairly high level during the major part of the sensitive period, and the susceptibility to auditory stimuli eliciting following even reaches its peak at an age far beyond the critical period. This is apparently a consequence of the conditions in nature, where the departure of the young from the nest may often not occur until after what under experimental conditions appears as the critical period, and where a successful accomplishment of the subsequent journey to the nearest water is dependent on the maintenance of a high responsiveness to stimuli eliciting following and particularly to the acoustic stimuli, on which they rely whenever visibility is restricted by dense vegetation.

Besides the critical period for maximum imprintability, there may also be other important subperiods within the sensitive period. Thus, there are observations indicating the existence of a period of maximum effect on the persistence and strength of the following response disregarding the development of discrimination, and it seems possible that other elements of the following response and imprinting may also be dependent on their own crucial periods. For a more accurate determination of these periods and a fuller understanding of their significance, it is necessary to overcome the difficulties caused by divergences in the terminology and in the technique of rearing, training and testing used by different authors, which often lead to considerable differences in their results.

References

BOYD, H. und E. FABRICIUS: Observations on the incidence of the following reaction elicited by visual and auditory stimuli in naive mallard ducklings *(Anas platyrhynchos)*. Behaviour (in preparation) • COLLIAS, N. E. (1952): The development of social behaviour in birds. Auk **69**, 127—159 • COLLIAS, N. E. und E. C. (1956): Some mechanisms of family integration in ducks. Auk **73**, 378—400 • FABRICIUS, E. (1951): Zur Ethologie junger Anatiden. Acta Zool. Fenn. **68**; 1—175 • Ders. (1962): Some aspects of imprinting in birds. Symp. Zool. Soc., London **8**,

139—148 • Ders. und H. Boyd (1954): Experiments on the following-reaction of ducklings. Rep. Wildfowl Trust 6, 84—89 • Gottlieb, G. (1961a): The following-response and imprinting in wild and domestic ducklings of the same species *(Anas platyrhynchos)*. Behaviour 18, 205—228 • Ders. (1961b): Developmental age as a baseline for determination of the critical period in imprinting. J. comp. physiol. Psychol. 54, 422—427 • Gottlieb, B. und P. H. Klopfer (1962): The relation of developmental age to auditory and visual imprinting. J. comp. physiol. Psychol. 55, 821—826 • Heinroth, O.: Beiträge zur Biologie, namentlich Ethologie und Physiologie der Anatiden. Verh. 5th Int. Ornithol. Kongr., Berlin 589—702 • Guiton, P. (1958): The effect of isolation on the following-response of brown leghorn chicks. Proc. Royal Physical Soc., Edinburgh 27, 9—14 • Ders. (1959): Socialization and imprinting in brown leghorn chicks. Anim. Behav. 7, 26—34 • Hess, E. H. (1956): Natural preferences of chicks and ducklings for objects of different colors. Psychol. Reports 2, 477—483 • Ders. (1957): Effects of meprobamate on imprinting in waterfowl. Ann. N. Y. Acad. Sci. 67, 724—732 • Ders. (1959a): Imprinting. Science 130, 133—141 • Ders. (1959b): Two conditions limiting critical age for imprinting. J. comp. physiol. Psychol. 52, 515—518 • Hinde, R. A., W. H. Thorpe und M. A. Vince (1956): The following-response of young coots and moorhens. Behaviour 9, 214—242 • James, H. (1959): An unconditioned stimulus for imprinting. Canad. J. Psychol. 13, 59—67 • Ders. (1960a): Imprinting with visual flicker. Canad. J. Psychol. 14, 13—20 • Ders. (1960b): Social inhibition of the domestic chick's response to visual flicker. Anim. Behav. 8, 223—224 • Jaynes, J. (1956): Imprinting: The interaction of learned and innate behaviour: I. Development and generalization. J. comp. physiol. Psychol. 49, 201—206 • Ders. (1957): Imprinting: The interaction of learned and innate behaviour: II. The critical period. J. comp. physiol. Psychol. 50, 6—10 • Ders. (1958a): Imprinting: The interaction of learned and innate behaviour: III. Practice effects on performance, retention and fear. J. comp. physiol. Psychol. 51, 234—237 • Ders. (1958b): Imprinting: The interaction of learned and innate behaviour: IV. Generalization and emergent discrimination. J. comp. physiol. Psychol. 51, 238—242 • Kaufmann, I. C. und R. A. Hinde (1961): Factors influencing distress calling in chicks, with special reference to temperature changes and social isolation. Anim. Behav. 9, 197—204 • Keenleyside, M. H. A. (1955): Some aspects of the schooling behaviour of fish. Behaviour 8, 183—248 • Klopfer, P. H. (1959a): An analysis of learning in young Anatidae. Ecology 40, 90—102 • Ders. (1959b): The development of sound-signal preference in ducks. Wilson Bull. 71, 262—266 • Klopfer, P. H., und G. Gottlieb (1962a): Learning ability and behavioural polymorphism within individual clutches of wild durcklings. Z. Tierpsychol. 19, 183—190 • Dies. (1962b): Imprinting and behavioural polymorphism: Auditory and visual imprinting in domestic ducks *(Anas platyrhynchos)* and the development of the critical period. J. comp. physiol. Psychol. 55, 126—130 • Lorenz, K. (1935): Der Kumpan in der Umwelt des Vogels. J. Ornithol. 83, 137—213, 289—413 • Ders. (1937): The companion in the bird's world. Auk 245—273 • Moltz, H. (1960): Imprinting: Empirical basis and theoretical significance. Psychol. Bull. 57, 291—314 • Ders., L. Rosenblum und

Nina Halikas (1959): Imprinting and level of anxiety. J. comp. physiol. Psychol. 52, 240—241 • Nice, Margaret M. (1953): Some experiments in imprinting ducklings. Condor 55, 33—37 • Ramsay, A. O. (1951): Familial recognition in domestic birds. Auk 68, 1—16 • Ders. und E. H. Hess (1954): A laboratory approach to the study of imprinting. Wilson Bull. 66, 196—206 • Salzen, E. A., und W. Sluckin (1961): The incidence of the following-response and the duration of the responsiveness in domestic fowl. Anim. Behav. 7, 172—179 • Schaefer, H. H. und E. H. Hess (1959): Color preferences in imprinting objects. Z. Tierpsychol. 16, 161—172 • Scott, J. P. (1962): Critical periods in behavioural development, Science 138, 949—958 • Smith, F. V. (1960): Towards a definition of the stimulus situation for the approach response in the domestic chick. Anim. Behav. 8, 197—200 • Smith, F. V. und P. A. Hoyes (1961): Properties of the visual stimuli for the approach response in the domestic chick. Anim. Behav. 9, 159—166 • Spalding, D. A. (1873): Instinct: With original observations on young animals. MacMillan's Magazine 27, 282—293. Reprinted in Brit. J. Anim. Behav., 1954, 2, 2—11 • Tinbergen, N. (1951): The study of instinct. Oxford Univ. Press, 1951 • Weidmann, U. (1958): Verhaltensstudien an der Stockente *(Anas platyrhynchos L.)*. II. Versuche zur Auslösung und Prägung der Nachfolge- und Anschlußreaktion. Z. Tierpsychol. 83, 277—300.

Zoology Department, Duke University, Durham, North Carolina, U. S. A.

Maternal "Imprinting" in Goats: fostering of alien young

P. H. and M. S. KLOPFER

Received 23. 10. 1967

Introduction

The stability and specificity of the relationship between mother and young in ungulates has been repeatedly discussed (e. g. ALTMANN 1963 and BUBENIK 1965). Once an attachment between a mother and her young is formed, it is rarely and only with difficulty disrupted. However, at least during the first few days after birth, this can hardly be due to any high degree of discrimination exercised by the young. Neonatal kids and fawns are as likely to approach and seek to nurse from an alien ♀ — even one of a different species — as from their natural parent. Their mothers, on the other hand, are generally more particular and may vigorously repulse alien kids. Perhaps the exceptions — ♀♀ prone to adopt aliens — are to be found principally among species which produce more than one young at a time. BUBENIK (1965) states that *Capreolus*, with more than one fawn per litter, does adopt aliens; *Cervus*, with only one, rejects them. Moose ♀♀ (*Alces*) which have lost their own calf may try to entice an alien calf to follow them, according to ALTMANN (1963), though except for these circumstances they will reject aliens. Domestic goats do not fit this pattern, of course, since they often produce 2 or even 3 kids per litter, but nonetheless usually limit their maternal solicitation to their own kids.

Another significant feature of the maternal-young bond in ungulates lies in the rapidity with which it is formed, reminiscent of the phenomenon of imprinting in fowl (LORENZ 1935). Often less than 5 minutes of post-parturitive contact suffices to establish a firm bond. Interference with the bonding process during this brief period may have lasting affects (COLLIAS 1956; KLOPFER, ADAMS & KLOPFER 1964; HERSCHER, RICHMOND & MOORE 1963).

We have previously proposed a hypothesis of olfactory imprinting to account for the establishment of the bond. Briefly stated, the hypothesis was that "... a ♀ responds initially to a labile and highly attractive element within the birth fluids, an element which may either be attractive at all times, or, as seems more probable, is only attractive to parturient females as a consequence of the physiological changes associated with parturition. Before this labile substance decomposes, the females' response becomes generalized to include associated chemical stimuli, particularly those unique to her kid and its effluvia". This hypothesis of "olfactory imprinting" accounts for the fact that a mother goat will accept all of her litter, though no aliens, so long as she has contact with one (though only one) of her kids immediately upon its birth. An experimental test using blindfolded goats whose olfactory mucosa was cocainized before, during, or after parturition revealed certain major deficiencies in the hypothesis. Specifically, these later results (KLOPFER & GAMBLE 1966) indicated the necessity for distinguishing between the evocation of maternal behavior, *per se*, and discrimination between own and alien young.

The latter is dependent on the integrity of the olfactory system, but the former is not. Apparently, the state of readiness to accept young is largely independent of cues provided by the young themselves. (This contrasts with ROSEN-BLATT's [1967] demonstration that the presence of infants sufficed to induce maternal behavior in rats). It is not excluded that *specific* cues from goat kids, particular odors or certain visually perceived behavior patterns, enhance the mother's interest. It does appear, however, that maternal attachments can be formed in the absence of such cues, provided only that the kid is present at the time directly after parturition. Presumably, any kid — even an alien of several days or weeks age — will be accepted in the same manner as the doe's own neonatal kid if it is present at parturition. The experiment described below was designed to test this assumption. The effect of presenting aliens of a different species will be the subject of a separate report.

Method

Our goats, purebred Toggenburgs, were allowed to select their own birthing sites within an ¼ acre enclosure where they had previously lived for at least 2 weeks. They were familiar and at ease with the observers. At the time of birth, the doe was assigned to one of two treatment groups: I. own kid removed at parturition and replaced by an alien; II. own kid retained, and an alien also presented. Assignment to the groups was random for primipara. For the multipara, the assignment was contrary to that which had been made the previous season (i. e. does which were previously involved in a test involving immediate removal of the offspring were this time allowed to retain their young).

The alien kids were also Toggenburgs, varying in age from 1 to 28 days. The kids had been kept in the same enclosure with the does. However, as they were either being hand-fed or were with their own mothers, they generally avoided the pregnant does and made only fortuitous and brief contact with them. It is to be noted, however, that the kids were not wholly strange to the does.

At parturition, i. e. as soon as emergence of the first kid was completed, the alien was placed before the doe and held until she sniffed or licked it. Thereupon, the timing of a 5-minute post-partum contact period commenced. The timing was interrupted if labor heralding the birth of a second kid intervened. Timing resumed on completion of the second birth. All kids after the first born were immediately removed. Where removal of even the first born was required (Group I), the neonatal kid was enveloped in towels as it emerged and then quickly taken out of sight and hearing to a nearby house. *The aliens being used for the test were kept from contact with birth fluids.*

Directly after the 5-minute contact period, the kids were removed to a distant building for a separation of 1—2 hours (half the animals being subjected to the shorter, half to the longer period). At the end of the separation period the alien kid was presented to the doe for a 10-minute test period. It was then removed and the doe's first-born own kid presented for another 10-minute period; finally both kids were presented together for 10 minutes. During this time, an observer noted the responses of the does towards the kids and *vice versa*. While a few instances of ambivalent behavior did occur, it was generally quite obvious whether a doe would tolerate a kid. Rejection behavior involved an abrupt withdrawal from the vicinity of the kid, or vigorous butting if the kid persisted in following or seeking to nurse. Acceptance involved avid licking of the kid, nuzzling, and maintenance of the nursing stance when suckling was attempted (details in: KLOPFER, ADAMS & KLOPFER 1964). Successful nursing could not be used as the criterion for acceptance in these experiments, since the hand-reared aliens never sought to suckle.

Results

The relevant data from the previous studies are summarized in Table I; the data of this experiment are summarized in Table II. These points stand out:

1. For normal goats, contact with young directly following parturition is a *sine qua non* for later acceptance (15/17 goats which had such contact accepted their kids vs. 1/14 which had been denied contact. These experiments involved "own" kids).

Table 1: Responses of Normal and Cocainized Goats to their own kids
(Summary of previously published results, KLOPFER & GAMBLE 1966)
Proportion of does that accepted their own kids after separation

A.	Does presented with their kids upon		no overlap of confidence intervals at 99 %*
B.	Does deprived of their kids upon parturition parturition	1/14 15/17	
C.	As A, but with does cocainized at parturition	8/9	no overlap of confidence intervals at 95 %
D.	As A, but with does cocainized during acceptance testing	3/7	

*TATE & CLELLAND, 1957

Table 2: Responses of Normal Goats to Alien Kids
Proportion of does that accepted kids after separation

		own kid	alien kid
A.	Does presented with aliens for 5 minutes directly after parturition:		
	alien alone presented —	4/5	5/5
	alien and own kid presented —	5/6	5/6
B.	Does presented with aliens continuously for 2 hours directly after parturition:		
	alien alone presented —	2/4	3/4

2. Blindfolds and partial olfactory anaesthesia do not reduce the effectiveness of the post-parturitive contact (8/9 of the cocainized does accepted their young).

3. Although not shown in the Tables, normal does which had been exposed to and had accepted their own young rarely failed to vigorously reject alien kids.

4. When a particular alien kid was presented directly after parturition it stood as good a chance of being accepted subsequently as did the does' own kid. (13/15 of the aliens were accepted, vs. 11/15 of own-kids). Other aliens were not accepted.

5. *Own-kids which were immediately removed at the time of birth might still be re-accepted later if, in the meantime, their mother had adopted an alien.* In 4/5 cases, the doe had been presented only an alien kid but nonetheless later accepted both that alien and her own.

6. The above result (5) was even obtained in 2/4 cases where the alien remained in continuous contact with the doe from parturition to the time of the test 2 hours later, even though the own-young had been immediately removed at birth.

Discussion

The results affirm the original presumption: events at the time of parturition alter the doe's receptivity. After completing labor, she is prepared to bestow her maternal affections even upon relatively old and reluctant kids. Indeed, on occasions where a doe produced stillborn kids and no alien was available for adoption the handler frequently found him- (or her-) self overwhelmed by lavishly bestowed licks from a suddenly loving nanny. The postulated attractant fluids, if they do exist, are not essential to the formation of the maternal attachment. It is to the internal changes, not the external releasers, that our attention must be particularly directed. At the same time, the role of signals emanating from the does' own neonatal kid cannot be wholly discounted. Consider these significant facts: if the doe is denied post-parturitive contact with her kid, even after only an hour's separation she will reject it. However, if she is allowed 5 minutes contact with one of her kids directly after its birth, the subsequent separation has no such fateful consequence. Under those circumstance she re-accepts her kid, and its littermates, but does not accept aliens. The contrary is not true. Denied her young but allowed 5 minutes post-parturitive contact with an alien, the doe not only accepts that alien (though not others), she then also accepts her own young! Her own kids obviously provide more potent stimuli than the aliens; not sufficiently potent to evoke maternal care in the absence of the post-parturitive experience, but sufficiently so as to assure acceptance when the maternal state is aroused. In this respect aliens and own young are clearly not equivalent. The difference, presumably, does lie in the character of the olfactory cues associated with the kids, since own-young/alien-young discriminations can be abolished by application of cocain to the olfactory mucosa. It will be of interest to discover what the nature of this cue is, how each kid is individually "coded", and how the related scent comes to be known. We might recall the work of BROWER, BROWER & CORVINO (1967), who showed that the palatability of certain butterflies (to birds) was a function of their food intake. Could not a similar model be invoked here?

Accepting the possible importance of stimuli provided by the kids must not blind us to the primacy of the transitory internal changes of the doe. What is happening in the space of those few minutes which makes her ready, then and only then, to attach herself to a kid? Once attached, she will display many of the human signs of distress when her kid is removed; spared an attachment, she seems to live as happily as any gay virgin. What could be happening?

During the final stage of labor, as the head of the fetus is presented, a large increase in the blood level of oxytocin, the posterior hypophyseal hormone (actually secreted in the hypothalamus), has been noted (FOLLEY & KNAGGS 1965). Indeed, the secretion of oxytocin can be induced by manual dilatation of the cervix (PEETERS et al. 1965). Within a few minutes after parturition, however, the oxytocin has fallen to its normal level. It is tempting to speculate that this hormone, which apparently brings on the final uterine spasms which deliver the kid, is also implicated in the induction of maternal behavior. Either acting directly or through intermediaries, the oxytocin could activate maternal "centers" in the hypothalamus or elsewhere.

Alternatively, it might alter the thresholds of peripheral receptors so as to temporarily sensitize the doe to certain elements of the world about her. In either event, these speculations, open as they are to experimental investigation, should prove valuable. Even if oxytocin is not the keystone of mother love, its action provides us with a most useful and exciting model.

Summary

If an alien kid is substituted for a doe's own newborn directly after parturition, a 5-minute period of contact suffices to establish the alien as an acceptable adoptee. The elicitation of maternal behavior is thus not dependent upon special olfactory cues emanating from the doe's own neonatal kid, even though such cues do exist and do enhance the attractiveness of the own-kid. A model is proposed that is based upon the production of oxytocin in response to cervical dilatation, with this neurohumor (or intermediates) also activating specific hypothalamic or peripheral structures related to maternal behavior.

Acknowledgements

P. H. KLOPFER received support from an NIH Career Development Award and NIH Grant #00453. We are indebted to J. Gamble and Dr. R. A. Castellanos for care given our animals, and to B. Gilbert for criticisms of the draft manuscript.

Literature cited

ALTMANN, M. (1963): Naturalistic studies of maternal care in moose and elk. In: Maternal Behavior in Mammals (H. RHEINGOLD ed.), J. Wiley & Sons • BROWER, L. P., J. V. E. BROWER & J. M. CORVINO (1967): Plant poisons in a terrestrial food chain. Proc. Nat. Acad. Sci. 57, 893—8 • BUBENIK, A. B. (1965): Beitrag zur Geburtskunde und zu den Mutter-Kind-Beziehungen des Rehs. Z. Säugetierkunde 30, 65—128 • COLLIAS, N. E. (1956): The analysis of socialization in sheep and goats. Ecology 37, 228—239 • FOLLEY, S. J. & G. S. KNAGGS (1965): Levels of oxytocin in the jugular vein blood of goats during parturition. J. Endocrin. 33, 301—315 • HERSCHER, L., J. B. RICHMOND & A. U. MOORE (1963): Maternal Behavior in sheep and goats. In: Maternal Behavior in Mammals (H. RHEINGOLD ed.), J. Wiley & Sons • KLOPFER, P. H., D. K. ADAMS, & M. S. KLOPFER (1964): Maternal Imprinting in Goats. Proc. Nat. Acad. Sci. 52, 911—914 • KLOPFER, P. H. and J. GAMBLE (1966): Maternal "Imprinting" in Goats: The role of chemical senses. Tierpsychol. 23, 588—592 • LORENZ, K. (1935): Der Kumpan in der Umwelt des Vogels. J. Ornithol. 83, 137—214 • PEETERS, G., M. DEBACKERE, M. LAURYSSENS, and E. KÜHN (1965): Studies in the release of oxytocin in domestic animals. Symposium on Advances in Oxytocin Research, 1964. (J. H. M. PINKERTON ed.), Pergamon Press • ROSENBLATT, J. (1967): Nonhormonal basis of maternal behavior in the rat. Science 156, 1512—1514 • TATE, M. W. & R. C. CLELLAND (1957): Nonparametric and shortcut statistics. Interstate Pubs.

Author's address: Prof. P. H. and M. S. KLOPFER Zoology Dept., Duke University, Durham, North Carolina/USA

Imprinting: Reversal of a Preference established during the Critical Period

Two distinctive features of "imprinting" originally emphasized by Lorenz[1] were that there was a critical period in which the preference for a particular species was established and that the preference established during this period was permanent and could not be changed by subsequent experience. These two features have been reiterated by Hess[2], who has added a primacy-recency feature, claiming that the first imprinting experience has priority over a subsequent one. These features of imprinting have been questioned by Sluckin and Salzen[3], who treated imprinting as a perceptual learning phenomenon in which the sensitive period is experience dependent and the stability of an imprinted preference is dependent on the amount of experience. More recent reviews by Sluckin[3] and Bateson[3] have supported this view. In particular the perceptual learning view of imprinting has been developed into a neuronal model hypothesis of imprinting by Salzen[4] and it predicts that object preferences established by the imprinting process should be subject to reversal given sufficient exclusive and enforced experience of new objects after the end of the so-called critical period. The present experiment demonstrates a reversal of this kind.

The experiment used Cornish × White Rock chicks hatched in separate boxes and transferred when 12–18 h old to isolation rearing cages. In the centre of each cage separate from the sources of food, water and heat, there was either a dark blue or a green cloth covered paper ball about 5 cm in diameter and hanging approximately 3 cm above the floor. The chicks quickly became strongly attached to the balls, spending much time beside them, and interacted with the balls by pushing, pulling, and pecking them. After three days (12 h light/dark cycle) the chicks were tested for their preference between blue and green balls. The balls were hung midway on opposite long sides of a box (45 × 90 cm). The chick under test was placed in the dark at the mid-point of a short side, a lamp was switched on above the box, and the chick was given 2 min in which to go to and stay with one of the balls. A preference was recorded if the chick after reaching a ball either contacted it, pecked and pulled it, and/or gave pleasure calls, or stayed close (1 in.) beside

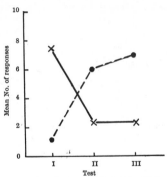

Fig. 1. Mean numbers of responses to the first-learned (×) and second-learned (●) coloured balls in the two-choice discrimination tests. Each of the twenty-two chicks had ten 2 min trials in each of three tests which were given at intervals of three days.

the ball and was silent or pleasure calling. The trial was ended when either of these criteria was reached or at the end of 2 min. The light was switched off, the chick was returned to a holding box and the positions of the objects were reversed ready for the next trial. Ten trials were made with each chick. After testing the chicks were returned to their cages and the balls exchanged so that each chick now had a new and different coloured ball. The chicks began to respond to the new balls on the same day. Three days later the chicks were again tested for their preference between green and blue balls. Then they were returned to their cages for a further three days but this time without any balls present. Finally, a third preference test was given. In this way twelve chicks were imprinted with a blue ball and then given reversal training with a green ball, while ten chicks were tested in the opposite manner.

The results are shown in Fig. 1 in terms of the mean number of responses made by the chicks to each ball in each preference test. The two colour treatments are combined because they were nearly balanced and gave similar results. The results show that at the end of the first 3 days the chicks had an almost exclusive preference for their familiar coloured ball ($p < 0.01$, Wilcoxon test). After the second three day period, this preference had been reversed ($p < 0.01$, Wilcoxon test). At the third test the new preference was maintained or even slightly increased because the responding to the preferred ball had increased significantly since the second test ($p < 0.02$, Wilcoxon test). Twenty-one of the twenty-two chicks made more responses to their familiar ball on the first test. On the second and third tests eighteen and seventeen of these twenty-one chicks made more responses to the newly experienced ball.

There can be no doubt that the period in which the first ball was experienced included any possible critical period for imprinting in chicks. The experience began

18 h after hatching, and Hess[5] has claimed that this period reaches its peak at this time for chicks. Furthermore, the second ball was experienced well after the end of the critical period of 24 h determined by Hess. Many studies[3] have shown that domestic chicks imprint with objects when exposed to them within the first 3 days after hatching. Thus the experiment shows that a strong preference established during this imprinting period can be completely reversed by subsequent experience. It also shows that this reversal was maintained intact after a period in which forgetting of both objects could have occurred. It cannot be said therefore that learning which takes place after the imprinting period is more rapidly forgotten than the learning during the imprinting period. Thus it would seem that the most recently learned preference predominated contrary to Hess's[2] claim of a primacy effect in imprinting. The recent test by Kaye[6] of a primacy effect gave an equivocal result, probably because of the very short training periods involved. The present test used stimulus objects that differed only in colours that were known from pilot studies to be equally easily learned and discriminated by chicks. The design was balanced for colour and similar results obtained with either colour. The training periods were long and the resulting preferences very strongly developed. Finally, the behaviour in the tests involved patterns of social interaction as well as the simple approach response. This study therefore represents the first closely controlled laboratory demonstration of reversibility of imprinting in precocial birds. It confirms the predictions of the neuronal model hypothesis of imprinting and agrees with the field observation of Steven[7]. In the field study by Schein[8] there appeared to be evidence for an irreversible preference for humans among human imprinted turkeys. It should be noted that these turkeys were always able to see humans as well as their later flock companions. Under these circumstances the neuronal model hypothesis would not necessarily predict a change in preference. The present demonstration of reversibility of imprinting in chicks agrees with the demonstration of a reversible social attachment in lambs[9]. Similar results have been obtained with a shape discrimination and a full account will be published elsewhere.

This work was supported by the National Research Council of Canada.

Eric A. Salzen
Cornelius C. Meyer

Department of Psychology,
University of Waterloo,
Waterloo, Ontario.

Received April 21; revised May 22, 1967.

[1] Lorenz, K. Z., Auk, 54, 245 (1937).
[2] Hess, E. H., Science, 130, 133 (1959).
[3] Sluckin, W., and Salzen, E. A., Quart. J. Exp. Psychol., 13, 65 (1961). Sluckin, W., Imprinting and Early Learning (Methuen, London, 1964), Bateson, P. P. G., Biol. Rev., 41, 177 (1966).
[4] Salzen, E. A., Symp. Zool. Soc. Lond., 8, 199 (1962).
[5] Hess, E. H., J. Comp. Physiol. Psychol., 52, 515 (1959).
[6] Kaye, S. M., Psychonom. Sci., 3, 271 (1965).
[7] Steven, D. M., Brit. J. Anim. Behav., 3, 14 (1955).
[8] Schein, M. W., Zeit. Tierpsychol., 20, 462 (1963).
[9] Cairns, R. B., and Johnson, D. L., Psychonom. Sci., 2, 337 (1965).

THE REINFORCING PROPERTIES OF CONSPICUOUS STIMULI IN THE IMPRINTING SITUATION

By P. P. G. BATESON & ELLEN P. REESE*

Sub-Department of Animal Behaviour, Madingley, Cambridge

The object with which a duckling or chick has been imprinted has been shown to act as a re-inforcing stimulus (Peterson 1960; Campbell & Pickleman 1961; Hoffman *et al.* 1966). Hoffman *et al.* (1966) found that when Peking ducklings were first presented with a model 9 to 10 days after hatching, the birds showed no signs of following and subsequently their pecking could not be reinforced by presenting the moving object. These authors conclude that the capacity of an imprinted stimulus to serve as a rein-forcement derive from events occurring during the sensitive period for imprinting. It was not possible to decide on the available evidence whether the range of reinforcing stimuli was *restricted* by imprinting or their properties were *acquired* as a consequence of the process.

In a recent study we showed that a flashing light, highly effective in eliciting social be-haviour, could also be used as a reinforcer in day-old domestic chicks and mallard ducklings that had not seen the light before (Bateson & Reese 1968). This suggests that the imprinting process *restricts* the range of visual stimuli acting as reinforcers. However, it has been argued that nonspecific sensory change is re-warding (e.g. Kish 1966) so our findings could be attributed to general properties of the stim-ulus rather than to its effectiveness as an im-printing object. Indeed, Eacker & Meyer (1967), who found that day-old chicks would learn to break an infrared beam in order to turn on an overhead light for 3 sec, related their results to general sensory reinforcement. Later, Meyer (1968) found that light onset in a visually com-plex environment was a much more effective reinforcer than light offset. The data, he felt, seriously questioned a stimulus change theory. However, the argument that the reinforcing properties of light onset is related to the effective-ness of the stimulus in the imprinting situation remained unsettled. In this study our concern was to discover whether chicks that had had an opportunity to work for a flashing light had developed a preference for it and whether some of the principal factors that determine the effectiveness of a stimulus in eliciting social behaviour also affect its reinforcing properties. The factors we examined were age at testing, experience prior to testing and the character-istics of the training stimulus. All these are known to affect the extent to which a chick will respond socially to a visual stimulus (see Bateson 1966).

General Methods

Subjects

Fertile eggs of a broiler strain (Chunkies) were obtained from a commercial hatchery 3 days before they were due to hatch. They were hatched in a dark incubator (Curfew) and were removed to a cooler incubator, also dark, within 3 hr of hatching. In experiment III some chicks were kept for 2 days in the cool incubator. Otherwise they were placed in rearing pens

*Present address: Mount Holyoke College, South Hadley, Mass. 01075.

within 12 hr of hatching. Socially-reared birds were kept in groups of three in pens approxim-ately 30 cm² and 30 cm high. Isolated chicks were kept singly in similar pens. All pens were painted grey and both socially-reared and iso-lated chicks were given chick crumbs and water *ad lib.* and kept under continuous illumination. A large number of batches were used but, as far as possible, equal numbers of chicks were drawn from a batch for each group when rearing conditions or testing conditions were varied.

Apparatus and Procedure

Operant conditioning apparatus. This was described in outline by Bateson & Reese (1968) and Bateson (1969) and shown working in a commercially available colour film ('Imprinting' from Appleton-Century-Crofts). The activity chosen for conditioning was stepping onto a pedal at floor level since it was easily performed by young chicks and did not require shaping by the experimenter. Furthermore, it was not necessary to handle a bird once it had been placed in the apparatus.

The area of the apparatus over which the birds could move measured 37 cm wide and 15 cm deep. At the front corners two pedals, 7·5 cm², were set into the floor (Fig. 1). The pedals were painted with black and white squares (2·5 cm²) in chess-board fashion; the remainder of the apparatus was painted grey. When a pedal was depressed it tilted slightly and an arm, connected to it and with a magnet on the other end, swung upward outside the apparatus. The magnet closed the contacts of a reed switch which in turn operated a relay. A flashing light was only turned on if a bird stepped onto the Active pedal; the other pedal (Control) measured any general changes in activity which might occur during a test.

The 37-cm-wide front of the apparatus was made of wire mesh (1·27 cm). Centred in front of this screen and 20 cm away was the flashing light—a modification of an Eisemann light for emergency vehicles. It consisted of a trans-lucent plastic box (18 cm long, 9 cm wide and 18 cm high) enclosing a 45 W, 12 V bulb. When the pedal controlling it was pressed, the bulb lit up and the box rotated on a vertical axis at 85 rev/min. The two smaller sides of the box were blacked out so that as it rotated the light ap-peared to flash. The flashing light remained on so long as a bird remained on the pedal. The light was highly effective in eliciting approach responses and was positioned between the pedals so that a bird would have to come off the pedal in order to approach it. As soon as a bird did so the light went out.

Chicks were placed singly in the apparatus. If a chick had not reached criterion (see below) within 1 hr it was removed. In experiment IV the time limit was lowered to 45 min. The apparatus was kept at 21 to 26°C. It was lit by one 60 W bulb placed approximately 1 m above and in front.

Choice alley. In several of the experiments it

254

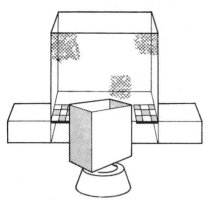

Fig. 1. Diagram of operant conditioning apparatus. In experiment IV the size of the pedals was reduced.

was necessary to test the preferences of chicks when given a choice between two stimuli. For this purpose an alley 120 cm long × 45 cm × 30 cm high was used with the stimuli placed behind mesh screens at either end. The alley was painted grey. The chicks were placed singly in the middle of the alley 60 cm from each end. They were left for 5 min and observed by means of a mirror placed above the alley. The apparatus was kept at 21 to 23°C. It was lit by two 60+W bulbs.

Measures

Each pedal of the operant conditioning apparatus controlled a channel on a polygraph and the time spent on the pedal operating the flashing light was automatically recorded on a digital timer. In addition records were taken of other aspects of the chicks' behaviour during testing. In order to make quantitative comparisons between groups treated in different ways, an arbitrary criterion for learning was devised. This took account of the rate of pressing the Active pedal (the one controlling the flashing light) and preferential pressing of the Active pedal. A chick was regarded as having reached criterion if, in eight of ten consecutive presses of the Active pedal, the interval between responses was less than 30 sec and if, in the intervals between pressing the Active pedal, the Control pedal was pressed no more than twice. Measurements were made of the *number of responses* from the first press of the Active pedal to the *first* of the ten presses in which criterion was reached. It was possible therefore for a rapid learner to reach criterion in one response. In some cases the *time* to reach criterion was measured. As might be expected this was correlated with the number of responses to criterion but in principle was less satisfactory as a measure since it also reflected the speed with which the chicks approached the flashing light.

In the choice alley the time from when the lights came on to when a chick crossed a line 15 cm from one of the wiremesh screens was recorded. While chicks do sometimes approach one stimulus and then turn round and approach the other stimulus in a choice situation, this never happened in the experiments described here. Once a chick had approached to within 15 cm of one end of the alley it stayed there. The chick was regarded as preferring the stimulus

which it approached and stayed by.

Experiment 1. Choice after Operant Conditioning

Methods

Fourteen chicks were kept in the dark until they were conditioned 20 to 24 hr after hatching. Half the chicks were rewarded with the flashing light already described with a primary red filter (Cinemoid No. 6 from Strand Electric) placed over the bulb. The other seven chicks were rewarded with a blue flashing light. This consisted of a translucent piece of plastic, 19·5 cm² mounted in front of a light blue filter (Cinemoid No. 18) and a 45 W, 12 V bulb. The square was divided into four triangular sectors, two of which were blacked out. When a bird stepped on the pedal controlling it, the bulb lit up and the square turned on a horizontal axis at 85 rev/min; the chick saw it rotating in two dimensions.

After conditioning each chick was marked with a felt-nib pen, so that it could be individually recognized, and returned to a dark incubator. After 14 to 18 hr each chick was placed singly in the choice alley. The red light ran continuously at one end and the blue light at the other end. The training condition of the chicks and the code for their markings were not known to the experimenter at the time of testing.

In addition to the trained chicks, twelve experimentally naive chicks were given a choice between the red and blue stimuli 18 to 24 hr after hatching.

Results

The results are shown in Table I. All the red-trained chicks preferred red and five of the blue-trained birds preferred blue—a difference which is statistically significant (Fisher test $P = 0.05$). None of the differences in the other measures is statistically significant. The two blue-trained birds that preferred red inadvertently received less overall experience with the blue light (245 and 271 sec) during conditioning than other members of the group. This is of interest because ten out of twelve experimentally naive day-old chicks approached the red light when given a choice between it and the blue light ($P<0.05$). Therefore in the operant conditioning situation a total exposure of at least 5 min to the blue light seemed to be necessary to overcome the initial preference for the red light.

Experiment II. Effects of Age

Methods

Forty-two socially-reared chicks were tested in the operant conditioning apparatus at various ages after hatching (Table II). In general the chicks were only tested once and if they had not reached criterion after being in the apparatus for an hour were removed. However, the group tested 48 hr after hatching were, with one exception, so slow in learning that they were given a second session in the apparatus—to no effect.

Results

The median reciprocals of the number of responses to reach criterion are plotted in Fig. 2. This method of plotting is used to make the data visually comparable with sensitive period data from the imprinting situation. An abrupt highly significant change occurred from 36 to 48 hr after hatching (Mann–Whitney U = 6, $P<0.01$). A significant change in the opposite direction occurred from 48 to 72 hr (U = 10, $P<0.05$).

Table I. Choice of Chicks after Their Pedal Pressing had been Reinforced by Either a Red or a Blue Flashing Light

Group	N	Mean exposure during conditioning (sec)	Mean approach latency (sec)	Number of chicks approaching Red	Blue
Red-reinforced	7	462·6	94·6	7	0
Blue-reinforced	7	375·4	122·9	2	5

Table II. Post-hatch Ages in Hours and Numbers of Chicks Used in Experiment II

Nominal age (hr)	24	36	48	60	72	96
Minimum	23	36	48	60	69	94
Maximum	25	37	48	63	75	96
N	7	7	7	7	7	7

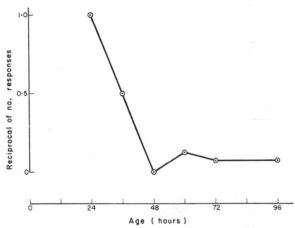

Fig. 2. Reciprocals of median number of responses to reach criterion in the operant conditioning apparatus. Data from experimentally-naive socially-reared chicks (N = 7 in each age group).

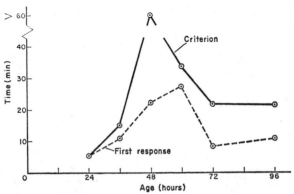

Fig. 3. Median times from being placed in the operant conditioning apparatus to making the first response and to reaching criterion. Data from experimentally-naive socially-reared chicks (N = 7 in each age group).

However, the older chicks pressed the pedal a significantly greater number of times before reaching criterion than the 36-hr old birds (36 v. 60: $U = 2$, $P<0.01$. 36 v. 72: $U = 10$, $P<0.05$. 36 v. 96: $U = 11$, $P<0.05$). Parallel changes occured in the median time from being placed in the apparatus to reaching criterion (Fig. 3). These changes can be partly attributed to changes in the time from being placed in the apparatus to making the first response. Nevertheless, there is a highly significant increase from 36 hr to 48 hr in the time from the first response to reaching criterion ($U = 2$, $P<0.01$), and a significant decline from 48 to 72 hr ($U = 10$, $P<0.05$).

Experiment III. Effects of Rearing Conditions
Methods

In addition to the seven 48-hr-old socially reared chicks whose behaviour was described in the last section, chicks were drawn from the same batches for two other rearing conditions. Seven chicks were reared in a dark incubator until the time of testing 47 to 48 hr after hatching and seven chicks were reared in isolation until testing at 48 to 51 hr.

Results

The medians of the number of responses to reach criterion are shown in Table III for the dark-reared and light-reared isolated chicks. The dark-reared birds all reached criterion on the first response and did so significantly before the isolated birds. The times to criterion also differed significantly but the times to the first response did not (see Table III). The isolated birds reached criterion significantly before the 48-hr socially-reared birds, whose performance is shown in Figs. 2 and 3 (for responses *and* time to criterion $U = 10$, $P<0.05$).

Experiment IV. Effects of Stimulus Characteristics
Methods

Fifty chicks were kept in the dark until testing 15 to 24 hr after hatching. The same flashing light was used as in experiments II and III except that in one condition an orange filter (Cinemoid No. 5 from Strand Electric) was placed over the bulb and in the other a light green filter (Cinemoid No. 23). The lights were not matched for intensity. They were picked because the orange light was preferred to the green one by experimentally naive day-old chicks placed between the stimuli in the choice alley. Seventeen out of twenty chicks approached the orange flashing light in preference to the green ($P<0.01$). Despite a strong preference for the orange light, the stimuli did not differ significantly in their eliciting properties when presented singly to experimentally naive day-old chicks. The median times taken to travel from a release point, 50 cm from one mesh screen in front of the stimulus in the alley to 15 cm from the screen, are shown in Table IV. The difference is very far from reaching statistical significance.

Since dark-reared chicks had been found to reach criterion very rapidly on the first day after hatching (Bateson & Reese 1968) the task was made slightly more difficult by decreasing the size of the pedals to 4 cm². These pedals were placed 2·5 cm from the side of the apparatus and 2·5 cm from the wire mesh front. By making the problem slightly more difficult we aimed to increase the spread in the scores.

The orange and green lights were used alternately. While equal numbers of chicks were tested with the two lights, records for two chicks rewarded with the orange light could not be used because the apparatus developed a fault.

Results

The number of responses to reach criterion are shown for each group in Fig. 4. Despite considerable variability within each group the chicks rewarded with the orange light reached criterion significantly before those rewarded with the green light (Mann–Whitney $U = 146$, $P<0.01$). It is noteworthy that when stimuli are presented singly to chicks a measure of their reinforcing properties discriminates more sensitively between them than a measure of their eliciting properties (compare Fig. 4 with Table IV).

Discussion

The results of these experiments can be summarized as follows. First, day-old chicks learned the characteristics of a flashing light at the same time as they learned to press a pedal that turned

Table III. Median Numbers of Responses and Median Times to Reach Criterion in the Operant Conditioning Apparatus of 48-hr-old Dark-reared and Isolated Light-reared Chicks

	N	responses to criterion	time to criterion (min)	time to first response (min)
Dark-reared	7	1	0·0	4·0
Isolated in light	7	6	6·9	11·3
Mann–Whitney U		0	0	16
P		0·001	0·001	ns

Table IV. Medians and Inter-quartile Ranges of Times Taken by Naive Day-old Chicks to Approach Orange and Green Flashing Lights in a Straight Alley

Group	N	Median (sec)	Inter-quartile range	Mann–Whitney U	P
Orange	28	212·5	161–342	361·5	>0·3
Green	28	256·5	122–514		

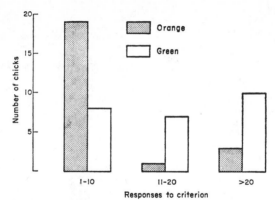

Fig. 4. The number of responses to reach criterion in the operant condition-ing apparatus by day-old chicks that were rewarded with either an orange flashing light (filled column) or a green flashing light.

it on; in other words imprinting and operant conditioning proceeded hand-in-hand.

Second, the rate of conditioning of socially-reared chicks declined up to the age of 48 hr and thereafter increased. The decline over the second day after hatching is very similar to the results obtained for the sensitive period for imprinting (Bateson 1966, 1969). The subse-quent increase is, on the face of it, dissimilar. However, this change over time does resemble the finding that the extent to which strange objects are avoided by isolated chicks decreases after the third day (Bateson 1964; Phillips & Seigel 1966). The causes of these changes over the second half of the first week after hatching are being investigated.

Third, the nature of their previous experience has a marked effect on the rate of conditioning in 48-hr-old chicks. Birds reared in the dark learned to press the pedal operating the flashing light as quickly as 24-hr-old birds (see Bateson & Reese 1968). Birds reared in the light but in isolation took significantly longer to reach criterion and six out of seven socially-reared birds failed to learn the problem in the time allowed. The effects of rearing conditions are very similar to those found in the imprinting situation where, broadly speaking, the more conspicuous stimuli in a young bird's im-mediate environment the more quickly it learns their characteristics and the less likely it is to respond socially to novel objects (see Bateson 1966).

Finally an orange flashing light that was pre-ferred to a green one by experimentally naive 1-day-old chicks was more effective as a rein-forcer. This result cannot be attributed to super-ior approach-eliciting properties of the orange flashing light since no difference in such proper-ties could be detected when the stimuli were presented singly to naive chicks. In any event the measure of the number of responses to reach criterion in the operant conditioning apparatus is not dependent on how long the chick takes to leave the pedal operating the light. The result indicates that those visual stimuli that are most effective in the imprinting situation are also most effective as reinforcers.

Taken together these results show that there is a close correspondence between the factors affecting the reinforcing properties of a con-spicuous visual stimulus and those affecting the elicitation of social behaviour by such a stim-ulus. We are, therefore, inclined to dismiss the view that the reinforcing properties of the flashing light can be attributed to non-specific stimulus-change. If our results are taken to-gether with those of Hoffman et al. (1966), we believe there is a strong case for supposing that imprinting narrows down the range of visual stimuli with reinforcing properties. The re-stricted range of stimuli with reinforcing proper-ties would not be expected to be any more stable than the acquired filial preference; and in the first week after hatching the filial prefer-ence of domestic chicks is much more labile than the term 'imprinting' suggests (Salzen & Meyer 1968). In the operant conditioning situ-ation once domestic chicks have been familiar-ized with a flashing light, they will readily work for it even though it differs markedly from the object with which they were originally imprinted (Reese, in preparation). For these reasons the effectiveness of a stimulus as a social reinforcer should be measured primarily in terms of the rate of acquisition of the conditioned response.

One aspect of the chicks' behaviour in the operant conditioning apparatus should be mentioned. Although day-old chicks learned to press the pedal operating the flashing light very quickly, the rate of responding characteristically tended to fall after the chicks had been in the apparatus for half an hour or so. At the same time the chicks peeped much more and in-creasingly tended to push themselves against the mesh that separated them from the flashing light. If, as we believe is justified, the flashing light is looked upon as having some of the properties of the natural mother, these observa-tions are not surprising. Under natural con-ditions a young bird's appetitive behaviour in the absence of its mother will increase the likelihood of it being able to see her and its approach behaviour will close the distance between them. The chick that is not yet fully able to regulate its own body temperature will generally crawl underneath its mother as soon as it has reached her side—particularly if it has been chilled. So while our flashing light has some of the reinforcing and eliciting properties of the natural parent, the situation is biologically inadequate in that it does not allow the completion of the response chain that is ended by tactile and thermal stimuli.

Summary

1. Day-old domestic chicks that had learned to press a pedal in order to be presented with either a red or a blue flashing light, subsequently approached the light used as a reinforcer when given a choice.

2. Socially-reared chicks most readily learned to press a pedal that turned on a flashing light when 24 hr old. Only one out of seven birds tested at 48 hr could be conditioned, but older birds could be conditioned more easily.

3. At 48 hr after hatching, dark-reared chicks could be conditioned with a flashing light more easily than birds reared in isolation in the light. The isolated birds could be conditioned more easily than birds reared in social groups in the light.

4. Day-old chicks could be conditioned more easily with an orange flashing light than with a green one. Seventeen out of twenty experimentally naive day-old chicks had previously been found to approach the orange light when given a choice between it and the green one.

5. These results suggest that the factors affecting the reinforcing properties of a conspicuous visual stimulus closely correspond with those affecting the elicitation of social behaviour by such a stimulus. Furthermore they suggest that imprinting can proceed hand-in-hand with operant conditioning and narrows down the range of visual stimuli with reinforcing properties.

Acknowledgments

We would like to thank Miss G. Seaburne-May for her help with one of the experiments. The work was supported by a grant from the Agricultural Research Council.

REFERENCES

Bateson, P. P. G. (1964). Changes in chicks' responses to novel moving objects over the sensitive period for imprinting. *Anim. Behav.*, **12**, 479–489.

Bateson, P. P. G. (1966). The characteristics and context of imprinting. *Biol. Rev.*, **41**, 177–220.

Bateson, P. P. G. (1969). The development of social attachments in birds and man. *Advmt Sci., Lond.*, **25**, 279–288.

Bateson, P. P. G. & Reese, E. P. (1968). Reinforcing properties of conspicuous objects before imprinting has occurred. *Psychon. Sci.*, **10**, 379–380.

Campbell, B. A. & Pickleman, J. R. (1961). The imprinting object as a reinforcing stimulus. *J. comp. physiol. Psychol.*, **54**, 592–596.

Eacker, J. N. & Meyer, M. E. (1967). Behaviorally produced illumination change by the chick. *J. comp. physiol. Psychol.*, **63**, 539–541.

Hoffman, H. S., Searle, J., Toffey, S. & Kozma, F. (1966). Behavioral control by an imprinted stimulus. *J. exp. Analysis Behav.*, **9**, 177–189.

Kish, G. B. (1966). Studies of sensory reinforcement. In *Operant Behavior: Areas of Research and Application* (ed. W. K. Honig). New York: Appleton-Century-Crofts.

Meyer, M. E. (1968). Light onset or offset contingencies within a simple or complex environment. *J. comp. physiol. Psychol.*, **66**, 542–544.

Peterson, N. (1960). Control of behavior by presentation of an imprinted stimulus. *Science, N.Y.*, **132**, 1395–1396.

Phillips, R. E. & Seigel, P. B. (1966). Development of fear in chicks of two closely related genetic lines. *Anim. Behav.*, **14**, 84–88.

Salzen, E. A. & Meyer, C. C. (1968). Reversibility of imprinting. *J. comp. physiol. Psychol.*, **66**, 269–275.

(*Received 1st May* 1968; *revised 15 September* 1969; *Ms. number:* 830)

Selection of Social Partners as a Function of Peer Contact during Rearing

Abstract. *Three groups of monkeys were raised with different degrees of contact with their peers. The first group was allowed no contact, the second only visual and auditory contact, and the third was allowed complete and normal contact with their peers. Animals of all three groups were allowed to interact socially; they were then tested for their preference for monkeys raised under the same conditions or for monkeys raised under different conditions. Monkeys raised under the same conditions preferred each other, even if the stimulus animals were completely strange to the test monkey.*

The early experiences of primates often have profound consequences on later behavior. In rhesus monkeys exploratory, maternal, sexual, and social behaviors appear extremely vulnerable to early social and sensory restric-

tion (*1*). Monkeys reared in isolation tend to withdraw from other animals and huddle by themselves in social situations. If such animals prefer each other over more normal monkeys, they may not be effectively exposed to the stimuli which lead to some degree of social adjustment. The fact that socially normal monkeys may avoid contact with monkeys reared in isolation further retards rehabilitation. We varied the amount of peer contact during rearing and investigated its effect on physical approach to a social partner, in order to determine whether monkeys reared under identical conditions prefer each other to monkeys reared under different conditions.

Three groups of rhesus monkeys were reared from birth in the laboratory without mothers. Each group contained four males and four females. Sets of three animals were matched across groups for age, sex, and test experiences after rearing was complete. The first group (A) was reared from birth to 9 months in individual closed cages. On the first 5 to 7 days they experienced physical, but minimal visual, contact with a human during feeding. No other physical or visual contact with humans or live monkeys occurred during rearing. Changing visual experiences throughout rearing were limited to presentation of pictures of monkeys engaged in various behaviors and pictures of people and inanimate objects (2). From months 9 through 18 the monkeys in group A were housed individually in bare wire cages from which they could see and hear other isolates and humans, but physical contacts were unavailable.

Subjects in the second group (B) were reared individually in a large nursery room in bare wire cages from birth to 9 months. Other monkeys and humans could be seen and heard, but physical contact was not available. From month 9 through 18 the monkeys in group B were housed in the same room as the monkeys in group A; they were in wire cages where they could see and hear, but not touch, one another.

The third group (C) lived in wire cages in peer groups of varying sizes during the first 18 months of life. Rearing conditions and social behavior tests provided physical peer contact during this period. In summary, group A had no early contact with live peers, group B had visual and auditory but no physical contact with peers, and group C had complete peer contact during the rearing period.

When they were 18 months old, sets of monkeys from all groups interacted during social behavior tests in a large playroom (3). Each animal was tested weekly for 12 weeks in three 30-minute sessions. In one weekly session a constant set of one group A, one group B, and one group C monkey of the same sex interacted together; the same animals were always tested together. On the two other weekly sessions constant pairs of groups A and B, A and C, and B and C subjects interacted in groups of four monkeys. After social testing, each subject had received equal playroom exposure to one monkey from its own rearing condition and to two monkeys from each of the other rearing conditions. After playroom testing was completed, the monkeys were tested for their preference for other monkeys reared under the same conditions or for those reared under different conditions.

Testing was done in the "selection circus" (Fig. 1), which consists of a central start compartment that bounds the entrances to six adjoining choice compartments. Wire-mesh cages for the stimulus animals were attached to the outside of appropriate choice compartments. The front walls of the stimulus cages, the outside walls of the choice compartments, and the guillotine doors separating choice compartments from the start compartment were all made of clear plexiglas.

For the testing, the subject was placed in the center start compartment with the plexiglas guillotine doors down for a 5-minute exposure period. The subject could see and hear the stimulus

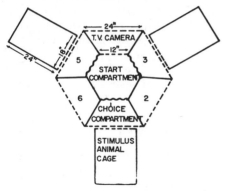

Fig. 1. Scheme of the "circus" which is constructed of aluminum channels containing plexiglas walls (dotted line), plywood walls (solid line), and plexiglas guillotine doors (wavy line). Wire-mesh stimulus cages with a single plexiglas wall are attached outside choice compartments. In testing, the subject is first placed in the start compartment. It can look into and through the choice compartments, but cannot enter them until the plexiglas guillotine doors are raised by a vacuum lift. Plywood walls block physical and visual access to choice compartments that are not used in the experiment.

Table 1. Mean number of seconds spent with each type of stimulus animal for each rearing condition, averaged over the two test trials.

Rearing condition of experimental animal	Rearing condition of stimulus animal		
	A (totally deprived)	B (partially deprived)	C (peer-raised)
A (totally deprived)	156	35	29
B (partially deprived)	104	214	103
C (peer-raised)	94	114	260

animals, but could not enter the choice compartments near them. Unused choice compartments were blocked off by plywood walls inserted in place of the plexiglas guillotine doors. After the exposure period, a 10-minute choice trial was given. The plex glas guillotine doors were raised by a vacuum system; this procedure allowed the subject to enter and reenter choice compartments or to remain in the start compartment. The total time spent in each choice compartment during the test trial was recorded over a closed-circuit TV system.

The monkey's entry into different choice compartments served as our index of social preference. This measure of preference involves visual orientation, but, more importantly, it also involves locomotion toward a specific social object. It may be argued that a measure of viewing time, such as that used by Butler (4) in which monkeys inspected various objects through a small window, is not a proper index of social preference. Although actual physical contact was not available to our subjects, a great deal of nontactile social interaction was possible. Thus, our measure of preference based on physical approach toward a social object seems to be more analogous to an actual social situation than would be a simple viewing response.

Two types of trials were given. In the first, the stranger trial, one stimulus animal from each of the rearing groups was randomly positioned in a stimulus animal cage outside choice compartments 1, 3, or 5. These stimulus animals had received no previous social contact with the test subject but they were the same age and the same sex. A second test was identical with the stranger trial except that the three stimulus animals had received extensive social experience with the test subject during the playroom tests. Before the start of these tests, all 24 subjects had been adapted to the circus during nonsocial exploration tests. The order of serving first as a stimulus animal or as a test subject was randomized across groups.

Analysis of variance of the total time spent in the choice compartment had rearing condition as an uncorrelated variable, and type of stimulus animal and degree of familiarity as correlated variables. Familiarity did not have a significant main effect, and it did not interact with the other variables (all $P > .20$). Rearing condition had a significant effect ($P < .001$), which indicated that total choice time in all compartments differed as a function of early peer contact. Group A subjects spent half as much time (average $=$ 220 seconds) in choice compartments as either group B (average $= 422$ seconds) or group C (average $= 468$ seconds) monkeys.

The interaction of rearing condition with type of stimulus animal was also significant ($P < .001$). Table 1 shows this effect, with choice times averaged over the trials with strange and familiar stimuli. These data show that like prefers like—each rearing condition produced maximum choice time for the type of stimulus animal reared under that condition. The data for individual subjects supports this averaged effect. In the group A, two of the eight monkeys did not enter choice compartments. Of the six remaining monkeys, five spent more time in the group A choice compartment than in the other two compartments (two-tailed binomial, $P = .038$, with $p = \frac{1}{3}$, $q = \frac{2}{3}$). In the groups B and C all subjects entered choice compartments, and seven out of eight in each group spent more time with the animal reared like themselves than with the other animals (both $P = .0038$, two-tailed binomial).

The data indicate that social preferences are influenced by rearing conditions. In playroom testing the group C monkeys were the most active and socially advanced groups studied. Therefore, it was not surprising that they discriminated and showed large preferences for both strange and familiar group C animals. The group A monkeys, however, were highly retarded in their playroom behavior, and they did not show much progress over the 12

weeks of social interaction. As expected, these animals did exhibit a low degree of choice time in this study. We also thought that group A monkeys would be least likely to show preferences for a particular type of animal. It was, therefore, surprising to find that they did prefer each other to animals reared under other conditions. The group B animals, which were intermediate in social adequacy in playroom testing, also preferred each other. This result seems to strengthen the idea that animals of equal social capability, whether or not they are familiar with each other, can discriminate themselves from others, and not only discriminate but approach each other.

These results have important implications for studies designed to rehabilitate primates from the devastating effects of social isolation. The fact that socially abnormal monkeys prefer each other poses difficulties in the design of social environments which contain experiences appropriate for the development of normal social responses. Further, the finding that socially normal monkeys do not choose to approach more abnormal ones compounds the problem of providing therapy for abnormal animals.

These data also have implications for attachment behavior in mammals. Cairnes (5) suggests a learning theory approach to the formation of attachments in which the subject will approach a social object as a function of having made many previous responses while the social object was part of the general stimulus situation. Thus, indices of social attachment toward an object are expected to be higher with increases in the probability that this object occurs as part of the stimulus field in the subject's overall repertoire of responses. Although this seems a reasonable approach, the present data present some difficulties for this view. During rearing, the monkeys in group A did not have the same opportunity to learn the characteristics of other monkeys as did the monkeys in groups B and C. Yet, the monkeys in group A did prefer each other to the alternative choices available. Thus, it is possible that the preference shown by group A monkeys was not based on the conditioning of approach behavior to specific social cues, as is suggested by the stimulus-sampling theory of attachment. It is possible that the behavior of group A was motivated by avoidance of cues contained in the social behavior or countenance of the other two types of monkeys. Thus, there may be at least two distinct kinds of processes in the choice of a social stimulus. The conditioning of specific social cues to the response systems of an animal may be one factor, and the avoidance of nonconditioned cues may be a second important factor in the formation of social attachments.

The specific cues used by the monkeys studied here are not known. Neither do we yet know how our animals differentiated between the stimuli. The discrimination may be based solely on differences in the gross activity of the stimulus animals, or on more subtle and specific social cues. Analysis of the specific stimulus components operating in this situation may clarify the nature of the social cues involved. The important question to be answered is whether the types of cues used in selecting a partner are qualitatively different for different rearing conditions, or whether the same aspects of stimulation are simply weighted differently as a function of an animal's rearing history.

CHARLES L. PRATT
GENE P. SACKETT

*Primate Laboratory, University
of Wisconsin, Madison 53706*

References and Notes

1. H. F. Harlow and M. K. Harlow, *Sci. Amer.* **207**, 136 (1962); G. P. Sackett, *Child Develop.* **36**, 855 (1965).
2. The rearing conditions are described fully by G. P. Sackett, *Science* **154**, 1468 (1966).
3. The playroom situation is described by H. F. Harlow, G. L. Rowland, G. A. Griffin, *Psychiat. Res. Rep.* **19**, 116 (1964).
4. R. A. Butler, *J. Comp. Physiol. Psychol.* **50**, 177 (1957).
5. R. B. Cairns, *Psychol. Rev.* **73**, 409 (1966).
6. Supported by NIMH grant MH-11894.

10 January 1967

Monkeys Reared in Isolation with Pictures as Visual Input: Evidence for an Innate Releasing Mechanism

Abstract. Monkeys reared in isolation from birth to 9 months received varied visual input solely from colored slides of monkeys in various activities and from nonmonkey pictures. Exploration, play, vocalization, and disturbance occurred most frequently with pictures of monkeys threatening and pictures of infants. From 2.5 to 4 months threat pictures yielded a high frequency of disturbance. Lever-touching to turn threat pictures on was very low during this period. Pictures of infants and of threat thus appear to have prepotent general activating properties, while pictures of threat appear to release a developmentally determined, inborn fear response.

Research on a wide variety of animals has shown that early experiences can be important determinants of later social and nonsocial behavior (*1*). Some of these experiences apparently must occur during a limited developmental period if the animal is to exhibit behavior patterns normal for its species.

Table 1. Overall responsiveness to pictures. Mean frequency of the five behavioral measures for all 2-minute periods, during the 9 months of testing.

Stimulus picture	Behaviors				
	Vocalization	Disturbance	Play	Exploration	Activity (climbing)
Threat	0.61	0.83	0.46	5.0	1.7
Infant	.48	.37	.54	4.8	1.8
Withdraw	.27	.20	.17	2.4	0.8
Fear	.27	.15	.26	2.3	.9
Play	.27	.21	.21	2.7	.8
Explore	.22	.19	.19	2.2	.8
Sex	.17	.24	.18	2.2	.8
Mother-infant	.29	.25	.19	2.5	.7
Nothing	.22	.21	.31	2.7	.9
Control	.14	.12	.16	2.6	.7

One important, but relatively neglected, area of study in primate behavior involves determination of the developmental importance of different types of sensory input early in life. The experiment reported here is part of a study examining the effects of visual social and nonsocial stimulation presented to monkeys otherwise reared in total social isolation. The present study asks if totally naive infant monkeys will show differential behaviors toward specific types of visual stimulation, and whether such differential behaviors mature at specific periods during the monkey's development.

Four male and four female rhesus monkeys (*Macaca mulatta*) were reared in individual wire cages (61 by 71 by 71 cm) from birth to 9 months. Three walls, the ceiling, and the area below the wire floor of each cage were covered by Masonite or aluminum panels blocking all visual access to the world outside of the cage. The rear wall of each cage was a rear projection screen, which also blocked visual access to the outside. The screen had a ground surface, preventing a mirror effect on the inner surface. Thus, reflections of the monkey's own image on the screen were minimized, although slight shadows did appear when the screen was brightly illuminated by the projector. A nonmovable brass lever, 0.6 cm in diameter, projected 7.6 cm into the cage at the bottom right corner of the screen. During rearing, the subjects never saw another monkey, and saw no humans after a hand-feeding period during the first 5 to 9 days of life. Sounds were not controlled, so the monkeys did hear other animals and humans.

On day 14, two types of visual stimulus presentations were begun, as follows.

Experimenter-controlled slides. In this procedure pictures of monkeys engaged in different activities and non-monkey control pictures were projected on the screen. Each individual picture was available for 2 minutes. Six monkey and two control pictures, randomly selected from a large pool, were projected in a daily test session. In these tests the subject had no direct control over the onset or duration of the picture.

Animal-controlled slides. In this procedure the subject could expose itself to pictures by touching the brass lever, which operated an electronic contact relay circuit. Lever-touching opened a shutter located in front of a Kodak Carousel slide projector, and also operated a printing counter that recorded the touching behavior. The standard schedule of six randomly selected monkey and two control pictures was used in each test session. Each picture was

Fig. 1. Examples of picture stimuli from the ten categories. The four categories selected for illustration here are (top left) fear, (top right) threat, (bottom left) infant, and (bottom right) control. The actual pictures were in natural color.

The 2- by 2-inch (5- by 5-cm) colored slides used as stimuli were grouped into ten categories (four of which are illustrated in Fig. 1). They include pictures of (i) threatening, (ii) playing, (iii) fearful, (iv) withdrawing, (v) exploring, and (vi) sexing monkeys, as well as pictures of (vii) infants, (viii) mother and infant together, and (ix) monkeys doing "nothing." Labels were applied, and stimuli were included for study, only when the pictures received a unanimous title by a panel of eight experienced monkey testers. The final category, (x) control pictures, included a living room, a red sunset, an outdoor scene with trees, a pretty adult female human, and various geometric patterns. Each of the ten categories had at least four different examples. Only one randomly chosen slide from each category was used in any individual test session. Complete randomness was restricted such that no single slide appeared more than once in a 7-day period. The monkey pictures were projected with an approximately life-size image.

In animal-controlled tests, the basic data were the number of lever touches producing shutter openings out of the 20 possible shutter openings in each 5-minute stimulus period. In experimenter-controlled tests data were collected on a checklist by an observer looking through a nonreflecting one-way viewing screen in one wall of the cage. These checklist data were frequencies per 2-minute stimulus period of (i) vocalization, (ii) disturbance behaviors including rocking, huddling, self-clasping, fear, and withdrawal, (iii) playing with the picture, (iv) visual and manual exploration of the picture, and (v) climbing on the walls of the cage. Sex, threat, and aggressive behaviors were also scored, but sexual responses never occurred, and only three threatening or aggressive responses were observed during the 9

potentially available for 5 minutes and 15 seconds. During the first 15 seconds the shutter automatically opened, exposing the subject to the picture that would be available for the next 5 minutes. During the next 5 minutes each lever touch turned the picture on for 15 seconds. If the subject continued to touch the lever, the picture still went off at the end of 15 seconds, and did not come on again until contact was broken and then the lever was touched again.

Up to the fourth month of life all subjects received a minimum of two experimenter- and two animal-controlled tests each week. At 4 months, four subjects received motion picture stimuli, but these monkeys were still exposed to at least one trial of experimenter-controlled slides each week. The motion picture data parallel the data for slides, and will not be treated here.

months of testing.

Evidence for behavioral differentiation of the ten types of stimuli during experimenter-controlled tests is shown in Table 1. These results can be summarized as follows. First, threat and infant pictures produced the greatest frequency of response on all measures of behavior. All differences between these two types of pictures and the other pictures taken individually were significant beyond the .01 level. Second, there was more vocalization and disturbance with threat than with infant pictures (both $p < .02$). Third, there were no significant differences between the remaining seven monkey pictures (fear, withdrawal, explore, sex, mother-infant, and nothing) on any measure (all $p > .10$). Tests of overall differences between any of these seven monkey pictures *for each month* during rearing also failed to reveal significant variation (all $p > .05$), indicating that these seven pictures were responded to similarly throughout rearing. Fourth, the control pictures had significantly lower frequencies than these remaining seven monkey pictures pooled together on the vocalization, disturbance, and play measures (all $p < .04$), but no significant differences appeared on exploration and climbing activity (both $p > .10$).

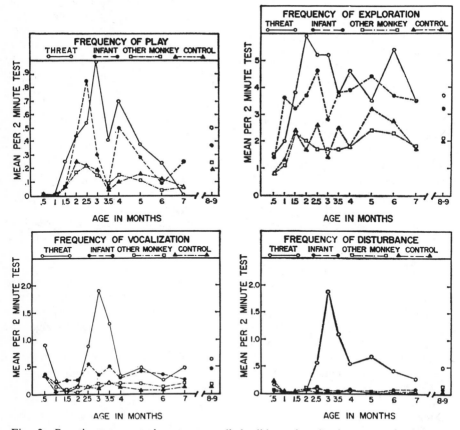

Fig. 2. Reactions to experimenter-controlled slides: the development of play, exploration, vocalization, and disturbance behaviors in response to pictures of threatening monkeys, infants, all other monkey pictures pooled, and control pictures.

The development of responding during experimenter-controlled tests is summarized in Fig. 2. In these data the seven monkey pictures that did not differ significantly from one another in overall frequency of eliciting responses are pooled together to form an "other-monkey" category. Disturbance behavior occurred at a uniformly low level throughout the 9-month period for all pictures except threat. Beginning at 2 to 2.5 months, and peaking at 2.5 to 3 months, disturbance behavior consisting primarily of fear, withdrawal, rocking, and huddling occurred at high levels whenever pictures of monkeys threatening appeared on the screen. At 3.5 months this apparently innate fear response to threat stimuli declined. The vocalization measure, a response that reflects disturbance but may also reflect contentment, showed a course of development similar to disturbance, except that vocalizations were relatively high with infant pictures. After the first month of life, pictures of threat and of infants received more exploration and play than did other-monkey or control pictures. Interestingly, the first stimulus pictures to receive a relatively high degree of play were threat, which were played with even during periods when disturbance responses to threat pictures were high. Climbing responses (Fig. 3), taken as an index of general activity, exhibited a large increase after the first month. Climbing was most frequent in response to threat and infant pictures from this time until the end of testing. Also illustrated in Figs. 2 and 3 is the finding that all measures for all stimuli generally leveled off at about 6 months and remained constant thereafter.

Figure 4 presents the data for animal-controlled pictures for all stimuli through the first 6 months of life. Lever-touching was equal for all pictures during month 1. During months 2 and 3 the subjects began exposing themselves more to pictures containing monkeys than to control pictures. About month 3, when the subjects were beginning to show disturbance to threat pictures in experimenter-controlled tests, lever-touching for threat declined markedly. However, responding for infant and other-monkey pictures continued to increase. During

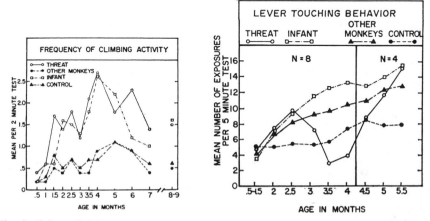

Fig. 3 (left). The development of climbing behavior during stimulation, taken as an index of general activity level.   Fig. 4 (right). Frequency of self-exposures to threat, infant, other monkey, and control pictures for the first 6 months of animal-controlled tests.

month 4 responding to threat pictures was depressed below the control-picture level, but lever-touching for threat did increase again during months 5 and 6. Lever-touching was generally higher for pictures of infants than for other-monkey pictures from month 2 until the end of testing. Although lever-touching may have been influenced by differential general activity with the various stimuli, it is unlikely that the decrease in response for threat pictures was the result of such a factor. As shown in Fig. 3, climbing activity was similar for both threat and infant pictures from months 2 to 5, yet infant pictures elicited a high level of lever-touching while touching for threat pictures declined markedly.

In general, the shapes of the curves in Figs. 2–4 were characteristic of the behavior of individual subjects. The individual curves tended to follow the major inflections shown in the averaged data, although there were discrepancies of up to 1 month in the exact age at which a given monkey might show a large increase or decrease in a given behavior. The most important case concerns disturbance behavior in response to threat pictures. Two monkeys showed a large increase in disturbance at 2 months of age, four animals showed increases at 2.5 months, and the remaining two subjects showed increased disturbance at 3 months. Kendall's Coefficient of Concordance was calculated to measure the degree of consistency in disturbance with threat pictures between subjects over age blocks. This measure revealed a very high degree of association between subjects ($W = .808$; $p < .001$), indicating that individual animals behaved in a very similar manner toward the threat pictures.

These data lead to several important conclusions. First, at least two kinds of socially meaningful visual stimuli, pictures of monkeys threatening and pictures of infants, appear to have unlearned, prepotent, activating properties for socially naive infant monkeys. From the second month of life these stimuli produced generally higher levels of all behaviors in all subjects. Second, the visual stimulation involved in threat behavior appears to function as an "innate releasing stimulus" for fearful behavior. This innate mechanism appears maturational in nature. Thus, at 60 to 80 days threat pictures release disturbance behavior, although they fail to do so before this age. These fear responses waned about 110 days after birth. This could be due to habituation, occurring because no consequences follow the fear behavior released by threat pictures—consequences that would certainly appear in a situation with a real threatening monkey.

One important implication of these results concerns the ontogeny of responses to complex social communication in primates. These data suggest that at least certain aspects of such communication may lie in innate recognition mechanisms, rather than in acquisition through social learning processes during interactions with other animals. Although the maintenance of responses to socially communicated stimuli may well depend on learning and some type of reinforcement process, the initial evocation of such complex responses may have an inherited, species-specific structure. Thus, these data suggest that innate releasing mechanisms such as those identified by ethologists (2) for insect and avian species may also exist in some of the more complex behaviors present in the response systems of primates.

GENE P. SACKETT

Primate Laboratory, University of Wisconsin, Madison 53715

References and Notes

1. See, for example, R. Melzack, in *Pathology*

and Perception (Grune and Stratton, New York, 1965); A. H. Riesen, in *Functions of Varied Experience*, D. W. Fiske and S. R. Maddi, Eds. (Dorsey Press, Homewood, Ill., 1961); M. R. Rosenzweig, *Amer. Psychol.* **21**, 321 (1966); G. P. Sackett, *Child Develop.* **36**, 855 (1965).
2. W. H. Thorpe, *Learning and Instinct in Ani-*
mals (Harvard Univ. Press, Cambridge, 1963).

3. Supported by grant MH-4528 from the National Institute of Mental Health. Portions of these data were reported at the 10th Interamerican Congress of Psychology, Lima, Peru, April 1966. I thank C. Pratt and L. Link for assistance with this research.

3 October 1966

EFFECTS OF SOCIAL DEPRIVATION ON MATERNAL BEHAVIOR OF RHESUS MONKEYS[1]

G. L. ARLING AND H. F. HARLOW

University of Wisconsin

The primary differences between the design of this experiment and that of Seay, Alexander, and Harlow (1964) concerning the maternal behavior of motherless mothers (MMs) were extending the observation period and balancing the groups for sex of the infants. As in the previous study, females separated at birth from their own mothers and deprived of early interaction with peers were distinctly deficient in basic patterns of maternal behavior when compared with feral-raised mothers. Also, MM infants were deficient in social play and sexual behavior and hyperaggressive in peer interaction as compared with infants of the feral mothers and infants in the Seay et al. study.

Grossly inadequate maternal behavior was observed in four female rhesus monkeys separated at birth from their mothers and deprived of interaction with other monkeys for the first 18 mo. of life (Seay, Alexander, & Harlow, 1964). Although the maternal behavior of two of these mothers was characterized as abusive (Harlow, Harlow, Dodsworth, & Arling, 1966) and the other two as indifferent, the social development of their infants was initially delayed but otherwise similar to that of four infants reared by adequate feral mothers.

The present study was designed both to replicate and to extend the previous investigation and differed in that (a) the period of observation was extended from 180 days to 240 days, and (b) the sex of the infants was balanced in the experimental and control groups, a condition which could not be achieved in the Seay et al. (1964) investigation because of an insufficient supply of infants.

---

[1] This research was supported by Grants MH-11894 and FR-0167 from the National Institutes of Health to the University of Wisconsin Primate Laboratory and Regional Primate Research Center, respectively.

METHOD

Subjects

The Ss were eight adult female rhesus monkeys (*Macaca mulatta*) and their infants. Four laboratory-reared primiparous "motherless mothers" (MM group) were assigned to the experimental group. Mother A-1 had been raised on a lactating cloth surrogate for the first 6 mo. of life (Harlow & Zimmermann, 1959) and then housed alone until she was placed with a cagemate at 10 mo. The other three mothers in the MM group were housed individually in wire cages for the first 2 yr. The two male and two female infants of the experimental group were delivered within a span of 34 days. The control group (FM group) was made up of four feral-reared females and their infants. The two male and two female infants of this group were delivered within a span of 19 days.

Apparatus

The mother-infant pairs of both groups were housed in a standard four-unit playpen apparatus described by Seay et al. (1964). Each living cage was a wire mesh compartment 36 × 36 × 36 in. with a 3.5 × 5.5 in. opening which allowed the infant access to a play area 60 × 60 × 30 in. while restraining the mother. The play area was divided into four separate compartments by means of removable mesh panels. A ladder, wooden toys, and raisins were provided for the infants during play sessions.

Procedure

Procedure

The mothers and infants were placed in the home-cage apparatus within 16 hr. of delivery. Two MM mothers, 16 and 27, would not allow their infants to nurse, and it was necessary to hand feed them in accordance with the standard laboratory schedule (Blomquist & Harlow, 1961). Motherless Mother 16 subsequently began nursing her infant at Day 30.

All *S*s were observed during two daily 1-hr. test sessions, one in the morning and one in the afternoon, 5 days per week. Throughout the first 15 days infants were allowed access to the playpen but were prevented by the mesh panels from interacting with other animals. At the beginning of each test session during the remaining 225 days, the panels between the facing playpen units were removed and the infant pairs were allowed free interaction for 1 hr. The infants also had access to their partner's home cage during this time. The infant pairings were balanced by means of a preordered weekly cage assignment rotation. Each mother-infant pair was observed for 15 min. of every test session in a balanced order.

A 97-category observation scheme was used to score behaviors occurring within successive 15-sec. periods. An *S*'s score for a 15-min. observation period in a particular behavior category was the number of 15-sec. intervals in which each behavior was observed. Pearson product-moment coefficients of correlation were used to determine reliability for each category based on data taken during 10 sessions beginning at approximately 120 days of age in which two *O*s scored the same mother-infant pair. A complete listing of all behavior categories is given by Hansen (1962); definitions and interobserver reliability of behavior categories for which graphs are presented in this paper are outlined below. The range of scores represents the high and low scores for any two of the four testers involved in the data collection. (a) *Mother-infant cradle:* supporting the infant in a contact position with one or both arms ($r = .88-.99$). (b) *Infant-mother clasp:* closure of the infant's hand on the skin or fur of the mother ($r = .84-.97$). (c) *Non-mutual contact play:* nonreciprocated mock fighting involving either wrestling, rapid biting without bloodletting, shifts in the locus of the biting, or head shaking movements while biting ($r = .63-.99$). (d) *Clasp-pull-bite:* any brief nip, cuff, or clasp-pull directed toward another infant ($r = .62-.90$).

The data were analyzed in 2-wk. blocks using repeated-measures analysis of variance, with the .05 level chosen as the criterion of significance. The data were graphed in 28-day blocks to illustrate developmental trends.

RESULTS

Mother-Infant and Infant-Mother Interactions

General observations. The maternal behavior of the MM group was characterized by wide variability. Motherless Mother 27 was abusive to her infant, refusing to allow him to nurse and responding to his attempts to establish physical contact by pushing him away or crushing him to the floor until he stopped struggling. Unprovoked attacks on the infant were frequently observed. Very often these attacks coincided with another infant's entering the home cage and attempting to contact MM 27. As was observed in the Seay et al. (1964) study, even though an infant was the victim of frequent rebuffs and violent attacks, he persisted in his attempts to gain contact with his mother during each observation session throughout the study.

Another mother, MM 16, refused to nurse her infant, rejected him, and became abusive when he approached her during the first 30 days. For no reason apparent to the *E*s, she began to nurse the infant during the second month and became extremely protective of him.

The other two motherless mothers, MM 32 and MM A-1, were classified as maternally adequate. Although MM 32 frequently positioned her infant inappropriately on her ventral surface and exhibited a higher than normal rate of rejection of the infant throughout the study, the *E*s' subjective impression was that her overall maternal behavior was within the normal range. No markedly aberrant maternal behavior was exhibited by MM A-1, which had had limited peer experience within the first year of life. Actually the objective data presented in this paper suggest that none of the MM mothers was normal. In contrast, all the mothers of the FM group were judged to be maternally adequate and the objective data are consistent with this evaluation.

Quantitative analysis. The data of the present study yielded statistically significant Group × Two-Week Block interactions for all the behavioral components of positive maternal behavior. Mother-infant cradle (Figure 1) was initially higher in the FM group than in the MM group. This same general result was found for the categories of infant-mother ventral contact, embrace, nipple contact, mother-infant approach, initiation of ventral contact, and visual contact with the infant.

The perseverance of the MM infant in seeking contact of any sort was partially reflected in the significantly greater number of manual explorations and clasps of the mother by MM infants than by FM infants, as illustrated by the clasp scores in Figure 2. The initially higher score for the FM infants resulted primarily from the fact that infants often clasp the mother's chest or arm while nursing; thus the clasp

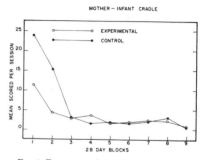

FIG. 1. Frequency of mother-infant cradle response.

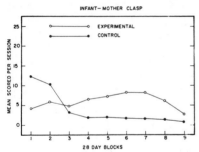

FIG. 2. Frequency of infant-mother clasp response.

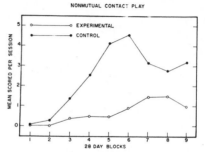

FIG. 3. Frequency of nonmutual contact play.

score would be expected to diminish as the frequency of nursing decreases and infant-infant interaction increases during observation periods. The relatively constant rate of clasp behavior observed in the MM group, however, reflected the desperate attempts of the infants to cling to the mother's back or side. A similar trend for infant-mother nonspecific contact was found to be significant and in the same general direction.

Infant-Infant Interaction

General observations. It was believed that the persistent attempts by the MM infants to gain and maintain contact with the mothers would militate against normal development of exploratory behavior, which initially provides a primary motivation for peer interaction (Harlow, 1962). However, the qualitative impression of the Os was that the social development of the infants was not distinctly different from that of infants of normal mothers.

Quantitative analysis. A number of important differences not apparent by general observation were revealed by the quantitative analyses. The number of periods the infants were observed to enter the playpen area was significantly higher for the FM infants than for the MM infants. Similar developmental trends were found for infant-partner nonspecific contact and visual contact. The FM infants scored significantly higher in all categories of appropriate sex behavior; similarly, their scores were higher in all categories of play behavior, in most instances significantly higher. The data for the development of nonmutual contact play are shown in Figure 3 and are illustrative of the play differences between groups. These differences were significant and paralleled those found for observed frequency of approach and avoidance noncontact play, which was also significant. The same trends are apparent for mutual contact and self-play although these effects are not significant.

Figures 4 and 5 provide an overview of the general differences between the males and females of both groups in the develop-

mental course of all types of sexual mounts and presents, appropriate or inappropriate, infantile or mature. These grouped scores were not analyzed for significance.

The MM infants exhibited significantly more infant-partner clasp-pull-bite responses than the FM infants (Figure 6). Although the highest frequency of this behavior was exhibited by the MM male infants, the mean scores for MM females exceeded those of FM males as well as FM females. Clasp-pull-bite responses were scored only when the behavior was judged to be an expression of aggression. If the behavior was observed in the course of normal infant play, it was not scored. This behavior pattern appears to be an early manifestation of peer aggression.

Mother and Infant Nonsocial Behavior

General observations. Each motherless mother exhibited a distinctive pattern of stereotypic pacing or backflipping similar to that shown by semisocial isolates in the Wisconsin Laboratory (Cross & Harlow, 1965). A striking finding was that three MM infants exhibited accurate copies of their own mother's stereotypic pattern. Such stereotypic behaviors were not observed in the adults or infants of the FM group. The motherless mothers frequently reacted to intensive infant-infant interactions involving their own infants with self-biting and cage shaking. The FM adults, on the other hand, initially reacted to these intensive interactions with threats toward the infant that was not their own. After approximately 3 mo. the FM mothers no longer reacted to the infant-infant play.

Quantitative analysis. The between-groups differences for self-grooming and self-biting were statistically higher in the adults of the experimental group. Although the mean scores for stereotypic behavior in the MM adult group were twice those of FM adults and the MM infants, scores were 20 times greater than those of the FM infants; the absolute scores for the infants were relatively low, and the effects were not significant.

In view of the quality of mother-infant

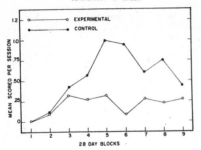

Fig. 4. Frequency of sexual mount by males.

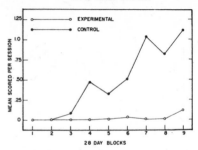

Fig. 5. Frequency of sexual present by females.

interaction in the MM group, it was expected that the MM infants would seek substitute oral and contact stimulation. Overall group differences in infant self-orality, self-clasp, and self-manipulation were significant and in the expected direction, the difference first appearing in the fourth month of age and increasing thereafter. The MM infants, as compared with the control infants, showed a significantly lower frequency of manual and oral exploration of physical objects, indicating a failure to follow the normal pattern of environmental exploration.

Discussion

A major difference between the motherless mothers observed by Seay et al. (1964) and those of the present experiment was that all four of the previous motherless mothers reacted with indifference or abusiveness toward their infants. At the outset of the present study, however, two of the laboratory-reared females, and, after a short time, a third female approached a modicum of adequate maternal behavior.

Possibly the behavioral differences between the two groups of motherless mothers stem from sampling errors in a highly variable population. Wide differences in maternal behavior toward firstborns have been found in a large group of socially deprived monkeys (see Harlow et al., 1966). Perhaps background differences between the groups have played a role in the behavioral differences. Both groups were comparable in experience up to 10 mo. of age; their experiences were comparable up to 21 mo. of age with the exception of MM A-1 of the present study, which was paired with another animal in a standard living cage. Also, both groups were tested with their infants in identical apparatus and under identical conditions. Nonetheless, there are differences in the mothers' histories after 21 mo. of age which could have been related to subsequent maternal behavior.

The statistical analyses of the present data indicate distinct and pervasive differences in maternal behavior between the feral-reared and laboratory-reared mothers that were similar to those reported by Seay et al. (1964). Although the behavior of two of the four motherless mothers of this group gave an overall, qualitative impression of adequacy from the start, there were significantly fewer occurrences of the basic infant-rearing responses such as cradling, nursing, and retrieving, commonly observed in normal monkey mothers. Thus, the differences between the feral-reared and laboratory-reared females of this study lie primarily on a quantitative continuum of maternal adequacy as opposed to the distinct qualitative differences observed in the previous study.

Actually a subtle qualitative maternal difference between groups was observed in the present study. There was an arbitrary quality about the maternal behavior of the motherless mothers as opposed to a predictability of maternal responsiveness in the feral mothers. Apparently through a variety of visual, vocal, or maturational cues, the FM infants were able to adequately respond to behavior patterns such as maternal rejection, which developed gradually and was gently administered in the FM group, allowing the infant to adapt slowly. However, in the MM group, even in those mothers whose behavior approached the normal range, maternal responsiveness was unsystematic and independent of any apparent cues. Devious and subtle methods of rejection were frequently used by these mothers. For example, MM 32 would press the head and back of her nursing infant solidly against the cage and slowly turn her body until the infant was forced off or pushed around to her dorsal surface. After a period of a few months the infants no longer became visibly upset by their mothers' capriciousness. This same arbitrary quality was also described by Seay et al. (1964).

The MM infants persisted in their at-

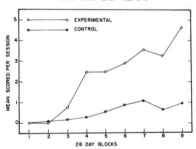

INFANT- INFANT CLASP-PULL-BITE

FIG. 6. Frequency of infant-infant clasp-pull-bite response.

tempts to gain physical contact with the mother even though the motherless mother often responded to such attempts with violent beatings. The two males that had to be initially hand fed by the nursery staff were more persistent than the nursed infants (females) in their attempts to attain any physical contact their mother would allow. Another finding of the previous study replicated here was that infants deprived of the normal amount of suckling indulged in some form of compensatory orality, self-directed in this study and peer directed in the previous study.

An extremely important difference between the results of the Seay et al. (1964) study and the present experiment was the marked deficit in social development suffered by the infants of our MM group. The previous researchers had expected a general depression of play behavior and a higher frequency of peer-directed aggression within the MM infant group, but the data failed to substantiate the aggression prediction and, except for the delay in peer interactions, revealed no significant deficits continuing in approach noncontact play and self-play. Significant differences in mutual contact play were no longer visible after 3 mo. In reexamining the results of the earlier investigation, the present authors found a number of nonsignificant differences in social development which were in the same direction as the significant differences reported above. In the present study the FM infants exhibited significantly higher frequencies in the categories of approach noncontact, avoidance noncontact, and nonmutual contact play. The same trend, though not significant, was also apparent in mutual contact and self-play. Conversely, infant-infant aggression as measured by clasp-pull-bite responses was observed with a significantly higher frequency in the MM group.

One possible reason for the peer interaction differences between these two studies is the differential group composition. Seay et al. (1964) observed a group of MM infants made up of three males and one female and an FM group of four male infants. The authors point out that their conclusions about the infant interactions were necessarily qualified by the difference in group composition. Subsequent findings (Sackett, 1965) of hyperaggressiveness in these same motherless-mother-reared animals at 3 yr. of age add weight to the hypothesis that the failure to uncover differences in the original investigation could have been a function of group composition and premature cessation of observations. An additional basis for the play differences may lie in the unusual behavior of the female in the Seay et al. (1964) group.

The deficiency in sexual behavior observed in the present MM infants strongly contrasts with the sexual precocity of the initial MM group. The lone female of the original group developed the female present pattern at an extremely early age and was judged at the time of observation to be persistent in seeking sexual stimulation from the three males. It is likely that her deviance led to the development of the high sex behavior scores of the group and also elevated the group's interaction scores. The replication group, on the other hand, had no sexually precocious member and was markedly depressed in play. There is reason to believe (Harlow, 1961) that infantile forms of sexual responses appear early in play and develop during the course of peer interaction into appropriate adult sexual behaviors. The second MM group, delayed and depressed in play and lacking a sexually aggressive member, lagged simultaneously in the development of play and sex behavior and thus developed in keeping with the predictions originally made for the Seay et al. (1964) MM group.

Previous studies (Alexander & Harlow, 1965) have found that animals deprived of mothers but given early and extensive peer experience make a relatively adequate social adjustment. Other reports (Alexander, 1966) indicated no persistent differences in play and sexual behavior between animals reared by normal mothers and allowed peer interaction from birth and two groups of infants reared by normal mothers but deprived of peer contact for 4 or 8 mo. However, Alexander (1966) reported that the 8-mo. peer-deprived group was hyperaggressive in its initial interaction with peers. Alexander also found that during the mother-infant isolation period, the mothers of the 8-mo. peer-deprived group were decidedly more punitive and threatening toward their infants. These findings clearly suggest that punitive and rejecting behaviors by the mothers produce hyperaggression in the infant either by some direct learning process or by impeding the infant's development of normal forms of social interaction.

The results of the present study support the conclusion that early social deprivation has a disrupting effect on the expression of adequate maternal behavior. They also suggest that quantity and quality of infant-mother interaction may play a decisive role in the development of the infant's social behavior.

REFERENCES

ALEXANDER, B. K. The effects of early peer deprivation on juvenile behavior of rhesus monkeys. Unpublished doctoral dissertation, University of Wisconsin, 1966.

ALEXANDER, B. K., & HARLOW, H. F. Social behavior of juvenile rhesus monkeys subjected to different rearing conditions during the first six months of life. Zool. Jb. Physiol., 1965, 71, 489–508.

BLOMQUIST, A. J., & HARLOW, H. F. The rhesus monkey program at the University of Wisconsin Primate Laboratory. Proc. Anim. Care Panel, 1961, 11, 57–64.

CROSS, H. A., & HARLOW, H. F. Prolonged and progressive effects of partial isolation on the behavior of macaque monkeys. J. exp. Res. Pers., 1965, 1, 39–49.

HANSEN, E. W. The development of maternal and infant behavior in the rhesus monkey. Unpublished doctoral dissertation, University of Wisconsin, 1962.

HARLOW, H. F. The development of affectional patterns in infant monkeys. In. B. M. Foss (Ed.), Determinants of infant behavior. New York: Wiley, 1961. Pp. 75–97.

HARLOW, H. F. Development of the second and third affectional systems in macaque monkeys. In T. T. Tourlentes, S. L. Pollack, & H. E. Himwich (Eds.), Research approaches to psychiatric problems: A symposium. New York: Grune & Stratton, 1962. Pp. 209–229.

HARLOW, H. F., HARLOW, M. K., DODSWORTH, R. O., & ARLING, G. L. Maternal behavior of rhesus monkeys deprived of mothering and peer associations in infancy. Proc. Amer. Phil. Soc., 1966, 110, 58–66.

HARLOW, H. F., & ZIMMERMANN, R. R. Affectional responses in the infant monkey. Science, 1959, 130, 421–432.

SACKETT, G. P. Effects of rearing conditions upon the behavior of rhesus monkeys (Macaca mulatta). Child Developm., 1965, 36, 855–868.

SEAY, B. M., ALEXANDER, B. K., & HARLOW, H. F. Maternal behavior of socially deprived rhesus monkeys. J. abnorm. soc. Psychol., 1964, 69, 345–354.

PART 5　Sensory Processes, Communication, and Orientation

Man has long been curious about the mental life of the creatures who share the earth with him, and he has posed many questions regarding the existence of "consciousness" and similar processes in animals. Some of these questions are forever unanswerable, but modern experimentation has conclusively demonstrated that many animals possess senses and means of communication and orientation that man does not have. Although experimentation on the topics included in this section is difficult and demanding, it can be most rewarding since many of the most interesting problems in animal behavior are found in these areas.

The first three selections are concerned with sensory processes. These papers illustrate three major methods available to us for the study of sensation in animals. One method involves training an animal to respond to a particular stimulus and then testing the limits of his perception in that modality. For example, the fact that many species can hear frequencies beyond the capacity of the human ear has been established in this fashion. A second method involves electrophysiological recording from receptors and relevant parts of the nervous system. This method has certain limitations. First, successful recording from a particular anatomical locus indicates that the system is operating up to that point, but tells us nothing of events further "upstream." Second, successful recording over the entire system offers only presumptive evidence that the animal perceives the stimulus. The method is most useful in working with animals that are difficult to condition, or in studying the electrophysiological responses of an animal whose sensory capacities are known. The third major method involves observation of an animal's "natural" responses to stimuli. The limitation here is that, while positive results indicate perception of the stimulus, lack of response does not mean that the animal is incapable of sensing the stimulus.

In the first reading, Catania presents behavioral and physiological evidence supporting the idea that pigeons are far-sighted when viewing objects located laterally to them and near-sighted for objects in front of them. Reading 37 concerns the question of hearing in turtles, a group that for many years was considered deaf. Gulick and Zwick present behavioral and electrophysiological evidence that turtles can, in fact, hear aerially conducted low-frequency sounds. In Reading 38, Gordon Burghardt makes use of the third method described above, that of observing the natural response of an animal to a stimulus. Different species of snakes prefer different kinds of prey. Burghardt shows that new-born, unfed snakes exhibit the same species differences in their responses to water extracts of the skin substances of various prey.

Our next major topic is that of animal communication. The sensory capacities of a species limit the range of stimuli to which that species can respond. But an animal usually responds to only a very restricted number of the many potential stimuli impinging on it at a given time. By one means or another, animals become particularly sensitive to, tuned to, certain stimuli. When these stimuli emanate from another animal and indicate to the recipient the emotional, motivational, or physiological state of the "sender," the process is called "communication." The various "displays" that members of certain species perform in particular circumstances are good examples. Such displays are considered by W. J. Smith in Reading 39. He proposes that, although the number of displays seen in a species may be considerably larger, the "messages" conveyed by the displays number only twelve.

Most of the displays described in Reading 39 involve visual or auditory communication. Animals are, of course, capable of communication by other senses. The chemical senses are particularly important in some species. A chemical produced by one animal and responded to by another of the same species is called a "pheromone." Much of the research on pheromones has involved insects. But pheromones are not the exclusive property of invertebrates, as we learn in Reading 40. Here Michael and Keverne demonstrate the operation of a pheromone in a primate.

It was noted above that communication is usually between members of the same species. But this is not always the case. Many animals respond to alarm reactions in members of other species. And man and his domestic animals have developed extensive interspecies communication. Attempts at developing even more sophisticated systems have involved home-raised chimpanzees. In Reading 41, W. N. Kellogg, a pioneer in the field, reviews such experiments, including the recent attempt to teach a chimpanzee the American sign language.

Science thrives on controversy. Providing that opposing theories are testable, nothing stimulates research better than disagreement. Such a dis-agreement has recently developed in regard to Karl von Frisch's classic studies of communication in honeybees. Do bees use the information con-tained in their dances? We enter in the middle of the argument with von Frisch responding to previous papers by D. L. Johnson and A. M. Wenner. Then Wenner and Johnson reply to von Frisch and, in Reading 44 with P. H. Wells, they provide further experimental evidence to support their position. Finally, Richard Dawkins offers an ingenious explanation of the findings reported in Reading 44. Can it account for the data? In a footnote in his recent book, *The Bee Language Controversy* (Educational Programs Improvement Corporation, 1971), Wenner writes that Dawkins' explanation requires that ". . . recruited bees would have to be misled both upwind and downwind from their 'intended' goals. The implication is that an animal could perceive an odor which is downwind from it." Is Wenner correct? This controversy is obviously not resolved to the satisfaction of all involved, and we can expect considerable research activity in the near future.

The last three papers in Part 5 are concerned with animal orientation. As the sun rises and sets, as the tides change, and with the turn of the seasons, animals move over the earth. This ceaseless motion occurs above, on, and under both land and water. What causes it? What guides it? We have learned much, but deep mysteries still exist.

In the first of the three papers, M. E. Meyer reviews four different hypotheses regarding bird orientation and navigation. Readings 47 and 48 concern overland orientation in newts. These papers reveal another scientific disagreement. In reading 47, Landreth and Ferguson indicate that these animals use a sun-compass mechanism in orientation, while, in the last selection, Grant, Anderson, and Twitty present evidence that homing orien-tation is accomplished by means of olfactory cues. Can both be correct?

ON THE VISUAL ACUITY OF THE PIGEON[1]

A. Charles Catania

SMITH KLINE AND FRENCH LABORATORIES

Several lines of evidence suggest that the pigeon is near-sighted for stimuli located in front of its beak and far-sighted for stimuli located to the sides of its head.

"The vision of the pigeon is of two types: for distant objects only one eye is used (monocular vision), while for grain or other close objects both eyes are used, looking forward (binocular vision)" (Levi, 1957, p. 378).

The effective use of an organism in behavioral research calls for a thorough understanding of its sensory systems. An examination of the pigeon's visual system, therefore, is prompted by the prominent role of visual stimuli in pigeon experiments (*e.g.*, Ferster and Skinner, 1957). The present note reviews some literature on visual acuity in the pigeon, and attempts to characterize its visual system in a useful way. Several lines of evidence suggest that the pigeon's eye contains a hyperopic or far-sighted region, used in lateral or "panoramic" viewing, and a myopic or near-sighted region, used in anterior or "binocular-stereoscopic" viewing.

Evidence for a hyperopic lateral field. A large part of the evidence for a hyperopic lateral field in the eye of the pigeon comes from casual observation, as in Levi: "The pigeon breeder, no doubt, has many times seen his birds cock their heads to one side and view with alarm some object in the distant sky. Many times the object is beyond the vision of the fancier or is a hawk or some other bird in flight so far distant as to be barely seen" (Levi, 1957, p. 249). In fact, lateral viewing by the pigeon seems to have been as much taken for granted by earlier investigators as anterior viewing is taken for granted by current investigators, who project stimuli on the response key at which the pigeon pecks. For example, lateral distance viewing is assumed rather than observed in this description: "When I observed the Pigeon as it squatted on the sill just in front of my window, about 40-50 feet above the ground, the eye facing me moved all the time, as probably also did the eye looking in the other direction toward the buildings opposite and the court below where people were moving about" (Polyak, 1957, p. 946). In some experiments, the assumption of distance viewing is stated in a fairly explicit way: "It was deemed necessary to have the fields removed from the point of choice sufficient to insure approximate distance accommodation" (Gundlach, 1933, p. 327), whereas the assumption of lateral viewing is implicit, if indicated at all. Accommodation for focus on the fovea, the effective region of the retina in lateral viewing, is implicit in Gundlach, Chard and Skahen's (1945) discussion of the mechanism of accommodation in the pigeon.

The available data on visual acuity in the pigeon come from experiments that probably involved only lateral distance viewing, and provide strong support for a hyperopic lateral field. Hamilton and Goldstein (1933) and Chard (1939), both using jumping stands, are in good agreement: "The near point of accommodation is between 31 and 66 cm." (Hamilton and Goldstein, 1933, p. 197); and, ". . . it seems likely that the near-point of accommodation has been approached or even passed at 40 cm." (Chard, 1939, p. 607). Hamilton and Goldstein supplemented their data with a skiascopic determination of the refraction of the eyes of their pigeons, which were between 0.5 and 1.5 Diopters hyperopic. Chard showed that the decrease in the pigeon's visual acuity (minimum separable), when stimuli were brought closer than the near point, was rapid. More recently, Catania (1963a) found it impossssible to establish discriminations of forms that were only 1 to 3 in. from the pigeon's eye, and concluded that "the pigeon cannot accommodate for lateral stimuli that are very close to its eye" (Catania, 1963a, p. 628).

Evidence for a myopic anterior field. One problem in the analysis of the pigeon's fields of view is the difficulty of seeing where the pigeon is looking. For example, Levine states: ". . . the experimenter was never able to detect by observation which eye the pigeon was using. The head movements were very rapid, and . . . [one] eye appeared to look at the stimulus as often as did the other" (Levine, 1945a, p. 123). Casual observation, in this case, provides conflicting evidence. An anterior myopic field has been noted by Levi, quoted above, by Chard and Gundlach, and by Polyak: "The pigeon undoubtedly possesses a visual field which affords binocular vision, although the bird appears to use mo-

[1]This note is an outgrowth of research conducted at the Psychological Laboratories, Harvard University, and supported by NSF Grant G8621 (B. F. Skinner, Principal Investigator). Reprints may be obtained from the author, Dept. of Psychology, New York University, University Heights, New York, N.Y. 10453.

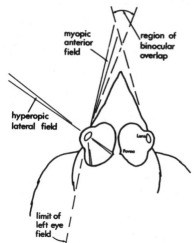

myopic
anterior
field

region of
binocular
overlap

hyperopic
lateral field

Lens

Fovea

limit of
left eye
field

Fig. 1. A highly schematic diagram of the visual fields of the pigeon. Angles are not drawn to scale. The two acute fields, arbitrarily shown subtending a small visual angle, are represented for the pigeon's left eye: the anterior myopic field, for stimuli in the region of the beak, and the lateral hyperopic field, for stimuli to one side of the head. These two fields are separated by a large but acute angle. The anterior myopic fields of the two eyes intersect in the region of the binocular overlap, at a locus presumably modifiable by either accommodation or eye movements. According to an oculist's measurement of a live pigeon (Chard and Gundlach, 1938), the region of binocular overlap is about 24°, or 12° beyond the midline for each eye, with maximal eye movements taken into account; the total field for each eye is a little more than 180°, and the blind region at the rear is therefore 18-20°. The hyperopic lateral fields of the two eyes form an angle of considerably less than 180°. The pecten and optic disk, temporal and ventral of the central fovea, have not been shown. It is unlikely that they are involved in vision in either the anterior or the lateral field (cf. Walls, 1942, p. 651).

nocular vision much of the time" (Chard and Gundlach, 1938, p. 256); ". . . it is evident from their behavior that they [pigeons] do possess a binocular field" (Chard and Gundlach, 1938, p. 271); ". . . the House Sparrow (*Passer domesticus*) and the Domestic Pigeon (*Columba livia*), with their laterally placed eyeballs, ordinarily use their eyes monocularly for observation. . . . In pecking grain or aiming at an angleworm just prior to seizing it, the final act that follows the critical examination, however, these birds use both eyes simultaneously in a binocular stereoscopic way" (Polyak, 1957, p. 946). Levine, on the other hand, would seem to rule out such a field: "When fixating an object, practically all birds, including the pigeon and chicken, do not look directly at it with both eyes but turn the head to one side. They thereby fixate the object with only one eye" (Levine, 1945a, p. 126).

The most convincing evidence for a myopic anterior field comes from the large body of operant research with the pigeon: stimuli projected on the response key at which the

pigeon pecks are generally directly in front of its beak, and these stimuli have been shown to exert a powerful control over the pigeon's key-pecking (*e.g.*, Ferster and Skinner, 1957; Skinner, 1960).

The "visual trident." Casual observations of pigeons in operant experiments support the notion that the pigeon is laterally hyperopic and anteriorly myopic. Stimuli projected on the response key tend to exert more powerful control than stimuli located at some distance behind the key; on the other hand, nearby lateral stimuli do not seem to be as effective as more distant lateral stimuli (Catania, 1963a). As an example of the effectiveness of distant lateral stimuli, the author has obtained excellent discriminative control of the pigeon's pecking with a row of lamps, ⅝-in. apart center-to-center, projecting from the front of the panel and located 10 in. to one side of the pigeon's response key.

The general characteristics of the pigeon's visual system, inferred from the present account, are illustrated in Fig. 1. The two acute fields are shown for the pigeon's left eye: the anterior myopic field, for stimuli in the region of the beak, and the lateral hyperopic field, for stimuli located to one side of the head. The acute anterior and lateral regions are shown subtending a small visual angle, by analogy with the small visual angle of the central area of acute vision in the eye of man. It has been argued, however, that acute vision is characteristic of the pigeon's entire visual field: "One had here a good demonstration of the tremendous advantage of a wide field of view, as the Pigeon has. The same is true of other Vertebrates which have panoramic, or rather largely panoramic, vision, practically amounting to a complete circle. It permits them to see simultaneously most of the horizon and to see it with about the same high acuity as that possessed by Man, as other observations of the Pigeons and Sparrows indicate" (Polyak, 1957, p. 947). This sort of account seems to stem more from the fine grain of the peripheral retina of the bird eye than from behavioral evidence, as Walls suggests: "The proverbial resolving power of the bird eye is based partly upon . . . the dense concentration of the cones and the high ratio of optic nerve fibers to visual cells" (Walls, 1942, p. 661).

In any case, the main point of Fig. 1 is that the pigeon's visual field includes both myopic and hyperopic regions, whatever the extent of these regions. It will be convenient to assume also that these are regions of high acuity relative to the rest of the visual field, although no evidence is available on this point. The acuity of the anterior field, however, does not have to be very great to account for the accurate discrimination of stimuli in front of the beak, because stimuli close to the eye necessarily subtend a relatively large visual angle. The region need be only somewhat more finely grained than other parts of the retina.

The visual system represented in Fig. 1 agrees well with Polyak's general characterization of the visual system of birds: "The avian visual apparatus represents a three-pronged mechanism with three visual axes—a common binocular axis directed forward and two monocular axes on the sides, the 'visual trident' of Rochon-Duvigneaud" (Polyak, 1957, p. 283).

Acuity, anatomy, and physiological optics. The validity of the present account depends in part on the structure of the pigeon's eye. Both its retina and its optical apparatus should be capable of resolving visual stimuli in the ways that have been discussed.

Polyak has commented on the diversity of the locally differentiated structures of bird's eyes: "Frequently two foveae are found in each eye: a central, nasal or anterior, and a lateral, temporal or posterior, area and fovea. . . . the two lateral foveae of both eyes apparently serve as an instrument in binocular stereoscopic vision, while the central foveae function independently" (Polyak, 1957, p. 283).[2] The pigeon, however, possesses only a single fovea in each eye, the central fovea (see Fig. 1). Probably the absence of a posterior fovea, to subserve acute vision in the binocular region, has been an important determinant of the assumption that the pigeon is a bird of predominantly "panoramic" rather than "binocular-stereoscopic" vision.

The absence of an anatomically distinct fovea does not rule out the possibility of a functionally distinct region on the pigeon's retina. Thus, it may be relevant that Chard and Gundlach, in discussing the diversity of the layers of the pigeon's retina, state: "One possible explanation of the diversity of these layers is the fact that the bird cannot move the eye in its socket a great deal for foveal vision. This might result in a structural differentiation of various parts so that some would, in part, take over some of the functions of the fovea" (Chard and Gundlach, 1938, p. 270). Walls has observed that: "The imperative need for accurate distance judgment . . . has lead to specializations of the temporal part of the retina. Some of these are slight, like the 'red field' of the hen; but in many different groups of birds, independently of each other, a second fovea has been differentiated in the temporal quadrant" (Walls, 1942, p. 307). It also may be significant that, in those birds with two foveae, the posterior fovea is usually less well-differentiated from the rest of the retina than the central fovea: "Except in the eagles and in *Apus apus*, the temporal foveae are inferior in construction to

the central ones" (Walls, 1942, p. 308); ". . . the grain of its photoreceptors [the posterior fovea of the barn swallow] also seems to be rougher than that in the central fovea" (Polyak, 1957, p. 856). These various observations call for a more detailed examination of the retina of the pigeon than is available at present.

The eyes of many birds provide certain advantages for anterior stimuli. In the barn swallow, for example, ". . . binocular convergence and fixation are [assisted by] . . . the position of the corneae, which face, as in the half-profile, in the antero-lateral direction . . . [and] a slight distortion of the corneal curvature similar to the 'anterior bulge' of the Fishes, because of which the more sharply curved anterior segment of the cornea is more favorable to the passage of rays coming from the direction of the beak" (Polyak, 1957, p. 853). The pigeon also possesses the former advantage, though it is not clear whether it possesses the latter. In any case, there appears to be no anatomical reason to reject the notion that the pigeon's optical apparatus is adequate for acute near vision in the binocular region.

A final suggestive property of the pigeon's optical system is its range of accommodation: ". . . the cornea itself provides a range of accommodation of something of the order of 17 Diopters. This is a very large figure when it is recalled that the maximal human range of accommodation is around 10 to 12 Diopters" (Gundlach, Chard and Skahen, 1945, p. 41). As mentioned above, the pigeon's eye is 0.5 to 1.5 Diopters hyperopic. Given this ametropic error and the 17 Diopter range of accommodation, the predicted near point of accommodation is about 6 cm (*cf.* Davson, 1963, p. 421), which is not in agreement with the experimentally-obtained near point of roughly 40 cm. The large range of accommodation, therefore, may indicate the involvement of an additional factor (in the eye of the turtle, for example, the 40-50 Diopter range of accommodation permits adequate refraction in both air and water). It may be that, in the eye of the pigeon, accommodation serves not only the central fovea but also, in binocular viewing, a differentiated region of the posterior retina.

Acuity and evolution. The conclusion that the pigeon is anteriorly near-sighted and laterally far-sighted is also supported by evolutionary considerations. The pigeon must be near-sighted if it is to see, directly in front of its beak, the food that it eats, whereas it must be far-sighted if it is to see, in the lateral "panoramic" field, the approach of predators from the distance. An organism with such a visual system might have a distinct competitive advantage. For this reason, the visual systems of other organisms with "panoramic" vision (*e.g.*, deer, rabbits) might be expected to have similar characteristics.

A related argument has been made to account for the correlation between frontality

---

[2]It should be noted that "lateral" has a different referent in "lateral field" than in "lateral fovea." A "lateral field" is lateral with respect to the pigeon's head; it is the field viewed by the central fovea. A "lateral fovea" is lateral with respect to the pigeon's eyeball; it is the fovea that views the anterior field. Confusion may be avoided by restricting the terms "lateral" and "anterior" to fields, and labelling the corresponding foveae "central" and "posterior," or "nasal" and "temporal."

and predacity: ". . . the hunters tend toward frontality so as to have the best vision of the prey they are pursuing, while the hunted tend to retain laterality of eye position so as to be able to detect an enemy coming from any direction" (Walls, 1942, p. 290). Such an argument, however, deals with the evolution of different degrees of frontality in different species, rather than with the evolution of different fields within a given species.

Horizon-fixation may also have been important in the evolution of the lateral field, but it has usually been cited to account for the extended or "troughlike" areae or foveae, primarily found in open plain or water birds (Pumphrey, 1961).

Acuity and attention. It is generally assumed that looking behavior is controlled in part by the location of objects in the field relative to the location of the acute regions on the retina: ". . . the presence of more than one small area of distinct vision suggests alternative regions of accurate fixation. The most reasonable determinant of the use of one of these regions would appear to be the location of the object fixated in the visual field of the bird" (Levine, 1945b, p. 141); "We infer that the shift in locus of the stimuli forced the bird to shift from one retinal fixation point to another" (Levine, 1952, p. 25). The present analysis indicates that both position in the field and distance may determine the "distinctiveness" of visual cues to the pigeon (*e.g.,* Jones, 1954).

Experiments on attention in the pigeon indicate that the extent to which a pigeon attends to one or another part of a stimulus complex is controlled by the relative locations of the parts of the complex. Reynolds (1961), for example, presented a stimulus complex made up of forms and colors projected on the response key, and lamps located to one side of the key. After an analysis of the control of the pigeon's pecking by various parts of this complex, Reynolds suggested that "the effective stimulus was the difference in the effects of the high and low side-lamp intensities upon the form and color combinations as they appeared on the response key" (Reynolds, 1961, p. 208). This implies that the pigeon attended to a nearby anterior stimulus, such as the glare of the lamps on the key, in preference to a nearby lateral stimulus, the lamps themselves.

Experiments on matching-to-sample behavior in the pigeon (Skinner, 1950) provide another relevant example. In these experiments, a stimulus is presented on the center key of three response keys. A peck on this key turns on stimuli on both side keys, one of which matches the center key stimulus. A peck on the matching key is then reinforced. The initial peck on the center key guarantees that the pigeon attends to the stimulus on that key; the present account suggests that this attention involves, at least to some extent, a simple kind of stimulus clarification, in that

the peck guarantees that the stimulus is in focus for the pigeon.

Acuity and interocular transfer. Levine (1945a, 1945b, 1952), in a series of experiments on interocular transfer in the pigeon, distinguishes between views in front of or below the bird's head: " 'Anterostral' will be used hereafter to refer to the position of stimuli when they are lying in front of the bird, and the line of regard between the stimulus and the eye forms as acute angle with the ground or is parallel to the ground. 'Subrostral' will be used to refer to the position of stimuli when they are lying directly below the head of the bird, so that the line of regard is approximately perpendicular to the ground" (Levine, 1945b, p. 138). This distinction was based on the finding that discriminations among subrostral stimuli transferred from one eye to the other, but discriminations among anterostral stimuli did not. Levine also was not able to demonstrate subrostral to anterostral transfer in a single eye. With different procedures, Catania (1963b) demonstrated complete interocular transfer. The present account may bear on Levine's findings.

Levine distinguished between anterostral and subrostral fields on the basis of the placement of stimuli in a modified Lashley jumping stand (*cf.* Halstead and Yacorzynski, 1938). This specification did not necessarily correspond to stimulated regions of the pigeon's retinae, determined by where the bird looked. Anterostral discriminations involved stimuli mounted vertically at the backs of the platforms to which the pigeons jumped, whereas subrostral discriminations involved stimuli mounted horizontally on the floors of the platforms. In most cases, the subrostral stimuli "were much closer to the eyes of the bird [and] . . . extended to a position directly below the bird's eyes" (Levine, 1945b, p. 136). This suggests that the pigeon viewed the anterostral stimuli laterally and the subrostral stimuli anteriorly. Thus, the difference in distance could have made generalization between anterostral and subrostral stimuli in a given eye less likely, even without taking into account a possible difference in the grain of the two retinal regions. Also, some loss in transfer may have depended on time the pigeon spent in learning to fixate stimuli in their new locations in a test for transfer.

The present analysis also may account for the more complex case, in which subrostral discriminations transferred completely from one eye to the other but anterostral discriminations did not. To respond appropriately to the distant anterostral stimuli in the jumping stand, the pigeon had to cock its head to one side, however briefly, at the time of jumping, to land on the "safe" platform (if the pigeon jumped to the incorrect stimulus, on the other platform, the platform collapsed, dropping the pigeon into a net). Thus, the pigeon learned to look and jump with a particular head and body orientation. When the blindfold was shifted from one eye to the other, in a test for transfer, the pigeon probably cocked its head to the usual side, at least for the first few trials, before learning to look and jump with the new eye. This might have confounded the test for transfer. With the subrostral stimuli, however, the pigeon probably looked at the stimuli, which were close by on the floor of the platforms, anteriorly and so binocularly. Consequently, it could look and jump with the same head and body orientation with either eye. Under these circumstances, the shift of the blindfold from one eye to the other could not have interfered with the test for transfer.

These interpretations may not account fully for Levine's findings, which were supplemented by a variety of control experiments. Nevertheless, the analysis suggests that the anterior-lateral distinction is more relevant to the proper interpretation of these experiments than the anterostral-subrostral distinction. Perhaps the results were determined more by the pigeon's looking behavior than by peculiarities of the hookups in its brain. It is interesting to note that, if the pigeon possessed two foveae in each eye, Levine's dichotomy between anterostral and subrostral fields would more likely have been a distinction between the anterior and lateral fields.

Conclusion. The present account has a practical bearing on ways to arrange apparatus for presenting visual stimuli to pigeons. Because the pigeon seems to be anteriorly near-sighted and laterally far-sighted, anterior stimuli should be located directly on the response key or, if behind it, not far from the pecking surface. Lateral stimuli, on the other hand, should be placed at a fair distance to one side of the key. The latter case provides some advantages over the usual presentation of stimuli on the key. For example, an effective stimulus continuum can be arranged simply by mounting a row of lamps to one side of the key. Other kinds of displays can be arranged laterally without the miniaturization, and its related optical problems, forced by the small area of the standard key.

These practical considerations drawn from the present account point up the importance of understanding an organism's sensory systems. Such an understanding depends on a knowledge of both the behavior of an organism and its anatomy and physiology, and may be crucial in an experiment at any point from the design of its apparatus to the interpretation of its results.

REFERENCES

Catania, A. C. Techniques for the control of monocular and binocular viewing in the pigeon. *J. exp. Anal. Behav.*, 1963, **6**, 627-629. (a)

Catania, A. C. Interocular transfer of discriminations in the pigeon. Paper read at the Eastern Psychological Assn., New York, 1963. (b)

Chard, R. D. and Gundlach, R. H. The structure of the eye of the homing pigeon. *J. comp. Psychol.*, 1938, **25**, 249-272.

Davson, H. *The physiology of the eye.* (2nd ed.) Boston: Little, Brown, 1963.

Ferster, C. B. and Skinner, B. F. *Schedules of reinforcement.* New York: Appleton-Century-Crofts, 1957.

Gundlach, R. H. The visual acuity of homing pigeons. *J. comp. Psychol.*, 1933, **16**, 327-342.

Gundlach, R. H., Chard, R. D., and Skahen, J. R. The mechanism of accommodation in pigeons. *J. comp. Psychol.*, 1945, **38**, 27-42.

Halstead, W. and Yacorzynski, G. A jumping method for establishing differential responses in pigeons. *J. genet. Psychol.*, 1938, **52**, 227-231.

Hamilton, W. F. and Goldstein, J. L. Visual acuity and accommodation in the pigeon. *J. comp. Psychol.*, 1933, **15**, 193-197.

Jones, L. V. Distinctiveness of color, form and position cues for pigeons. *J. comp. physiol. Psychol.*, 1954, **47**, 253-257.

Levi, W. M. *The pigeon.* Columbia, S. C.: R. L. Bryan Co., 1957.

Levine, J. Studies in the interrelations of central nervous structures in binocular vision: I. The lack of bilateral transfer of visual discriminative habits acquired monocularly by the pigeon. *J. genet. Psychol.*, 1945, **67**, 105-129. (a)

Levine, J. Studies in the interrelations of central nervous structures in binocular vision: II. The conditions under which interocular transfer of discriminative habits takes place in the pigeon. *J. genet. Psychol.*, 1945, **67**, 131-142. (b)

Levine, J. Studies in the interrelations of central nervous structures in binocular vision: III. Localization of the memory trace as evidenced by the lack of inter- and intraocular habit transfer in the pigeon. *J. genet. Psychol.*, 1952, **81**, 19-27.

Polyak, S. *The vertebrate visual system.* Chicago: Univ. of Chicago, 1957.

Pumphrey, R. J. Sensory organs: vision. In Marshall, A. J. (ed.) *The biology and comparative physiology of birds.* Vol. 2. N. Y.: Academic Press, 1961, 55-68.

Reynolds, G. S. Attention in the pigeon. *J. exp. Anal. Behav.*, 1961, **4**, 203-208.

Skinner, B. F. Are theories of learning necessary? *Psychol. Rev.*, 1950, **57**, 193-216.

Skinner, B. F. Pigeons in a pelican. *Amer. Psychologist*, 1960, **15**, 28-37.

Walls, G. L. *The vertebrate eye.* Bloomfield Hills, Mich.: Cranbrook Press, 1942.

(37) AUDITORY SENSITIVITY OF THE TURTLE[1]

W. L. GULICK[2] AND HARRY ZWICK
University of Delaware

Auditory sensitivity functions were obtained by electro-physiological methods for the turtle, *Pseudemys scripta,* and these were compared to behavioral threshold data obtained under comparable stimulation conditions. The turtle can hear tones between 20 and 1000 cps with maximum sensitivity in the range from 200 to 700 cps. Data support the electrical hypothesis of auditory nerve action.

As a consequence of meager attention, little is known about the functional status of the ear of the turtle. In 1915 Andrews demonstrated hearing in the turtle by means of an avoidance conditioning paradigm. Yet a replication of her study by Kuroda (1923, 1925) failed to obtain any evidence of hearing. Likewise, the experiments of Karimova (1958) and Chernomordikov (1958) indicate that the turtle is deaf. A review of the literature on hearing in the turtle led Munn (1955) to conclude that they are deaf.

In 1960 McGill wrote, perhaps more cautiously, that, ". . . hearing in the turtles is still a question" (p. 167). His caution was probably well-advised because of the electrophysiological data which suggest functional activity of the turtle's auditory system up to and including the auditory nerve.

Wever and Bray (1931) obtained synchronized responses from the auditory nerve of the painted turtle for tones between 100 and 1,200 cps, although responses to stimuli above 500 cps were feeble. Adrian, Craik, and Sturdy (1938) obtained responses from the auditory nerve to stimuli between 50 and 500 cps with maximum sensitivity at 100 cps. More recently, Wever and Vernon (1956 a, b, c,) found the cochlear response for several species of turtle uniformly sensitive to tones in the region from 100 to 700 cps. Weaker potentials were obtained for stimuli above 700 cps, and beyond 3000 cps injurious intensities were required to produce measurable responses.

Behavioral and electrophysiological data concerning hearing in the turtle are not in agreement with each other. Whereas the behavioral data, although somewhat contradictory, favor the conclusion that turtles are deaf, the electrophysiological literature is surprisingly consistent in its indication that the auditory system of the turtle is a

1 This research was supported by the University of Delaware Research Foundation and was done in the Physiology Laboratory, Department of Psychology, University of Delaware. Data cited on behavioral measures of auditory sensitivity in the turtle were obtained by Dr. W. C. Patterson in the Delaware laboratory as a doctoral dissertation. A full treatment of his method and data will be published elsewhere.
2 Now at Department of Psychology, Dartmouth College.

functional system. Both the cochlear and auditory nerve potentials show maximum sensitivity in the frequency range from 100 to approximately 700 cps.

Although Wever and Venon have demonstrated the general nature of the cochlear response in the turtle, the purpose of the present study was to obtain electrophysiological data from the cochlea of the turtle and compare them with behavioral auditory thresholds obtained in this laboratory (Patterson, 1965) under comparable stimulation conditions.

METHOD

Subjects

Four adult turtles, *Pseudemys scripta,* each weighing approximately 1.9 kg were used. The turtles were housed in aquaria in which the water temperature was maintained at 32° C. Weekly diets consisted of 150 mg of raw beef and fish distributed over three feedings.

Surgery

Anesthesia was produced with sodium pentobarbital (Nembutal-Abbott, 50/cc) administered intraperitoneally in a dosage of 0.7 cc/kg. A midline skin incision on the dorsal surface of the head gave access to the temporalis muscle which was retracted laterally to expose the suture between the paroccipital and supraoccipital bones. Midway along this suture a small hole was drilled which accommodated a hollow tube through which passed the active electrode insulated except at its tip. The indifferent electrode was affixed to the exposed temporalis muscle.

Apparatus

Pure tones were generated with an audio-oscillator (Hewlett-Packard, 200 AB) the output of which fed through an attenuator (Hewlett-Packard, 350 B) to a driver unit (University, ID-60). Sound was conducted to the tympanic membrane through a closed tube which terminated one millimeter away from the side of the turtle's head. Sound pressure was measured with a condensor microphone equipped with a probe tube located at the tympanic membrane. Signals picked up from the cochlea passed through a low-level preamplifier (Tektronix, 122) and were measured with an audio spectrometer (Brüel and Kjaer, 2019), used as a selective voltmeter. Oscillator signals were tuned for maximum transmission through the filter networks of the spectrometer.

During stimulation and recording procedures each animal was isolated in an electrically shielded room.

Procedure

Intensity functions were obtained for each turtle for frequencies of 100, 200, 320, 400, 500, 640, 800, 1000, and 2000 cps. Each function was obtained by increasing the sound intensity in 5 db steps and recording the amplitude of the cochlear response. The order of frequencies studied was different for each animal. So as not to injure the ear, each intensity function was terminated before the response reached its maximum but after it ceased to show linearity.

RESULTS

The data from the present experiment indicate that the turtle can hear aerial sound from 20 to 1000 cps with maximum sensitivity in the range of 200 to 600 cps. Above 600 cps sensitivity decreases rapidly until at 1000 cps evidence of hearing, as determined electrophysiologically, was obtained only at extremely high intensities. In Figure 1 the broken line represents the intensity required at each of several frequencies to produce a cochlear response of 0.3 microvolts. The solid

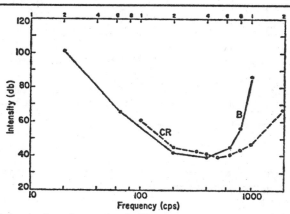

Fig. 1. Behavioral auditory threshold curve (B) and an equal cochlear response curve (CR) for the turtle *Pseudemys scripta*. Each curve based on data from four turtles. Intensity is expressed in db re: 0.0002 dyne/cm². The cochlear response magnitude was constant at 0.3 microvolts.

line represents an averaged absolute auditory threshold based on four turtles, and it is representative of each. Variability of the behavioral threshold (solid line) upon repeated measures after a 30-day lapse was surprisingly small (±3 db). The fact that the two functions parallel each other through the frequency range of 100 to 640 cps suggests that the magnitude of the cochlear response at threshold is a constant value in the turtle, regardless of frequency except at the upper extreme where hearing is worse than would be expected if the cochlear response were the sole determinant of auditory sensitivity.

In Figure 2 are presented individual sensitivity functions for each of four turtles showing the intensity required to produce a 0.3 microvolt cochlear response at various frequencies. These data are similar but not identical to those obtained by Wever and Vernon (1956) for the same species, as shown in Figure 3.

The cochlear potential shows a progressive and regular increase with intensity until the higher levels when overloading leads to negative acceleration. Typical intensity functions are shown in Figure 4. These functions show an abbreviated range of linearity compared with the mammals and birds. One would expect, therefore, that such a restricted dynamic range would characterize an auditory system that was inferior in mediating loudness discriminations inasmuch as the

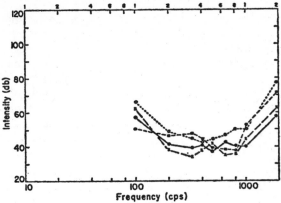

Fig. 2 Sensitivity functions for each of four turtles showing the intensity in db re:
0.0002 dyne/cm² required to produce a 0.3 microvolt cochlear response at various
frequencies.

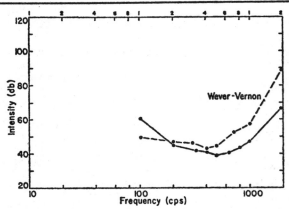

Fig. 3 Comparison of equal cochlear response curves (0.3 microvolt). Solid
circles represent data from this experiment (n = 4), whereas open circles summarize
data from Wever and Vernon (n = 3). All turtles are *Pseudemys scripta*.

cochlear potential from threshold magnitude (0.3 μV) to maximum
(3.0 μV) represents only a 20 db increase.

Wever and Vernon (1956) have presented similar functions insofar
as range and slope are concerned. There is, however, one marked
difference between the intensity functions of Figure 4 and those obtained
by them. Our functions are linear through most of the range, whereas
their functions begin to depart from linearity much earlier. We believe
inner ear temperature to be an important factor which might account
for this difference in linearity. We observed that warming the ear
extended the limit of linearity.

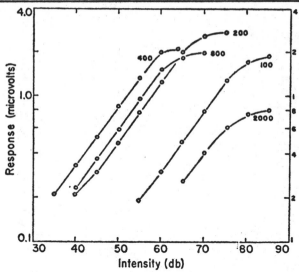

Fig. 4 Representative intensity functions showing the progressive increase in cochlear response with sound intensity (db re: 0.0002 dyne/cm²) for each of several frequencies.

DISCUSSION

The evidence obtained in this experiment clearly indicates that the turtle can hear low frequency sounds borne by air, and that cochlear response magnitude bears a systematic relationship to behavioral thresholds. Maximum sensitivity of the acoustic mechanism of the turtle is the same whether determined behaviorally or electrophysiologically. This certainly adds considerable weight to Wever's claim of the relationship of the cochlear response to hearing. Departure of the two different types of sensitivity curves (Figure 1) at high frequencies suggests that the upper limit of frequency sensitivity as determined behaviorally is due to some factor other than the action of the hair cells of the cochlea. Behavioral data obtained with the head submerged would undoubtedly alter the shape of the behavioral absolute threshold function obtained in this experiment, particularly at the higher frequencies. The nature of the turtle's sensitivity to water-borne sound, however, remains to be determined.

In an experiment on the relationship between auditory sensitivity and the magnitude of the cochlear potential, McGill (1959) demonstrated with the cat that at behavioral threshold the cochlear response was no greater than 0.01 μV over most of the frequency range studied. Our estimate of the threshold response for the turtle at 0.3 μV seems, therefore, erroneously high. Let us consider briefly why the threshold trigger required by the turtle is so much greater than that found by McGill for the cat.

McGill (1959) found that, "a more sensitive animal generally produces a cochlear potential of greater magnitude for a given sound-pressure level than a less sensitive animal produces, and a more sensitive animal generally produces a cochlear potential of lesser magnitude for behavioral-threshold sound-pressure level than a less sensitive animal produces" (p. 206). He was, of course, referring to animals within a species. Nevertheless, the same line of reasoning which he used and which Wever and Lawrence (1954) have used, applies across species as well. Data from the present experiment are certainly consistent with his conclusion.

An important factor which certainly influences the magnitude of the cochlear response at behavioral threshold is the distribution of energy along the basilar membrane. In an ear like that of the turtle, one would expect a general spread of energy along the membrane rather than, as would be expected in the mammalian ear, a concentration of energy varying in location with frequency. When the spread of energy is broad, more energy is required to reach neural thresholds. Wever (1949) anticipated this when he suggested that, ". . . it is more advantageous when the quantity of energy is small, to focus it on only a few (neural) elements rather than to spread it over a great many." Accordingly, in the mammal one would expect the cochlear potential magnitude at behavioral threshold to be highest for the low tones where the spread of energy is greatest, lowest for the high tones where the spread of energy is most restricted, and intermediate for the middle tones. This is exactly what McGill found in his study of the cat.

The implication for the turtle's auditory mechanism is as follows: the spread of energy is probably broad for all tones to which the turtle responds because of the nature of the mechanical action of the ear. This supposition is consistent with the fact that the trigger level is relatively high, and with the fact that the potential at threshold does not vary in magnitude as a function of frequency.

Even in its frequency range of maximum sensitivity (200 to 700 cps), the turtle requires sound pressures above those required for human threshold. Nevertheless, the ear appears sufficiently sensitive to suggest that hearing may play some functional role in the turtle's normal behavior. Two situations are apparent: namely, protection and mating. The role of vibratory sensibility remains to be determined in detail, but Patterson (1965) has shown unequivocally that the turtle is sensitive to bodily vibration even when the columellar bones are bilaterally transected. The relative utility of hearing and sensing body vibration is unknown.

Carr (1952) indicates that there is some evidence that certain species of turtle vocalize with a bark or grunt, ". . . as a regular and perhaps functional feature of their mating program . . ." (p. 17). Certainly most instances of a "voice" credited to turtles is unjustified and probably represents sounds produced during exhalation or noise from mutual contact of parts of the body. Nevertheless, a careful study of the frequency components of sounds emitted by the turtle might be well worth the undertaking.

REFERENCES

ADRIAN, E. D., CRAIK, K. J. W. & STURDY, R. S. 1938. The electrical response of the auditory mechanism in cold-blooded vertebrates. *Proc. Roy. Soc. London, B.*, 125, 435-455.

ANDREWS, O. 1915. The ability of turtles to discriminate between sounds. *Bull. Wisc. Nat. Hist. Soc.*, 13, 189-195.

CARR, A. 1952. *Handbook of Turtles.* Ithaca, New York: Comestock.

CHERNOMORDIKOV, V. V. 1958. On the physiology of the auditory analyzer in turtles. *Zh. vyssh. nervn. Deiatel.*, 8, 109-115.

KARIMOVA, M. M. 1958. On the conditioned reflex characteristics of the auditory analyzer in turtles. *Zh. vyssh. nervn. Deiatel.*, 8, 103-108.

KURODA, R. 1923. Studies in audition reptiles. *J. comp. Psychol.*, 3, 26-36.

KURODA, R. 1925. A contribution to the subject of hearing in tortoises. *J. comp. Psychol.*, 5, 285-291.

McGILL, T. E. 1959. Auditory sensitivity and the magnitude of the cochlear potential. *Annals Otol., Rhinol., Laryngol.*, 68, 1-15.

McGILL, T. E. 1960. A review of hearing in amphibians and reptiles. *Psychol. Bull.*, 57, 165-168.

MUNN, N. L. 1955. *The Evolution and Growth of Human Behavior.* New York: Houghton Mifflin.

PATTERSON, W. C. 1965. Hearing in the turtle. Unpublished doctoral dissertation, University of Delaware.

POLIAKOV, K. L. 1930. The physiology of the olfactory and auditory analyzers in the turtle. *Russian J. gen. Psychol.*, 13, 161-178.

WEVER, E. G. & BRAY, C. W. 1931. Auditory nerve responses in the reptile. *Acta Oto-laryngol.*, 16, 154-159.

WEVER, E. G. & LAWRENCE, M. 1954. *Physiological Acoustics.* New Jersey: Princeton University Press.

WEVER, E. G. & VERNON, J. A. 1956. The sensitivity of the turtle's ear as shown by its electrical potentials. *Proc. Nat. Acad. Sci.*, 42, 213-220. (a)

WEVER, E. G. & VERNON, J. A. 1956. Sound transmission in the turtle's ear. *Proc. Nat. Acad. Sci.*, 42, 292-299. (b)

WEVER, E. G. & VERNON, J. A. 1956. Auditory responses in the common box turtle. *Proc. Nat. Acad. Sci.*, 42, 962-965. (c)

Chemical-Cue Preferences of Inexperienced Snakes: Comparative Aspects

Abstract. *Different species of new-born, previously unfed snakes will respond with tongue flicking and prey-attack behavior to water extracts of the skin substances of various small animals. However, there are clear species differences in the type of extract responded to by previously unfed snakes, even within the same genus. These differences correspond to the normal feeding preferences shown by the various species.*

It has often been noted that animals can selectively respond to certain highly specific perceptual cues without the benefit of previous experience with those cues (1). The stimuli involved usually represent but a small fraction of the entire stimulus situation and are termed sign stimuli or releasers. In many instances the resulting response is also quite specific and stereotyped. For instance, newborn, previously unfed garter snakes (*Thamnophis s. sirtalis*) will respond with prey-attack behavior to extracts of the surface substances of normally eaten prey when these extracts are presented on cotton swabs (2). Similar specificity to chemical cues has been demonstrated in many forms of invertebrates and, to a lesser extent, in vertebrates (1).

Beyond the existence and analysis of such stimulus–response relations in a particular species looms the broader evolutionary implications. I here report the chemical perception aspects of feeding behavior in a number of species of neonate colubrid snakes.

I presented a variety of extracts from the surface substances of small animals to litters of individually isolated newborn snakes. The animals used in preparing extracts for the testing were: nightcrawler (*Lumbricus terrestris*), leafworm (*Lumbricus rubellus*), redworm (*Eisenia foetida*), turtle leech (*Placobdella parasitica*), slug (*Deroceras gracile*), cricket (*Acheta domestica*), minnow (*Notropis atherinoides acutus*), guppy (*Lebistes reticulatus*), goldfish (*Carassius auratus*), larval salamander (*Ambystoma jeffersonium*), metamorphosed salamander (*Ambystoma jeffersonium*), cricket frog (*Acris crepitans blanchardi*), and newborn mouse (*Mus musculus*). An extract was made by placing one or more of the intact animals in distilled water (10 ml of water per 1.5 g of body weight) at 50°C for 1 minute and stirring the water gently. The animal was then removed and the resulting liquid centrifuged and refrigerated until use. Extracts for any one experiment were always prepared on the same day.

The snakes were from litters or eggs borne by gravid females captured in the field and maintained in captivity until parturition or egg-laying. Shortly after birth or hatching the snakes were weighed, measured, and then isolated in glass tanks measuring 23 by 14 by 17 cm. Each tank was placed on white shelf paper and the four outside walls were covered with white partitions. The floor of the tank was bare except for a small plastic petri dish containing water. Except for testing periods, the aquaria were covered with glass tops. The temperature of the room in which the snakes were housed never varied more than between 22° to 26°C; during testing the temperature was maintained at

24° to 25°C.

Each member of a given litter of newborn snakes was tested only once on a series of extracts of the surface substances of potential prey. Usually twelve or thirteen different extracts were used. Distilled water was the control. Each subject received a different ordering of the test extracts, systematically balanced insofar as possible for each litter. Testing was carried out over 2 or 3 successive days beginning on the 3rd or 4th day of life and always before any previous feeding or exposure to the extracts (3). The testing procedure consisted of dipping a 15-cm cotton swab into the extract or control, slowly introducing it into the tank, and bringing it within about 2 cm of the snake's snout. If the swab was not attacked within 30 seconds, it was moved closer until it touched the snout gently three times, as actual contact with the lips of the snake is sometimes necessary to elicit an attack. If no attack was made at the end of 1 minute, the swab was removed and the total number of tongue flicks emitted in the 1-minute interval recorded. If the swab was attacked, the elapsed time, measured to the nearest 0.1 second, was recorded (4).

An extract, when not actually eliciting a prey-attack response, would often elicit a large number of tongue flicks over and above that elicited by distilled water. It appeared as though the frequency of tongue flicking was correlated with the intensity of arousal by or interest in the swab. Since previous experiments indicated that the prey-attack response in snakes is mediated by the tongue–Jacobson's organ system (3, 5), tongue-flick data can reasonably be considered along with the attack data in assessing the relative releasing value of various extracts on different species of snakes. The control swab (distilled water) never elicited a prey-attack response in an inexperienced

snake, although sometimes a large number of flicks would occur. In most of the species studied here, aggressive behavior was never shown by the newborn snakes; and, indeed, it was impossible to provoke such behavior. A conservative scoring system was used to score the extract given to each snake. The scoring system was based on the assumptions that an actual attack is more definitive than any number of tongue flicks and that a more potent stimulus will lead to an attack with a shorter latency than will a weaker stimulus. The base unit was the maximum number of tongue flicks given by any individual of the litter tested to any of the test stimuli (the maximum was invariably given to a swab containing an extract). A snake which did not attack was given a score identical with the number of tongue flicks it emitted in the 1-minute test period. If the snake did attack, it was given a score identical with the base unit (for that litter) plus one point or fraction for every second or fraction less than 1 minute that it responded. The score for an attacking subject can be represented by base unit + (60 − response latency), measured in seconds.

Figure 1 shows an example of the type of profile obtained when a litter is presented with a series of extracts. The species represented is the eastern plains garter snake, *Thamnophis r. radix*. The 22 living young from a litter of 24 born to a female captured at the Palos Forest Preserve were tested. Each of the previously unfed snakes was presented once with extracts prepared from earthworms, leeches, slugs, crickets, fish, amphibians, and baby mice. Responses to all extracts were significantly higher than those to the control except for those to the baby mouse, slug, cricket, and metamorphosed salamander extracts ($P < .01$, t-test). Although no extensive ecological studies have been done on this species,

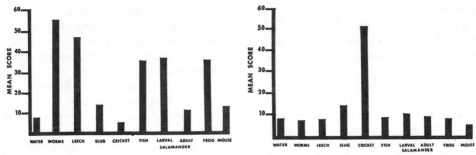

Fig. 1 (left). Response profile of 22 newborn, previously unfed eastern plains garter snakes (*Thamnophis r. radix*) to water extracts from the surface substances of various small animals. The results for the three species of earthworms and the three species of fish have been averaged together.   Fig. 2 (right). Response profile of five newly hatched, previously unfed western smooth green snakes (*Opheodrys vernalis blanchardi*). The snakes were the same age as those in Fig. 1 and were tested at the same time and with the same extracts.

it appears that earthworms, amphibians, fish, and leeches are readily eaten, with worms being probably most common in the natural diet (6). The present results with inexperienced newborn snakes on isolated chemical cues are in remarkably close agreement. Worms as a class were more effective than fish as a class, as there was no overlap in the mean scores for the various worm and fish species. The increased releasing value of the larval salamander over the metamorphosed form ($P < .0005$, *t*-test) is a relationship that has been found frequently in most species of newborn snakes tested that include amphibians in their normal diet. A chemical change in the skin during metamorphosis is probably responsible for the difference.

In sharp contrast to these results were results obtained from the western smooth green snake, *Opheodrys vernalis blanchardi*. This species is oviparous, and five young from a clutch of seven eggs laid by a female captured on the Palos Forest Preserve were tested. The eggs hatched on the same day that the plains garter snakes were born. The green snakes were tested along with the plains garter snakes on the same extracts at the same time. Although each green snake received a different ordering of the extracts, each

sequence was identical to one used with a plains garter snake. In Fig. 2 the results for the green snake are presented for the same extracts as shown for the plains garter snake. The cricket extract was the most potent; indeed, it was the only extract to which actual attacks were made and the only one with a score significantly higher than that of the control ($P < .004$, Mann-Whitney U test, one-tailed). This result becomes more meaningful when it is realized that the cricket extract is the only one which represents an organism eaten by the green snake. In fact, this species apparently will eat only insects, spiders, and perhaps small soft-bodied arthropods.

With literally every procedural detail controlled, clear differences were found in the chemical perception of food objects in the two species of inexperienced snakes. In contrast to the green snake, the plains garter snake does not show any interest in insects as food and the cricket extract received the lowest score of all the extracts. Likewise the green snake was uninterested in those extracts which elicited significant responses in the plains garter snake.

To test these results further, three more closely related forms were studied in the same manner, although only differentiating results for the three earthworm, three fish, and slug extracts will be presented. The eight surviving young of a litter of ten born to a midland brown snake (*Storeria dekayi wrightorum*) captured on the Palos Forest Preserve were tested. Of the above three classes of prey—earthworms, fish, and slugs—this species is known to eat only worms and slugs. The second species tested was Butler's garter snake (*Thamnophis butleri*). A litter of 15 was obtained from a female caught in southern Michigan. In captivity, Butler's garter snake readily eats worms and fish but not slugs. The third species was the aquatic garter snake, *Thamnophis elegans aquaticus*. A litter of nine was tested which were born to a female found in southern California. Of the three classes of prey, this species is known to eat only fish.

The inexperienced young of the three species were tested on the seven extracts representing worms, fish, and slugs (Fig. 3). All scores for the midland brown snake (*Storeria*) were doubled so as to bring them up to the same scale as the two species of *Thamnophis*. For a given species of snake, all scores above 25 are significantly higher than scores below 25 ($P < .05$, t-test). The responses of the different species of inexperienced snakes to skin extracts parallels the feeding habits of specimens captured in the wild. The generally lower scores shown by the midland brown snake are due mainly to the fact that the frequency of tongue flicking was lower than for the two *Thamnophis* species. This may be an important difference also.

These results clearly indicate that chemical perception in newborn young

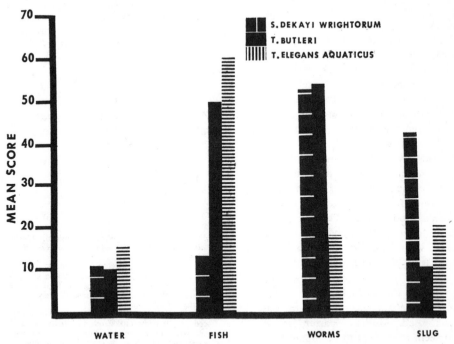

Fig. 3. Differential results for three species of newborn, previously unfed snakes with extracts from the surface substances of three classes of potential prey. Three species of worms and three species of fish were used. All scores for the midland brown snake (*Storeria dekayi wrightorum*) have been doubled to bring them up to the same scale as the two species of *Thamnophis*.

is species-specific. That these are related to the natural feeding ecology of the species is equally clear. But an inexperienced snake will respond to chemical cues that cannot or do not figure in the normal feeding behavior of the species. For instance, the aquatic garter snake (*T. elegans aquaticus*) rarely, if ever, encounters the guppy in nature, yet the inexperienced young readily responded to the guppy extract. Since the aquatic garter snake normally eats fish, however, it is probable that the guppy possesses chemical cues similar or identical to those found in fish which the snake normally eats. In Butler's garter snake (*T. butleri*), the situation is a little more complex, for fish do not constitute any part of the species' normal diet (6). Yet specimens readily eat fish in captivity and newborn young, as shown here, respond significantly to fish extracts. It is, therefore, apparent that the normal feeding habits and ecology of a species are not sufficient to explain the response to chemical cues in newborn young. In this case Butler's garter snake may retain the perceptual side of releasing mechanism that appears to be of no selective advantage in its present mode of life. Of course, retention of the potential to respond to chemical cues from fish by inexperienced snakes would be advantageous if a change in the environment occurred such that fish became a necessary or more easily obtainable food source. The same situation is found with amphibians in this species. Amphibian extracts are responded to by newborn snakes but amphibians also do not form a part of the normal diet of Butler's garter snakes. Therefore, in relation to the extracts used, Butler's garter snake would seem to possess more innate perceptual responsivity than does the aquatic garter snake, which did not respond to any of the worm extracts. Butler's garter snake is generally considered as having evolved from the plains garter snake which not only innately responds to extracts from fish and amphibians, but also normally eats them (7).

The results are open to an evolutionary interpretation. Highly specific stimulus-response information is probably genetically coded in the organism and must in part, at least, be expressed by an innate filtering mechanism at the level of Jacobson's organ or even within the central nervous system itself. This does in no way, of course, rule out the possibility that subsequent feeding experiences (or perhaps even maternal feeding) can influence the feeding preferences of newborn snakes. Indeed, something akin to food imprinting, such as already demonstrated in turtles, may take place (8). In any event, the present data show that innate perceptual differences can be useful in the study of closely related as well as more distantly related forms, and that the analysis of the chemical perceptual mechanisms involved should consider evolution and ecology.

GORDON M. BURGHARDT

W. C. Allee Laboratory of Animal Behavior, University of Chicago, Chicago, Illinois 60637

References and Notes

1. P. R. Marler and W. J. Hamilton, *Mechanisms of Animal Behavior* (Wiley, New York, 1966), pp. 228–315.
2. G. M. Burghardt, *Psychon. Sci.* **4**, 37 (1966).
3. More complete details concerning the subjects, the experimental procedures, and the results are recorded in G. M. Burghardt, thesis, University of Chicago (1966).
4. To check the reliability of the testing procedure, 20 trials (10 water and 10 nightcrawler) were later run on different snakes with a second observer independently timing attack latencies and counting tongue flicks. This second observer did not know which extract was being presented. The average tongue-flick count discrepancy for a given trial was less than 1 and the average latency discrepancy less than 0.5 second. The rank correlation of the 20 trials was highly significant ($r_s = .997$).

5. G. Naulleau, thesis (P. Fanlac, Paris, 1966); W. S. Wilde, *J. Exp. Zool.* **77**, 445 (1938).
6. Information concerning feeding habits in the field and in captivity was gleaned from the following, in addition to personal experience: C. C. Carpenter, *Ecol. Monogr.* **22**, 235 (1952); R. L. Ditmars, *The Reptiles of North America* (Doubleday, New York, 1936); P. W. Smith, *Ill. Nat. Hist. Surv. Bull,* **28**, Art. 1 (1961); R. C. Stebbins, *Amphibians and Reptiles of Western North America* (McGraw-Hill, New York, 1954); H. W. Wright and A. A. Wright, *Handbook of Snakes of the United States and Canada* (Comstock, Ithaca, 1957),

2 vols.
7. K. P. Schmidt, *Ecology* **19**, 396 (1938).
8. G. M. Burghardt and E. H. Hess, *Science* **151**, 108 (1966); G. M. Burghardt, *Psychon. Sci.* **7**, 383 (1967).
9. Assisted by NIH grants MH 776 and MH 13375. I thank E. Lace and other naturalists at the Palos Division, Cook County Forest Preserve, P. Allen, and H. Campbell for providing the gravid females and newborn young; E. H. Hess, E. Klinghammer, G. S. Reynolds, T. Uzzell, and D. Wake for assistance.

13 April 1967

Messages of Vertebrate Communication

In communicating, most birds and mammals appear to use a very limited set of referents.

W. John Smith

Animals possess in their behavioral repertoires acts that have become specialized in the course of evolution to convey information and are called "displays;" these acts include postures, movements, vocalizations and other sounds, the release of volatile chemicals, and so on (*1*). Each species has from about 15 to 40 or 45 displays, and most displays of one species differ in form from those of another. Although certain general features of the form of displays recur with some regularity, for the most part it is difficult

The author is associate professor of biology at the University of Pennsylvania, Philadelphia. An earlier version of this article was presented 28 December 1967 at the New York meeting of the AAAS.

to establish homologies at the genus or higher taxonomic level; thus the list of different displays of animals is very long. Yet it is beginning to appear that the "messages" of displays [the "messages" are the information carried (*2*)] are not nearly so diverse or numerous as the displays themselves. All birds and mammals, and perhaps other vertebrates, may encode as messages selections from the same small set of referent classes. I propose here a list that could include most or all of the messages conveyed by nonlinguistic vertebrates (that is, vertebrates other than man) with social patterns of more than minimal complexity. I suggest why the total set is small, and what circumstances may foster the evolution of displays carrying exceptional messages.

Displays do not resemble the words of our languages, and the messages of displays are not closely similar to the referents of most words. Most display messages make the behavior of the communicator to some degree more predictable by the recipient of the message. The information conveyed probably permits the recipient to select appropriate behavior. But natural selection can have acted only if the response to the message conveyed meets the needs not only of the recipient but of the communicator as well.

Not surprisingly, it is not always easy for us to deduce what the messages of a given display are. Consider a vocal display of a small North American bird, the eastern phoebe (3). This brief call sounds like "twh-t" and is uttered in several different sorts of situations: by unmated males while foraging alone and patrolling their newly defined territories, early in the spring; by mated males just after singing in the predawn twilight, in the period in which their rather aggressive mates approach and sometimes permit copulation; by a male warily associating with his mate, if one of his foraging flights should take him close to her; by either member of a pair, when watching a potential predator in the vicinity of the nest; and by a male following a defeated intruder from his territory. In this variety of circumstances there is one important consistency about the way in which the call is used: It almost always comes just as the bird alights, or when it appears hesitant about continuing its flight. But the call is not associated with all flights. For instance, a great many flights are simply ordinary foraging flights, and on these the bird is silent. Because of the broad range of situations in which the call is made, we cannot conclude that any particular motivation, excitatory or inhibitory, is always present. Without seeing the bird we can know only (i) that it is hesitant about flying and (ii) that it is an eastern phoebe, since the form of the display is species-specific.

Many other birds have displays with patterns of use quite similar to that of the "twh-t" display. This leads us to suspect that information about the probability of locomotion is important to these birds. When one considers the circumstances under which the displays are used and the kinds of contextual information (2, 4) that is available to recipients, one readily sees why the information is valuable. For instance, only unmated, territorial phoebes do much flying and stopping along an extensive perimeter in early spring. They are hard to see, but newly arrived migrant female phoebes could easily locate them by their calls. A phoebe uttering the "twh-t" call in the nest area is upset by a potential danger to the nest, and if the mate is aware of this and comes, the two of them may be able to harry and drive off the predator. In each context, the information that the communicator may or may not cease flying indicates a certain type of situation.

The search for a general set of messages entails comparison of the display repertoires of animals with similar and different social behaviors, since the display repertoire, and the use made of it, in any species presumably evolves to facilitate social behavior, and social behavior in different species involves different forms of pair-bonding, of flocking, of seasonal changes, and so forth. Further, since it is not obvious that all species must solve their problems of communication in the same ways, a range of comparisons over different phylogenetic distances is required. Finally, the different sound environments, habitats, and other ecological factors associated with different species influence some aspects of the evolution of displays and must be taken into account in studying messages. In a large number of species of the same family as the phoebe (Tyrannidae), the messages of displays have now been studied (5), although not all the analyses have been completed. The large size and unusual diversity of this family makes it especially suited for such comparisons. Outside this family, analysis of displays for message content has so far been completed for only one species, the winter-flocking Carolina chickadee (6), but work on bird species in three other families is in progress. In mammals, studies of the displays of captive prairie dogs and young captive gorillas are being made (7).

This comparative base is still weak, and the provisional list of messages given here is more a progress report than a confident statement. Changes in the list will be required, but some clear trends have emerged. Some difficulties remain—that of ensuring the comparability of messages found in the course of the comparative studies, and that of matching these messages with messages derived from communication studies reported in the literature. Moreover, the complete range of uses of a display must usually be known before the messages the display carries can be determined, and learning this range is difficult in the field and perhaps impossible for animals in captivity. Further, it often appears necessary to isolate small details of behavior, like the correlation of a phoebe's "twh-t" with the act of alighting. Since most studies reported in the literature were designed for purposes other than that of developing a comparative list of messages, the data reported are necessarily incomplete and must always be reinterpreted. For present purposes I have limited my use of the literature to some particularly detailed examples.

The Message Set

When we speak of the messages of a display we mean the information available to an individual as a result of having received just the display; all other sources of information are considered contextual. The messages, it is believed, specify or predict classes of activities that the communicator may perform at about the time of displaying, or specify a probable change in his activities. Because most messages indicate some selection within the behavioral repertoire of the communicator, an investigator recognizes each message by the particular class of behavior consistently correlated with the displays that encode it. The remaining messages are effectively modifiers, and every display encodes two modifiers plus one or more of the other messages.

1) *Identification.* The identification message is a modifying message, specifying the categories or classes to which the communicator belongs and the behavioral repertoires of members of these classes. In some extreme cases, like that of the convergent vocalizations often called predator alarm calls, a class may be definable only as, say, small birds. At the other extreme is the class represented by one individual. The most common classes are probably species, sex, maturity, and one individual.

Any act within a particular repertoire will be performed in a fashion typical of, or at least possible for, a member of the class having that repertoire. Furthermore, once a communicator is identified, the classes of individuals with which he is prepared to interact socially is known, so the identification message facilitates what Marler (8) has called the specification (that is, selection) of recipients.

We recognize identification messages by comparing the form of the displays of communicators belonging to different communicator classes. It is assumed that the behavior typical of each communicator class will be in some senses unique. Actually, comparing in detail the behaviors typical of these communicator classes would be very tedious, although comparable with the methods used to determine other messages.

No display encodes only identification, but the identification message is present in all displays. Because of its universality, usually I do not mention it here in giving examples of displays to illustrate the encoding of other messages.

2) *Probability*. The probability of occurrence of each behavioral act specified by a display is indicated in the display. These indications yield the relative probabilities of occurrence of the acts predicted by a single display, and also the relative probabilities of occurrence of acts predicted by different displays that carry similar messages. For instance, when a greenbacked sparrow, *Arremonops conirostris*, uses the "chuck notes" display, attack is less probable than escape; when the sparrow uses the "medium hoarse notes" display, attack is as probable as escape (*9*); and when it uses the "hoarse scream" display, attack and escape are, again, equally probable, and more probable than they are when the sparrow utters the "medium hoarse notes." In this example, three different displays combine the same attack and escape messages with different probability information. In other species the form of a display may be varied to indicate changing probabilities. For instance, as the "repeated vocalization" of the eastern kingbird gets harsher, attack becomes more probable (*5*), whereas a rise in pitch in the cawing of a rook, *Corvus frugilegus*, correlates with increasing probability of escape behavior (*10*).

Finally, some displays are not graded and indicate only a range of probabilities; a recipient then needs contextual sources as an aid in predicting relative probabilities. Contextual sources include the manner of displaying: for example, an alteration in the rate of repetition of the display (*11*).

3) *General set*. Many species have one or two displays which are used in association with a number of different activities that range from maintenance activities (foraging, preening, resting, and so on) to most social activities, and which appear, therefore, to refer unselectively to the whole set of behavior patterns in the species' repertoire. For example, the "tsit" display of tanagers (of the genus *Chlorospingus*) is used at all seasons, by birds of both sexes; the communicator may be "performing any type of locomotory or prelocomotory movements, or sitting or standing in almost any type of unritualized posture" (*12*). The very fact that such displays are used so widely and so abundantly makes the gathering of sufficient quantitative data on their occurrence or absence in association with different acts and in different situations very time-consuming, and none of these displays has as yet been fully studied. Although present evidence about the message implies a lack of information permitting prediction of which act the communicator will select within its general set of acts, further research will probably show the message to be somewhat less broad than it seems. One possibility, for instance, is that the message specifies that a change in the type of the communicator's activity is likely. In addition, the message may always be combined with modifiers indicating probability; for example, the "tsit" mentioned above is rarely used by solitary tanagers and indicates that association behavior is probable, relative to other possibilities.

298

The general-set message is sometimes encoded in displays together with another, more selective message. Examples are given under the headings "Locomotion" and "Escape."

4) *Locomotion.* Some displays are used only during locomotion, or at the beginning or end of locomotion. The function of the locomotion is largely irrelevant; it may be foraging, patrolling, following a mate or parent or flock member, avoiding, attacking, chasing, fleeing, and so on. In well-understood cases there is usually indication that displays are also associated with behavior conflicting with the initial locomotory behavior. Such displays usually come primarily at the end of locomotion (when the bird alights and sings, eats, or does something else which requires perching) or during slowing or turning, as described above for the "twh-t" of the eastern phoebe. In cases of slowing or turning, the conflicting behavior may itself be locomotory, with orientation opposed to that of the initial locomotion. (Examples are a bird's approach to copulate as opposed to its flight to escape; its following of a mate as opposed to its return to the nest.) Three vocalizations described by Smith (6) for the Carolina chickadee can be ranked in order of descending probability of correlation with flight and in order of increasing probability of correlation with other behavior; "high tee" is usually uttered in flight or, less often, during rapid pivoting on a perch; "chick" is uttered on alighting or during rare, extraordinarily erratic flight; and "dee" is usually uttered from a perch, often immediately after alighting. (The three vocalizations often occur in succession as a bird is alighting, and constitute the sound commonly called "chickadee.")

Typical of these "locomotory hesitance" displays is the fact that the function of the associated locomotion and of the behavior in conflict with the initial locomotion differs in different usages. Thus, in these displays a locomotory message is compounded with the general-set message. (If the chickadee's "high-tee" can be shown to have an escape message, it will have to be reclassified.)

Many displays reported in the literature may be locomotory hesitance displays or may encode only locomotory messages. Moynihan (12) described wing-flicking and tail-flicking displays of tanagers (of the genus *Chlorospingus*) which are restricted to preflight situations in which the probability of the bird's taking flight is usually increasing (13). Blurton Jones (14) says that "the Canada Goose seems to have . . . special calls given whenever locomotion (to whatever purpose) is blocked." In other cases, while both locomotory and other behavioral possibilities are typically associated with most presentations of a display, sometimes there may not be conflicting possibilities. For example, the "tit flight-call" of buntings (15) and the "flight call" of the chaffinch (16) are both used in flight, even though they are more commonly used on taking flight. Night monkeys use "gulps" and "sneeze-grunts" displays throughout periods when they are very active (17). Perhaps the situations in which such calls are made during locomotion have not yet been examined in sufficient detail to rule out the possibility that these are locomotory hesitance displays, or perhaps locomotory behavior may be specified in the absence of opposing behavioral possibilities. In either case, the message does not indicate a very narrow selection of possible communicator behavior.

5) *Attack.* Of the various acts more closely specified than locomotion, the most common are probably agonistic or hostile acts, a class comprising attack, escape, and ambivalent behavior when both attack and escape are pos-

sible. The attack message is encoded when the communicator is attacking or is making "intention movements" toward an object or other animal which are sometimes followed by attack. (Ethologists refer to movements that appear to be incomplete forms of other, identifiable movements of any sort—for example, flight, striking, nest-building, and so forth—as "intention movements." The term is misleading; it is intended to be simply descriptive and not to imply that a motivational analysis has been made.) Both attack and escape messages are commonly encoded in the same display.

6) *Escape*. A display used when a communicator is escaping, is gradually withdrawing, or is making oriented movements away from an aversive stimulus carries an escape message. Often the probability of other acts nearly balances the probability of escape in the case of a particular display, and this near-balance leads to observed behavior that satisfies the criteria for locomotory hesitance except for the fact that escape per se is always specified as one of the alternatives. For example, the "jump-yip" display of black-tailed prairie dogs occurs when attack, nonaggressive social behavior, or maintenance activity is likely to be interrupted or prevented by escape behavior. The display is usually used just as the prairie dog stops running or just as he appears to be about to start, or about to emerge from a burrow (7). It thus carries the general-set and escape messages, with relative probabilities of occurrence nearly equal for the two.

7) *Nonagonistic subset*. A nonagonistic subset is a large subset within the general set of behavior. It is not uncommon for a display to carry both the nonagonistic subset message and an escape message. The "tseet" call of the Carolina chickadee (6) is given in a variety of circumstances—when the communicator may flee or withdraw, may associate with a flock mate, forage, continue eating, and so on, but will not attack. I once viewed messages of this sort as a distinct category—anxiety messages (5). I now believe anxiety messages to be simply a compound of weak escape messages and this message specifying a wide range of other, nonagonistic acts.

8) *Association*. Some displays occur when one individual associates with another by approaching and remaining near (but not attempting to make contact) while at the same time avoiding approaches made by the other (but not escaping from it). Or the communicator may passively permit another individual to approach. The association message is carried by the "chatter vocalization" of most tyrannid species studied, but apparently usually in combination with another message indicating that the association is directed only toward mates. The "lisping tee" display of the Carolina chickadee is used by birds associating with mates, families, or members of foraging flocks (6).

The complex "jingle vocalization" of the spice finch (18) appears to carry an association message. The call is used by a male separated from his companion or companions, or clumped with companions but separated from his mate. Sometimes a lone "jingling" bird is approached by another spice finch. He continues to "jingle" only so long as he remains perched, and he trys to avoid letting the other bird initiate contact behavior. Finally, a male will "jingle" before mounting his mate for copulation, but he always remains beside her while using this display and mounts after completing a "jingle." In all these remarkably varied usages the communicator lacks, avoids, or delays some form of contact with an individual of the same species.

Some birds belonging to the order Galliformes have an array of intergrading vocal displays best known for their occurrence in a social activity called "tidbitting" (19). In the chukar partridge three vocal displays are recognized, the most variable of which (the "food call," which is not restricted to events involving food) overlaps the other two in form. It appears to encode association and general set messages, being used by a male associating with another male in an agonistic encounter, or used in various encounters between a male and a female, or by a bird showing novel food to other birds of particular classes. The remaining two vocal displays of the chukar partridge are discussed below.

9) *Bond-limited subset.* The bond-limited subset of the behavioral repertoire comprises acts occurring between mates, between parents and offspring, and among members of larger organized groups, which are permitted because of the persistent behavioral convention that I call a "bond." The behavior included in this convention is behavior that fosters cohesion between individuals. Different species have different social relationships, but in general the bond-limited subset includes association, grooming of other individuals, huddling, caring for others (that is, feeding them, guarding them), copulation, and the like. As a message category, this subset is poorly understood and may be an artifact of the current inadequacy of our understanding of some displays. For instance, the message sometimes refers to the probability of occurrence of some act in the subset and at other times it seems to be only a modifier of a narrower message —such as association.

There are displays, like the courtship calls of the chaffinch (16), which appear to be largely mate-oriented and more or less restricted to the period of what is usually called "courtship" behavior (20). This period is characterized primarily by mate association, and perhaps some such displays carry only association messages. Most are clearly not associated solely with copulation or with precopulatory behavior, although they are often called "sexual." Many genera of tyrannid flycatchers have a "chatter vocalization" and a visible "nest-site-showing" display in which there is often ritualized nest-building behavior (3, 5). Communicators associate with other birds when using this display, or remain at a site and permit association if the partner appears. A closely similar vocalization is found in galliforms as one of the three displays of the "tidbitting" group of displays; this vocalization is associated with a nest-building display, under circumstances similar to those observed for tyrannids. In fact, such calls (usually staccato series) and nest displays are unusually widespread in birds and occur in several families.

In addition, there are displays that appear to encode a similar sort of message, are used within a larger, bonded group, and are not restricted to a "courtship" period. Grooming of other individuals is seen in many social birds and mammals (21) and is usually considered to be at least partially a display. Such allogrooming is apparently limited to individuals who recognize each other; it reduces agonistic acts within the groups, and it may indicate a probability that the communicators will select further behavior from a bond-limited subset of behavioral acts. It apparently does not help create or reinforce status distinctions, but minimizes the potentially adverse effects of such distinctions.

10) *Play.* It is apparent that, among bonded individuals, various nonaggressive contact activities are often initiated and sustained with little or no displaying (22). However, displays associated only with play are known, especially in primates. Most resemble in form a parody of elements of non-play fighting. Among the best understood is the

"relaxed open-mouth face" display (23). Other primarily facial displays, often called play signals (for example, laughter), usually occur in various non-play situations as well.

11) *Copulation.* Displays used only before or during copulation occur in a number of species, although apparently not in tyrannid flycatchers or chickadees. The chaffinch, for instance, has a special variant of song—"congested song"—associated with copulation (16), and a male chukar partridge running to mount a female uses a "copulation-intention call" display (19). This call is the third of the "tidbitting" group of vocalizations mentioned above; the three appear to encode, respectively, association, the bond-limited message, and the copulation message. Perhaps the copulation message is characteristically encoded in displays that are relatively minor variants of other displays, the responses to which would not be entirely inappropriate should a recipient fail to distinguish correctly.

12) *Frustration.* Some displays are used only when some particular behavior would occur if the opportunity were available, or when the opportunity for a particular behavior that has been occurring has gone (24). The substituted behavior differs from case to case, although it often shows orientation components related to the pattern of the behavior that is not possible. The substitute may be a display, or it may be accompanied by a display, and one message of such a display is taken to be "frustration." Because frustration cannot be recognized except in relation to the frustrated behavioral possibility, the message must be combined with at least one other message.

Displays encoding frustrated escape are used when the communicator is trapped or cornered. Screams occasionally heard from a prey animal held by a predator, or by birds caught in mist nets (nets woven of very fine threads) are probably good examples. And animals often "freeze" in stereotyped poses when they are cornered by dominant individuals. The distinctive "cowering" posture of gorillas appears to be a display of this sort. According to Schaller (25), this posture is assumed by individuals "attempting to escape the slap of displaying males" or behaving submissively, and by a small infant terminating vigorous play with a larger infant. A young gorilla in the Philadelphia Zoo "cowered" after escaping from her cage into a hallway; she then responded with infantile clinging when picked up. The younger of the zoo's two males was once attacked by the older while mounting the latter's female cage-mate. He quickly dismounted and "cowered" (7). Similar cowering displays occur in many other species; for example, a gull too young to fly and under vigorous pecking attack from an older gull may alternate escape behavior and the "bill-down crouch" posture (26).

There are also displays that encode the message combination "frustrated attack." Kingbirds have a "tumble flight" display (5) used primarily by territorial males, usually in the absence of an appropriate opponent (that is, an opponent visible and within the territory). The "swoop and soar" display of the black-headed gull is probably closely similar (27). Two displays of male parrots of the genus *Agapornis* appear to encode "frustrated copulation" messages (28). Several species of New World songbirds of the genera *Arremonops* (9), *Ramphocelus* (29), and *Chlorospingus* (12) have "plaintive notes" displays which appear to encode "frustrated association" messages. Probably other messages are combined with the "frustration" message in the displays of some species.

Why There Are Few Messages

These 12 message categories are all I have identified as yet, and it seems likely that not many more will be found. If this is the case, then a very few messages have a great deal of work to do in facilitating social interactions.

Of course, the fact that messages are combined in many ways in different displays, and that one of the messages in each display is a probability modifier, is important. Different species use different combinations of messages and specify different probabilities in coping with their species-specific problems. Yet 12 messages, two of them (identification and probability) modifiers of the other ten, constitute a very small set.

Interestingly, within any one species the number of displays is also quite small—usually between 15 and 45, when all modes of displaying, in all of the species so far studied, are counted. In some species there is much intergrading of displays, but even when allowance is made for personal preferences in splitting up such continua, one can rarely recognize more than about 50 displays and functionally similar activities of different evolutionary status. Although there is not a one-to-one correspondence between the number of messages and the number of displays, the latter is only slightly larger.

It is not clear why each species has so few displays. One plausible explanation is that displays must be sufficiently distinct from one another to be recognizable by the recipient. Since the number of ways of producing displays is limited, there must be limits on the range of forms the displays can take. But there is little reason to think that selection acting to keep displays distinct would set as low a limit as we find. Moynihan (30) has argued that limitations on the acceptable range of elaboration, and on the frequency of occurrence of the rarer displays, will also act to limit the number of displays.

Whatever the evolutionary explanation of the small number of displays per species, there are clearly more functions served by displaying than there are displays. This augmentation of function appears to result from the use of most displays under more than one set of circumstances. That is, vertebrate communication appears to require extensive use of contextual information by the recipient of a display. Most of the 12 message categories listed above are broad, and probably the recipient must depend heavily on context if he is to make appropriate responses. Contextual information greatly extends the set of events concerning which there can be communication by means of displays (31).

It is not clear whether the small number of displays per species is the cause of the small number of messages or its result, or whether both have some other cause. However, in most arguments about the small size of specific display repertoires the number of available messages is not seen as limiting. Probably it is the converse that is true: because each species can have few displays, natural selection has favored the messages which can be used most broadly (that is, in the greatest number of contexts) and which can thus generate the maximum number of different responses. Of the messages that could evolve, those that can be used very broadly are probably rare, so it is not suprising that we have as yet empirically demonstrated only 12, and it would not be surprising if we were to find only a few more.

Circumstances Fostering Exceptional Messages

Again, the basic assumptions of this article are (i) that each message must do a great deal of work and serve in the maximum number of contexts because the number of available displays in the repertoire of any species is severely limited, and (ii) that much communication is more effective (more free of errors) when signaling is stylized. Examination of these assumptions leads to the prediction of other possibilities in certain cases.

1) Context-dependent messages may not always provide sufficiently unambiguous information, and evolution of the display repertoire may favor the inclusion of more precise messages ("exceptional messages") to elicit a particular response in the shortest possible time. It might, for instance, sometimes be very difficult for an animal to initiate play-fighting if the recipient of the message could not determine whether or not the first animal's approach was attack. For the same reason it might be difficult for an animal to initiate mounting for copulation, the other case for which a specific message is clearly known. There are other possibilities. Many highly social animals may be gregarious in part because the group provides them with an efficient predator-detection device, and a relatively finely divided set of messages about escape probabilities would have a high selective value in the evolution of the display repertoire. In any case in which a message is precise, however, the precision is achieved at the cost of tying up one of the few displays available to the species.

2) Certain circumstances limit, sometimes severely, the availability of contextual information. For instance, much contextual information is obtained visually, and a recipient belonging to a nocturnal species has a relatively context-poor environment; such a recipient may need relatively precise messages.

3) There may be ways of circumventing the size limitations of the display repertoire—ways other than communication through human speech. Two displays may be used in such a way as to provide contexts for each other and thus modify each other's messages, but such modification seems to be primarily modification of the probability message (32). It appears that new classes of messages are not generated by this technique. In two cases cited above, however (the galliform "tidbitting" group of vocalizations and the song and "congested song" of the chaffinch), new messages were encoded in minor variants of a display that encoded a broad, context-dependent message. In both cases the new message was copulation, a particular nonattack contact message with a very restricted range of usage; in both cases the new message was encoded by a variant of a display which encoded an "association" or "bond-limited" message. Adding a new message to the repertoire through minor variation of a display is perhaps the communicator's only economical way of encoding a message that is so narrowly defined as to be nearly independent of context. The risk that the recipient will fail to distinguish between the original display and its variant is relatively high, but when the responses to the message carried by the original display and that carried by the variant are sufficiently compatible as to make such failure of little significance, the display repertoire may evolve to include the variant.

4) Finally, there are species in which the number of types of social interaction is so limited that the display repertoire includes fewer displays than are potentially available, and each display may then be very specific. One would expect this to be the case in many nocturnal, nonterritorial frogs. Even the bullfrog, however, uses at least some of its approximately six vocalizations in more than one context (33).

It is difficult to make an a priori evaluation of the extent to which these potential sources of exceptional messages are operative. Empirically, however, it appears that very precise messages are few in number and even totally lacking from the displays of many birds and mammals, and that even nocturnal species use many displays in more than one context. Assessment of the use of minor display variants is a fairly difficult problem, as is the detailed study of relatively asocial animals. Nonetheless, it does seem that the basic list of message classes given above, or some list that is similar to it in many respects, is likely to be very generally representative. If it is, then there are broad implications both for the evolution of patterns of communication (including at least the origins of language) and for the evolution of social systems.

References and Notes

1. M. H. Moynihan, *Proc. Int. Ornithol. Congr. 12th* (1960), pp. 523–541.
2. W. J. Smith, *Amer. Naturalist* 99, 405 (1965).
3. ——, *Behaviour*, in press.
4. ——, *Amer. Naturalist* 97, 117 (1963); ——, in *Animal Communication*, T. A. Sebeok, Ed. (Univ. of Indiana Press, Bloomington, 1968).
5. ——, "Communication and Relationships in the Genus Tyrannus," *Nuttall Ornithol. Club, Cambridge, Mass., Pub. 6* (1966), pp. 1–250.
6. S. T. Smith, thesis, Harvard University (1968).
7. The studies of captive mammals are being made at the Philadelphia Zoo by me and the following members of my group: S. L. Smith, L. Oppenheimer, and J. G. deVilla (prairie dog studies); A. Maizel (gorilla studies). I am making additional studies of infant mammals with C. Ristau and studies of abnormal displaying with M. Bernstein. The types of overt behavior observed in these latter studies present special problems which are not dealt with here.
8. P. Marler, *Science* 157, 769 (1967).
9. M. H. Moynihan, *Auk* 80, 116 (1963).
10. C. J. F. Coombs, *Ibis* 102, 394 (1960).
11. For a discussion of grading, see M. Konishi, *Z. Tierpsychol.* 20, 349 (1963).
12. M. H. Moynihan, *Auk* 79, 310 (1962).
13. Movements, such as these flickings of wing and tail, which resemble postures or movements representative of the acts of taking flight or landing are common in displays [see A. Daanje, *Behaviour* 3, 48 (1951)]. The form alone, however, does not necessarily indicate that a locomotory message is encoded by the display.
14. N. G. Blurton Jones, *Wildfowl Trust Ann. Rep. 11th* (1960), pp. 46–52.
15. R. J. Andrew, *Ibis* 99, 27 (1957).
16. P. Marler, *ibid.* 98, 231 (1956); ——, *Behaviour* (Suppl.) 5, 1 (1956).
17. M. H. Moynihan, *Smithsonian Inst. Misc. Collections* 146, No. 5, 1 (1964).
18. —— and M. F. Hall, *Behaviour* 7, 33 (1954).
19. A. W. Stokes, *Condor* 63, 111 (1961); ——, *Animal Behaviour* 11, 121 (1963); ——, *Auk* 84, 1 (1967); H. W. Williams, A. W. Stokes, J. C. Wallen, *ibid.* 85, 464 (1968).
20. D. Morris, in *L'instinct dans le comportement des animaux et de l'homme*, M. Autori, Ed. (Masson, Paris, 1956).
21. J. Sparks, in *Primate Ethology*, D. Morris, Ed. (Morrison and Gibb, London, 1967), pp. 148–175.
22. There may or may not be a message specifying the general subset of nonattack contact behavior patterns. And although there are some narrowly predictive messages each specifying the probability of only one type of contact, these appear to be few and rarely encoded. In addition to play and copulation messages, some authors have proposed food-finding or food-giving messages. Acts, like allogrooming, which are only partly displays remain hard to interpret. Some other iconic gestures (that is, gestures resembling acts that have functions other than communication) may or may not be displays. For further discussion of these gestures, see W. J. Smith, *Semiotica*, in press.
23. J. A. R. A. M. van Hoof, in *Primate Ethology*, D. Morris, Ed. (Morrison and Gibb, London, 1967), pp. 7–68.
24. These are two of the three criteria for motivational thwarting proposed by D. Morris [*Behaviour* 9, 75 (1956)].
25. G. B. Schaller, *The Mountain Gorilla* (Univ. of Chicago Press, Chicago, 1963), pp. 1–431.
26. M. H. Moynihan, *Behaviour* 14, 214 (1959).
27. This display has been studied by M. H. Moynihan [*Behaviour* (Suppl.) 4, 1 (1955)] and G. H. Manley [*Ardea* 48, 37 (1960)]. The greeting ceremony which usually precedes this aerial display appears to Moynihan and to me to contain many real attack components; Manley feels that intra-pair hostility "may be more apparent than real."
28. W. C. Dilger, *Z. Tierpsychol.* 17, 649 (1960).
29. M. H. Moynihan, *Auk* 79, 655 (1962).
30. ——, in preparation.
31. Apart from its use in specialized communication, contextual information has been shown to be of profound importance in modifying the response of monkeys to all sorts of stimuli [see E. W. Menzel, in *Naturalistic Viewpoints in Psychological Research*, E. P. Willems and H. L. Raush, Eds. (Holt, Rinehart and Winston, New York, 1969)].
32. See, for example, the modification of the "regularly repeated vocalization" display of the eastern phoebe by changes in the relative numbers of the display's two components (W. J. Smith, *Behaviour*, in press) or the hostile displays of the green-backed sparrow [M. H. Moynihan, *Auk* 80, 116 (1963)].
33. R. R. Capranica, *MIT (Mass. Inst. Technol.) Press Res. Monogr.* 33, 1 (1965).
34. This study is based on research done under the following grants: National Science Foundation grants G19261, GB2904, and GB6108; Air Force Office of Scientific Research grant F-44620-67-0057; and National Institutes of Health grant FR-07083-01. I thank S. T. Smith, C. Snowdon, and D. L. Anderson for criticizing the manuscript.

Pheromones in the Communication of Sexual Status in Primates

by
R. P. MICHAEL
E. B. KEVERNE

Primate Research Centre,
Institute of Psychiatry,
Monks Orchard Road,
Beckenham, Kent

Anosmic male rhesus monkeys showed no interest in females receiving oestrogen until their olfaction was restored, when they pressed a lever 250 times to gain access to the females. These findings indicate the communication of information about the females' endocrine state by means of a pheromone.

UNLIKE hormones, which are secreted into the blood stream, ectohormones[1] or pheromones are substances secreted by an animal externally with specific effects on the behaviour or physiology of another individual of the same species[2,3]. These substances may be secreted rather generally by the skin or by specialized glands and, similarly, their detection by the recipient individual may be simply by ingestion or by specialized chemoreceptors such as those on the antennae of the silkworm moth, *Bombyx mori*. The importance of this mode of communication has been thoroughly established in several invertebrate forms, particularly among the social insects. A distinction is usually made between pheromones and other chemical releasers[4]—those, for example, involved in the detection of food or prey, for the latter substances are not usually produced by an individual of the same species. Territorial demarcation substances would, however, come within the pheromone category, where they are used to attract receptive females or warn away competing males, as would the trail-marking substances of termites and ants[5].

Pheromones in Insects

The role of an olfactorily acting sexual pheromone has been studied in detail in such insects as *B. mori*, where it is found in the sacculi laterales of the last abdominal segments of the female. Males react to an extract of these glands with high excitement and with copulatory attempts on objects impregnated with it. The silkworm pheromone has been identified as *trans*-10, *cis*-12-hexadecadien-1-ol[6] and is active at 10^{-12} μg. It is detected by olfactory receptors on the antennae of males from which specific action potentials can be recorded at 10^{-3} those producing behavioural responses[7,8]. Males orient their flight up-wind to air currents bearing this pheromone, responding to the concentration gradient across considerable distances. The sex pheromone of the gipsy moth, *Porthetria dispar*, has also been isolated as *d*-10-acetoxy-*cis*-7-hexadecen-1-ol[9,10]; it, too, is active at 10^{-12} μg.

Although closely resembling Butenandt's compound, both being unsaturated, 16-carbon, straight-chain alcohols, these attractants are species specific. Olfactory sex pheromones have now been established in more than thirty species of moth, butterfly, fly, beetle and cockroach[11], and synthetic analogues have become important commercially for insect pest control[12]. In general, males are attracted to females, but in the case of the boll weevil, *Anthonomus grandis*, the males produce the attractant[13], and in other cases aggregations occur in which both sexes are brought mutually together by these substances. Of considerable interest in the present context are the aphrodisiacs of many *Lepidoptera* and *Hymenoptera*: these are usually produced by the male after it has responded to the attractant of the female, and they stimulate the copulatory behaviour of the female which is essential for successful mating[14].

Pheromones in Mice

No mammalian pheromone has so far been identified chemically, but conclusive evidence for their role in reproductive physiology and behaviour has been obtained in recent years[15,16]. The following more notable effects have been demonstrated in laboratory mice. (1) Female

mice maintained in groups show a higher incidence of anoestrus and pseudopregnancy than when caged individually; the effect on pseudopregnancy can be prevented by removal of the olfactory bulbs[17–20]. (2) The oestrous cycle can be shortened and spontaneous pseudopregnancy prevented by the presence of males[21], an effect that is not caused by visual, auditory or tactile stimulation. Because removal of the olfactory bulbs completely abolishes oestrous cycles in mice, the final demonstration that olfaction was involved was only obtained by introducing male mouse urine into the nares of females with the same result as the presence of males[22]. (3) If males are given access to groups of female mice that have been previously isolated from them, the maximum incidence of oestrus is three nights later; a synchronization of oestrus and mating thus results[20,23,24]. (4) If males from a different strain are introduced for 2–3 days on the day following mating, 70–80 per cent of recently mated females returned to oestrus within a week, and genetic marking shows that any offspring that do result are sired by the second male, the original pregnancy having been blocked by the alien male[25,26]. A similar effect was observed when newly mated females were transferred to cages contaminated by urine from a group of alien males that had recently occupied them[27]. Pregnancy block in mice fails to occur with anosmic females[28] and with castrated males[29] and cannot be induced after implantation has occurred. All these observations suggest the existence of substances in excretions that influence pituitary gonadotrophin secretion through the olfactory sense. Although analogous phenomena have not been found in laboratory rats[30], closely similar effects were described in deermice, *Peromyscus maniculatus bairdii*[31]. Furthermore, the synchronization of lambing has been reported when rams were introduced into flocks of ewes previously maintained in isolation from males[32].

Olfactory Stimuli in Mammals

The few studies that have been made on the behavioural effects of olfactory stimuli in mammals derive chiefly from the breeding of farm animals. Effects appear to be exerted by each sex on the other. Thus the odour of the boar elicits, with other stimuli, the immobilization reflex in oestrous sows so that they stand rigidly while being mated[33,34]. The presence of the male cat evokes the pattern of rolling and rubbing, and also the oestrual crouch and treading of oestrous females. This behaviour is released when oestrous females are placed in a cage recently occupied and marked by an active male: it does not occur if the cage is first washed with disinfectant (Michael, unpublished observations). The release by males of specialized postural responses essential for coitus in female mammals is similar to the "aphrodisiac" action on females of certain male insects. There are several instances of the olfactory influence of the female on the male. Dogs are attracted over distances to oestrous bitches[35] and also to their urine[36]. Similarly, the urine of oestrous mares sexually stimulates, in particular, the young stallion[37,38], and olfactory cues are of considerable importance in sexually arousing bulls during semen collection[39]. Rams can differentiate between oestrous and non-oestrous ewes by their scent[40,41], and careful studies have shown that male rats, too, exhibit a preference for the odour of receptive as compared with non-receptive females[42-44], an effect not shown by pre-pubertal or by castrated males, although their ability to discriminate odours is unimpaired[45]. The evidence is therefore gradually accumulating that olfactory communication plays a part in the integration of reproductive behaviour in mammals even though olfactory bulb ablation may not entirely abolish it.

Olfactory Communication between Primate Sexes

Among primates, the prosimians provide the clearest evidence for communication between the sexes by olfaction: many possess specialized, apocrine scent-glands used for territorial marking, for self-marking and for marking the females by males (in *Loris tardigradus lydekkerianus*[46], in *Lemur catta*[47-49]). Closely similar behaviour has been described in the marmoset, *Oedipanidus spixi*[50], which possesses specialized perineal and genital glands that become functional at puberty. In the view of Marler[51], olfactory communication plays little part in the distance communication of monkeys and apes, although he points out that the urine of oestrous females seems to convey information about their condition to males in the group: this is reminiscent of the observations of Beach and Gilmore[36] that dogs spend more time investigating urine from receptive than from non-receptive bitches. Certainly, the strong-smelling vaginal discharge of toque macaques, *Macaca sinica*, during certain days of the menstrual cycle can be detected by the human observer[52]. In several species of macaques—*M. radiata*[53], *M. irus*[54], *M. nemestrina*[55]—field studies have revealed that scenting the female's anogenital region by males is an almost routine occurrence.

The possible role of olfaction in microsmatic, higher primates has not been investigated experimentally. The many field observations and the frequent scenting of the female's genital region by male rhesus monkeys during controlled mating tests (personal observations), however, led us to study the problem in laboratory conditions. The sexual behaviour of male rhesus monkeys undergoes rhythmic variations in relation to the menstrual cycles of the females with which they are paired[56,57]. These variations are abolished by ovariectomy, and the sexual behaviour of males can be restored by injecting ovarian hormones into the female. These findings provide clear evidence that the males are aware of their partners' endocrine status. When progesterone is injected into ovariectomized females receiving oestrogen, the sexual activity of the pair declines[58]. Two distinct mechanisms appear to underlie this decline: the first depends on a decrease in the receptivity of females indicated by increased refusals of male mounting attempts; the second depends on a decline in the attractiveness of females, indicated by the relative failure of her sexual invitations to stimulate male mounting behaviour[59]. While the first mechanism seems to depend on a change in a hormone-dependent mechanism within the brain of the female, the second mechanism requires the mediation of the distance receptors of the male.

Michael and Saayman[60] found that when small doses of oestrogen were administered intravaginally they were more effective in stimulating the sexual interest of males than similar doses given subcutaneously. They used doses too small to cause a significant increase in female receptivity (that is, in the number of sexual presentations). This pointed to an oestrogen-dependent vaginal mechanism capable of stimulating male sexual activity, and to one that could do so independently of any change in female receptivity. Unfortunately, these experiments did not distinguish clearly between tactile and olfactory transmission of information, because males had access to the females. We have now considered the possibility that olfactory cues are involved.

Experiments with Monkeys

Three adult male rhesus monkeys of known sexual potency were first trained to press a lever for food reward on a fixed ratio schedule while confined in primate chairs.

When high rates of pressing were consistently achieved, the animals were transferred to a free-cage situation in which each side of a large, twin-compartment cage was equipped with a lever, and where animals could be observed from behind a one-way vision mirror. Operating the levers 250 times activated a servo motor which raised a dividing partition between the two compartments. Initially, the reinforcement was food and, when all the males were thoroughly familiar with the situation, the reinforcement was a female rhesus monkey. If males pressed rapidly 250 times, they obtained access to females for 1 h, during which their behaviour was scored; the animals were then separated. The females were untrained and not able to raise the partition. One male never performed consistently and results are based on the behaviour of the other two. Each male was paired with three ovariectomized females on alternate days, and one of these (the control) received subcutaneous injections of oestradiol (10 µg/day) throughout the experiment. The two other ovariectomized (anhormonal) females initially received no treatment. Both males regularly pressed to criterion and obtained access to the control female (pressed in all of fourteen tests) during a 22 day period but did so only intermittently for the anhormonal females (pressed in six out of twenty-eight tests) during the same period. This demonstrated that the males were prepared to work more consistently for oestrogenized than for non-oestrogenized partners. At this point, the males were rendered anosmic by plugging the nasal olfactory area with gauze impregnated with bismuth–iodoform–paraffin paste and by cutting the nerve supply to the organ of Jacobson. The plugs were inserted so as to leave a clear nasal airway which permitted the animals to breathe normally. With the males rendered anosmic, testing was continued as previously with both control and experimental females: presumably because of their previous experience with the females, the males continued to press for, and gain access to, the one receiving oestrogen but did not do so for the other two. Use was then made of the observation[11] that administration of oestrogen intravaginally markedly increased male sexual interest and mounting activity[60]. With the males anosmic, oestrogen was administered intravaginally (5 µg/day) to the two previously anhormonal females. As a further control procedure, testing with a normal male was carried out to demonstrate that, after a few days, both these females were stimulating mounting activity and ejaculations. Although the two anosmic males were pressing to criterion for the control female receiving subcutaneous oestrogen (eleven out of fourteen tests), the administration of intravaginal oestrogen to the other two females induced no changes in the behaviour of the anosmic males which continued to respond to them as though they were anhormonal; lever pressing to criterion occurred in only one out of twenty-eight tests. Between 5 and 8 days after removing the nasal plugs (approximately the time required for the restoration of olfactory acuity in similarly treated human subjects), however, both males commenced lever pressing for the two females receiving intravaginal oestrogen. Because in two pairs the male had previously never pressed or obtained access to females during the "pre-blocking" and "blocked" periods, the onset of lever pressing for the first time after unblocking occurred in the absence of any previously rewarding sexual experience of these females (Fig. 1). It was important to distinguish between olfactory cues and tactile information received from the vagina, and so physical access to their female partners was denied males until they had pressed to criterion on three separate occasions. It was probable that their operant behaviour would rapidly extinguish in the absence of any reward, and so they were then allowed access to the females when a normal mounting sequence with ejaculation immediately occurred (Table 1).

The intravaginal dose administered was insufficient to produce any changes in the invitational motor behaviour of these females or any changes in the coloration of their sexual skin: the fact that there were no changes in the males' behaviour until the anosmia was reversed made it unlikely that they were influenced by visual, behavioural cues. Experiments with progesterone have indicated that its administration to females depresses the lever pressing behaviour of males, and that this effect is reversed when the hormone is withdrawn.

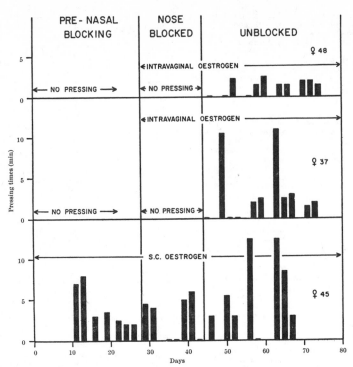

PRE - NASAL BLOCKING | NOSE BLOCKED | UNBLOCKED

Fig. 1. Effect of reversible anosmia on the lever-pressing behaviour of a male rhesus monkey when pressing 250 times gave access to each of three ovariectomized female partners. Female 45 (control) received subcutaneously 10 μg/day of oestradiol throughout. Females 48 and 37 received 5 μg/day of oestradiol intravaginally only during and after the period of the male's anosmia. The male responded and obtained access to females 48 and 37 only after the anosmia was reversed—indicating that the sexual attractiveness of these females was communicated to the male by olfaction.

Table 1. EFFECT OF ANOSMIA ON THE LEVER-PRESSING PERFORMANCE AND SEXUAL BEHAVIOUR OF TWO MALE RHESUS MONKEYS EACH PAIRED WITH THREE FEMALES (126 TESTS)

	Pre-nasal blocking		Noses blocked		Noses unblocked	
Male No.	41	38	41	38	41	38
Female No.						
	Percentage of tests in which lever pressing to criterion occurred					
37 (exptl)	14	0	0	0	100*	100
48 (exptl)	86	0	14	0	100	100
45 (control)	100	100	100	57	100	86
	Mean time for 250 lever presses (min)					
37	4·00†	—	—	—	2·83 ± 0·32*	3·50 ± 1·26
48	3·58 ± 0·28*	—	4·00†	—	2·28 ± 0·21	1·78 ± 0·14
45	3·42 ± 0·36	4·00 ± 0·93	5·50 ± 0·36	4·87 ± 0·42‡	3·71 ± 0·37	7·16 ± 1·78*
	Mean latent period to first lever press (min)					
37	13·50†	—	—	—	5·00 ± 2·46*	7·50 ± 0·48
48	9·41 ± 2·83*	—	6·00†	—	6·00 ± 2·73	10·92 ± 2·92
45	1·42 ± 0·13	14·85 ± 3·52	5·28 ± 1·81	17·62 ± 3·38‡	5·00 ± 0·85	16·60 ± 2·66*
	Mean No. of mounts per test					
37	2·3 ± 0·5	1·9 ± 0·7	0	0	8·6 ± 1·8	9·0 ± 0·9
48	0	1·7 ± 0·5	0	0	5·7 ± 1·6	13·1 ± 0·9
45	12·0 ± 1·3	5·7 ± 0·6	10·8 ± 0·4	6·1 ± 0·5	13·0 ± 0·9	7·6 ± 0·9
	Mean No. of ejaculations per test					
37	0	0	0	0	0·4 ± 0·2	1·6 ± 0·2
48	0	0	0	0	0·4 ± 0·2	1·7 ± 0·2
45	2·6 ± 0·2	2·1 ± 0·1	2·6 ± 0·2	2·0 ± 0·00	1·9 ± 0·1	2·4 ± 0·2
	Mean time for ejaculation to occur (min)					
37	—	—	—	—	18·0 ± 6·7§	6·3 ± 1·1
48	—	—	—	—	26·5 ± 10·0§	8·9 ± 2·4
45	2·0 ± 0·2	0·9 ± 0·2	1·6 ± 0·3	1·4 ± 0·2	3·5 ± 0·7	0·9 ± 0·1

—, No data; *responses in 6 tests; †in 1 test; ‡in 4 tests; §in 3 tests.
All means are based on seven tests except where indicated.
Female 45 (control) received subcutaneously 10 μg/day of oestradiol throughout: females 37 and 48 (experimental) received intravaginally 5 μg/day of oestradiol only during and after the period of the males' anosmia.

Pheromones in Monkeys

These studies provide strong evidence that sexual excitation and activity in male rhesus monkeys are mediated in certain cases by a hormone-dependent, olfactorily acting pheromone, possibly of vaginal origin. Communication over even short distances that serves to identify females in the society with ovulatory follicles would have the obvious selective advantage of increasing the likelihood of fertile matings.

In women, changes in olfactory acuity to pleasant, musk-like odours ('Exaltolide') occur in relation to the menstrual cycle[61,62] and, more specifically, in relation to ovulation[63]. Furthermore, there is evidence that progesterone changes the quality of odours emitted[64].

Although in humans, olfactory influences may frequently be below the threshold of consciousness, it is now clear that in certain microsmatic, infra-human primates they play a larger part in determining interactions between the sexes than was previously suspected.

We thank Mr Peter McKelvie for his advice. This work was supported by grants from the National Institute of Mental Health and the Bethlem Royal and Maudsley Hospital Research Fund.

[1] Bethe, A., *Naturwissenschaften*, **20**, 177 (1932).
[2] Karlson, P., and Butenandt, A., *Ann. Rev. Entomol.*, **4**, 39 (1959).
[3] Kalmus, H., *Proc. Second Intern. Cong. Endocrinol. Symp.* 7, 188 (1964).
[4] Wilson, E. O., *Sci. Amer.*, **208**, 100 (1963).
[5] Carthy, J. D., *Behaviour*, 3, 275 (1951).
[6] Butenandt, A., Beckmann, R., and Hecker, E., *Hoppe-Seyler's Z. Physiol. Chem.*, **324**, 71 (1961).
[7] Schneider, D., *Z. Vergl. Physiol.*, **40**, 8 (1957).
[8] Schneider, D., *Proc. First Intern. Symp. on Olfaction and Taste*, 85 (London, 1963).
[9] Jacobson, M., Beroza, M., and Jones, W. A., *Science*, **132**, 1011 (1960).
[10] Jacobson, M., Beroza, M., and Jones, W. A., *J. Amer. Chem. Soc.*, **83**, 4819 (1961).
[11] Butler, C. G., *Biol. Rev.*, **42**, 42 (1967).
[12] Beroza, M., in *Agents Affecting Fertility* (edit. by Austin, C. R., and Perry, J. S.), 136 (Churchill, London, 1965).
[13] Keller, J. C., Mitchell, E. B., McKibben, G., and Davich, T. B., *J. Econ. Entomol.*, **57**, 609 (1964).
[14] Wigglesworth, V. B., in *The Principles of Insect Physiology*, sixth ed. (Methuen, London, 1965).
[15] Bruce, H. M., and Parkes, A. S., in *Agents Affecting Fertility* (edit. by Austin, C. R., and Perry, J. S.), 124 (Churchill, London, 1965).
[16] Whitten, W. K., in *Advances in Reproductive Physiology*, 1 (edit. by McLaren, A.), 155 (Academic Press, New York, 1966).
[17] Lee, S. van der, and Boot, L. M., *Acta Physiol. Pharm. Neerl.*, **4**, 442 (1955).
[18] Lee, S. van der, and Boot, L. M., *Acta Physiol. Pharm. Neerl.*, **5**, 213 (1956).
[19] Whitten, W. K., *Nature*, **180**, 1436 (1957).
[20] Whitten, W. K., *J. Endocrinol.*, **18**, 102 (1959).
[21] Whitten, W. K., *J. Endocrinol.*, **17**, 307 (1958).
[22] Marsden, H. M., and Bronson, F. H., *Science*, **144**, 1469 (1964).
[23] Whitten, W. K., *J. Endocrinol.*, **13**, 399 (1956).
[24] Lamond, D. R., *J. Endocrinol.*, **18**, 343 (1959).
[25] Bruce, H. M., *Nature*, **184**, 105 (1959).
[26] Bruce, H. M., *J. Reprod. Fertil.*, **1**, 96 (1960).
[27] Parkes, A. S., and Bruce, H. M., *J. Reprod. Fertil.*, **4**, 303 (1962).
[28] Bruce, H. M., and Parrott, D. M. V., *Science*, **131**, 1526 (1960).
[29] Bruce, H. M., *J. Reprod. Fertil.*, **10**, 141 (1965).

[30] Hughes, R. L., *CSIRO Wildlife Res.*, **9**, 115 (1964).
[31] Eleftheriou, B. E., Bronson, F. H., and Zarrow, M. X., *Science*, **137**, 764 (1962).
[32] Schinckel, P. G., *Austral. Vet. J.*, **30**, 189 (1954).
[33] Signoret, J. P., and du Mesnil du Buisson, F., *Proc. Fourth Intern. Cong. Anim. Reprod.*, 171 (The Hague, 1961).
[34] Signoret, J. P., and Mauleon, P., *Ann. Biol. Anim. Biochem. Biophys.*, **2**, 167 (1962).
[35] Fuller, J. L., and Dubuis, E. M., in *The Behaviour of Domestic Animals* (edit. by Hafez, E. S. E.), 247 (Baillière, Tindall and Cox, London, 1962).
[36] Beach, F. A., and Gilmore, R. W., *J. Mammal.*, **30**, 391 (1949).
[37] Berliner, V. R., in *Reproduction in Domestic Animals* (edit. by Cole, H. H., and Cupps, P. T.), 267 (Academic Press, New York, 1959).
[38] Wierzbowski, S., and Hafez, E. S. E., *Proc. Fourth Intern. Cong. Anim. Reprod.* (The Hague, 1961).
[39] Hart, G. H., Mead, S. W., and Regan, W. M., *Endocrinology*, **39**, 221 (1946).
[40] Kelley, R. B., *Bull. Counc. Sci. Indust. Res. Austral.*, No. 112 (1937).
[41] Lindsay, D. R., *Anim. Behav.*, **13**, 75 (1965).
[42] Le Magnen, J., *Arch. Sci. Physiol.*, **6**, 295 (1952).
[43] Carr, W. J., Loeb, L. S., and Dissinger, M. L., *J. Comp. Physiol. Psychol.*, **59**, 370 (1965).
[44] Carr, W. J., Loeb, L. S., and Wylie, N. R., *J. Comp. Physiol. Psychol.*, **62**, 336 (1966).
[45] Carr, W. J., and Caul, W. F., *Anim. Behav.*, **10**, 20 (1962).
[46] Ilse, D. R., *Anim. Behav.*, **3**, 118 (1955).
[47] Montagne, W., *Ann. NY Acad. Sci.*, **102**, 190 (1962).
[48] Petter, J. J., in *Primate Behaviour* (edit. by DeVore, I.), 292 (Holt, Rinehart and Winston, New York, 1965).
[49] Jolly, A., in *Social Communication among Primates* (edit. by Altmann, S. A.), 3 (The University of Chicago Press, 1967).
[50] Epple, G., *Folia Primatol.*, **7**, 37 (1967).
[51] Marler, P., in *Primate Behaviour* (edit. by DeVore, I.), 544 (Holt, Rinehart and Winston, New York, 1965).
[52] Jay, P., in *Behaviour of Non-Human Primates* (edit. by Schrier, A. M., Harlow, H. F., and Stollnitz, F.), 525 (Academic Press, New York, 1965).
[53] Simonds, P. E., in *Primate Behaviour* (edit. by DeVore, I.), 175 (Holt, Rinehart and Winston, New York, 1965).
[54] Ellefson, J., thesis, Univ. California, Berkeley (1968).
[55] van Hooff, J. A. R., *Symp. Zool. Soc.*, **8**, 97 (1962).
[56] Michael, R. P., *Proc. Roy. Soc. Med.*, **58**, 595 (1965).
[57] Michael, R. P., Herbert, J., and Welegalla, J., *J. Endocrinol.*, **39**, 81 (1967).
[58] Michael, R. P., Saayman, G., and Zumpe, D., *Nature*, **215**, 554 (1967).
[59] Michael, R. P., Saayman, G., and Zumpe, D., *J. Endocrinol.*, **39**, 309 (1967).
[60] Michael, R. P., and Saayman, G., *J. Endocrinol.*, **41**, 231 (1968).
[61] Le Magnen, J., *CR Acad. Sci.*, **228**, 947 (1949).
[62] Le Magnen, J., *Arch. Sci. Physiol.*, **6**, 125 (1952).
[63] Vierling, J. S., and Rock, J., *J. Appl. Physiol.*, **22**, 311 (1967).
[64] Kloek, J., *Psychiat. Neurol. Neurochir.*, **64**, 309 (1961).

Communication and Language in the Home-Raised Chimpanzee

The gestures, "words," and behavioral signals of home-raised apes are critically examined.

Winthrop N. Kellogg

Oral speech develops in the human infant as an outgrowth of his contact with older humans who are continuously using language. A deaf mute fails to speak because he never hears the acoustic patterns which make up words. He has no sound patterns to follow, no models to imitate. If the ear itself is functioning but the child is mentally retarded, he may be able to hear but not to imitate. Again, he does not learn to speak. A normal ear, a normal brain and speech organs, the continuous hearing of spoken language, and a great deal of imitation are necessary for the completion of the process.

The author is professor emeritus of experimental psychology at Florida State University, Tallahassee.

The ear, the speech mechanism, and the capacity to imitate are furnished by the child. The linguistic models come from the human environment in which he lives. Also furnished by the child—perhaps as a result of, or in connection with, his imitation—is a long prespeech period in which he produces both vowels and consonants, but not words. This period of prattling and babbling seems to be a necessary forerunner of the words to come. Children who acquire normal speech habits do so as a kind of outgrowth and expansion of this developmental phase (1). In the terminology of the experimental psychologist, it may be thought of as a period of "preconditioning" or "pretraining."

If special requirements such as these are necessary for speech to occur in a young human, does any other organism below man possess them? The chimpanzee certainly has a good enough ear, as measurements of auditory sensitivity have demonstrated (2). So far as the larynx and speech parts are concerned, the general assumption has been that these also are sufficiently well developed to permit the articulation of words—although Kelemen (3) takes exception to this position. The chimpanzee is a great imitator of the movements and activities it sees performed, although it is not as good an imitator as the child (4, 5). It does not naturally imitate sounds and noises, like the parrot or the myna bird, which can reproduce human word sounds but are less apt at nonvocal imitation. Also, the development of the chimpanzee brain as compared with that of man remains in doubt.

But has a chimpanzee (or any of the other apes, for that matter) ever been given a really adequate opportunity to learn and to imitate human speech signals as they occur in their natural context? Has a chimpanzee been exposed to the environmental sound-models which are necessary—for as long a time and in the same way as human children?

The Ape-Rearing Experiment

The ape-rearing experiment should furnish an answer to such questions. If communication were ever to evolve, it would seem that the environment of a human household would offer the most favorable conditions. To be sure, the keeping of infrahuman primates as pets or playthings is by no means a novel practice and can be traced historically as far back as the ancient Greeks and Egyptians (6). Apes as household pets are not uncommon today and several books by lay authors attest to the problems involved (7). Such ventures have never given any indication of the development of human language. But pet behavior is not child behavior, and pet treatment is not child treatment.

It is quite another story, therefore, for trained and qualified psychobiologists to observe and measure the reactions of a home-raised pongid amid controlled experimental home surroundings. Such research is difficult, confining, and time-consuming. Too often, unfortunately, its purpose is misunderstood. Since 1932 reports of five such experiments by qualified investigators have been published in the United States and one in Russia. Four of the U.S. studies were sponsored by the Yerkes Laboratories of Primate Biology at Orange Park, Florida (8). The animals used in all instances were chimpanzees.

The Russian research and two of those conducted in America had a human child or children as permanent in-house controls. In the other experiments the chimps were raised in a household with adult humans alone. Table 1 gives some of the characteristics of the different experiments, including the approximate duration of each,

Table 1. Prinicipal chimpanzee-raising experiments.

Publication date	Investigator	Approx. duration	Approx. age of chimp at start	Sex and name of chimp	No. of child controls
1932	Jacobsen, Jacobsen, and Yoshioka (20)	1 year	A few days	F; Alpha	0
1932–67	Kellogg and Kellogg (5, 10–12)	9 months	7½ months	F; Gua	1
1935	Kohts (9)	2½ years	1½ years	M; Joni	1
None	Finch	3 years	3 days	M; Fin	2
1951–54	Hayes and Hayes (4, 14–18)	6½ years	3 days	F; Viki	0
1967	Gardner and Gardner (19)	In progress	9–15 months	F; Washoe	0

the number of child controls, the ages of the chimpanzees, and the names of the investigators. In the present article we shall deal only with those aspects of these researches having to do with communication and language. The work of Kohts (9), Kellogg and Kellogg (5, 10–12), C. Hayes (13), Hayes and Hayes (4, 14–18), and Gardner and Gardner (19) is of special importance in this connection. The observations of Jacobsen et al. (20) do not deal with this topic, and Finch himself never published any of his findings.

The Pronunciation of Words

The results of such projects show in general that the infant chimp, when properly handled in the home situation, reacts in many ways as a young child does. It adapts rapidly to the physical features of the environment (11, 18), shows a strong attachment for its caretaker or experimental mother, passes a good many of the preschool developmental tests designed for children, and imitates acts performed by adults without special training. Up to the age of perhaps 3 years, its "mental age" is not far behind that of a child. At the same time, its skeletal and muscular development are much more rapid than those of a child.

With regard to the problem of communication, the results at first glance are disappointing. For even in the experimentally controlled environment in which a home-raised chimpanzee is given the same linguistic and social advantages as a human baby, the chimp displays little evidence of vocal imitation. Despite its generally high level of imitative behavior, it never copies or reproduces human word sounds. Yerkes has written with reference to this matter that in neither the studies of Kellogg nor of Finch "were attempts to imitate speech or other indications of learning to use human language observed" (21). Kohts noted also that her home-raised chimpanzee displayed not the slightest evidence of trying to reproduce any human vocalizations (9, p. 576).

Moreover, no ape has ever been known to go through the long period of babbling and prattling which, in the human baby, seems to be the necessary prerequisite to the subsequent articulation of word sounds. Vocalized play of this sort was absent in the Kelloggs' chimp, who made no sounds "without some definite provocation . . . and in most cases this stimulus was obviously of an emotional character" (5, p. 281). The Hayeses noted also that their ape was much "less vocal" and was relatively silent as compared to a child

(*15*, p. 106; *16*).

Despite these observations, the usual chimpanzee noises—such as the food-bark, the "oo oo" cry, and screeching or screaming—were present in all of these experiments and were vigorously employed. The use of these and other sounds as natural communicative signals has been examined by Goodall (*22*) for chimpanzees in the wild, and by Yerkes and Learned (*23*) for captive animals. It is a question whether such sounds can be modified or shaped to fit the human language pattern.

On the positive side belong the remarkable cases of so-called talking apes. A trained chimpanzee studied by Witmer as far back as 1909 was reported to be able to pronounce the word "mama" but only with great difficulty. The "m" of "mama" was well done, but the "ah" was not voiced (*24*).

A few years later, Furness (*25*), working diligently with a young orang-utan, finally succeeded in getting it to say "papa" and "cup." In training the animal to say "papa," Furness found it necessary to place his fingers on the animal's lips and to open and close them in the proper rhythm.

The best known and most successful of these linguistic efforts is that of the Hayeses (*13*), who were able to get their chimpanzee Viki to emit recognizable versions of the words "papa," "mama," and "cup." A beginning was also made toward the sound of "up." Viki thereby exceeded the vocabulary level of either of the other apes, although interestingly enough, she pronounced the same words that they had. She had only one vowel for all of her word sounds, a hoarse and exaggerated stage whisper.

The first step in Viki's speech training was designed to teach her to produce a sound—any sound—on demand. This was done by reinforcing whatever noises she made during the training session, such as the pleasure barks elicited by showing her food, or the "oo oo" which resulted from withdrawing the food. It was 5 months, however, before the animal could emit a sound promptly on cue, and the noise she made then was a new one: a hoarse "ah," quite unlike the normal chimpanzee vocalizations which had been previously rewarded.

The Hayeses taught Viki to say "mama" by manipulating her lips as she said "ah," then gradually reduced the amount of manipulation as she learned to make the lip movements herself. In this way the animal finally came to say "mama," softly and hoarsely, and without help (although she persisted in putting her own forefinger on her upper lip). Viki's later words were learned more quickly, making use of existing consonant-like mouth sounds which she had often produced in play. Fortunately, her articulation and vocal behavior have been preserved in a sound motion picture film (*14*).

These then, "mama," "papa," "cup," and possibly "up," represent the acme of chimpanzee achievement in the production of human speech sounds. But they were learned only with the greatest difficulty. And, even after she could reproduce them, the animal's words were sometimes confused and were used incorrectly. The most important finding of the Hayeses was perhaps not that their chimp could enunciate a few human sounds. It lay rather in the discovery that these sound patterns were extremely hard for the ape to master, that they never came naturally or easily, and that she had trouble afterward in keeping the patterns straight.

Comprehension of Language

The ability of a home-raised chimpanzee to "understand" or react characteristically to spoken words or phrases is perhaps best illustrated by the Kelloggs' ape Gua. These investigators kept a daily record of the language units which both the chimpanzee and her human control were able to discriminate. In the case of the chimpanzee, the words reacted to varied from such relatively simple commands as "No no" and "Come here" to statements like "Close the door," "Blow the horn" (of a car), "Don't put that in your mouth," and "Go to Daddy," "Go to Mama," "Go to Donald" (as the case might be). In the first 4 months of the study, the chimp was slightly ahead of the child in the total number of spoken phrases to which she could respond correctly. This was no doubt due to her superior locomotor ability since, in the beginning, the human subject was obviously unable to comply with such commands as "Get up on the chair." During the last 5 months of the period of comparison, the child surpassed the ape in comprehension. The total score for the entire 9 months was 68 specific response patterns for the child and 58 for the chimpanzee (5).

Although the ape was only slightly behind her human control at the end, it is noteworthy that she had earlier scored higher than he. This means that she was overtaken by the child, who accelerated at a more rapid rate. Had the comparison continued for a longer period, all indications are that the human subject would have left the animal far behind in the comprehension of words.

Spontaneous Gesturing

Does an anthropoid ape, maintained in the human household, ever use or develop any system of motions or gestures which carry special significance or meaning? The answer is "yes," the amount and type of gesturing depending upon the particular home environment and the particular animal. Regarding this matter, the Hayeses have written about Viki that she "makes relatively little use of gestures of the hand alone" (17, p. 299). She would nevertheless take hold of the experimenter's hand and lead him where she wanted to go, an activity earlier observed by Yerkes (26) in an orangutan with which he worked.

Mrs. Kohts reports that gestures were commonly employed by her chimpanzee Joni and, surprisingly, that many of the chimp gestures were like those used by her son. "Both infants sometimes show a nearly similar gesture language. Thus 'request' is expressed by extending hand forward, 'rejection of food' by turning face and head aside, 'thirst' by putting hand to mouth, 'desire to draw attention to oneself' by tugging at dress" (9, p. 544).

The Kelloggs' chimpanzee Gua also employed a kind of language of gesture or of action, but in this instance the gesturing of the ape was generally different from that of the child. Most of Gua's gestures consisted of movement patterns which occurred regularly just before or in advance of some subsequent or final act. In this way they served as preparatory signals for the terminal response to come later. Viewed objectively, these signaling movements can be interpreted as anticipatory reactions which were consistent with and occurred in specific situations. It need not be presumed, therefore, that they necessarily represented conscious or purposeful efforts on the part of the animal to "tell" others what she wanted. Their reliability was confirmed by numerous repetitions. The principal instances of this language of action are given in Table 2.

The most significant of the gestures listed in Table 2 are probably those for "sleep" or "sleepiness," those indicating bladder and bowel needs, and

Table 2. Early gesture signals of chimpanzee Gua.*

Behavior pattern	Human interpretation
Biting or chewing at clothing or fingers of experimenter	"Hungry"
Climbing into high chair	Same
Protruding lips toward cup	"Drink"
Pushing cup away	"Enough"
Removing bib from her neck	"Finished eating"
Taking hand of experimenter and hanging on it	"Swing me"
Throwing self prone on floor	"Sleepy" or "Tired" (goes to sleep at once when put to bed for nap)
Pulling hand of experimenter to coke bottle	"Help me" or "Lift this for me"
Holding of genitalia	"Need to urinate (or defecate)"

* Adapted from Kellogg and Kellogg (5, pp. 275–278).

the "help me" signal in drinking a coke. The latter occurred spontaneously during a minor test problem. The animal was seated upon the floor with legs spread apart, and a bottle of Coca Cola with cap removed was placed between her feet. Although she could hold the bottle at the proper angle while drinking, she had not yet learned how to transport it from the floor to her mouth. Unsuccessful attempts consisted of licking or sucking at the opening of the bottle and of overturning it in the crude attempt to pick it up. Finally, after staring at the bottle and looking up at the experimenter, she took his hand in one of her own and drew it gently down to the base of the bottle. This was by no means an isolated instance, since it appeared several times during repetitions of the test. Similar reactions of placing the experimenter's hand on objects to be manipulated were also observed by the Hayeses with their chimpanzee Viki.

Two-Way Communication by Gesture

The spontaneous use of gesture movements by chimpanzees raises the question whether this ability to gesture can be developed into something more. Could an intelligent animal learn a series of regular or standardized signals—as a sort of semaphore system? Even though a chimp may lack the laryngeal structure or neural speech centers of man, it does not necessarily follow that it has deficiencies in general motor activity. Might it therefore be able to communicate back and forth by a series of hand movements, arm signals, and postures? Is two-way communication by gesture possible? This is the question which has recently been asked by the Gardners (19) and is now under active investigation by them.

It should be understood, however, that the signs and signals employed by the Gardners constitute a systematic and recognized form of voiceless communication. The alphabet language devised for the deaf, in which each word is spelled out by individual hand and finger movements, would obviously be unsuitable. What the Gardners are using is a series of more general or more encompassing hand and arm movements (not involving spelling) which serve as substitutes for entire words, phrases, or sentences. The American Sign Language meets these requirements. This is an accepted form of human language and is in active use today in Canada and the United States, principally by the deaf (27).

The chimpanzee subject of the Gardners' study, a young female named Washoe, has been undergoing training in the understanding and transmitting of sign-language signals since June 1966. The animal lives in a fully furnished house trailer and also has access to children's toys and equipment, as well as to extensive play areas. The human beings who come into contact with Washoe communicate with each other in Washoe's presence only by means of sign language. She hears no human words except those spoken inadvertently by workmen or others not associated with the project. Conditioning methods have been used to establish many of the signs which are employed.

In support of this new approach is the fact that both chimpanzees and gorillas in the wild state are known to use specific gestures and postures (along with noises) for communicating among themselves (22, 28). Chimpanzees in laboratory experiments will also adopt characteristic attitudes as a means of communication. An example is the posture of imploring or begging observed by Wolfe (29). As for the home-raised chimp, the gestures of both Mrs. Kohts' Joni and the Kelloggs' Gua have already been noted (see Table 2). There would seem, therefore, to be considerable promise in the gesture method.

After 16 months of training, Washoe was able to use 19 signs reliably. Five more signs were in the developmental stage. A good many of the movements used by the animal are standard American Sign Language signals. Some are variants of the standard and a few are chimpanzee originals. There is evidence that she understands a great many more signs than she can use herself. Some of the gestures employed by Washoe are given in Table 3.

The most significant thing about these gesture signals is that they are by no means confined to the names of specific persons or things. (They are not all nouns.) Some of them—for example, "please," "hurry," "sorry"— are verbs and adjectives which apply in varying social contexts and are used effectively in different situations of the same class. As such they are far in advance of all previous chimpanzee efforts to communicate with human beings.

Summary

Although often misunderstood, the scientific rationale for rearing an anthropoid ape in a human household is to find out just how far the ape can go in absorbing the civilizing influences of the environment. To what degree is it capable of responding like a child and to what degree will genetic factors limit its development? At least six comprehensive studies by qualified investigators have been directed wholly or partly to this problem. All of these studies employed young chimpanzees as subjects and some also had in-house child controls whose day-to-day development could be compared directly with that of the experimental animal. In general, the results of this sort of research show that the home-raised chimp adapts rapidly to the physical features of the household. It does many things as well as a human child and some of them better (for example, those involving strength and climbing).

By far the greatest deficiency shown by the ape in the human environment is its lack of language ability. This eliminates the verbal communication which humans enjoy, and with it the vast amount of social intercourse and learning which are dependent upon language. Even amid human surroundings a chimp never prattles or babbles

Table 3. Some significant gesture-language signs used by chimpanzee Washoe.

Meaning of sign	Description	Context
Come-gimme	Beckoning, with wrist or knuckles as pivot.	To persons, dogs, etc.; also for objects out of reach such as food or toys.
Up	Point up with index finger.	Wants a lift to reach object such as grapes on vine, leaves, etc., or wants to be placed on someone's shoulders.
Hear-listen	Index finger touches ear.	For loud or strange sounds: bells, car horns, sonic booms, footsteps, etc.
Toothbrush	Using index finger as brush, rub front teeth.	At end of meals. Once when Washoe noticed toothbrush in strange bathroom.
Hurt	The extended index fingers are jabbed toward each other. Can be used to indicate location of pain.	To indicate cuts and bruises on herself or on others. Can be elicited by red stains on a person.
Hurry	Shaking open hand at the wrist. [Correct ASL (American Sign Language) form: use index and second fingers extended side by side.]	Frequently follows signs such as "come-gimme," "out," "open," "go."
Sorry	Rub bent hand across chest. (Correct ASL form: rub fisted hand, circular motion.)	After biting someone, or when someone has been hurt in some other way (not necessarily by Washoe). When told to apologize for mischief.
Please	Rub open hand on chest, then extend in a begging gesture. (Correct ASL form: use fingertips and circular motion.)	Asking for objects and activities. Frequently combined: "Please go," "Out please," "Please drink," etc.

as a young child does when beginning to talk. Although it imitates the behavior of others readily, it seems to lack the ability for vocal imitation. The neural speech centers of the brain are no doubt deficient in this respect and it is possible also that the larynx and speech organs are incapable of producing the complex sound patterns of human language. One long-time attempt to teach a home-raised chimp to pronounce human words succeeded only in getting the animal to mouth unvoiced whispers of the words "mama," "papa," "cup," and "up."

At the same time, a chimpanzee in the home, as in the wild state, uses gestures or movements as communicating signals. This suggests the possibility of training a home-raised ape to employ a standardized system of gestures as a means of two-way communication. Such an investigation is now under way, using a gesture language devised for the deaf. Considerable progress has already been made in both the receiving and sending of gesture signals by this method. The technique seems to offer a much greater likelihood of success than other methods of intercommunication between chimpanzees and humans.

References and Notes

1. F. L. Smith and G. A. Miller, Eds., *The Genesis of Language* (M.I.T. Press, Cambridge, Mass., 1966).
2. J. H. Elder, *J. Comp. Psychol.* 17, 157–183 (1934); *Amer. J. Physiol.* 112, 109 (1935).
3. G. Kelemen, *J. Morphol.* 82, 229–256 (1948); *Arch. Otolaryngol.* 50, 740 (1949).
4. K. J. Hayes and C. Hayes, *J. Comp. Physiol. Psychol.* 45, 450 (1952).
5. W. N. Kellogg and L. A. Kellogg, *The Ape and the Child: A Study of Environmental Influence on Early Behavior* (Hafner, New York, 1967; originally published by McGraw-Hill, 1933).
6. R. Morris and D. Morris, *Men and Apes* (McGraw-Hill, New York, 1966).
7. B. Harrisson, *Orang-utan* (Collins, London, 1962); L. Hess, *Christine the Baby Chimp* (Bell, London, 1954); A. M. Hoyt, *Toto and I: A Gorilla in the Family* (Lippincott, New York, 1941); C. Kearton, *My Friend Toto: The Adventures of a Chimpanzee and the Story of His Journey from the Congo to London* (Arrowsmith, London, 1925); G. D. Lintz, *Animals Are My Hobby* (McBride, New York, 1942).
8. Now the Yerkes Regional Primate Research Center of Emory University at Atlanta, Georgia.
9. N. Kohts, *Infant Ape and Human Child* (Museum Darwinianum, Moscow, 1935).
10. W. N. Kellogg and L. A. Kellogg, *Comparative Tests on a Human and a Chimpanzee Infant of Approximately the Same Age* (16-mm silent film) (Pennsylvania State Univ., Psychol. Cinema Register, University Park, 1932); *Experiments upon a Human and a Chimpanzee Infant after Six Months in the Same Environment, ibid.* (1932).
11. ———, *Some Behavior Characteristics of a Human and a Chimpanzee Infant in the Same Environment, ibid.* (1933); *Some General Reactions of a Human and a Chimpanzee Infant after Six Months in the Same Environment, ibid.* (1933).
12. ———, *Facial Expressions of a Human and a Chimpanzee Infant Following Taste Stimuli, ibid.* (1945).
13. C. Hayes, *The Ape in Our House* (Harper, New York, 1951).
14. K. J. Hayes and C. Hayes, *Vocalization and Speech in Chimpanzees* (16-mm sound film) (Pennsylvania State Univ., Psychol. Cinema Register, University Park, 1950).
15. ———, *Proc. Amer. Phil. Soc.* 95, 105 (1951).
16. ———, *J. Comp. Physiol. Psychol.* 46, 470 (1953).
17. ———, *Human Biol.* 26, 288 (1954).
18. ———, *The Mechanical Interest and Ability of a Home-Raised Chimpanzee* (16-mm silent film) (Pennsylvania State Univ., Psychol. Cinema Register, University Park, 1954).
19. R. A. Gardner and B. T. Gardner (parts I and II), *Psychonomic Bull.* 1, (2), 36 (1967); ———, personal communication; ———, unpublished proposal and progress report, Univ. of Nevada, Reno (1967).
20. C. F. Jacobsen, M. M. Jacobsen, J. G. Yoshioka, *Comp. Psychol. Monogr.* 9 (No. 1), 1–94 (1932).
21. R. M. Yerkes, *Chimpanzees. A Laboratory Colony* (Yale Univ. Press, New Haven, 1943), p. 192.
22. J. Goodall, in *Primate Behavior*, I. Devore, Ed. (Holt, Rinehart & Winston, New York, 1965), pp. 425–473.
23. R. M. Yerkes and B. W. Learned, *Chimpanzee Intelligence and Its Vocal Expressions* (Williams & Wilkins, Baltimore, 1925).
24. L. Witmer, *Psychol. Clinic* (Philadelphia) 3, 179–205 (1909).
25. W. H. Furness, *Proc. Amer. Phil. Soc.* 55, 281 (1916).
26. R. M. Yerkes, *Behav. Monogr.* 3, 1–145 (1916).
27. W. C. Stokoe, D. Casterline, C. G. Croneberg, *A Dictionary of American Sign Language on Linguistic Principles* (Gallaudet College Press, Washington, D.C., 1965).
28. G. B. Schaller, *The Mountain Gorilla: Ecology and Behavior* (Univ. of Chicago Press, Chicago, 1963).
29. J. B. Wolfe, *Comp. Psychol. Monogr.* 12 (5), 1–72 (1936).
30. I am indebted to Dr. Keith J. Hayes who has read most of the material in this article in its preparatory stages and has made a number of helpful suggestions. We are also grateful to Dr. R. A. Gardner and Dr. B. T. Gardner for permission to publish information, from one of their research proposals (see *19*), concerning the progress of the chimpanzee, Washoe, for the first part of their experiment. Further development of the chimpanzee in this remarkable research is anticipated. However, the subject matter as presented here is solely my responsibility.

Honeybees: Do They Use Direction and Distance Information Provided by Their Dancers?

My experiments on the language of the bees (1) received new impetus when I discovered that successful forager bees upon their return to the hive inform their hive mates of the location of the feeding place by wagging dances (2, 3). The direction of the goal in relation to the sun's position and to the polarized light of the sky is indicated by means of the straight part in the wagging run. The distance to the feeding place is announced by the speed of the dance movement (2, 3).

Recently Johnson (4) and Wenner (5) have expressed a different view. They agree that the dancers in the hive indicate the distance as well as the direction of the goal, but they believe that the hive mates do not make any use of the indication of distance (5) and that the information about direction is not used (4) to the accuracy stated in my publications. They propose that the newcomers in their search for the goal are guided by local scents at the feeding site.

I thought the same when I first observed the straight flight of the newcomers toward a distant feeding place. I found that a forager, upon its return to a rich feeding place, will evert its scent organ; this scent is attractive to other bees and is far more intense to their sense of smell and hence is perceived for a greater distance than any other relevant odor (6, pp. 517–520 and Table 44, p. 520). Thus the recruits might follow the odor of the abdominal scent organ. However, I have not been able to confirm this hypothesis. Sealing of the openings of the scent organs, while not impairing the collecting and dancing activities of the treated bees, prevents them from everting their glands so that no odor is given off; nevertheless, recruits alarmed by these dancers still find the feeding place with surprising speed and precision (3, pp. 30–32; 6, pp. 53, 128, 228).

A comprehensive survey of our methods and results has been published (6). I shall relate a few of the experiments, the results of which show that, for the discovery of a good feeding place by recruits, the distance and direction given by the dancers are essential.

1) Whenever a feeding place is close to the hive, foragers upon their return perform round dances. These contain no information about the distance or direction of the food source (6, p. 85). However alerted recruits, closely following the dances learn the odor of the visited blossoms because it clings to the body of the dancers. In most of our experiments, such an odor was the scent of some volatile oil added to the feeding place. Consequently, the newcomers start swarming out in all directions in the neighborhood of their hive in search of this scent, visiting in about equal numbers all the scented foodless plates set up around the hive. If the feeding place is now moved stepwise to greater distances from the hive, an indication of distance and direction from about 25 m becomes recognizable in the dance. This becomes clearer the greater the distance is, and it is quite pronounced at 100 m. By then the round dance has turned into a wagging dance. Accordingly, from a distance of 25 m and up, the recruits begin to search preferably in the direction of the feeding place, while at a distance of about 100 m there are hardly any newcomers searching in the wrong direction or at the wrong distance (6, pp. 150–152). The whole

318

arrangement has not changed except for the increase in distance, which certainly would make it not easier but more difficult for the newcomers to be attracted by the scent organ of the foragers or by any other local odors. The distances stated refer to carniolan bees (*Apis mellifera carnica*). Other races begin indicating direction at even smaller distances (*6*, pp. 294–295, Fig. 251).

2) Inside their dark hive, bees dancing on a vertical comb transpose the solar angle into the gravitational angle; in this way, even without seeing the sky, they inform their companions about the direction they must take in relation to the sun when flying out. After the observation hive is tilted horizontally, the dancing bee simply retains the angle which she kept in relation to the sun during her flight to the feeding place; thus the wagging run points directly to the goal. When the sun and the blue sky are screened off, her dances at once become disoriented and indicate neither a certain distance nor direction (*6*, p. 133). Even these disoriented dances arouse her companions, which now behave as if alarmed by round dances, searching in all directions in the vicinity of the hive (*6*, p. 152, Fig. 132). If the hive is tilted up again into its previous vertical position—all other external and internal factors remaining the same—in a few minutes the disoriented swarming of the recruits turns into an oriented search for the goal (*6*, pp. 154–157, Figs. 134 and 135).

3) In our detour experiments, a mountain ridge or a high building lay between bee hive and feeding place. When we established these feeding places the numbered bees were guided around these obstacles along a hairpin curve; they remained faithful to this route during their foraging flights.

Dancing inside the hive they had a remarkable ability to integrate the actually flown detour by indicating the direction of the "beeline." Observers at the top of the obstacle noticed that recruits sent out by these foragers indeed followed the beeline, overcoming the obstacle by flying over its top to reach the feeding place on the other side. There had been no chance for them to perceive any scent marks of the feeding site from this side of the obstacle nor could they have followed a trail of scent left in the air by foragers who had actually followed quite a different route. Hence there had been nothing to guide them but the information obtained inside their hive (*6*, pp. 177–186, Figs. 164 and 167). Many more of our observations cannot be reconciled with the opinions of Johnson and Wenner. However, the three mentioned above should suffice to clear up the situation.

If one compares Johnson's and Wenner's experimental procedures with ours it can be explained why their results differ from ours. To find out how accurately the recruits follow the direction information, we carried out fan experiments. After setting up an observation hive in a plain, open field, we establish a feeding place at a distance of, for example, 600 m from the hive; this is visited by numbered foragers. As long as this group of bees is gradually moved away from the hive to the 600-m mark the sugar solution offered as food is kept so weak that the bees hardly, if at all, dance upon return and hence arouse no recruits. This procedure requires constant and accurate observation of the bees at the feeding place, as well as inside the hive. Both Wenner and Johnson refer to Wenner's training method (*7*). When gradually bringing the bees to the goal, he offers a strong sucrose solution from

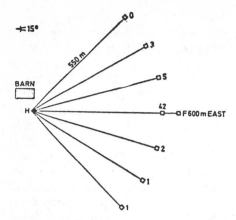

Fig. 1. Fan experiment, 30 August 1955, in a plain, open field. H, beehive; F, feeding place 600 m to the east. White squares represent scent plates 550 m from the hive; added are the numbers of visits by recruits during the first 50 minutes counted from the beginning of the experiment. Weak winds from east-northeast.

the very beginning. Consequently newcomers are continuously aroused; many of them, judging from our own experience, may loose contact with the group while it is moved along. During the next days of testing when food is offered, these bees can be rearoused by feeding, and they go searching all over the surroundings, so providing a serious source of error to the experiments.

At the start of our experiment, seven scent plates without food are set up in the form of a fan, at a distance of 550 m at an angular separation of 15° (Fig. 1). Only now, strongly concentrated sugar solution provided with the same scent as at the scent plates is offered at the feeding place. And only now the foragers begin to dance vividly within the hive; the recruits, following the dances, go searching for the scent they perceived at the dancers' bodies. The number of bees appearing at the various scent plates reveals the direction in which the recruits are searching. In assessing the results we have, in contrast to Johnson and

Wenner, not taken into account the number of visitors appearing at the actual, more distant feeding place (600 m) since conditions here are different owing to the presence of foragers using their scent organs. Moreover, the additional attractiveness of the bee scent may vary greatly for it depends on the degree to which the scent organ is used during the experiment and on wind conditions.

Up to now we have carried out twelve fan experiments (6, pp. 85–96). They show clearly that newcomers in fact do search in the direction of the goal. Johnson carried out some experiments of a similar kind, stating that with this experimental setup he, too, has obtained results expected according to the "dance language," for 78 percent of his recruits arrived in the correct direction of the feeding place. However, this figure is not comparable to results of our experiments since he has summed up the numbers of visits counted at two different places in the direction of training: above all one of them was the feeding place, naturally favored by the coming and going foragers and the attractive odor of their scent organs. In the two other directions there was only one scented plate, without foraging bees (Fig. 2; $M+A$ against N and S, or $N+B$ against M and S). If, as we ourselves have done, one does not take into account the number of visits at the feeding place, in Johnson's experiments not more than 56 percent of the recruits came to the scent plate in the direction of training.

Johnson states that our experiments lack an essential control since the scent plates are not uniform. First, he says, the newcomers could have been attracted in this direction by the feeding foragers. To rule this out I had in control experiments eliminated the strong-

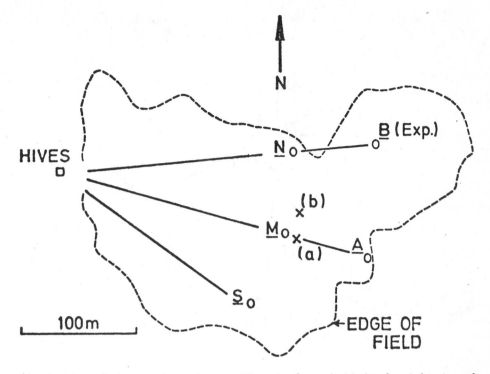

Fig. 2. Map of the experimental area. The experimental (dark-colored bees) and control hives (light-colored bees) were adjacent to one another at the edge of a football practice field (outlined by the broken line). The experimental site in the first series of experiments was *A*; in the second series *B*. The three sites, north (*N*), middle (*M*), and south (*S*) served as controls and had dishes of sugar solution to which recruits could come. Points *a* and *b* indicate the geometric center of each set of four feeding sites for each experimental series. [After Johnson (*4*, Fig. 1)]

est attractant, the odor of the scent organ. Besides, as long as there is only one feeding station, it is easy to check the influence of local scent factors by taking the wind conditions into consideration. Second, he states that the recruits might have aimed at the place in the middle of the fan, this being the geometric center of all feeding places; however, he does not say why they did so. He does not note that in our first experiments on direction information the feeding place was established, not in the center of the fan, but on its outer margin, or even farther outward. The newcomers arrived in this case in this direction and not at the center (*3*, pp. 27–29). When the feed-

ing place, which at the beginning was close to the center of the fan, was transferred 15° to the outside, under otherwise identical conditions the stream of newcomers turned correspondingly (*6*, p. 157) to this new direction.

The control experiments carried out by Johnson differed from ours. To create more uniform conditions at all the different stations he set up a second colony of bees with lighter color at the side of the first. While he fed the dark bees at their usual feeding place (*A* in Fig. 1), he offered food to the light bees at all four places simultaneously. In another series of experiments, he removed the second

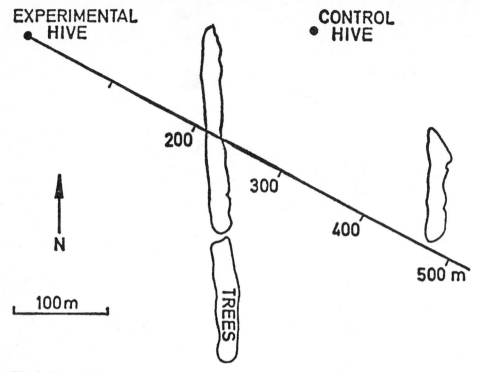

EXPERIMENTAL HIVE

CONTROL HIVE

200

300

400

500 m

N

100 m

TREES

Fig. 3. Map of the experimental area, showing placement of experimental hive (dark-colored bees) and control hive (light-colored bees) in relation to the four training sites. Bees from the experimental hive were trained to forage at either the 400- or 500-m site, depending upon the particular experiment. Trained bees from the control hive foraged at none, three, or four of the sites in different experiments. [After Wenner (5, Fig. 1)]

colony and kept feeding groups of dark bees at all four places. If he moved the feeding place, at 270 m, from *A* to *B*, most of the recruits still appeared in a central direction in both series of experiments, a fact which he ascribes to an effect of the geometric center. However, a simpler explanation takes into account the strong wind from the south, prevailing during his experiments. This wind must have carried along scent from those bees foraging at the central station toward the recruits flying in the direction of *B*; many of these may have been led astray by it to the central station. In our fan experiments we have observed examples of such deviations even with volatile oils

with less intense odors (6, pp. 156–163, Fig. 136).

While Johnson's tests included visits of newcomers in only three different directions, we usually checked a much wider field, setting up a fan, as a rule consisting of at least seven scent plates. Moreover, while he established his feeding places at distances not exceeding 200 m and 270 m, respectively, from the hive, in our control experiments the distances between hive and feeding place amounted to 600 m (Fig. 1) and even to 1250 m. With such great distances, it is not likely that the direction of the newcomers' flights could have been influenced by local scent marks of the feeding place. We are well informed about the capability of their organs of smell (6, pp. 517–22). While those scent plates lying in the direction of the goal received a great number of visits from recruits, the rest were but poorly visited in our experiments. Both facts are equally remarkable, showing that no stray recruits were roaming about, as seems to have been the case in Johnson's experiments.

While bees were fed at a feeding place 400 m from Wenner's experimental hive, (5) three more places were being provided with the same food and scent, but were not yet frequented by any foragers (Fig. 3). Out of a total of 123 recruits counted arriving at the various stations, the percentages were as follows: 74 at the feeding place itself (400 m), 10 at 200 m, 14 at 300 m, 2 at 500 m. While he maintains that these figures do not differ fundamentally from those to be expected according to the distance communication in the dance "language" hypothesis, they do not really contribute anything to the solution of this question. The visits to the feeding place at 400 m may have been due just as well to distance information as to the

attractiveness of the scent organ of the foragers there (and only there). For this reason we carried out our experiments in a different way (Fig. 4).

Here the distance between hive and feeding place was 300 m. Only those recruits visiting the seven scent plates without any food have been evaluated. The number of visitors given at each site in the figure show clearly that the recruits had followed the distance indication. If in this experiment there had been an attractive effect of the scent organ at the adjacent scent plates 50 m to both sides of the feeding station, we should have expected a greater number of recruits arriving at 350 than at 250 m, since a soft wind (north-northwest to northwest) had been blowing.

Wenner's controls consisted of a second colony of bees of lighter color set up 150 m to the north of the line of flight (Fig. 3); 25 and 26 of these bees were fed at the 200- and 300-m sites, respectively, while 13 dark bees together with 13 light-colored ones were frequenting the 400-m site. Now it appears as if the newcomers of the dark race hardly followed the distance in-

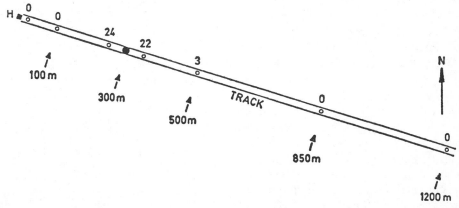

Fig. 4. Step experiment of 3 September 1962. *H*, beehive. Feeding-site (black dot) at 300 m from the hive. Scent plates (white rings) with numbers of visits by recruits during the time of the experiment (2.5 hours).

formation given by their foragers since 18 percent of their recruits paid visits to the light bee's feeding place at 200 m, and 48 percent visited the 300-m site; only 33 percent visited the one at 400 m, that is, the original feeding site of their own colony. However, we could have predicted such a result. Those recruits who had been given the 400-m information were bound to fly over the nearer feeding places at 200 and 300 m located in the same line, and were therefore likely to be attracted to them by the sight of the foraging bees as well as the odor of their scent organs and the scent used for training, particularly with strong southerly winds prevailing there at the time of the experiment (9 knots, or about 4.6 m/sec). Whenever the wind is that strong, bees will keep close to the ground, and attraction by the odor of the scent organ or the training scents at the closer sites will be favored (6, pp. 95–96 and Table 12). In one of our experiments a wind with force similar to that in Wenner's experiments caused the bees to fly close to the ground and to pay more visits than usual to the scent plates (in our case only scented and no foragers visiting) situated nearer to the hive. For this reason, we selected calm weather whenever possible. Results can be spoiled by wind conditions in step as well as in fan experiments.

We still have to discuss the behavior of recruits belonging to the control hive set up sideways. After groups of its lighter bees were fed at the 200-, 300-, and 400-m sites, the light-colored recruits appeared, similar to the results with dark bees, in the following proportion: 12 percent at 200 m, 62 percent at 300 m, and 26 percent at 400 m. As an explanation, Wenner also refers to an assumed geometric center, without going into details about this relation.

After a glance at Fig. 3, we may suspect other causes to have been at work. The fact that the site at 200 m was screened by trees offers a possible explanation for the scarce visitation by bees from the control hive. Because of its direction, the wind (220 degrees), blowing the odor of the scent plates as well as of the foragers' scent organs across the path of recruits flying to the 400-m site, might well have misled these bees to the 300-m site. Wenner's third experiment, being only a variation of the second, does not add any fundamentally new aspect.

Wenner's experiments, just as Johnson's, extended only over a small distance (500 m). In our own step experiments the distance from hive to feeding place has often been much greater: 750 m, 1050 m, 2000 m, and 4400 m (6, pp. 89–95, Figs. 84–89). Again I must state that local scent marks cannot possibly be held responsible for the arrival of recruits at the proper place over such great distances.

Some of my colleagues, having read the two papers published in this journal, spontaneously declared their readiness to repeat the crucial experiments in collaboration with Johnson and Wenner and neutral observers. I sincerely hope that this can be done.

KARL V. FRISCH

References and Notes

1. K. v. Frisch, *Zool. Jahrb. Physiol.* **40**, 1 (1923).
2. ———, *Experientia* **2**, 397 (1946): *The Dancing Bees* (Methuen, London, 1966).
3. ———, *Österreichische Zool. Z.* **1**, 1 (1946).
4. D. L. Johnson, *Science* **155**, 844 (1967).
5. A. M. Wenner, *ibid.*, p. 847.
6. K. v. Frisch, *Tanzsprache und Orientierung der Bienen* (Springer-Verlag, New York, 1965). English translation in press at Harvard Univ. Press, Cambridge, Mass.
7. A. M. Wenner, *Bee World* **42**, 8 (1961).
8. I thank Prof. Dr. M. Lindauer, Dr. H. Markl, and Dr. W. Rathmayer for reading the manuscript.

26 June 1967

43

Reply to Karl von Frisch

Our experimental analysis of the dance-language hypothesis during the past 3 years has led us to a new and tentative interpretation of all available evidence. A statement of this interpretation has not yet appeared in print (1, 2). A sketch of it is as follows:

We find that the hive, its surrounding environment, and its past history are part of a dynamic system and must be studied as such. In discussing recruitment of bees to a source in the field, for example, one must first distinguish between those recruits that have previously fed at the same site visited by a successful forager and those that have not been there before (preferably, those that have not even been in the same area before). The importance of this distinction is not clear in the literature (2, 3).

Bees experienced at visiting a given source can rely upon their memory of the location and can be recruited by means of a conditioned response to either food odor or location odor brought back into the hive by hive mates (3–5). The time spent searching for a source, no matter how long, is negligible compared to the time spent exploiting such a source. Thus, we conclude that the experienced bees, which require no language for re-recruitment (3), are basically responsible for providing the food for their colony.

Those bees that have never been to a source before apparently experience a great deal of difficulty in finding it—their ability to use a variety of odors and wind patterns enables them to do so. Even then, only a small percentage of those that leave the hive succeed in finding a point source (3). Most of those that do succeed in finding the source appear to have spent enough time after leaving the hive to have searched a considerable area before finding the site, even up to 10 minutes for a site at a distance having a direct flight time of 30 seconds (6). Our work to date indicates that naive recruits function in the following manner:

1) Recruits stimulated to leave the hive associate a number of location odors, first sensed on the recruiters, with a potential source of food. These include odor of the food, both from the bee which stimulated the recruit to leave and from other bees successful at the same source; and other odors in the locality visited by successful foragers (which may adhere to them) including those of other flowers, those of various associated plants, and any inorganic odors.

2) Recruits leave the hive and drop 200 m, 300 m, or more downwind from the hive before commencing their search, depending on wind speed and on individual differences among bees. In strong winds they drop further downwind. This maneuver permits them to: negate the influence of their own hive odor and find those potential sources which are closest to the hive—those which are downwind as well as those which are in other directions.

3) Recruits search for the proper combination of odors. In addition to those odors which they have previously associated with the food source, they search for the odor of other bees which are feeding on crops, particularly the crop most impressed on them while in the hive. This search pattern is complicated by: (i) attractance of hive-

specific odors of feeding bees from the same hive, (ii) repellency of hive-specific odors of feeding bees from other hives, and (iii) Nasanoff gland attractance. Covering this gland with the strong odor of shellac may even increase the discrepancy between odor of the experimental site and odor of control sites (3). The use of shellac on experienced bees does not eliminate this factor, since newly arriving recruit bees often expose their Nasanoff gland before landing.

Apparently, the disagreement in interpretation which has arisen stems largely from the question of adequate control in experimental design. After wrestling with the problem of "proof" over the past few years, we have had to agree with various statements (7) that one cannot obtain absolute verification for any hypothesis, no matter how many times experiments are repeated (also, apparently, any attempt to establish the "truth" of a hypothesis introduces an unwelcome bias). Progress apparently depends, rather, upon the sharpening of experimental design and the use of ever better controls, when such controls are found to be necessary. In this context, a hypothesis is best considered as an interim statement until a better hypothesis can be formulated. In that sense the contribution of von Frisch (8) was a dramatic step forward in its incorporation of controls, in the use of logic, and in the reserved interpretation of results.

We would like to emphasize, therefore, that we consider that our results (9) do not disprove of the dance-language hypothesis (since this is never possible), but indicate that a more simple interpretation exists for previous experimental results.

The third experiment of Wenner (Fig. 3 of von Frisch's letter) provides an excellent example for weighing the relative efficacy of the two interpretations provided in these letters. This experimental design is particularly valuable in that each hive serves as a control against the other.

Individually marked bees from the experimental hive foraged only at the 500-m site, while individually marked bees of a different color from the control hive foraged at all four sites. Under these conditions foragers visiting the 500-m site from the experimental hive could provide only a 500-m distance information in their hive by means of their waggle dances. Bees foraging at all four site from the control hive, on the other hand, could collectively furnish distance and direction information about all four sites in their hive. Yet, when the experiment was run, the distribution of recruits at the four stations from the experimental hive was identical to the distribution of recruits that had come from the control hive.

When sets of results not predicted by a particular hypothesis arise, one has to choose a course of action. Either he can keep the hypothesis intact and rationalize that in this case the bees have been "misled," or he can trust the data furnished by the bees and proceed accordingly. Whereas von Frisch (and many others, apparently) has chosen the former course, we have chosen to explore the alternative. It is for this reason that we pay such close attention to the similarity between the distribution of bees from the experimental hive at the four stations (6, 43, 42, and 9 percent) and a potential multinomial distribution about the geometric center of all sites (12, 38, 38, and 12 percent). To us, the data are more suggestive of a probablistic search pattern than of a goal-directed flight.

We conclude that while the classic dance-language hypothesis has been a reasonable interpretation for results obtained in the past, it is not necessarily an exclusive interpretation. Our results indicate, instead, the validity of the more simple interpretation outlined above and forms the basis for a fruitful line of research. Some questions which must now be studied include (i) What is the disposition of recruits unsuccessful at finding a source in the field? (ii) How long does an unsuccessful recruit search before returning to the hive? (iii) Why are recruits more successful at finding one site than at finding another apparently identical site? (iv) What are the relative contributions to the attractiveness of a site of location odor, food odor, and bee odor? (v) What are the effects of the duration of an experiment upon recruitment?

Although these are difficult problems, we believe that progress toward an understanding of bee behavior will be more rapid if experimental design is not restricted by the assumption that bees have a "language." The assumption of the language notion would, in fact, prohibit the study of some questions.

The history of biology is replete with predicaments similar to that indicated in this exchange. We hope that our results and interpretation will be welcomed as a stimulus to further and more critical experimentation and that. others will repeat both our experiments and the classic experiments and ponder. the question of controls. On the basis of our work, the following seem necessary: (i) Control and experimental sites must be in areas with nearly identical locality odors (5). (ii) An equal number of bees must be feeding at each control site and at the experimental site. (iii) The experimental site must not be near the center of a cluster of sites, since this is also the center of the odor field. (iv) Bees arriving at the experimental site must be tallied and considered, since they have obviously been recruited. When this is done, recruit performance in the field is considerably better than the accuracy of dance information (see 10). (v) All recruits must be caught and killed at control as well as at experimental stations (see 10). (vi) Ideally, recruits should never before have been in the locality of the experimental site. (vii) The duration of the experiment must be short enough to eliminate the possibility that recruits can repeatedly leave the hive and learn where not to go. For those who cannot repeat the experiments we urge a study of the experimental design of the various studies alluded to above as a basis for a decision on whether the controls specified by us are necessary (11).

ADRIAN M. WENNER
*Department of Biological Sciences,
University of California, Santa Barbara*
DENNIS L. JOHNSON
*Department of Chemistry and
Physiology, U.S. Air Force Academy,
Colorado Springs, Colorado*

References

1. D. L. Johnson. thesis, University of California, Santa Barbara (1967).
2. A. M. Wenner. in *Animal Communication—Techniques of Study and Results of Research,* T. A. Sebeok, Ed. (Indiana Univ. Press, Bloomington, in press).
3. D. L. Johnson and A. M. Wenner, *Anim. Behav.* 14, 261 (1966).
4. A. M. Wenner and D. L. Johnson, *ibid.,* p. 149.
5. D. L. Johnson, *ibid.,* in press.
6. A. M. Wenner, unpublished data.
7. C. Bernard. *An Introduction to the Study of Experimental Medicine* (Dover Press, New York, 1957); W. S. Beck. *Modern Science and the Nature of Life* (Doubleday Anchor. New York. 1961); K. R. Popper, in *British Philosophy in the Mid-Century: A Cambridge Symposium,* C. A. Mace, Ed. (Macmillan, New York, 1957), pp. 155–91; T. S. Kuhn, *The Structure of Scientific Revolutions* (Univ. of Chicago Press, Chicago, 1962).
8. K. v. Frisch, *Österreichishe Zool. Z.* 1, 1 (1946).
9. D. L. Johnson, *Science* 155, 844 (1967); A. M. Wenner, *ibid.,* p. 847.
10. A. M. Wenner. *Anim. Behav.* 10, 79 (1962).
11. We thank D. Davenport. L. Friesen, and P. Wells for reading the manuscript.

28 August 1967

Honey Bee Recruitment to Food Sources: Olfaction or Language?

Abstract. *Honey bee recruits locate food sources by olfaction and not by use of distance and direction information contained in the recruitment dance. Recruitment efficiency increases as odor of the food source accumulates in the hive, from hour to hour and from day to day. Flight patterns, landing patterns, bee odor, and Nassanoff secretion apparently do not aid in recruitment of bees.*

When von Frisch generated the "dance language" hypothesis of honey bee recruitment (*Apis mellifera* L.) (*1*), it was based on the results of elegantly simple experiments and withstood the tests of repeatability and "proof" by verification (*2*). Inadequacies in this explanation have been revealed (*3*) through studying the nature of correlations between behavioral and environmental parameters. Wenner and Johnson (*4*) documented the existence and relevance of simple conditioning during recruitment, just as Lopatina (*5*) had earlier.

This demonstration led to a questioning of the assumption that the "language" was an "instinctive" act. Challenging a basic assumption (*6*), Wells and Giacchino (*7*) found that altering the sugar concentration did not alter the amount of solution ingested by foragers.

Furthermore, the language hypothesis has failed the more critical test of refutation (*8*) in that experimentation with controls not incorporated in the early experiments yielded results other than those predicted by the hypothesis (*9*). In the later experiments, recruited bees arrived at sites in the field in apparent disregard of any dance information that they could have acquired before leaving the hive.

Such data are not only incompatible with a language hypothesis but also provide a basis for the a posteriori generation of an alternative hypothesis (*10*): Potential recruits stimulated to leave the hive search the field for the odor (or odors) carried into the colony by successful foragers.

That bees locate a food source by olfaction is especially possible in view of the extremely low recruitment rate of regular foragers collecting unscented sucrose at an unscented site. On 25 July 1968, for instance, in the absence of a major nectar source for the colony, we received only five recruits from a hive of approximately 60,000 bees after ten bees had foraged at each of four stations for a total of 1374 round trips during a 3-hour period.

Although the olfaction hypothesis can explain most (if not all) of these results, no a priori experimental design has contrasted the two hypotheses. We felt that such a test was necessary and should be possible with the use of a single hive.

Despite the difficulties in designing such an experiment (*10*), some unexpected results obtained during the summer of 1967 provided the basis for just such a test. In the experimental series of 1967, ten individually marked bees routinely visited each of two clove-scented sources (0 to 0.26 ml of oil of clove per liter of 1.5 molal sucrose solution), 200 m in opposite directions from the hive. Each new recruit landing at a dish was killed in a covered jar of alcohol.

We had expected a constant number of recruits per unit time, but an increasing number of new bees arrived and were killed as the experiment progressed (Fig. 1). Since the number of new arrivals reflected the cumulative number of trips by experienced foragers, we concluded that a recruit more readily locates a site in the field as a direct consequence of odor in the hive. Further-

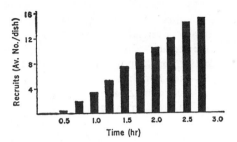

Fig. 1. Daily pattern of recruitment during 26 days in the summer of 1967. Each bar represents the mean number of new recruits killed per 15 minutes in the course of nearly 3 hours, while 20 foragers made regular round trips between the hive and feeding dishes.

more, the data gathered on 1 day were not independent of the previous day's manipulations.

If odor accumulates in the hive and contributes to the relative success of a recruit searching in the field, a rationale exists for designing an experiment. Bees visiting certain scented sources in the field for 1, 2, or 3 days accumulate odor in the hive and continue to visit the same locations on a subsequent day, even if no scent is used in the solution. The day after odor is used in the food, then, one can run an experiment by using the scented food at a third (control) site which is not visited by any foragers.

This design permits the formulation of mutually exclusive predictions from the two competing hypotheses. If the dance language hypothesis is valid, then recruits should arrive at the sites visited by the regular foragers. However, if the olfaction hypothesis is valid, one should obtain the recruits at a control station if it contains the odor brought into the hive on the previous day, even if no foragers visit such a site.

The experimental design also provides the basis for a second prediction. If an olfaction hypothesis is the correct

interpretation for the set of results obtained in 1967 (Fig. 1), then the number of recruits caught per unit time should not increase on days when experienced foragers collect unscented sucrose solution.

We have now run such a series of experiments. A two-story standard hive with approximately 50,000 Starline hybrid bees was moved onto the "Storke Ranch" area of the University of California, Santa Barbara, on 21 June 1968, and was used during the course of the summer. We selected two experimental sites (Nos. 1 and 3), 280 m from each other and 200 m from the hive (Fig. 2). An intermediate control site (No. 2) at the same distance from the hive was also selected. This choice of experimental and control sites precluded the possibility that new recruits could be simultaneously "misled" by wind patterns to the control site from the two experimental sites (11). These distances are approximately equivalent to those used by von Frisch (1).

The experimental series began 8 August and ran 24 consecutive days, including 5 days of a related study near the end of the series. Each day's session ran from 8:30 to 11:30 (Pacific Daylight Time). No changes were made in the format during any 1 day. Ten foragers routinely visited each experimental site, with a normal turnover of about ten bees per week. Each dish contained 1.5 molal unscented or scented sucrose solution [20 drops (0.26 ml) of oil of clove per liter of solution]. To control against odor artifacts, a clean dish with fresh solution was used each 15 minutes; each dish rested on a disk of filter paper (also replaced each 15 minutes) on a vinyl-topped feeding platform; each platform was washed at least once each day; and all scented materials were sealed in airtight plastic bags immediately after use.

The format for the first 17 days varied according to a schedule (Table 1) to provide for odor accumulation in the hive for 1 or 2 days and to permit an experimental day subsequent to a day of odor accumulation. Throughout the series we tallied (i) the number of new arrivals per unit time; (ii) the number of trips of individual foragers per 15 minutes; and (iii) the number of times the scent gland (Nassanoff gland) was exposed by each forager in each 15 minutes [some component of the scent gland secretion reportedly attracts searching bees (12)]. After being counted, each new recruit was placed in a covered jar of alcohol. At no time did any bees fill at station No. 2 and return to the hive.

Initially, we found that some recruits landed only reluctantly at the control station. According to Kalmus (13), this is due to a lack of adequate visual and olfactory stimuli generated by the flight activity and odors of foraging bees. To prevent bees from inspecting and rejecting the middle station because of the lack of a necessary "landing factor," we lowered an insect net over the reluctant recruits as they hovered near the dish. This prevented them from arriving at the control station and proceeding upwind to one of the experimental sites (usually No. 1). However, most recruits landed at the dish, attracted in part by the visual stimulus of bee-sized pieces of cellulose sponges placed around the inside circumference

Table 1. Total number of recruits received per day and the experimental procedure at the three sites. Foragers never visited the control site (No. 2), and ten bees made a relatively constant number of trips per unit time to the experimental sites (Nos. 1 and 3). On day 7 only five of the regular foragers arrived at site No. 3. On day 16 a second scent (0.13 ml of oil of peppermint per liter of 1.5 molal sucrose solution) was used at each experimental site (no peppermint scent had accumulated in the hive previous to this time). The number of times the Nassanoff gland was exposed is the average for sites 1 and 3.

Day	Procedure	Recruitment (No. at each site)			Nassanoff exposure
		No. 1	No. 2	No. 3	
1	Scent at 1 and 3	42		71	31.0
2	No scent at 1 and 3, scent at 2	15	38	3	134.5
3	Scent at 1 and 3	89		76	71.5
4	No scent at 1 and 3	20		7	182.0
5	Scent at 1 and 3	87		90	94.5
6	Scent at 1 and 3	70		55	82.0
7	No scent at 1 and 3, scent at 2	4	51	0	139.5
8	Scent at 1 and 3	111		101	136.5
9	No scent at 1, 2, or 3	0	3	17	223.0
10	Scent at 1 and 3	44		90	149.0
11	Scent at 1 and 3	159		89	160.0
12	No scent at 1 and 3, scent at 2	4	91	5	253.0
13	Scent at 1 and 3	102		61	92.0
14	No scent at 1, 2, or 3	6	2	5	161.5
15	Scent at 1 and 3	93		87	87.5
16	2nd scent at 1 and 3, 1st scent at 2	2	44	0	82.0
17	Scent at 1 and 3	71		29	55.5
18–22	[Separate experimental series, scent at 1 and (or) 3]				
23	Scent at 1 and 3	68		32	168.5
24	Scent, but no bees at 1, 2, and 3	1	0	0	0.0

of the dish. Care used in transferring bees to the alcohol bottle prevented the release of alarm odor (14).

Our results (Table 1) support the olfaction hypothesis and contradict the dance language hypothesis (Table 1 and Fig. 3). Recruits came to the site marked by the food odor but not necessarily to the sites presumably indicated in the hive by the dance maneuvers of

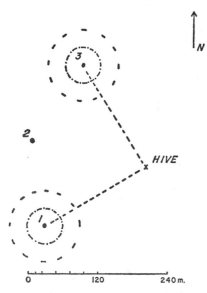

Fig. 2. Relative locations of hive, experimental sites (Nos. 1 and 3), and the control site (No. 2). All three stations were located on relatively level open grassland (dry annual grasses) with no trees between hive and stations. The broken circles around the experimental sites represent approximately one and two standard deviations, respectively, for the "dance language" information. These values were derived by studying "dance" maneuvers in the hive (17). The control station (No. 2), therefore, is well outside the areas where the "language" hypothesis predicts recovery of recruits. Wind direction during the series normally rotated slowly from the southeast through the south and to the southwest during the course of each experimental period. The wind never blew from the control station (No. 2) toward the hive. No measurable amount of rain fell during the summer.

returning foragers. This was true, even when the odor had not been used since the previous day. Other experiments with a different hive in another location, in which experimental and control sites were at different distances (370 and 150 m, respectively), yielded comparable results (15).

Our results also support the odor accumulation hypothesis. The linear increase in recruitment per unit time occurred when scent was used at the experimental sites (Fig. 4), but did not occur at the control site when foragers collected unscented sucrose at the experimental sites (Fig. 3).

Neither the odor of feeding bees nor the odor from the scent gland provided the problems anticipated (10). No site had odor in the food on days 4, 9, and 14; and recruitment of bees was lowest on each of these days. This indicates that searching bees had to be very close to feeding and landing bees before they could use either the odor or the visual pattern of flying or feeding bees. Apparently, the attraction afforded by foraging bees (13) was used only after the

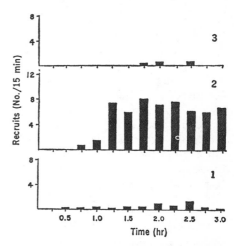

Fig. 3. The average daily recruitment at the three sites on days 2, 7, 12, and 16 of the experiment (Table 1). The control site (No. 2) had scented solution of the type used on the previous day at the experimental sites. No bees foraged at site No. 2.

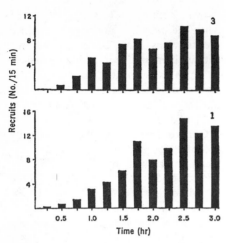

Fig. 4. The average daily recruitment at the experimental sites (Nos. 1 and 3), when no control site (No. 2) existed (that is, days 1, 3, 5, 6, 8, 10, 11, 13, 15, 17, and 23). The steady increase in the number of recruits caught per unit time (after start of experiment) matches the data obtained in the 1967 series (Fig. 1).

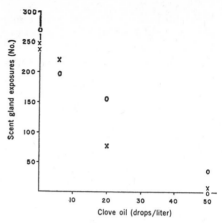

Fig. 5. Data obtained from preliminary experiments testing the effect of the amount of scent in the food on the incidence of Nassanoff gland exposure (days 18 through 22). Station No. 1 (O) had 50, 6, 0, 20, and 50 drops of oil of clove per liter of solution; and station No. 3 (X) had 0, 20, 50, 6, and 0 drops per liter, respectively, on the 5 days of odor variation.

recruits had chemotactically oriented to the food odor (or distinctive location odor) at that site.

The degree of exposure of the scent gland varied inversely with recruitment (Table 1), and it appeared that the use of unscented sucrose solution contributed to a high rate of gland exposure. To determine whether there is a relation between amount of odor in the food and rate of gland exposure, we varied the amount of odor in the solution at the two experimental sites during a 5-day period after our 17-day sequence. The results (Fig. 5) indicate that the level of exposure of the scent gland can be adjusted by altering the amount of odor in the food. This may also explain why bees do not expose their scent glands when visiting natural food sources such as flowers (16).

Three concepts have been examined in the above experiments: odor accumulation in the hive, attractiveness of Nassanoff secretion, and the usefulness of the olfaction hypothesis in predicting the field distribution of recruited bees. Our results show that, although elements of the dance maneuver in the hive do correlate with the distance and direction traveled by regular foragers in the field, the presence of this information in the hive does not appear to contribute to the ecology of foraging or recruitment (3).

ADRIAN M. WENNER
*Department of Biological Sciences,
University of California,
Santa Barbara 93106*
PATRICK H. WELLS
*Department of Biology, Occidental
College, Los Angeles, California 90041*
DENNIS L. JOHNSON
*Department of Life Sciences,
U.S. Air Force Academy,
Colorado Springs, Colorado 80840*

References and Notes

1. K. von Frisch, *Osterr. Zool. Z.* **1**, 1 (1946); translation, *Bull. Anim. Behav.* **5**, 1 (1947).
2. K. von Frisch, *Tanzsprache und Orientierung der Bienen* (Springer, New York, 1965), translation, *The Dance Language and Orientation of Bees* (Harvard Univ. Press, Cambridge, Mass., 1967).
3. A. M. Wenner, P. H. Wells, F. J. Rohlf, *Physiol. Zool.* **40**, 317 (1967).
4. A. M. Wenner and D. L. Johnson, *Anim. Behav.* **14**, 149 (1966); D. L. Johnson and A. M. Wenner, *ibid.*, p. 261; D. L. Johnson, *ibid.* **15**, 487 (1967).
5. N. G. Lopatina, *Pchelovodstvo* **84**, 34 (1964).
6. K. von Frisch, *Z. Vergl. Physiol.* **21**, 1 (1934).
7. P. H. Wells and J. Giacchino, *J. Apicult. Res.* **7**, 77 (1968).
8. K. R. Popper, in *British Philosophy in the Mid-Century*, C. A. Mace, Ed. (MacMillan, New York, 1957).
9. D. L. Johnson, *Science* **155**, 844 (1967); A. M. Wenner, *ibid.*, p. 847.
10. A. M. Wenner and D. L. Johnson, *ibid.* **158**, 1076 (1967).
11. K. von Frisch, *ibid.*, p. 1072.
12. M. Renner, *Z. Vergl. Physiol.* **43**, 411 (1960); D. A. Shearer and R. Boch, *J. Insect Physiol.* **12**, 1513 (1966).
13. H. Kalmus, *Brit. J. Anim. Behav.* **2**, 63 (1954).
14. R. A. Morse and A. W. Benton, *Bee World* **45**, 141 (1964).
15. L. J. Friesen and M. Iacaboni, unpublished results.
16. C. R. Ribbands, *The Behaviour and Social Life of Honeybees* (Dover, New York, 1964).
17. E. M. Schweiger, *Z. Vergl. Physiol.* **41**, 272 (1958); A. M. Wenner, *Anim. Behav.* **10**, 79 (1962).
18. Supported by NSF grant GB-6448. We thank P. Craig, J. Fawcett, L. Friesen, and M. Iacaboni for technical assistance and D. Davenport and D. Smith for reviewing the manuscript.

22 October 1968; revised 31 December 1968

Bees Are Easily Distracted

Wenner and his colleagues (*1*) presume to challenge findings of a great biologist. There is of course nothing wrong with this as such, but reliance on an elementary logical fallacy in doing so should not be encouraged in your journal.

In a characteristic quotation they state: "Recruited bees arrived at sites in apparent disregard of any dance information that they could have acquired before leaving the hive. Such data are not only incompatible with a language hypothesis. . . ." This non-sequitur is akin to one which faced von Frisch (*2*) earlier in his career, when von Hess asserted that bees were color-blind because he had found an experimental situation in which they ignored color.

Suppose a man tells me there is a bar three blocks down the street on the right. I set off thirsty, but on the way a strong smell of beer distracts me to another bar hidden up a side alley. Does this prove that human language does not communicate information?

Von Frisch and Lindauer (*3*) did an experiment in which a terrestrial landmark, the edge of a forest, competed with the sun as an orientation cue for bees. They found circumstances in which such a terrestrial cue overruled the sun: the bees appeared to ignore the sun completely. To conclude from this that bees do not use a sun compass would have been wrong, even if there had been no other evidence for a sun compass. The fact is of course that bees have alternative methods of orientation.

Similarly, it is entirely reasonable to suppose that bees have alternative ways of finding food—among them, the dance, smell, and the presence of other bees—and that each of these cues may predominate under different circumstances. For example, the artificial use of strong scent might cause olfactory cues to prevail, while the artificially engineered presence of large crowds of bees at control feeding stations might well distract foragers from other cues.

In brief, bees are easily distracted.

This modest and uncontroversial conclusion is all that can be drawn from the experiments purporting to disprove von Frisch's classic work.

RICHARD DAWKINS
Department of Zoology,
University of California, Berkeley 94720

References

1. A. M. Wenner, P. H. Wells, D. L. Johnson, *Science* 164, 84 (1969).
2. K. von Frisch, *Bees, Their Vision, Chemical Senses, and Language* (Cornell Univ. Press, Ithaca, N.Y. 1950), p. 4.
3. M. Lindauer, *Communication Among Social Bees* (Harvard Univ. Press, Cambridge, Mass., 1961), p. 126.

 STIMULUS CONTROL FOR BIRD ORIENTATION[1]

MERLE E. MEYER
University of Washington

During the last 2 decades there have developed 4 experimental lines of approach toward the understanding of the stimulus control of bird orientation and navigation: sun-compass-orientation, star-navigation, sun-navigation, and what might be called nonvisual hypotheses. Each position has yielded important evidence which has in turn led to sharper definitions of problems and more rigorous appraisal of theory. The intention of this paper is to review the research findings and conclusions concerning each of the positions.

The stimulus control of navigation and migration by birds has constituted one of the most challenging problems for the student of animal behavior. This general topic has always aroused the imaginative and the curious, but it has only been during the past 20 years that impetus has been given to the development of new explanations and new methods of investigation. During this time four lines of approach have emerged. The sun-compass-orientation hypothesis set forth by Kramer and his co-workers has established that diurnal migrating birds maintain their direction by orientation with respect to the sun. With Sauer's work and the development of the star-navigation hypothesis, there is evidence that nocturnal migrating birds orient and navigate by means of star patterns. Matthews' sun-navigation hypothesis has been put forward to account for the evidence that birds can use observations of the sun for true bicoordinate navigation, and lastly the nonvisual hypothesis, orientation and navigation by sensitivities to magnetic

[1] This paper was written while the author was on a National Science Foundation Faculty Fellowship and on leave from Whitman College. The writer wishes to express his thanks to Geo. P. Horton, Paul E. Fields, Donald M. Baer, Bert Forrin, Robert Lockard, Gordon H. Orians, and Frank Richardson, all of whom read the paper and made valuable comments.

and "Coriolis" forces, has been proposed. This review concerns itself with the advances and conclusions made by each position.

SUN-COMPASS-ORIENTATION HYPOTHESIS

Virtually nothing was known of the mechanisms which organisms use for orientation prior to 1949. Since that time it has been shown that several species of birds, arthropods, fish, and reptiles possess the ability to find compass directions with the help of the sun and to keep that direction despite the "movement" of the sun during the day.

The sun-azimuth orientation consists in the determination of the compass directions by the sun position regardless of the time of day; hence, it requires mainly the ability to correct for the sun's daily azimuth displacement. Generally it has been assumed that only the azimuth of the sun's position is used as the basis for orientation. The sun's azimuth, that is the projection of the sun's position onto the horizon, however, changes during the day with varying speed. In order to maintain one's compass direction accurately, the correction for the azimuth movement has to vary with the same rhythm. The azimuth movement varies, not only during the course of the day, but also with the seasons and with various latitudes. An organism which uses only the sun's azimuth for keeping a compass direction has, therefore, to compensate for different azimuth movements in equal time intervals at different times of the day, at different seasons, and at different latitudes if it migrates.

It has been suggested by Kramer (1961) and by Wallraff (1960a, 1960b) that two kinds of orientation occur in nature, one-direction orientation and goal orientation. In the former case, no matter where the animal is, it tries to go in a given compass direction; in the latter case, it tries to go towards a "home" goal. According to the hypothesis, the direction to be taken is in many cases unlearned, while the location of a goal area, on the other hand, must be learned or imprinted through experience. Navigation is the ability to recognize displacement in unfamiliar surroundings and to choose the correct homing direction.

Kramer (1950a, 1950c) found that his captive starlings Sturnus vulgaris which lived in an outdoor aviary got restless at migration time and would cling to the side of the cage or make short sallies in the direction they would take if free to migrate. The starlings' visual field was restricted to that of the sky above by a round aviary which excluded the sight of the horizon. Kramer noted that the diurnal fluttering remained oriented in the species-specific migration direction only when the sun or the sky near it was unobscured by cloud cover. This directional tendency was manifest even in a round cage of a diameter of about 2 feet. Only the overhead sky and the features of the apparatus remained as visual cues and only the former provided constant directional information, since the apparatus was regularly rotated. At the same time, it was clear that the birds were able to correct for the sun's movement during the day, for they showed the ability to take time into account by holding the same direction in spite of passing time. However, individual starlings differed in appraising the hourly angle of displacement in spite of their being constantly exposed to the natural sun. Birds that were allowed the sight of the blue sky through one window only, tended to react as if this window represented the sun and took their directions accordingly. If the incidence of light was changed by the use of mirrors, the direction chosen by the starlings changed correspondingly. When the magnetic field around the experimental chambers was greatly altered by masses of iron, the response of a compass was drastic, but this change in the magnetic field had no effect on the direction of orientation.

In a series of experiments based upon direction learning without the migratory urge, Kramer (1952, 1953) and his co-workers (Kramer & Riese, 1952; Kramer & von St. Paul, 1950) trained starlings to a compass direction in order to be free from the restrictions of the seasons and hours of migration. A circular training cage was used. The birds first learned to go to 1 of 12 containers placed about the circumference for food. The compensation for the sun's motion during the day could be demonstrated by observing that birds which had been trained at a restricted time of day to expect food at a definite angle to the sun chose the same compass direction in critical tests at other times of the day. Similar experiments (Kramer, 1953), but with an artificial sun, have shown that birds alter their absolute direction by changing their angle to the fixed light source. A number of deviations were observed; these errors did not disappear when adjustments of the diameter of the projected sun and the altitude to that of the natural sun were made. It became evident that the starlings were evaluating only the azimuth, and that it made no difference how high or low the sun was.

In an experiment (Kramer, 1953) with birds raised under sunless conditions, one starling was raised without seeing the sun and trained and tested with a fixed artificial sun. This bird compensated for a clockwise movement it had never experienced. However, when the length of day was adjusted to the fall season and latitude, the bird compensated for a sun-azimuth movement as it occurs in June. All "sunless" starlings raised in 2 subsequent years, however, showed a simple constant angle orientation when tested at times different from training.

The ability of sun-azimuth orientation has been demonstrated experimentally in the starling, red-backed shrike

Lanius collurio, and warblers (Kramer, 1949, 1950a, 1950b, 1951). In a series of experiments, von St. Paul (1953, 1956) was able to demonstrate orientation in the barred warbler *Sylvia nisoria,* the red-backed shrike, and in the western meadowlark *Sturnella neglecta.* This has also been shown with homing pigeons *Columbia livia* (Kramer, 1957, 1959).

Hamilton (1962b) reared pintails *Dafila acuta,* blue-winged teal *Anas discors,* and green-winged teal *Anas crecca* from eggs laid by wild birds. The eggs were hatched in incubators, and when the ducks were 24 hours old, they were transferred to test cages. To test the ability of ducks to tell direction by the sun, the birds were reared in an environment lacking constant direction save that of the sun and overhead sky. The birds were allowed to obtain water in only one direction, and by the time the birds were 3 weeks old their ability to locate the water source was well developed. In critical tests the experimental birds were removed from the apparatus and deprived of water. In daytime tests with the sun obscured or in twilight periods at dawn and dusk, the birds made random choices, but with the sun directly visible accurate choices were the rule.

The field experiments of Griffin and Goldsmith (1955) showed that common terns *Sterna hirundo* released inland regularly fly southeast for as far as they can be observed. The direction is maintained regardless of the actual home site. When the sky had an overcast, as in previous studies, no orientation could be seen. Similar results were found by Bellrose (1958) with wild mallards *Anas platyrhynchos.* The birds showed a strong tendency to fly north on clear days and nights; the orientation was random with overcast skies. Matthews (1961) observing nonmigratory mallards suggests that the birds upon release flew northwest regardless of the distance and direction of release, season, and length of captivity. Such flights occurred at any time, and with birds of any age, or either sex. These observations suggest sun orientation.

The biological clock which is normally in phase with the astronomical day-night cycle can be controlled and shifted by an artificial light-dark cycle. Starlings studied by Kramer (1957) showed deviation of their clock by producing determinate direction choices. The direction choices were equal to those produced by birds kept in outdoor conditions if the artificial light-dark change was synchronized with the astronomical day-night cycle. They deviated in a predictable manner if the artificial cycle was shifted. A shift of 6 hours resulted in a final directional deviation of roughly 90 degrees. An exposure of 4–12 days to the phase-shifted light-dark cycle was sufficient to attain the full shift of the internal clock. Other experiments have confirmed these findings (Hoffmann, 1960; Schmidt-Koenig, 1960a).

It is well known that all birds do not migrate during the day. Kramer (1950) suggested the functioning of the sun compass at night. His experiments on directional findings in nocturnal migrants done with Old World shrikes and warblers suggested that orientation was possible only if birds were allowed to see the sun around sunset or earlier. However, Hoffmann's studies (1960) indicated that birds are not able to compensate for the sun's motion during the night and suggested that some other stimulus control was at work.

Studies that do not negate the sun-compass hypothesis but do complicate it have been made by Perdeck (1957), Tinbergen (1956), and Tinbergen and Fijlstra (1954). Perdeck, using Kramer's round cage method, demonstrated that a starling, caught in the autumn, displayed a satisfactory precision in its southwest tendency as long as the sun was visible. However, when the sky became overcast, the bird was at first disoriented but managed to orient again when the sky remained heavily overcast for several days. Observations by Tinbergen of the directional flight of migrating starlings revealed increased scatter on a number of successive cloudy days, but sharp orientation on a cloudy morning following an afternoon when the sun shone for a brief time. This finding would support a celestial clue hypothesis as the oriented flights under overcast can be attributed to a carryover of orientation which was achieved under clearer conditions.

STAR-NAVIGATION HYPOTHESIS

It has been noted that warblers along with most small passerines migrate chiefly at night so that the sun is not what guides them. In specially designed cages, Sauer and Sauer (1955) began looking for other factors in orientation. They observed that warblers reared in closed, soundproof chambers under summerlike conditions still got restless at the time when they would have begun their migrations.

Sauer and Sauer (1955) also tested blackcaps *Sylvia atricapilla* and garden warblers *Sylvia borin,* night migrants, for nocturnal migratory directional tendencies. In the autumn migration period, birds were put singly into a circular cage which could be rotated and was screened on all sides so that no surrounding landscape could be seen below an angle of 68 degrees. Definite nocturnal orientation was observed under clear or partly cloudy skies, even if the birds had never seen the sky before the experiment. The fluttering birds kept facing in their natural migration direction, for example, towards the south-southwest and southwest. As long as the brightest stars were still visible through a veil of clouds, the direction of migration orientation was unimpaired. In a diffusely illuminated room, under polarized light, or under a cloudy sky, the birds were completely disoriented. It was noted that the birds showed positive phototropic responses to the moon, bright meteorites, and directed artificial light. In similar experiments during spring migration, blackcaps chose the species-specific direction of migration, north-northeast and northeast.

Further experiments by Sauer and Sauer (1959) with the common whitethroat *Sylvia communis*, garden warbler, wood warbler *Phylloscopus sibilatrix*, and lesser grey shrike *Lanius minor* were made in Southwest Africa, and the birds took up roughly the directions which would be expected. It was suggested that the birds recognized when they had arrived at the end of their migration by the star pattern. The effect of overcast skies was again stressed. Whitethroats still tended to the south, however, even though they were already 2,000 miles south of their normal winter quarters.

Sauer (1956, 1957a, 1957b) followed his hypothesis of birds' orientation by stars by taking birds into a planetarium. In a Zeiss planetarium, under diffuse illumination, the direction of migration was random. Under an artificial replica of the starlit spring sky a blackcap faced north-northeast and northeast. A lesser whitethroat faced towards the south-southeast and southeast under an artificial autumn sky. An inexperienced lesser whitethroat presented with the starry skies of different latitudes faced between southeast-east in a way which exactly corresponds to the known behavior of experienced birds in nature. The presentation of an autumn sky during spring and vice versa caused the birds to alternate rapidly between the direction of spring and autumn migration. Under a winter or a summer sky during autumn, a lesser whitethroat was completely disoriented. If the constellations were changed to correspond with an eastward or westward displacement of the birds, they were able to compensate partly for this and would have found their way back to their summer

or winter quarters. It was suggested that the birds were able to see a part of the star pattern known to them.

A lesser whitethroat (Sauer, 1957b) was presented with an artificial sky as would appear at the latitude of the southern Mediterranean. The bird changed the direction of its movements from southeast to south in the same way as these birds are known to change their course when reaching the eastern end of the Mediterranean, indicating true bicoordinate navigation. It must be noted, however, that such correction was not observed in cases where the westward displacement was simulated.

Orientation of two garden warblers and three blackcaps studied with progressive shifts of the star pattern (forward in time through a total of 24 hours) led to compensation for reorientation, disorientation conflicts between the appropriate migration direction and its reverse, disorientation, and, finally, to normal orientation again. The results were not always consistent and were not duplicated by shifting the pattern backwards in time. Changes in apparent latitude did not seem to affect the conflict type of orientation (Sauer & Sauer, 1960).

In making an evaluation of birds' reactions to simulated changes of position, Kramer (1961) noted that the artificial sky stood still and its time adjustment was consistently retarded in a manner corresponding to a westerly displacement of as much as 15 degrees longitude or more. In addition, the testing apparatus had to be placed excentrically in the planetarium, as the center was occupied by the projector. In general, the cage was placed south of the room center and as the dome was only 6 meters in diameter, parallactic distortions were unavoidable. It must be pointed out that even the displacement of the bird in the cage as it moved must have caused gross visual changes. The net results of these technical problems may have caused marked changes in the behavior of the bird.

Sauer (1961) concluded from his research that birds not only use the stars to determine a fixed compass direction, but also to derive further information, particularly with respect to the seasons, from the temporal arrangements of the constellations. He suggested that various species possess a mechanism of migration orientation which enables them, independent of local topography and their individual experience, to determine, with the help of their ability to assess time, their species' course of migration while steering by starlit sky. This implies that birds may use a bi-coordinate system of star navigation when displaced spatially. But, as yet, it has not been possible to ascertain what celestial features are the principal cues for the bird. In all of Sauer's work the sky zone lower than approximately 35 degrees above the horizon was not shown. If the sky was overcast so that the Milky Way could not be seen but the major stars were yet visible, the bird's orientation was not disrupted. The cues that were used were in all probability of some configurational nature.

The conclusions of Sauer, however, have been complicated by a recent observation of Agron (1962), who has pointed out that Sauer has neglected the evolutionary implications of the relatively rapid changes in the star positions. The stars and seasons reverse their relationships completely every 13,000 years because of the earth's axial precession, and also there are slower changes in star pattern due to "proper motion" of stars. Agron suggested that for birds to navigate by the stars, they must be continuously evolving at a rate which is not incompatible with the ratio of celestial changes.

Using the white-crowned sparrow *Zonotrichia coronata*, Mewald and Gose (1960) observed in an experimental setting that these birds showed strong orientation of nocturnal but not diurnal activity toward the north in the spring and the south in the fall. A more diffuse orientation in the fall was ascribed to the birds being close to their normal wintering area.

Hamilton (1962a) using North Dakota bobolinks *Dolichonyx oryzivorus* under a clear, moonless fall sky in San Francisco reported a remarkable uniformity in preferred direction. The most frequent response under overcast was waning, nondirected response intensity, and subsequent termination of activity; direction was lacking. Response amplitude faded when bright stars were no longer visible. The moon disrupted the directional tendency. When the migratory call notes were recorded and played back, inactive birds could be stimulated to activity and the birds already active to longer than normal activity.

Pintails, blue-winged teal, and green-winged teal under a clear moonless sky consistently made accurate direction choices although some birds could not be induced to respond at all. With the moon in the sky some birds diverted direction of choice toward the moon, others were not affected (Hamilton, 1962b).

Fromme (1961) and Merkel and Fromme (1958), using European robins *Enithacus rubecula*, redbacked shrikes, and whitethroats, observed that the birds preferred a direction in nocturnal migration which corresponded to the natural migratory direction appropriate to the time of year. These observers reported that orientation was just as good without optical points of reference and proposed that these birds must have a means of orientation other than the star pattern shown by Sauer (1956) to be important to other species. They suggested that electromagnetic radiations from celestial bodies could be excluded, however, for investigations (Merkel & Fromme, 1958) with an artificial magnetic field were ambiguous. Migratory direction was completely lost though, when the birds were put into steel chambers. Fromme and Merkel's observations, that birds remained oriented without optical reference points, can not be explained by any of the present theories and are contrary to the findings of others.

Two papers by Wallraff (1960a, 1960c) include detailed criticisms of Sauer's (1956) claims that warblers detect changes in latitude and longitude from corresponding shifts in star patterns. Sauer's data have been recalculated and regrouped with the result that changes in orientation with different latitudes now do appear somewhat less convincing. Changes with differences in longitude are shown to have inconsistencies and are explained as due to the azimuthal compensation of a star compass imposed by a change in time. It must be noted, however, that there is a strong tendency for the grouping of data until very small differences achieve a given level of significance. It is highly conceivable that much of the controversy has its roots well buried in the ground of statistical method.

SUN-NAVIGATION HYPOTHESIS

About the time of Kramer's original work on the sun orientation hypothesis, Matthews in England was studying the critical problem of stimulus control of navigation. This area has been one of the most difficult problems for the student of animal behavior. True navigation involves the ability in animals of "knowing" where they are in unfamiliar surroundings.

Three studies may exemplify this point. Kenyon and Rice (1958) removed 18 adult Layson albatrosses *Diomedea exulans* from nests at Midway Atoll. Fourteen of these returned from widely spaced points of release. The greatest distance of release was 4,120 miles from the nest, and the bird returned in 32 days. Mazzeo (1953) provided an account of a Manx shearwater *Procellaria puffinus* that homed

from Boston to its colony off Wales in less than 13 days. This shearwater returned from outside the range of the species along an east-west route at right angles to its normal migration. Recently, Hamilton (1962c) described a report in which a captive bobolink escaped during the fall at Berkeley, California. This bird had been taken from its breeding grounds in North Dakota during the previous summer. The following summer this same bird was recaptured at the location where it had originally been trapped in North Dakota. Since California is not on the migratory pathway of bobolinks, the eventual return of the bird implies some capacity of navigation.

From Matthews' early work (1951, 1953c) the suggestion has come that homing pigeons get their orientation for navigation from the sun. This must be the case, it is argued, for the performance of the birds was not as good under overcast skies. Under this condition the birds scattered randomly when released, and homing was very much better when the sky was clear. The same general findings hold for the Manx shearwater (Matthews, 1953a) and also for gulls (Matthews, 1952). Matthews (1951) has shown that pigeons are able to fly in a given direction when released at unknown points. When released in unknown areas at right angles to, or in the opposite direction from, the original line of training, a good proportion of the birds returned to the loft. It has been emphasized by Matthews (1953b) that homing and initial orientation are two distinct events. Using young and untrained birds, he reported orientation toward the home loft. However, such birds homed poorly. It was thought that practice affected the return rather than the determination of direction bearing. From his studies Matthews hypothesized that homing birds determine latitude on the basis of the sun's altitude and longitude on the basis of time.

Matthews (1955a) stated:

> The essential feature is the sun arc. This is inclined at an angle from the horizontal which is constant for a given place and is a measure of the latitude of that place. . . . The speed at which the sun moves round its arc is, for practical purposes, constant at 15° an hour. When it has reached a particular point on this arc at home, it will have advanced further to an observer in the east, and less far to one in the west, the difference in arc angle (the angle round the arc from the noon position) being directly proportional to the change in longitude. At home the bird will become familiar with the features of the sun arc and the sun's position on it at different (local) times. These will be related to the internal "chronometer" which is also an essential part of the hypothesis. In unfamiliar surroundings the bird will have to construct the sun-arc from observation. The suggestion is that it observes the sun's movement over a small part of its arc and extrapolates to obtain the highest point. Measurement of the altitude of this point, the angle from the horizontal and comparison with the remembered value for home, say, the previous day, will give the latitude change. The arc angle from the observed sun to this highest point when compared with that obtained at home for the same chronometer time will give the longitude change [pp. 92–94].

In support of his assumption of the chronometer, Matthews (1955b) conducted an experiment on that part of the sun-navigation hypothesis which suggests that birds can detect longitude displacement by comparison of home time with local time estimated from the highest point of the sun's arc. Pigeons were exposed for 10 days to an artificial day which was 3 hours in advance of the normal day. When tested, the birds showed no loss in time orientation. Continuing the research, the birds were then exposed to 4 or 5 days of irregular light-dark sequences followed by 11 days of regular sequences, advanced or retarded with respect to normal days. The tests from west, east, and north indicated that the chronometers of the birds had been affected. The pigeons tended to fly in the predicted false direction, east, after an advanced day and west after a retarded one.

These results support the general theory. Much of the supporting evidence for sun navigation suggested by Matthews has been criticized, although his studies have not been reproduced by other investigators.

It has been observed that birds show a "position effect," in that they do not find their way equally well from all directions. Kramer (1957); Pratt and Wallraff (1958); Kramer, Pratt, and von St. Paul (1958); and Schmidt-Koenig (1960) have found that birds homed and showed more accurate orientation by flying toward the north than the birds flying toward the south. This northerly orientation may also be related to the postfledgling movements of many birds. This "nonsense orientation" in pigeons, and birds in general, Matthews (1961) argues, has caused confusion in research studies on navigation. The fact that there are directional effects in different geographical localities was thought by Kramer as possibly due to selective differences in the pigeon stock that was used. Hoffmann's (1958) research seems to have eliminated this possibility. Using both English and German stock in his experiments, Hoffmann found no differences between the two. The differences from the original studies, it was suggested, seemed to be due to some unknown aspect of the locality. Wallraff (1960c), in studying the relationship between homing ability of pigeons and meteorological and geophysical factors, found that low wind velocities and clouding had a negligible effect on homing ability, though air temperatures and barometric pressures had a great influence. In time, it may be discovered that the position effect can be explained by a critical analysis of the homing locale. However, Kramer (1961) noted day-to-day variations in homing success which could not be explained in terms of traditional meteorology.

Homing ability also shows marked

seasonal fluctuations. Kramer and von St. Paul (1956) and Kramer (1957, 1959) observed that homing was much poorer in winter than in summer at least in Northern Germany. The very poor results obtained in winter over very short distances showed that the birds did not use visual information from the surroundings.

Kramer (1959) and Wallraff (1959) have studied orientation independent of landmarks. Pigeons which were raised in open aviaries exhibited homeward orientation when released. No such orientation was displayed by birds which were raised in walled aviaries allowing vision only of the sky down to 30 degrees above the horizon, in aviaries allowing a view of a sector of the northern sky and horizon, or in aviaries surrounded by palisades in such a manner that free sight of the sky was not allowed except for a zone of elevation 3 degrees above the horizon. Using the bank swallow *Chaetura pelogica* Sargent (1962) tested birds in a portable orientation cage. The birds showed preferences of direction at distances up to 25 miles provided a view of surroundings was available to them during transit, but showed no such tendencies at greater distances or if not permitted to observe surroundings during transit.

The sun-arc navigation theory requires observation of the sun's movement for extrapolation. Kramer (1953) denied pigeons the observation of the sun's path. He demonstrated that the birds quickly oriented themselves even if they were released at the time of day when the elevation of the sun, at the release site, was the same as that of the home loft.

In testing aspects of Matthews' theory, Pratt and Thouless (1955) allowed their pigeons to see the sun for varying periods of time before release, while other birds were screened until release. They observed that both groups oriented towards home with equal accuracy and with such prompt headings

after release that there was some question that the birds were judging the trend of the sun's arc. Pratt (1955) and Pratt and Thouless (1955), using both trained and untrained birds, found that both groups showed a significant tendency to fly in the homeward section of the release circle. Likewise, both groups homed with about the same speed and success. This similarity was contrary to the results obtained by Matthews. Like Kramer, Pratt (1955) attributed the differences in results to stock differences. It has also been pointed out that another possible interpretation lies in the fact that Matthews did not give free range to his birds in the loft, whereas Pratt allowed such activity. The restricted birds, upon arrival in the vicinity of the loft, may not have been able to recognize their home territory.

Hoffmann (1954, 1958, 1960) and Schmidt-Koenig (1960a, 1960b) reported a number of findings with pigeons whose biological clocks were shifted. These data showed that the sun was definitely involved in orientation, but only to the extent that it served as a compass. In the sun-arc theory, following a shift of the bird's chronometers 6 hours clockwise, only at one particular time of day, at 9 A.M., do the altitudes of the anticipated and realized sun agree. All birds that were released before that time should have taken their heading toward the east to southeast, and all birds released after that time toward the north to northwest. This was clearly not the case for there was a deviation to the left with reference to the headings of the control birds, no matter what time and from which direction or distance the birds were released. This evidence was more in keeping with an orientation reaction rather than true navigation. Wallraff (1960a), after summarizing the literature on navigation, concluded by stating:

It has not yet been possible to demonstrate navigation on a purely astronomical basis in any animal. At the present the hypothesis of sun navigation is to be regarded as disproved, at least in pigeon homing, that of star navigation as not proven [p. 459].

Whether migratory flight is governed by goal or directional orientation has been the subject of a whole series of field displacement experiments with the European starling (Kratzig & Schuz, 1936; Perdeck, 1954, 1957), hooded crow *Corvus cornix* (Ruppell, 1944), American crow *Corvus brachyrhynchos* (Rowan, 1946), European sparrow hawk *Accipter nisus* (Dorst, 1939), and European white stork *Ciconia ciconia* (Schuz, 1949, 1950, 1951; Thienemann, 1931). In all of the tests, birds of the same year flew parallel to the normal migratory route; whereas older birds displayed a stronger tendency to home towards the normal distribution area of their population.

Perdeck (1958) suggested that the birds possess at least two different mechanisms for orientation. He observed on the basis of recovery of banded birds that juvenile starlings displaced transversely to their normal route before or during their first migration, flew in the original direction after displacement. He concluded that what they used for orientation must have been a sort of compass to find their direction. Adult birds headed straight to their wintering areas if displaced, though they flew in directions that differed from their normal migratory course over long areas unknown to them.

There seems to be adequate support for the conclusion that there are great differences among species in the capacity to navigate. In surveying many tests of homing ability in the nonmigratory titmice *Paridae*, Hinde (1952) concluded that these birds can find their way home up to a maximum of 7 miles. The coming into home territory seemingly determines the rate of return. In a similar study, Wojtusiak (1949), experimenting with the European tree sparrow *Passer montanus*, also nonmigratory, found no birds returned home from distances greater than 7 miles. The extraordinary abilities in certain migratory sea birds, have, on the other hand, been demonstrated. Lack and Lockley (1938) have reported Manx shearwaters removed from their nesting borrows returned successfully to the colony from points as remote as 930 miles and from areas outside their normal range.

Pennycuick (1960a) has criticized the sun-arc hypothesis from a theoretical point of view. He suggested that a change of azimuth can only be measured by reference to some object which does not move sideways. A bird, then, could only make the measurement of a change in azimuth by reference to a fixed object when the bird is stationary on the ground. Over the sea it is not physically possible to measure it at all without some kind of compass. However, he pointed out that birds do navigate over water. Therefore, Pennycuick saw Matthews' theory as untenable on the grounds of the physical impossibility of making one of the measurements. When Matthews considered errors of position, he assumed that they would appear as errors in latitude. Pennycuick questioned how meridian altitude data could be calculated by Matthews' theory.

Pennycuick's arguments were shown by Pumphrey (1960) to be fallacious. What the bird needs, according to Pumphrey, is an indication of the direction on the horizontal plane long enough to allow the change of azimuth. It may be assumed that a flying bird could obtain the necessary information in flights over the sea, and does not need a fixed object. It was conceded by Pennycuick (1960b) that the rate of change of the sun's azimuth could, at least in principle, be measured by possible reference to, and from analysis of, the waves on the sea. Wave patterns are, under some conditions, more or less regular, but in general seem to be too irregular to be used for measurement of sun angles.

It can be held that Matthews' theoretical position has not been proven in that there is currently little evidence in its support. Nonetheless, there is no doubt that given species do navigate over great distances, and some form of bicoordinate sun navigation cannot be ruled out as the method.

A simpler sun-navigation hypothesis has in turn been suggested by Pennycuick (1960a). It was supposed that upon release the bird measures the sun's elevation and its rate of change and compares these with the conditions at home. Schmidt-Koenig (1961) commented on Pennycuick's theory and argued that the experimental evidence from previous research does not agree with the theory. Under given aspects of a phase shift of the chronometer, birds came to expect a decrease in altitude but did in fact observe an increase in altitude. Instead of an eastern heading, as would be predicted by the theory, there was a left deviation.

From Pennycuick's theory of sun navigation follows the possibility of the use of stars for orientation. Theoretically the use of stars for navigation should be easier than use of the sun. He has pointed out that the altitudes of two different stars can be used simultaneously as two referent points and that there is no need to measure the rates of change, as viewed from Sauer's planetarium experiments in which the star pattern did not move.

Furthermore, it is a well-known phenomenon that under given situations the human observer can detect some of the brighter stars during the day, and if, by chance, the bird is capable of such observations under "normal" circumstances, a new much more simple navigation theory would be possible. At the present time it is not possible to make any reliable statement about the discriminative basis for navigation. It has been conjectured that vision is responsible, but this can scarcely be more than

a generalization as no data are available for the quantities the bird is supposed to be measuring.

OTHER ATTEMPTS TO EXPLAIN TRUE NAVIGATION

Wojtusiak (1946, 1949), reporting on studies made in Poland, brought forth the theory that birds may be sensitive to the infrared visual spectrum. If the theory holds, birds could see through fog and also at night. There is no satisfactory experimental support that birds use the infrared frequencies (Matthews & Matthews, 1939). Watson and Lashley (1915), Lashley (1916), Hecht and Pirenne (1940), and recently Blough (1957) have evidence that birds' visual spectrum is approximately that of man, and therefore, there appears to be no evidence for the theory.

Ising (1946) proposed that the navigation of birds may depend upon the Coriolis force. The Coriolis force is a mechanical effect which results from the rotation of the earth; the strongest force is at the poles and is zero at the equator. As a result of the rotation of the earth, a flying bird's weight changes depending on the direction of flight and its latitude. Theoretically a bird could judge latitude. Wynne-Edwards (1948) has shown, however, that a change of speed from 40 to 39 miles per hour in the bird's flight could alter the Coriolis effect by 2.5%, and this same change would correspond to a displacement of about 150 miles. The Coriolis force is very small and could be offset by many confusing circumstances such as the effect of variable winds and air turbulences. The measurement of the changes that are required by the theory seems outside the organ sensitivity of the bird (de Vries, 1948; Griffin, 1955; Thorpe & Wilkinson, 1946).

Since the nineteenth century, various theories of navigation based on the geomagnetic field have been in circulation, but as yet no one has produced experimental evidence that any animal is sensitive to the magnetic field. Nonetheless, Yeagley (1947, 1951) reported accounts of his experiments with homing pigeons designed to show use of both magnetism and the Coriolis force. He suggested that birds determine the latitude by the effects of the Coriolis force and the longitude from the variations in strength of the earth's magnetic field. The variation in these two forces may be thought of as constituting a grid in North America; one set of lines, equaling the Coriolis force, being the parallels of latitude, and the other being arcs drawn about the North Magnetic Pole as a center. He reported an experiment with pigeons that had been trained to return to a loft in Pennsylvania. These birds were then released in Nebraska where the lines of the two forces intersect as they do at the loft in Pennsylvania. In actuality only a very few birds even reached the general area of the Nebraska loft. However, Yeagley considers that the results showed a significant tendency to fly in that direction. Yeagley also reported positive evidence for his position when comparing homing abilities of two groups, one with magnets attached to the wings, which was to prevent any measurement of magnetism, and a second group with unmagnetized copper bars attached in similar fashion. It was stated that the magnets produced a magnetic field of about the same intensity as the vertical component of the earth's field. Birds without magnets returned more rapidly and in greater numbers. On subsequent tests Yeagley failed to find any differences between the groups. This was explained on the basis of magnetic disturbances occurring on the testing day.

Several other investigators have attempted to replicate the experiment but have found no significant differences between birds with and without magnets (Matthews, 1951; Van Riper & Kalmbach, 1952). Griffin (1955), examining the Yeagley study, has pointed out dif-

ferences in method of attachment of the magnets and copper and has shown that several magnets dropped off the birds in one group while all the metal remained attached in the control group. Differences in attachment may have resulted in differences in irritation and injury. Griffin (1955) and Orgel and Smith (1954) reported negative outcomes of attempts to elicit given responses to a magnetic field in the laboratory. It has also been shown that responses of orientation were not affected (Fromme, 1961; Kramer, 1950a, 1950b). Wynne-Edwards (1948), Thorpe (1949), Griffin (1952, 1955), and Matthews (1955) have presented fundamental criticisms of Yeagley's work. Yeagley's theory appears disproved because it has not withstood critical replication.

However, the theory may not be completely dismissed. It has been reported by Stewart (1957) that electric conditions are created by air friction on the moving bird's feathers. The magnetic field surrounding it cannot help but react to the earth's magnetic fields. This in turn could cause the tips of the wings to move, and thus, the bird may detect this movement. It is thought by Stewart that a bird in flight could correct its direction from these magnetic cues. Nonetheless, evidence for orientation and navigation without the use of celestial clues is not very convincing.

REFERENCES

AGRON, S. L. Evolution of bird navigation and the earth's axial precession. *Evolution*, 1962, **16**, 524–527.

BELLROSE, F. C. Celestial orientation by wild mallards. *Bird Band.*, 1958, **29**, 75–90.

BLOUGH, D. S. Spectral sensitivity in the pigeon. *J. Opt. Soc. Amer.*, 1957, **47**, 827–833.

DE VRIES, H. L. Die Reizschwelle der Sinnesorgane als physikalisches Problem. *Experientia*, 1948, **4**, 205–213.

DORST, R. Über den Einfluss von Verfrachtungen zur Herbstzugzeit auf den Sperber, *Accipiter nisus* (L.). *Proc. 9th Int. Ornithol. Congr. Rouen*, 1939, **100**, 503–521.

FROMME, H. G. Untersuchungen über das

Örientierungsvermögen nächtlich ziehender Kleinvögel. *Z. Tierpsychol.*, 1961, **18**, 205–220.

GRIFFIN, D. R. Bird navigation. *Biol. Rev.*, 1952, **27**, 359–393.

GRIFFIN, D. R. Bird navigation. In A. Wolfson (Ed.), *Recent studies in avian biology*. Urbana: Univer. Illinois Press, 1955. Pp. 154–197.

GRIFFIN, D. R., GOLDSMITH, T. H. Initial flight directions of homing birds. *Biol. Bull.*, 1955, **108**, 264–274.

HAMILTON, W. J., III. Bobolink migratory pathways and their experimental analysis under night skies. *Auk*, 1962, **79**, 208–233. (a)

HAMILTON, W. J., III. Celestial orientation in juvenal waterfowl. *Condor*, 1962, **64**, 19–33. (b)

HAMILTON, W. J., III. Does the bobolink navigate? *Wilson Bull.*, 1962, **74**, 357–366. (c)

HECHT, S., & PIRENN, M. H. The sensibility of the nocturnal long-eared owl in the spectrum. *J. gen. Physiol.*, 1940, **23**, 709–717.

HINDE, R. A. The behavior of the great tit (*Parus major*) and some other related species. *Behaviour*, 1952, Suppl. No. 2.

HOFFMANN, K. Versuche zu der im Richtungsfinden der Vögel enthaltenen Zeitschätzung. *Z. Tierpsychol.*, 1954, **11**, 453–475.

HOFFMANN, K. Repetition of an experiment on bird orientation. *Nature, London*, 1958, **181**, 1435–1437.

HOFFMANN, K. Experimental manipulation of the orientational clock in birds. *Cold Spr. Harb. Symp. quant. Biol.*, 1960, **25**, 379–387.

ISING, G. Die physikalisch Möglichkeit eines tierischen Orientierungssinnes auf Basis der Erdrotation. *Ark. Mat. Astron. Fys.*, 1946, 32A(No. 18).

KENYON, K. W., & RICE, T. W. Homing of the Layson albatross. *Condor*, 1958, **60**, 3–6.

KRAMER, G. Über Richtungstendenzen bei der nächtlichen Zugunruhe gekäfigter Vögel. In E. Mayr & E. Schüz (Ed.), *Ornithologie als Biologische Wissenschaft*. Heidelberg: Winter, 1949. Pp. 269–283.

KRAMER, G. Orientierte Zugaktivität gekäfigter Singvögel. *Naturwissenschaften*, 1950, **37**, 188. (a)

KRAMER, G. Weitere Analyse der Faktoren, welche die Zugaktivität des gekäfigten Vögels orientieren. *Naturwissenschaften*, 1950, **37**, 377–378. (b)

KRAMER, G. Eine neue Methode zu Erforschung der Zugorientierung und die bisher damit erzielten Ergebnisse. *Proc. 10th Int. Ornithol. Congr. Uppsala*, 1951, 269–280.

KRAMER, G. Experiments on bird navigation. *Ibis*, 1952, **94**, 265–285.

KRAMER, G. Die Sonnenorientierung der Vögel. *Verh. zool. Gesellsch. Frieburg*, 1953, 72–84.

KRAMER, G. Experiments on bird orientation and their interpretation. *Ibis*, 1957, **99**, 196–227.

KRAMER, G. Recent experiments on bird orientation. *Ibis*, 1959, **100**, 399–416.

KRAMER, G. Long-distance orientation. In A. J. Marshall (Ed.), *Biology and comparative physiology of birds*. Vol. 2. New York: Academic Press, 1961. Pp. 341–371.

KRAMER, G., PRATT, J. G., & VON ST. PAUL, U. Neue Untersuchungen über den "Richtungseffekt." *J. Ornithol.*, 1958, **99**, 178–191.

KRAMER, G., & RIESE, E. Die Dressur von Brieftauben auf Kompassrichtung in Wahlkäfig. *Z. Tierpsychol.*, 1952, **9**, 245–251.

KRAMER, G., & VON ST. PAUL, U. Stare (*Sturhus vulgaris*) lassen sich auf Himmelsrichtungen dressieren. *Naturwissenschaften*, 1950, **37**, 526–527.

KRAMER, G., & VON ST. PAUL, U. Weitere Erfahrungen über den "Wintereffekt" beim Heimfindvermögen von Brieftauben. *J. Ornithol.*, 1956, **97**, 353–370.

KRÄTZIG, H., & SCHÜZ, E. Ergebnis der Versetzung Ostbaltischer Stare ins Binnenland. *Vogelzug*, 1936, **7**, 163–175.

LACK, D., & LOCKLEY, R. M. Stokholm Bird Observatory homing experiments: I. 1963–37. Puffins, storm-petrels and Manx shearwaters. *Brit. Birds*, 1938, **31**, 242–248.

LASHLEY, K. S. The color vision of birds: I. The spectrum of the domestic fowl. *J. anim. Behav.*, 1916, **6**, 1–26.

MATTHEWS, G. V. T. The experimental investigation of navigation in homing pigeons. *J. exp. Biol.*, 1951, **28**, 508–535.

MATTHEWS, G. V. T. An investigation of homing ability in two species of gulls. *Ibis*, 1952, **94**, 243–264.

MATTHEWS, G. V. T. Navigation in the Manx shearwater. *J. exp. Biol.*, 1953, **30**, 370–396. (a)

MATTHEWS, G. V. T. The orientation of untrained pigeons: A dichotomy in the homing process. *J. exp. Biol.*, 1953, **30**, 268–276. (b)

MATTHEWS, G. V. T. Sun navigation in homing pigeons. *J. exp. Biol.*, 1953, **30**, 243–267. (c)

MATTHEWS, G. V. T. *Bird navigation*. Cambridge: University Press, 1955. (a)

MATTHEWS, G. V. T. An investigation of the "chronometer" factor in bird navigation. *J. exp. Biol.*, 1955, **32**, 39–58. (b)

MATTHEWS, G. V. T. "Nonsense" orientation

in mallard *Anas Phatyhnchas* and its relation to experiments on bird navigation. *Ibis*, 1961, **103**, 211–230.

MATTHEWS, L. H., & MATTHEWS, B. H. C. Owls and infra-red radiation. *Nature, London*, 1939, **143**, 983.

MAZZEO, R. Homing of the Manx shearwater. *Auk*, 1953, **70**, 200–201.

MERKEL, R. W., & FROMME, H. G. Untersuchungen über das Orientierungsvermögen nächtich ziehender Rotkelchen. *Naturwissenschaften*, 1958, **45**, 499–ɔ00

MEWALD, L. D., & GOSE, R. G. Orientation of migratory restlessness in the white-crowned sparrow. *Science*, 1960, **131**, 105–106.

ORGEL, A. R., & SMITH, J. C. Test of the magnetic theory of homing. *Science*, 1954, **120**, 891–892.

PENNYCUICK, C. J. The physical basis of astro-navigation in birds: Theoretical consideration. *J. exp. Biol.*, 1960, **37**, 573–593. (a)

PENNYCUICK, C. J. Sun navigation by birds. *Nature, London*, 1960, **188**, 1127–1128. (b)

PERDECK, A. C. Jaarverslag 1953. *Jversl. Vogeltrekst. Texel*, 1954, 3–13.

PERDECK, A. C. Stichting Vogeltrekstation Texel Jaarverslag over 1956. *Limosa*, 1957, **30**, 62–75.

PERDECK, A. C. Two types of orientation in migrating starlings, *Sturnus Vulgaris* L., and chaffinches, *Fringilla coolebs* L., as revealed by displacement experiments. *Ardea*, 1958, **46**, 1–37.

PUMPHREY, R. J. Sun navigation by birds. *Nature, London*, 1960, **188**, 1127.

PRATT, J. G. An investigation of homing ability in pigeons without previous homing experience. *J. exp. Biol.*, 1955, **32**, 70–73.

PRATT, J. G., & THOULESS, R. H. Homing orientation in pigeons in relation to opportunity to observe the sun before release. *J. exp. Biol.*, 1955, **32**, 140–157.

PRATT, J. G., & WALLRAFF, H. G. Zweirichtungs-Versuche mit Brieftauben: Langstreckenflüge auf der Nord-Süd Achse in Westdeutschland. *Z. Tierpsychol.*, 1958, **15**, 332–337.

ROWAN, W. Experiments in bird navigation. *Trans. Roy. Soc. Canada*, 1946, **40**, 123–235.

RUPPELL, W. Versuche über das Heimfinden ziehender Nebelkrähen nach Verfrachtung. *J. Ornithol.*, 1944, **92**, 106–132.

SARGENT, T. A study of homing in the bank swallow. *Auk*, 1962, **79**, 234–246.

SAUER, E. G. F. Further studies on stellar orientation of nocturnally migrating birds. *Psychol. Forsch.*, 1961, **24**, 224–244.

SAUER, E. G. F., & SAUER, E. M. Star navigation of nocturnal migrating birds.

Cold Spr. Harb. Symp. quant. Biol., 1960, **25**, 463–473.

SAUER, F. Zugorientierung einer Mönchsgrasmücke (*Sylvia a. atricapilla*, L.) unter künstlichem Sternenhimmel. *Naturwissenschaften*, 1956, **53**, 231–232.

SAUER, F. Astronavigatorische Orientierung einer unter künstlichem Sternenhimmel verfrachteten Klappergrasmücke, *Sylvia C. currca* (L.). *Naturwissenschaften*, 1957, **44**, 71. (a)

SAUER, F. Die Sternenorientierung nächtlich ziehender Grasmücken (*Sylvia atricapilla, borin* und *curruca*). *Z. Tierpsychol.*, 1957, **14**, 29–70. (b)

SAUER, F., & SAUER, E. Zur Frage der nächtlichen Zugorientierung von Grasmücken. *Rev. Suisse Zool.*, 1955, **62**, 250–259.

SAUER, F., & SAUER, E. Nächtliche Zugorientierung europäischer Zugvögel in Südwestafrika. *Vogelwarte*, 1959, **20**, 4–31.

SCHMIDT-KOENIG, K. Internal clocks and homing. *Cold Spr. Harb. Symp. quant. Biol.*, 1960, **25**, 389–393. (a)

SCHMIDT-KOENIG, K. The sun-azimuth compass: One factor in the orientation of homing pigeons. *Science*, 1960, **131**, 826–828. (b)

SCHMIDT-KOENIG, K. Sun navigation in birds. *Nature, London*, 1961, **190**, 1025–1026.

SCHÜZ, E. Die Spätauflassung ostpreussischer Jungstörche in Westdeutschland 1933. *Vogelwarte*, 1949, **15**, 63–78.

SCHÜZ, E. Früh Auflassung ostpreussischer Jungstörche in Westdeutschland durch die Vogelwarte Rossitten 1933-1936. *Bonn. zool. Beitr.*, 1950, **1**, 239–253.

SCHÜZ, E. Überblick über die Orientierungsversuche der Vogelwarte Rossitten (jetz: Vogelwarte Radolfzug). *Proc. 10th Int. Ornithol. Congr. Upsala*, 1951, 249–268.

STEWART, O. J. A birds inborn navigational device. *Trans. Ky. Acad. Sci.*, 1957, **18**, 78–84.

THIENEMANN, J. Von Vogelzug in Rossitten. *J. Neumanns, Neudamm*, 1931.

THORPE, W. H. A discussion on the orientation of birds on migratory and homing flights: Recent biological evidence for the methods of bird orientation. *Proc. Linn. Soc. Lond.*, 1949, **160**, 85–94.

THORPE, W. H., & WILKINSON, D. H. Ising's theory of bird orientation. *Nature, London*, 1946, **158**, 903–904.

TINBERGEN, N. Field observations of migration and their significance for the problems of migration. *Ardea*, 1956, **44**, 231.

TINBERGEN, N., & FIJLSTRA, J. J. De veldwaarnemingen: Een schakel die ontrak. *Jversl. Vogeltrekst. Texel*, 1954, 14–22.

VAN RIPER, W., & KALMBACH, E. R. Homing not hindered by wing magnets. *Science,* 1952, **115**, 577–578.

VON ST. PAUL, U. Nachweis der Sonnenorientierunger bei nächtlich ziehenden Vögeln. *Behaviour,* 1953, **6**, 1–7.

VON ST. PAUL, U. Compass directional training of western meadowlarks (*Sturnella neglecta*). *Auk,* 1956, **73**, 203–209.

WALLRAFF, H. G. Örtlich und zeitlich bedingte Variabilität Heimkehr verhaltens von Brieftauben. *Z. Tierpsychol.,* 1959, **16**, 513–544.

WALLRAFF, H. G. Does celestial navigation exist in animals? *Cold Spr. Harb. Symp. quant. Biol.,* 1960, **25**, 451–461. (a)

WALLRAFF, H. G. Können Grasmücken mit Hilfe des Sternenhimmels navigeren? (Kritische Bearbeitung einiger Planetariumsversuche von F. Sauer.) *Z. Tierpsychol.,* 1960, **17**, 165–177. (b)

WALLRAFF, H. G. Über Zusammenhänge des Heimkehrverhaltens von Brieftauben mit meteorologischen und geophysikalischen Faktoren. *Z. Tierpsychol.,* 1960, **17**, 82–113. (c)

WATSON, J. B., & LASHLEY, K. S. Homing and related activities of birds. *Pap. Tortugas Lab.,* 1915, **7**, 1–104.

WOJTUSIAK, R. J. Hypothesis of sensibility to infra-red rays as an attempt to explain some problems of orientation in animals. *CR Sci. Math. Nat. Acad. Polon.,* 1946, 28–29.

WOJTUSIAK, R. J. Polish investigations on homing in birds and their orientation in space. *Proc. Linn. Soc. Lond.,* 1949, **160**, 99–108.

WYNNE-EDWARDS, V. C. Yeagley's theory of bird navigation. *Ibis,* 1948, **90**, 606–611.

YEAGLEY, H. L. A preliminary study of a physical basis of bird navigation. *J. appl. Physiol.,* 1947, **18**, 1035–1063.

YEAGLEY, H. L. A preliminary study of a physical basis of bird navigation. Part 2. *J. appl. Physiol.,* 1951, **22**, 746–760.

Newts: Sun-Compass Orientation

Abstract. *Rough-skinned newts, captured from breeding ponds, oriented on courses that would have intersected the familiar shorelines at right angles, when released in a circular arena on land under the sun or moon. Pondward migrants oriented similarly. Reorientation failed under complete cloud cover and after 7 days of darkness in an environmental chamber, but persisted in newts whose eyes were excised and in those displaced more than 27 kilometers in darkness. Both normal and blind animals compensated for displacement in sunshine. Preliminary evidence suggests that alternative light receptors in blinded animals may be associated with the optic tectum. No evidence of olfactory guidance was observed.*

Several anuran amphibians employ a sun-compass mechanism for guidance in activities associated with the home shore (*1*) and in migratory movements (*2*). The toad *Bufo woodhousei fowleri* can learn an escape route relative to a light cue, and the directional choice can be altered by manipulation of the daily light-dark regime (*3*). Terrestrial salamanders migrate long distances to particular breeding sites (*4, 5*).

Although these movements appear to be guided (*6*), the mechanism involved is in doubt. The ability of the newt *Taricha rivularis* to home after extirpation of the eyes led Twitty to conclude that olfactory cues were used in orientation (*7*). In laboratory experiments *T. granulosa* used a sun-compass mechanism to determine direction of a goal, but olfactory cues appeared to confirm the goal's identity (*8*).

We now report field studies in which rough-skinned newts, *T. granulosa,* oriented by the sun during the breeding season. Newts from breeding ponds, when tested on land with only celestial cues visible, moved in directions that would have returned them to water at the home shore. *Taricha granulosa,* captured en route to a breeding site, maintained the same compass course when released 27.6 km away, presumably beyond the reach of familiar odors; they failed to select an expected compass course under cloudy skies or after 7 days in darkness. Under the sun, surgically blinded newts moved in the expected direction as well as did normal animals.

Our experimental animals came from a population of *T. granulosa* breeding in fish ponds (9); a test site was established nearby (10). Their directional choices were tested in a circular arena (13.4 m in diameter; walls, 1.98 m) constructed of black plastic (No. 55 Griffolyn) nailed to posts (5 by 10 cm) driven into the ground. They were released in the center of the arena and recovered from drop-traps (4-liter cans sunk to ground level) located at 15° intervals around the wall. The ground inside the arena was bare, and the walls obscured all landscape; the arena has been described (2). Although most newts were tested on the day of capture, some late afternoon collections were held overnight.

Altogether 1001 newts were captured with a dip net along straight segments of shore at the breeding ponds and placed in black plastic bags, pending release in sunshine. Equal numbers were taken from the four shores representing the four basic compass points. Newts from a north shore went southward (Fig. 1a), those from a south shore went northward (Fig. 1b), those from an east shore went westward (Fig. 1c), and those from a west shore went eastward (Fig. 1d). The mean angle of the scores, computed vectorially (11) (Fig. 1, a–d), is within 44° of the expected direction; the newts generally moved in directions that would have taken them to water at the home shore, not toward the ponds. The test arena was about 0.4 km from the breeding ponds, presumably within range of olfactory cues.

More newts (172) were taken from the water along the same four shores and treated similarly, except that they were released at night in five tests in moonlight. When all the diagrams of these results are rotated so that the directions toward water coincide (Fig. 1e), the directional choices are toward water relative to the home shore, and the mean angle of the scores is within 2° of the expected direction.

Several groups of *T. granulosa* from the north shores of these ponds were handled in the manner described, but were released under cloudy skies lacking celestial cues. These 312 newts tested moved in random directions (Fig. 1f); they responded slowly, often remaining stationary for more than 1 hour. Animals released during showers of hail or snow, however, left the center of the pen faster in an apparent search for cover.

Animals must know local time in order to use the sun as a compass, and prolonged darkness should affect this sense of time. A group of 129 newts, captured along a north shore, were placed in an environmental chamber in total darkness at 20° to 21°C for 7 days before being taken to the test pen in black plastic bags and released in sunshine; their directional choices were random rather than toward water at the home shore (Fig. 1g). More newts (65) were kept similarly in darkness for 7 days before being exposed for 1 week to a light-dark regime equivalent to outdoors but initiated 6 hours after sunrise each day. At the home shore these newts would have had to move northward to find water, but, if their time sense had been altered by 6 hours, they would have moved eastward. The directional choices in these tests were scattered, but many went either northward or eastward (Fig. 1h). Although there was marked difference in the responses in comparison with those of newts tested after 7 days in darkness, the expected shift of directional choices was incomplete.

Taricha granulosa were captured in a small pond located 27.68 km west by air of the test arena, brought there immedi-

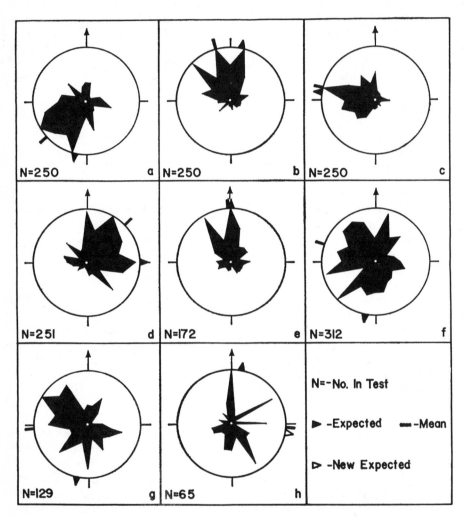

Fig. 1. Responses in the test arena of newts captured in breeding ponds. Animals were from shores having water located southward (a), northward (b), westward (c), eastward (d). Newts were tested in moonlight (e), under cloudy skies (f), after 7 days in constant darkness (g), and after 7 days in darkness followed by 7 days in a 12-hour: 12 hour light-dark regime initiated 6 hours after sunrise (h). The largest number of newts caught in a single trap is represented by the radius; the number in each of the other 23 traps is a radial line of proportional length in the appropriate direction; connection of distal points on the 24 radii encompasses the shaded area. When the data in all diagrams were analyzed statistically with the Rayleigh test, a hypothesis of random distribution was rejected (P, .01) in all instances but (f) and (g). Arrows point northward.

ately in black bags, and released in sunshine; they were caught along a straight shore having water to the east. Their directional choices (Fig. 2a) were eastward, with a mean angle of scores within 18° of this direction, and opposite the direction of the nearest ponds. The results were similar to those with animals that were captured near the test site, where familiar odors were likely (Fig. 2).

Although the preceding evidence establishes that newts can use celestial cues to associate land-water positions, it does not show that migrating animals use the mechanism. A large migration of *T. granulosa* approaching a breeding pond was fortuitously encountered, and their directional response was tested in the arena. A group of 58 females was captured by hand, within 9 m of the water, on a straight segment of shore; in black bags they were taken to the test arena to be released the following day. Most of their directional choices corresponded to the direction traveled

Table 1. Recaptures of marked newts in a series of parallel drift fences after 229-m displacement from the breeding ponds. Individuals trapped at the first fence were considered on course; those trapped only at a subsequent fence were termed off course.

Condition of displacement	Number of newts moved		Newts recaptured					
			On course			Off course		
			Number		Per- cent- age	Number		Per- cent- age
	♂	♀	♂	♀		♂	♀	
In black bag	142	206	23	41	18.4	3	8	3.2
Under cloud	112	94	32	28	29.1	8	14	10.7
In sunshine, normal	138	123	28	18	17.6	0	0	0.0
In sunshine, blinded	43	87	3	13	12.3	0	0	0.0
Totals								
	435	510	86	100	19.7	11	22	3.5

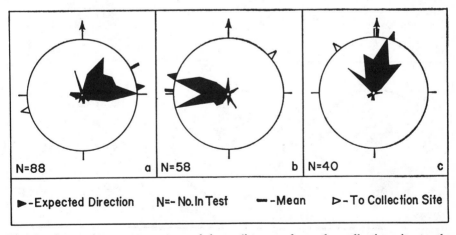

N=88 a N=58 b N=40 c

▶-Expected Direction   N=- No. In Test   ▬-Mean   ▷- To Collection Site

Fig. 2. Scores by newts transported long distances from the collection site to the test arena; they were captured in a breeding pond 27.68 km westward (a), on land as they approached a pond 6 km northeastward (b), or in a drift fence at a site 27.6 km northwestward (c). When all data were analyzed with the Rayleigh test, a hypothesis of randomness was rejected (*P*, 0.1). Arrows point northward.

before capture; they were not toward the pond (Fig. 2b). Forty more newts were captured by drift fences and traps as they approached a pond 27.60 km by air from the test site; their directional choices in the test arena corresponded to the course they had been traveling when trapped (Fig. 2c).

The following experiments tested the awareness of *T. granulosa* to displacements imposed upon them. Altogether 278 newts were captured from various shores, placed in light-tight containers, and taken to the arena. Before testing, the animals were placed in a clear plastic container, walked on a straight course (east to west) for 183 m, returned to the light-tight containers, and taken to the center of the arena for release. Most of them moved in a direction opposite the displacement (Fig. 3a). Animals from a shore having

water in a direction opposite the direction of displacement scored with greater accuracy. Newts (127) from a west shore were treated similarly except that both eyes were excised and they were held for 24 hours before displacement in sunshine; all were held and transported in light-tight plastic bags. Their directions were generally eastward, in a direction opposite the displacement (Fig. 3b). The directional choices of these newts were away from the ponds, and their performance compared favorably with the precision of normal animals in the expected direction. This finding reduces the probability that olfactory cues were used, and suggests that blind newts can ascertain the sun's position (Fig. 3).

Normal (Fig. 3c) and blinded animals (Fig. 3d) were used to repeat the last two series of tests; they were dis-

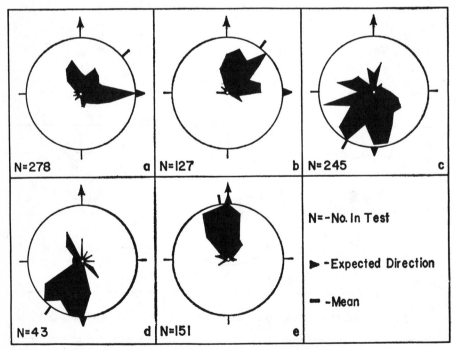

Fig. 3. Response of newts displaced 183 m on a compass course in sunshine before testing: westward displacement of normal (a) and blinded newts (b); northward displacement of normal (c) and blinded animals (d); blinded newts displaced southward (e). Random distribution was rejected (Rayleigh test) in all tests (*P*, .01). *Expected direction*: direction opposite the displacement. Arrows point northward.

placed northward for 183 m in bright sunshine. The scoring patterns in both series were generally in the expected direction—opposite the displacement. A final group of 151 newts, from a south shore, were blinded and displaced 183 m southward before testing; the results show a precise northward pattern (Fig. 3e). A blinded newt usually held its head high and positioned it in different directions as it moved; although these animals moved back and forth on a chosen course, they ultimately reached the wall in the expected direction.

The movements of T. granulosa in their habitat were compared with movements in the test arena by translocating them from the breeding pond and releasing them behind a system of drift fences. A series of three plastic drift fences (55 m long, 61 cm high), with drop-traps, was arranged with one fence 23 m from the ponds and with the others parallel and at 91-m intervals; each fence was centered on a line extending westward from the ponds. The 945 newts were individually marked, translocated 228 m from the ponds, over the center of each fence, and released; the spatial relations were optimal for use of olfactory cues. Table 1 shows the recaptures of normal animals moved in sunshine, in light-tight containers, and under cloudy skies, as well as the recaptures of blinded newts (eyes excised) translocated in sunshine. The positions of recaptured animals were noted, and each newt was released on the opposite (pondward) side of the fence. During these experiments the weather became dry and warm, interrupting natural breeding migrations. The percentages of recaptures were not significantly different among the four groups, but the numbers of newts recaptured off course (those that missed the first fence) correlate with the nature of the translocation. All normal or blinded newts moved in sunshine were captured on a direct line heading for the ponds. Although the distance to the first fence was only 23 m, newts transported in black bags and under cloudy skies were often captured initially at the second or third fence. Two newts transported and released under cloud cover were recaptured in a drift fence 0.4 km eastward and at right angles to the system of fences. The T. granulosa denied celestial cues during displacement may have used random movements in attempting to locate familiar areas (Table 1).

The responses of T. granulosa thus indicate that a course is determined relative to celestial cues. Awareness of newts to translocation in sunshine suggests that a sun compass may function in local movements and in migrations; their directional choices were affected under cloudy skies, after exposure to darkness for long periods, and after subjection to altered light regimes, but not by excision of both eyes. Observations did not indicate that blinded newts relied on olfactory or other cues, but did suggest awareness of the sun's position. Taricha granulosa appear to obtain information with vitiated visual sensory equipment and do not abandon the sense for another. We made no attempt to determine the site of reception—such as exposed nerves in the socket, or skin receptors. Twitty (4, 7) witnessed homing by blinded T. rivularis, but he did not test a hypothesis of light reception without eyes (12).

Our newts relied on a sun-compass mechanism in the absence of other cues, but presumably the same animals use all available cues for orientation in their natural habitat. The sun is a dominant feature in the environment, and many amphibians can use it for direction finding (1–3). We postulate that a sun compass is a basic mechanism in orientation of amphibians.

HOBART F. LANDRETH*
DENZEL E. FERGUSON

*Department of Zoology, Mississippi
State University, State College 39762*

References and Notes

1. D. Ferguson, H. Landreth, M. Turnipseed,
Copeia **1965**, 58 (1965); H. Landreth and D.
Ferguson, *Herpetologica* **22**, 106 (1966); **23**,
81 (1967).
2. D. Ferguson and H. Landreth, *Behaviour* **26**,
105 (1966).
3. H. Landreth and D. Ferguson, *ibid.*, in press.
4. V. Twitty, D. Grant, O. Anderson, *Proc. Nat.
Acad. Sci. U.S.* **51**, 51 (1964).
5. ———, *ibid.* **56**, 864 (1966).
6. V. Twitty, *Science* **130**, 1735 (1959).
7. ———, *Of Scientists and Salamanders* (Freeman, San Francisco, 1966).
8. H. Landreth and D. Ferguson, *Nature* **215**,
516 (1967).
9. Owned by Oregon State University.
10. On Soap Creek, 16 km north of Corvallis,
Oregon, 8 March 1967.
11. E. Batschelet, "Statistical methods for the
analysis of problems in animal orientation
and certain biological rhythms," Amer. Inst.
Biol. Sci. monogr., Washington, D. C., 1965.
12. Preliminary laboratory investigations provide
some insight into the nature of light reception
in blind newts. Using techniques and apparatus described (*8*), we trained 24 newts to
move in a particular direction under an artificial "sun." Equal numbers of the trained
newts were subjected to surgery to produce
experimental groups that were blind, blind
with severed olfactory tracts, and blind with
destroyed optic tecta. On testing, directional
training relative to the light cue persisted in
the blind, blind anosmic, and sighted anosmic
animals, but not in the blind group lacking
optic tecta. Newts with eyes excised were
alert, demonstrated responsiveness to light
cues by head motions and attitudes, and exhibited deliberate directional choices. Those
lacking optic tecta showed no evidence of
visual stimulation.
13. Supported by NSF grant GB 3991. We thank
R. M. Storm and his students (Oregon State
University) for assistance in the field. Elizabeth Crosby and Henry Hoffman (University
of Alabama Medical School) provided assistance and facilities for surgery.
* Present address: Department of Biology,
Southwestern State College, Weatherford, Oklahoma 73096.

24 August 1967

Homing Orientation by Olfaction in Newts (Taricha rivularis)

Abstract. Newts displaced after perfusion of the olfactory epithelium with formaldehyde failed to orient toward home, whereas control animals subjected to oral perfusion with formaldehyde oriented as readily as did untreated controls. Newts with surgically extirpated olfactory nerves failed to home unless their nerves had regenerated. These results strongly suggest a critical role for olfaction in homing behavior.

The newt *Taricha rivularis* is able to
return to its home area after being displaced for distances as great as 8.0 km.
This feat is accomplished by direct,
oriented migration toward the home
area, regardless of its compass direction
or the ruggedness of the intervening
mountain terrain (*1*). Moreover, newts
take correct initial homeward headings
upon leaving the release site, even when
the displacement distance is as great
as 12.8 km (*2*). The maximum distance
at which *T. rivularis* can orient its initial migratory movements has yet to be
established, though we have found that
the farther a newt is displaced, the
more likely it is to leave the release
site in a random, nonoriented direction.
Since blinded animals can home successfully (*3*), it seems unlikely that
vision is essential for orientation, although the possible existence of alternate photosensory systems has not been
tested.

The experiments we report here provide evidence that in these animals olfaction plays a major role in initial
orientation and in the eventual return
to the home site.

In the first experiments designed to
assess the importance of olfaction in
homing, we effected anosmia surgically

by extirpating a section of the olfactory nerves. Of 617 such operated newts displaced from Pepperwood Creek to Jim Creek (about 3.2 km displacement distance), only 15 are known to have returned home. These were killed and dissected, and each proved to have regenerated olfactory nerves. The control group for this homing study consisted of 692 normal animals that experienced the same displacement. Of these, 564 were later recaptured at their home sites along Pepperwood Creek. Daily patrols of the stream and frequent collections in the land traps adjacent to Pepperwood Creek preclude the possibility that large numbers of animals could have returned undetected. Although the total return of operated newts was too small to permit any broad conclusions, it is at least clear that not one newt with unregenerated nerves was recaptured at the home location.

In similar experiments designed to test initial orientation rather than complete homing performance, we compared surgically treated anosmic newts with a control group in which an identical opening was made in the skull but the olfactory nerves were left intact. Members of both groups showed random orientation at the release site. Since in the salamander the cerebral hemispheres are predominantly olfactory in function (4), the sham operation may have produced anosmia through traumatization of this region. Thus, though the surgical experiments gave unclear results, they did suggest that interventions involving olfactory regions of the central nervous system produced deficits in the ability to take correct initial headings and to complete a homing performance.

We were thus encouraged to attempt more controlled and rigorous lesions in the olfactory system, this time testing initial orientation. We rendered newts anosmic by perfusing the nasal cavities with a 10 percent solution of formaldehyde. A blunted hypodermic syringe was inserted into each external naris, and the solution was injected until it flowed freely from the internal nares into the oral cavity. Excess formaldehyde in the oral cavity was immediately flushed away with fresh water. Histological examination of animals treated in this way showed that the olfactory epithelium had become necrotic.

In another large group of newts only the oral cavity was perfused with 10 percent formaldehyde, which was immediately flushed out with fresh water. A third group was used as a standard with which to compare initial orientation.

All were collected from the same segment of stream and released on land about 1.2 km upstream (Fig. 1). Displacements were made early in the breeding season and each release consisted of approximately equal numbers of anosmic animals and treated controls selected randomly from the total collected each day. The normal control group had experienced the same displacement and recapture routine 1 year earlier. All three groups were marked distinctively by coded toe clipping: 502 anosmic animals, 451 treated controls, and 617 normal controls were released.

Recapture fences were constructed of ¼-inch mesh hardware cloth, arranged so as to funnel migrating newts into escape-proof traps. They were arranged predominantly on the steep, wooded hillside that forms the south bank of Pepperwood Creek in Sonoma County, California. Three fences (30.48 m long) were spaced 41.1, 91.4, and 219.4 m from—and perpendicular to—the stream (Fig. 1). We built a fourth fence on the north side of Pepperwood Creek on flat, open terrain where little migration of newts occurs. Complete four-fence networks of this type were located 228.5 m downstream and 228.5 m upstream from the release point. Captures in two additional fences, one in a densely wooded area farther upstream on the north bank and a comparable one farther downstream augmented the number of recaptures in the main fence networks. In the present tests we made all of our displacements from a downstream collecting site (about 1.2 km) (Fig. 1).

The newt's initial orientation movements upon its departure from the release site were measured by comparing the number of captures in the traps upstream from the release site with the number of captures in the downstream traps. The newts were allowed as much as 3 months to choose their migratory direction when leaving the release site.

The reason for conducting these experiments over long periods and in a large test area is related to our observation, over many years of experimenting with displaced newts in test enclosures, that *T. rivularis* is subject to great changes in behavior through handling. In early displacement tests, the enclosures were small (18.3 to 30.48 m across), and the displacement distances were short, requiring a minimum of handling. The results in these short-time,

short-distance tests were satisfactory. But with greater displacement distances, longer periods of confinement during processing, and added handling for operating and coding, we found that results in small test enclosures were unsatisfactory. Many animals refused to leave the release site; those that did leave appeared to be seeking escape or shelter regardless of the home direction. We eliminated these difficulties by using larger test areas and allowing more time. The newts may remain immobile for long periods, but then have an opportunity to probe the release area seeking homing cues without committing themselves to capture in a trap. Once the directional choice is made, the newt must travel in the chosen direction for at least 228.5 m before encountering a trap.

The first trap captures in each group occurred about 2 weeks after release, when a few test animals encountered the fences. Captures mounted steadily through the next month, then fell off with the onset of hot, dry weather in late spring when newts cease migrating and seek underground hiding places to

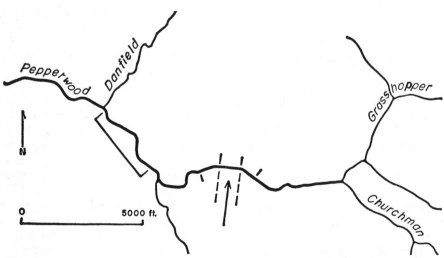

Fig. 1. Newts were collected from the portion of Pepperwood Creek indicated by the bracket and displaced upstream to the release site (arrow) midway between land traps perpendicular to the stream. The displacement distance is approximately 1.2 km.

avoid summer desiccation.

Although the treated newts did not move completely at random, accuracy in orienting toward the home area was greatly reduced (Fig. 2). The treated controls oriented with the same accuracy as the normal controls.

Studies of amphibian orientation and homing have produced several hypotheses concerning the sensory basis of this phenomenon. Landreth and Ferguson have shown that newts and frogs use a

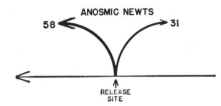

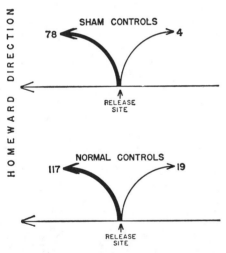

Fig. 2. The distribution of displaced anosmic newts released between the two trap networks is significantly different ($P = .01$) from the distributions of the two control groups. The distribution of the treated control group does not differ significantly from that of the normal controls (test based upon normal approximation to the binomial distribution). Actual release and recapture figures: 502 anosmic released, 89 recaptured; 451 treated controls released, 82 recaptured; 617 normal controls released, and 136 recaptured.

sun-compass mechanism in maintaining a compass course (y-axis) that bisects the home shore at right angles (5). Frogs tested in an aquatic arena failed to orient under cloud cover or when the sky was of uniform light intensity, indicating a visual mechanism. Shoop, on the other hand, found that the salamander *Ambystoma maculatum* does most of its migrating during cloudy and rainy nights (as does *T. rivularis*) when no celestial cues are available. He doubts that visual cues could guide these migrations (6). When the frog *Pseudacris triseriata* was tested in a T-maze, 71 percent chose odors from a breeding habitat rather than upland forest odors (7). Our own earlier results (3) give no indication that the homing performance of blinded newts is impaired.

It appears from the results with *T. rivularis* treated with formaldehyde, in which only olfactory tissue is destroyed, that odor plays an important, though not necessarily exclusive, role in initial orientation. The fact that anosmic newts did not distribute themselves completely randomly suggests that other mechanisms may partially take over when olfaction fails. This is consistent with Ferguson's proposal that orientation is probably not dependent on one sense exclusively.

An olfactory basis for homing presupposes a stable source of odorant capable of remaining recognizable year after year. Because normal newts orient toward home before and after, as well as during, their aquatic breeding season, and because their migration is terrestrial, it seems unlikely that anything in the water attracts them to the home territory. Terrestrial odors from trees, smaller plants, and decaying plant material could provide such long-term odors. Even a microsmatic biologist can easily differentiate between that portion of Pepperwood Creek bounded by fir trees and another stretch where California laurel predominates. The odor complex which identifies an area must be a composite of numerous individual odors, which can maintain its collective identity over long periods.

DAVID GRANT
OSCAR ANDERSON
VICTOR TWITTY*

*Department of Biological Sciences,
Stanford University,
Stanford, California 94305*

References and Notes

1. V. C. Twitty, D. Grant, O. Anderson, *Proc. Nat. Acad. Sci. U.S.* **56**, 864 (1966); *ibid.* **51**, 51 (1964).
2. ———, *ibid.* **57**, **342** (1967).
3. V. C. Twitty, *Of Scientists and Salamanders* (Freeman, San Francisco, 1966),, pp. 134–38.
4. C. J. Herrick, *The Brain of the Tiger Salamander* (Univ. of Chicago Press, Chicago, 1948).
5. H. Landreth and D. Ferguson, *Nature* **215**, 516 (1967); *Herpetologica* **23**, 81 (1967); *Science* **158**, 1459 (1967).
6. C. R. Shoop, *Science* **149**, 558 (1965).
7. B. S. Martof, *Physiol. Zool.* **35**, 270 (1962).
8. Supported by NSF grant GB-4164. We thank D. Kennedy (Stanford) for his editorial advice and especially for his efforts in arranging the continuation of this research following the death of Victor Twitty. We also thank J. Ware for help with the statistical analysis.
* Died 22 March 1967 before the completion of these experiments.

10 May 1968

PART 6 Learning

Now that we have studied the genetics, physiology, and development of animal behavior, with an excursion into sensory processes, communication, and orientation, we turn to what has historically been the psychologist's favorite topic: learning. The literature on animal learning is vast and selection of representative papers is particularly difficult. Many of those who have studied animal learning were really interested in *human* learning. They were using animals as substitutes for humans in a search for laws of learning that could apply across species.

Others have approached the topic from a different point of view. It should be obvious, at this point, that learning is a biological adaptation. It is just as much a product of evolution as any other character. Therefore, learning may be studied as a process that may operate in the behavior of an animal in its natural environment. The reports that follow are primarily of this sort.

Part 6 begins with a paper by Neal E. Miller called "Laws of Learning Relevant to Its Biological Basis." Since his first publication in 1934, Miller has made many major contributions to the study of learning and motivation. In the present selection he reviews some basic facts about these topics. Included is a report of some of the recent, exciting work from his laboratory on instrumental conditioning of the autonomic nervous system, a phenomenon that was previously thought to be impossible.

Reading 50 considers an old problem in psychology, that of phyletic differences in learning. In this selection, M. E. Bitterman describes a series of experiments on this problem. Reading 51 is a related study. Here Bresler and Bitterman report the fascinating finding that fish with experimentally produced greater-than-normal amounts of brain tissue perform like "higher animals" in a series of habit reversals. The conclusions drawn in Reading 50 were criticized by Hodos and Campbell in Reading 2, and the student will want to review those criticisms after considering Readings 50 and 51.

It has been said that farmers know many things about animal behavior and some of them are even correct. In actuality, it generally pays to listen carefully to those whose livelihood depends upon animals. In an increasing number of cases this scientifically unacceptable, anecdotal lore of animal behavior has proven correct. We shall cover two examples. The first concerns the proposition that animals learn from one another, or, more specifically, that mothers educate their young. In Reading 52, Phyllis Chesler presents experimental evidence that kittens are indeed more apt to imitate their mother than they are a strange cat. Note that this particular experiment does not prove that mother cats actively educate their young (although this may well occur), but rather indicates that the young can be educated by observation and imitation of the mother. Examples of such observational learning in field studies of primates are found in Reading 61 in Part 7. The existence of observational learning in the natural situation provides the basis for cultural transmission of information from one generation to the next.

Our second example is related to stories that certain animals can become "poison-shy." This seemed particularly difficult to believe because it violated widely accepted principles of learning. Consider what is required. An animal begins to eat food that is poisoned, but, for some reason, eating behavior is interrupted before a lethal dose has been ingested. Some time later, the animal sickens but does not die. Henceforth, he avoids the food that previously tasted good. The learning principles that are involved are discussed by Miller in Reading 49 in a section called Effective Temporal Sequences. In the summary of that paper the following statement (amply supported by experimental evidence) appears: "Learning is dependent on close temporal association between stimulus and response, and at least in conditioning situations, forward associations seem to be established much more easily than backward ones, if indeed the latter are possible, a point which needs further experimental clarification." The fact that the aversive consequences of eating the food occur some time after its ingestion violates the requirement of close temporal association, at least if rapid learning is to occur. Yet, for an animal to become poison-shy, rapid learning is required since the animal will not survive repeated trials. Of course if such learning is simply a myth, one does not need to be concerned about explaining it. Unfortunately for the theorists (and for the food-growers), learning closely approximating that required for the avoidance of poisoned bait has been demonstrated in the laboratory. Examples from two different species are given by Wilcoxon, Dragoin, and Kral in Reading 53. Can such learning be explained without violation of generally accepted principles of learning, or have the principles been established in situations that are foreign to the evolutionary history and natural behavior patterns of the animals?

Reading 54 is related to this problem. Can frogs learn standard laboratory escape and avoidance tasks? Boice clearly shows that the answer depends on which species is tested and, further, that the ability to learn is related to the natural activity level of the species. Such items need much more attention in comparative learning studies.

Part 6 ends with a paper by Campbell and Jaynes that provides experimental support for a new principle of retention. The authors describe the principle, called *reinstatement*, as "obvious and disarmingly simple," and the reader will probably agree. Nevertheless, this is the first clear statement and description of a phenomenon that is doubtless of great importance both to animals in their natural environments and to man.

49

LAWS OF LEARNING RELEVANT TO ITS BIOLOGICAL BASIS[1]

NEAL E. MILLER

Professor, Rockefeller University

(Read April 21, 1967, in the Symposium on Memory and Learning)

As THE first step in looking for the biological basis of learning, it is logical to review some of its chief characteristics. These should help one to determine whether or not a specific experiment actually is dealing with learning; furthermore, certain of the characteristics of learning may narrow down the range of mechanisms that could account for it. In a short talk of this type, one of the difficulties is the fact that so much work has been done on learning. One book (Kimble, 1961), which primarily summarizes studies of animal conditioning, contains more than 1,700 references, and another book (McGeogh and Irion, 1962), which emphasizes human verbal learning, lists 748 different authors, many of whom contribute a considerable number of publications. I shall have to try to select a few of the main facts that appear to me to be the most relevant, but in doing so may well ignore much significant material. If, from the enormous number of studies in the literature I seem to cite a disproportionate number of ones from my own laboratory, it is not solely for the reason that you may suspect; it happens also that on short notice suitable slides summarizing the results of those studies were more readily available.

Most of the work on learning has been done on mammals, and this is the work with which I am most familiar. Therefore, I shall deal only with mammalian learning and only with phenomena that all investigators will agree are learning. To the extent that lower animals show the same phenomena, we shall be reasonably confident that we are dealing with something like the learning that occurs in mammals. On the other hand, it is entirely possible that certain lower forms may display different kinds of learning which might even have a different physical basis from that occurring in mammals. It is also possible that other phenomena, such as the habituation of an innate response to a stimulus, the more rapid production of enzymes with repeated demand, the supersensitivity following denervation, the addictive effects of certain drugs, or possibly even immune reactions to foreign proteins, may turn out to have some elements in common with learning and may provide the key to an understanding of its physical basis. After we understand the physical mechanisms of learning, we shall be in a much better position to define it. While I choose to take a somewhat limited approach to the problem, concentrating on phenomena that all students of mam-

malian behavior will agree is learning, I want to be perfectly clear that in our state of ignorance we cannot afford dogmatically to discard any approaches.

DEFINITION OF LEARNING

My definition of learning will involve a group of characteristics rather than any single characteristic. Indeed, all of the laws of learning may be considered to be a part of its definition; the more of these laws a given phenomenon is known to follow, the more certain we can be that it is a genuine example of learning.

The most important characteristic of a learned response (R) is that it can be made specific to any arbitrarily selected stimulus (S) within the animal's repertoire. Actually, there may be some practical limitations to this proposition; for example, it may be difficult to attach an approach response to an extremely strong electric shock, but if we are dealing with true learning, it should be possible to establish a wide range of reasonably specific S-R combinations. Stated abstractly, this means that our learning procedures should be able to cause S_1 to elicit R_1, S_2 to elicit R_2, and S_3 to elicit R_3, or S_1 to elicit R_2, S_2 to elicit R_3, and S_3 to elicit R_1, etc.[2]

As far as I know, phenomena that will pass the foregoing test of learning, with a sufficient number of arbitrary S-R combinations, will also be found to pass the following tests; and phenomena that will pass a number of the following tests will pass this one. This fact increases our confidence that we are dealing with useful definitions of a significant phenomenon rather than with something trivial. It also gives us a certain amount of practical flexibility in defining learning in various ways which are more convenient in different experiments.

Learning may also be defined as the product of a previous association between a stimulus and a response and/or between a response and a reward. The escape from an aversive stimulus serves as a reward. As far as I know, the

[1] Supported by U. S. Public Health Service Research Grant MH 13189 from the National Institute of Mental Health. This paper inevitably will be similar to one recently written for a similar purpose (Miller, 1967); for a slightly different statement, see that paper.

[2] If one limits oneself to a single pair of stimuli and responses, as the author did in a preceding paper (Miller, 1967), one can imagine circumstances under which experimental manipulations other than learning could produce the different S-R combinations. For example, let S_1 be pure water and S_2 be 2 per cent saline, R_1 be drinking and R_2 be not drinking. Then water deprivation could cause S_1 to elicit R_1, S_2 to elicit R_2, while adrenalectomy plus preloading with water could cause S_1 to elicit R_2, and S_2 to elicit R_1. This set of operations, however, would not qualify on the basis of some of our other tests of learning. Furthermore, I believe it would be impossible to achieve all of the combinations among a larger group of stimuli and responses by means other than learning.

potentiality for producing the arbitrary *S-R* connections demanded in the foregoing criterion can be produced only by the procedures described in this one, and any connections set up by this procedure can be made to achieve the demanded arbitrary specificity.

Finally, in the absence of conflicting training, learning is relatively permanent, lasting for days or years rather than seconds or minutes, but it can be reversed by specific retraining.

Combining the foregoing considerations, we arrive at the definition that *learning is a relatively permanent tendency for a stimulus to elicit a response that is based on previous association between the stimulus and the response and/or the response and a reward, that can be established between any one of a considerable number of arbitrarily selected S-R combinations, and that can be reversed by specific retraining.*

Briefly in passing, I should say that stimulus and response are used broadly to refer to independent and dependent variables which may include direct electrical stimulation of certain neural structures and direct recording from them. This liberalized definition has been discussed in greater detail elsewhere (Miller, 1959). The phrase "tendency for a stimulus to elicit a response" means that, other things being equal, there is a higher probability that the stimulus will elicit the response; sometimes the phrase "stimulus-response connection" is used to refer to the same observation. We are tentatively assuming that reduced probabilities of the occurrence of a response are produced by strengthened tendencies to an incompatible response, but these are details which need not concern us at the moment.

At this point it will be useful to distinguish pseudo-conditioning, or as it is sometimes called, "sensitization" from true learning. If a strong unconditioned stimulus or a reward is administered a number of times, it will sometimes be found that other, previously neutral stimuli will elicit a new response. That this new stimulus-response connection is not the product of new learning can be demonstrated by the fact that it is transient, cannot be made specific to any arbitrarily selected stimulus, and that it was not dependent on close association between either a specific stimulus and a response or a specific response and a reward. The procedure to test for pseudo-conditioning is to present one group with trials in which the conditioned stimulus is immediately followed by the unconditioned stimulus (that elicits the response to be learned), and another group with trials in which the conditioned and unconditioned stimuli are presented separately. If tests show that the conditioned stimulus is reliably more likely to elicit the response in the paired than in the unpaired group, learning has occurred, but if equal changes have been produced in both groups, the results cannot be attributed to learning. A similar type of control can be secured by pairing a response with reward

in one group, but presenting an equal number of rewards not associated with the response to another group. Only changes specific to the response-reward association are considered to be true learning, and indeed I believe that only such responses will show all of the other attributes of learning. Other examples of phenomena not qualifying as learning have been discussed elsewhere (Miller, 1967).

ONE VERSUS MORE TYPES OF LEARNING

In the definition of learning, I spoke of the association between a stimulus and a response and/or between a response and a reward. The stimulus-response association is the most obvious feature of one type of learning situation, called classical conditioning, and the response-reward association is the most obvious feature of another type of learning situation, called operant conditioning, trial-and-error learning, or instrumental learning. The strong traditional belief has been that glandular and visceral responses, mediated by the presumably more primitive autonomic nervous system, could be modified only by classical conditioning, believed to be a more primitive type of learning, in contrast with instrumental learning, supposed to be a more sophisticated type possible only for skeletal responses, mediated by the presumably superior cerebro-spinal system.[3] If true, such a difference between the capacities of a more primitive and a more advanced component of the nervous system for a more primitive and a more advanced type of learning would have deep implications for the biological basis of learning.

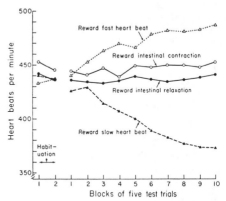

Fig. 1. When increases or decreases, respectively, in the heart rates of curarized rats are rewarded, the rates change in the appropriate direction; when a different response, intestinal contraction, is rewarded, heart rate is unaffected. (From Miller and Banuazizi, 1968.)

---

[3] For example, Kimble's (1961) authoritative summary states: " ... for autonomically mediated behavior, the evidence points unequivocally to the conclusion that such responses can be modified by classical, but not instrumental, training methods" (p. 100).

Recent work from my laboratory, however, has secured persuasive evidence against this strongly held, traditional view. Experiments on thirsty dogs have shown that their rate of spontaneous salivation can be either increased or decreased by rewarding the appropriate change with water which does not elicit any unconditioned salivary response (Miller and Carmona, 1967). Other experiments have shown that the heart rate of rats, maintained on artificial respiration and with skeletal responses completely paralyzed by curare, can be increased or decreased, respectively, by rewarding the appropriate changes by direct electrical stimulation of rewarding areas in the brain (Trowill, 1967; Miller and DiCara, 1967). Figure 1 shows the result of a study which Mr. Banuazizi and I (Miller and Banuazizi, 1968) have performed on deeply curarized rats maintained on artificial respiration. You can see that the heart rate increases when increases are rewarded, decreases when decreases are rewarded, and remains unchanged when either intestinal contraction or relaxation is rewarded. Conversely, figure 2 shows that intestinal contractions increase when they are rewarded, decrease when relaxation is rewarded, but remain unchanged when either increases or decreases in heart rate are rewarded. Thus, each of these two different types of autonomically mediated responses can be instrumentally learned, and such learning is quite specific. Additional experiments (DiCara and Miller, 1968; Banuazizi, 1968) show that such learning is not limited to reward by direct electrical stimulation of the brain; deeply curarized rats can learn to change either their heart rates or their intestinal contractions when the reward is escape from mild electric shock. In the face of such evidence it is hard to retain the strongly held traditional view that instrumental learning is fundamentally differ-ent from classical conditioning in that it is restricted to the supposedly superior cerebro-spinal nervous system.

Another venerable distinction, namely, the assertion that classically conditioned responses are elicited while operantly conditioned (i.e., instrumental) ones are emitted (Skinner, 1938) has been eliminated by modern experimental evidence on stimulus control (Terrace, 1966). I believe it is highly probable that other alleged differences between classical conditioning and instrumental learning will turn out to be the effects of different conditions in the learning situation rather than of basic differences in the laws involved (Miller, 1967). Nevertheless, as long as there is any doubt whatsoever about this fundamental problem, it should be unequivocally clarified by further experimental work.

There are a number of people (Tolman, 1949; Hilgard, 1956) who believe that the characteristically human capacities, which we modestly call higher, involve superior types of learning and that there are a number of inferior types. I believe that these differences are not the product of fundamental differences in the basic mechanism of learning, namely, the production of the long-term memory trace, but are instead consequences of increased numbers of traces which can be stored and increased capacities for performance resulting from superiorities in the complex neural networks for processing information after it is received from the sense organs but before it is stored, or after it has been retrieved from storage and is involved in the initiation of behavior. To this latter category, I would assign such properties of learned behavior as stimulus generalization, positive and negative induction (sometimes called behavioral contrast), secondary reinforcement, effects of schedules of reinforcement and of correlated reinforcement, learning to learn, concept formation, insight, reasoning, problem solving, and probably the capacity for delayed reaction and short-term memory. Therefore, I shall not be concerned with such phenomena, except short-term memory, in this paper. In making the foregoing assumptions, I hope to have raised a significant problem clearly, even though I may turn out to have been wrong about its ultimate solution.

LONG- VERSUS SHORT-TERM MEMORY

There is a debate about whether the short-term memory (that we exhibit during the time between looking up and dialing a new phone number) and the long-term memory (that we exhibit for a phone number that we have memorized) are merely the extreme ends of a continuum or are fundamentally different processes. Within the past few years, a great deal of experimental work has been performed on short-term memory by students of human verbal learning (Hilgard and Bower, 1966). The results of these investigations seem to be indicating that there are some fundamental differences between these two processes

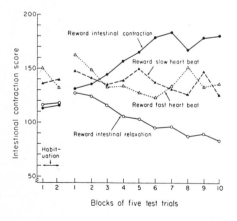

FIG. 2. When increases or decreases, respectively, in the spontaneous intestinal contractions of curarized rats are rewarded, changes in the appropriate direction are produced; when a different response, heart rate, is rewarded, intestinal contractions are unaffected. (From Miller and Banuazizi, 1968.)

(Symposium on Short-term and Long-term Memory, Moscow, 1966). Perhaps the simplest convincing evidence comes from studies of human patients with bilateral lesions in the medial temporal lobes of the brain. Milner (1959, 1962) has shown that such patients have a good memory for events occurring a sufficient time before their lesion and for events within their immediate span of attention, but have great difficulties in acquiring new long-term memories. For example, when one of these patients heard that a close friend had been killed in an automobile accident, he was extremely distressed and talked about it for some time. But, as soon as his attention was distracted to another topic, he completely forgot so that when the friend's name came up a short time later, he referred to him as if he were still living and showed the same shock and dismay when told that he had been killed. Exactly the same thing happened many times without producing any retrievable long-term memory. It was as if the patient had lost the capacity to transfer memory from a short-term to a long-term store. The specificity of the deficit which these patients can show suggests that two different mechanisms are involved in long- and short-term memory.

In addition to short-term memory, there is evidence for an apparently different kind of storage which ordinarily does not last for more than a half-second (Auerbach and Correll, 1961). This storage is presumably central, because an image momentarily exposed to one eye can be erased by a flash given to the opposite eye one-tenth of a second later. The extremely brief duration of this store, the way it can be erased, and yet other characteristics, suggest that it probably is purely sensory though central, being different from either long- or short-term memory.

You will remember that one of my criteria for true learning is relative permanency. According to this definition, true learning must involve long-term memory, although one or more intervening stages of short-term storage may turn out to be essential steps in the biological basis for such learning.

LEARNING AND INITIAL CONSOLIDATION CAN OCCUR QUICKLY

Under many conditions learning can be a painfully slow process, but under favorable conditions it can occur very quickly, and any biological mechanism for learning must be able to account for these rapid instances.

A good example of rapid learning is the one-trial passive avoidance procedure, which has been used in a considerable number of experiments. If a tame albino rat is placed in a short, narrow compartment leading out into a considerably larger one, he will step out into the larger area within a few seconds. If he is then immediately given a strong electric shock through the grid floor of the larger compartment and then removed

from it, he will be extremely hesitant about stepping out again when given another test on a subsequent day. He has learned in a single trial.

The foregoing type of situation has been used to test the effects of electroconvulsive shock on the consolidation of learning (Chorover and Schiller, 1965). In one typical experiment, Quartermain, Paolino and I (1965) gave rats a 1 ma. shock to their feet via the grid floor for 2 seconds immediately after they stepped out into the larger compartment. The rats were prevented from retreating back into the narrow start-box by a guillotine door. All of the rats had electrodes clipped onto their ears, through which a strong electroconvulsive shock to the brain (100 ma. for 0.3 second) was delivered shortly after the shock to the feet. In human subjects, such an electroconvulsive shock produces immediate unconsciousness, and in rats it appears to have the same effect. It also produces a massive convulsion which would be expected to disrupt any reverberatory circuits which might be storing the information in the brain, much as one repeats a telephone number to oneself in an effort to retain or to learn it more permanently.

Different groups of rats were given the *ECS* at different times after the shock to the feet. Their memory was tested by placing them back in the same situation on the next day without any grid shock or *ECS*. The results are shown in figure 3. At the extreme right-hand side, you can see that when there was no *ECS,* all of the subjects remembered as indicated by the fact that none of them stepped out into the large compartment within 2 minutes on the second day. When the *ECS* was delayed for 1 minute after the painful foot shock, the memory was practically as good. When the *ECS* was delivered 15 seconds after the shock to the rat, some of the rats showed impaired memory, stepping out into the place where their feet had been shocked, but most of them remembered. This means that the memory had been

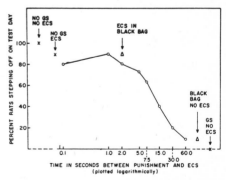

Fig. 3. Effects of electroconvulsive shock (*ECS*), as a function of the time it was administered after a grid shock (*GS*) to the feet of rats. Amnesia is shown by stepping off into the place where the grid shock was received. (From Quartermain, Paolino and Miller, 1965.)

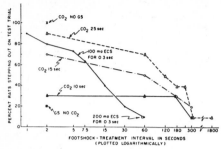

FIG. 4. Effects of three different durations of CO_2 exposure, administered at different intervals after a learning trial with grid shock (*GS*) on amnesia as indicated by the per cent of rats stepping out on test trials into the place where they received grid shock. Temporal gradient for treatment by electroconvulsive shock (see fig. 3) is presented for comparison. (From Paolino, Quartermain and Miller, 1966.)

consolidated well enough within these 15 seconds to withstand the drastic effects of the *ECS*. Even if one thinks of the rats as rehearsing their painful experience or storing it in reverberating circuits in the brain, most of them have learned within 15 seconds and practically all of them have learned within 60 seconds. On the other hand, when the *ECS* occurred within 1 second of the shock to the feet, it wiped out the memory as shown by the fact that almost all of the rats stepped out into the compartment where they previously had received the strong electric shock. Thus, a certain amount of time seems to be necessary to consolidate the memory enough so that it can withstand the effects of *ECS*. Perhaps such consolidation involves transfer from a short- to a long-term memory mechanism. Whatever the biological processes are that are responsible for learning, they must be subject to disruption by an electroconvulsive shock occurring almost immediately after the learning experience but be able to resist the effects of such a shock (at least, under the conditions of this experiment) when it is delayed approximately 15 seconds after the learning experience.

It would be much simpler if the same curve for the temporal course of consolidation occurred in all experiments. Unfortunately, this is not the case. For example, in another experiment Paolino, Quartermain, and I (1966) trained the same strain of rats in the same apparatus in the same way, but instead of convulsing them by *ECS*, we anesthetized them by plunging them into an atmosphere of CO_2. This treatment was given at different times after the single trial with the foot shock. Figure 4 shows the results. For purposes of comparison, the curve of the original experiment is repeated. You can see that the learning can be wiped out by CO_2 anesthesia a considerable time after its susceptibility to amnesia by *ECS* is gone. Treatments with different strengths of

ECS and different exposures to CO_2 strongly suggest that there is a real difference in the temporal course of the curve that cannot be accounted for by the strength of treatments administered. Other experiments using different types of learning situations and/or different types of amnesia-inducing treatments have secured still longer gradients of retrograde amnesia (Kopp *et al.*, 1966; Flexner *et al.*, 1966; Deutsch and Leibowitz, 1966). Because most of these experiments differ in a variety of respects, it is difficult to draw any detailed generalization from the temporal pattern of results, except for the two limiting ones, that the biological mechanisms responsible for the consolidation of the memory trace must be able to account for the fact that (*a*) in some cases, memory can survive when strong *ECS* is given as soon as 15 seconds after the learning experience, and (*b*) in other cases, it can be affected by a treatment given hours or days later. You will hear more about some of these experiments in subsequent talks which will show how they are revealing additional clues to the biological basis of learning.

PERMANENCE OF LEARNING

While the effects of learning can be wiped out by certain traumatic treatments and can be reversed by conflicting training, under other circumstances it can last a long time. Using the simple one-trial learning that has just been described, Miller and Kushel (unpublished data) secured the retention curves presented in figure 5. You will note that the rats that were given their first test 23 days after the one trial of receiving a single electric shock remembered as well as the

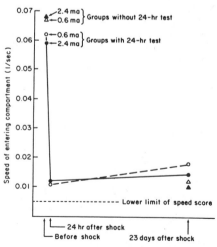

FIG. 5. The memory of rats for a single trial on which they received electric shocks upon entering a distinctive compartment. Learning and retention is shown by reduced speed in entering compartment. (Unpublished data by Miller and Kushel.)

rats that were tested 24 hours later. When the latter rats were given a second test 23 days after the shock, they also remembered very well; the slight apparent improvement is not statistically reliable. In fact, all 60 of the rats given a brief electric shock in the large compartment were slower in stepping out into it when tested 23 days later.

From the foregoing experiments on one-trial learning you can see that a lower mammal like the rat can form simple associations very quickly and retain them quite well. The general finding seems to be that man and the lower mammals do not differ in the speed of forming simple associations. This is one of the reasons for tentatively attributing the obvious differences in their capacities to other factors, such as differences in information-processing mechanisms and in the size of the memory store available, rather than to fundamental differences in the basic mechanism for memory storage.

Other experiments in which animals have been trained for a number of trials show good retention after a period of several years without any opportunity for practice. Rigorously controlled experiments involving still longer periods of retention are extremely rare, as might be expected from the 7-year rule on Ph.D. candidates and the publish-or-perish policy for the faculty. Relatively reliable anecdotal evidence is, however, available. For example, when inducted into the Air Force in 1942 I stopped playing tennis and did not have a racket in my hand until my son urged me to play with him in 1963. Although speed and endurance were reduced by increased age and weight, when I stepped onto the court for the first time in 21 years, I found to my delight that there had been very little deterioration in the complex skills involved in the basic strokes which could not have been practiced during the intervening time without court, ball, or racket. Such retention seems to be characteristic of many motor skills. It also seems to occur when one returns to a place or meets a friend after an absence of many years.

It is quite clear that the physical mechanisms for learning and memory have to be capable of retention and retrieval after long intervals during which most of the components of the body have turned over many times. Therefore, the physical basis for learning must reside either in one of the relatively rare bodily components that do not turn over with time or in some self-maintaining structure, self-replicating molecule, or self-perpetuating system. Thus, it may be no accident that the neurons are among the rare types of mammalian cells that show very little, if any, cell reproduction after early stages of development. This unique characteristic may be related to the mechanism for memory storage. If memories are indeed stored in specific anatomical or functional connections between neurons, one can imagine how the repro-duction and growth of new neurons could confuse the effects of earlier learning.

FORGETTING PRODUCED BY INTERFERENCE

If learning can be so permanent, how does it happen that we so often forget? A large number of experimental studies indicate that much, and perhaps almost all, of ordinary forgetting of long-term memories is produced by various sources of interference. If a subject learns the association A-B and then subsequently is taught the interfering association A-C, this second, interfering training will greatly reduce his retention of the originally learned association. This phenomenon is called retroactive inhibition. Its importance is increased considerably by the fact that the stimulus situations designated by A do not have to be identical in the A-B and A-C instances of learning; they need to have only some elements of similarity in common, with more interference being introduced the more elements they have in common. Similarly, the responses B and C do not have to be completely different.

One of the reasons why I remembered tennis so well probably is the fact that, during the 21 years, I was not practicing any similar sport that could be a source of retroactive interference. If I had been playing other racket games or, worse still, playing tennis with an opponent who was so poor that I had merely to pat the ball to him, the skill would have deteriorated much more than it did with complete disuse.

Interference can be produced also by learning that has occurred before the association that is forgotten. In the example that we have just given, the fact that the subject had previously learned A-B will make him less likely to remember A-C than he would be if he had only learned the latter association. Interference can also be generated by conflicts among different parts of a task sequence.

While it is difficult to be certain that absolutely no forgetting occurs with mere disuse, and indeed some forgetting might be expected from the death of neurons, the general conclusion from a large amount of experimental work is that most of the forgetting which occurs under normal circumstances probably is the product of interference, and that the interfering habits supersede rather than delete the forgotten one. Thus an apparently forgotten memory can often be retrieved by appropriate measures and, even after a habit seems to be completely gone, there typically is some trace as evidenced by a considerable saving in relearning it. For these reasons, it seems unwise to design experiments in which one hopes to produce phenomena analogous to true forgetting by inducing disuse through such treatment as cutting a tendon to a muscle, or to devise hypothetical mechanisms which would account for the disappearance of much of the physical basis for memory with the mere passage of time.

EFFECTIVE TEMPORAL SEQUENCES

Many studies indicate that conditioning is most effective when the unconditioned stimulus (UCS) follows the conditioned stimulus (CS) by an interval of approximately a half-second. Longer delays are progressively less effective. Absolute simultaneity seems to be much poorer, producing little or no learning, and there is considerable question about whether backward association (with the UCS preceding the CS) produces any learning at all.

In investigating the effects of backward conditioning, one has to be careful to control for the effects of sensitization, which you will remember refers to the fact that when a strong response has been elicited several times recently by a UCS the animal may be sensitized to make this response so that it is likely to be elicited by other stimuli which have not been specifically associated with the UCS. The situation is much like that of a runner, crouched to begin a 100-yard dash, who may make a false start to any novel stimulus. In other cases, one has to be alert for the possible overlapping of stimuli and of their immediate after-effects, so that the onset of a subsequent CS may actually precede some of the after-effects of a previous UCS. Certainly, some of the earlier experiments which seemed to indicate a transient phase of backward conditioning did not control adequately for such factors. It is difficult to be certain whether the few later experiments which seem to indicate such conditioning (Beritoff, 1965; Morrell, 1967; Tenen, 1967) had completely eliminated all such factors.

If we could be sure that only forward associations are possible in the fundamental elements of learning, this would place important constraints on the physical mechanisms responsible for its biological basis. Therefore, it is important to try to design experiments that can unequivocally clarify this problem. In the meantime, there is enough evidence in favor of an advantage for forward associations to ask what unique physico-chemical conditions are present at the synapse between neuron 1 and neuron 2 when the CS firing neuron 1 has been followed by the UCS firing neuron 2.

There is a great deal of evidence that the effects of a reward in strengthening a response are greater the sooner the reward comes after the response. This fact has been referred to as a gradient of reinforcement. The length of the effective gradient of reinforcement varies in a systematic way with certain characteristics of the experimental situation. It is known that a stimulus immediately associated with reward acquires the capacity to function as a reward. This phenomenon is called secondary reinforcement. Spence's (1947) careful analysis of a whole series of experimental studies has shown that, when there are good opportunities for secondary reinforcing stimuli to be immediately associated with the performance of the correct response and then immediately associated with the primary reward, a considerable delay in the primary reward can be tolerated, or in other words, the gradient of reward extends over a considerable period of time. On the other hand, when the possibilities for secondary reinforcement are reduced, the gradient of reward becomes very short, so that a delay of a few seconds can make efficient learning and performance impossible. Subsequent work, summarized by Kimble (1961), seems to confirm this conclusion. It is tempting to wonder whether there is any similar mechanism underlying the short temporal gradient for ECS and that for reward when the effects of secondary reinforcement are removed.

Some early work by Thorndike (1933) seemed to show that responses occurring immediately after reward, as well as those occurring immediately before it, were strengthened, but Sheffield (1949) showed that this conclusion was based on an artifact, the statistical effect of sequences of guessing habits. One of my students, Nagaty (1951a, 1951b) has performed two simple but convincing experiments on this problem. In order to be able reliably to secure a response immediately after a reward, hungry rats were trained to press a rod as soon as it was inserted into the apparatus. They always received a pellet of food for pressing the rod. During the latter part of training the rod was withdrawn if the rat did not press it immediately. Thus they learned to press it promptly. The rats sometimes received a pellet of food immediately before the rod was inserted. The results are shown in figure 6. When the pellet before presentation of the rod was omitted and the delivery of the pellet after pressing it was delayed for 2 seconds, the habit was maintained indefinitely. Under the opposite conditions, when the pellet after pressing the rod was omitted and one was always given within 2 seconds before the rod was pressed, the habit was extinguished at the same rate as it was when a pellet was given between trials so that it was not associated with pressing the rod.

In another similar experiment, rats were taught to rotate a wheel in order to avoid electric shocks. Then they were given extinction trials during which the shocks given if the rats did not turn the wheel in time were omitted. Half of the rats received a brief shock immediately before the CS and the other half received a shock between trials. They all reacted to this shock by rotating the wheel, but the close association between the shock and the immediately subsequent warning signal had no effect on the extinction of the response of wheel-turning. Both of these experiments agree in showing that the effects of reinforcement act in only one direction.

DRIVE AND REWARD

If there were not some powerful selective factor somewhere in the learning or retrieval mechanism, all mammals would be hopelessly bogged down in total recall. It is an empirical fact that, in most

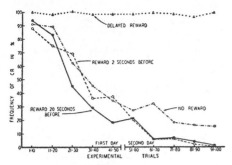

FIG. 6. A reward of food delayed for 2 seconds after hungry rats press a bar maintains their response, but one administered 2 seconds before allows it to extinguish at the same rate as control rats without any association between bar pressing and reward. (From Nagaty, 1951b.)

practical learning situations where a variety of stimuli are competing for attention and a variety of responses for performance, drive and reward play an important selective role, so that motivation coupled with appropriate reward is an important factor in determining what is learned and how efficiently it is learned. This fact is of practical importance to any experimenter who wants to secure efficient learning in order to investigate its biological basis. This fact also may well turn out to have important theoretical relevance for the biological basis of learning, but, until we know more details about the mechanism of how drive and reward affect learning, we cannot make unequivocal statements. It may be that the memory engram is based solely upon association and that the effects of drive and reward are exerted indirectly by determining which stimuli the organism pays attention to and which responses he performs, thereby determining which ones are available for association. On the other hand, it is conceivable that drive and reward function mainly to determine which memories are retrieved at a given time. Finally, it is possible that drive and reward operate more directly on the laying down of the memory engram. In any event, one should not expect that efficient learning will inevitably occur in their absence.

SOME ADDITIONAL FACTS

In conclusion, I want to mention briefly some additional significant facts which cannot be discussed adequately in the remaining time.

A variety of lines of evidence suggest that learning reaches an upper limit or asymptote, a fact which must have implications for the mechanism of learning. It also provides an opportunity to differentiate the effects of mere use of neural circuits in the performance of a specific habit from those unique to the process of learning that habit. These matters are discussed in more detail elsewhere (Miller, 1967).

Extensive work, especially by Lashley (1950), has failed to eliminate any specific memory by any specific lesion in the brain. Such results have been interpreted as indicating that memory is distributed equally over considerable areas of the cortex and perhaps is a function of the cortex acting as a whole. On the other hand, attempts to test a field-theory hypothesis of memory storage and retrieval have also yielded negative results (Lashley et al., 1951). An alternative view is that memories are stored in specific connections but that, especially in the case of complex habits, there are large numbers of redundant circuits scattered through different parts of the brain. This view is made somewhat more attractive by the fact that studies, such as those of Hubel and Wiesel (1963), are showing that certain phenomena of visual perception which once were thought to be inexplicable in terms of specific connections, can now be explained in terms of such connections. Finally, extensive and provocative work summarized by Penfield and Perot (1963) shows that, with certain types of epileptic patients, it is possible to elicit what appear to be specific memories by stimulating specific points on the brain.

SUMMARY

Learning is defined by a variety of attributes. It is a relatively permanent tendency for a stimulus to elicit a response that is based on a previous association between that stimulus and that response and/or that response and a reward; it can be established between any one of a considerable number of arbitrarily selected S-R combinations, and it can be reversed by specific retraining. The biological mechanism of learning has to be able to account for the fact that under favorable circumstances it, and the initial stages of its consolidation, can occur very quickly and can last for a very long time. Extremely short-term, short-term and long-term memory probably involve at least somewhat different mechanisms. I have chosen to demand long-term memory as one of the criteria of true learning. Forgetting seems to be produced largely by interference rather than by mere disuse. Stimulus and response are broadly defined as independent and dependent variables. Learning is dependent on close temporal association between stimulus and response, and at least in conditioning situations, forward associations seem to be established much more easily than backward ones, if indeed the latter are possible, a point which needs further experimental clarification. Drives and relevant rewards are of great practical importance in learning, although their mechanism of action is unclear and needs further clarification. A reward preceding a response seems to be ineffective, while one following a response is more effective the more immediately it follows. The degree of delay which is tolerable seems to depend on the possibilities for secondary reinforcement. When the possibilities for sec-

369

ondary reinforcement are remote, the temporal gradient for reward is approximately of the same brief duration as that of retrograde amnesia produced by electroconvulsive shock. Learning reaches an upper limit, or asymptote; it seems impossible to eliminate specific memories by specific lesions in the brain, but in certain people suffering from temporal lobe epilepsy it does seem possible to elicit specific memories by stimulating specific points on the brain.

REFERENCES

AUERBACH, E., and A. S. CORRELL. 1961. "Short-term Memory in Vision." *Bell Syst. Tech. Jour.* **40:** pp. 309–328.

BANUAZIZI, A. Ph.D. dissertation, in preparation.

BERITOFF, J. S. 1965. *Neural Mechanisms of Higher Vertebrate Behavior* (W. T. Liberson, Translator and Editor), (Boston, Little, Brown & Co.).

CHOROVER, S. L., and P. H. SCHILLER. 1965. "Short-term Retrograde Amnesia in Rats." *Jour. Comp. Physiol. Psychol.* **59:** pp. 73–78.

DEUTSCH, J. A., and S. F. LEIBOWITZ. 1966. "Amnesia or Reversal of Forgetting by Anticholinesterase, Depending Simply on Time of Injection." *Science* **153:** pp. 1017–1018.

DICARA, L. V., and N. E. MILLER. "Changes in Heart Rate Instrumentally Learned by Curarized Rats as Avoidance Responses." *Jour. Comp. Physiol. Psychol.* In press.

FLEXNER, L. B., J. B. FLEXNER and R. B. ROBERTS. 1966. "Stages of Memory in Mice Treated with Acetoxycyclohexamine Before or Immediately After Learning." *Proc. Nat. Acad. Sci.* **56:** pp. 730–735.

HILGARD, E. R. 1956. *Theories of Learning* (2nd Ed., New York, Appleton-Century-Crofts).

HILGARD, E. R., and G. H. BOWER. 1966. *Theories of Learning* (3rd Ed., New York, Appleton-Century-Crofts).

HUBEL, D. H., and T. N. WIESEL. 1963. "Receptive Fields, Binocular Interaction and Functional Architecture in the Cat's Visual Cortex." *Jour. Physiol.* **160:** pp. 106–154.

KIMBLE, G. A. 1961. *Hilgard and Marquis' Conditioning and Learning* (2nd Ed., New York, Appleton-Century-Crofts).

KOPP, R., A. BOHDANECKY, and M. E. JARVIK. 1966. "Long Temporal Gradient of Retrograde Amnesia for a Well-discriminated Stimulus." *Science* **153:** pp. 1547–1549.

LASHLEY, K. S. 1950. "In Search of the Engram." In: *Symp. Soc. Exp. Biol.,* No. 4 (Cambridge, Eng., Cambridge Univ. Press): pp. 454–482.

LASHLEY, K. S., K. L. CHOW, and J. SEMMES. 1951. "An Examination of the Electrical Field Theory of Cerebral Integration." *Psychol. Rev.* **58:** pp. 123–136.

MCGAUGH, J. L., *et al.* 1966. "Symposium on Short-term and Long-term Memory." In: *Abstracts of Proc. International Congress of Psychology, Moscow* **2:** pp. 231–252.

MCGEOCH, J. A., and A. L. IRION. 1952. *The Psychology of Human Learning* (2nd Ed., New York, Longmans, Green & Co.).

MILLER, N. E. 1959. "Liberalization of Basic S-R Concepts: Extensions to Conflict Behavior, Motivation and Social Learning." In: *Psychology: A Study of a Science,* Study 1, Vol. 2 (S. Koch, Ed.), (New York, McGraw-Hill Co.), pp. 196–292.

——. 1967. "Certain Facts of Learning Relevant to the Search for Its Physical Basis." In: *The Neurosciences: A Study Program* (New York, The Rockefeller University Press). In press.

MILLER, N. E., and A. BANUAZIZI. "Instrumental Learning by Curarized Rats of a Specific Visceral Response, Intestinal or Cardiac." *Jour. Comp. Physiol. Psychol.* In press.

MILLER, N. E., and A. CARMONA. 1967. "Modification of a Visceral Response, Salivation in Thirsty Dogs, by Instrumental Training with Water Reward." *Jour. Comp. Physiol. Psychol.* **63:** pp. 1–6.

MILLER, N. E., and L. DICARA. 1967. "Instrumental Learning of Heart-rate Changes in Curarized Rats: Shaping, and Specificity to Discriminative Stimulus." *Jour. Comp. Physiol. Psychol.* **63:** pp. 12–19.

MILNER, B. 1959. "The Memory Defect in Bilateral Hippocampal Lesions." *Psychiat. Res. Rept.* **11:** 43–51.

——. 1962. "Les Troubles de la memoire accompagnant des lésions hippocampiques bilatérales." *Physiologie de l'hippocampe.* Colloques Internationaux du Centre National de la Recherche Scientifique, No. 107 (Paris), pp. 257–272.

MORRELL, F. 1967. "Electrical Signs of Electrical Coding." In: *The Neurosciences: A Study Program* (New York, The Rockefeller University Press). In press.

NAGATY, M. O. 1951a. "The Effect of Reinforcement on Closely Followed S-R Connections: I. The Effect of a Backward Conditioning Procedure on the Extinction of Conditioned Avoidance." *Jour. Exp. Psychol.* **42:** pp. 239–245.

—— 1951b. "The Effect of Reinforcement on Closely Followed S-R Connections: II. Effect of Food Reward Immediately Preceding Performance of an Instrumental Conditioned Response on Extinction of That Response." *Jour. Exp. Psychol.* **42:** pp. 333–340.

PAOLINO, R. M., D. QUARTERMAIN, and N. E. MILLER. 1966. "Different Temporal Gradients of Retrograde Amnesia Produced by Carbon Dioxide Anesthesia and Electroconvulsive Shock." *Jour. Comp. Physiol. Psychol.* **62:** pp. 270–274.

PENFIELD, W., and P. PEROT. 1963. "The Brain's Record of Auditory and Visual Experience. A Final Summary and Discussion." *Brain* **86:** pp. 595–696.

QUARTERMAIN, D., R. M. PAOLINO, and N. E. MILLER. 1965. "A Brief Temporal Gradient of Retrograde Amnesia Independent of Situational Change." *Science* **149:** pp. 1116–1118.

SHEFFIELD, F. D. 1949. "'Spread of Effect' Without Reward or Training." *Jour. Exp. Psychol.* **39:** pp. 575–579.

SKINNER, B. F. 1938. *The Behavior of Organisms* (New York, Appleton-Century-Crofts).

SPENCE, K. W. 1947. "The Role of Secondary Reinforcement in Delayed Reward Learning." *Psychol. Rev.* **54:** pp.1–8.

TENEN, S. S. "Recovery Time as a Measure of CER Strength; the Effects of Benzodiazepine, Amobarbital, Chlorpromazine and Amphetamine." *Psychopharmacologia.* In press.

TERRACE, H. 1966. "Stimulus Control." In: *Operant Behavior: Areas of Research and Application* (W. H. Honig, Ed.), (New York, Appleton-Century-Crofts), pp. 271–344.

THORNDIKE, E. L. 1933. "A Proof of the Law of Effect." *Science* **77:** pp. 173–175.

TOLMAN, E. C. 1949. *Purposive Behavior in Animals and Men* (New York, Appleton-Century-Crofts; also, University of California Press).

TROWILL, J. A. 1967. "Instrumental Conditioning of the Heart Rate in the Curarized Rat." *Jour. Comp. Physiol. Psychol.* **63:** pp. 7–11.

50

PHYLETIC DIFFERENCES IN LEARNING [1]

M. E. BITTERMAN

Bryn Mawr College

ONE way to study the role of the brain in learning is to compare the learning of animals with different brains. Differences in brain structure may be produced by surgical means, or they may be found in nature—as when the learning of different species is compared. Of these two approaches the first (the neurosurgical approach) has been rather popular, but the potentialities of the second still are largely unexplored. Students of learning in animals have been content for the most part to concentrate their attention on a few closely related mammalian forms, chosen largely for reasons of custom and convenience, which they have treated as representative of animals in general. Their work has been dominated almost from its inception by the hypothesis that the laws of learning are the same for all animals—that the wide differences in brain structure which occur in the animal series have a purely quantitative significance.

The hypothesis comes to us from Thorndike (1911), who more than any other man may be credited with having brought the study of animal intelligence into the laboratory. On the basis of his early comparative experiments, Thorndike decided that however much animals might differ in "what" they learned (which could be traced, he thought, to differences in their sensory, motor, and motivational properties), or in the "degree" of their learning ability (some seemed able to learn more than others, and more quickly), the principles which governed their learning were the same. Thorndike wrote:

If my analysis is true, the evolution of behavior is a rather simple matter. Formally the crab, fish, turtle, dog, cat, monkey and baby have very similar intellects and characters. All are systems of connections subject to change by the laws of exercise and effect [p. 280].

[1] This paper was presented in March 1964, under the auspices of the National Science Foundation and of the National Institute of Mental Health, at the Institut de Psychologie in Paris, the Institute of Experimental Psychology in Oxford, the Institut für Hirnforschung in Zurich, and the Nencki Institute of Experimental Biology in Warsaw. The research described was supported by Grant MH-02857 from the National Institute of Mental Health and by Contract Nonr 2829(01) with the Office of Naval Research.

Although Thorndike's hypothesis was greeted with considerable skepticism, experiments with a variety of animals began to turn up functional similarities far more impressive than differences, and before long there was substantial disagreement only as to the *nature* of the laws which were assumed to hold for all animals. As acceptance of the hypothesis grew, the range of animals studied in experiments on learning declined—which, of course, was perfectly reasonable. If the laws of learning were the same everywhere in the animal series, there was nothing to be gained from the study of many different animals; indeed, standardization offered many advantages which it would be foolish to ignore. As the range of animals declined, however, so also did the likelihood of discovering any differences which might in fact exist.

It is difficult for the nonspecialist to appreciate quite how restricted has been the range of animals studied in experiments on animal learning because the restriction is so marked; the novelty of work with lower animals is such that two or three inexpressibly crude experiments with a flatworm may be better publicized than a hundred competent experiments with the rat. Some quantitative evidence on the degree of restriction was provided about 20 years ago by Schneirla, whose conclusion then was that "we do not have a comparative psychology [Harriman, 1946, p. 314]." Schneirla's analysis was carried further by Beach (1950), who plotted the curves which are reproduced in Figure 1. Based on a count of all papers appearing between 1911 and 1948 in the *Journal of Animal Behavior* and its successors, the *Journal of Comparative Psychology*, and the *Journal of Comparative and Physiological Psychology*, the curves show how interest in the rat mounted while interest in submammalian forms declined. By the '30s, a stable pattern had emerged: about 60% of papers on the rat, 30% on other mammals (mostly primates), and 10% on lower forms. The set of points at the extreme right, which I have added for the decade after 1948, shows no change in the pattern. You will note that these curves are based on papers published only in a single line of journals, and on all papers in those journals—not only the ones which deal with learning; but most of the papers *do* deal with learning, and I know of no other journal which is a richer source of information about learning in submammalians or which, if included in the tabulation, would alter the conclusion that what we know about learning in animals we know primarily from the intensive study of a small number of mammalian forms.

How widespread is the acceptance of Thorndike's hypothesis by contemporary theorists and systematists may be judged from a set of writings recently assembled by Koch (1959). Skinner is quite explicit in his assumption that which animal is studied "doesn't matter." When due allowance has been made for differences in sensory and motor characteristics, he explains, "what remains of . . . behavior shows astonishingly similar properties [Koch, 1959, p. 375]." Tolman, Miller, Guthrie, Estes, and Logan (representing Hull and Spence) rest their perfectly general conclusions about the nature of learning on the data of experiments with a few selected mammals—mostly rat, monkey, and man—skipping lightly back and forth from one to another as if indeed structure did not matter, although Miller "does not deny the possibility that men may have additional capacities which are much less well developed or absent in the lower mammals [Koch, 1959, p. 204]." Harlow alone makes a case for species differences in learning, pointing to the unequal rates of improvement shown by various mammals (mostly primates) trained in long series of discriminative problems, but he gives us no reason to believe that the differences are more than quantitative. While he implies clearly that the capacity for interproblem transfer may be absent entirely in certain lower animals—in the rat, he says, it exists only in a "most rudimentary form [Koch, 1959, p. 505]"—submammalian evidence is lacking.

Although I have been considering thus far only the work of the West, I do not think that things have been very different on the other side of the Curtain. The conditioning has been "classical" rather than "instrumental" in the main, and the favored animal has been the dog rather than the rat, but the range of animals studied in any detail has been small, at least until quite recently, and the principles discovered have been generalized widely. In the words of Voronin (1962), the guiding Pavlovian propositions have been that

The conditioned reflex is a universal mechanism of activity acquired in the course of the organism's individual life . . . . [and that] In the course of evolution of the animal world there took place only a quantitative growth or complication of higher nervous activity [pp. 161–162].

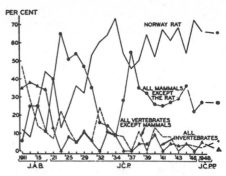

Fig. 1. Percentage of papers dealing with animals in each of four categories which appeared between 1911 and 1948 in the *Journal of Animal Behavior*, the *Journal of Comparative Psychology*, and the *Journal of Comparative and Physiological Psychology* (Beach, 1950). (The points at right, for the decade after 1948, were added by me.)

These propositions are supported, Voronin believes, by the results of some recent Russian comparisons of mammalian and submammalian vertebrates. On the basis of these results, he defines three stages in the evolution of intelligence which are distinguished in terms of the increasing role of learning in the life of the individual organism, and in terms of the precision and delicacy of the learning process. He hastens to assure us, however, that there is nothing really new even at the highest stage, which differs from the others only quantitatively.

The results of the experiments which I shall now describe support quite another view. I began these experiments without very much in the way of conviction as to their outcome, although the formal attractions of the bold Thorndikian hypothesis were rather obvious, and I should have been pleased on purely esthetic grounds to be able to accept it. I was convinced only that the hypothesis had not yet received the critical scrutiny it seemed to warrant, and that it was much too important to be taken any longer on faith. With the familiar rat as a standard, I selected for comparative study another animal—a fish—which I thought similar enough to the rat that it could be studied in analogous experiments, yet different enough to afford a marked neuroanatomical contrast. I did not propose to compare the two animals in terms of numerical scores, as, for example, the number of trials required for (or the number of errors made in) the mastery of some problem, because such differences would not necessarily imply the operation of different learning processes. I proposed instead to compare them in terms of *functional relations*—to find out whether their performance would be affected in the same way by the same variables (Bitterman, 1960). Why I chose to begin with certain variables rather than others probably is not worth considering—the choice was largely intuitive; whatever the reasons, the experiments soon turned up some substantial differences in the learning of fish and rat. I shall describe here two of those differences, and then present the results of some further experiments which were designed to tell us what they mean.

One of the situations developed for the study of learning in the fish is illustrated in Figure 2. The animal is brought in its individual living tank to a black Plexiglas enclosure. The manipulanda are two Plexiglas disks (targets) at which the animal is trained to strike. The targets are mounted on rods set into the needle holders of phonograph cartridges in such a way that when the animal makes contact with one of the targets a voltage is generated across its cartridge. This voltage is used to operate a set of relays which record the response and control its consequences. The targets are illuminated with colored lights or patterns projected upon them from behind; on any given trial, for example, the left target may be green and the right one red, or the left target may show a triangle and the right one a circle. The reward for correct choice is a *Tubifex* worm discharged into the water through a small opening at the top of the enclosure—the worm is discharged from an eyedropper whose bulb is compressed by a pair of solenoid-operated jaws. When a worm is dropped, a magazine light at the rear of the enclosure is turned on for a few seconds, which signals that a worm has been dropped and provides some diffuse illumination which enables the animal to find it. All of the events of training are programed automatically and recorded on tape.[2]

I shall talk about two kinds of experiment which have been done in this situation. The first is concerned with *habit reversal*. Suppose an animal is trained to choose one of two stimuli, either for a fixed number of trials or to some criterion level of correct choice, and then the positive and negative

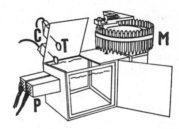

FIG. 2. A situation for the study of discrimination in the fish. (T, targets which are lowered into the water as the cover of the enclosure is brought down; C, phonograph cartridges which hold the targets and register contacts with them; P, projectors for projecting various stimuli on the targets; M, live-worm dispenser.)

stimuli are reversed; that is, the previously unrewarded stimulus now is rewarded, and the previously rewarded stimulus is unrewarded. After the same number of trials as were given in the original problem, or when the original criterion has been reached in the first reversal, the positive and negative stimuli are reversed again—and so forth. In such an experiment, the rat typically shows a dramatic improvement in performance. It may make many errors in the early reversals, but as training proceeds it reverses more and more readily.

In Figure 3, the performance of a group of African mouthbreeders is compared with that of a group of rats in a series of spatial reversals. (In a spatial problem, the animal chooses between a pair of stimuli which differ only with respect to their position in space, and reinforcement is correlated with position, e.g., the stimulus on the left is reinforced.) The apparatus used for the rat was analogous to the apparatus for the fish which you have already seen. On each trial, the animal was offered a choice between two identically illuminated panels set into the wall of the experimental chamber. It responded by pressing one of the panels, and correct choice operated a feeder which discharged a pellet of food into a lighted food cup. The fish were trained in an early version of the apparatus which you have already seen. For both species,

righteously, "*I* like to *watch* my animals." I explain that the automated techniques were developed after a good deal of watching to determine what was worth watching, and that they simply transfer a good part of the watching function to devices more sensitive and reliable than the experimenter, but that they do not rule out the possibility of further watching. In fact, freed of the necessity of programing trials and of recording data, the experimenter now can watch more intently than ever before. The United States has seen great advances in mammalian technique during recent years, while submammalian technique (except for the Skinnerian work with pigeons) has remained terribly primitive. A systematic comparative psychology will require some parallel advances in submammalian technique.

there were 20 trials per day to the criterion of 17 out of 20 correct choices, positive and negative positions being reversed for each animal whenever it met that criterion. Now consider the results. The upper curve of the pair you see here is quite representative of the performance of rats in such a problem—rising at first, and then falling in negatively accelerated fashion to a low level; with a little more training than is shown here, the animals reverse after but a single error. The lower curve is quite representative of the performance of fish in such a problem—there is no progressive improvement, but instead some tendency toward progressive deterioration as training continues.

How is this difference to be interpreted? We may ask first whether the results indicate anything beyond a quantitative difference in the learning of the two animals. It might be contended that reversal learning simply goes on more slowly in the fish than in the rat—that in 10 or 15 more reversals the fish, too, would have shown progressive improvement. In fact, however, the training of fish has been carried much further in later experiments, some animals completing more than 150 reversals without any sign of improvement. I invite anyone who remains skeptical on this point to persist even longer in the search for improvement.

Another possibility to be considered is that the difference between fish and rat which is reflected in these curves is not a difference in learning at all, but a difference in some confounded variable—sensory, motor, or motivational. Who can say, for example, whether the sensory and the motor demands made upon the two animals in these experiments were exactly the same? Who can say whether the fish were just as hungry as the rats, or whether the bits of food given the fish were equal in reward value to those given the rats? It would, I must admit, be a rare coincidence indeed if the conditions employed for the two animals were exactly equal in all of these potentially important respects. How, then, is it possible to find out whether the results obtained are to be attributed to a difference in learning, or to a difference in sensory, or in motor, or in motivational factors? A frank critic might say that it was rather foolish to have made the comparison in the first place, when a moment's thought would have shown that it could not possibly have any meaningful outcome. It is interesting to note that neither Harlow nor Voronin shows any appreciation of this problem. We may doubt, then, whether they have evidence even for quantitative differences in the *learning* of their various animals.

I do not, of course, know how to arrange a set of conditions for the fish which will make sensory and motor demands exactly equal to those which

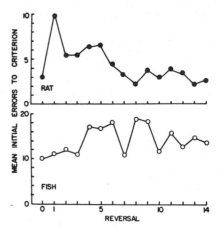

Fig. 3. Spatial habit reversal in fish and rat. (The fish data are taken from Bitterman, Wodinsky, & Candland, 1958; the rat data are from Gonzalez, Roberts, & Bitterman, 1964.)

are made upon the rat in some given experimental situation. Nor do I know how to equate drive level or reward value in the two animals. Fortunately, however, meaningful comparisons still are possible, because for *control by equation* we may substitute what I call *control by systematic variation*. Consider, for example, the hypothesis that the difference between the curves which you see here is due to a difference, not in learning, but in degree of hunger. The hypothesis implies that there is a level of hunger at which the fish *will* show progressive improvement, and, put in this way, the hypothesis becomes easy to test. We have only to vary level of hunger widely in different groups of fish, which we know well how to do. If, despite the widest possible variation in hunger, progressive improvement fails to appear in the fish, we may reject the hunger hypothesis. Hypotheses about other variables also may be tested by systematic variation. With regard to the question of reversal learning, I shall simply say here that progressive improvement has appeared in the rat under a wide variety of experimental conditions—it is difficult, in fact, to find a set of conditions under which the rat does not show improvement. In the fish, by contrast, reliable evidence of improvement has failed to appear under a variety of conditions.

I cannot, of course, prove that the fish is incapable of progressive improvement. I only can give you evidence of failure to find it in the course of earnest efforts; and the point is important enough, perhaps, that you may be willing to look at some more negative results. The curves of Figure 4 summarize the outcome of an experiment in which the type of problem was varied. Three groups of mouthbreeders were given 40 trials per

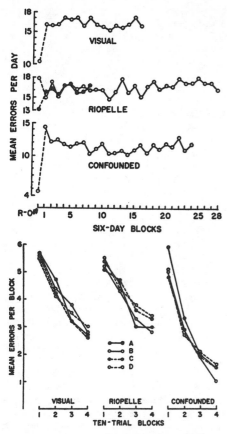

Fig. 4. Visual habit reversal in the fish. (The upper curves show between-sessions performance in each of three problems; the lower curves show within-sessions performance at various stages of training—A, early, D, late—in each problem. These data are taken from some as yet unpublished experiments by Behrend, Domesick, and Bitterman.)

day and reversed daily, irrespective of their performance. In the visual problem, reinforcement was correlated with color and independent of position, which varied randomly from trial to trial; e.g., red positive on odd days and green positive on even days. In the confounded problem, reinforcement was correlated both with color and position; e.g., red always on the left, green always on the right, with red-left positive on odd days and green-right positive on even days. The Riopelle problem was like the visual problem, except that each day's colors were chosen from a group of four, with the restriction that there be no more than partial reversal from one day to the next; i.e., yesterday's negative now positive with a "new" color negative, or yesterday's positive now negative with a "new" color now positive. The upper curves show that

there was no improvement over days in any of the three problems (the suggestion of an initial decline in the confounded curve is not statistically reliable). The lower curves show that there was a considerable amount of learning over the 40 trials of each day in each problem and at every stage of training, but that the pattern of improvement over trials did not change as training continued. Negative results of this sort now have been obtained under a variety of conditions wide enough, I think, that the burden of proof now rests with the skeptic. Until someone produces positive results, I shall assume that the fish is incapable of progressive improvement, and that we have come here upon a difference in the learning of fish and rat.

Experiments on *probability learning* also have given different results for rat and fish. Suppose that we train an animal in a choice situation with a ratio of reinforcement other than 100:0; that is, instead of rewarding one alternative on 100% of trials and the other never, we reward one alternative on, say, a random 70% of trials and the other on the remaining 30% of trials, thus constituting what may be called a *70:30 problem*. Under some conditions, rat and fish both "maximize" in such a problem, which is to say that they tend always to choose the more frequently reinforced alternative. Under other conditions—specifically, under conditions in which the distribution of reinforcements is exactly controlled—the rat continues to maximize, but the fish "matches," which is to say that its distribution of choices approximates the distribution of reinforcements: In a 70:30 problem, it chooses the 70% alternative on about 70% of trials and the 30% alternative on the remaining trials.

Figure 5 shows some sample data for a visual problem in which the discriminanda were horizontal and vertical stripes. In the first stage of the experiment, response to one of the stripes was rewarded on a random 70% of each day's 20 trials, and response to the other stripe was rewarded on the remaining 30% of the trials—a 70:30 problem. In the second stage of the experiment the ratio of reinforcement was changed to 100:0, response to the

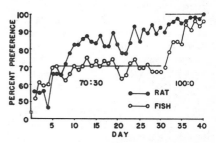

Fig. 5. Visual probability learning in fish and rat (from Bitterman, Wodinsky, & Candland, 1958).

375

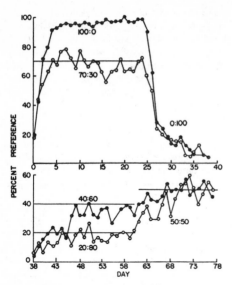

FIG. 6. Probability matching in the fish (from Behrend & Bitterman, 1961).

70% stripe of the first stage being consistently rewarded. The curves shown are plotted in terms of the percentage of each day's responses which were made to the more frequently rewarded alternative. The fish went rapidly from a near-chance level of preference for the 70% stimulus to about a 70% preference, which was maintained from Day 5 until Day 30. With the beginning of the 100:0 training, the preference shifted rapidly upward to about the 95% level. The preference of the rats for the more frequently reinforced stimulus rose gradually from a near-chance level at the start of the 70:30 training to about the 90% level on Day 30. In the 10 days of 100:0 training, this preference continued to increase gradually, as it might have done irrespective of the shift from inconsistent to consistent reinforcement. Some further evidence of the close correspondence between choice ratio and reward ratio, which is easy to demonstrate in the fish, is presented in Figure 6. The upper portion shows the performance of two groups of mouthbreeders; one trained on a 100:0 and the other on a 70:30 confounded (black-white) problem, and both then shifted to the 0:100 problem (the less frequently rewarded alternative of the first phase now being consistently rewarded). The lower portion shows what happened when one group then was shifted to 40:60 and the other to 20:80, after which both were shifted to 50:50.

Two characteristics of these data should be noted. First, the probability matching which the fish curves demonstrate is an individual, not a group phenomenon—that is, it is not an artifact of averaging. All the animals in the group behave in much

the same way. I make this obvious point because some averaged data which have been taken as evidence of matching in the rat are indeed unrepresentative of individual performances.[3] Second, the matching shown by the fish is random rather than systematic. The distribution of choices recorded in the 70:30 problem looks like the distribution of colors which might be obtained by drawing marbles at random from a sack of black and white marbles with a color ratio of 70:30—that is, no sequential dependency is to be found in the data. While the rat typically maximizes, it may on occasion show a correspondence of choice ratio and reward ratio which can be traced to some systematic pattern of choice, like the patterns which are displayed in analogous experiments by human subjects. For example, a correspondence reported by Hickson (1961) has been traced to a tendency in his rats to choose on each trial the alternative which had been rewarded on the immediately preceding trial. Quite the opposite tendency, which also tends to produce a correspondence between choice ratio and reinforcement ratio, has been found in the monkey —a tendency to *avoid* the rewarded alternative of the preceding trial (Wilson, Oscar, & Bitterman, 1964a, 1964b). The matching shown by the fish, which I shall call *random matching*, is a very different sort of thing.

Here then, are two striking differences between rat and fish. In experiments on habit reversal, the rat shows progressive improvement while the fish does not. In experiments on probability learning, the fish shows random matching while the rat does not. These results suggest a number of interesting questions, of which I shall raise here only two: First, there is the question of how the two differences are related. From the point of view of parsimony, the possibility must be considered that they reflect a single underlying difference in the functioning of the two animals—one which has to do with adjustment to inconsistent reinforcement. Inconsistency of reinforcement certainly is involved in both kinds of experiment, between sessions in reversal learning and within sessions in probability learning. It also is possible, however, that the results for reversal learning reflect one functional difference and the results for probability learning quite another. A second question concerns the relation between the observed differences in behavior and differences in brain structure. We may wonder, for example, to what extent the cortex of the rat is responsible for its progressive improvement in habit reversal, or for its failure to show random matching.

[3] The averaged data are cited by Estes (1957). The distribution of individual performances is given by Bitterman, Wodinsky, and Candland (1958).

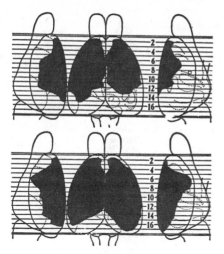

FIG. 7. Extent of cortical destruction in two rats operated at the age of 15 days and sacrificed at the age of 150 days. (The two brains are selected to illustrate the range and general locus of injury produced by the operation. From Gonzalez, Roberts, & Bitterman, 1964.)

In an effort to answer such questions we have begun to do some experiments, analogous to those which differentiate fish and normal rat, with a variety of other animals, and with rats surgically deprived in infancy of relevant brain tissues.

I shall describe first some results for extensively decorticated rats (Gonzalez et al., 1964). The animals were operated on at the age of 15 or 16 days in a one-stage procedure which resulted in the destruction of about 70% of the cortex. Two sample lesions, one relatively small and one relatively large, are shown in Figure 7. The experimental work with the operates, like the work with normals, was begun after they had reached maturity—at about 90 days of age. From the methodological viewpoint, work with a brain-injured animal is perfectly equivalent to work with a normal animal of another species, and rats operated in our standard fashion are treated in all respects as such, with systematic variation employed to control for the effects of sensory, motor, and motivational factors. The substantive relation of the work with decorticated rats to the work with normal animals of different species is obvious: We are interested in whether extensive cortical damage will produce in the rat the kinds of behavior which are characteristic of precortical animals, such as the fish, or of animals with only very limited cortical development.

The results for decorticated rats emphasize the importance of the distinction between spatial and visual problems. In a pure spatial problem, you will remember, the two alternatives are identical except for position in space, and reinforcement is correlated with position, e.g., the alternative on the left is reinforced. In a pure visual problem, the two alternatives are visually differentiated, each occupying each of the two positions equally often, and reinforcement is correlated with visual appearance—e.g., the green alternative is reinforced independently of its position. The behavior of the decorticated rat is indistinguishable from that of the normal rat in spatial problems, but in visual problems it differs from the normal in the same way as does the fish.

The criterion-reversal performance of a group of decorticated rats trained in a spatial problem is shown in Figure 8 along with that of a group of normal controls. There were 20 trials per day by the correction method, and the criterion of learning was 17 out of 20 correct choices. As you can see, the performance of the two groups was very much the same in the original problem. In the first 10 reversals the operates made more errors than did the normals, but (like the normals) they showed progressive improvement, and in the last 10 reversals, there was no difference between the two groups. The results for two additional groups, decorticated and normal, trained under analogous conditions in a visual problem (a brightness discrimination) are plotted in Figure 9. Again, the performance of normals and operates was much the same in the original problem. In the subsequent reversals, the error scores of the normal animals rose at first and then declined in characteristic fashion, but the error scores of the operates rose much more markedly and showed no subsequent tendency to decline.

In spatial probability learning the performance of the operates was indistinguishable from that of normals, but in visual probability learning the operates showed random matching. The asymptotic preferences of operates and normals, first in a 70:30 and then in a 50:50 brightness discrimination, are

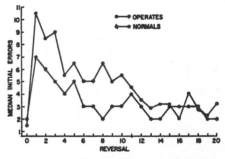

FIG. 8. Spatial habit reversal in normal rats and in rats extensively decorticated in infancy (from Gonzalez, Roberts, & Bitterman, 1964).

-377

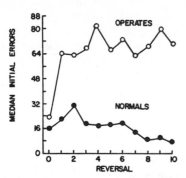

FIG. 9. Visual habit reversal in normal rats and in rats extensively decorticated in infancy (from Gonzalez, Roberts, & Bitterman, 1964).

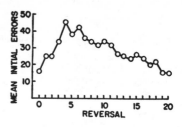

FIG. 10. Visual habit reversal in the pigeon (from Stearns & Bitterman, 1965).

TABLE 1

PREFERENCES OF DECORTICATED RATS (O) AND NORMAL CONTROLS (N) FOR THE MORE FREQUENTLY REINFORCED ALTERNATIVE IN A 70:30 VISUAL PROBLEM AND FOR THE SAME ALTERNATIVE IN A SUBSEQUENT 50:50 PROBLEM

Subject	70:30 problem	50:50 problem
O-1	68.0	49.5
O-2	69.5	53.0
O-3	71.5	47.0
O-4	73.5	57.0
O-5	76.0	62.0
N-1	64.5	CP
N-2	79.0	CP
N-3	89.5	86.0
N-4	90.0	CP
N-5	90.0	80.0

Note.—CP means choice of one position on 90% or more of trials. Data from Gonzalez, Roberts, and Bitterman (1964).

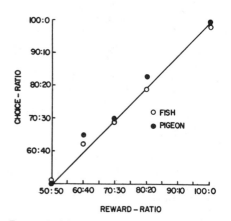

FIG. 11. Probability matching in fish and pigeon. (The points for the fish are based both on spatial and on visual data, while those for the pigeon are based only on visual data.)

shown in Table 1. In the 70:30 problem, the operates came to choose the 70% stimulus on about 70% of trials (the mean was 71.7%); in the 50:50 problem they chose the two stimuli about equally often (the mean preference for the former 70% stimulus was 53.7%). No sequential dependencies could be found in their behavior. By contrast, the normal animals tended to maximize in the 70:30 problem. The two whose preferences came closest to 70% adopted rigid position habits (CP) in the 50:50 problem, while one of the others also responded to position, and two continued in the previously established preference. In both spatial experiments, then, the decorticated rats behaved like normal rats, while in both visual experiments they behaved like fish.

These results are compatible with the hypothesis that the cortex of the rat is responsible in some measure for its progressive improvement in habit reversal and for its failure to show random probability matching, at least in visual problems. They are compatible also with the hypothesis that the behavioral differences between fish and rat which appear in the two kinds of experiment are reflections of a single functional difference between the two species. The latter hypothesis is contradicted, however, by some results for the pigeon which I shall now describe. I need not go into any detail about the experimental situation, because it is a fairly familiar one. Suffice it to say that the Skinnerian key-pecking apparatus was adapted for discrete-trials choice experiments directly analogous to those done with fish and rat. The bird, in a darkened enclosure, pecks at one of two lighted keys, correct choice being rewarded by access to grain. Contingencies are programed automatically, and responses are recorded on tape.

In experiments on habit reversal, both visual and

378

spatial, the pigeon behaves like the rat; that is, it gives clear evidence of progressive improvement (Bullock & Bitterman, 1962a). Shown in Figure 10 is the criterion-reversal performance of a group of pigeons trained in a blue-green discrimination. There were 40 trials per day to the criterion of 34 correct choices in the 40 trials, with positive and negative colors reversed for each animal whenever it met that criterion. The results look very much like those obtained in analogous experiments with the rat: There is an initial increase in mean errors to criterion, followed by a progressive, negatively accelerated decline. Now what can we say of the behavior of the pigeon in experiments on probability learning? Figure 11 gives evidence of a correspondence between choice ratio and reward ratio as close in the pigeon as in the fish, and statistical analysis shows that the matching is random. The points for the pigeon, like those for the fish, represent the pooled results of a variety of experiments, both published and unpublished, which were carried out in my laboratory. Unlike the points for the fish, however, the points for the pigeon are based only on *visual* data, because the pigeon shows random matching only in visual problems; in spatial problems it tends to maximize (Bullock & Bitterman, 1962b; Graf, Bullock, & Bitterman, 1964).

The results for the pigeon, then, are in a sense intermediate between those for the rat and for the fish. Like the rat, the pigeon shows progressive improvement in habit reversal, but, like the fish, it shows random probability matching—in visual problems if not in spatial ones. One conclusion which may be drawn from these results is that experiments on habit reversal and experiments on probability learning tap somewhat different processes. If the processes were the same, any animal would behave either like the fish, or like the rat, in both kinds of experiment. We have, then, been able to separate the processes underlying the two phenomena which differentiate fish and rat by a method which might be called *phylogenetic filtration*. It is interesting, too, that the visual-spatial dichotomy which appeared in work with the decorticated rat appears again in the probability learning of the pigeon. In experiments on habit reversal, the pigeon behaves like a normal rat; in experiments on probability learning, the pigeon behaves, not like a fish, but like an extensively decorticated rat.

Now let me show you some comparable data for several other species. Being very much interested in the reptilian brain, which is the first to show true cortex, I have devoted a good deal of effort to the development of a satisfactory technique for the study of learning in the painted turtle. After some partial success with a primitive T maze (Kirk & Bitterman, 1963), I came finally to the situation

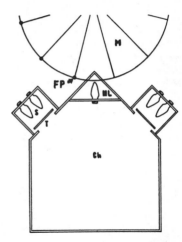

Fig. 12. A situation for the study of discrimination in the turtle. (Ch, animal's chamber; T, target; S, lamps for projecting colored lights on the targets; M, feeder which rotates a pellet of food, FP, into the chamber; ML, magazine lamp which is turned on to signal the presentation of food. From Bitterman, 1964.)

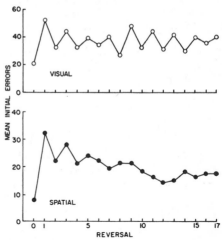

Fig. 13. Visual and spatial habit reversal in the turtle. (The data are taken from some as yet unpublished experiments by Holmes and Bitterman.)

diagramed in Figure 12. As in our latest apparatus for monkey, rat, pigeon, and fish, the turtle is presented with two differentially illuminated targets between which it chooses by pressing against one of them. Correct choice is rewarded with a pellet of hamburger or fish which is rotated into the chamber on a solenoid-driven tray. Some experiments on habit reversal now under way in this situation have yielded the data plotted in Figure 13. One group of turtles was trained on a spatial problem (both targets the same color) and another group on a visual problem (red versus green). There were 20 trials per day, with reversal after every 4 days. As you can see, progressive improvement has appeared in the spatial problem, but not in the visual problem. Some experiments on probability learning also are under way in this situation. In spatial problems, only maximizing and nonrandom matching (reward following) have been found, but in visual problems, random matching has begun to appear. This pattern of results, you will remember, is exactly that which was found in decorticated rats. Insofar as performance in these tests is concerned, then, extensive decortication in infancy turns rats into turtles.

I come now to some work with invertebrates. Diagramed in Figure 14 is a Y maze for the cockroach used in the experiments of Longo (1964). The technique is a much cruder one than those used for vertebrates, but it represents, I think, a considerable advance over anything that has yet been done with the cockroach. The motive utilized is shock avoidance: Ten seconds after the animal is introduced into the starting box, shock is turned on, and remains on, until the animal enters the goal box, which is its home cage; if the animal reaches the goal box in less than 10 seconds, it avoids shock entirely. Choices are detected objectively by photocells, but complete automation is not possible, because no satisfactory alternative to handling the animal has been found. The results of an experiment on spatial probability learning in the cockroach, which was patterned after those done with vertebrates, are plotted in Figure 15. Like the fish —but *unlike any higher vertebrate*—the cockroach shows random matching under spatial conditions. The results of an experiment on spatial habit reversal in the cockroach are plotted in Figure 16. Three groups of animals were given 10 trials per day—one group reversed each day, another group reversed every 4 days, and a control group never reversed

during the stage of the experiment for which data are plotted. Although the 4-day group showed no significant improvement (its curve hardly declines at all beyond the first point, which is for the original problem), the daily group did show significant improvement (its curve declining in much the same way as that of the control group). What does this result mean? Have we found in the primitive cockroach a capability which does not exist in the fish? A consideration of some results for the earthworm will help to answer this question.

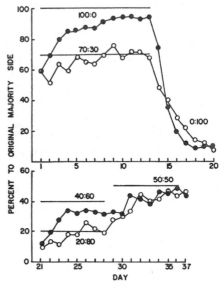

Fig. 15. Spatial probability matching in the cockroach (from Longo, 1964).

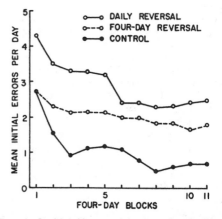

Fig. 16. Spatial habit reversal in the cockroach (from Longo, 1964).

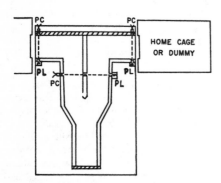

Fig. 14. A Y maze for the cockroach. (PC, photocell; PL, photocell lamp; S, starting compartment. From Longo, 1964.)

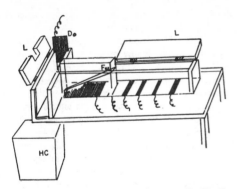

FIG. 17. A T maze for the earthworm. (L, lid; Do, metal door which converts one arm of the maze into a cul and delivers shock for erroneous choice; Fu, funnel to reduce retracing; HC, home container. From Datta, 1962.)

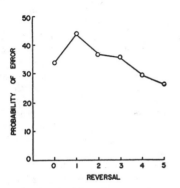

FIG. 18. Spatial habit reversal in the earthworm (from Datta, 1962).

Diagramed in Figure 17 is a T maze developed for the earthworm by Datta (1962). The stem of the maze is bright, warm, and dry, and the animal occasionally is shocked in it. A correct turn at the choice point carries the animal to its dark, moist, cool, shock-free home container, while an incorrect turn is punished with shock from a metal door which converts one arm of the maze into a cul. When the animal is shocked for contact with the door, a sensitive relay in the circuit is energized, thereby providing an objective index of error. This technique, again, is a crude one by vertebrate standards, but it seems to give reliable results. Some sample data on spatial habit reversal are plotted in Figure 18. The worms were given five trials per day and reversed every 4 days. Note that the mean number of errors rose in the first reversal, and thereafter declined progressively, the animals doing better in the fourth and fifth reversals than in the original problem. In a further experiment, how-

ever, this improvement was found to be independent of reversal training per se and a function only of general experience in the maze: A control group, trained always to the same side while an experimental group was reversed repeatedly, did not differ from the experimental group when eventually it, too, was reversed. This test for the effects of general experience is feasible in the earthworm, because the turning preferences which it develops do not persist from session to session. The analysis of the progressive improvement shown by the cockroach is, however, a more difficult matter, and I must be content here simply to state Longo's opinion that it reflects, as in the earthworm, not an improvement in reversal capability, but an improved adjustment to the maze situation. The course of that general improvement is traced by the curve for the control group, which parallels that of the daily group. Nonspecific improvement probably is not as evident in the vertebrate data because general adjustment to the experimental situation proceeds rapidly and is essentially complete at the end of pretraining.[4]

The results of these experiments on habit reversal and probability learning in a variety of animals are summarized in Table 2. Spatial and visual problems are categorized separately because they give different results. The rows for all the subjects except one are ordered in accordance with the conventional scale of complexity—monkey at the top and earthworm at the bottom. The only subject whose place in the table is not based on preconceived complexity is the decorticated rat, whose placement (with the turtle, between the pigeon and the fish) is dictated by experimental outcomes. The differences between fish and rat which provided points of departure for the subsequent work with other organisms also provide a frame of reference for reading the table: R means that the results obtained in a given kind of experiment with a given subject are like those for the rat (that is, progressive improvement in habit reversal and failure of random matching), while F means that the results obtained are like those for the fish (that is, random matching and failure of progressive improvement). It should be understood that these entries are made with

[4] A possibility to be considered is that a portion at least of the cockroach's improvement was due to improvement in the experimenter, of whom the conduct of the experiment required considerable skill. The same may be said of the first in the series of experiments with the fish by Wodinsky and Bitterman (1957) which was the only one to show anything like progressive improvement and whose results have not been replicated in work with automated equipment; the pattern of improvement was, incidentally, quite unlike that found in mammals. A study of another arthropod (the Bermuda land crab) in a simple escape situation, by Datta, Milstein, and Bitterman (1960), gave no evidence of improvement.

TABLE 2

BEHAVIOR OF A VARIETY OF ANIMALS IN FOUR CLASSES OF
PROBLEM WHICH DIFFERENTIATE RAT AND FISH EX-
PRESSED IN TERMS OF SIMILARITY TO THE BE-
HAVIOR OF ONE OR THE OTHER OF THESE
TWO REFERENCE ANIMALS

Animal	Spatial problems		Visual problems	
	Reversal	Probability	Reversal	Probability
Monkey	R	R	R	R
Rat	R	R	R	R
Pigeon	R	R	R	F
Turtle	R	R	F	F
Decorticated rat	R	R	F	F
Fish	F	F	F	F
Cockroach	F	F	—	—
Earthworm	F	—	—	—

Note.—F means behavior like that of the fish (random probability matching and failure of progressive improvement in habit reversal). R means behavior like that of the rat (maximizing or nonrandom probability matching and progressive improvement in habit reversal). Transitional regions are connected by the stepped line. The brackets group animals which have not yet been differentiated by these problems.

varying degrees of confidence. Where there are no data, there are no entries, but an entry is made even where, as in the case of the turtle, the data are yet fragmentary and incomplete. All entries are based on data from my laboratory, except those for reversal learning in the monkey, which are based on the literature.

The table is an orderly one. In each column there is a single transition from F to R as the scale of subjects is ascended, although the point of transition varies from column to column, suggesting a certain functional independence: Rat-like behavior in spatial problems of both kinds appears first in decorticated rat and turtle, rat-like behavior in visual reversal learning appears first in pigeon, and rat-like behavior in visual probability learning appears first in rat. The eight subjects fall into four different groupings: monkey and rat in one; pigeon in a second; turtle and decorticated rat in a third; fish, cockroach, and earthworm in a fourth. Monkey and rat fall into the same grouping because they are not differentiated by these experiments when all failures of random probability matching are classified as R. The data for the two mammals do, however, show different kinds of sequential dependency in experiments on probability learning, reward following in the rat giving way in the monkey to the opposite strategy (avoiding the rewarded alternatives of the preceding trial). It is interesting to note that this new strategy of the monkey has been manifested thus far only with respect to the spatial locus of reward, even when the alternatives have been visually distinct. This finding fits the generalization suggested at other points in the table: that as we ascend the phyletic

scale new modes of adjustment appear earlier in spatial than in visual contexts.

It is of some interest to ask whether R modes of adjustment are in any sense more effective than F modes, and for habit reversal, at least, the answer is clear. Progressive improvement is on its face a superior adjustment, representing a flexibility that cannot help but be of value in an animal's adjustment to changing life circumstances. The answer for probability learning is less clear, although it can be said that maximizing produces a higher percentage of correct choice than does matching. In a 70:30 problem, for example, the probability of correct choice is .70 for maximizing but only .58—$(.70 \times .70) + (.30 \times .30)$—for matching. Nonrandom matching is no more successful than random matching by this criterion, but we know that in human subjects it is the outcome of an effort to find a principle that will permit 100% correct choice; the hypotheses tested reflect the observed reward ratio, and they produce a corresponding choice ratio. To the degree that nonrandom matching in infrahuman subjects is based on an emerging hypothetical or strategic capability, it represents a considerable functional advance over random matching.

The table does, of course, have certain obvious limitations. Clearly, I should like to be able to write *bird* rather than *pigeon,* I should like by *fish* to mean more than *mouthbreeder,* and so forth. It will be interesting to discover how representative of their classes are the particular species studied in these experiments—whose choice was dictated largely by practical considerations—and to extend the comparisons to other classes and phyla. I can say, too, that the behavioral categories used in the table almost certainly will need refining; already the R-F dichotomy is strained by the data on probability learning (with R standing for maximizing, for near maximizing, and for nonrandom matching of several different kinds), while better techniques must be found for isolating the various constituents of progressive improvement in habit reversal. The uncontaminated linear order which now appears in the table, while undeniably esthetic, is rather embarrassing from the standpoint of the far-from-linear evolutionary relationships among the species studied; nonlinearities are perhaps to be expected as the behavioral categories are refined and as the range of tests is broadened.

Whatever its limitations, the table is useful, I think, not only as a summary of results already obtained, but as a guide to further research. Almost certainly, the order in the table will permit us to reduce the amount of parametric variation which must be done before we are satisfied that some phenomenon for which we are looking in a given animal is not to be found. Suppose, for example, that we had begun to work with the turtle before the pigeon, and suppose that we had sought persistently, but in vain, for evidence of random matching in spatial probability learning, being satisfied at last to enter an R for the turtle in the second column of the table. Turning then to the pigeon, we should be prepared after many fewer unsuccessful efforts to enter an R. I do not mean, of course, that systematic parametric variation is no longer important in comparative research; we must continue to do a great deal of it, especially at points of transition in the table, and wherever the entries fail to reflect gross discontinuities in the evolutionary histories of the organisms concerned. I do think, however, that the table will save us some parametric effort *in certain regions*—effort which may be diverted to the task of increasing the range of organisms and the range of tests represented. It does not seem unreasonable to expect that, thus expanded, the table will provide some useful clues to the evolution of intelligence and its relation to the evolution of the brain.

REFERENCES

BEACH, F. A. The snark was a boojum. *American Psychologist*, 1950, 5, 115–124.

BEHREND, E. R., & BITTERMAN, M. E. Probability-matching in the fish. *American Journal of Psychology*, 1961, 74, 542–551.

BITTERMAN, M. E. Toward a comparative psychology of learning. *American Psychologist*, 1960, 15, 704–712.

BITTERMAN, M. E. An instrumental technique for the turtle. *Journal of the Experimental Analysis of Behavior*, 1964, 7, 189–190.

BITTERMAN, M. E., WODINSKY, J., & CANDLAND, D. K. Some comparative psychology. *American Journal of Psychology*, 1958, 71, 94–110.

BULLOCK, D. H., & BITTERMAN, M. E. Habit reversal in the pigeon. *Journal of Comparative and Physiological Psychology*, 1962, 55, 958–962. (a)

BULLOCK, D. H., & BITTERMAN, M. E. Probability-matching in the pigeon. *American Journal of Psychology*, 1962, 75, 634–639. (b)

DATTA, L. G. Learning in the earthworm, *Lumbricus terrestris*. *American Journal of Psychology*, 1962, 75, 531–553.

DATTA, L. G., MILSTEIN, S., & BITTERMAN, M. E. Habit reversal in the crab. *Journal of Comparative and Physiological Psychology*, 1960, 53, 275–278.

ESTES, W. K. Of models and men. *American Psychologist*, 1957, 12, 609–616.

GONZALEZ, R. C., ROBERTS, W. A., & BITTERMAN, M. E. Learning in adult rats with extensive cortical lesions made in infancy. *American Journal of Psychology*, 1964, 77, 547–562.

GRAF, V., BULLOCK, D. H., & BITTERMAN, M. E. Further experiments on probability-matching in the pigeon. *Journal of Experimental Analysis of Behavior*, 1964, 7, 151–157.

HARRIMAN, P. L. (Ed.) *Twentieth century psychology*. New York: Philosophical Library, 1946.

HICKSON, R. H. Response probability in a two-choice learning situation with varying probability of reinforcement. *Journal of Experimental Psychology*, 1961, 62, 138–144.

KIRK, K. L., & BITTERMAN, M. E. Habit reversal in the turtle. *Quarterly Journal of Experimental Psychology*, 1963, 15, 52–57.

KOCH, S. *Psychology: A study of a science*. Vol. 2. *General systematic formulations, learning, and special processes*. New York: McGraw-Hill, 1959.

LONGO, N. Probability-learning and habit-reversal in the cockroach. *American Journal of Psychology*, 1964, 77, 29–41.

LONGO, N., & BITTERMAN, M. E. Improved apparatus for the study of learning in fish. *American Journal of Psychology*, 1959, 72, 616–620.

LONGO, N., & BITTERMAN, M. E. An improved live-worm dispenser. *Journal of the Experimental Analysis of Behavior*, 1963, 6, 279–280.

SIDOWSKI, J. (Ed.) *Experimental methods and instrumentation in psychology*. New York: McGraw-Hill, 1965.

STEARNS, E. M., & BITTERMAN, M. E. A comparison of key-pecking with an ingestive technique for the study of discriminative learning in pigeons. *American Journal of Psychology*, 1965, 78, in press.

THORNDIKE, E. L. *Animal intelligence*. New York: Macmillan, 1911.

VORONIN, L. G. Some results of comparative-physiological investigations of higher nervous activity. *Psychological Bulletin*, 1962, 59, 161–195.

WILSON, W. A., JR., OSCAR, M., & BITTERMAN, M. E. Probability learning in the monkey. *Quarterly Journal of Experimental Psychology*, 1964, 16, 163–165. (a)

WILSON, W. A., JR., OSCAR, M., & BITTERMAN, M. E. Visual probability-learning in the monkey. *Psychonomic Science*, 1964, 1, 71–72. (b)

WODINSKY, J., & BITTERMAN, M. E. Discrimination-reversal in the fish. *American Journal of Psychology*, 1957, 70, 569–576.

51

Learning in Fish with Transplanted Brain Tissue

Abstract. *Material taken from fish embryos during gastrulation was implanted at prospective tectal sites in host embryos of the same age and species. When mature, the hosts were trained in a series of habit reversals. Two of six animals showed progressive improvement in reversal (a phenomenon not typically found in fish, but characteristic of higher animals), two showed unusually few errors, and two behaved normally. Differences in performance were correlated with differences in brain structure.*

One way to study the role of the brain in learning is to study the learning of animals with less than the normal amount of brain tissue. The function of the missing tissue is inferred from differences in the learning of normal animals and animals whose brains are altered by ablation. The ablation method has been used to analyze differences in the learning of vertebrates of different classes (*1*). For example, adult rats, extensively decorticated at an early age, show fishlike behavior with respect to habit reversal. Now it is possible to reverse the logic of the ablation experiment—to study the learning of animals with more than the normal amount of brain tissue. The first results of such a "supplementation" experiment suggest that transplantation of brain tissue may facilitate learning in simple vertebrates and even endow them with capabilities normally present only in more complex forms.

Although transplantation has not yet been accomplished in adult animals, Oppenheimer in work with *Fundulus* has shown that brain tissue can be supplemented by grafting during early stages of development (*2*). In some cases, the grafting procedure produced suppression or rearrangement of primary brain structures; in others, there was duplication of structure. Oppenheimer described certain aspects of the behavior of her altered embryos, but killed them for histological study soon after they hatched (*3*). We report here some observations on the learning of supplemented animals which we reared to maturity.

Our work was done with *Tilapia macrocephala* (the African mouthbreeder), a species of fish more easily bred in the laboratory than *Fundulus* and about whose learning more is known (*4*). The surgical technique was a modification of the one developed by Oppenheimer. Embryos at stages 10 through 12 (*5*) were removed from the mouth of an adult male and rinsed repeatedly in sterile aquarium water to reduce bacteria. The specimens were placed in a dish of sterile water, and the operation was performed aseptically under high-power magnification of a dissecting microscope. Watchmaker's forceps sharpened to needlepoints were used to dechorionate host and donor embryos. Material from posterior regions of the donor embryo was removed with steel needles sharpened to knife-edges and implanted in the prospective tectal tissue of the host.

Healing was so rapid that no mechanical device was necessary to keep the implant in place. The host then was transferred to a large covered petri dish containing a 1 percent solution of sulfadiazene in sterile aquarium water. After absorption of their yolk, the fry were fed, first Micrograin, and later trout chow. As they grew in size, the animals were transferred to progressively larger containers.

Although survival rates increased as the surgical technique was perfected, postoperative mortality was at best rather high. Many embryos starved because the grafting interfered with the normal development of mouthparts. In others, the grafts differentiated into nonnervous tissue (notochord, eye, or ear) which may have suppressed the development of brain structures necessary for survival. Tectal abnormalities may also have resulted in respiratory failure (6). We reared only ten experimental subjects to sexual maturity. Of the ten, two died from unknown causes while they were being trained to strike a target and take worms from an automatic feeder, and two failed to adjust satisfactorily to the experimental situation. The six remaining animals were trained in a series of habit reversals.

Our choice of task was related to our choice of the prospective tectum as a grafting site. Higher vertebrates (reptiles, birds, and mammals) show progressive improvement in habit reversal, but fish typically do not (7). Since the tectum of the fish is regarded as homologous to the cortex of mammals (8), and since the results of ablation experiments suggest that the mammalian cortex plays an important role in progressive improvement (9), we thought that reversal learning in the fish might be enhanced by tectal supplementation.

Our fully automated training apparatus has been described (10). Each animal was carried in its individual living tank to a black Plexiglas enclosure.

On each trial, two circular Plexiglas targets were illuminated with colored lights, and the response of the animal was to strike at one of them. Correct choice was rewarded with a live *Tubifex* worm; incorrect choice produced a period of darkness, after which the correct target alone was illuminated and the animal was rewarded for response to it. After learning to strike a target and to take worms from the feeder (7), three of the animals (Nos. 1, 4, and 6) were trained to discriminate between red and green targets, and choice of red (the less preferred color) was rewarded; the positions of the two colors were changed from trial to trial in balanced order. The other animals (Nos. 8, 9, and 10) were trained in a position discrimination; both targets were red, and choice of the left target was rewarded. There were 40 trials per day, and each animal was trained to the criterion of six or fewer errors per day, with no more than three errors in the last 20 trials.

As each animal reached the criterion of learning in the original problem (R_0), the correct and incorrect stimuli were reversed—the choice of green now was rewarded for the first three animals, and choice of right for the others. After reaching criterion in this first reversal (R_1), each animal was reversed again, and so on (R_2, R_3. . . . R_n). Training was terminated when the animals contracted a disease which also affected unoperated mouthbreeders living in other parts of the laboratory. Five of the animals died, and the remaining subject (No. 4) was killed with a 3 percent urethane solution. All specimens were fixed in Bouin's solution. Then their brains were removed, embedded in Paraplast, sectioned at 10 μ, and stained by Davenport's modification of the Bodian silver-impregnation technique (11). The brains of 24 control animals of the same age and parentage were prepared for study in the same way.

Of the six experimental animals, two had brains which were indistinguishable from those of the control animals, and four showed marked tectal abnormalities. The normal brains were those of Nos. 1 and 6. Three coronal sections through the mesencephalon of No. 1 are sketched in Fig. 1. Section B was taken about 0.5 mm from the cephalic end of the tectum, section D from the middle region, and section F about 1 mm from the caudal end. Although abnormalities in brain structure can be produced in fish embryos by mechanical injury (2) and by antibiotics (12) the fact that these two brains were normal suggests that the changes in structure found in the other four were not due to such secondary aspects of the operative procedure. As Oppenheimer noted, grafted tissue fails occasionally to effect a junction with the nervous system of the host, and may be sloughed off or absorbed into the host tissue (2); that perhaps is what happened here. Whatever the reason for our failure to alter the tecta of these animals, they serve the function of sham-operated controls.

Three kinds of tectal abnormality found in the brains of the other four animals are illustrated in Fig. 1. The brain of No. 10 showed a supplementary layered structure, about 1 mm in longitudinal extent, overlying the anterior third of the tectum. The new structure may be seen clearly in section A, which was taken at the same (relatively anterior) level as the normal section B. The brain of No. 4 showed a substantial increase in tectal thickness, which may be seen in section C, taken at the same (medial) level as the normal section D. The thickening was evident in all regions of the tectum of this animal al-

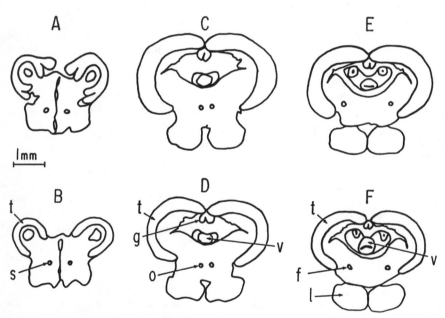

Fig. 1. Coronal sections through the mesencephalon showing (A) a supplementary tectal structure in animal No. 10; (C) tectal thickening in animal No. 4; (E) tectal thickening in animal No. 8; and (B, D, F) the normal brain of animal No. 1 at corresponding levels; (t) tectum opticum; (s) tractus striothalamicus and hypothalamicus; (g) torus longitudinus; (o) tractus octavothalamicus; (v) valvula cerebelli; (f) fasciculus longitudinus lateralis; and (l) inferior lobes.

though other brain structures were of normal size, and it could be traced to an increase in the width of the tectal layers rather than to an increase in the number of layers. The brains of Nos. 8 and 9, both very much alike, also showed tectal thickening, which was confined principally to the posterior third of the tectum. The thickening may be seen in section E, which was taken from the brain of No. 8 at the same (relatively caudal) level as the normal section F. Nothing remotely like these tectal abnormalities was found in the control brains. The supplementary tectum of No. 10 was, of course, unique, and the enlargements in the brains of the other three animals were evident to the naked eye. A simple ranking test (with the two normal brains assigned median ranks) shows the sample of six experimental brains to be different from the control sample at the 1 percent level of confidence. The locus of abnormality in the experimental brains corresponded to the locus of implant.

Individual learning curves plotted in terms of errors to criterion over reversals (Fig. 2) show that all of the animals (whose training was begun at different times) reached criterion in the original problem and at least five subsequent reversals. The curves also show three kinds of performance. Those for animals Nos. 1 and 6 illustrate the inefficient reversal performance typically found in normal mouthbreeders (7). Those for animals Nos. 4 and 10 show significant progressive improvement (*P* < .05 in each case by Fisher's exact test), and examination of the fine grain of the performance (analysis of errors over blocks of trials) shows it to be indistinguishable from that found in rats (*13*). The curves for animals Nos. 8 and 9 show another kind of performance which is unusual in fish—not progressive improvement, but error scores which are very low throughout. In experiments with large numbers of normal fish, an occasional animal does give some indication of improvement over reversals. Behrend and Bitterman (7) reported "two or three" in a sample of 75. If we take 4 percent as the population value, the probability of two or more such animals in a sample of six is only about 3 percent. Animals with low error scores like those of animals Nos. 8 and 9 are at least as rare, and the probability of two such animals in a sample of six is therefore at least as low. To find four such deviant animals in a sample of six is even less likely.

The best evidence that our grafting procedure affected both the brains and the behavior of our experimental animals may be found in the correlation between the brain structure and the behavior. The two animals with normal brains (Nos. 1 and 6) behaved normally. The probability of this correspondance alone is only about 2 percent. Furthermore, the two animals with unusually low error scores (Nos. 8 and 9) showed tectal thickening which was restricted to the caudal region, whereas

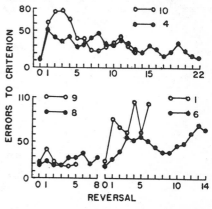

Fig. 2. The performance of the six animals plotted in terms of errors per reversal. Reversal 0 is the original problem. The curves for animals Nos. 4 and 10 (above) show progressive improvement. The curves for animals Nos. 8 and 9 (lower left) show error scores which are unusually low throughout. The curves for animals Nos. 1 and 6 (lower right) are characteristic of normal mouthbreeders.

the two animals with progressive improvement (Nos. 4 and 10) showed changes in the anterior tectum (No. 10 a new structure; and No. 1, a general thickening that included the anterior region). Our results thus suggest that supplementation experiments have an important role to play in the analysis of brain function.

DAVID E. BRESLER

Department of Psychology,
University of California,
Los Angeles 90024

M. E. BITTERMAN

Department of Psychology,
Bryn Mawr College,
Bryn Mawr, Pennsylvania 19010

References and Notes

1. M. E. Bitterman, *Amer. Psychol.* **20**, 396 (1965).
2. J. M. Oppenheimer, *J. Exp. Zool.* **115**, 461 (1950); *ibid.* **129**, 649 (1955); ——— and N. Vassady, *Proc. Nat. Acad. Sci. U.S.* **42**, 785 (1956).
3. J. M. Oppenheimer reports (personal communication) that animals were quite unlikely to survive after the depletion of their yolk sacs because the operation usually produced peripheral anomalies, such as faulty mouthparts, which might have led to death from starvation.
4. That the behavioral technique used here for *Tilapia* is appropriate also to *Fundulus* was demonstrated about 10 years ago. The behavior of *Fundulus* was examined out of interest in the possibility of just such experiments as are reported here. See N. Longo and M. E. Bitterman, *Amer. J. Psychol.* **72**, 616 (1959).
5. E. S. Shaw and L. R. Aronson, *Bull. Amer. Mus. Nat. Hist.* **103**, 375 (1954).
6. *Tilapia* seems to be particularly sensitive to tectal injury, according to unpublished studies by L. R. Aronson and D. S. Liang. Even very small unilateral lesions invariably result in death from respiratory failure. See L. R. Aronson, in *Sharks and Survival*, P. W. Gilbert, Ed. (Heath, Boston, 1963), pp. 165–241.
7. E. R. Behrend, V. B. Domesick, M. E. Bitterman, *J. Comp. Physiol. Psychol.* **60**, 407 (1965).
8. E. G. Healey, in *The Physiology of Fishes*, M. E. Brown, Ed. (Academic Press, New York, 1957), vol. 2, pp. 1–119; L. R. Aronson, in *Sharks and Survival*, P. W. Gilbert, Ed. (Heath, Boston, 1963); D. J. Ingle, *Perspect. Biol. Med.* **8**, 241 (1965).
9. R. C. Gonzalez, W. A. Roberts, M. E. Bitterman, *Amer. J. Psychol.* **77**, 547 (1964).
10. M. E. Bitterman, in *Experimental Methods and Instrumentation in Psychology*, J. Sidowski, Ed. (McGraw-Hill, New York, 1966), pp. 451–484.
11. H. A. Davenport, *Histology and Histological Technics* (Saunders, Philadelphia, 1960), p. 261.
12. P. D. Anderson and H. I. Battle, *Can. J. Zool.* **45**, 191 (1967).
13. F. Gatling, *J. Comp. Physiol. Psychol.* **45**, 347 (1952).
14. This work was performed at Bryn Mawr College and supported by NIH grant MH02857. We thank Miss J. M. Oppenheimer for advice on operative and histological procedures.

29 October 1968

Maternal Influence in Learning by Observation in Kittens

Abstract. *Kittens who observed their mothers perform a stimulus-controlled response (lever pressing to a visual stimulus for food) acquired and discriminated that response sooner than kittens who observed a strange female cat's performance. Kittens exposed to a trial and error condition never acquired the response. Initial differences in attentiveness to demonstrator performances disappeared by the second day. "Altruism" (food sharing) and other forms of social behavior were exhibited by both mother and stranger demonstrators.*

In several animal species, including man, mothers care for their young for a long time after birth. During this time, the young develop sensory and motor functions and acquire skills which are necessary for survival. The mother's role in teaching her young a specific skill, such as acquisition of food, has often been observed (*1*) but has not been experimentally demonstrated. Several investigators have suggested that infant mammals may learn from their mothers (*2*), and from their elders (*3*), primarily by observation. We have previously shown that learning by observation in adult cats is a more efficient method of learning than conventional shaping procedures (*4*). In this study, we undertook to determine whether the speed and efficiency of observation learning is improved by the use of a mother cat as demonstrator.

The subjects were 18 kittens, all between 9 and 10 weeks old when observation began. Each kitten lived with its mother and littermates in a home or homelike laboratory environment, or both, from birth until the end of the experiment. Group I consisted of six kittens who observed their mother's performance (M kittens); group II consisted of six kittens who observed the same strange female's performance (S kittens); group III consisted of six kittens exposed to a trial and error condition (TE kittens). The members of a given litter were randomly distributed to at least two of these three groups,

and where possible, to all three groups. All littermates began testing on the same day. Five female demonstrator cats (three mothers and two strangers) were used. Their task performances were equivalent and practically without error throughout the experiment.

The task was a lever press performed within 20 seconds after onset of a flickering light (4 cycle/sec). The lever was made of plexiglass and extended 12.5 cm beyond the front panel of a standard operant conditioning cage. A plexiglass partition divided the cage evenly into a demonstrator and observer compartment. A dipper that delivered a blended mixture of milk and meat was located 3.75 cm away from the lever in the demonstrator compartment.

After being familiarized with the cage, a kitten that had been deprived of food for 24 hours was placed in the demonstrator compartment alone and given one "free" food reward. The demonstrator cat (mother or strange female) was then introduced and performed ten stimulus-controlled lever presses. Although both M and S kittens had physical access to the food during these ten observation trials, they generally did not eat at this time. In fact, the occasional one, or at most two, rewards eaten by an M or S kitten during these ten trials, does not seem to constitute a determinant in their motivation or attentiveness. After these observation trials, the kitten was removed to the adjacent observer compartment for the opportunity to observe 30 more lever presses. The number of times the kitten oriented toward (paid attention to) the demonstrator cat was recorded for the 40 observation trials.

The demonstrator cat was then removed, and the kitten was placed back in the demonstrator compartment. Using a blind procedure, an assistant presented ten randomly spaced trials of the visual stimulus. This overall procedure was repeated daily until the kitten had pressed the lever in eight of the ten trials. When this occurred, it was given 20 additional presentations. When the kitten achieved 90 percent criterion for these 30 trials, acquisition was considered to have taken place and it was removed. Thirty trials were then presented daily, without further observation, until stimulus discrimination was achieved. Discrimination was decided to have taken place when the kitten made five or fewer interstimulus presses each day for three consecutive days. No kitten remained just below criterion in acquiring the response. Every kitten stabilized at or above the criterion level. All kittens were tested for 30 days or until they had discriminated the response.

The TE kittens were subjected to the same procedure except that no demonstrator cat was present. A TE kitten received one "free" food reward in the demonstrator compartment and ten presentations of the stimulus, after which it was placed in the observer compartment for 30 trials. During this time in the observer compartment, the stimulus was presented at random intervals and was terminated with the sound of the food dipper, as if a demonstrator cat were performing. The kitten was then placed back in the demonstrator compartment and presented with ten trials. This procedure was abbreviated any time a kitten started to press the lever spontaneously during the first ten observation trials when it had access to the lever. The demonstrator cat (if any) was removed, the 30 additional observation trials were bypassed, and the kitten was tested alone. Three M kittens and three S kittens achieved criterion performance in this way.

The M kittens acquired the lever-pressing response faster (median of 4.5 days) than did S kittens (median of 18.0 days) (Fig. 1). One M kitten performed the response at criterion on the first day after observing 29 demonstrator performances. A second M kitten spontaneously performed the response at criterion on the second day, after having observed 16 demonstrator performances on the first day. Two S kittens never acquired the response. No TE kitten ever acquired the response. Once lever pressing was achieved, M kittens brought it under stimulus control within a median of 3.5 days as compared to 14.0 days for S kittens. The M kittens never fell below acquisition criterion once it was reached; two of the four S kittens did so briefly before they discriminated the response.

Kittens acquire and discriminate a lever-pressing response more rapidly and efficiently by observing their mothers than by observing a strange female or by a trial and error procedure. Such rapid learning on the part of M kittens, occurring with relatively little prior reinforcement or practice, suggests that some unique representational process is operative during their observation period. However, it is likely that a representational process also exists in S kittens. Despite the variable rate with which M and S kittens acquired the response, if and when the response appeared, it was accompanied and defined by specific and identical behavior in all kittens: (i) Both M and S kittens made their initial lever presses at criterion with a directness, sureness, and minimum latency indicative of informationally motivated behavior. For example, the average latency of the first

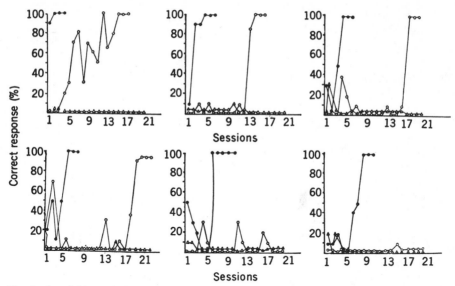

Fig. 1. Acquisition of an approach response (lever press) by observation learning in 18 kittens. Solid circles, kittens who observed their mothers (M kittens); open circles, kittens who observed strangers (S kittens); triangles, trial and error (TE) kittens.

lever press made on the first day of response acquisition was 3.5 seconds for both M and S kittens. (ii) Both M and S kittens were similarly attentive—in terms of body orientation and eye movements —to those demonstrator performances that directly preceded their own response acquisition. (iii) With one exception, both M and S kittens had a characteristically sharp response-acquisition curve (Fig. 1). All observing kittens acquiring the response moved from lever pressing at or below 50 percent to lever pressing at 90 percent or criterion as a step function. Thus, whereas the speed, efficiency, and success of response acquisition and discrimination were influenced by whether the kitten observed his mother or a strange female, when the response appeared it was invariably accompanied by the above behavior.

The mother may function as a more effective demonstrator for several reasons. These include her having nursed the kittens, having provided contact proximity, having some kind of maternal "teaching instinct" (5), providing a still lactating and therefore stimulating or arousing presence during the observation period (6), and providing a familiar and therefore rewarding or relaxing presence during the observation period. All or any combination of the above might constitute a social or affective bond that enhances learning by observation.

Perhaps response acquisition depends on the existence of or, in the case of S kittens, on the eventual formation of an affective or social bond with the demonstrator. In fact, both M and S kittens displayed what are considered friendly relations (7) with the demonstrator cat. Both mothers and strangers were generally nonaggressive toward the kittens, licked them, and exhibited "altruistic" behavior by pressing the lever and either sharing or allowing the kitten to eat the entire reward. Also, whereas M kittens observed a mean of 16 demonstrator performances on the first day, as compared with a mean of 7 for the S kittens, this initial difference in attentiveness disappeared by the second day, when M kittens observed a mean of 18 demonstrator performances and S kittens a mean of 16. This suggests that any distraction caused by the strange demonstrator's presence was quickly reduced or eliminated.

In conclusion, these data show that a mother cat may function as an important vehicle for information transmission, via observation. Perhaps the suggested primacy of learning by observation in the adult cat (8) and in other mammals (9), as opposed to trial and error learning or operant conditioning, stems from the particular social and biological responses developed in the infant by a period of mother-dependence (10).

PHYLLIS CHESLER

Brain Research Laboratory, New York Medical College, New York and
Department of Psychology,
Richmond College, City University
of New York, Staten Island 10301

References and Notes

1. R. G. Burton, *The Book of the Tiger* (Hutchinson, London, 1933); R. F. Ewer, *Nature* **222**, 698 (1969); R. F. Ewer, *Z. Tierpsychol.* **20**, 570 (1963); K. R. C. Hall, *Brit. J. Psychol.* **54 (3)**, 201 (1963); K. Imanishi, *Psychologia* **1**, 47 (1957); P. Leyhausen, *Z. Tierpsychol. Beineft,* 2, (1956); H. L. Rheingold, Ed., *The Maternal Behavior of Mammals* (Wiley, New York, 1963); G. B. Schaller, *The Deer and the Tiger* (Univ. of Chicago Press, 1967); T. C. Schneirla, J. S. Rosenblatt, E. Tobach, in *The Maternal Behavior of Mammals,* H. Rheingold, Ed. (Wiley, New York, 1963); E. F. V. Wells, *Lions, Wild and Friendly* (Viking Press, New York, 1934); C. Wilson and E. Weston, *The Cats of Wildcat Hill* (Duell, Sloan and Pearce, New York, 1947).
2. Z. Y. Kuo, *J. Comp. Psychol.* **11**, 1 (1930); *ibid.* **25**, 1 (1938); see also K. R. C. Hall *(1)* and K. Imanishi *(1)*.
3. E. J. Corner, *Proc. Roy. Inst.* **36**, 1 (1955); H. W. Nissen and M. P. Crawford, *J. Comp. Physiol. Psychol.* **22**, 283 (1936).
4. E. R. John, P. Chesler, I. Victor, F. Bartlett, *Science* **159**, 1489 (1968).
5. R. F. Ewer, *Nature* **222**, 698 (1969).
6. One of the mothers responded to nursing attempts by her kittens by walking away or by cuffing them. She continued to press the lever, indifferent to the kitten's meowing.
7. H. Winslow, *J. Comp. Psychol.* **37**, 297 (1944).
8. H. A. Adler, *J. Genetic Psychol.* **86**, 159 (1955); M. J. Herbert and C. M. Harsh, *J. Comp. Psychol.* **37**, 81 (1944); see also E. R. John *et al.* (4).
9. A. L. Bandura, in *Nebraska Symposium on Motivation,* M. R. Jones, Ed. (Univ. of Nebraska Press, Lincoln, 1962); ———, in *Advances in Experimental Social Psychology,* S. Berkowitz, Ed. (Academic Press, New York, 1965), vol. 2; J. A. Corson, *Psychon. Sci.* **7**, 197 (1967); M. P. Crawford and K. W. Spence, *J. Comp. Psychol.* **27**, 133 (1939); K. K. Hayes and C. Hayes, *J. Comp. Physiol. Psychol.* **45**, 450 (1952); W. N. Kellogg and L. A. Kellogg, *The Ape and the Child* (Hafner, New York, 1967 reprint of the 1933 edition); D. Mainardi and A. Pasquali, *Soc. Ital. Sci. Natur. Milan.* **107**, 2 (1968); C. J. Warden and T. A. Jackson, *J. Genet. Psychol.* **46**, 103 (1935); C. J. Warden, H. A. Fjeld, A. M. Koch, *ibid.* **56**, 311 (1940).
10. K. R. C. Hall, *Brit. J. Psychol.* **54 (3)**, 201 (1963).
11. I thank E. R. John, A. Rabe, N. Chesler, N. Jody, F. Burgio, and P. Walker for their assistance. Supported by PHS grant MH 08579 and by the New School for Social Research.

30 June 1969; revised 10 September 1969

53 Illness-Induced Aversions in Rat and Quail: Relative Salience of Visual and Gustatory Cues

Abstract. *Bobwhite quail, like the rat, learn in one trial to avoid flavored water when illness is induced by a drug ½ hour after drinking. In contrast to the rat, quail also learn to avoid water that is merely darkened by vegetable dye. The visual cue is even more salient than the taste cue in quail.*

Earlier work on illness-induced aversions to eating and drinking shows rather clearly that the rat, at least, must have either a gustatory or an olfactory cue in order to learn to avoid ingesting a substance if the illness that follows ingestion is delayed by ½ hour or more. Visual, auditory, and tactual cues, even though conspicuously present at the time of ingestion, do not become danger signals for the rat in such circumstances (*1, 2*). On the other hand, blue jays (*Cyanocitta cristata bromia* Oberholser, Corvidae) easily learn to reject toxic monarch butterflies (*Danaus plexippus* L., subfamily Danainae) on sight, although the model suggested for this learning gives emetic reinstatement of taste during illness a prominent, mediating role (*3*).

Impetus for our experiments came from the general view that the behavior of an organism, including what it can and cannot readily learn, is largely a product of its evolutionary history. In view of the rat's highly developed chemical senses, nocturnal feeding habits, and relatively poor vision, its ability to learn to avoid toxic substances on the basis of their taste or smell, rather than their appearance, is not surprising. But how general is this phenomenon across species? Might we not expect a diurnal bird, with its superior visual equipment and greater reliance upon vision in foraging for food and drink, to show a different pattern? Perhaps such birds, even in situations involving long delay between the time of ingestion of some food and the onset of illness, can learn to avoid ingesting substances that are distinctive in appearance only.

We report here two experiments which show that bobwhite quail (*Colinus virginianus*) can associate a purely visual cue with a long-delayed, illness consequence. In the first experiment we investigated the relative salience of a visual cue and a gustatory cue in both rats and quail. In the second experiment, in which we used quail only, we controlled for two variables which, unless accounted for, would not have allowed clear-cut interpretation of the first experiment.

Forty 90-day-old male Sprague-Dawley rats and 40 adult male bobwhite quail were subjects (*4*) in the first experiment. All were caged individually and had free access to food throughout the experiment. At the start, both species were trained over a period of several days to drink all of their daily water from 30-ml glass Richter tubes. Water was presented at the same time each day, and the time allowed for drinking was gradually reduced to a 10-minute period. Baseline drinking was then measured for 1 week, after which experimental treatments were imposed.

On treatment day, subgroups of each

species received an initial 10-minute exposure to water that was either dark blue ($N = 8$), sour ($N = 8$), or both blue and sour ($N = 24$). Water was made blue by the addition of three drops of vegetable food coloring to 100 ml of water. Sour water consisted of a weak hydrochloric acid solution (0.5 ml per liter). One-half hour after removal of the distinctive fluid all subjects were injected intraperitoneally with the illness-inducing drug, cyclophosphamide. The dosage for the rats was 66 mg/kg, a dosage known to be effective for establishing one-trial aversions to distinctive tastes in the rat. We used a larger dose (132 mg/kg) for the quail, however, because exploratory use of the drug with the birds showed that the larger dose was necessary in order to produce the primary symptom of illness that rats exhibit, namely, extensive diarrhea.

For 2 days after treatment all subjects drank plain water at the regular 10-minute daily drinking period. This allowed them time to recover from the illness, as evidenced by remission of diarrhea and a return to baseline amounts of water consumption. Extinction tests were then begun to determine whether aversive conditioning had been established to the cues present in the water on treatment day. Five 10-minute tests were conducted, one every third day, with 2 days intervening between tests during which subjects were allowed to drink plain water to re-establish the baseline.

Animals that drank sour water on treatment day were tested with sour water (S : S); those that drank blue water on treatment day received blue water in the extinction tests (B : B). However, the 24 animals of each species that had drunk blue-sour water on treatment day were divided into three subgroups for testing. One group of each species was tested on blue-sour water (BS : BS), another on sour water (BS : S), and the third on blue water (BS : B).

Figure 1 shows a comparison of the amount of water drunk by rats and quail over five extinction trials for each of the five treatment : test conditions. Differences between mean drinking scores on treatment day and the first extinction trial (E_1) were assessed for statistical significance by the t-test. Results in the S : S condition show that the sour taste by itself was an effective cue for avoidance in both rat ($P < .02$) and quail ($P < .05$). Only the quail, however, showed reduced drinking ($P < .01$) of water that was colored blue on treatment and test days (B : B). In the BS : BS condition, both species again showed significantly reduced drinking in the tests ($P < .001$).

Perhaps the most striking results were shown by the last two subgroups for which the compound cue (BS) of the treatment day conditioning trial was split for separate testing of each component. In the latter two conditions (BS : S and BS : B) rats and quail showed a remarkable difference with respect to the salience of gustatory and visual cues. When the sour element of the compound conditioning stimulus was the test cue (BS : S), rats avoided it ($P < .001$) but quail did not. On the other hand, when the blue color was the element tested (BS : B), quail avoided it ($P < .01$) but rats did not. The behavior of the quail in these split-cue tests is especially informative. Although the quail learned the aversion to taste alone (S : S condition), removal of the visual element from the compound conditioning stimulus (BS : S condition) apparently constituted such a radical change in stimulus for them that it rendered the remaining taste element ineffective. The results demonstrate, therefore, not only that quail can associate a visual cue with long-delayed illness, but also that a visual cue can be so salient as to overshadow

Fig. 1. Comparison of the amount of water consumed by quail (solid lines) and rats (dashed lines) expressed as a ratio of the amount consumed on a given day to the amount consumed on treatment day (TD); E_1 through E_5 are the five extinction trials given at 3-day intervals after the single conditioning trial on TD. (A) Group S : S; (B) group B : B; (C) group BS : BS; (D) group BS : S; (E) group BS : B.

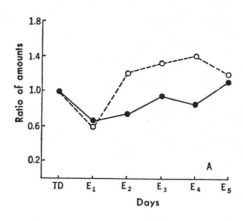

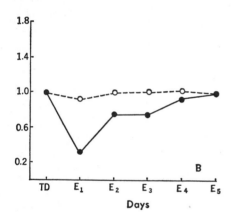

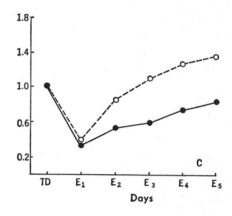

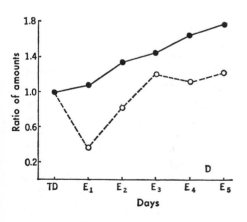

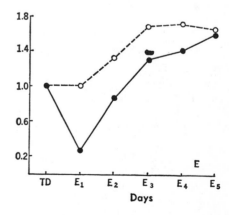

Table 1. Means and standard deviations (S.D.) of drinking scores in all groups of both experiments from the last baseline day through the first extinction test (E_1). Probabilities (P) of differences between means of the treatment day (TD) and E_1 were calculated by the t-test for repeated measures.

Group	N	Last baseline day		TD		First recovery day		Second recovery day		E_1		P
		Mean (ml)	S.D.	Mean (ml)	S.D.	Mean (ml)	S.D.	Mean (ml)	S.D.	Mean (ml)	S.D.	
					Experiment 1							
S : S quail	8	12.9	3.16	9.1	3.24	9.8	4.49	12.6	3.75	6.0	3.77	< .05
S : S rat	8	17.8	4.60	10.6	2.31	17.6	2.04	19.0	3.16	6.2	3.99	< .02
B : B quail	8	12.4	2.52	14.1	2.83	9.5	4.50	11.4	1.90	5.1	3.66	< .01
B : B rat	8	17.4	2.71	19.6	3.70	13.1	2.60	17.6	2.27	18.1	3.71	
BS : BS quail	8	13.0	1.80	6.8	2.49	12.2	3.03	13.0	2.35	2.2	2.68	< .001
BS : BS rat	8	20.4	2.30	13.1	2.29	15.9	3.38	19.4	3.09	5.0	2.92	< .001
BS : S quail	8	13.2	3.07	6.6	3.03	13.2	4.81	12.2	2.59	7.1	3.61	
BS : S rat	8	17.9	2.90	12.0	2.24	17.6	2.53	17.8	2.17	4.5	2.96	< .001
BS : B quail	8	11.5	2.55	8.8	3.19	11.8	3.70	11.9	2.06	2.2	3.19	< .001
BS : B rat	8	18.5	3.08	12.2	3.73	15.9	1.93	17.5	2.96	12.2	4.35	
					Experiment 2, quail only (tinted tube)							
Drug-treated	20	14.1	2.61	13.2	3.58	9.5	3.24	11.4	3.44	7.0	3.63	< .001
Saline-treated	20	13.3	2.86	13.5	3.98	13.0	3.87	13.5	3.30	12.5	3.10	

taste when the two cues are compounded.

The most important result of this experiment is that quail were somehow able to associate blue water with a subsequent illness which we induced arbitrarily ½ hour after removal of the drinking tube. Failure of the rats used in our experiments to do so does not, of course, constitute a powerful argument that this species cannot associate a visual cue over a long delay. It is conceivable, although we think it unlikely, that rats see no difference between plain and dark blue water. In any event, Garcia and his co-workers (1) have reported much more convincing evidence than ours that rats do not utilize a visual cue in delayed-illness avoidance learning. Thus, our main concern after the first experiment was whether the results for quail were unequivocal, rather than whether rats could actually see our visual cue.

In the second experiment we attempted to answer two questions: (i) Could the quail have been relying on some subtle taste of the dyed water rather than solely upon its appearance?; and (ii) Was the effective consequence that produced aversion to blue water really the drug-induced illness, or was it the considerable trauma of being caught, handled, and injected?

Birds from each of the five earlier subgroups were assigned to one of two groups, assignment being random except for the restriction that the groups be balanced with respect to prior treatment and test conditions. Procedural details were the same as in the first experiment. On treatment day, however, both groups drank from tinted blue tubes filled with the same plain water to which they were accustomed. One group ($N = 20$) was then injected with cyclophosphamide ½ hour after drinking, whereas the other group ($N = 20$) was injected with normal saline.

Figure 2 shows the result. Birds that received the illness-inducing drug drank less from the tinted tube when they next encountered it ($P < .001$), whereas those injected with saline did not.

Although Figs. 1 and 2 give a clear picture of the relative changes in drinking occasioned by treatment-day and test conditions, they give no information on the absolute amounts ingested or the degree of variability. Accordingly, means and standard deviations are shown in Table 1 for all groups each day from the last baseline day through the first extinction test. Comparison of baseline scores with those of treatment day shows that sour water, whether blue or not, was somewhat aversive to both species at first encounter, that is, before induction of illness; blue water alone was not. The amount of plain water drunk on the

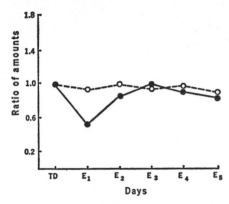

Fig. 2. A comparison of the amount of plain water drunk from tinted tubes by drug-treated quail (solid line) and saline-treated quail (dashed line). The amount drunk is expressed as a ratio of the amount ingested on a given day to the amount consumed on treatment day (TD).

two recovery days after treatment shows a return to baseline levels. Effects of the delayed-illness conditioning trial are seen best by comparing scores of treatment day with those of the first extinction test.

Despite the controls introduced in the second experiment, it could be argued that the results represent not true associative learning but only the birds' increased wariness of strange-looking fluids as a result of recent illness. However, studies now completed in our laboratory (5) show that, although such sensitization or heightened neophobia contributes to the effect, there is a significant associative learning component as well. We are confident, therefore, that at least one avian

species can associate a purely visual cue with a delayed illness without mediation by means of peripheral mechanisms such as reinstated taste.

It seems reasonable to expect that this capacity will be widespread among animals whose visual systems are highly developed and whose niches demand great reliance upon vision in foraging. If so, the implications for ecology, behavior theory, and evolutionary theory are of considerable importance.

HARDY C. WILCOXON
WILLIAM B. DRAGOIN*
PAUL A. KRAL†
Department of Psychology,
George Peabody College for Teachers,
Nashville, Tennessee 37203

References and Notes

1. J. Garcia and R. A. Koelling, *Psychonom. Sci.* 4, 123 (1966); J. Garcia, B. K. McGowan, F. R. Ervin, R. A. Koelling, *Science* 160, 794 (1968).
2. P. Rozin, *J. Comp. Physiol. Psychol.* 67, 421 (1969).
3. L. P. Brower, W. N. Ryerson, L. L. Coppinger, S. C. Glazier, *Science* 161, 1349 (1968); L. P. Brower, *Sci. Amer.* 220, 22 (Feb. 1969).
4. We thank Dr. G. McDaniel of Auburn University for supplying the quail and Dr. P. Tavormina of Mead Johnson Research Center for experimental samples of cyclophosphamide.
5. H. C. Wilcoxon, W. B. Dragoin, P. A. Kral, in preparation.
6. This research is part of the program of the John F. Kennedy Center for Research on Education and Human Development, George Peabody College for Teachers, Nashville, Tennessee, under a Biomedical Sciences Support grant from the National Institutes of Health.
* Present address: Department of Psychology, Auburn University, Auburn, Alabama 36830.
† Present address: Parsons State School and Hospital, Parsons, Kansas 67357.

2 November 1970; revised 3 December 1970

54 AVOIDANCE LEARNING IN ACTIVE AND PASSIVE FROGS AND TOADS[1]

ROBERT BOICE[2]

University of Missouri, Columbia

To test Van Bergeijk's notion that behavioral passivity in some salientians is incompatible with the arbitrary nature of shuttle-box jumping, this study compared one-way shuttle-box escape and avoidance in frogs and toads selected for differences in behavioral passivity. Markedly passive toads (*Scaphiopus hammondi*) and frogs (*Rana pipiens*) never avoided shocks. Moderately active frogs (*Rana clamitans*) showed marginal avoidance, and toads (*Bufo woodhousei*) which are active hunters in the wild showed reliable evidence of escape and avoidance learning.

Unsuccessful attempts to condition salientians may have involved an error of forcing an arbitrary response on a normally passive animal (Van Bergeijk, 1967). For example, the normally inactive leopard frog fails, eventually, to escape shock in a shuttle box (McGill, 1960). In contrast, the persistent walking gait of some species of toads should be more appropriate where arbitrary locomotion such as shuttle-box negotiation is required (Noble, 1967; Thorpe, 1956). The present study compared escape and avoidance conditioning of a one-way shuttle response in four types of frogs and toads which differ in terms of natural passivity. Two of these, the leopard frog (*Rana pipiens*) and the spadefoot toad (*Scaphiopus hammondi*) are markedly passive. The spadefoot toad is fossorial, coming out of hibernation only when rain pools are present in its environment. The third type, the green frog (*Rana clamitans*), is somewhat more active and terrestrial than the leopard frog. The fourth type, the Woodhouse's toad (*Bufo woodhousei*), is an especially active hunter for the greater part of the year.

[1] This paper was presented at the 1968 meetings of the Psychonomic Society, St. Louis. Initial phases of this research were supported by National Institute of Mental Health Grant 10316-01 to Frank A. Logan.

[2] Requests for reprints should be sent to Robert Boice, Department of Psychology, 209 McAlester Hall, University of Missouri, Columbia, Missouri 65201.

METHOD

Subjects

The *S*s were 20 adult members of each species: leopard frogs (*Rana pipiens*); spadefoot toads (*Scaphiopus hammondi*); green frogs (*Rana clamitans*); and Woodhouse's toads (*Bufo woodhousei*). All *S*s were collected from road surfaces in New Mexico and Ohio during rains, were housed in individual terraria, and were forcefed redworms weekly.

Apparatus

The shuttle box had two chambers, each 18 × 6 × 18 in., one white and one black, separated by a guillotine door. Stainless-steel grids, spaced ½-in. center to center, were connected in series of five by neon bulbs (NE 2). Shock at 100 v. dc and 200 μa. illuminated the bulbs until *S*, offering less resistance than the bulbs, contacted any two grids. Electronic timers and relay circuitry controlled the CS-US interval and ITI and measured response latency.

Procedure

Each *S* received 20 one-way trials per daily session. The intertrial interval was always 120 sec., most of which *S*s spent upon a wet towel in the safe side. Trials in the first three sessions did not include shock and were used to test for spontaneous jumps to the door (the CS). A trial began with the positioning of *S* directly facing and ½ in. away from the door. The door was then opened. In test trials, spontaneous jumps were counted during the 4 sec. following the opening of the door. If *S* had not crossed the center grid within 14 sec. following door opening, it was then placed into the safe side for the remainder of the interval.

In the 10 acquisition sessions which followed, each species group was randomly divided into experimental (*n* = 10) and control (*n* = 10) groups. If *S* in an experimental group failed to cross (avoid) to the opposite chamber within 4 sec.

after the opening of the door, shock was delivered to that chamber until S escaped. The subjects in the control group were treated identically except that they received unescapable shock in either chamber equivalent in duration to that received by a matched S in the experimental group which could escape shock. The purpose of the control procedure was to test for possible effects of shock upon unconditioned (i.e., sensitized) responding to the CS. In either case shock duration was limited to 10 sec. per trial. All groups were conterbalanced so that half of the Ss started in the white and half in the black chamber.

RESULTS AND DISCUSSION

Figure 1 depicts spontaneous jumping during test trials followed by acquisition of anticipatory jumping.

Measures of spontaneous jumps correspond with relative estimates of activity for each species obtained in natural observations of frogs and toads in experimental groups. The leopard frogs and spadefoot toads showed no avoidance responding. Escape latencies for the leopard frogs usually varied between 7–10 sec. Escape latencies, however, did not deteriorate as found by McGill (1960), perhaps because shock duration was limited to 10 sec. per trial in the present study. Escape latencies for the spadefoot toads were relatively invariant and remained at about 5 sec. over sessions.

Avoidance responding in the Woodhouse's toads was significantly more reliable than that in the green frogs ($F = 135.09$, $df = 1/18$, $p < .01$). Avoidance responding in the

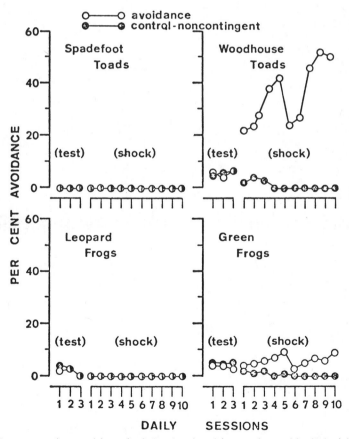

FIG. 1. Spontaneous jumps with no shock (test) and anticipatory jumps (shock) in daily sessions of 20 trials each.

green frogs was significantly higher than in the group which did not respond ($F = 29.14$, $df = 1/18$, $p < .01$) but was marginal in terms of improvement over days ($F = 1.76$, $df = 9/162$). The marked drop in avoidance responding between the fifth and sixth sessions (Figure 1) followed a 2-day break in experimentation. This decrement points out the impermanence of avoidance learning in these salientians. Similarly, Crawford and Langdon (1966) have noted that Southern toads (*Bufo terrestris*) seem to require relearning in each of daily sessions in one-way shuttle training. The Woodhouse's toads in this study showed a drop in mean latency of escape responding from over 5 sec. to less than 1 sec. in the course of each session. The subsequent reestablishment of avoidance responding in each session seems to have limited asymptotic performance to about 50% of all shocks avoided. Escape latencies in the green frogs, in contrast, typically lengthened within sessions from means of less than 2 sec. to more than 5 sec. Avoidance responses in the green frogs were apparently inhibited by tendencies to become inactive during shock late in sessions. There was no obvious effect in any group of using the black or white chamber as the safe side. The control procedure for sensitization produced noncontingent anticipatory jumping only with the Woodhouse's toads and green frogs. Sensitized responses to the door did not occur on more than 6% of session trials and were absent in later sessions (Figure 1).

The striking difference between the active and passive salientians in shuttle-box responding was not unexpected in view of general terraria behaviors. The Woodhouse's toads of this study moved frequently while the spadefoot toads were immobile except to bury themselves. Activity in the green frogs seemed to be directed at escape from their terraria, while the leopard frogs rarely moved except at objects within range of their tongues. Although phylogenetic differences in learning ability must be considered, this study supports Van Bergeijk's (1967) emphasis on using "natural" responses for meaningful study of conditioning in passive salientians. Leopard frogs will, for instance, show the development and retention of reliable feeding hierarchies (Boice & Witter, 1969).

REFERENCES

BOICE, R., & WITTER, D. W. Hierarchical feeding behavior in the leopard frog (*Rana pipiens*). *Animal Behavior*, 1969, 17, 474–479.

CRAWFORD, F. T., & LANGDON, J. W. Escape and avoidance responding in the toad. *Psychonomic Science*, 1966, 6, 115–116.

McGILL, T. E. Response of the leopard frog to electric shock in an escape learning situation. *Journal of Comparative and Physiological Psychology*, 1960, 53, 443–445.

NOBLE, G. K. *The biology of the amphibia*. New York: McGraw-Hill, 1967.

THORPE, W. H. *Learning and instinct in animals*. Cambridge: Harvard University Press, 1956.

VAN BERGEIJK, W. A. Anticipatory feeding behaviour in the bull frog (*Rana catesbeiana*). *Animal Behaviour*, 1967, 15, 231–238.

(Received January 7, 1969)

THEORETICAL NOTE

REINSTATEMENT [1]

BYRON A. CAMPBELL AND JULIAN JAYNES

Princeton University

Reinstatement is defined as periodic partial repetition of an experience such that it maintains the effects of that experience through time. This principle is demonstrated in a developmental study on the effects of early fear in rats, and is then discussed in relation to clinical and developmental theory.

In most of the phyla from arthropods to man early experience exerts a multiplicity of effects on adult behavior (Beach & Jaynes, 1954; Scott, 1962). Sometimes such effects are the simple persistence in adult behavior of habits formed early in life. In other instances it may be that early experience influences later behavior by structuring the individual's perceptual or response capacities. And in still others, there is a critical period of development during which some aspect of behavior, on which later behaviors depend, is learned and molded for life.

In this paper we suggest yet another mechanism. Although obvious and disarmingly simple, it yet seems to the authors of such neglected importance as to warrant this note and the coining of a term for it. By *reinstatement* we denote a small amount of partial practice or repetition of an experience over the developmental period which is enough to maintain an early learned response at a high level, but is not enough to produce any effect in animals which have not had the early experience. The following experiment is meant as a demonstration of this phenomenon in a commonly studied instance of learning.

METHOD

The subjects were 30 albino rats of the Wistar strain born and raised in the Prince-

[1] This research was supported in part by Public Health Service Grant M-1562 from the National Institutes of Mental Health and by National Science Foundation Grant GB 2814.

ton colony. They were divided into three groups of 10 each, with an equal number of males and females in each. The apparatus used was one commonly used in fear experiments (Campbell & Campbell, 1961). It consisted of two compartments separated by a door, a black one with a grid floor, and a white compartment with a solid metal floor. Shock could be administered to the grid of the black compartment. To two of the three groups an early fear-arousing experience was given in the black compartment. This consisted of placing the rat just after weaning, when approximately 25 days old, on the grid side of the apparatus with the door fixed so that the rat could not escape, then giving the rat 15 2-second 170-volt shocks on a 20-second variable interval schedule, taking aproximately 5 minutes, then removing the animal and placing him on the nonshock side for 5 minutes, and then repeating this entire procedure once. Thus each animal received a total of 30 shocks. At the end of this period the rat was removed and placed in a home cage. A third control group was run through this procedure without any shock being administered to the grid. During the next month a total of three shocks—the reinstatements—were given to one of the early experience groups and to the control group. These shocks were administered 7, 14, and 21 days after the original training session. The procedure was to administer, at some random number of seconds up to a minute after the animal was placed on the grid side of the apparatus, a single 2-second shock of the same intensity as before. The rat was then placed in the white compartment for an identical period of time and then returned to its home cage. On alternate weeks the animal was placed first on the nonshock side of the cage and then on the shock side, with half of the animals being placed on the shock side for the first reinstatement procedure and half on the safe side. Otherwise this procedure was precisely the same as the training procedure except that only 1 instead of 30 shocks was administered. The second pretrained group was given the same procedure except that no shock was administered. One week after the third reinstatement procedure, when the animals were 53 days of age, they were all tested for the effects of their early experience. This was done by placing them individually in the black compartment (where all of them had been shocked at one time or another) with the door removed so that the animal could run freely into the white compartment. The time spent in the white compartment over the ensuing hour was then recorded.

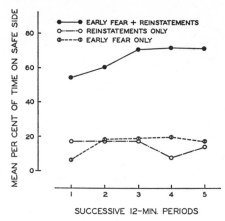

FIG. 1. The effect of reinstatement of early fear on later behavior.

RESULTS AND DISCUSSION

The results were unequivocal. As seen in Figure 1, the group that had received the early fearful experience followed by three 2-second shocks administered at weekly intervals, spent an increasing percentage of its time in the white compartment during the 1-hour test period, thus showing the effects of the early fearful experience with the black compartment. In contrast, the group that had had a similar early experience just after weaning, but no reinstatement of it in the intervening month, failed to show any significant fear of the black compartment, spending on the average all but about 10 minutes of the hour on that side. Similarly the group which had not had any early traumatic experience, but had received the three brief shocks over the month, failed to acquire any significant fear of the black compartment. The difference between the first group and the other two groups is, as it appears on the graph, highly reliable statistically ($p < .01$, Mann-Whitney U test).

There is nothing dramatically surprising about this finding. It is indeed what anyone thinking carefully about learning and practice would expect, namely, that there is some small amount of practice over certain time intervals which could maintain a previously learned response and yet not be enough to train naïve animals to perform that response. The possibility that this mechanism of reinstatement has wide and important applicability in the ontogeny of behavior in many vertebrate species seems beyond question.

In theoretical analyses of human growth and development traumatic events in infancy and childhood have long occupied a central, if controversial, role. In Freud's early analyses, traumatic events in childhood were considered a major cause of adult behavior disorders. With time, this view was gradually modified such that White writing in 1956 summed up current opinion by stating:

Undoubtedly it is true that some adult neuroses have their origin in violently frightening events. . . . The theory has long since been abandoned, however, that all neuroses, or even a majority of neuroses, take their start from traumatic events [1956, p. 238].

The early trauma theory has inconsistencies with certain facts of memory and learning as well. First, on a mere phenomenological level, we know that memory becomes more and more dim the further back into our childhood we try to remember. Second, in rats, the earlier in life that a fearful experience is given the animal, the more likely it is to be forgotten in adulthood (Campbell & Campbell, 1962). Third, in chickens, the earlier in the critical period that the chick is imprinted, the more likely it is to be forgotten when the animal reaches the juvenile stages (Jaynes, 1957). This evidence seems to indicate that the organism is constantly forgetting, time or neurological maturation or perhaps other processes constantly changing the mnemonic traces of events and feelings. And all the evidence suggests that the earlier the experience has occurred, the more profound and the faster the forgetting.

In this context reinstatement is proposed as a major mechanism by which the effects of early experiences can be perpetuated and incorporated into adult personality. Following an early experience, either pleasant or unpleasant, three developments may occur. First, the experience may be gradually forgotten as described above. Second, it may be remembered and persist indefinitely if it is occasionally reinstated. The language-based cultures of human societies are particularly rich in methods of such reinstatement, including ones so simple as occasionally reminding a child of a previous event or feeling. Even the child may occasionally reinstate the experience himself under the prompting of his ethical value system. A third possibility is the active repression of the experience, and we suggest here that the repression itself —as well as the experience—may undergo either forgetting or maintenance by reinstatement in exactly the same way. Again, the language-based cultures of man contain many reinstatement-of-repression mechanisms such as parental conversational taboos, etc., which determine what repressions are maintained into adult life. In a general sense, we propose that any learned response, whether acquired in infancy or adulthood,

conscious or unconscious, instrumental or autonomic, joyful or traumatic, can be maintained at a high level by an occasional reinstatement.

Moreover, reinstatement as a principle has considerable adaptive significance, particularly in the learning of fear. Young organisms, at least after a short initial period of apparent fearlessness in some species, become highly vulnerable to the acquisition of fears. These fears have, of course, great survival value in keeping the young organism away from danger. But if they all persisted and could not be forgotten, they would imprison the animal in his own prior experience, making adult adaptive behavior impossible. It is thus essential to adult activity that most early experiences be forgotten, and that only those experiences which are periodically reinstated by a particular habitat or culture be retained.

REFERENCES

BEACH, F. A., & JAYNES, J. Effects of early experience upon the behavior of animals. *Psychological Bulletin,* 1954, **51,** 239–263.

CAMPBELL, B. A., & CAMPBELL, E. H. Retention and extinction of learned fear in infant and adult rats. *Journal of Comparative and Physiological Psychology,* 1962, **55,** 1–8.

JAYNES, J. Imprinting: The interaction of learned and innate behavior: II. The critical period. *Journal of Comparative and Physiological Psychology,* 1957, **50,** 6–7.

SCOTT, J. P. Critical periods in behavioral development. *Science,* 1962, **138,** 949–958.

WHITE, R. W. *The Abnormal Personality.* (2nd ed.) New York: The Ronald Press, 1956.

(Early publication received March 21, 1966)

PART 7 Social Behavior

Much of the animal behavior that we observe results from an individual's interaction with members of its own species. Such interactions are called "social behavior." Social behavior exists in several diverse groups of animals because it has biological adaptiveness. Thus, questions concerning the evolutionary past, and present function, of the behavior are particularly appropriate in this area. For this reason, ethologists have been interested in social behavior, and much of their research has been concerned with it. Many of the readings included in Part 7 are examples of such research.

Part 7 begins with a paper dealing with the behavior of one of the ethologist's favorite subjects: the three-spined stickleback. (Indeed, this fish has been so popular in ethological research that it has been referred to as the "three-spined rat.") This reading is an excellent illustration of ethological analysis and methods, including the use of animal models. Animals sometimes encounter situations in which opposing "drives" are simultaneously aroused. Often in such a situation an animal will perform a bit of behavior that seems irrelevant to both tendencies. These behaviors are called *displacement activities*. Wilz presents examples of displacement activities in the courtship behavior of the three-spined stickleback and discusses their role in the behavior pattern.

A *social response* has been defined as ". . . a behavioral response made by a group-living animal to another in its group but not to animals or objects which are not members of the group" (W. Etkin, *Social Behavior from Fish to Man,* University of Chicago Press, 1967, p. 4). Some of these responses are fairly specific, predictable motor-patterns that are made to the movements, calls, odor, and / or appearance of the other species member. The characteristic responded to is then called a *sign stimulus* or a *releaser.* (Similar phenomena exist between species, for example, the response of certain predators to their prey and vice versa.) Releasers have been most frequently found and studied in nonmammalian species. However, they do exist in mammals, as Grant, Mackintosh, and Lerwill report in Reading 57. In a most interesting experiment they demonstrate that enlarging the dark spot on the chest of a male golden hamster with hair dye results in that animal defeating hamsters who had previously defeated him.

Territoriality is an important aspect of social behavior in the lives of many animals. The functional advantages of holding a territory have been the subject of considerable speculation. Territoriality may act as an antipredator device; it may aid in the protection of the young; it may reduce the likelihood of the spread of disease. The spacing out of individuals by the establishment of territories may insure enough food, nest material, or space to conduct reproductive displays, or it may increase a territory-holding male's chances of successful mating. In Reading 58, Stephen Emlen describes territorial behavior in male bullfrogs. In this species, a male who holds a territory close to other territory-holding males has an increased chance of mating.

Many animals that do not establish individual territories instead develop dominance hierarchies within a group occupying a common space. As with territoriality, these hierarchies probably have different functions in different species. In Reading 59, Le Boeuf and Peterson report that male elephant seals maintain such a social system. Furthermore, they show that elephant seals high in the hierarchy engage in much more copulatory acactivity than do animals lower in status. As the authors note, such a social system may have important genetic consequences. On the positive side, most pups are being fathered by the most vigorous males. However, if the same few males continued to sire all pups season after season, the genetic variability of the population would be greatly reduced, and the species might not survive an environmental change.

In the next reading Rabb, Woolpy, and Ginsberg describe observational studies of a group of captive wolves over several breeding seasons. They report that, unlike elephant seals, the alpha male wolf (the most dominant) does not always engage in the most sexual behavior. Note also the interesting mate preferences that exist.

One of the most important recent developments in the study of animal social behavior has been the large number of field studies devoted to the behavior of primates. In Reading 61, three investigators in this area, Washburn, Jay, and Lancaster, provide a succinct review of the findings of many such studies.

Field studies are particularly important for threatened species. In Reading 62, Valerius Geist summarizes some of his observations on the North American mountain sheep. The author points out that the social behavior of this species is a major reason why their numbers are not increasing. (For more information about these interesting animals, see Geist's book, *The Mountain Sheep*, University of Chicago Press, 1971.)

Studies of the social behavior of animals assumed great importance after Darwin pointed out the continuity of animal life, including man. The structures of several different animal societies have been used as models to explain human society, as it is or as it is supposed to be. However, as observations accumulated, it became apparent that a great variety of animal societies exist. Even among nonhuman primates there are major differences from species to species. Moreover, anthropological studies have shown large differences among various human cultures. Yet, are these differences only variations on a theme? Are there underlying similarities such as territoriality, dominance relationships, and, consequently, aggressive responses? Several scientists think so and have written books, designed for the general public, in which the findings of research on animal behavior have been extrapolated to man. In our final reading, the distinguished ethologist Niko Tinbergen discusses two of these books in a paper appropriately titled "War and Peace in Animals and Man."

REPRINT No. 199 from *Animal Behaviour*, **18**, 1, February, 1970

Anim. Behav., 1970, **18**, 115–124

CAUSAL AND FUNCTIONAL ANALYSIS OF DORSAL PRICKING AND NEST ACTIVITY IN THE COURTSHIP OF THE THREE-SPINED STICKLEBACK *GASTEROSTEUS ACULEATUS*

By KENNETH J. WILZ*

University of Oxford

The courtship behaviour of the three-spined stickleback, *Gasterosteus aculeatus*, is frequently referred to in the ethological literature (Tinbergen 1951; Marler & Hamilton 1966). Normally it consists of a chain of stimulus–response events in which the male and female play alternating roles. The female appears in the territory of a nest-owning male, and, in reaction to the male's zig-zag dance, she approaches. The male responds to this by leading to the nest, and the female follows. The male then shows the nest entrance, the female enters, the male quivers on the female's tail region, and the sequence concludes with spawning and fertilization.

There are, however, several departures from this 'idealized' sequence which have received far less attention. One of these is the performance by the male of a behaviour known as dorsal pricking (ter Pelkwijk & Tinbergen 1937). This pattern consists of a somewhat jerky pushing of the female towards the water's surface with the dorsal side, often accompanied by rapid circular movements (circling). It occurs almost exclusively in response to female approach as revealed by a detailed quantitative analysis of uninterrupted male-female interactions (Wilz in prep.). In this analysis 24 per cent cent of the male responses to female approach consisted of pricking, 53 per cent of leading, and the remainder of biting. It has no obvious function, as it is clearly not the shortest possible route to successful mating. Also, careful observation revealed that the female stimulus situations releasing pricking and leading responses are identical, suggesting that the male's internal state controls whether it will occur or not. For these reasons experiments using models were designed to study the causal basis and the function in the courtship structure of the pricking response.

A second departure which often occurs is the male's performance of various activities at the nest. The incorporation of these actions, which normally function in the nest-building or parental phase of the male's reproductive cycle, has often been cited as an example of the displacement phenomenon (Tinbergen & van Iersel 1947; Sevenster 1961). There is good evidence, from the analysis of male–female sequences, that these activities do not in any manner arouse

*Present address: Department of Biology, Williams College, Williamstown, Mass.

or direct the female (see also Tinbergen & van Iersel 1947). Yet their frequency in courtship (normally occurring in response to the female's holding or waiting in the 'head-up' posture) is very striking. It was decided, therefore, to analyse these activities as they occur in sexual behaviour. As in the case of dorsal pricking, attention focussed on the causal basis of these activities and any possible function that they might serve in the sequence.

Materials and Maintenance

The sticklebacks (*Gasterosteus aculeatus*) used in this study were obtained from the streams and canals in and around Oxford. Fish were collected at almost any time of the year and stored in a cool room in large zinc baths. They were given 8 hr illumination daily. As they were required for study, individuals were transferred into large tanks under conditions of 16 hr of light and higher, but not precisely controlled temperatures. Later, as signs of aggression and nest-building activity appeared, males were transferred singly into tanks of 45×25^2 cm or $37^2 \times 60$ cm. Here they were encouraged to build nests by providing nest materials and loose sand. Both males and females were fed almost daily on a diet of *Tubifex* and *Daphnia*.

Many of the observations and experimental manipulations were made from behind a collapsible hide (122 cm^2 × 53 cm) covered with a black cloth and provided with a long narrow slit in the front. The model fish used extensively in this study were made of barbola paste, and many were kindly provided by Dr Esther Cullen. In many of the experiments an individual was used more than once. This was necessary due to the limited number of model-responding males available. The number of individuals used and the number of total cases are always stated clearly in the tables.

Experimental Methods and Results

I. Motivational Aspects of Dorsal Pricking

To measure the strength of the dorsal pricking response a model female was employed attached to the end of a taut wire connected to a short bamboo pole. This model was introduced into the male's tank and moved manually in the direction of the male (the equivalent of the live female's approach). It continued to follow the male in this manner, and the amount of time spent in pricking before the male leads the model to the nest was recorded. This 'dorsal pricking time' varies considerably, and this test, therefore, provided a useful measure of the response strength. (There is lag time of approximately one second before any male response is evoked. A few bites also occur during the test (see later), but these take up a negligible amount of time.)

To study the causal basis of this response, then, this procedure was preceded by various experimental manipulations. In the first series of tests the effect of a 10-min 'aggression test' (male in a narrow tube at a fixed distance from the nest) was compared to a control where no male was present in the tube. Each fish tested was presented with both situations twice. The tests were run in pairs in a randomized order, with each set of two tests preceded by a 10-s pricking test in order to stimulate the males sexually. (See Fig. 1(a) for a representation of the experimental design.)

Table I. The Effect of an Aggression Stimulus on Dorsal Pricking Time

Condition	N	Cases	Pricking time (median)	Significance
Aggression stimulus	8	16	41 s	
				$P<0.005$ (Wilcoxon test, 1-tailed; Siegel 1956)
Control	8	16	7 s	

The results of this experiment, presented in Table I, show that the male proceeds to lead almost immediately under the control conditions. In marked contrast to this, the aggression stimulus increases the pricking time to a median of 41 s, a very significant difference. It appears, therefore, that a high aggressive tendency (independent experiments show that the tendency to bite is increased at the conclusion of the aggression stimulus presentation; Wilz 1967) is positively correlated with dorsal pricking response strength. It should also be noted that these results can be interpreted in terms of an inhibition of leading behaviour.

In another experiment the effect of a model female presentation at a fixed distance from the nest on dorsal pricking was investigated. This model was presented for 1 min and run alternatively in a random order with a control period, where no such test was given. Each of these two situations was followed immediately by the pricking test, and the tests were spaced at intervals of 120 min. Each series of two tests was again preceded by a priming test situation (Fig. 1b).

During the 'sex test' the male performs numerous zig-zags, a number of leads, and also some nest actions. Following such a test it is known that the animal remains in a state of sexual arousal for some time as measured, for instance, by the number of 'vacuum' zig-zags performed (Sevenster 1961; Nelson 1965) or by the ease with which the show nest response can be evoked (Wilz 1967). The female model presentation, on the other hand, almost totally excludes any pricking, and the lead occurs almost at once. In contrast to this, the pricking

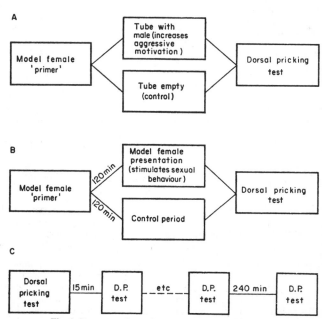

Fig. 1. Representations of the three dorsal pricking tests.

tests following the control period yield a considerable amount of dorsal pricking. These results are summarized in Table II.

Table II. The Effect of a 'Sex-test' on Dorsal Pricking Time

Condition	N	Cases	Pricking time (median)	Significance
'Sex test'	5	10	2 s	$P < 0.005$ (Wilcoxon, 1-tailed)
Control	5	10	36·5 s	

A third experiment studied the recovery of dorsal pricking time after sexual arousal. In this experiment a pricking test was performed until the male leads and shows the nest. (Fig. 1c). (It will be stated later that sometimes no lead was evoked over a 2-min period. If this occurred, and it was rare in this series, the model was caused to hold for a brief time. Leading was 'hen evoked without delay.) This constitutes the priming and no score was recorded. Fifteen minutes were then allowed to elapse, and a dorsal pricking score was then obtained. Following this another pricking test was performed after 30 min, and successive tests followed at 60 min, 120 min, and 240 min, each time measured from the end of the previous test. In this manner each successive score is preceded by a pricking test culminating in a lead and a show nest display, the pricking test here constituting the sexual stimulation since it can be shown normally to have the same qualitative effects on the male's motivational system as the 1-min presentations used in the previous experiment. (To ensure considerable sexual arousal two leads and two show nests are elicited at the conclusion of each test.) The results obtained for this experiment, using a total of nine males (and eleven total cases), are summarized in Fig. 2.

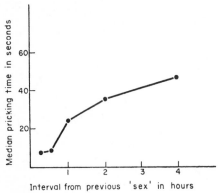

Fig. 2. The recovery of dorsal pricking time after sexual arousal.

This figure shows that with increasing intervals between tests the dorsal pricking score increased from a median of 7 s following a 15-min interval to a median of 47 s following a 240-min period of isolation. This trend was evident in all the males studied.

In this experiment it could be argued that later scores in the series might be influenced by the fact that they have been preceded by more pricking tests than the earlier ones. Since such tests (especially when followed by the elicitation of several leads and show nests) normally have the same qualitative effects on the male's motivational state as the 1-min female presentations, such an influence would have the effect of successively reducing the response strength of dorsal pricking. Figure 2, however, shows that the response strength is markedly increased with successive trials, so that any influence of a larger number of earlier tests, if there is one, must be largely overruled by the increasing time between trials. To check this interpretation a variation on the above test was designed in which alternating intervals of 15 min and 240 min were compared, the tests run in pairs preceded by a primer pricking test. Three of the males used in the previous test were the subjects, and the results (twelve total cases for each condition) showed a median pricking time of 44·5 s for the 240-min interval and a 4-s median time for the 15-min interval.

These experiments, together with others which support the results described here, demonstrate something about the motivational basis of the dorsal pricking response. It occurs in response to female approach, instead of the lead, either when the aggressive tendency has been aroused directly or when it is activated in a relative sense due to the lack of any sexual stimulation. (More bites occur following the longer inter-stimulus intervals. They are also very common during the first few seconds of a test where a female model is placed at a distance from the nest, precisely when sexual arousal would be expected to be relatively low. See Wilz 1967.) A sexual stimulus, shown to facilitate the actions zig-zag, lead, and show nest, on the other hand, eliminates dorsal pricking almost entirely,

II. The Function of Dorsal Pricking

In the experiment described above I said that pricking scores following a 10-min aggression stimulus were at a median level of 41 s. It is important to note, however, that many of the scores obtained in this and other experiments far exceed this 41 s, pricking often extending to 120 s in reaction to continuous female following. At this point, in fact, tests were broken off and labelled an 'infinity response', because tests carried beyond this point (to 180 s or more) revealed no further leads. Also, the frequency of biting (see Table III, data from males consistently performing 'infinity responses' following short periods of sexual isolation) tends to increase as the pricking test proceeds. This would seem to indicate a decreased likelihood of a lead in view of the inhibition demonstrated for the biting tendency on the lead response. Such findings indicate that, under certain conditions, the female's continuous following decreases rather than increases the likelihood of male sexual behaviour.

Consideration of such infinity responses, in fact suggests a function for the dorsal pricking display. Focusing on the results of data collected from the male-female interactions, one

Table III. The Incidence of Biting During Consecutive Minutes of a Dorsal Pricking Test

Condition	N	Cases	Mean bites	Significance
Minute 1	4	16	1·5	$P<0·01$ (Wilcoxon 2-tailed)
Minute 2	4	16	6·0	

finds that the pricking in the vast majority of cases quickly and efficiently induces the female to adopt a holding or waiting posture. To show this and other effects the sequence of events was recorded on a tape recorder as an alternation of behavioural events between partners, the records consisting of a succession of male–female–male–female . . . behaviour patterns. With results collected in this manner, one can demonstrate the effect that a male dorsal prick has in inducing a female to switch from approaching to waiting. This is shown in the following transition table where the probability of female waiting is computed, given the approach-pricking sequence:

Female approach–male prick–female wait = 67/112 = 0·60

Thus, in 60 per cent of cases the female immediately readopts the waiting postures. This is strikingly different from the effect that a lead or a bite has on an approaching female, where following to the nest and fleeing respectively are much more common (Wilz 1967). In addition, in 36 per cent of cases the female continues to approach in reaction to an initial dorsal pricking stimulus. If the female does continue to approach however, the male is very likely to renew pricking, and the female is then commonly persuaded to adopt a waiting posture. These points are illustrated in the following tables, calculated as before:

Male prick–female continued approach–male prick = 49/66 = 0·74

Female continued approach–male prick–female wait = 48/75 = 0·64

Dorsal pricking, then, effectively induces the female's switch from approaching to waiting. In all, of the 112 recorded approaches followed by the pricking response 97 (87 per cent) result in the female's readoption of the waiting posture.

This waiting by the female permits a temporary separation of the partners. I considered, therefore, that, when aggressive motivation is high, the temporary separation of the fish achieved by dorsal pricking facilitates the male's switch to a greater sexual motivation, thereby permitting such sexual behaviours as leading and showing the nest to occur freely. The severity of aggressive encounters between territorial males under natural conditions is known to be great (van den Assem 1967) and it has been shown experimentally that this highly aggressive state can seriously inhibit the zig-zag dance and the showing display as well as the lead (Wilz 1967; Sevenster 1961). On the other hand, the sudden approach of a female is a relatively rare event, and adjustment in motivation would be required for the male to respond appropriately. This shift is critical to the success of the courtship, and any mechanism that encourages this transition would be of considerable advantage.

This hypothesis was subsequently tested. Results on five males produced ten infinity responses (that is, no lead) when the male's pricking to a model did not have its usual effect of inducing the female to wait. Characteristically, the males became more aggressive toward the end of a test, and, when the female model finally did wait, the males often continued to bite and it was some time before sexual responses could be released. In contrast, in cases where the female was caused to wait in response to the initial dorsal prick, a short separation occurred, and ten leads were induced upon the male's return to the female. This whole procedure took only a mean time of 28·0 s measured from the initiation of the female's first approach. These tests were run 12 hr apart, randomized, and each pair of tests was preceded by 12 hr by a 'priming' 10-s dorsal pricking test. It is thus clear that the male's sexual behaviour is considerably facilitated by this short period of separation.

III. The Role of the 'Displacement Activities'

During this brief 'breathing space' achieved through dorsal pricking it was noted, both in model experiments and in the interactions involving live females, that the male almost invariably performs certain activities at the nest, the so-called 'displacement actions'. It seemed possible, therefore, that these activities are themselves implicated in achieving the motivational shift (from an aggressive to a sexually responsive state). Indeed, qualitative observations in pilot tests suggested that the shift in motivation is not so much correlated with the duration of the separation of the partners, but with the completion of the nest activities. I decided, therefore, to study these actions in some detail in order to determine their role in the present context.

The first stage in this analysis was to examine the frequency and patterning of male courtship, including all the nest activities and biting, in reaction to a model female placed in a waiting posture at a distance of 40 cm from the nest site. Such experimental situations commonly release, of course, the zig-zag dance (recorded in bouts), the lead response (more rarely), and biting. Of the nest activities the fanning action, the subject of Sevenster's (1961) detailed study, is the most common. This behaviour normally functions in the parental phase to aerate the eggs, but, of course, no eggs are present at this time. Creeping through (CT) the nest (Nelson 1965) also occurs. This action is performed toward the end of the nest-building phase to create a nest tunnel and also occurs following the female's spawning, when sperm are released to fertilize the eggs. Other actions which occur include gluing, a secreting of a kidney substance over the nest which binds the nest together, bringing of material, pushing at the nest structure, and boring into the nest entrance. All these latter actions occur in the nest-building phase of the reproductive cycle.

Pattern analysis of these activities reveals that two of the nest activities, creeping through and fanning (usually preceded by a bore and followed by a glue and defined as including them, if they occur), are of particular interest because their occurrence is commonly preceded by a high biting frequency and a relatively low level of zig-zag and lead and followed by relatively little biting and high levels of zig-zag and lead. This is precisely the shift a male must undergo when confronted with a suddenly approaching female. Creeping through and fanning are, it is important to point out, the two behaviours which occur most frequently during a nest visit following dorsal pricking performance.

To show these shifting effects each behavioural action is treated as one unit of the sequence, and an equal number of units (ten in this case) preceding and following a fanning bout complex, or a creeping through, is compared. Results treated in this manner for creeping through are shown in Table IV. The figures quoted are an expression of percentage total units, and the results are based on data from ten males (and eighty-one total cases).

Table IV. The Relative Frequencies of Behaviours Preceding and Following Creeping Through

	Preceding creep through (% total units)	Following creep through (% total units)
Bite	0·27	0·08
Zig-zag	0·30	0·47
Lead	0·08	0·16

These results, all the differences being highly significant (Wilcoxon), clearly show that there is a marked switch in relative frequency from bite to zig-zag and lead when the activity creeping through is interposed. It is also noteworthy that the fanning frequency decreases substantially following creeping through (Table V with 81 total cases; see also Sevenster 1961; Nelson 1965). As shown in Table V, not only does the frequency of fanning per ten units

Table V. Measures of Fanning Preceding and Following Creeping Through

	Preceding creep through	Following creep through
Total fanning bouts	81	34
Fanning (s) /bout	6·2	2·6
Fanning bout/nest visit	0·90	0·27

diminish substantially, but also the mean bout length and the probability of fanning given a nest visit.

A similar switch in relative frequency from biting to zig-zag and leading occurs around a fanning bout. The effect is particularly striking if fanning bouts of longer duration (more than 3 s) are analysed.

It is clear, therefore, that creeping through and fanning, the two nest actions which very commonly occur immediately after dorsal pricking, are closely correlated with a transition resulting in a change in the internal situation favourable to courtship. The more interesting question, whether or not the performance of these two nest actions is in some way causally involved in the motivational switch, remain open for further experimentation. The abruptness of the changes which occur is already suggestive, however.

Both Tinbergen (1952) and Nelson (1965) have previously argued that fanning and/or creeping through probably play a causal role, though without linking the phenomenon to dorsal pricking and without direct experimental evidence. Tinbergen of course suggested that 'displacement activities' widely serve a function of motivational catharsis. Since then, however, the physiological model with which he and other ethologists of that time were working has been extensively criticized, and the suggestion has been largely abandoned (Zeigler 1964). More recently, however, Nelson (1965), without any underlying physiological assumptions, has revived interest in the possibility by suggesting that the performance of creeping through, in its non-fertilization context, can markedly influence the behaviour that follows it. He states: 'In the past, creeping through has usually been regarded as an indication rather than a cause of changes in motivation (Sevenster 1961; Sevenster-Bol 1962). The implication has been that the shift to a more sexual state, as measured by zig-zag, which is found to occur at creeping through would also occur in its absence. However, the very abruptness of the changes accompanying creeping through reinforces the impression that its role in those changes is a causal one.'

I decided, therefore, as a next step in the analysis, to perform an experiment based on qualitative observations made during the course of the previous work. If a male's creeping through is blocked, or even partially prevented, by, for instance, a hardening of the sand in the nest area, the male does not undergo, in the course of the courtship, the transition to a more sexual behaviour expected under conditions where the creeping through is successful. In a series of tests, therefore, the nest tunnel was blocked artificially on alternate trials, and the male's behaviour towards a model female following this was compared to that when creeping through was permitted. When blocking the nest passage care had to be taken to disturb the male's normal behaviour as little as possible. A bent, cryptic wire was placed perpendicular to the line of the tunnel in such a way that the male, able to bore but not to creep through, was not able to perceive any strange object in the nest area.

The procedure was to perform a dorsal pricking test once every 2 hr, removing the model immediately afterwards. In this circumstance the male almost invariably attempts to creep through during the next 2 min. This is either blocked in the manner described, or permitted. A model female was then introduced immediately at the standard distance from the nest and the male's behaviour to this model recorded over a 3-min period. Tests were, of course, fully randomized and run in pairs with a 'primer' as before.

The results are consistent with the hypothesis that creeping through has a causal role. In cases where creeping through is permitted, biting is relatively low in frequency and the zig-zag and lead responses very high. Under conditions where the creeping through is blocked, however, biting remains high and zig-zag and lead relatively low. Also, in accordance with the previous results for creeping through, fanning is almost totally absent when creeping through is allowed, whereas it remains high in the other cases. These differences are all significant ($P < 0.025$, Wilcoxon, 1-tailed) and are summarized in Table VI from data on two males (12 cases). It should further be reported that, under conditions where creeping through is blocked, neither additional attempts at creeping through during the test by the male nor abnormal manipulations of the nest structure were observed.

Table VI. The Effect of Creeping Through Prevention on Behaviour

| | Behaviour after creep through attempt | |
	CT blocked	CT permitted
Mean bites	5·0	2·7
Mean zig-zag bouts	13·6	24·5
Mean leads	2·1	8·7
Mean fanning time (s)	31·5	7·3

These findings, therefore, argue that the switch that normally occurs around creeping through cannot take place in its absence and that creeping through is something more than a mere by-product of an underlying motivational change. A further discussion of this critical consideration, however, will be left until two further experiments, consistent with these results and involving less artificial manipulation, are reported.

In the next experiment a similar approach was used except that attempts were made to emulate more closely the dorsal pricking situation itself and to prevent the performance of either fanning or creeping through. More precisely the procedure was, following a 10-min aggression stimulus presentation, to elicit pricking in the usual manner and to cause the model female to wait for 10 s away from the nest site, which is the normal response of the female to dorsal pricking. The male then, as explained earlier, proceeds almost immediately to the nest. Under the control conditions he performs either a long fanning bout, usually followed by a glue, or, more rarely, a creeping through. In the other half of the trials, however, this fanning or creeping through was prevented by placing a small transparent beaker over the nest site immediately before the test began. In both situations 30 s was then allowed to elapse. Towards the middle or end of this period the male, having performed activity at the nest or having had this blocked by the beaker, returned to the female and the model was made to initiate a second approach. (If in either case the male was still at the nest at the end of the 30 s, possibly as a result of a second nest visit, the female was manipulated slightly in order to attract the male away from the nest.) The dorsal pricking time was then recorded and compared under the two test situations. Tests were again run in sets of two, randomized and each set was preceded by a primer.

In this manner the role of the fanning complex and creeping through can be studied with a minimum disruption of the normal courtship structure. Another advantage of the test is that the male has the same opportunity for stimulus separation from the female and thus the role of the disengagement of partners and that of the performance of nest activities can be distinguished. Finally, in the control series a glass beaker was always placed along one side of the nest structure. By doing this the male in both the control and the experimental situation returns to the nest to find a novel object in the nest area, and it would thus seem unlikely that some feedback of 'nest unsuitable' could have produced the effects shown. (Or at least, if such a stimulus situation were preventing the switch from occurring one would expect some reduction in ability to undergo the motivational transition when the beaker is placed along one side of the nest entrance. However, no difference between this procedure and tests where the nest area was left completely open were ever detected). Also, any fear the object might evoke is controlled for, although there was never any evidence of fearful behaviour.

The results of this experiment are clear. If fanning and creeping through occur, the male leads the female to the nest. The lead could be evoked as soon as the fanning complex or creeping through was completed and rarely required 30 s. On the other hand, if free access to the nest entrance was prevented (in which case fanning and creeping through do not occur and the male's 30 s are occupied by attempts to reach the entrance and by the performance of circling, biting, and zig-zagging, as well as no response) the male's tested were seen to perform bouts of dorsal pricking exceeding 2 min in all but one of the trials made (when leading followed some additional pricking). The results are summarized in Table VII.

Table VII. The Effect of 'Displacement Activity' Blockage on Pricking Time. Entrance Blocked by Transparent Glass				
Condition	N	Cases	Pricking time (median)	Significance
Fanning—CT prevented	4	8	>120 s	
				$P<0.005$ (Wilcoxon 1-tailed)
Fanning—CT permitted	4	8	1 s	

Table VIII. The Effect of 'Displacement Activity' Blockage on Pricking Time. Entrance Blocked by Model Female				
Condition	N	Cases	Pricking time (median)	Significance
Fanning—CT prevented	6	12	>120 s	
				$P<0.005$ (Wilcoxon 1-tailed)
Fanning—CT permitted	6	12	1 s	

Finally, a variation on the above experiment was designed in order to eliminate the need of disturbing the nest site in any way. In this series, the same procedure was used as before with one important exception. Following the 10 s of dorsal pricking the female took up one of two positions with respect to the nest. In one case the model was placed on top of the nest structure. In this situation the male goes to the nest to fan or creep through (again, more rarely) during the 30-s interval. In the other trials, in contrast, the female was placed at the nest entrance itself, effectively presenting a show nest stimulus situation to the male. Under those circumstances fanning and creeping through at the nest entrance are prevented by the presence of the female and no response, zig-zag, bite, and circle occur instead. At the end of the 30-s interval in both cases the female was moved vertically above the nest structure and caused to approach the male a second time, the male by now being away from the nest site in both experimental situations. The dorsal pricking time was then recorded and compared under the two situations.

Thus, in this experiment the nest activities were again prevented and compared with a control. With this design, however, no manipulation of the nest structure or introduction of objects other than the female were necessary. Additionally, the nest structure, though blocked for the positioning required for fanning and creeping through, was plainly visible and the male obtained as much information about the state of the nest as by performing a fanning bout followed by a glue. A similar disengagement of the partners was also possible in both the experimental condition and the control. Finally, by positioning the female at the nest entrance in half the cases, one might expect that this would have a greater sexually stimulating effect on the male, since this is the nest stage in the courtship sequence. The results (Table VIII), however, based on comparisons in six males, reveal that the opposite is true.

These findings are similar to those obtained in the previous experiments. The male, having crept through or performed the fanning complex, leads the female to the nest immediately in all twelve cases. Again, the full 30 s are rarely required. When the nest activities are prevented by the presence of the female, however, some further pricking is present in all cases and the majority exceed 120 s.

Discussion

The observations reported in this paper suggest that the activities creeping through and fanning, found commonly in male courtship and referred to as 'displacement activities', play a valuable role in adjusting the male's motivation. Usually thought of as an indicator of motivational balance and transition, an epiphenomenon of internal events, it now seems that these activities are instrumental in effecting a motivational switch to a state favourable to sexual activity. Their role in producing the changes in behaviour which follow, so vital to courtship success, is thus seen as a causal one.

A function for the dorsal pricking response is thus indicated. When the sexual responses are under a certain degree of inhibition, dorsal pricking serves as a temporary discouragement to an approaching female, preventing any possibility of further activation of the aggressive tendency. More important, however, the separation achieved by the pricking allows the male an opportunity to perform activities at the nest which are directly involved in effecting a shift in internal states. These could not have occurred had the females been at the nest entrance, since her presence there would have prevented their occurrence much as the model does. Following the performance of such activities the male returns to his prospective mate and courts effectively.

The findings outlined here raise a number of points that require further investigation. Tinbergen (1954) has argued that a major function of animal courtship is 'to suppress non-sexual responses in the partner'. It appears now that this statement must be interpreted more broadly to include not only the suppression of such tendencies in the mate, but the suppression of conflicting tendencies in the performer as well. Disruptive tendencies may appear as overt behaviour, or, at sub-threshold, they may inhibit the expression of appropriate behaviour in the individual courting. This self-regulation of motivation is similar to Chance's (1962) concept of 'cut-off', as applied to certain agonistic and courtship displays. Chance argues that such displays at least provide for a greater flexibility of behaviour or for an actual change from one type of motivation to another. This approach has yet to receive adequate experimental attention. Yet it may prove to be an important function of certain agonistic and courtship displays.

Also, the experimental analysis of the nest activities raises a number of points related to the general problems of motivational theory and the 'displacement activity'. It reawakens interest in both the causal and functional aspects of displacement activities (see also Delius 1967). This is not to claim, however, that all displacement activities have such an apparent function. It has been pointed out many times recently that the category 'displacement activity' is a heterogeneous one (Hinde 1966).

This consideration of function, in turn, indicates certain limitations of the disinhibition hypothesis (Sevenster 1961; Zeigler 1964) as a causal explanation for certain displacement-like actions. Other findings related to the male stickleback's nest activities are also difficult to interpret under the disinhibition hypothesis (Wilz, in prep.).

Summary
The causal and functional aspects of a display known as dorsal pricking performed during the courtship of the three-spined stickleback (*Gasterosteus aculeatus*) were examined. This behaviour, a somewhat jerky pushing of the female with the dorsal side, is sometimes incorporated as a reaction to female approach in place of the leading to the nest action. In experiments using models it was found that pricking is incorporated when aggressive motivation is relatively high. Further studies demonstrated that, by inducing the female to cease following, the dorsal pricking display functions to facilitate the male's switch from high aggression to a greater sexual motivation. It seems, therefore, to be a mechanism for self-adjustment of motivation.

During the brief separation of male and female induced by the pricking the male performs 'displacement' nest activities. These actions, therefore, were studied in detail in order to determine whether their performance plays a causal role in the switch from high aggression to a state conducive to sexual behaviour. A series of experiments demonstrated that the performance of certain nest activities directly affects the adjustment that occurs.

Acknowledgments
I wish to thank Professor J. W. S. Pringle, F.R.S., for agreeing to accommodate me in the Zoology Department, Oxford University, and the Professor of Animal Behaviour, Dr N. Tinbergen, F.R.S. for giving me the opportunity of working in the animal behaviour unit.

Dr J. M. Cullen supervised this D.Phil. research and read this manuscript in its original form, and my most sincere thanks are extended to him. I am also grateful to the many other people who have shown an interest in the development of this research.

REFERENCES
Assem, J. van den (1967). Territory in the three-spined stickleback. *Behaviour*, Suppl. XVI.
Chance, M. R. A. (1962). An interpretation of some agonistic postures; the role of 'cut-off' acts and postures. *Symp. zool. Soc. Lond.*, **8**, 71–89.
Delius, J. D. (1967). Displacement activities and arousal. *Nature, Lond.*, **214**, 1259–1260.
Hinde, R. A. (1966). *Animal Behaviour*. New York: McGraw-Hill.
Marler, P. R. & Hamilton III, W. J. (1966). *Mechanisms of Animal Behavior*. New York: John Wiley & Sons.
Nelson, K. (1965). After-effects of courtship in the male three-spined stickleback. *Z. vergl. Physiol.*, **50**, 569–597.
Pelkwijk, J. J. ter & Tinbergen, N. (1937). Eine Reizbiologische Analyse einiger Verhaltensweisen von *Gasterosteus aculeatus* L. *Z. Tierpsychol.*, **1**, 193–204.
Seigel, S. (1956) *Nonparametric Statistics for the Behavioural Sciences*. New York: McGraw Hill.
Sevenster, P. (1961). A causal analysis of a displacement activity (fanning in *Gasterosteus aculeatus* L.). *Behaviour*, Suppl. IX.
Sevenster-Bol, A. C. A. (1962). On the causation of drive reduction after a consummatory act. *Arch. neerl. Zool.*, **15**, 175–236.
Tinbergen, N. (1951). *The Study of Instinct*. Oxford: Clarendon Press.
Tinbergen, N. (1952). Derived activities: their causation, biological significance, origin and emancipation during evolution. *Q. Rev. Biol.*, **27**, 1–32.
Tinbergen, N. (1954). The origin and evolution of courtship and threat display. In *Evolution as a Process*. London: George Allen & Unwin.
Tinbergen, N. & Iersel, J. J. A. van (1947). Displacement reactions in the three-spined stickleback. *Behaviour*, **1**, 56–63.
Wilz, K. (1967). The organization of courtship behaviour in sticklebacks. D.Phil. Thesis University of Oxford.
Zeigler, H. P. (1964). Displacement activity and motivation theory, A case study in the history of ethology. *Psychol. Bull.*, **61**, 362–376.

(Received 27 March 1969; revised 8 August 1969; MS. number: 886)

Sonderdruck aus „Zeitschrift für Tierpsychologie"
[Z. Tierpsychol., 27, 73—77, 1970]
Alle Rechte, auch die des auszugsweisen Nachdruckes, der photomechanischen Wiedergabe und der Übersetzung, vorbehalten
Verlag Paul Parey, Berlin u. Hamburg

The Effect of a Visual Stimulus on the Agonistic Behaviour of the Golden Hamster

By E. C. Grant[1]), J. H. Mackintosh[2]) und C. J. Lerwill[3])

With one figure

Received: 19. 12. 1968

Introduction

Grant and Mackintosh (1963) suggested that the black marking on the chest of the golden hamster, *Mesocricetus auratus*, was a morphological sign stimulus indicating aggression. This assumption was based on the observation that these marks are displayed in offensive postures and hidden by the light coloured forearms in defensive postures. One of the authors in the course of a study of the social behaviour (Lerwill 1968) carried out a pilot study based on this suggestion. In this he found that if the markings were exaggerated by dying the under side of some hamsters black, these animals would win their agonistic encounters with normal hamsters even if they had previously lost to these individuals.

The present paper describes a more detailed study of this finding.

Material and Methods

Male golden hamsters were obtained from two separate stocks within the University. These animals were approximately three months old at the time of the experiments. When they were brought into the laboratory they were immediately put into a reversed lighting regime, i. e. a red light during the day, 9.00—18.00 hours, and a bright white light the rest of the time. A week later half the animals in each group were dyed with a commercial hair dye ("Incecto rapid black") on the chest and forearms (Fig. 1). At this time they were isolated into wire cages 29 × 16 × 10 cm., where they remained for a further week. At all times food and water was supplied *ad libitum*.

The experimental technique was to introduce one animal into the home cage of another. In half of these introductions, a marked animal was introduced into the home of an unmarked animal and in the other half the situation was reversed. Each animal was used twice, once on each of two consecutive days, meeting a different partner on the second occasion. This gave twelve introductions from twelve animals in Part. 1. Part 2 was a repeat of Part 1 giving us a further ten introductions from ten animals. These introductions each lasted ten minutes and in all cases there were two observers each recording the behavior of one of the interacting animals on a stereophonic tape recorder. The elements of agonistic behaviour in the hamster have been described and analysed (Grant and Mackintosh 1963; Mackintosh and Grant, in press). For the purposes of this experiment, these elements were grouped into a number of broad categories as follows:

Aggression: Offensive Upright, Offensive Sideways, Chase, Attack, Bite, Threat.
Ambivalence: Upright Posture, Sideways Posture. *Flight:* Crouch, Retreat, Evade, Defensive Sideways, Defensive Upright, Freeze, Submissive Posture, Flee, Tail Up, Pull Faeces.

---

[1]) Department of Psychiatry, Medical School, Birmingham, 15.
[2]) Sub-Department of Ethology, Medical School, Birmingham, 15.
[3]) Science Department, North-East Essex Technical College and School of Art, Colchester, Essex.

The elements occurring in these categories were scored for each animal in each encounter. We have at other times recorded both duration and frequency of elements and have shown that, especially in agonistic behaviour, these measures give substantially the same results in comparisons of this type. The effect of using duration is to exaggerate the difference between experimental and control groups and, therefore, only frequencies have been used in this paper.

Fig. 1: The black mark on the chest of the hamster. Left: intensified. Right: normal

Results

A test/retest correlation between Part 1 and Part 2 had a value of 0.95 and therefore the results of both are treated together. Tab. 1 shows the frequency of elements in each behavioural category for each animal for each introduction and Tab. 2 summarises the results given in Tab. 1.

A non-parametric statistic, the Mann Whitney U, was selected because of the non-normal distribution of the data and the probability values given in the results are derived from this test. These show that the marking had a highly significant effect on the agonistic behaviour. Unmarked animals show much more flight behaviour than marked ones and the marked animals show more aggression. The other important effect shown depends on whether the unmarked animal is at home or introduced during the encounter. When the unmarked animal is at home, the total amount of agonistic behaviour is significantly reduced.

It is possible, on the basis of our previous analysis, to differentiate between more and less intense forms of flight behaviour. If this is done, it can be seen that the unmarked animal not only shows more flight but shows proportionally more of the intense forms of this behaviour (Tab. 3).

Table 1: Individual scores

	Introduction	Marked Animal			Unmarked Animal		
		Aggression	Ambivalence	Flight	Aggression	Ambivalence	Flight
Marked animal at home.	1	12	2	2	0	1	8
	2	15	2	0	0	0	27
	3	2	1	2	0	0	0
	4	77	6	3	0	0	123
	5	41	4	0	0	3	61
	6	47	6	3	5	5	50
	7	18	19	20	22	17	8
	9	11	2	2	3	2	9
	10	4	4	47	7	2	8
	11	40	1	2	!	1	40
Marked animal introduced	12	22	4	1	0	1	95
	13	7	0	1	0	1	6
	14	0	4	10	0	0	0
	15	0	0	0	0	0	0
	16	9	0	0	0	0	51
	17	2	6	7	4	5	5
	18	24	5	4	3	12	13
	19	1	1	3	1	1	7
	20	0	0	1	5	2	1
	21	10	1	1	0	2	39
	22	9	1	2	4	1	12

Table 2: Summary of results

Position of marked animal:	Marked Animal			Unmarked Animal			Total Agonistic
	Aggres.	Ambiv.	Flight	Aggres.	Ambiv.	Flight	
Home	323	53	83	38	35	421	955[4]
Introduced	84	22	30	17	25	229	407[4]
Total	407[1]	75[2]	113[3]	55[1]	60[2]	650[3]	

1,1. P = 0.00016   3,3. P = 0.007
2,2. P = 0.13 N. S.   4,4. P = 0.028

Table 3

	Low intensity	High intensity
Flight behaviour in marked animals	70	43
" " " unmarked animals	185	465

Discussion

As was said in the introduction, we have previously made the observation that the black mark on the chest of the hamster was displayed in aggressive postures and we suggested that it might have signal value. The results of the experiments described here are consistent with this suggestion. When agonistic

Note: In Table 1 the following figures should be insert between lines 7 and 9:
8   56   6   2   0   4   87

encounters occur between hamsters in which the black marking is intensified and hamsters in which it is not, then the marked animals show a predominance of aggressive behaviour and the unmarked animals a predominance of flight behaviour. Although visual signals have been inferred to be operative in the agonistic encounters of many animals, direct experimental evidence is frequently lacking. The comb in hens (COLLIAS 1947; MARKS, SIEGEL and KRAMER 1960) would seem to have a similar function to the black mark in the hamsters, as hens with small combs are less likely to win a fight than those with large ones and comb removal also depresses fighting ability. In most other cases that have been experimentally studied, e. g., the red breast of the chaffinch (MARLER 1956) and of the robin (LACK 1939) and also the red belly of the stickleback (PELKWIJK & TINBERGEN 1937), there is a difference from the present results in that the main effect demonstrated is that animals with the mark are attacked. That is, the sign releases rather than inhibits aggression in the other animal. This is similar to the olfactory releaser of aggression that we have previously demonstrated in mice (MACKINTOSH and GRANT 1966).

It is unlikely that the mark has a direct effect on the animal bearing it, so that the immediate result is presumably to precipitate flight behaviour in the unmarked animal. This is supported by the results. In the situation where the marked animal is introduced it is relatively unlikely to initiate an encounter and in this situation the proportion of flight elements shown by the unmarked animal to aggressive elements shown by the marked one is of the order of 3 : 1. This is significantly greater than in the alternative situation where the marked animal is at home and is likely to be aggressive. Here the ratio is approximately 4 : 3. That is, in the first situation the unmarked animals were showing more flight than one would expect from the amount of aggression displayed towards them. From observation it was clear that the flight response was often initiated by a non-agonistic movement which fortuitously displayed the black mark. The marked animals do, however, show a considerable amount of aggression which appears as a response to the flight behaviour of the other animal. This is of interest, as it emphasises the reciprocal relationship between flight and aggression; as would be expected, much flight occurs as a response to aggression but here we can see that the reverse is also true. A similar situation was described in rats (GRANT 1963) where it was shown that the behaviour of the flight motivated animals largely determined the course of the encounters.

In general when one hamster is introduced into the home cage of another the home animal shows most aggression. In half of the encounters described here the introduced animal carried a black mark which, as indicated by the results of this paper, has the effect of increasing flight behaviour in the other animal. The home animal is then in a situation which would potentiate both flight and aggression, that is one would expect an increase in ambivalent behaviour. This does not occur. The main characteristic of this situation is a highly significant reduction in all agonistic behaviour. This effect is the result of a cut-off activity (CHANCE 1962, GRANT and MACKINTOSH 1963) on the part of the home animal. This cut-off was not so much shown in discrete postures but was the result of a general avoidance of contact. For example, one home unmarked hamster spent eight minutes out of the ten-minute encounter chewing at a piece of food pellet while crouching in the corner of the cage with its back towards the introduced animal.

As well as showing an increase in flight behaviour the unmarked animal showed a proportionately greater increase in the high intensity forms of flight behaviour (Tab. 3 in the results). This would indicate that the response that we are showing is an increasing tendency to flee rather than the potentiation of a particular response pattern. Clearly there are many factors still to be investigated, e. g. whether position or pattern of this black mark has an effect on the response, and further experimentation is in progress.

Summary

Experiments are described which confirm an earlier suggestion that the display of the black mark on the chest indicates aggression in the golden hamster. Normal ♂♂ showed an increase in flight behaviour when paired with ♂♂ in which the black mark had been intensified by dying.

Literature cited

CHANCE, M. R. A. (1962): An interpretation of some agonistic postures: the role of "cut-off" acts and postures. Symp. Zool. Soc. Lond. 8, 71—89 • COLLIAS, N. E. (1943): Statistical analysis of factors which make for success in initial encounters between hens. Amer. Nat. 77, 519—538 • GRANT, E. C. (1963): An analysis of the social behaviour of the male laboratory rat. Behaviour 11, 260—281 • GRANT, E. C, and J. H. MACKINTOSH (1963): A description of the social postures of some laboratory rodents. Behaviour 21, 246—259 • LACK, D. (1939): The behaviour of the robin, I and II. Proc. Zool. Soc. Lond. A. 109, 169–178 • LERWILL, C. G. (1968): Agonistic Behaviour and Social Dominance in the Golden Hamster, *Mesocricetus auratus auratus* (Waterhouse). M. Sc. thesis. University of Wales • MACKINTOSH, J. H., and E. C. GRANT (in press): An analysis of the social behaviour of some laboratory rodents • MACKINTOSH, J. H., and E. C. GRANT (1966): The effect of olfactory stimuli on the agonistic behaviour of laboratory mice. Z. Tierpsychol. 23, 584—587 • MARKS, H. L., P. B. SIEGEL and C. Y. KRAMER (1960): The effect of comb and wattle removal on the social organisation of mixed flocks of chickens. Anim. Behav. 8, 192—196 • MARLER, P. (1956): Studies of fighting in Chaffinches. 3. Proximity as a cause of aggression. Brit. J. Anim. Behav. 4, 23—30 • PELKWIJK, J. J. ter, and N. TINBERGEN (1937): Eine reizbiologische Analyse einiger Verhaltensweisen von *Gasterosteus aculeatus* L., Z. Tierpsychol. 1, 193—200.

Territoriality in the bullfrog, *Rana catesbeiana*

STEPHEN T. EMLEN

During the breeding season, adult male bullfrogs, *Rana catesbeiana*, establish territories from which conspecific males are aggressively excluded. Stereotyped postures, approaches, and physical encounters all function in the defense of such areas. It is proposed that the highly polygamous social system present in this species creates an intense intermale competition for females, and that possession of a territory directly influences an individual male's chances of successful mating.

INTRODUCTION

THE tendency for an animal to restrict its activities to a specified area and to defend this area against other members of its species is known as territoriality. Although such behavior is extremely widespread among almost all groups of vertebrates, there are few reports of its occurrence within the class Amphibia. Unequivocal evidence for the existence of such aggressive behavior in urodeles is lacking. Among anurans, individuals of several species have been shown to inhabit specific home ranges to which they often return upon short-distance displacement (Bogert, 1947; Martof, 1953b; Jameson, 1957; Kikuchi, 1958; Ferguson, 1963; Dole, 1965). In addition, field and laboratory observations of apparent agonistic behavior have been described for several species of tropical dendrobatids (Test, 1954; Sexton, 1960; Duellman, 1966) and pipids (Rabb and Rabb, 1963a, b), as well as for *Leptodactylus insularum* (Sexton, 1962) and *Hyla faber* (Lutz, 1960). But among temperate zone species, only the green frog (*Rana clamitans*) is known to exhibit what Martof (1953a) has described as a "primitive type of territory."

During the breeding season male bullfrogs (*Rana catesbeiana*) commonly space themselves at regular intervals along the shores of millponds, small lakes, and streams, and individuals frequently remain at specific locations for periods of two to three weeks (Noble, 1931:404–405; Wright and Wright, 1949:445). The purpose of this report is to demonstrate that the areas surrounding such male bullfrogs do in fact constitute territories that are actively defended from other males by stereotyped, aggressive behaviors.

MATERIALS AND METHODS

During the summers of 1965 and 1966 I studied a population of approximately 200 bullfrogs inhabiting a five-acre pond on the University of Michigan's Edwin S. George Reserve near Ann Arbor. The frogs overwintered in an adjacent marsh area and entered the pond through a narrow inlet stream during May and early June. Individual bullfrogs were trapped as they entered the pond, sexed, measured, and toe-clipped for identification. Males were additionally marked by placing colored and/or numbered nylon elasticized bands around their waists. These permitted rapid individual recognition from a distance, without the necessity of capture and consequent disturbance.

Observations were made during the evenings from late May, when the frogs first called from the pond, until late July, by which time the majority of the females had spawned. Behavioral interactions were recorded with the aid of binoculars and a Bolex H16 movie camera from both the shore line and a small rowboat. Nightly censuses were also conducted and the positions of marked males were accurately mapped.

OBSERVATIONS AND DISCUSSION

The frogs commonly spent the daylight hours in cracks or crevices in the overhanging bank of the pond or in the shallow water near shore. Calling was infrequent (except on two overcast, rainy days), and social interactions were rarely observed.

At dusk, the majority of the males left the bank and took up regular calling stations, where they remained throughout the evening, and to which they returned on consecutive nights. During the early part of the summer these stations characteristically were located in a band within 50 ft from shore, at a water depth of two–five ft. But by mid-June, when immigration had increased the male population to its peak of approximately 100 individuals, large choruses of from 14 to 37 males were formed. These aggregations extended into deeper water, farther from shore.

Males occupying stations adopted a characteristic "high" posture in which the lungs were greatly inflated with air. This caused the animals to float very high in the water with the entire head, most of the abdomen, and the dorsal portions of the hind legs resting above the water's surface. The head was raised slightly, exposing the brilliant yellow gular area.

Males exhibiting this posture called at frequent intervals and aggressively excluded other males from the areas surrounding them. The size of these defended areas varied from individual to individual, and appeared to be influenced by the availability of suitable shore-line. Measurements taken in June 1966, show the average distance between a frog and its closest male neighbor within a chorus (both exhibiting the "high" posture) to be 17.8 ft (standard deviation = 5.9 ft; n = 94). This implies an average minimum territory radius of approximately nine ft.

If an inflated neighboring male approached closer than this distance, a stereotyped challenge ensued. The resident gave a sudden, short, staccato "hiccup" vocalization, turned abruptly, faced the intruder, and swam a few feet toward him. This "hiccup" challenge was observed several hundred times and almost invariably accompanied intermale aggressive encounters. (The few exceptions occurred in the absence of any stimulus discernible to me.)

The behavior that followed this initial challenge depended upon the response of the intruding male. If he turned away and returned to his previous station, no further interaction occurred. However, if he called, continued to advance, or both, the resident continued his approach via a series of discrete challenges. Each challenge consisted of the "hiccup" note and an advance of a few ft toward the intruder; each was followed by a motionless pause, often lasting for one min or more, during which one or both males usually called. As the distance between frogs decreased, the swimming approach was replaced by a slower crawling movement through the water until the frogs came to rest only inches apart.

It should be emphasized that this sequence could be broken at any time, should either male turn away from his challenger and leave the immediate vicinity. In fact, of 79 encounters observed over a five-night period in June 1966, 58 (73.5%) terminated in this manner without physical contact.

However, if neither individual withdrew, a confrontation occurred when the distance between the males decreased to three or four inches. In this situation, one frog occasionally jumped directly at or upon the other, but much more commonly the two individuals simultaneously pushed against one another and became locked, throat to throat and venter to venter, with the fore-arms of each tightly grasped around the inflated pectoral region of the other. Locked in this manner, the frogs engaged in a violent struggle, kicking with the hind legs until one individual was forced over onto its back, at which time contact was broken. The force exerted during this struggle pushed the two males vertically out of the water until only the posterior third of the abdomen and the hind legs remained submerged.

Such struggles generally lasted only 15–20 sec, but bouts continuing for four and five min were occasionally observed. Following an encounter, the frog which successfully out-pushed its opponent remained in the "high" posture and called. By contrast, the other individual stayed submerged

for several sec and, upon surfacing, adopted an entirely different, "low" posture in which the lungs were deflated and only the upper portion of the head was visible above the water. If he surfaced within one or two ft of his opponent, he was usually rechallenged and responded by rapidly exiting from the vicinity. Far more commonly, however, the "low" individual swam some distance under water, surfacing several ft away. In these instances, although the deflated frog often was still within the defended area, further aggressive behavior was rare, suggesting that deflation characterizes a submissive posture which inhibits attack.

The behavior of "non-established" males, individuals which either did not possess territories or which inhabited areas far from active choruses, lends additional support to this hypothesis. The population under study included many such individuals and each evening several would move into the choruses. These males consistently maintained the "low," deflated posture when approaching and entering a chorus, and in this manner they moved among the established males without evoking any aggressive response. Yet, when such a male inflated himself and called, he was challenged and attacked immediately. Occasionally the invaders succeeded in supplanting a resident, but more frequently they were forced from the chorus, or at least to its periphery.

There is also evidence suggesting that the "high" posture functions directly as a threat. The inflated body form is undoubtedly a necessary prerequisite for effective vocalization since air is forced from the lungs through the larynx into the vocal sacs during calling. But this posture was maintained throughout the night, even during long, noncalling periods. Preliminary experiments measuring the intensity of males' aggressive responses to a model bullfrog suggest that the inflated posture (which maximizes the apparent size of the caller) is an effective stimulus eliciting aggressive challenges. The model used in these tests was a painted, latex cast of a bullfrog mounted over a styrofoam base. The "high" and "low" postures could be simulated by attaching various weights to the base, thereby altering the buoyancy of the model. When placed inside an established territory in the "high" position, the model evoked prompt challenges from six of eight resident males tested. The remaining two individuals deflated, assuming the "low" posture, and no aggressive behavior was noted. By contrast, no behavioral responses occurred when the same model was presented floating low in the water (n = 12). Playbacks of tape recordings of both the "hiccup" vocalization and the normal male call (neither of which are given by males in the "low" posture) also consistently evoked aggressive responses.

The adaptive significance of bullfrog territoriality is best understood in conjunction with the breeding biology of the species. Unlike many North American anurans, in which members of a given population attain peak reproductive condition synchronously and mating occupies only a brief period of days or weeks, male bullfrogs remain reproductively active throughout much of the summer. Each female, however, is sexually receptive for only a short time, and the long breeding season results from the great variation in the dates at which different females attain this state (Raney, 1940; Emlen, unpubl. obs.). In the Michigan population studied, gravid females were encountered from mid-June until late July.

The behavior of the females varied in accordance with their reproductive condition. Prior to ovulation, they were quite secretive, remaining hidden along the shore or in a shallow marsh adjacent to the breeding pond. When ripe, however, females immigrated into the pond via the small inlet stream, left the cover of the shoreline, and approached the male choruses. These approaches evidently were guided at least in part by the sound of the males' calling, since females could be attracted to a tape recorder by playbacks of chorusing. However, direct observation revealed that females were *not* strongly attracted to males calling from isolated territories; in all observed instances (n = 16) females passed by such males and continued on to the large choruses.

Once a chorus was reached, a female adopted an extreme "low" posture and moved from territory to territory without eliciting any noticeable response from the resident males. After many hours of remaining "low" in first one territory and then another, the female appeared to select a mate, swimming up to him and seemingly making physical contact. Only then would the male respond, by immediately seizing her in amplexus.

It is apparent from this information that an individual male bullfrog maximizes his chances of contributing genetically to the next generation by 1) congregating with other males in a large chorus, and 2) remaining in a sexually active state throughout the season when females become ripe.

Although it is assumed that all mature females in a population breed, it was only rarely that more than one or two individuals entered a chorus during the course of an evening. Consequently, the ratio of responsive males to receptive females at any one time is enormous—on the order of 40–50 to 1 in the population studied. As a result of this, male competition for females must be extremely intense.

This social system is quite similar to the "leks" present in several species of polygamous birds and mammals in which males establish territories in a communal display ground or arena (see Armstrong, 1964:431–433). Females come to these display areas and, after moving among the males, select a mate and copulate. In males of these species, as with male bullfrogs, there must be a strong selective premium placed upon rapid attraction of the opposite sex.

I suggest that the possession of a territory is one important factor increasing a male bullfrog's chance of successful mating. Perhaps this advantage is accrued by the creation of a buffer zone around the holder which allows females to approach and select a male without interference from numerous, nearby, competing males. Such buffer zones might also yield a measure of stability to a chorus, thereby resulting in an overall decrease in energy expended in aggressive interactions. In addition, some aspect of a territory, such as its size or location, might directly enhance the attractiveness of its holder. It is even possible that the agonistic interactions associated with territoriality help maintain the prolonged state of sexual responsiveness present among males.

At present these suggestions are highly speculative. Future experiments examining the factors operative in a female bullfrog's selection of a mate will be required to provide an empirical test of this hypothesis—that the possession of a territory helps to maximize the reproductive potential of the individual holder.

ACKNOWLEDGMENTS

I thank C. F. Walker for his helpful suggestions and H. W. Ambrose, T. Eisner, and W. T. Keeton for commenting upon the manuscript. This study was supported by a National Science Foundation Graduate Fellowship.

LITERATURE CITED

ARMSTRONG, E. A. 1964. Lek display. *In*: A new dictionary of birds. A. L. Thomson, ed. McGraw-Hill, New York.

BOGERT, C. M. 1947. A field study of homing in the Carolina toad. Am. Mus. Novit. No. 1355, 24 pp.

DOLE, J. W. 1965. Summer movement of adult leopard frogs, *Rana pipiens* Schreber, in northern Michigan. Ecology 46:236–255.

DUELLMAN, W. E. 1966. Aggressive behavior in dendrobatid frogs. Herpetologica 22:217–221.

FERGUSON, D. E. 1963. Orientation in three species of anuran amphibians. Ergebn. Biol. 26:128–134.

JAMESON, D. L. 1957. Population structure and homing responses in the Pacific treefrog. Copeia 1957(3):221–228.

KIKUCHI, T. T. 1958. On the residentiality of a green frog, *Rana nigromaculata* Hallowell. Jap. J. Ecol. 8:20–26.

LUTZ, B. 1960. Fighting and an incipient notion of territory in male tree frogs. Copeia 1960(1):61–63.

MARTOF, B. S. 1953a. Territoriality in the green frog, *Rana clamitans*. Ecology 34:165–174.

————. 1953b. Home range and movement of the green frog, *Rana clamitans*. *Ibid.* 34: 529–543.

NOBLE, G. K. 1931. The biology of the amphibia. McGraw-Hill, New York.

RABB, G. B. AND M. S. RABB. 1963a. On the behavior and breeding biology of the African pipid frog *Hymenochirus boettgeri*. Zeits. Tierpsychol. 20:215–241.

———— AND ————. 1963b. Additional observations on breeding behavior of the Surinam toad, *Pipa pipa*. Copeia 1963(4):636–642.

RANEY, E. C. 1940. Summer movements of the bullfrog, *Rana catesbeiana* Shaw, as determined by the jaw-tag method. Am. Midl. Nat. 23: 733–745.

SEXTON, O. 1960. Some aspects of the behavior and of the territory of a dendrobatid frog, *Prostherapis trinitatus*. Ecology 41:107–115.

————. 1962. Apparent territorialism in *Leptodactylus insularum* Barbour. Herpetologica 18:212–214.

TEST, F. H. 1954. Social aggressiveness in an amphibian. Science 120:140–141.

WRIGHT, A. H. AND A. A. WRIGHT. 1949. Handbook of frogs and toads of the United States and Canada. Cornell Univ. Press, Ithaca, New York.

DEPARTMENT OF ZOOLOGY AND MUSEUM OF ZOOLOGY, UNIVERSITY OF MICHIGAN, ANN ARBOR 48104. *Present address*: SECTION OF NEUROBIOLOGY AND BEHAVIOR, DIVISION OF BIOLOGICAL SCIENCES, CORNELL UNIVERSITY, ITHACA, NEW YORK 14850.

(59) Social Status and Mating Activity in Elephant Seals

Burney J. LeBoeuf and Richard S. Peterson

Abstract. *Individually marked male elephant seals, Mirounga angustirostris, observed on an island off central California participate in a social hierarchy resembling the peck order of domestic chickens. Individuals achieve status by fighting and maintain it by stereotyped threat displays. The higher the status of a male, the more readily he approaches and copulates with females. Four percent of the males inseminated 85 percent of the females.*

Patterns of social organization in vertebrates have been generally categorized as territories or social hierarchies (*1*). Many pinnipeds are territorial; a few males defend specific sites where breeding females gather in "harems" (*2*). *Mirounga angustirostris* and *M. leonina,* the northern and southern elephant seals, are exceptions. Males of these species establish social hierarchies in which the males of highest rank remain near the breeding females but do not defend specific sites (*3*). Previous studies of the hierarchies were severely limited since few animals were recognizable as individuals, and since an observer must know the members of a group individually to obtain accurate data on social order. During the 1967–1968 breeding season of *M. angustirostris* at Año Nuevo Island, San Mateo County, California, we marked virtually all of the males that landed; thus we are able to provide the first quantitative description of the hierarchy and to relate individual status to breeding success.

In December of each year male elephant seals land at Año Nuevo Island, and many of them remain there continuously until March (*4*). In January, after many males have been on land for several weeks, the adult females come ashore, give birth, suckle their young for an average of 28 days, breed, and depart. We observed this population, on an average, for 6.0 hours per day, from 10 December 1967 to 15 March 1968, from blinds overlooking two beaches. We put individual markings on 93 of approximately 115 males as they landed on the island, and on 46 of 225 females (*5*). The males that we did not mark were immature transients rarely seen near the females.

As they came ashore, the adult males exhibited mutual rivalry which kept them apart from each other. Rivalry was evidenced most often by stereotyped threat patterns; a male elevated his forequarters, reared back his head allowing his proboscis to hang into his opened mouth, and emitted a series of

Fig. 1. Two northern elephant seal bulls fighting.

loud, low-pitched, gutteral sounds (6). Normally, the threatened male halted his approach or retreated. If, instead, he held his ground or answered the display with one of his own, a confrontation often followed in which the males came together and attempted to butt, bite, and slash each other on the neck (Fig. 1). We saw only 90 clashes, but more than 6000 threat displays. Fights lasted from a few seconds to 15 minutes and ended when one participant turned and fled.

We determined the direction of dominance between pairs of marked animals by noting which individual retreated after every threat or fight. Some pairs of individuals interacted as often as 65 times in 10 days. The social rank of an individual was determined by the number and identity of animals from which he retreated when threatened.

The relations between the seven top-ranking males on area 17, one of the two study areas, when displayed at 10-day intervals, demonstrates the dynamic nature of the social system (Table 1). The hierarchies were either linear (28 February to 8 March, Table 1), or complicated by triangular relations. An example of the latter occurred from 19 to 28 January when subject NIC moved subject GL, GL moved CLS, and CLS moved NIC. The direction of dominance between a pair of males did not change unless a fight occurred between them. The relation reversed when the previously dominant male retreated. The animals recognized each other individually.

The most important animal in the system was the alpha bull, the male that dominated all others on the beach. Activity centered around him since he usually remained in or near the aggregation of females toward which the other males were also oriented. Much of the alpha bull's activity involved

Table 1. Social rank and copulation frequency of highest ranking males on area 17. Each male .dominates those listed below it; deviations from a linear hierarchy are indicated by arrows. Dotted arrows denote a change in relation which occurred toward the end of the 10-day period. Copulation frequencies are in parentheses.

21 Dec. to 30 Dec.	30 Dec. to 8 Jan.	9 Jan. to 18 Jan.	19 Jan. to 28 Jan.	29 Jan. to 7 Feb.	8 Feb. to 17 Feb.	18 Feb. to 27 Feb.	28 Feb. to 8 Mar.	Total copulations (No.)
NIC	NIC	CLS*	NIC(1)	GL(6)	GL(15)	GL(19)	GL(5)	46
UG	UG†	NIC	GL(1)	CLS(13)	CLS(7)	CLS(9)	CLS(1)	31
GL	GL--	GL*	CLS(2)	NIC‡	GLS(4)	GLS(8)	GLS(1)	15
WN	WN	GLS	GLS(1)	GLS(5)	TWO(2)	PIN	PIN	8
HSN	TWO	TWO	TWO(2)	TWO(1)	PIN(3)--	YLN(3)	YLN	9
TWO	YDB	PIN	PIN	PIN	YLN(3)	TWO‡	BLB	3
BRS	PIN	YLN	YLN	YLN(1)	BO	BLB(2)	BO	3
Copulations (No.)								
0	0	0	7	26	34	41§	7	
Females present (range)								
0–2	2–21	24–58	66–102	70–89	54–79	19–51	6–15	
Males present (range)								
15–27	19–26	19–28	22–29	24–34	24–34	23–35	24–31	

* Indeterminate relation during period despite two bloody fights.   † Moved to area 3 after losing fight to YLN at end of period.   ‡ Left island during period and did not return.   § Three other copulations were observed during this period; two by BO, one by WN.

keeping other males away from the females.

Copulation frequencies (in parentheses, Table 1) show that social rank was highly correlated with breeding success (7). We estimate that four of the highest ranking males (GL, CLS, GLS, and YLN), representing 6 percent of 71 individuals observed in area 17, inseminated 88 percent of the 120 females on that beach. The alpha bull from 29 January to 8 March (GL) copulated more frequently than any other male.

Among the four males that copulated most frequently, high rank was positively correlated with (i) demonstrating dominance over other males, (ii) preventing others from mounting and copulating, and (iii) mounting and copulating without interruption (Table 2).

On the other beach under study, area 3, one individual maintained the alpha position during the entire breeding season. This bull was involved in 73 percent of the copulations observed on area 3.

The extent to which social structure restricted mating to only a few males is illustrated by the combined statistics of the entire island. The four highest ranking males on area 17, plus the alpha bull on area 3, accounted for 123 of 144 copulations observed during the season. Thus 4 percent of the males apparently inseminated 85 percent of the females.

Social hierarchies exist in several mammalian species (8), but the type we observed in male elephant seals is especially comparable to that of domestic fowl (9). In both systems, the hierarchy may be linear, or may show triangular relations. The relations between individuals are stable unless fighting leads to reversals. However, among male fowl, high status confers access to food and roosting and nesting sites as well as to females, whereas in elephant seals the competition during the breeding season relates primarily to females. A male elephant seal shows no preference for a particular site, except one close to the females. As the females shift location, the males follow them. High-ranking males do not eat during the 3-month haul-out, and therefore do not compete for food. In addition, all the male elephant seals in our population exhibited a dominance relation with each other, whereas "no-contest" relations occur between some individuals in chicken peck orders.

A social system in which only a few males mate might have important genetic consequences for the evolution of the species, particularly if the same males continue to mate for more than one season. We do not know how many

Table 2. Correlates of social rank in four males on area 17 during the period when GL was the alpha male.

Males (in order of rank)	Times other males moved by threats (No.)	Mounts prevented by male (No.)	Copulations interrupted by male (No.)*	Mounts prevented by others (%)	Copulations interrupted by others (%)
GL	726	213	15	0	0
CLS	332	52	5	24	15
GLS	332	23	1	71	47
YLN	215	9	0	83	57

* Taken from all copulations observed, a total of 152.

seasons one male successfully competes for females, or whether he fertilizes all those with whom he mates (*10*).

BURNEY J. LE BOEUF

Crown College, University of California, Santa Cruz 95060

RICHARD S. PETERSON

Stevenson College, University of California, Santa Cruz 95060

REFERENCES

1. A. M. Guhl, in *The Behavior of Domestic Animals*, F. S. E. Hafez, Ed. (Bailliere, Tindall, and Cox, London, 1962), p. 96.
2. G. A. Bartholomew and P. G. Hoel, *J. Mammal.* **34**, 417 (1953); H. R. Hewer and K. M. Backhouse, *J. Zool. Proc. Zool. Soc. London* **134**, 157 (1960); A. W. Cameron, *Can. J. Zool.* **45**, 161 (1967); R. W. Rand, *Invest. Rep. Div. Sea Fish. Un. S. Afr.* **60**, 1 (1967); R. S. Peterson and G. A. Bartholomew, *The Natural History and Behavior of the California Sea Lion* (American Society of Mammalogists, Spec. Publ. No. 1, 1967); R. J. Schusterman and R. G. Dawson, *Science* **160**, 434 (1968).
3. G. A. Bartholomew, *Univ. Calif. Publ. Zool.* **47**, 369 (1952); M. Angot, *Mammalia* **15**, 1 (1954); R. M. Laws, *Falkland Is. Dependencies Sur. Sci. Rep.*, No. 13 (1956); R. L. Carrick, S. E. Csordas, S. E. Ingham, *Commonw. Sci. Ind. Res. Organ. Wildlife Res.* **7**, 161 (1962).
4. K. W. Radford, R. T. Orr, C. L. Hubbs, *Proc. Calif. Acad. Sci. 4th Ser.* **31**, 601 (1965); R. T. Orr and T. C. Poulter, *ibid.* **32**, 377 (1965).
5. Our best marks were obtained by slowly dripping 30 percent hydrogen peroxide, mixed with a cosmetic emulsifier, on the pelage of sleeping animals. The marks were easily recognizable from the blinds and lasted throughout the breeding season. We thank Clairol, Inc., for providing the emulsified "Lady Clairol Ultra Blue."
6. G. A. Bartholomew and N. E. Collias, *Anim. Behav.* **10**, 7 (1962).
7. Copulation frequencies include only the first of a female's copulations that we observed. Additional copulations by the same female are excluded because we assumed that insemination occurred most likely as a result of the initial mating.
8. For example: J. A. Kaufmann, in *Social Communication among Primates*, S. A. Altmann, Ed. (Univ. of Chicago Press, Chicago, 1967), p. 73; A. M. Guhl and F. W. Atkeson, *Trans. Kans. Acad. Sci.* **62**, 80 (1959).
9. A. M. Guhl, in *The Behavior of Domestic Animals*, F. S. E. Hafez, Ed. (Bailliere, Tindall, and Cox, London, 1962), p. 491.
10. We attached permanent monel metal tags to many of the seals to identify them in future seasons and study the reproductive rates of males and females.
11. Our studies in Año Nuevo State Reserve were authorized by the California Department of Parks and Recreation, W. P. Mott, Jr., director; and permission to tag seals was granted by the California Department of Fish and Game, W. T. Shannon, director. We acknowledge the field assistance of M. Skeel, D. Ramsey, G. Eaton, and R. Gentry.

27 June 1968

Am. Zoologist, 7:305-311 (1967).

Social Relationships in a Group of Captive Wolves

GEORGE B. RABB

Chicago Zoological Park, Brookfield, Illinois

JEROME H. WOOLPY, and BENSON E. GINSBURG

University of Chicago

SYNOPSIS. The social organization of a group of wolves in a large outdoor enclosure was followed through several breeding seasons. During the breeding season conflicts become more frequent and the social hierarchy obvious. The more dominant animals restrict courtship activities by inferior wolves of their own sex. However, apparently as a correlate of their position, two alpha males have shown less mating activity than other males. Mate preferences exhibited by animals of both sexes also limit the number of matings. The preferences appear related to the social hierarchy existing when an animal matures. Cultural transmission of social status is suggested by some changes in ranking of wolves raised in the woods at Brookfield. Temporary removal of the original alpha male and death of the original alpha female appear to have promoted changes in social order and an increase in actual mating combinations. The probable consanguineous nature of wolf groups and facets of the social behavior suggest that some form of group selection could be operative in the wild.

The basic relationships and activities of a group of wolves held captive at the Chicago Zoological Park, Brookfield, have been reported in previous film showings and summaries (Rabb, *et al.*, 1962; Ginsburg, 1965). The present paper is an abbreviated account of the social relations within this group during the mating season and the changes that have taken place over the years.

The wolf woods at Brookfield is ¾ acre enclosed by a chain link fence. In this area, there are several large native trees, a moated open viewing area, an artificial waterfall and pool, and a cement block shelter. The wolves dig their own burrows. There are no other caged animals nearby. The wolves are not tame. They recognize the keepers, but shy away when one enters the enclosure. They are fed chunks of horse meat, canned dog food, and ground meat in mid-afternoon, and visitors ply them with marshmallows. Perhaps because of the feeding regime and daytime activity in the park, the wolves are largely diurnal, in contrast to some situations in the wild. In general, our observations agree with what little is known of group relations in the wild, principally that recorded by Adolph Murie

Supported by the Chicago Zoological Society and U. S. P. H. S. Grant MY-03361. We gratefully acknowledge the considerable observational work done by Mary S. Rabb in recent seasons and earlier work by Susan Andrews and other students.

(1944) and Mech (1966). Thus, the Brookfield wolves have cooperated in raising the young of a single mother, they gang up on an outcast, they have a leader to whom all defer, etc.

The Brookfield females come in heat during the cold weather at the beginning of February. Intense courtship activity starts a week before and continues for three weeks. Most of this activity takes place in mid-afternoon, although there have been late morning matings. During the breeding season, we usually watch and make film records for 5 or 6 hr each day from across the moated viewing area. Observations made through binoculars from a nearby building indicate that our usual proximity has no apparent effect on the wolves' behavior. Except on Sundays, the few winter visitors and the non-scientific voyeurs rarely distract the animals. We and keepers have checked at night and found little activity and no courtship behavior then. As used in this paper, courtship actions include sniffing, licking, pawing, dancing, mounting, presenting, and certain kinds of nipping. The elements of communication used in these and other social activities have been well described by Schenkel (1947).

The group originally consisted of 2 males and 3 females, surviving offspring of six born in April, 1957 to a common father and two mothers, all of whom were then 2 years old. The parents, of Canadian stock, had come to Brookfield as pups. One mother was a very white animal, and it is likely that four of the young, who were similarly light, came from her. The other parents and the other young were well marked with dark features.

The exact early social relations in the group in the wolf woods, to which they were transferred in 1958, are not known. However, two of the females had young of their own when they were 2 years old. These two litters were brought by their mothers to a common shelter, the concrete block den. Amiable relations lasted one night. The next night all of the pups were killed, most of them being neatly pulled in half.

In subsequent seasons, only a single female mated successfully and gave birth. This bitch dominated the other two females by assaulting them physically or psychically whenever they solicited a male or were receptive to a male. The other females were confined by intimidation to small areas of the woods (Fig. 1). Consequently, only one of the others mated, and then only once, when the chief bitch was herself in copulatory tie. The alpha bitch, ♀1, preferred the alpha male, ♂1, and actively courted and solicited him (Fig. 2). So did ♀3. ♂1 reciprocated ♀3's attentions, but rebuffed ♀1. ♀1 thereupon accepted ♂2. ♂1 punished ♂2 while he was tied, as did ♀1. However, the punishment was not severe or lasting. ♂1 discouraged many mounting attempts by ♂2 simply by approaching the

FIG. 2. Alpha female unsuccessfully soliciting alpha male, 1963 season. Left to right: ♂1, ♀1, ♂3?, ♂2.

pair. Despite the increase of conflict in the mating season and restriction of lesser females' movements, the sociability of the group was maintained.

Change was built into this situation in that some of the pups produced were allowed to remain with the group. These included a male and a female from 1961, two males from 1962, and a female from 1963, all of them ♀1's offspring. However, there was no change in the relationships among the old adults in the mating seasons through 1963 (Fig. 3).

In 1964, we removed ♂1 shortly before the females showed vaginal blood, the sign of impending estrus. ♀1 accommodated quickly. She tied with ♂2 three times, and briefly with both of the 2-year-old males. However, ♀4, now 3 years old, and ♀2, one of the subordinate older females, were courted by the males. As in the past, intimidation by ♀1 prevented actual mating by them. Often the lesser females simply sat down when mounted, effectively terminating the mating attempt. As before, there were some cross-sexual dominance actions, principally ♀1 dominating the lesser males.

♂1 broke a lower canine tooth while in solitary confinement. Perhaps partly because of this, as well as his absence during a critical period, he was no longer dominant the following season. Although he still patrolled the area, deference went to ♂2. We had next planned to remove ♀1 to determine how complete a release in mating activities would result for the other animals. However, this was done for us in a natural fashion at the end of 1964 in the period of pre-

FIG. 1. Low-ranking female wolf in a restricted area deferring to alpha bitch, 1963 season. Alpha animal, ♀1, is being followed by males. The squatting position of ♀2 often was succeeded by further fawning, including a belly-up posture on the ground, if ♀1 turned directly toward her.

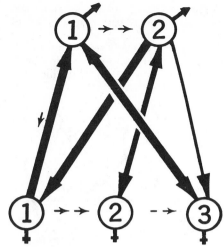

FIG. 3. Relations of original group of wolves at Brookfield in mating season, 1963. Small arrows indicate direction of dominance actions; large arrows, courtship actions. Relative frequency of courtship actions is suggested by width of lines.

FIG. 4. Alpha female rejecting suitors, 1965 season. Left to right: ♂5, ♂2, ♀4, ♂4. ♂5 has one paw on the female's back. If males persisted after initial snarl, ♀4 often whirled upon them in a snapping attack.

mating rivalries and status adjustment (cf. Schenkel, 1947, p. 84-86). ♀1 died from infection of leg wounds apparently inflicted by the most repressed animal, ♀3, as she was being badgered by ♀1. Despite suppression by ♀4, who was now the alpha female, ♀3 mated eight times with ♂1 in the 1965 season. ♂2 mated with ♀3 twice. ♂1 generally rebuffed the attentions of ♀4, and she in turn rebuffed her two young suitors, ♂4 and ♂5 (Fig. 4). ♀3 gave birth to a litter, which was cared for by ♀2 and ♀4.

In the 1966 season ♀5, a 3-year-old, was very important because of her new alpha status in partly restricting the other females' activities, but particularly in thwarting continuing dominance by ♀4. All of the animals mated except ♂3 and ♀5 (Fig. 5). In addition to ties in the reciprocal courtship relations, two males succeeded in tying with two females who did not court them and usually rejected them. All three females that mated gave birth.

Among points worth noting from our observations is the effect of dominant animals in restricting the courtship activities of lesser animals. This applies not just to the alpha animals, but to other relationships, such as ♀4 in the 1966 season to ♀2 and ♀3 (Fig. 6). Or ♂5 to ♂1: for the 1965 and 1966 seasons, ♂5, the beta male, was chiefly responsible for repressing ♂1.

A second point is the lasting nature of mate preferences, which is outstanding in the case of ♂1 and ♀3 (Table 1). Mate preferences seem to be related to the order of dominance in the group when the young first become mature. Thus, ♀4 prefers ♂1, and ♀5 prefers ♂2. ♂4 and ♂5 preferred ♀1, but switched to ♀4 when ♀1 was no longer available (about ⅓ of their recorded courtship actions were directed to ♀4 in 1964, ⅔ in 1965, and 9/10 in 1966). The relation of ♂3 to ♀2 is apparently also linked indirectly to the dominance hierarchy. In 1963 he split his attentions between ♀1 and ♀2. He later concentrated on ♀2 after his initial rebuffs and domination by ♀1. These younger males, of course, were not very experienced

TABLE 1. Mate preference in Brookfield wolves, mainly based on frequency of courtship activity.

Season	♂1	♂2	♂3	♂4	♂5
1961	c ♀3	a ♀1			
1962	c ♀3	a ♀1	—		
1963	c ♀3	a ♀1	a ♀1	a ♀1	—
1964		a ♀1	c ♀2	a ♀1	a ♀1
1965	d ♀3	c ♀2	c ♀2	a ♀4	a ♀4
1966	c ♀3	c ♀3	d ♀2	b ♀4	b ♀4

	♀1	♀2	♀3	♀4	♀5
1961	a ♂1	?	a ♂1		
1962	a ♂1	?	a ♂1	—	
1963	a ♂1	b ♂2	a ♂1	a ♂1	
1964	a ♂2	a ♂2	0	0	—
1965		a ♂2	e ♂1	e ♂1	a ♂2
1966		a ♂2	d ♂1	d ♂1	a ♂2

—, animal was present but not mature; 0, animal present but no preference evident; ?, data lacking.

Letters before individual symbols indicate dominance rank within sex.

431

TABLE 2. *Changes in dominance rankings of Brookfield wolves. Separate rankings within sexes.*

Wolf	Birth year	1961	1962	1963	1964	1965	1966
♂1	57	A	A	A	—	E	D
♂2	57	B	B	B	A	A	A
♂3	61	—	C	C	B	B	E
♂4	62	—	—	D	D	D	C
♂5	62	—	—	D	C	C	B
♀1	57	A	A	A	A	—	—
♀2	57	B	B	C	C	C	D
♀3	57	C	D	D	D	D	C
♀4	61	—	C	B	B	A	B
♀5	63	—	—	—	?	B	A

?, animal present (*contra* report in Ginsburg, 1965) but not enough interactions with other animals to assign rank (definitely below ♀1).

competitors for ♀1's favor. However, lesser males can, and do, partly thwart a superior male's attentions to a mutually preferred female by blocking and fawning maneuvers.

Also noteworthy is that some kind of filial or allegiance-bond is seen in males. Thus, ♂3 has always sided with ♂1, protecting him when he was being attacked while in tie. Likewise, ♂4 and ♂5 seem to shield ♂2 from other animals at such critical times. These allegiances may be related to the dominance hierarchy when the young males mature. The recent decline of ♂3 in the rank order may thus be in part a result of the fall of ♂1. In respect to this, Table 2 is slightly misleading in giving linear rankings—♂3 was not truly dominant to ♂1 in 1965 in terms of conflict, but he definitely was superior to ♂4 and ♂5 at that time. The rapid rises in rank of ♀4 and then ♀5 also suggest cultural transmission of status. As pups they apparently adopted their alpha mother's attitude to the other adult females, and upon growth were able to enforce this attitude.

We previously remarked on the lesser mating activity of the alpha male, when we had evidence from only one animal (Ginsburg, 1965). However, in the 1966 season, the second alpha male in the group's history tied only once, and was the most inactive of all the males in courting activity, continuing a trend from his previous two alpha seasons. Admittedly, his preferred female was no longer in the group in 1965 and 1966. In both of these seasons, he tied with the first female to come fully into heat, and thereafter showed relatively little interest in the proceedings. Conversely, in the last two seasons, the former alpha male has increased his courtship activity (Table 3.)

Not enough young have grown up in the woods at Brookfield to give many clues to social relations between maturing litter

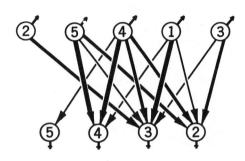

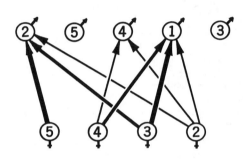

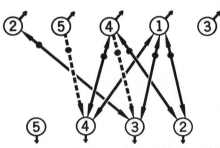

FIG. 5. Summaries of courtship relations in wolves at Brookfield, 1966 mating season. Top, male actions; middle, female actions; bottom, reciprocal courtships and ties. In top and middle, width of lines indicates relative frequency of courtship. In bottom, bulbs on arrows represent copulatory ties; dashed arrows are non-reciprocal courtships that resulted in ties. Symbols for individuals arranged in order of dominance, alpha animals at left.

432

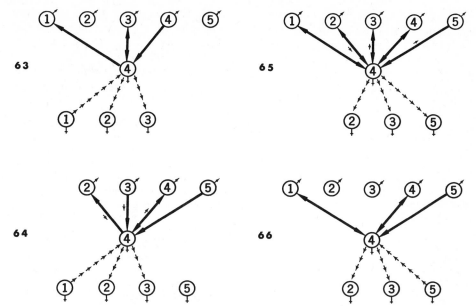

FIG. 6. Principal relations of ♀4 to other wolves at Brookfield in four mating seasons. This female became mature in 1963. Small arrows, dominance actions; large arrows, courtship actions.

mates. For the first 3 years, the brother and sister of 1961, ♂3 and ♀4, had a mutually tolerant and rather playful relation. He was dominant to her, but also he fended off some courting attentions to her by younger males. In the midst of the 1965 mating season, ♀4 somehow, and for unknown cause, subjugated her brother. This gave rise to amusing failures in communication as the younger males mistook his submissive gestures for deference to themselves. Between these younger males, ♂4 and ♂5, there has been strong, and even savage, rivalry. However, in the 1966 sea-

son, there was more tolerance, and even some evidence of mutual support.

Fig. 6 shows graphically the relationships of one of these young, ♀4, through four mating seasons to give an idea of the changes that occur and the complexity of the social structure. However, graphs cannot convey the flavor of each wolf's personality, which displays some characteristics not linked to the hierarchical order. For example, ♂4 was sexually precocious compared to his brother, ♂5, and has always been more acceptable to the females. Simple effects of density or crowding are

TABLE 3. *Courtship actions and number of ties in Brookfield wolves. Courtship figures are percentages of total bouts recorded for each season. Active indicates animal initiated behavior, passive, that animal was object of courtship.*

Season	Behavior	♂1	2	3	4	5	N	♀1	2	3	4	5	N
1966	Active	23	7	10	34	26	279		12	47	16	25	146
	Passive	54	38	0	7	1	146		17	39	43	1	279
	Ties	2	1		3	2	8		2*	3*	3*		8
1965	Active	9	18	19	36	18	363		15	50	32	3	117
	Passive	81	14	2	3	0	117		23	16	60	1	363
	Ties	8	2				10			10*			10
1964	Active		31	9	35	25	187	40	35	5	20	0	20
	Passive		45	35	10	10	20	59	19	2	20	0	187
	Ties		3		1	2	6	6*					6
1963	Active	14	47	19	16	4	135	43	16	35	6		49
	Passive	70	14	16	0	0	49	69	15	13	3		135
	Ties	1	5		1		7	6*		1			7

* Female subsequently gave birth.

not obvious in the reproduction of this captive group, where food is amply provided. Seven litters have ranged in size from 3 to 6, average 4.3; a total of 12 young was born in 1966 when three females gave birth. However, females born after the group was established have not bred or even shown full estrus in their second year, despite high social ranking.

The Brookfield wolves are not in a natural situation, but there are indications from the literature that similar relationships and behavior are seen in the wild. For example, judging from Murie's account, the dominant male of his most closely studied pack was not the father of the young. Similarly, Ognev (1931) reported that N. A. Dmitriev-Mamonov found that a female mated for four consecutive years with a small, lame male in apparent preference to other males in the area. Other studies in captivity also lend support. Mr. George Wilson of St. Louis, Missouri, who has kept two males and two females outdoors in a rather natural setting, has told us that the dominant male was not the father in his group. In the group of five studied by Frädrich and Göltenboth (1965), the mother was the beta female.

The significance of these matters in the biology of wolves is not fully clear. However, the existence of strong mate preferences alone patently restricts the reproductive potential of a pack. Dominance within the sexes also has contraceptive value, but the actions of the alpha male do not necessarily amount to psychological castration of the lesser males, as has been suggested by Etkin (1964, p. 275) on the basis of studies of the dog. However, our chief bitch, for all practical purposes, did achieve this state of control over lesser females. When the original strong dominance hierarchy broke down, there were relatively numerous cross-sexual combinations, although the result was obviously not a wholly promiscuous or random mating situation (Fig. 5).

It appears that captive groups composed of litter mates untutored by their parents can show complex group organization, which we infer arises through genetically determined behavior (cf. Scott and Fuller, 1965, p. 415). The group at Brookfield, despite persecution of an occasional outcast, shows strong evidence of natural cohesiveness in assembling for greeting ceremonies,

in howling together in response to artificial wolves in the form of local sirens, through group assaults, etc. Again, there is close correspondence to behavior reported in the wild, which even includes situations where outcasts do not leave the group (see Mech, 1966, p. 63-64).

The ritualized group activities, the altruism shown in the care and raising of the young by non-parents, and the low level of reproductive activity apparent in some male leaders suggest that wolves have evolved their social structure with some selective pressure for traits of value to the group, and not just the individual.

It may be impractical or impossible to determine whether such selection operates mainly on individual wolves as adaptive units within a social environmental unit (Wiens, 1966), or as bearers of common genes in a kinship group (Williams, 1966). It has been presumed that the basic social unit in wild wolves is composed of litter mates (e.g., Scott and Fuller, 1965, p. 416). But is it? Does a litter that starts hunting together become an enduring reproducing group? Even if so, what are the genetic and social relationships to the basic group of the apparent strangers that are accepted and rejected on occasion? There is obviously a need to know much more about the formation of wolf groups in the wild.

The natural and induced changes of social structure in the wolves at Brookfield demonstrate that a fascinating range of relationships is possible in a captive group. We hope this and related work on similar groups (e.g., Schönberner, 1965) will provide reference points for studies in the wild, where biotelemetry and marking techniques promise eventually to give a definitive picture of wolf life.

If we need additional stimulus to tackle problems implied and touched on in this report, the ideas of recent years concerning man's early evolution from a pack-hunting primate seem an ample challenge to us. The social organizations of wolves, lions, and Cape hunting dogs may be more relevant than those of most primates to the human situation.

REFERENCES

Etkin, W. 1964. Types of social organization in birds and mammals, p. 256-297. *In* W. Etkin, [ed.], Social behavior and organization among vertebrates. Univ. Chicago Press, Chicago, Ill.

Frädrich, H., and R. Göltenboth. 1965. Aufzucht von Wölfen im Rudel. D. Zool. Garten (NF) 30: 274-278.

Ginsburg, B. E. 1965. Coaction of genetical and nongenetical factors influencing sexual behavior, p. 53-75. In F. A. Beach, [ed.], Sex and behavior. John Wiley and Sons, Inc., New York, N. Y.

Mech, L. D. 1966. The wolves of Isle Royale. U. S. Natl. Park Serv., Fauna Ser. 7. 210 p.

Murie, A. 1944. The wolves of Mt. McKinley. U. S. Natl. Park Serv., Fauna Ser. 5. 238 p.

Ognev, S. I. 1931. Mammals of Eastern Europe and Northern Asia. Vol. II. Carnivora (Fissipedia). Transl. 1962, Israel Prog. Sci. Transl., Natl. Sci. Foundation, Washington, D. C.

Rabb, G. B., B. E. Ginsburg, and S. Andrews. 1962. Comparative studies of canid behavior. IV. Mating behavior in relation to social structure in wolves. Bull. Ecol. Soc. Am. 43:79.

Schenkel, R. 1947. Ausdrucks-Studien an Wölfen. Behaviour 1:81-129.

Schönberner, D. 1965. Beobachtungen zur Fortpflanzungsbiologie des Wolfes, Canis lupus. Z. Säugetierkunde 30:171-178.

Scott, J. P., and J. L. Fuller. 1965. Genetics and the social behavior of the dog. Univ. Chicago Press, Chicago, Ill.

Wiens, J. A. 1966. On group selection and Wynne-Edwards' hypothesis. Am. Scientist 51:273-287.

Williams, G. C. 1966. Adaptation and natural selection. Princeton Univ. Press, Princeton, N. J.

 61

Field Studies of Old World Monkeys and Apes

Recent prolonged field studies have led to radical revisions of our knowledge of primate behavior.

S. L. Washburn, Phyllis C. Jay, and Jane B. Lancaster

For many years there has been interest in the evolutionary roots of human behavior, and discussions of human evolution frequently include theories on the origin of human customs. In view of the old and widespread interest in the behavior of our nearest relatives, it is surprising how little

Dr. Washburn is professor of anthropology at the University of California, Berkeley. Dr. Jay is assistant professor of anthropology, University of California, and assistant research anthropologist, National Center for Primate Biology, Davis. Mrs. Lancaster is acting instructor of anthropology, University of California, Berkeley.

systematic information was collected until very recently. At the time (1929) Yerkes and Yerkes collected data for their book on the great apes (1), no one had devoted even one continuous month to the systematic study of the behavior of an undisturbed, free-ranging nonhuman primate. Apparently scientists believed that the behavior of monkeys and apes was so stereotyped and simple that travelers' tales or the casual observations of hunters formed a reliable basis for scientific conclusions and social theorizing. As a part of the program of the Yale Laboratories of Comparative Psychology, Yerkes encouraged a series of field studies of the chimpanzee (2), the mountain gorilla (3), and the howling monkey (4). These first studies proved so difficult that Yerkes could write, in the introduction to Carpenter's study, "His is the first reasonably reliable working analysis of the constitution of social groups in the infrahuman primates, and of the relations between the sexes and between mature and immature individuals for monkey or ape" (4, p. 4). Zuckerman, quite independently, had realized the importance of field observations and had combined some field work with physiology and the older literature to produce two very influential volumes (5). From this beginning, only Carpenter continued to make field studies of behavior, and his study of the gibbon (6) is the first successful study of the naturalistic behavior of a member of the family Pongidae. Hooton summarized (7) what was then known about the primates, particularly stressing the importance of behavior and the work of Carpenter and Zuckerman.

The war stopped field work, and no major studies were undertaken for some 15 years. Then, in the 1950's, investigators in Japan, England, France, Switzerland, and the United States independently started studies on the behavior of a wide variety of free-ranging primates. For the history of science it would be interesting to examine the reasons for this burst of parallel activity. Field studies were undertaken at more or less the same time, and publications start in the late 1950's and accelerate rapidly in the 1960's. This trend is still continuing and is well shown by the pattern of frequency of citations in a recent review by Hall (8). The review cites the papers of Bingham, Carpenter, Köhler (9), Nissen, Yerkes, and Zuckerman, but there are no references to additional field studies in the period 1941–1951, and most of the references are to papers appearing in 1960 or later.

The increased interest in primates, and particularly in the behavior of free-ranging primates, has given rise to several symposiums, and results of the new studies have been published almost as soon as they have been completed. Data from the recent field studies are included in volumes edited by Buettner-Janusch (10), Washburn (11), Napier and Barnicot (12), and, especially, DeVore (13). The volume edited by DeVore is devoted entirely to recent field studies and their evaluation. It includes accounts of the behavior of five kinds of monkeys, of chimpanzees, and of gorillas. Each chapter is by the person who did the field work, and in addition there are eight general chapters. Two new journals also are devoted to primates. *Primates*, published by the Japan Monkey Centre, is now in its 5th year, and *Folia Primatologica* has completed volume 3. Carpenter's field studies and general papers have been reprinted so that they are now easily available (14). Southwick has published a collection of readings in primate social behavior (15), and Eimerl and DeVore contributed a volume on the primates to the Life Nature Library (16). Field studies have recently been reviewed by Jay (17), and proceedings of a symposium organized and edited by Altmann should appear shortly (18). This abundance of published material makes it hard to believe that only 2 years ago a course on primate social behavior was difficult to teach because of the lack of easily available, suitable reading material.

The New Field Studies

Obviously, with so much new data a complete review is impossible, and readers wishing more information and bibliography are referred to Jay (*17*) and to the symposiums previously noted. Here we wish to direct attention to the nature of the recent field studies and to a few of their major contributions. Perhaps their greatest contribution is a demonstration that close, accurate observation for hundreds of hours is possible. Prior to Schaller's field work, reported in 1963 (*19*), it was by no means clear that this kind of observation of gorillas would be possible; previous investigators had conducted very fragmentary observations, and Emlen and Schaller deserve great credit for the planning and execution of their study. A field study of the chimpanzee that seemed adequate in the 1930's now seems totally inadequate, when compared to Goodall's results (*20*). Today a field study is planned to yield something of the order of 1000 hours of observations, and the observer is expected to be close to the animals and to recognize individuals. A few years ago observations of this length and quality were thought unnecessary, if not impossible.

The importance of studies in which groups are visited repeatedly and animals are recognized individually may be illustrated by the problems they make it possible to study. For example, during one season of the year chimpanzees "fish" for termites by breaking off sticks or stiff grasses and sticking the prepared implement into a termite hole (*21*), and this whole complex of nest examination, tool preparation, and fishing is learned by the young chimpanzee. It can be seen at only one time of the year and can be appreciated only by an observer whose presence no longer disturbs the animals. Habituation to the observer is a slow and difficult process. Goodall reports (*20*) that after 8 months of observations she could approach to no closer than 50 meters of the chimpanzees and then only when they were in thick cover or up a tree; by 14 months she was able to get within 10 to 15 meters of them. The problem of tool use in nonhuman primates has been reviewed by Hall (*22*), but the essential point here is that the amount of throwing and object manipulation in the monkeys (Cercopithecidae) was greatly exaggerated in travelers' tales, which were uncritically accepted, and it took years of observation in a favorable locality to reveal the complexity of this kind of behavior in the chimpanzee (*23*).

Predation

Another example of the value of continued observations is in the study of deliberate hunting by baboons. In three seasons of field work and more than 1500 hours of observation DeVore had seen baboons catch and eat small mammals, but apparently almost by chance, when the baboon virtually stepped on something like a newborn antelope and then killed it (*24, 25*). But in 1965 DeVore saw repeated incidents of baboons surrounding, hunting, and killing small mammals (*26*).

The whole matter of predation on primates has been difficult to study. Rare events, such as an attack by an eagle (*27*) may be very important in the survival of primates, but such attacks are seldom observed, because the presence of the human observer disturbs either the predator or the prey. We think that the present de-emphasis of the importance of predation on primates arises from these difficulties of observation and from the fact that even today most studies of free-ranging primates are made in areas where predators have been reduced or eliminated by man. Most predators are active at night, and there is still no adequate study of the nocturnal behavior of any monkey or ape.

Predation probably can best be measured by studying the predators rather than the prey.

Recognition of individual animals is necessary for the study of many problems, from the first stages of the analysis of a social system to observations of social continuity or constancy of group membership; such observations are exceedingly difficult under most field conditions. For example, understanding of the dominance system implies repeated recognition of a number of animals under sufficiently various conditions so that the patterns of interaction become clear. Again, to be sure that a group has lost or gained a member, the observer must know the whole composition of the group.

Long-continued observations have proved to be important in many unexpected ways. For example, rhesus monkeys have been observed in several of their many very different habitats, and it has been found that young rhesus play more in cities than in some kinds of forest and play in the forest more at some seasons than at others. These differences are due in part to the amount of time which must be spent in getting food; the same forest troop may play more when fruits are available and hunger may be rapidly satisfied than at times of the year when the diet is composed of tiny seeds which take a long time to pick. Extracting the small seeds of sheesham pods during the months when rhesus troops spend most of their time in the sheesham trees takes many hours of the day (28). What might easily have been described in a short-term study as a species-specific difference of considerable magnitude turns out to be the result of seasonal and local variations in food source. It is essential to sample behavior in several habitats to gain an understanding of the flexibility of the built-in behavior patterns of a species, flexibility which precludes the need for development of new forms of genetically determined behavior to cope successfully with different habitats.

The long-term study in which many groups of a species are observed in different, contrasting localities, and in which at least some groups are known so well that most of the individuals can be recognized, will correct many false notions and will make valid generalizations possible. Although so far there have been only a few major investigations of this sort, some important generalizations seem possible.

Environment and Social Behavior

Nowhere is the extent to which the behavior of a species is adaptable and responsive to local conditions more apparent than among groups of rhesus living in India. Rhesus occur naturally in such diverse environments as cities, villages, roadsides, cultivated fields, and many types of forest ranging to altitudes of over 2400 meters. Contact with man varies in these habitats from constant and close to rare and incidental.

Where rhesus groups are subjected to pressures of trapping, harassment, and high incidence of infectious disease, groups are tense and aggression is high. These pressures are found in areas where there is most contact and interaction with man, such as in cities and at places of pilgrimage. The animals are in generally poor physical condition, and numerous old and new wounds are evidence of a high rate of intragroup fighting. Tension among groups occupying adjacent areas of land is similarly high where there is insufficient space for normal movement and behavior, and where there may be intense competition for a limited supply of food and water. This is in sharp contrast to those groups living away from man where normal spacing among groups can be effected by the means evolved by the species. In the latter environments, such as forests, the rhesus are in excellent physical condition and what aggressive behavior occurs functions to maintain stable social groups and relationships among the members of the group; wounds are substantially fewer, and disease appears to be rare.

There has been considerable controversy in discussions of the relationships among social groups of the same species as to whether or not the geographical area occupied by a group should be called a territory or a home range. The point we wish to emphasize is that, within one species, populations living in different habitats may act quite differently toward neighboring groups. Populations may be capable of a wide variety of behavior patterns ranging from exclusive occupation of an area which may be defended against neighboring groups to a peaceful coexistence with conspecifics in which wide overlap in home ranges is tolerated. Because local populations of a species may maintain their ranges in different ways it is necessary to investigate all variations in group spacing in diverse habitats before attempting to describe characteristic behavior patterns for any species.

Not unexpectedly, population and group composition reflect these differences in habitat and stress. Groups living on the Gangetic plains, where trapping, harassment, and disease are important factors, are smaller, and the proportion of young members is also significantly smaller (28, 29). The long-term effects of pressures on different rhesus populations in northern and central India are now being investigated by a team of anthropologists of the National Center for Primate Biology.

A city presents a very different set of challenges to a rhesus group than does a forest. Often there are no trees to sleep in; living space must be shared with man and his domestic animals. Food is not available in the form common to other habitats, and monkeys may have to depend on their skill in stealing food from man. Often the food has been prepared by man for his own consumption, or it consists of fruits and vegetables pilfered from houses, shops, and streets. Garbage is picked through and edible portions are consumed. It is essential that the monkeys learn to differentiate between those humans who represent a real threat to their safety and those who are safe to approach. They must react quickly and learn to manipulate doors, gates, and other elements of the physical environment unique to their urban habitat. This is a tremendously different setting from that in which most rhesus live. City rhesus are more manipulative, more active, and often more aggressive than are forest rhesus. Clearly, the same species develops quite different learned habits in different environments.

Annual Reproductive Cycle

The belief, which has been widely maintained, that there is no breeding season in monkeys and apes gave rise to the theory that the persistence throughout the year of groups, or highly organized troops, was due to continuous sexual attraction. The evidence for a breeding season has been reviewed by Lancaster and Lee (30) who found that in many species of monkeys there is a well-marked breeding season. For example, Mizuhara has presented data (31) on 545 births of Japanese macaques of Takasakiyama. There were on the average approximately 90 births per year over six consecutive years. The average length of the birth season was 125 days, but it varied from 95 to 176 days. The majority of the births occurred in June and July. Copulations were most frequent in November to March and were not observed during the birth season, and in spite of this the highly organized group continues as a social unit throughout the year.

The birth season has been studied in other groups of Japanese macaques, and in general the situation is similar. There is no doubt that both mating and birth seasons are highly restricted in the Japanese macaque. The birth season is spring and summer, but its onset and duration vary considerably. If observations were limited and combined for the whole species, as they were in early studies, the birth season would appear to be much longer than in fact it is for an individual group, and it is the events within the local group, not averages of events for the species, that bear upon the role of sexual attraction in holding primate society together.

Under very different climatic conditions, in India, rhesus macaques also have a birth season, but copulations were observed in all months of the year, although probably not with equal frequency (29). Among rhesus on a small island off Puerto Rico births occur from January to June, and copulations are restricted to July–January (32). These data confirm the point that a birth season will be more sharply defined in a local group than in a species as a whole. There is a mating season among rhesus introduced on the island, but only a peak of mating in the same species in their native India (29). It is clear that survey data drawn from many groups over a wide area must be used with caution when the aim is to interpret the behavior of a single group. Since the birth season is an adaptation to local conditions, there is no reason to expect it to be the same over the entire geographical distribution of a species, and under laboratory conditions rhesus macaques breed throughout the year.

No data comparable to those for the macaques exist for other primates, and, since accurate determination of mating and birth seasons requires that reasonable numbers of animals be observed in all months of the year and that groups be observed in different localities, really adequate data exist for only the Japanese macaque. However, Lancaster and Lee were able to assemble data on 14 species of monkeys and apes. They found that probably the most common situation is a birth peak, a time of year at which births tend to be concentrated, rather than sharply limited mating and birth seasons. This is highly adaptive for widely distributed species, for it allows the majority of births to occur at the optimum time for each locality while maintaining a widely variable basic pattern. The birth season may be a more effective adaptation to extreme climatic conditions. There may be a birth peak in the chimpanzee (20), and there may be none in the mountain gorilla (19), but, since we have no more data than are necessary to clarify the reproductive pattern in a single species of macaque, we can conclude only that, while birth seasons are not present in either gorillas or chimpanzees, a peak is possible in chimpanzees, at least for those living near Lake Tanganyika.

Prior to the recent investigations there was a great deal of information on primate reproduction, and yet as late as 1960 it was still possible to maintain that there were no breeding seasons in primates and that this was the basis of primate society. Until recently the question of seasonality was raised without reference to a birth season as distinguished from a birth peak, or to a limited mating season as distinguished from matings throughout the year with a high frequency in a particular period.

Frequency of Mating

Obviously many more studies are needed, and one of the intriguing problems is the role of potency. Not only does the frequency of mating vary through the year, but also there appear to be enormous differences in potency between species that are reproducing at a normal rate. In nearly 500 hours of observation of gorillas, Schaller (*19*) saw only two matings, fewer than might be seen in a troop of baboons in almost any single morning. The redtail monkey (*Cercopithecus ascanius*) mates rarely (*27*), but the closely related vervet (*Cercopithecus aethiops*) does so frequently. To a considerable extent the observed differences are correlated with structure (*33*), such as size of testes, and all these species seem to be reproducing at an adequate and normal rate. There is no evidence that langurs (*Presbytis entellus*) are less successful breeders than rhesus, but the langurs copulate less frequently (*34*).

Now that more adequate data are becoming available, the social functions of sexual behavior should be reinvestigated. The dismissal of the theory that sexual attraction is *the* basis of primate society should open the way for a more careful study of the multiple functions of sexual behavior. The great differences among the primate species should provide data to prove or disprove new theories. In passing it might be noted that the human mating system without estrous cycles in the female and without marked seasonal variations is unique.

Systems of Mating

Mating systems, like the presence or absence of seasonality in breeding and the frequency of copulation, are extremely variable in monkeys and apes. Eventually the relation of these variations to species adaptations will be understandable; at present it is most important to note that monkeys do not necessarily live either in harems or in promiscuous hordes as was once assumed. Restrictive mating patterns such as the stable and exclusive pair-bond formed between adult gibbons (*6*) and the harem system of the Hamadryas baboon (*35*) are comparatively rare. The most common mating pattern of monkeys and apes is promiscuity more or less influenced by dominance relationships. In species in which dominance relations are not constantly at issue, such as langurs (*34*), chimpanzees (*20*), or bonnet macaques (*36*), matings appear to be relatively promiscuous and are often based on the personal inclination of the estrous female. When dominance relationships are constantly at issue, as in baboons (*37*), Japanese macaques (*38*), and rhesus macaques (*39, 40*), sex often becomes one of the prerogatives of dominant rank. In such species dominant males tend to do a larger share of the mating than do more subordinate animals, but it is only in unusual situations that subordinate animals are barred from the mating system altogether. Mating systems probably support the general adaptation of the species to its environment. In most baboons and macaques the tendency for a few males to do much of the mating may be partly a by-product of natural selection for a hierarchy of adult males which dominates the troop so that in a dangerous terrestrial habitat external dangers will be met in an orderly way. Selection is not only for a male which can impregnate many females but it may also have favored a dominance-oriented social organization in which sexual activity has become one of the expressions of that dominance.

Dominance Relationships

Long-term field studies of monkeys and apes in their natural habitats have emphasized that social relationships within a group are patterned and organized in very complex ways. There is no single "monkey pattern" or "ape pattern"; rather, there is great variability, both among different species. and among different populations of the same species, in the organization and expression of social relationships. A difference in the relative dominance of individuals is one of the most common modes of social organization in monkey and ape societies. Dominance is not synonymous with aggression, and the way dominance is expressed varies greatly between species. In the gorilla, for example, dominance is most often expressed by extremely attenuated gestures and signals (19); a gentle nudge from the dominant male is more than enough to elicit a submissive response from a subordinate, whereas, in baboons, chases, fights, and biting can be daily occurrences (37). In many primates there is a tendency for the major age-sex classes to be ranked in a dominance order; for example, in baboons, macaques, and gorillas, adult males as a class are usually dominant over adult females, and females are dominant over young. This may not always be true, for in several species of macaques some females may outrank some adult males (36), although groups dominated by a female (such as the Minoo-B troop of Japanese macaques) are extremely rare (41). Dominance relationships may be quite unstructured, as in the chimpanzee (20), where dominance is expressed in interactions between individuals but where these relationships are not organized into any sort of hierarchy. A much more common situation is one in which dominance relations, among males at least, are organized into linear hierarchies that are quite stable over time, as in baboons (37), langurs (34, 42), and macaques (43, 44). Sometimes these dominance hierarchies are complicated by alliances among several males who back each other up very effectively (37) or even by an alliance between a male and a female (36). Although dominance varies widely among monkeys and apes both in its form and function, it is certainly one of the most important axes of social organization to be found in primate societies.

Genealogical Relationships

Recognition of individual animals and repeated studies of the same groups have opened the way to the appreciation of other long-continuing social relationships in monkeys and apes which cannot be interpreted in terms of dominance alone. Long-term studies of free-ranging animals have been made on only two species of nonhuman primates, Japanese macaques, which have been studied since 1950 by members of the Japan Monkey Center, and Indian rhesus macaques living free on Cayo Santiago, Puerto Rico, the island colony established by Carpenter in 1938. In these studies, when the genealogy of the animals has been known, it has been obvious that genetic relationships play a major role in determining the course and nature of social interactions (41, 45–47). It becomes clear that bonds between mother and infant may persist into adult life to form a nucleus from which many other social bonds ramify. When the genealogy of individual animals is known, members of commonly observed subgroupings, such as a cluster of four or five animals grooming or resting together, are likely to be uterine kin. For example, members of a subgroup composed of several adult animals, both male and female, as well as juveniles and infants, may all be offspring of the same female (47). These relations continue to be very important in adult life not only in relaxed affectional relationships but also in dominance interactions. Sade saw a female rhesus monkey divert the attack of a dominant male from her adult son and saw another adult female protect her juvenile half-sisters (paternity is not determinable in most monkey societies). There is a very high frequency of grooming between related animals, and many animals never seek grooming partners outside of their own genealogies.

It should be stressed that there is no information leading us to believe that these animals are either recognizing genetic relationships or responding to any sort of abstract concept of family. Rather these social relationships are determined by the necessarily close association of mother with newborn infant, which is extended through time and generations and which ramifies into close associations among siblings. We believe that this pattern of enduring social relations between a mother and her offspring will be found in other species of primates. Because of their dramatic character, the importance of dominance and aggression has been greatly exaggerated compared to that of continuing, positive, affectional relations between related animals as expressed by their sitting or feeding together, touching, and grooming. Much of this behavior can be observed easily in the field, but the extent to which it is in fact an expression of social genealogies has been demonstrated only in the studies cited above.

Positive, affectional relations are not limited to relatives. Male Japanese macaques may take care of young by forming special protective relationships with particular infants (48), but whether these males have any special relationship to the infants as either father or brother is uncertain, and the mating system is such that paternity cannot be known either to the observer or to the monkeys. MacRoberts (49) has recorded a very high frequency of care of infants by males in the Gibraltar macaque. In addition, he has demonstrated that these positive protective relations are very beneficial to the juvenile. Two juveniles which had no such close relationship were forced to be peripheral, were at a great disadvantage in feeding, and were groomed much less than other juveniles in the group.

The status of the adult can be conferred on closely associated young (frequently an offspring when the adult is female), and for this reason the young of dominant animals are more likely to be dominant. This inheritance of rank has been discussed by Imanishi (45) for the Japanese macaque and by Koford (46) for the rhesus. Sons of very dominant females seem to have a great advantage over other males both because their mothers are able to back them up successfully in social interactions and because they stay with their mothers near the other dominant animals at the center of the group. They may never go through the stage of being socially and physically peripheral to the group which is typical for young males of these species. A male cannot simply "inherit" high rank; he must also win this position through his own abilities, but his chances of so doing are greatly increased if he has had these early experiences of associating with and being supported by very dominant animals.

There could hardly be a greater contrast than that between the emerging picture of an orderly society, based heavily on affectionate or cooperative social actions and structured by stable dominance relationships, and the old notion of an unruly horde of monkeys dominated by a tyrant. The 19th-century social evolutionists attributed less order to the societies of primitive man than is now known to exist in the societies of monkeys and apes living today.

Communication

Research on the communication systems of monkeys and apes through 1962 has been most ably summarized and interpreted by Marler (50). Most of the data represent work by field observers who were primarily interested in social structure, and the signals, and their meanings, used to implement and facilitate social interactions were more or less taken for granted. Only in the last year or so have communication systems themselves been the object of careful study and analysis (see, for example, *18*). Marler has emphasized both the extraordinary complexity of the communication systems of primates and the heavy dependence of these systems on composite signals (*50*). Most frequently it is not a single signal that passes between two animals but a signal complex composed of auditory, visual, tactile, and, more rarely, olfactory signals.

Communication in some monkey species is based on a system of intergrading signals, whereas in others much more use is made of highly discrete signals. For example, most vervet sounds (described by Struhsaker, *51*) are of the discrete type, there being some 36 different sounds that are comparatively distinct both to the human ear and when analyzed by a sound spectrograph. In contrast, Rowell and Hinde have analyzed the sounds of the rhesus monkey (*52*) and found that of 13 harsh noises, 9 belonged to a single intergrading subsystem expressing agonistic emotions.

As more and more study is done on primates it will probably be shown that their communication systems tend to be of mixed form in that both graded and discrete signals are used depending on the relative efficiency of one or the other form in serving a specific function. In concert this use of both discrete and intergrading signals and of composites from several sensory modes produces a rich potential for the expression of very slight but significant changes in the intensity and nature of mood in the signaling animal. Marler has emphasized (*50*) that, except for calls warning of danger, the communication system is little applied to events outside the group. Communication systems in monkeys and apes are highly

evolved in their capacity to express motivation of individuals and to facilitate social relationships. Without this ability to express mood, monkeys and apes would not be able to engage in the subtle and complicated social interactions that are a major feature of their adaptations.

Social Learning

Harlow and Harlow's experiments (*53*) show the importance of learning in the development of social life; however, monkeys and apes are so constituted that, except in the laboratory, social learning is inevitable. They adapt by their social life, and the group provides the context of affection, protection, and stability in which learning occurs. No one factor can explain the importance of social behavior, because society is a major adaptive mechanism with many functions, but one of the most important of these functions is the provision of a rich and protected social context in which young mature. Field observations, although mainly observations of the results of learning rather than of the process itself, provide necessary clues as to the nature of the integration of relevant developmental and social factors. These factors can then be estimated and defined for subsequent intensive controlled research in a laboratory or colony.

It has become clear that, although learning has great importance in the normal development of nearly all phases of primate behavior, it is not a generalized ability; animals are able to learn some things with great ease and other things only with the greatest difficulty. Learning is part of the adaptive pattern of a species and can be understood only when it is seen as the process of acquiring skills and attitudes that are of evolutionary significance to a species when living in the environment to which it is adapted.

There are important biological limitations which vary from species to species and which do not reflect differences in intelligence so much as differences in specializations. For example, Goodall (21) has observed young chimpanzees learning to fish for termites both by their observation of older chimpanzees and by practice. It takes time for the chimpanzee to become proficient with these tools, and many mistakes are made. Chimpanzees are not the only primates that like termites, and Goodall has observed baboons sitting near chimpanzees watching and waiting while the latter are getting termites. The baboons are just as eager as the chimpanzees to eat termites but are unable to learn how to fish for termites for themselves.

It is likely that there are important variables among groups of a single species that make it possible for the acquisition of new patterns of behavior or the expression of basic learned species patterns to vary from group to group and from one habitat to another. For example, the nature of the integration and operation of a social unit vary in the extent to which it depends on the personalities of individuals in the group—this is another dimension of our understanding of how social behavior may affect species survival. Particularly aggressive adult males can make the behavior of their groups relative to that of adjacent groups with less assertive males substantially different. For example, a group with very aggressive males can control a larger geographic area than is occupied by a group with much less aggressive males. The tenor of life within a group may be tenser or more relaxed depending on personalities of adults in the group.

Imprinting has traditionally been distinguished from other learning processes by the fact that in imprinting the young animal will learn to follow, to be social (54), without an external or immediate reward (55). However, among monkeys and apes, simply being with other animals is a reward, and learning is reinforced by the affectional, attentive, supportive social context of the group (56). Butler was the first to use the sight of another monkey as a reward in psychological experiments (57). The field worker sees sick and practically disabled animals making great efforts to stay with their group. Among ground-living forms, animals that have lost or broken limbs or are so sick that they collapse as soon as the group stops moving, all walk along as the troop moves. Instances of wounded rhesus macaques' moving into langur groups after the rhesus have left or been forced out of their own group have been recorded. Clearly, it is essential for the young monkey or ape to mature in a social setting in which it learns appropriate skills and relationships during early years and in which it continues to learn during adulthood. "Where the individual primate is, in temporary isolation, learning a task without reference to any other member of its species, the learning is not normal" (58).

Future Primate Studies

At present many long-term studies are in process and major films are being edited (Goodall on chimpanzee and DeVore on baboon). There will be about twice as many major accounts available in 2 years as there are now. Since it is now clear that detailed descriptive studies of undisturbed free-ranging primates can be made, and since available data show that there are substantial differences in the behavior of the different species, more species should be investigated. So far studies have concentrated for the most part on the larger ground-living forms which are easier to study. There is no study of *Cercocebus*, little on *Colobus* (59), and nothing on the numerous langurs (*Presbytis*) of southeast Asia. New World monkeys have been investigated very little, and there are numerous genera that have not been the subjects of a major field study. Also, since

445

local variation is important, forms such as the chimpanzee and gorilla should be studied in more and contrasting localities.

Once the general characteristics of the behaviors of several species are known, then interest can shift to topics such as detailed ecology, birth, infant behavior, peer groups, affectionate behaviors, sex, or dominance, to mention only a few. The behavior of a whole species is a large problem, and description has to be at a very general level when the goal is a first general statement. A problem-oriented study permits choice of species and elaboration of techniques. A further advantage of the problem-oriented approach is that it allows the close coordination of the field work with experimental work in the laboratory. Fortunately, no division has developed between those doing the field work and those involved in the experimental analysis of behavior. Many scientists have done both controlled experiments and field studies. The interplay between naturalistic observation and controlled experiment is the essential key to the understanding of behavior (60). The character of the natural adaptation of the species and the dimensions of the society can be determined only in the field. Many topics, such as geographic range, food, predation, group size, aggression, and the like, can be seen only under field conditions. But the mechanisms of the observed behavior can be determined only in the laboratory, and this is the more complicated task. The relation of a field study to scientific understanding is like the relation of the observation that a man walks or runs to the whole analysis of locomotion. The field worker lists what the animals eat, but this gives no understanding of nutrition. The kinds of interactions may be charted in the field, but their interpretation requires the laboratory. Field workers saw hours devoted to play, but it was Harlow's experiments that showed how essential this activity was

to the development of behavior. As the field studies develop it is to be hoped that they will maintain a close relation to controlled experiment. It is most fortunate that the present studies are being carried on by anthropologists, psychologists, and zoologists. An understanding of behavior is most likely to come from the bringing together of the methods and interests of many sciences, and we hope that the field studies remain a part of general behavioral science and do not become independent as workers and problems become more and more numerous.

Even now, in their preliminary state, the field studies can offer some conclusions that might be pondered by students in the multiplicity of departments now dividing up the study of human behavior. Behavior is profoundly influenced by the biology of the species, and problems of perception, emotion, aggression, and many others cannot be divorced from the biology of the actors in the social system. Early learning is important, and an understanding of the preschool years is essential to an understanding of behavior. Play is tremendously important, and a species that wastes the emotions and energies of its young by divorcing play from education has forfeited its evolutionary heritage—the biological motivation of learning. Social behavior is relatively simple compared to the biological mechanisms that make the behavior possible. Ultimately a science of human behavior must include both biological and social factors, and there is no more reason to separate the study of human behavior into many compartments than there would be to separate the field studies from the intellectual enrichment coming from the laboratory.

REFERENCES

1. R. M. Yerkes and A. W. Yerkes, *The Great Apes, A Study of Anthropoid Life* (Yale Univ. Press, New Haven, 1929).
2. H. W. Nissen, "A Field Study of the Chimpanzee," *Comp. Psychol. Monogr. No. 8*

(1931).

3. H. C. Bingham, "Gorillas in a Native Habitat," *Carnegie Inst. Wash. Publ. No. 426* (1932).

4. C. R. Carpenter, "A Field Study of the Behavior and Social Relations of Howling Monkeys," *Comp. Psych. Monogr. No. 10* (1934).

5. S. Zuckerman, *The Social Life of Monkeys and Apes* (Routledge and Kegan Paul, London, 1932); *Functional Affinities of Man, Monkeys and Apes* (Routledge and Kegan Paul, London, 1933).

6. C. R. Carpenter, "A Field Study in Siam of the Behavior and Social Relations of the Gibbon, *Hylobates lar.*," *Comp. Psychol. Monogr. No. 16* (1940).

7. E. A. Hooton, *Man's Poor Relations* (Doubleday, Garden City, N. Y., 1942).

8. K. R. L. Hall, *Proc. Zool. Soc. London* 14, 265 (1965).

9. W. Köhler, *The Mentality of Apes* (Harcourt Brace, New York, 1925).

10. J. Buettner-Janusch, Ed., "The Relatives of Man," *Ann. N.Y. Acad. Sci.* 102, 181–514 (1962); J. Buettner-Janusch, Ed., *Evolutionary and Genetic Biology of Primates* (Academic Press, New York, 1963–1964).

11. S. L. Washburn, Ed., *Classification and Human Evolution*, Viking Fund Publications in Anthropology No. 37 (Aldine, New York, 1963).

12. J. Napier and N. Barnicot, Eds., "The Primates," *Symp. Zool. Soc. London No. 10* (1963).

13. I. DeVore, Ed. *Primate Behavior: Field Studies of Monkeys and Apes* (Holt, Rinehart and Winston, New York, 1965).

14. C. R. Carpenter, *Naturalistic Behavior of Nonhuman Primates* (Pennsylvania State Univ. Press, University Park, 1964).

15. C. H. Southwick, Ed., *Primate Social Behavior* (Van Nostrand, Princeton, 1963).

16. S. Eimerl and I. DeVore, *The Primates* (Time, Inc., New York, 1965).

17. P. Jay, in *Behavior of Nonhuman Primates*, A. M. Schrier, H. F. Harlow, F. Stollnitz, Eds. (Academic Press, New York, 1965), pp. 525–591.

18. S. A. Altmann, Ed., "Social Communication among Primates," (Univ. of Chicago Press, Chicago, in press).

19. G. Schaller, *The Mountain Gorilla: Ecology and Behavior* (Univ. of Chicago Press, Chicago, 1963).

20. J. Goodall, *Primate Behavior: Field Studies of Monkeys and Apes*, I. DeVore, Ed. (Holt, Rinehart and Winston, New York, 1965), pp. 425–473.

21. ———, *Nature* 201, 1264 (1964).

22. K. R. L. Hall, *Current Anthropol.* 4 (5), 479 (1963).

23. J. B. Lancaster, "Chimpanzee tool use," paper presented at Southwestern Anthropological Association annual meeting, Los Angeles, Calif. (Apr. 1965).

24. I. DeVore and K. R. L. Hall, in *Primate Behavior: Field Studies of Monkeys and Apes* (Holt, Rinehart and Winston, New York, 1965), pp. 20–52.

25. "Baboon Behavior," motion picture produced by I. DeVore and S. L. Washburn, University Extension, Univ. of California, Berkeley (1961).

26. I. DeVore, personal communication (1965).

27. A. J. Haddow, *Proc. Zool. Soc. London* 122 (II), 297 (1952).

28. P. Jay and D. Lindburg, "The Indian Primate Ecology Project (September 1964–June 1965)," unpublished manuscript.

29. C. H. Southwick, M. A. Beg, M. R. Siddiqi, *Ecology* 42, 538 (1961); *ibid.*, p. 698.

30. J. B. Lancaster and R. B. Lee, in *Primate Behavior: Field Studies of Monkeys and Apes*, I. DeVore, Ed. (Holt, Rinehart and Winston, New York, 1965), pp. 486–513.

31. H. Mizuhara, personal communication (1965), quoted by Lancaster and Lee (*30*).

32. C. B. Koford, in *Primate Behavior: Field Studies of Monkeys and Apes*, I. DeVore, Ed. (Holt, Rinehart and Winston, New York, 1965), pp. 160–174.

33. A. H. Schultz, *Anat. Rec.* 72, 387 (1938).

34. P. Jay, in *Primate Behavior: Field Studies of Monkeys and Apes*, I. DeVore, Ed. (Holt, Rinehart and Winston, New York, 1965), pp. 197–249.

35. H. Kummer and F. Kurt, *Folia Primatologica* 1, 4 (1963).

36. P. E. Simonds, in *Primate Behavior: Field Studies of Monkeys and Apes*, I. DeVore, Ed. (Holt, Rinehart and Winston, New York, 1965), pp. 175–196.

37. K. R. L. Hall and I. DeVore, in *Primate Behavior: Field Studies of Monkeys and Apes*, I. DeVore, Ed. (Holt, Rinehart and Winston, New York, 1965), pp. 53–110.

38. K. Tokuda, *Primates* 3, 1 (1961–62).

39. C. H. Conaway and C. B. Koford, *J. Mammal.* 45, 577 (1965).

40. C. Southwick, in *Primate Behavior: Field Studies of Monkeys and Apes*, I. DeVore, Ed. (Holt, Rinehart and Winston, New York, 1965), pp. 111–159.

41. M. Yamada, *Primates* 4, 43 (1963).

42. S. Ripley, in "Social Communication among Primates," S. Altmann, Ed. (Univ. of Chicago Press, Chicago, in press).

43. S. A. Altmann, *Ann. N.Y. Acad. Sci.* 102, 338 (1962).

44. J. Itani, R. Tokuda, Y. Furuya, K. Kano, Y. Shin, *Primates* 4, 1 (1963).

45. K. Imanishi, *Current Anthropol.* 1, 393 (1960).

46. C. B. Koford, *Science* 141, 356 (1963).

47. D. S. Sade, *Am. J. Phys. Anthropol.* 23, 1 (1965).

48. J. Itani, *Primates* 4, 1 (1959).

49. M. MacRoberts, "Gibraltar macaques," paper presented at Southwestern Anthropological Association annual meeting, Los Angeles, Calif. (Apr. 1965).

50. P. Marler, in *Primate Behavior: Field Studies of Monkeys and Apes*, I. DeVore, Ed. (Holt, Rinehart and Winston, New York, 1965), pp. 544–584.

51. T. T. Struhsaker, in "Social Communication among Primates," S. A. Altmann, Ed. (Univ. of Chicago Press, Chicago, in press).

52. T. E. Rowell and R. A. Hinde, *Proc. Zool. Soc. London* 138, 279 (1962); T. E. Rowell, *Symp. Zool. Soc. London* 8, 91 (1962).

53. H. F. Harlow and M. K. Harlow, in *Behavior of Nonhuman Primates*, A. M. Schrier, H. F. Harlow, F. Stollnitz, Eds. (Academic Press, New York, 1965), vol. 2, pp. 287–334.

54. N. E. Collias, in *Roots of Behavior*, E. L. Bliss, Ed. (Harper, New York, 1962), pp. 264–273.

55. W. Sluckin, *Imprinting and Early Learning* (Aldine, Chicago, 1965).

56. K. R. L. Hall, *Brit. J. Psychol.* 54, 201 (1963).

57. R. A. Butler, *J. Exp. Psychol.* 48, 19 (1954).

58. K. R. L. Hall, unpublished manuscript.

59. W. Ullrich, *Zool. Garten* 25, 305 (1961).

60. W. A. Mason, in *Primate Behavior: Field Studies of Monkeys and Apes*, I. DeVore, Ed. (Holt, Rinehart and Winston, New York, 1965), pp. 514–543.

61. Supported by USPHS grant MH 08623. We thank Anne Brower, John Ellefson and Lewis Klein for reading the preliminary version of the manuscript and for helpful criticisms.

A Consequence Of Togetherness

The inability of the North American mountain sheep

to disperse into new habitat stems from

the inheritance of social traditions

by Valerius Geist

During the last century, large populations of bighorn sheep grazed widely from central British Columbia to northern Mexico, and from the coastal mountains of California to the Black Hills of the Dakotas. But with the opening of the West, the bighorns (*Ovis canadensis*) dwindled in number and finally disappeared from most of their former range. Protective measures enacted at the turn of the century failed to reverse their fortunes, and ever since they have existed only in small, widely scattered bands. Some of these relic populations have occasionally increased in size, but they have never recolonized the large amount of former living space available to them. Although the ranges of Dall's and Stone's sheep (*O. dalli* and *O. d. stonei*) are remote and less vulnerable to human invasion, a similar predicament exists for these animals. In short, the North American mountain sheep appear to be incapable of dispersal.

In contrast to the sheep, moose (*Alces alces*) and white-tailed deer (*Odocoileus virginianus*) have made spectacular acquisitions of new territory and have succeeded in increasing their numbers throughout most of their North American range. Why this differential success in acquiring new living space between the sheep and these ungulates?

We know that the former ranges are still acceptable to sheep, for reintroduced populations have generally done well. From twenty-nine reintroductions made on this continent, whose success can be evaluated today, twenty-two have proven successful. And the failure of others may have been due to improper release methods rather than to unsatisfactory range conditions. However, reintroduced populations behave much like the natural relic populations. They remain small in number and generally fail to spread far from the release sites, although an occasional animal may be seen a great distance from his companions.

Nor are sheep physically limited from dispersing. They are most capable migrants and in their travels often swim lakes or rivers and cross over rock rubble and cliffs. In late winter they often travel from mountain to mountain on frozen snow crusts without breaking through. They can go anywhere deer or moose can, and many places they cannot.

Apparently, sheep dislike entering timber, and it is thought that wooded valleys act as barriers to dispersion. Bighorns, for instance, which had become so tame that they followed me at heel as I conducted my field research, rarely went more than one hundred paces into the timber before they left me and returned to the open slopes. Similarly, migratory routes tend to take the shortest distance between mountains and to skirt forest; yet, during regular, seasonal migrations of natural populations, sheep may cross miles of dense timber.

The North American sheep's failure to disperse away from established ranges becomes the more unusual when we remember that, on a worldwide basis, sheep have distributed over a great area. They are found from southwestern Europe, through Asia Minor, the Himalayas, central Asia, eastern Siberia, Alaska, western Canada, the western United States, and Mexico. No other living bovid equals, let alone surpasses, such a distribution. Since sheep have spread through so vast a range, why are they failing in North America today?

Between 1961 and 1966, field studies of several natural populations of North American sheep suggested an answer to their inability to extend their ranges. During this period, my observations indicated that sheep maintain their areas of distribution by passing on home ranges from generation to generation as a living tradition. Each generation of sheep inherits the home ranges of its elders; that is, they acquire the same habits of living in certain areas at specific seasons, and of using the same migratory routes. Exploration apparently plays a most insignificant part in establishing the home range of an individual. Moose and deer, however,

extend their areas of distribution via individual exploration. Neither traditions nor a means of passing them are discernible in the life history of these two species.

If home range traditions are to exist, then there must be a continuous association between donors and receivers, a condition satisfied by sheep. Moreover, sheep society provides for leadership by the elders, reinforces acquired habits, and, by minimizing disruptions in social life, provides no impetus for independent exploration. A comparison between the separation of mother and young in moose and sheep is instructive in this regard.

While the cow moose forms a close relationship with her calf, the female sheep and her lamb live in a rather loose association. But in an abrupt change of behavior, when the female moose is about to give birth to another calf she turns on her yearling and drives it off. The life of the young animal is changed suddenly and violently. Within a few days it changes from a social to a solitary existence, for no cow moose will tolerate the yearling close by and the bulls are little better. The calf is now on his own, and begins the wanderings that eventually lead to the establishment of a new home range.

In contrast, the young sheep experiences no such upheaval. About one week after birth, the lamb begins to associate with other lambs in a band. After it is weaned, the bond with its mother commences to weaken, and the young sheep will follow other animals, preferably an old, barren female, which may even run and play with the youngster. Eventually, the lamb loses all preference for its mother over other sheep.

The important feature of this separation is that the offspring is not chased away and thus does not lose contact with other sheep. Of 283 bighorn yearlings observed between May 15 and June 30, in 1964 and 1965, 76 per cent followed some adult ewe, 15.5 per cent followed an adult ram, 5 per cent followed a subadult sheep (two years old), 3.2 per cent followed other yearlings. Only 1 per cent were seen alone.

Observation of tagged or marked sheep has shown that females, but not males, acquire the home ranges of the female band they are born in. Only rarely do young females leave their band and accept the traditions of another group. When after a prolonged absence I returned to my Stone's sheep study area, I found known female sheep in the expected localities. They were feeding on the same slopes, resting in the same favorite beds, and entering the same caves they had frequented three years previous. In fact they behaved so much in the familiar manner that I felt I had never been away from them.

Young males gradually break with the movement pattern of their female band, by joining male bands that have other, equally stable home ranges. In his third summer, when the young ram begins to search out male bands, he shows a weak, but discernible, wandering phase. In July and August, up to one third of all such little rams may be seen alone, or in the company of a companion of equal age. After his third summer, the ram is again a dedicated follower of older sheep—and remains such till, with increasing age, he gradually becomes more independent and is then followed in turn.

Generally the leader of a ram band is an animal at least eight years old, with long, massive horns. By following these older sheep, the younger rams get to know the wintering areas, the salt licks, the rutting grounds, the summer ranges, and the migratory routes, which have been passed on through the generations. In general, by following the choices of their leaders, younger males acquire those habits that allowed their leaders to grow old: habits that are constant and predictable. Thus, it is evident that sheep society is virtually designed for the passage of habits.

Two-year-old rams can and do stray into areas uninhabited by sheep, yet they will not remain unless accompanied by other animals. If we observe such a single, wandering ram we will note that he often climbs on elevated sites and scans the country below. He calls loudly—which all lone sheep do when traveling. These young rams are apparently searching for other sheep. If they do hit upon unoccupied good habitat, they are not likely to remain, for a habitat without companions is simply not a suitable place for a sheep to live. Furthermore, young rams cannot lead other animals into a newly discovered range, for they have not yet become leaders of a band. Thus, the range extension performed by dispersing juvenile moose will not occur in mountain sheep.

Unlike moose or deer, mountain sheep seem able to disperse only as groups, if they disperse at all. We have no direct data on this, save one introduced population that moved, as a whole, twenty-five to thirty miles to a different locality, but field observations revealed a possible means by which this might have been accomplished. In spring, groups of young rams occasionally go on long excursions into the valleys. Apparently, the "group spirit" of such a band is a strong enough factor to permit the sheep to overcome their reluctance to enter even small patches of timber. Thus, a band may leave an inhabited mountain to visit a nearby, unpopulated area, if intervening timber is not particularly dense. Once a visit has been made, the rams are almost certain to return, since they experienced the new habitat in the presence of companions. However, these group excursions can only occur if the sheep population is large enough to provide large bands of young rams that will discover and retain the new range.

How is it that sheep have developed one system of range establishment and retention, while moose have adopted quite different methods? This question appears particularly apt when we consider that sheep are faring relatively poorly compared to moose. The answer seems to stem from the fact that the habitats of these two species have shaped the evolution of different social systems, which in turn have determined the means by which these animals acquire living space.

Throughout much of its range in America, the moose is found in communities of deciduous shrubs and trees, which follow in the wake of forest fires. Such moose habitat flourishes some years after a fire and allows moose to build up large populations in response to the rich food supply. As coniferous climax forests slowly displace the deciduous species on which the animals feed, the populations decline and vanish. Mature timber, hot summers, and lightning storms assure moose new living space, albeit a rather temporary one. Today, man-made forest fires and logging operations play an important role in the creation of new habitat, although man's intrusion is a relatively recent influence that probably had little effect upon the animal's social evolution.

We find moose not only in the short-lived "burn habitat" created by forest fires but also in small areas with permanent shrub communities, such as on rich alluvial soils along watercourses—particularly in deltas—and on south-facing mountain slopes above timber line, as in northern British Columbia. These limited localities assure a small amount of permanent living space to moose, where they can survive in the absence of habitat created by forest fires.

Under these conditions, the practice of juvenile dispersion serves an important function in maintaining and extending the moose population. Young animals wander out on their own, chance upon burn habitat, establish new ranges, and become the ancestors of large populations that will remain in an area until the habitat disappears. Since the vast majority of moose habitat is short-lived, traditions of range retention would be useless to them. Such traditions would return the animals to increasingly poorer habitat and finally to no habitat at all. Moreover, sizable herds of moose—needed to transmit such traditions—could not be maintained on small patches of permanent habitat. Moose are large animals, and where a few can survive, a dozen would eat themselves out of house and home. Thus, if moose were to develop a social tolerance for one another as sheep have, the resulting "group living" might cause their extinction.

Sheep habitat, whether in California's Death Valley or beyond the Arctic Circle in Alaska's Brooks Range, is always characterized by an open, mountainous landscape and stable plant communities. Most sheep are found on grasslands, which regenerate themselves and do not vanish within a few sheep generations as moose burn habitat does. Today sheep habitat is usually found in small, often widely dispersed patches. These may be separated by brush flats, glaciers, lakes, or wide belts of timber in the valleys. Natural populations of sheep link such patches of habitat via migratory routes inherited from their ancestors.

The distribution of sheep tells us that today's habitat is only the remnant of much larger grasslands that existed shortly after the glaciers withdrew. In later millennia, forests spread along the valleys and ascended mountain slopes, thereby dividing and squeezing mountain grasslands into ever smaller patches. Much sheep habitat vanished, but the remainder was retained by the sheep's home range and migratory traditions—the animals continued to exploit all available patches of habitat. Under these conditions, there is no selection in favor of dispersing juveniles since all the habitat they would normally encounter is already occupied. By leaving adults and moving off through miles of unsuitable territory, juveniles would only increase their chances of getting killed. In relic populations that make long migrations between patches of habitat, selection will favor those animals that remain in the company of others. Any behavior that disrupts this association between young and old sheep will be selected against. Traditions of habitat retention are therefore desirable for sheep, whereas juvenile dispersal is not.

Upon the sheep's evolved habits of range retention, however, must be superimposed the recent intrusion of man. After climatic and vegetal changes had forced sheep to link patches of suitable habitat by means of migratory routes, the coming of man destroyed many of these links—as well as the sheep. Thus, in much of North America, sheep now live in scattered populations, despite the presence of nearby habitat. But this set of conditions is a man-made artifact not previously encountered by the species and to which it lacks a meaningful response. When sheep are exterminated or alienated from certain mountains, the migratory traditions die out, for no surviving adult will return to where it is harassed and no young sheep will be led to it. Once an area has been "forgotten" by a population, sheep are then incapable of returning, even if the area is close at hand. Furthermore, reintroductions appear to me as only a partial solution. Once sheep are stocked on an unfamiliar mountain, the animals' lack of familiarity with the new habitat tends to make them cling to the immediate vicinity. Their exploration is limited to open territory connected to the original area of introduction. They rarely cross timbered valleys and other barriers that may separate them from nearby, potential range. While in natural populations, the males move off to their own areas; in the introduced populations, they share the area (which may be a single mountain) with the ewes. This limits the available food supply via competition and prevents significant growth in numbers. The ideal solution would necessitate a knowledge of access routes to nearby habitat, but this knowledge does not exist. Thus, dispersal is unlikely. The problem is further complicated if men inhabit nearby areas, for this will generally frighten sheep and restrict their activity to the undisturbed parts of a range.

Thus it seems that the evolution of the mountain sheep's means of maintaining its population has not prepared the species for coexistence with man. The contraction of suitable habitat following the glacial retreat has brought about the traditions of range establishment and migration, which have recently been disrupted by human interference. If this interference persists, sheep face an uncertain future. But if a means is found to re-establish migratory routes between patches of available habitat, I believe the animals will overcome their earlier setbacks.

EDITOR's NOTE: After forty-three months spent in the field researching the mountain sheep. Valerius Geist found that these animals would eat from his hand, follow him about, even play "hide and seek" with him. This behavior conflicts with the rather stereotyped notion that sheep are wild and unapproachable. However, it suggests an answer to the problem mentioned in his article—

the sheep's inability to spread into new habitat from their established home ranges. In a recent letter, Dr. Geist stated: "A little patience, tact and delicacy can turn these shy creatures into pets, or even into a nuisance. Although I have not yet tried to lead a band of sheep into an area it does not regularly visit. I am sure it can be done. I believe they can be tamed and made to use salt licks that are progressively moved into new territory, thereby establishing migratory routes which would be followed by succeeding generations."

On War and Peace in Animals and Man

An ethologist's approach to the biology of aggression.

N. Tinbergen

In 1935 Alexis Carrel published a best seller, *Man—The Unknown* (1). Today, more than 30 years later, we biologists have once more the duty to remind our fellowmen that in many respects we are still, to ourselves, unknown. It is true that we now understand a great deal of the way our bodies

Dr. Tinbergen is professor of animal behavior, Department of Zoology, University of Oxford, Oxford, England. This article is the text of his inaugural address, 27 February 1968.

function. With this understanding came control: medicine.

The ignorance of ourselves which needs to be stressed today is ignorance about our behavior—lack of understanding of the causes and effects of the function of our brains. A scientific understanding of our behavior, leading to its control, may well be the most urgent task that faces mankind today. It is the effects of our behavior that begin to endanger the very survival of our species and, worse, of all life on earth. By our technological achievements we have attained a mastery of our environment that is without precedent in the history of life. But these achievements are rapidly getting out of hand. The consequences of our "rape of the earth" are now assuming critical proportions. With shortsighted recklessness we deplete the limited natural resources, including even the oxygen and nitrogen of our atmosphere (2). And Rachel Carson's warning (3) is now being followed by those of scientists, who give us an even gloomier picture of the general pollution of air, soil, and water. This pollution is seriously threatening our health and our food supply. Refusal to curb our reproductive behavior has led to the population explosion. And, as if all this were not enough, we are waging war on each other—men are fighting and killing men on a massive scale. It is because the effects of these behavior patterns, and of attitudes that determine our behavior, have now acquired such truly lethal potentialities that I have chosen man's ignorance about his own behavior as the subject of this paper.

I am an ethologist, a zoologist studying animal behavior. What gives a student of animal behavior the temerity to speak about problems of human behavior? Of course the history of medicine provides the answer. We all know that medical research uses animals on a large scale. This makes sense because animals, particularly vertebrates, are, in spite of all differences, so similar to us; they are our blood relations, however distant.

But this use of zoological research for a better understanding of ourselves is, to most people, acceptable only when we have to do with those bodily functions that we look upon as parts of our physiological machinery—the functions, for instance, of our kidneys, our liver, our hormone-producing glands. The majority of people bridle as soon as it is even suggested that studies of animal behavior could be useful for an understanding, let alone for the control, of our own behavior. They do not want to have their own behavior subjected to scientific scrutiny; they certainly resent being compared with animals, and these rejecting attitudes are both deep-rooted and of complex origin.

But now we are witnessing a turn in this tide of human thought. On the one hand the resistances are weakening, and on the other, a positive awareness is growing of the potentialities of a biology of behavior. This has become quite clear from the great interest aroused by several recent books that are trying, by comparative studies of animals and man, to trace what we could call "the animal roots of human behavior." As examples I select Konrad Lorenz's book *On Aggression* (4) and *The Naked Ape* by Desmond Morris (5). Both books were best sellers from the start. We ethologists are naturally delighted by this sign of rapid growth of interest in our science (even though the growing pains are at times a little hard to endure). But at the same time we are apprehensive, or at least I am.

We are delighted because, from the enormous sales of these and other such books, it is evident that the mental block against self-scrutiny is weakening —that there are masses of people who, so to speak, want to be shaken up.

But I am apprehensive because these books, each admirable in its own way, are being misread. Very few readers give the authors the benefit of the doubt. Far too many either accept uncritically all that the authors say, or (equally uncritically) reject it all. I believe that this is because both Lorenz and Morris emphasize our knowledge rather than our ignorance (and, in addition, present as knowledge a set of statements which are after all no more than likely guesses). In themselves brilliant, these books could stiffen, at a new level, the attitude of certainty, while what we need is a sense of doubt and wonder, and an urge to investigate, to inquire.

Potential Usefulness of Ethological Studies

Now, in a way, I am going to be just as assertive as Lorenz and Morris, but what I am going to stress is how much we do not know. I shall argue that we shall have to make a major research effort. I am of course fully aware of the fact that much research is already being devoted to problems of human, and even of animal, behavior. I know, for instance, that anthropologists, psychologists, psychiatrists, and others are approaching these problems from many angles. But I shall try to show that the research effort has so far made insufficient use of the potential of ethology. Anthropologists, for instance, are beginning to look at animals, but they restrict their work almost entirely to our nearest relatives, the apes and monkeys. Psychologists do study a larger variety of animals, but even they select mainly higher species. They also ignore certain major problems that we biologists think have to be studied. Psychiatrists, at least many of them, show a disturbing tendency to apply the *results* rather than the *methods* of ethology to man.

None of these sciences, not even their combined efforts, are as yet parts of one coherent science of behavior. Since behavior is a life process, its study ought to be part of the mainstream of biological research. That is why we zoologists ought to "join the fray." As an ethologist, I am going to try to sketch how my science could assist its sister sciences in their attempts, already well on their way, to make a united, broad-fronted, truly biological attack on the problems of behavior.

I feel that I can cooperate best by discussing what it is in ethology that could be of use to the other behavioral sciences. What we ethologists do not want, what we consider definitely wrong, is uncritical application of our results to man. Instead, I myself at least feel that it is our method of approach, our rationale, that we can offer (6), and also a little simple common sense, and discipline.

The potential usefulness of ethology lies in the fact that, unlike other sciences of behavior, it applies the method or "approach" of biology to the phenomenon behavior. It has developed a set of concepts and terms that allow us to ask:

1) In what ways does this phenomenon (behavior) influence the survival, the success of the animal?

2) What makes behavior happen at any given moment? How does its "machinery" work?

3) How does the behavior machinery develop as the individual grows up?

4) How have the behavior systems of each species evolved until they became what they are now?

The first question, that of survival value, has to do with the effects of behavior; the other three are, each on a different time scale, concerned with its causes.

These four questions are, as many of my fellow biologists will recognize, the major questions that biology has been pursuing for a long time. What ethology is doing could be simply described by saying that, just as biology investigates the functioning of the organs responsible for digestion, respiration, circulation, and so forth, so ethology begins now to do the same with respect to behavior; it investigates the functioning of organs responsible for movement.

I have to make clear that in my opinion it is the comprehensive, integrated attack on all four problems that characterizes ethology. I shall try to show that to ignore the questions of survival value and evolution—as, for instance, most psychologists do—is not only shortsighted but makes it impossible to arrive at an understanding of behavioral problems. Here ethology can make, in fact is already making, positive contributions.

Having stated my case for animal ethology as an essential part of the science of behavior, I will now have to sketch how this could be done. For this I shall have to consider one concrete example, and I select aggression, the most directly lethal of our behaviors. And, for reasons that will become clear, I shall also make a short excursion into problems of education.

Let me first try to define what I mean by aggression. We all understand the term in a vague, general way, but it is, after all, no more than a catchword. In terms of actual behavior, aggression involves approaching an opponent, and, when within reach, pushing him away, inflicting damage of some kind, or at least forcing stimuli upon him that subdue him. In this description the effect is already implicit: such behavior tends to remove the opponent, or at least to make him change his behavior in such a way that he no longer interferes with the attacker. The methods of attack differ from one species to another, and so do the weapons that are used, the structures that contribute to the effect.

Since I am concentrating on men fighting men, I shall confine myself to intraspecific fighting, and ignore, for instance, fighting between predators and prey. Intraspecific fighting is very common among animals. Many of them fight in two different contexts, which we can call "offensive" and "defensive." Defensive fighting is often shown as a last resort by an animal that, instead of attacking, has been fleeing from an attacker. If it is cornered, it may suddenly turn round upon its enemy and "fight with the courage of despair."

Of the four questions I mentioned before, I shall consider that of the survival value first. Here comparison faces us right at the start with a striking paradox. On the one hand, man is akin to many species of animals in that he fights his own species. But on the other hand he is, among the thousands of species that fight, the only one in which fighting is disruptive.

In animals, intraspecific fighting is usually of distinctive advantage. In addition, all species manage as a rule to settle their disputes without killing one another; in fact, even bloodshed is rare. Man is the only species that is a mass murderer, the only misfit in his own society.

Why should this be so? For an answer, we shall have to turn to the question of causation: What makes animals and man fight their own species? And why is our species "the odd man out"?

Causation of Aggression

For a fruitful discussion of this question of causation I shall first have to discuss what exactly we mean when we ask it.

I have already indicated that when thinking of causation we have to distinguish between three subquestions, and that these three differ from one another in the stretch of time that is considered. We ask, first: Given an adult animal that fights now and then, what makes each outburst of fighting happen? The time scale in which we consider these recurrent events is usually one of seconds, or minutes. To use an analogy, this subquestion compares with asking what makes a car start or stop each time we use it.

But in asking this same general question of causation ("What makes an animal fight?") we may also be referring to a longer period of time; we may mean "How has the animal, as it grew up, developed this behavior?" This compares roughly with asking how a car has been constructed in the factory. The distinction between these two subquestions remains useful even though we know that many animals continue their development (much slowed down) even after they have attained adulthood. For instance, they may still continue to learn.

Finally, in biology, as in technology, we can extend this time scale even more, and ask: How have the animal species which we observe today—and which we know have evolved from ancestors that were different—how have they acquired their particular behavior systems during this evolution? Unfortunately, while we know the evolution of cars because they evolved so quickly and have been so fully recorded, the behavior of extinct animals cannot be observed, and has to be reconstructed by indirect methods.

I shall try to justify the claim I made earlier, and show how all these four questions—that of behavior's survival value and the three subquestions of causation—have to enter into the argument if we are to understand the biology of aggression.

Let us first consider the short-term causation; the mechanism of fighting. What makes us fight at any one moment? Lorenz argues in his book that, in animals and in man, there is an internal urge to attack. An individual does not simply wait to be provoked, but, if actual attack has not been possible for some time, this urge to fight builds up until the individual actively seeks the opportunity to indulge in fighting. Aggression, Lorenz claims, can be spontaneous.

But this view has not gone unchallenged. For instance, R. A. Hinde has written a thorough criticism (7), based on recent work on aggression in animals, in which he writes that Lorenz's "arguments for the spontaneity of aggression do not bear examination" and that "the contrary view, expressed in nearly every textbook of comparative psychology . . ." is that fighting "derives principally from the situation"; and even more explicitly: "There is no need to postulate causes that are purely internal to the aggressor" (7, p. 303). At first glance it would seem as if Lorenz and Hinde disagree profoundly. I have read and reread both authors, and it is to me perfectly clear that loose statements and misunderstandings on both sides have made it appear that there is disagreement where in fact there is something very near to a common opinion. It seems to me that the differences between the two authors lie mainly in the different ways they look at internal and external variables. This in turn seems due to differences of a semantic nature. Lorenz uses the unfortunate term "the spontaneity of aggression." Hinde takes this to mean that external stimuli are in Lorenz's view not necessary at all to make an animal fight. But here he misrepresents Lorenz, for nowhere does Lorenz claim that the internal urge ever makes an animal fight "in vacuo"; somebody or something is attacked. This misunderstanding makes Hinde feel that he has refuted Lorenz's views by saying that "fighting derives principally from the situation." But both authors are fully aware of the fact that fighting is started by a number of variables, of which some are internal and some external. What both authors know, and what cannot be doubted, is that fighting behavior is not like the simple slot machine that produces one platform ticket every time one threepenny bit is inserted. To mention one animal example: a male stickleback does not always show the full fighting behavior in response to an approaching standard opponent; its response varies from none at all to the optimal stimulus on some occasions, to full attack on even a crude dummy at other times. This means that its internal state varies, and in this particular case we know from the work of Hoar (8) that the level of the male sex hormone is an important variable.

Another source of misunderstanding seems to have to do with the stretch of time that the two authors are taking into account. Lorenz undoubtedly thinks of the causes of an outburst of fighting in terms of seconds, or hours— perhaps days. Hinde seems to think of events which may have happened further back in time; an event which is at any particular moment "internal" may well in its turn have been influenced previously by external agents. In our stickleback example, the level of male sex hormone is influenced by external agents such as the length of the daily exposure to light over a period of a month or so (9). Or, less far back in time, its readiness to attack may have been influenced by some experience gained, say, half an hour before the fight.

I admit that I have now been spending a great deal of time on what would seem to be a perfectly simple issue: the very first step in the analysis of the short-term causation, which is to distinguish at any given moment between variables within the animal and variables in the environment. It is of course important for our further understanding to unravel the complex interactions between these two worlds, and in particular the physiology of aggressive behavior. A great deal is being discovered about this, but for my present issue there is no use discussing it as long as even the first step in the analysis has not led to a clearly expressed and generally accepted conclusion. We must remember that we are at the moment concerned with the human problem: "What makes men attack each other?" And for this problem the answer to the first stage of our question is of prime importance: Is our readiness to start an attack constant or not? If it were—if our aggressive behavior were the outcome of an apparatus with the properties of the slot machine—all we would have to do would be to control the ex-

ternal situation: to stop providing three-penny bits. But since our readiness to start an attack is variable, further studies of both the external and the internal variables are vital to such issues as: Can we reduce fighting by lowering the population density, or by withholding provocative stimuli? Can we do so by changing the hormone balance or other physiological variables? Can we perhaps in addition control our development in such a way as to change the dependence on internal and external factors in adult man? However, before discussing development, I must first return to the fact that I have mentioned before, namely, that man is, among the thousands of other species that fight, the only mass murderer. How do animals in their intraspecific disputes avoid bloodshed?

The Importance of "Fear"

The clue to this problem is to recognize the simple fact that aggression in animals rarely occurs in pure form; it is only one of two components of an adaptive system. This is most clearly seen in territorial behavior, although it is also true of most other types of hostile behavior. Members of territorial species divide, among themselves, the available living space and opportunities by each individual defending its home range against competitors. Now in this system of parceling our living space, avoidance plays as important a part as attack. Put very briefly, animals of territorial species, once they have settled on a territory, attack intruders, but an animal that is still searching for a suitable territory or finds itself outside its home range withdraws when it meets with an already established owner. In terms of function, once you have taken possession of a territory, it pays to drive off competitors; but when you are still looking for a territory (or meet your neighbor at your common boundary), your chances of success are improved by avoiding such established owners. The ruthless fighter who "knows no fear" does not get very far. For an understanding of what follows, this fact, that hostile clashes are controlled by what we could call the "attack-avoidance system," is essential.

When neighboring territory owners meet near their common boundary, both attack behavior and withdrawal behavior are elicited in both animals; each of the two is in a state of motivational conflict. We know a great deal about the variety of movements that appear when these two conflicting, incompatible behaviors are elicited. Many of these expressions of a motivational conflict have, in the course of evolution, acquired signal function; in colloquial language, they signal "Keep out!" We deduce this from the fact that opponents respond to them in an appropriate way: instead of proceeding to intrude, which would require the use of force, trespassers withdraw, and neighbors are contained by each other. This is how such animals have managed to have all the advantages of their hostile behavior without the disadvantages: they divide their living space in a bloodless way by using as distance-keeping devices these conflict movements ("threat") rather than actual fighting.

Group Territories

In order to see our wars in their correct biological perspective one more comparison with animals is useful. So far I have discussed animal species that defend individual or at best pair territories. But there are also animals which possess and defend territories belonging to a group, or a clan (10).

Now it is an essential aspect of group territorialism that the members of a group unite when in hostile confronta-tion with another group that approaches, or crosses into their feeding territory. The uniting and the aggression are equally important. It is essential to realize that group territorialism does not exclude hostile relations on lower levels when the group is on its own. For instance, within a group there is often a peck order. And within the group there may be individual or pair territories. But frictions due to these relationships fade away during a clash between groups. This temporary elimination is done by means of so-called appeasement and reassurance signals. They indicate "I am a friend," and so diminish the risk that, in the general flare-up of anger, any animal "takes it out" on a fellow member of the same group (11). Clans meet clans as units, and each individual in an intergroup clash, while united with its fellow-members, is (as in interindividual clashes) torn between attack and withdrawal, and postures and shouts rather than attacks.

We must now examine the hypothesis (which I consider the most likely one) that man still carries with him the animal heritage of group territoriality. This is a question concerning man's evolutionary origin, and here we are, by the very nature of the subject, forced to speculate. Because I am going to say something about the behavior of our ancestors of, say, 100,000 years ago, I have to discuss briefly a matter of methodology. It is known to all biologists (but unfortunately unknown to most psychologists) that comparison of present-day species can give us a deep insight, with a probability closely approaching certainty, into the evolutionary history of animal species. Even where fossil evidence is lacking, this comparative method alone can do this. It has to be stressed that this comparison is a highly sophisticated method, and not merely a matter of saying that species A is different from species B

(*12*). The basic procedure is this. We interpret differences between really allied species as the result of adaptive divergent evolution from common stock, and we interpret similarities between nonallied species as adaptive convergencies to similar ways of life. By studying the adaptive functions of species characteristics we understand how natural selection can have produced both these divergencies and convergencies. To mention one striking example: even if we had no fossil evidence, we could, by this method alone, recognize whales for what they are—mammals that have returned to the water, and, in doing so, have developed some similarities to fish. This special type of comparison, which has been applied so successfully by students of the structure of animals, has now also been used, and with equal success, in several studies of animal behavior. Two approaches have been applied. One is to see in what respects species of very different origin have convergently adapted to a similar way of life. Von Haartman (*13*) has applied this to a study of birds of many types that nest in holes—an anti-predator safety device. All such hole-nesters center their territorial fighting on a suitable nest hole. Their courtship consists of luring a female to this hole (often with the use of bright color patterns). Their young gape when a general darkening signals the arrival of the parent. All but the most recently adapted species lay uniformly colored, white or light blue eggs that can easily be seen by the parent.

An example of adaptive divergence has been studied by Cullen (*14*). Among all the gulls, the kittiwake is unique in that it nests on very narrow ledges on sheer cliffs. Over 20 peculiarities of this species have been recognized by Mrs. Cullen as vital adaptations to this particular habitat.

These and several similar studies (*15*) demonstrate how comparison reveals, in each species, systems of interrelated, and very intricate adaptive features. In this work, speculation is now being followed by careful experimental checking. It would be tempting to elaborate on this, but I must return to our own unfortunate species.

Now, when we include the "Naked Ape" in our comparative studies, it becomes likely (as has been recently worked out in great detail by Morris) that man is a "social Ape who has turned carnivore" (*16*). On the one hand he is a social primate; on the other, he has developed similarities to wolves, lions and hyenas. In our present context one thing seems to stand out clearly, a conclusion that seems to me of paramount importance to all of us, and yet has not yet been fully accepted as such. As a social, hunting primate, man must originally have been organized on the principle of group territories.

Ethologists tend to believe that we still carry with us a number of behavioral characteristics of our animal ancestors, which cannot be eliminated by different ways of upbringing, and that our group territorialism is one of those ancestral characters. I shall discuss the problem of the modifiability of our behavior later, but it is useful to point out here that even if our behavior were much more modifiable than Lorenz maintains, our cultural evolution, which resulted in the parceling-out of our living space on lines of tribal, national, and now even "bloc" areas, would, if anything, have tended to enhance group territorialism.

Group Territorialism in Man?

I put so much emphasis on this issue of group territorialism because most writers who have tried to apply ethology to man have done this in the wrong way. They have made the mistake, to which I objected before, of uncritically extrapolating the results of animal studies to man. They try to explain man's behavior by using facts that are valid only of some of the animals we studied. And, as ethologists keep stressing, no two species behave alike. Therefore, instead of taking this easy way out, we ought to study man in his own right. And I repeat that the message of the ethologists is that the methods, rather than the results, of ethology should be used for such a study.

Now, the notion of territory was developed by zoologists (to be precise, by ornithologists, 17), and because individual and pair territories are found in so many more species than group territories (which are particularly rare among birds), most animal studies were concerned with such individual and pair territories. Now such low-level territories do occur in man, as does another form of hostile behavior, the peck order. But the problems created by such low-level frictions are not serious; they can, within a community, be kept in check by the apparatus of law and order; peace within national boundaries can be enforced. In order to understand what makes us go to war, we have to recognize that man behaves very much like a group-territorial species. We too unite in the face of an outside danger to the group; we "forget our differences." We too have threat gestures, for instance, angry facial expressions. And all of us use reassurance and appeasement signals, such as a friendly smile. And (unlike speech) these are universally understood; they are cross-cultural; they are species-specific. And, incidentally, even within a group sharing a common language, they are often more reliable guides to a man's intentions than speech, for speech (as we know now) rarely reflects our true motives, but our facial expressions often "give us away."

If I may digress for a moment: it is humiliating to us ethologists that many nonscientists, particularly novelists and actors, intuitively understand our sign language much better than we scientists ourselves do. Worse, there is a category of human beings who understand intuitively more about the causation of our aggressive behavior: the great demagogues. They have applied this knowledge in order to control our behavior in the most clever ways, and often for the most evil purposes. For instance, Hitler (who had modern mass communication at his disposal, which allowed him to inflame a whole nation) played on both fighting tendencies. The "defensive" fighting was whipped up by his passionate statements about "living space," "encirclement," Jewry, and Freemasonry as threatening powers which made the Germans feel "cornered." The "attack fighting" was similarly set ablaze by playing the myth of the Herrenvolk. We must make sure that mankind has learned its lesson and will never forget how disastrous the joint effects have been—if only one of the major nations were led now by a man like Hitler, life on earth would be wiped out.

I have argued my case for concentrating on studies of group territoriality rather than on other types of aggression. I must now return, in this context, to the problem of man the mass murderer. Why don't we settle even our international disputes by the relatively harmless, animal method of threat? Why have we become unhinged so that so often our attack erupts without being kept in check by fear? It is not that we have no fear, nor that we have no other inhibitions against killing. This problem has to be considered first of all in the general context of the consequences of man having embarked on a new type of evolution.

Cultural Evolution

Man has the ability, unparalleled in scale in the animal kingdom, of passing on his experiences from one generation to the next. By this accumulative and exponentially growing process, which we call cultural evolution, he has been able to change his environment progressively out of all recognition. And this includes the social environment. This new type of evolution proceeds at an incomparably faster pace than genetic evolution. Genetically we have not evolved very strikingly since Cro-Magnon man, but culturally we have changed beyond recognition, and are changing at an ever-increasing rate. It is of course true that we are highly adjustable individually, and so could hope to keep pace with these changes. But I am not alone in believing that this behavioral adjustability, like all types of modifiability, has its limits. These limits are imposed upon us by our hereditary constitution, a constitution which can only change with the far slower speed of genetic evolution. There are good grounds for the conclusion that man's limited behavioral adjustability has been outpaced by the culturally determined changes in his social environment, and that this is why man is now a misfit in his own society.

We can now, at last, return to the problem of war, of uninhibited mass killing. It seems quite clear that our cultural evolution is at the root of the trouble. It is our cultural evolution that has caused the population explosion. In a nutshell, medical science, aiming at the reduction of suffering, has, in doing so, prolonged life for many individuals as well—prolonged it to well beyond the point at which they produce offspring. Unlike the situation in any wild species, recruitment to the human population consistently surpasses losses through mortality. Agricultural and technical know-how have enabled us to grow food and to exploit other natural resources to such an extent that we can still feed (though only just) the enormous numbers of human beings on our crowded planet. The result is that we now live at a far higher density than that in which genetic evolution has molded our species. This, together with long-distance communication, leads to far more frequent, in fact to continuous, intergroup contacts, and so to continuous external provocation of aggression. Yet this alone would not explain our increased tendency to kill each other; it would merely lead to continuous threat behavior.

The upsetting of the balance between aggression and fear (and this is what causes war) is due to at least three other consequences of cultural evolution. It is an old cultural phenomenon that warriors are both brainwashed and bullied into all-out fighting. They are brainwashed into believing that fleeing —originally, as we have seen, an adaptive type of behavior—is despicable, "cowardly." This seems to me due to the fact that man, accepting that in moral issues death might be preferable to fleeing, has falsely applied the moral concept of "cowardice" to matters of mere practical importance—to the dividing of living space. The fact that our soldiers are also bullied into all-out fighting (by penalizing fleeing in battle) is too well known to deserve elaboration.

Another cultural excess is our ability to make and use killing tools, especially long-range weapons. These make killing easy, not only because a spear or a club inflicts, with the same effort, so much more damage than a fist, but also, and mainly, because the use of long-range weapons prevents the victim from reaching his attacker with his appeasement, reassurance, and distress signals. Very few aircrews who are willing, indeed eager, to drop their bombs "on target" would be willing to strangle, stab, or burn children (or, for that matter, adults) with their own hands; they would stop short of killing, in response to the appeasement and distress signals of their opponents.

These three factors alone would be sufficient to explain how we have become such unhinged killers. But I have to stress once more that all this, however convincing it may seem, must still be studied more thoroughly.

There is a frightening, and ironical paradox in this conclusion: that the human brain, the finest life-preserving device created by evolution, has made our species so successful in mastering the outside world that it suddenly finds itself taken off guard. One could say that our cortex and our brainstem (our "reason" and our "instincts") are at loggerheads. Together they have created a new social environment in which, rather than ensuring our survival, they are about to do the opposite. The brain finds itself seriously threatened by an enemy of its own making. It is its own enemy. We simply have to understand this enemy.

The Development of Behavior

I must now leave the question of the moment-to-moment control of fighting, and, looking further back in time, turn to the development of aggressive behavior in the growing individual. Again we will start from the human problem. This, in the present context, is whether it is within our power to control development in such a way that we reduce or eliminate fighting among adults. Can or cannot education in the widest sense produce nonagressive men?

The first step in the consideration of this problem is again to distinguish between external and internal influences, but now we must apply this to the growth, the changing, of the behavioral machinery during the individual's de-velopment. Here again the way in which we phrase our questions and our conclusions is of the utmost importance.

In order to discuss this issue fruitfully, I have to start once more by considering it in a wider context, which is now that of the "nature-nurture" problem with respect to behavior in general. This has been discussed more fully by Lorenz in his book *Evolution and Modification of Behaviour* (18); for a discussion of the environmentalist point of view I refer to the various works of Schneirla (see *19*).

Lorenz tends to classify behavior types into innate and acquired or learned behavior. Schneirla rejects this dichotomy into two classes of behavior. He stresses that the developmental process, of behavior as well as of other functions, should be considered, and also that this development forms a highly complicated series of interactions between the growing organism and its environment. I have gradually become convinced that the clue to this difference in approach is to be found in a difference in aims between the two authors. Lorenz claims that "we are justified in leaving, at least for the time being, to the care of the experimental embryologists all those questions which are concerned with the chains of physiological causation leading from the genome to the development of . . . neurosensory structures" (*18*, p. 43). In other words, he deliberately refrains from starting his analysis of development prior to the stage at which a fully coordinated behavior is performed for the first time. If one in this way restricts one's studies to the later stages of development, then a classification in "innate" and "learned" behavior, or behavior components, can be considered quite justified. And there was a time, some 30 years ago, when the almost grotesquely environmentalist bias of psychology made it imperative for ethologists to stress the extent to which behavior patterns could appear in perfect or near-perfect form without the aid of anything that could be properly called learning. But I now agree (however belatedly) with Schneirla that we must extend our interest to earlier stages of development and embark on a full program of experimental embryology of behavior. When we do this, we discover that interactions with the environment can indeed occur at early stages. These interactions may concern small components of the total machinery of a fully functional behavior pattern, and many of them cannot possibly be called learning. But they are interactions with the environment, and must be taken into account if we follow in the footsteps of the experimental embryologists, and extend our field of interest to the entire sequence of events which lead from the blueprints contained in the zygote to the fully functioning, behaving animal. We simply have to do this if we want an answer to the question to what extent the development of behavior can be influenced from the outside.

When we follow this procedure the rigid distinction between "innate" or unmodifiable and "acquired" or modifiable behavior patterns becomes far less sharp. This is owing to the discovery, on the one hand, that "innate" patterns may contain elements that at an early stage developed in interaction with the environment, and, on the other hand, that learning is, from step to step, limited by internally imposed restrictions.

To illustrate the first point, I take the development of the sensory cells in the retina of the eye. Knoll has shown (20) that the rods in the eyes of tadpoles cannot function properly unless they have first been exposed to light. This means that, although any visually guided response of a tadpole may well, in its integrated form, be "innate" in Lorenz's sense, it is so only in the sense of "nonlearned," not in that of "having

grown without interaction with the environment." Now it has been shown by Cullen (21) that male sticklebacks reared from the egg in complete isolation from other animals will, when adult, show full fighting behavior to other males and courtship behavior to females when faced with them for the first time in their lives. This is admittedly an important fact, demonstrating that the various recognized forms of learning do not enter into the programing of these integrated patterns. This is a demonstration of what Lorenz calls an "innate response." But it does not exclude the possibility that parts of the machinery so employed may, at an earlier stage, have been influenced by the environment, as in the case of the tadpoles.

Second, there are also behavior patterns which do appear in the inexperienced animal, but in an incomplete form, and which require additional development through learning. Thorpe has analyzed a clear example of this: when young male chaffinches reared alone begin to produce their song for the first time, they utter a very imperfect warble; this develops into the full song only if, at a certain sensitive stage, the young birds have heard the full song of an adult male (22).

By far the most interesting aspect of such intermediates between innate and acquired behavior is the fact that learning is not indiscriminate, but is guided by a certain selectiveness on the part of the animal. This fact has been dimly recognized long ago; the early ethologists have often pointed out that different, even closely related, species learn different things even when developing the same behavior patterns. This has been emphasized by Lorenz's use of the term "innate teaching mechanism." Other authors use the word "template" in the same context. The best example I know is once more taken from the development of song in certain birds.

As I have mentioned, the males of some birds acquire their full song by changing their basic repertoire to resemble the song of adults, which they have to hear during a special sensitive period some months before they sing themselves. It is in this sensitive period that they acquire, without as yet producing the song, the knowledge of "what the song ought to be like." In technical terms, the bird formed a *Sollwert* (*23*) (literally, "should-value," an ideal) for the feedback they receive when they hear their own first attempts. Experiments have shown (*24*) that such birds, when they start to sing, do three things: they listen to what they produce; they notice the difference between this feedback and the ideal song; and they correct their next performance.

This example, while demonstrating an internal teaching mechanism, shows, at the same time, that Lorenz made his concept too narrow when he coined the term "innate teaching mechanism." The birds have developed a teaching mechanism, but while it is true that it is internal, it is not innate; the birds have acquired it by listening to their father's song.

These examples show that if behavior studies are to catch up with experimental embryology our aims, our concepts, and our terms must be continually revised.

Before returning to aggression, I should like to elaborate a little further on general aspects of behavior development, because this will enable me to show the value of animal studies in another context, that of education.

Comparative studies, of different animal species, of different behavior patterns, and of different stages of development, begin to suggest that wherever learning takes a hand in development, it is guided by such *Sollwerte* or templates for the proper feedback, the feedback that reinforces. And it becomes clear that these various *Sollwerte*

are of a bewildering variety. In human education one aspect of this has been emphasized in particular, and even applied in the use of teaching machines: the requirement that the reward, in order to have maximum effect, must be immediate. Skinner has stressed this so much because in our own teaching we have imposed an unnatural delay between, say, taking in homework, and giving the pupil his reward in the form of a mark. But we can learn more from animal studies than the need for immediacy of reward. The type of reward is also of great importance, and this may vary from task to task, from stage to stage, from occasion to occasion; the awards may be of almost infinite variety.

Here I have to discuss briefly a behavior of which I have so far been unable to find the equivalent in the development of structure. This is exploratory behavior. By this we mean a kind of behavior in which the animal sets out to acquire as much information about an object or a situation as it can possibly get. The behavior is intricately adapted to this end, and it terminates when the information has been stored, when the animal has incorporated it in its learned knowledge. This exploration (subjectively we speak of "curiosity") is not confined to the acquisition of information about the external world alone; at least mammals explore their own movements a great deal, and in this way "master new skills." Again, in this exploratory behavior, *Sollwerte* of expected, "hoped-for" feedbacks play their part.

Without going into more detail, we can characterize the picture we begin to get of the development of behavior as a series, or rather a web, of events, starting with innate programing instructions contained in the zygote, which straightaway begin to interact with the environment; this interaction may be discontinuous, in that periods of predominantly internal development alternate with periods of interaction, or sensitive periods. The interaction is enhanced by active exploration; it is steered by selective *Sollwerte* of great variety; and stage by stage this process ramifies; level upon level of ever-increasing complexity is being incorporated into the programing.

Apply what we have heard for a moment to playing children (I do not, of course, distinguish sharply between "play" and "learning"). At a certain age a child begins to use, say, building blocks. It will at first manipulate them in various ways, one at a time. Each way of manipulating acts as exploratory behavior: the child learns what a block looks, feels, tastes like, and so forth, and also how to put it down so that it stands stably.

Each of these stages "peters out" when the child knows what it wanted to find out. But as the development proceeds, a new level of exploration is added: the child discovers that it can put one block on top of the other; it constructs. The new discovery leads to repetition and variation, for each child develops, at some stage, a desire and a set of *Sollwerte* for such effects of construction, and acts out to the full this new level of exploratory behavior. In addition, already at this stage the *Sollwert* or ideal does not merely contain what the blocks do, but also what, for instance, the mother does; her approval, her shared enjoyment, is also of great importance. Just as an exploring animal, the child builds a kind of inverted pyramid of experience, built of layers, each set off by a new wave of exploration and each directed by new sets of *Sollwerte,* and so its development "snowballs." All these phases may well have more or less limited sensitive periods, which determine when the fullest effect can be obtained, and when the child is ready for the next step. More important still, if the opportunity for the next stage is offered either too early or too late, development may be damaged, including the development of motivational and emotional attitudes.

Of course gifted teachers of many generations have known all these things (25) or some of them, but the glimpses of insight have not been fully and scientifically systematized. In human education, this would of course involve experimentation. This need not worry us too much, because in our search for better educational procedures we are in effect experimenting on our children all the time. Also, children are fortunately incredibly resilient, and most grow up into pretty viable adults in spite of our fumbling educational efforts. Yet there is, of course, a limit to what we will allow ourselves, and this, I should like to emphasize, is where animal studies may well become even more important than they are already.

Can Education End Aggression?

Returning now to the development of animal and human aggression, I hope to have made at least several things clear: that behavior development is a very complex phenomenon indeed; that we have only begun to analyze it in animals; that with respect to man we are, if anything, behind in comparison with animal studies; and that I cannot do otherwise than repeat what I said in the beginning: we must make a major research effort. In this effort animal studies can help, but we are still very far from drawing very definite conclusions with regard to our question: To what extent shall we be able to render man less aggressive through manipulation of the environment, that is, by educational measures?

In such a situation personal opinions naturally vary a great deal. I do not hesitate to give as my personal opinion that Lorenz's book *On Aggression,* in spite of its assertativeness, in spite of factual mistakes, and in spite of the many possibilities of misunderstandings that are due to the lack of a common language among students of behavior—that this work must be taken more seriously as a positive contribution to our problem than many critics have done. Lorenz is, in my opinion, right in claiming that elimination, through education, of the internal urge to fight will turn out to be very difficult, if not impossible.

Everything I have said so far seems to me to allow for only one conclusion. Apart from doing our utmost to return to a reasonable population density apart from stopping the progressive depletion and pollution of our habitat, we must pursue the biological study of animal behavior for clarifying problems of human behavior of such magnitude as that of our aggression, and of education.

But research takes a long time, and we must remember that there are experts who forecast worldwide famine 10 to 20 years from now; and that we have enough weapons to wipe out all human life on earth. Whatever the causation of our aggression, the simple fact is that for the time being we are saddled with it. This means that there is a crying need for a crash program, for finding ways and means for keeping our intergroup aggression in check. This is of course in practice infinitely more difficult than controlling our intranational frictions; we have as yet not got a truly international police force. But there is hope for avoiding all-out war because, for the first time in history, we are afraid of killing ourselves by the lethal radiation effects even of bombs that we could drop in the enemy's territory. Our politicians know this. And as long as there is this hope, there is every reason to try and learn what we can from animal studies. Here again they can be of help. We have already seen that animal opponents meet-ing in a hostile clash avoid bloodshed by using the expressions of their motivational conflicts as intimidating signals. Ethologists have studied such conflict movements in some detail (26), and have found that they are of a variety of types. The most instructive of these is the redirected attack; instead of attacking the provoking, yet dreaded, opponent, animals often attack something else, often even an inanimate object. We ourselves bang the table with our fists. Redirection includes something like sublimation, a term attaching a value judgment to the redirection. As a species with group territories, humans, like hyenas, unite when meeting a common enemy. We do already sublimate our group aggression. The Dutch feel united in their fight against the sea. Scientists do attack their problems together. The space program —surely a mainly military effort—is an up-to-date example. I would not like to claim, as Lorenz does, that redirected attack exhausts the aggressive urge. We know from soccer matches and from animal work how aggressive behavior has two simultaneous, but opposite effects: a waning effect, and one of self-inflammation, of mass hysteria, such as recently seen in Cairo. Of these two the inflammatory effect often wins. But if aggression were used successfully as the motive force behind nonkilling and even useful activities, self-stimulation need not be a danger; in our short-term cure we are not aiming at the elimination of aggressiveness, but at "taking the sting out of it."

Of all sublimated activities, scientific research would seem to offer the best opportunities for deflecting and sub-limating our aggression. And, once we recognize that it is the disrupted relation between our own behavior and our environment that forms our most deadly enemy, what could be better than unit-ing, at the front or behind the lines, in the scientific attack on our own behavioral problems?

I stress "behind the lines." The whole population should be made to feel that it participates in the struggle. This is why scientists will always have the duty to inform their fellowmen of what they are doing, of the relevance and the importance of their work. And this is not only a duty, it can give intense satisfaction.

I have come full circle. For both the long-term and the short-term remedies at least we scientists will have to sublimate our aggression into an all-out attack on the enemy within. For this the enemy must be recognized for what it is: our unknown selves, or, deeper down, our refusal to admit that man is, to himself, unknown.

I should like to conclude by saying a few words to my colleagues of the younger generation. Of course we all hope that, by muddling along until we have acquired better understanding, self-annihilation either by the "whimper of famine" or by the "bang of war" can be avoided. For this, we must on the one hand trust, on the other help (and urge) our politicians. But it is no use denying that the chances of designing the necessary preventive measures are small, let alone the chances of carrying them out. Even birth control still offers a major problem.

It is difficult for my generation to know how seriously you take the danger of mankind destroying his own species. But those who share the apprehension of my generation might perhaps, with us, derive strength from keeping alive the thought that has helped so many of us in the past when faced with the possibility of imminent death. Scientific research is one of the finest occupations of our mind. It is, with art and religion, one of the uniquely human ways of meeting nature, in fact, the most active way. If we are to succumb, and even if this were to be ultimately due to our own stupidity, we could still, so to speak, redeem our species. We could at least go down with some dignity, by using our brain for one of its supreme tasks, by exploring to the end.

REFERENCES

1. A. Carrel, *L'Homme, cet Inconnu* (Librairie Plon, Paris, 1935).
2. AAAS Annual Meeting, 1967 [see *New Scientist* 37, 5 (1968)].
3. R. Carson, *Silent Spring* (Houghton Mifflin, Boston, 1962).
4. K. Lorenz, *On Aggression* (Methuen, London, 1966).
5. D. Morris, *The Naked Ape* (Jonathan Cape, London. 1967)
6. N. Tinbergen. *Z. Tierpsychol.* **20**, 410 (1964).
7. R. A. Hinde, *New Society* **9**, 302 (1967).
8. W. S. Hoar, *Animal Behaviour* **10**, 247 (1962).
9. B. Baggerman, in *Symp. Soc. Exp. Biol.* **20**, 427 (1965).
10. H. Kruuk, *New Scientist* **30**, 849 (1966).
11. N. Tinbergen, *Z. Tierpsychol.* **16**, 651 (1959); *Zool. Mededelingen* **39**, 209 (1964).
12. ———, *Behaviour* **15**, 1–70 (1959).
13. L. von Haartman, *Evolution* **11**, 339 (1957).
14. E. Cullen, *Ibis* **99**, 275 (1957).
15. J. H. Crook, *Symp. Zool. Soc. London* **14**, 181 (1965).
16. D. Freeman, *Inst. Biol. Symp.* **13**, 109 (1964); D. Morris, Ed., *Primate Ethology* (Weidenfeld and Nicolson. London, 1967).
17. H. E. Howard, *Territory in Bird Life* (Murray, London, 1920); R. A. Hinde *et al.*, *Ibis* **98**, 340–530 (1956).
18. K. Lorenz, *Evolution and Modification of Behaviour* (Methuen, London, 1966).
19. T. C. Schneirla, *Quart. Rev. Biol.* **41**, 283 (1966).
20. M. D. Knoll, *Z. Vergleich. Physiol.* **38**, 219 (1956).
21. E. Cullen, *Final Rept. Contr. AF 61 (052)-29.* USAFRDC. 1–23 (1961).
22. W. H. Thorpe, *Bird–Song* (Cambridge Univ. Press, New York, 1961).
23. E. von Holst and H. Mittelstaedt, *Naturwissenschaften* **37**, 464 (1950).
24. M. Konishi, *Z. Tierpsychol.* **22**, 770 (1965); F. Nottebohm, *Proc. 14th Intern. Ornithol. Congr.* 265–280 (1967).
25. E. M. Standing, *Maria Montessori* (New American Library, New York, 1962).
26. N. Tinbergen, in *The Pathology and Treatment of Sexual Deviation*, I. Rosen, Ed. (Oxford Univ. Press, London, 1964), pp. 3–23; N. B. Jones, *Wildfowl Trust 11th Ann. Rept.*, 46–52 (1960); P. Sevenster, *Behaviour, Suppl.* **9**, 1–170 (1961); F. Rowell, *Animal Behaviour* **9**, 38 (1961).

Indexes

AUTHOR INDEX

* Numbers in parentheses indicate that the author is referred to by that reference number, rather than by name, on the page indicated.

Hobbson, A., 140(5)
Hodos, W., 9, 27
Hoel, P. G., 425(2)
Hoffman, H. S., 254, 258
Hoffmann, K., 337, 341–342
Holst, E. C., 84
Holst, E., von, 39, 47–48, 464(23)
Hooton, E. A., 436(7)
Hormann-Heck, S. von, 71
Hovda, R. B., 236(7)
Howard, E., 7
Howard, H. E., 461(17)
Hoyes, P. A., 239
Hoyt, A. M., 310(7)
Hsu, T. C., 72
Hubbs, C. L., 425(4)
Hubel, D. H., 369
Huber, G. C., 11
Hudgens, G. A., 236
Hudspeth, W. J., 114
Hughes, R. L., 306(30)
Hunsaker, D., 73
Hunt, J. M., 197(2), 205(2)
Hutchinson, R. R., 131
Huxley, J. S., 7, 24–26

I

Iacaboni, M., 331(15)
Iersel, J. J. A., van, 36, 408
Ikonen, M., 176(46)
Ilse, D. R., 307(46)
Iltis, H., 60
Imanishi, K., 389(1,2), 442–443(45)
Ingham, S. E., 425(3)
Irion, A. L., 362
Ising, G., 344
Itani, J., 442(44), 443(48)

J

Jackson, T. A., 392(9)
Jacobsen, C. F., 311(20)
Jacobsen, M. M., 311(20)
Jacobsohn, D., 165(10)
Jacobson, M., 306(9,10)
Jaffrey, J. S., 80
Jakway, J. S., 70

James, H., 238–240, 242
Jameson, D. L., 421
Jarvik, L. F., 65
Jarvik, M. E., 115, 366
Jasper, H. H., 137
Jay, G. E., 114
Jay, P., 307(52)
Jay, P. C., 435, 436(17), 438–439 (28), 440(34)
Jaynes, J., 4, 24, 238–240, 244–245, 401–402
Jennings, R. D., 113
Jensen, D., 225
Johannessen, N. B., 126(6)
John, E. R., 389(4), 392(8)
Johnson, D. C., 165(15)
Johnson, D. L., 253(9), 318–324(4), 325–327(1,3–5,9), 328(9,10), 333
Jolly, A., 307(49)
Joly, H., 5
Jones, C. N., 15
Jones, F. G. W., 43, 45
Jones, J. K., 16
Jones, L. V., 281
Jones, N. B., 467(26)
Jones, R. L., 84
Jones, W. A., 306(9,10)
Joos, M., 219, 224
Jost, H., 67

K

Kaada, B. R., 126(4–7)
Kahan, S., 118
Kakihana, R., 111
Kalmbach, E. R., 345
Kalmus, H., 306(3), 330–331(13)
Kano, K., 442(44)
Karas, G. G., 236(10)
Karczmar, A. G., 188, 196
Karimova, M. M., 283
Karlson, P., 306(2)
Kato, M., 118
Katz, D., 23
Kaufmann, I. C., 240
Kaufmann, J. A., 427(8)
Kavanau, J. P., 194–195
Kaye, S. M., 253(6)

Kearton, C., 310(7)
Keenleyside, M. H. A., 242
Keesey, R. E., 140(11)
Kelemen, G., 310(3)
Keller, J. C., 306(13)
Kelley, R. B., 306(40)
Kellogg, L. A., 310(5), 311(10–12), 392(9)
Kellogg, W. N., 309, 310(5), 311(5,10–12), 313(5), 392(9)
Kenyon, K. W., 340
Keverne, E. B., 306
Kiess, H. D., 131, 135–137
Kikuchi, T. T., 421
Kimble, G. A., 362–363, 368
Kimball, S., 80
King, J. A., 19, 180(12), 188, 193, 197(6)
Kirk, K. L., 379
Kish, G. B., 254
Kline, N. J., 174(44)
Kling, J. W., 140(11)
Klock, J., 308(64)
Klopfer, M. S., 248
Klopfer, P. H., 15–16, 72, 239, 241, 244, 248
Knoll, M. D., 464(20)
Koch, A. M., 392(9)
Koch, S., 372
Koelling, R. A., 393(1), 396(1)
Koford, C. B., 32, 39, 46, 440(32), 441(39), 442–443(46)
Köhler, W., 436(9)
Kohts, N., 311(9), 314(9)
Konishi, M., 225, 234(4), 464(24)
Koopman, K. F., 73, 81
Kopp, R. A., 366
Kozma, F., 254, 258
Knaggs, G. S., 251
Knight, G. R., 81
Kral, P. A., 397(5)
Kramer, C. Y., 419
Kramer, G., 334–345
Kramer, S., 34, 37–38
Krätzig, H., 343
Krech, D., 62, 118, 195(5), 236(11)
Kruuk, H., 459(10)
Kuenen, D. J., 37

Kuhn, E., 251
Kuhn, T. S., 59, 326(7)
Kummer, H., 441(35)
Kuo, Z. Y., 214, 237, 389(2)
Kurt, F., 441(35)
Kuroda, R., 283
Kurokawa, M., 118

L

Lack, D., 27, 343, 419
Lamond, D. R., 306(24)
Lancaster, J. B., 435, 437(23), 439(30)
Landreth, H. F., 348(1–3,8), 349(2), 353(1–3), 357(5)
Lane, P., 114
Langdon, J. W., 400
Lanyon, W., 234(6)
Lashley, K. A., 7, 344, 369
Lauprecht, C. W., 126(2), 129(2)
Laursen, A. M., 129(12)
Lauryssens, M., 251
Lawrence, M., 288
Lawrence, N., 169(32)
Laws, R. M., 425(3)
Learned, B. W., 312(23)
Leblond, C. P., 146(2)
LeBoeuf, B. J., 424
Lee, R. B., 439(30)
Lee, S. van der, 306(17,18)
LeGros Clark, W. E., 13, 15
Lehrman, D. S., 34, 42–43, 46–47, 146(1), 149–150, 152, 214, 225
Leibowitz, S. F., 366
LeMagnen, J., 307(42), 308(61,62)
Lennox, W. G., 67
Lerwill, C. G., 416
Lerwill, C. J., 416
Lessac, M. S., 198(13), 207(13), 209(13)
Levi, W. M., 278
Levine, J., 278–282
Levine, L., 111
Levine, S., 165–176(6,7,17,22,26,27,34,36–38,42), 177–178(1), 236(10)
Levinson, G., 162(15)
Levy, J. V., 180(12)

478

Wright, A. H., 421
Wright, H. W., 292(6), 294(6)
Wurtman, R. J., 141(13)
Wyers, E. J., 126(2), 129(2)
Wylie, N. R., 307(44)
Wynne-Edwards, V. C., 344–345
Wyrwicka, W., 132

Y

Yacorzynski, G., 281
Yamada, M., 442(41)
Yates, F. E., 172(39)
Yeagley, H. L., 345
Yen, C. Y., 181
Yerkes, A. W., 435(1)

Yerkes, R. M., 311(21), 312(23), 314 (26), 435(1)
Yoshioka, J. G., 311(20)
Young, J. Z., 11, 13–14, 226, 228
Young, W. C., 153(2), 164(2,3), 165 (12), 168(3)

Z

Zarrow, M. N., 236(9)
Zarrow, M. X., 236, 306(31)
Zeigler, H. P., 412, 415
Zigler, E., 197(1)
Zimmermann, R. R., 269
Zuckerman, S., 436(5)
Zwick, H., 283

SUBJECT INDEX